Texas
Guide

Travel Guides to Planet Earth!

OPEN ROAD TRAVEL GUIDES SHOW YOU
HOW TO BE A TRAVELER – NOT A TOURIST!

*Whether you're going abroad or planning a trip in the United States, take Open Road along on your journey. Our books have been praised by **Travel & Leisure, The Los Angeles Times, Newsday, Booklist, US News & World Report, Endless Vacation, American Bookseller, Coast to Coast**, and many other magazines and newspapers!*

Don't just see the world – experience it with Open Road!

About the Authors

Lauri Hoese is an attorney, writer, and enthusiastic dabbler who has traveled throughout Russia, Greece, France, the Caribbean, Great Britain, Germany, and the United States. She has lived in Austin, Texas since 1988.

Judy Moore is a professional travel writer who makes her home in Austin, Texas. She is the co-author of *Teach Central Europe*, an educational directory for those interested in teaching opportunities in Eastern and Central Europe. She is also the author of Open Road's *Vietnam Guide*.

Open Road -
Travel Guides to Planet Earth!

Open Road Publishing has guide books to exciting, fun destinations on four continents. As veteran travelers, our goal is to bring you the best travel guides available anywhere!

No small task, but here's what we offer:

• All Open Road travel guides are written by authors with a distinct, opinionated point of view – not some sterile committee or team of writers. Our authors are experts in the areas covered and are polished writers.

• Our guides are geared to people who want to make their own travel choices. We'll show you how to discover the real destination – not just see some place from a tour bus window.

• We're strong on the basics, but we also provide terrific choices for those looking to get off the beaten path and experience the country or city – not just see it or pass through it.

• We give you the best, but we also tell you about the worst and what to avoid. Nobody should waste their time and money on their hard-earned vacation because of bad or inadequate travel advice.

• Our guides assume nothing. We tell you everything you need to know to have the trip of a lifetime – presented in a fun, literate, no-nonsense style.

• And, above all, we welcome your input, ideas, and suggestions to help us put out the best travel guides possible.

Texas
Guide

Travel Guides to Planet Earth!

Lauri Hoese & Judy Moore

Open Road Publishing

For BB

3rd Edition

Cover photos copyright Paris Permenter and John Bigley. Maps by Rob Perry.

The authors have made every effort to be as accurate as possible, but neither they nor the publisher assume responsibility for the services provided by any business listed in this guide; for any errors or omissions; or any loss, damage, or disruptions in your travels for any reason.

Judy would like to extend a big Texas thanks to: Dean Barrera, Brenda Baylor, Francis Blatt, Marci Buck, Dr. Christopher Champion, Dr. and Mrs. Minuth of El Paso, Mike Minuth, Mr. and Mrs. Michael of Houston, Susan Michael of Austin, Mr. and Mrs. Moore and Tess, Dr. Pringle of St. Edward's University in Austin, Daniel Springer, Tony Yardley, Cynthia Wilberts, Mr. and Mrs. Wright of Dallas.

Lauri would like to thank Bonnie Hubert and Jeff Oswald, without whose love and patience this book would never have been finished. More warm gratitude to Frank and Cynthia Hubert, Amy and Pat Freund, Frank Hubert III, Mary Elizabeth Hubert and my perfect nieces and nephews, for providing still more love, support, diversion, and the occasional reality check. Non-electronic thanks to George Rizk for keeping me aware of the future. Finally, I was fortunate enough to enjoy the cameraderie and friendship of traveling companions extraordinaire Dan Goff, Susan Michael, and Cindy Crawford.

Texas Guide

c o n t e n t s

7. Basic Information   73

8. Sports & Recreation   77

9. Taking the Kids   83

10. Major Events   86

Sidebars

Maps

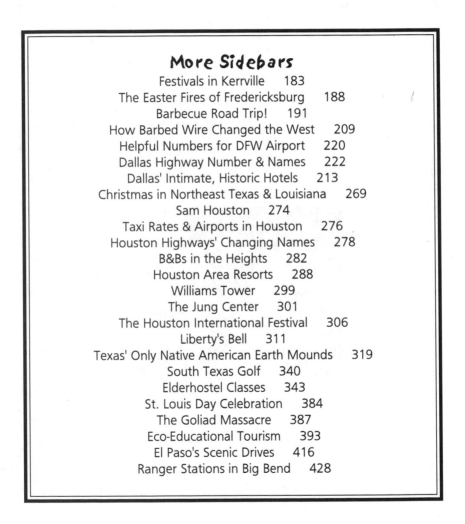

More Sidebars

Chapter 1

introduction

To the casual tourist, Texas means cowboys and cattle, oil barons and gushers, wide-open spaces and a brash frontier spirit. But to the traveler willing to take the time to delve beneath its celebrated image, Texas offers something much more rewarding—complexity, diversity, and a surprising modernity mixed with careful preservation of tradition.

Within its sprawling borders, Texas contains numerous smaller lands, each with its own unique character. Many native Texans have yet to venture to the distant corners of the state. The very size of Texas sets it apart, more than one-fifth of the continental United States. El Paso, in the far western corner of the state, sits closer to Los Angeles than to Houston.

Three of the nation's largest metropolitan centers, Dallas, Houston and San Antonio, entice with their own exciting styles of art, music, and entertainment. Outside the big cities, many versions of paradise await the nature lover. The sweeping coastline of the Gulf of Mexico boasts year-round fishing and protected wetlands. The rugged hills of Central Texas, home of three-peat Tour de France champion Lance Armstrong, offer excellent routes for bicycle touring. Four national forests and the Big Thicket National Preserve are found in the woodlands of East Texas. Easy hikes near Lake Amistad lead to some of the oldest cave paintings on the continent.

From glittering cities to desert solitude, history to legend, the many landscapes of Texas can satisfy all tastes. Whether you yearn for the new west of Luckenbach or the Old West of Amarillo, Texas remains unlike any other place in the world.

**O
v
e
r
v
i
e
w**

Chapter 2

The enduring legends of cowboys and oil barons live on in a modern state with some of the most progressive and cosmopolitan cities in the world. On a trip to Texas you will find breathtaking landscapes, rich history, and entertainment for every taste.

Its newness is perhaps the most striking aspect of Texas compared to other areas of the world. The various Native American cultures of the area were hunter-gatherers rather than cultivators, and did little to change the face of the landscape. Not until hundreds of years after its discovery by Europeans did development in Texas begin. Most of the oldest buildings in the state date from the eighteenth century, barely a tick away on history's clock.

Texas is the second largest state in area, behind Alaska, and the second largest in population, behind California. In the 1990s, Texas overtook the state of New York in population. Today over 19 million people call Texas home. Only one century ago over eighty percent of Texans led a rural life. Today this has reversed and over eighty percent of Texans live in urban areas.

You can find the strangest things in the least expected places. Getting off the beaten track on Texas' own slice of Route 66 leads to the quirky **Cadillac Ranch**. Eccentric millionaire Stanley Marsh III's version of public art consists of ten vintage Cadillacs buried askew on the Panhandle Plains. Texas has its share of mysteries as well. In West Texas people swear to the existence of native UFOs, the "**Marfa Lights**," luminous globes that hover just above the horizon at dusk. A more infamous and somber mystery can be explored at the **Conspiracy Museum** in Dallas – did Oswald act alone when he assassinated President John F. Kennedy?

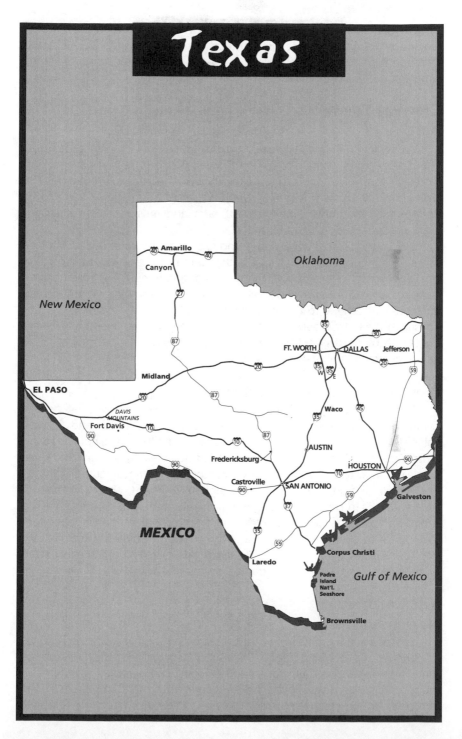

As you might expect given its size, Texas could be divided into many regions by distinctive geographical and cultural characteristics. Each is different enough to be a country within itself, yet they are united under the same large Texas sky.

Central Texas

Austin

Limestone hills and the constant thrum of music mark the heart of Texas. The state capital, Austin, is a center of higher learning, seat of government, high-tech center and one of the fastest growing regions in the nation. The **University of Texas** brings renowned artists of international scale to its performance programs. The diverse theater and music scenes reflect the avant-garde attitude of Austinites.

Live music fills coffeehouses, trendy restaurant-bars and dusty honky-tonks. Austin may be the only city in the country to have its own television station devoted to local music. Many extraordinary musicians rose to fame here, including Janis Joplin and Stevie Ray Vaughn. On any given night you can find those who hope to follow in their footsteps playing the many venues housed in the historic buildings along Sixth Street. During ten days in March the **South by Southwest (SXSW) Festival** makes Austin the center of the alternative music universe.

Brenham & Washington-on-the-Brazos

Thick woodlands characterize this region, which has a great deal in common with its eastern neighbor, Louisiana. Both French and Spanish colonists coveted beautiful east-central Texas, but neither could hold on to this crossroads of culture. The densely wooded acres along the **Brazos River** cradle the small towns where the Texas independence movement took shape.

The great frontiersmen of Texas legend — Davy Crockett, Stephen F Austin, and Sam Houston - were drawn to this land. And here in small log cabins and plank houses, they embarked on the creation of an independent state. Later European immigrants transformed the rich soil of the bottomlands into farms. Brenham offers a bucolic landscape of rolling green hills dotted with white fences, stables, and dairies.

Hill Country

New Braunfels

European immigrants from countries such as Germany and Czechoslovakia founded the charming cities of the Hill Country. Skilled craftsmen used the materials available to them to produce modest but well-built structures of wood and stone. These lovely houses, churches, and farms built by the European settlers bestow a distinct character to the hills of central Texas. At

The Largest Texas Cities
Houston 1,953,631
San Antonio 1,171,700
Dallas 1,069,338
Austin 656,562
El Paso 563,662
Fort Worth 490,000

one time central Texas was actually the western frontier. The isolated communities that thrived here retain much of the atmosphere and heritage of old Europe.

This is paradise for nature lovers. In the crystal-clear rivers of the region you can enjoy days of kayaking, fishing, or snorkeling. In the evenings you can enjoy southwestern and German cuisine in charming restaurants.

Music flourishes here, and the old traditions remain strong. You can still listen and dance to bands that include polkas and waltzes in their repertoires. It isn't all oom-pah-pah and fiddles, though. In **Gruene**, the oldest dance hall in the state draws nationally acclaimed country, folk, and rock musicians.

Kerrville

The Hill Country is a popular retreat for native Texans and tourists alike. In the southern region the towns of **Bandera** and **Kerrville** offer country retreats where the most refined urbanite can become a cowboy for a few days. Vacation ranches offer horseback riding, golf, hiking, and many other diversions. The Kerrville Folk Festival, one of the foremost celebrations of native music, presents exceptional talent showcased under the open skies.

Just north of Kerrville lies an amazing section of dramatic, winding hills and vast lakes. Driving through the Hill Country is not only breathtaking but also full of hidden surprises. Orchards and vineyards surround the historic town of **Fredericksburg**.

The beauty and serenity of this area attracts nature lovers and sportsmen. **Enchanted Rock**, a giant granite dome surrounded by stone faced hills, was regarded as sacred by the Native Americans who inhabited the region. Enchanted Rock State Park remains the premier rock climbing and rappelling spot in the state.

Panhandle Plains

The true grit of the Old West thrived in this region, where rolling plains and steep canyons provided a backdrop for cattle drives and outlaw hideouts. Apache and Comanche once dominated the dry prairies; their legacy colors history. Immense ranches that stretched across the horizon, seemingly to the end of the world itself, shaped the face of Texas forever.

Amarillo

Only in Texas can you find the largest ranch on earth. The **XIT Ranch**, as big as a state in itself, has a legendary history. The story of its founding sounds like a tale spun over a cowboy's campfire. When Texans decided to construct a capitol, the building was so grandiose that the only way to pay for it was to trade three million acres of land for the building. That chunk of land became the XIT. Every year modern-day cowboys meet here to test their skills at the XIT Rodeo.

The northernmost region of Texas, part of the Great Plains, is called the Panhandle. The area is a dream destination for an old-fashioned road trip. Old Route 66 crosses this land, and the nation's second largest canyon is near by.

Amarillo stands on the vast prairies of the northern region of the panhandle. The stark Texas plains dramatically give way to the red rock-face of **Palo Duro Canyon** in the northernmost lands. You can hike along the burnt orange canyon and stay in a cabin in a land where buffalo still roam the range.

Lubbock

The proud inheritors of these lands took diverse paths to greatness. For example, Buddy Holly, whose rock and roll music changed our culture, hailed from Lubbock. That city keeps the southern music traditions alive in its vibrant nightlife and active live music scene.

The richness of Texas' ancient history also is evident in Lubbock. The **Lubbock Lake Archaeological Site** has yielded evidence of Native American culture that flourished over 12,000 years ago. The park offers hiking trails that lead to archaeology excavations and a museum that explains these amazing finds.

North Texas

Forth Worth

The first cattle drives came through Fort Worth, giving cowboys a place to forever call home. The city evolved from the original cow town to a true gem of culture. The **Kimbell Museum** receives the finest traveling exhibitions; its permanent collection is known as one of the finest in the world.

In the saloons of **Hell's Half-Acre** in Fort Worth the most menacing and notorious outlaws once mingled. Bonnie and Clyde are said to have passed through, evading lawmen on their infamous race to death. Doc Holliday practiced dentistry in nearby Dallas.

Some of the less notorious residents were more brave than fierce. Rugged settlers, hungry for the opportunities of a new frontier, survived sparse vegetation, dramatic weather, and hostility to carve out cities against all odds. Desolate army forts still stand as a tribute to those who took on this life. The settlers would be proud to see the modern ranges tamed by prosperous suburbs, rich farmland, and vineyards that produce some of the state's finest wine.

Dallas

Dallas stands on the borderlands of east and north Texas, overlooking both. Dallas is a new breed of city, offering the pleasure of both urban and suburban lifestyles. The monumental architecture of downtown Dallas fills the eye and boggles the mind.

For a city of its great size, Dallas is easy to visit as a tourist. **Dealy Plaza** where President Kennedy was assassinated is a short walk from the animated restaurants of the colorful West End area. You can take the light rail into downtown and to the **Dallas Museum of Art**. The district known as **Deep Ellum** offers magical nightlife and many live music clubs. Well-respected ballet, symphony, and theater can satisfy the most sophisticated taste.

East Texas
Houston

Houston, the second largest metropolitan area in the state, is the heart of East Texas. Nowhere is the contrast between old and new more apparent than in Houston. The city erupted with a gush of Texas crude oil and grew into an immense metropolitan center. In Houston you will never run out of diversions. The city offers a thriving cultural scene and a large museum district. You will discover new worlds in Houston, like exciting amusement parks, and **NASA's Visitors Center**.

Houston, an illuminated masterpiece of modern development, is a tribute to all that Texans have become. Fine stores, extraordinary restaurants, and vibrant clubs compare to the world's best. An exciting nightlife, world-class hotels, and shopping are all within proximity of the beautiful Gulf coast.

Nacogdoches & The National Forests

The **Caddo**, Native Americans of the Mississippian culture who settled near the Big Thicket, left unique cultural monuments. Although the Caddo have long since vanished from Texas, the earth mounds they built have survived the centuries. The name Tejas, from which Texas is derived, is a Caddo word meaning "friendship."

Gulf Coast
Galveston

The beautiful Victorian homes of Galveston testify to the historic grandeur of the city. At the turn of the century it was the largest port on the Texas coast, with an affluent social scene to match. Today when you visit the **Strand** Galveston's main street, you'll feel transported to a Victorian city.

Early last century, a devastating hurricane whipped through the city and left it frozen in time. Only the most magnificent of the buildings remained, and the city never regained its status as a port city. Today Galveston has the beauty of a Victorian resort town. Numerous tourists enjoy the beaches and seafood, especially on summer weekends when Houstonians drive in for a day or weekend.

Corpus Christi

Along the warm waters of the Gulf of Mexico, life in Corpus Christi seems to move at a slower, more tropical pace. The riches of nature are within your grasp. Deep-sea fishing, surfing, and swimming are but a few ways to spend time here. You can also enjoy exceptional windsurfing in Corpus Christi Bay. Migratory birds inhabit the area's wetlands, making it a birder's paradise. Fresh seafood, miles of coastal nature preserves, and tropical foliage attract visitors from around the world. The city is just a few hours' drive from bustling Mexican border towns.

Kingsville

Texas cowboys originated at the **King Ranch**, just south of Corpus Christi. As one of the first ranches in North America its unique traditions date back centuries. This is where the word "cowboy" was defined. Borrowing from the dress and gear used further south by Mexican *vaqueros*, Texans began to blaze new trails across their own land. The vast flatlands of coastal Texas proved a good habitat for Spanish longhorn steer.

South Padre Island

South Texas shines from the vibrant cultural mix of Mexico and Texas, and it is most apparent in the resort town of South Padre Island. Spectacular dune-filled beaches provide the backdrop to a host of resort hotels on the tip of Padre Island. Here the seafood is freshest, water sports most exciting, and atmosphere most inviting. Just a few miles away are the cities of **Brownsville** and neighboring **Matamoros, Mexico**. Filled with history and awash in natural beauty, this part of the state attracts thousands of winter sun worshippers.

South Texas

South Texas is proud to be a land where the cultures and histories of two nations meet. No symbol could better represent Texas than the rugged old façade of the **Alamo**, which remains almost in defiance of the modern buildings that surround it. The region is cloaked in history, from the jazz-age architecture of downtown San Antonio to the ancient Spanish missions in the countryside.

San Antonio

The gorgeous **River Walk**, in the heart of downtown, is famous for its appealing restaurants, music, and entertainment. An amazing cache of culture and history awaits you in San Antonio. From ancient missions to modern art, the city proudly celebrates the past and future. This is probably the most Texan of any city, simply because the Alamo makes it so. You can easily spend an entire day at the Alamo and in the beautiful downtown area.

In the evening river taxis buzz through the city center and free shows are presented on the outdoor stage at the **River Center**. The beautiful River Walk lined with restaurants, cafes, bars and live music blossoms at night. During any time of the year you visit San Antonio cultural activities abound. The warm people of San Antonio may be the friendliest, in a state known for hospitality.

West Texas

El Paso

The enchantment of West Texas is characterized by rich sunsets on the wide horizon. Standing on the hills overlooking El Paso you have four hundred years of history within your gaze. The **missions** of West Texas are the state's oldest structures, dating from the time of Imperial Spain. The buildings of downtown blossom next to the El Paso arts district.

A truly international city, El Paso is the gateway to the west for Texas. Its twin city, **Juarez**, is the largest city on the Texas-Mexico border. From El Paso, you can embark on a journey to the magnificent Guadalupe Mountains and then on to New Mexico, or head south to the spectacular Copper Canyon and Mexican Pacific coast.

Big Bend & Beyond

The **Chihuahuan Desert** is awash in flowering cacti and rocky ledges. The stark desert landscape was once Comanche territory. The epic struggles of settlement - war, railroads, and outlaws - are the life story of West Texas. Tickle your imagination by walking through the real frontier forts and small settlement houses. The evidence of the past that remains standing is most dramatic because it survived against hostile and disruptive forces and was born of modest beginnings.

Big Bend, named for the long winding stretch of the Rio Grande River that passes through two canyons, lies in the remotest part of the state. Hundreds of miles from the nearest large city, Big Bend is an isolated paradise. Desert gives way to verdant mountains teeming with wildlife. Camping options range from backcountry hiking paths to a cozy lodge nestled in a mountain gap. You can watch for bears, mountain lions, and all types of flora and fauna. The park has an extensive array of nature walks and classes for all ages and abilities.

To the north, the majestic **Davis Mountains** rise through the desert to one of the clearest horizons on earth. You can venture into the galaxy at the **McDonald Observatory**. The state-of-the-art research facility offers its telescopes for regular public viewing of the sun and the night sky. Whether you choose to stay a few days or a lifetime, the adventure of being in Texas continues.

Chapter 3

There is so much to do and see in Texas, that you could easily spend a few weeks just getting to the basics. Most visitors—and natives—get around the state by driving. Probably the easiest way to combine in-depth sightseeing with as much ground as you care to cover is to either combine air and car travel or spend your time in one area.

The following itineraries have at least two weeks of options packed into one week. They are designed for a person arriving at the major urban center of one of the areas in the state. The basics are covered, then a "weekend" extension is offered. These weekend extensions take you to the most popular and representative spot within a day's drive. If you have the time, extend the weekends for travel at a slower pace or to cover more territory.

Some of the suggestions are geared for special interests, such as history or nature. Again, the pace of the schedules is fast because there is much to do. If you plan to travel between cities by plane, you can easily mix and match pieces of the itineraries to suit your timetable and schedule. If you choose not to rent a car you can still see everything of interest by taking a bus. The routes are extensive and the cost very economical.

Central Texas

Day One: Arrive in Austin. Take a leisurely stroll down Congress Avenue and historic Sixth Street. Dine in the downtown area.

Day Two: Tour the State Capitol Complex. Begin at the visitor's center building, then the Capitol itself, and finish with the Governor's Mansion. Take in some live music on Sixth Street in the evening.

Day Three: Enjoy the outdoors at Zilker Park and the Austin Nature Center. Walk along Town Lake. Drive to the Wildflower Research Center in the afternoon to enjoy the native flowers and nearby biking and skating trails.

Day Four: Visit The University of Texas campus and the LBJ Library and Museum. Spend some time on Guadalupe Street, also called the Drag, at the heart of student life. Attend a cultural performance at the university.

Day Five: Enjoy the arts with a visit to the Laguna Gloria Art Museum. Take time to enjoy the museum's lakefront grounds. Follow this by going to the Austin Art Museum downtown. Dine at a trendy restaurant and enjoy the nightlife in the Warehouse District.

Extended Tour

Day Six: Drive through the Hill Country to Fredericksburg. Stop at the LBJ State and National Park to take the tour of the Johnson family home. Spend the night in a quaint bed & breakfast in Fredericksburg.

Day Seven: Visit Enchanted Rock. Bring a picnic lunch and spend the day at this serene park.

East Texas

Day One: Arrive in Houston. Drive through or go shopping in the Galleria and Post Oak Area. Dine at one of the many international restaurants there.

Day Two: Visit Allen's Landing Park to enjoy the historic stories that document the beginnings of the city. Walk downtown and check out the pedestrian tunnel system. You can visit the monumental buildings downtown via the tunnels, thus avoiding the strong sun. Dine downtown in the theater area and take in a play.

Day Three: Visit NASA and Clear Lake. The NASA tour will take a few hours and it will be time well spent. Dine at a casual lakeside restaurant. If you have time (preferably an extra day) drive to the Astrodome and take a tour, or check out the new home of the Houston Astros, Astros Field.

Day Four: Visit Hermann Park; choose from the museums and gardens or the zoo. In the evening, hit a hot spot in Market Square or the downtown Westheimer area.

Day Five: Indulge in a day of fine art with a visit to the Houston Museum of Fine Arts and the Menil Collection.

Extended Tour

Day Six: Drive to Galveston. Walk along the sea wall and have lunch or dinner on the historic Strand.

Day Seven: Enjoy the beach by engaging in some water sports, taking a nature walk or bird watching.

North Texas

Day One: Arrive in Dallas. Visit the West End or Deep Ellum area and dine there.

Day Two: Visit the Dallas Museum of Art. Walk downtown to enjoy the monumental architecture with stops at the Water Gardens Building and original Neiman Marcus. In the evening, go to Greenville Avenue for food and fun.

Day Three: Visit Fort Worth. Check out the Kimbell Museum and the cultural district. Go to the Stockyards in the evening. If possible, spend the night.

Day Four: Spend the day in Dallas visiting the Kennedy Memorial, the Sixth Floor Museum and the Conspiracy Museum. Take the trolley to McKinney Avenue for dinner.

Day Five: Spend the day at State Fair Park visiting the museums and fairgrounds.

Extended Tour

Day Six: Fly to Amarillo. Tour the city and drive on Texas' own slice of Route 66.

Day Seven: Spend the day at Palo Duro Canyon. Hike along the nature trails and enjoy the breathtaking sunset.

South Texas

Day One: Arrive in San Antonio. Take a boat tour of the San Antonio River. Stroll along the River Walk and spend the evening dining and enjoying the festive atmosphere.

Day Two: Tour the Alamo. Return to the River Walk and visit the River Center for shopping and dining. In the evening watch a show at the outdoor theater or at the IMAX.

Day Three: Take a tour of the Spanish Missions. If you have time, visit the Institute of Texan Cultures to gain a perspective of what life inside the missions and around the state was once like. In the evening, enjoy a cultural performance downtown.

Day Four: Make a day trip to Castroville to see the many historic buildings preserved in this Hill Country town.

Day Five: Spend the day at Brackenridge Park enjoying the museums and botanical gardens. Visit the San Antonio Art Museum.

Extended Tour

Day Six: Drive to Laredo to visit the animated Texas-Mexico border. Eat dinner at Victoria's in Nuevo Laredo.

Day Seven: Visit San Augustine Square in Laredo. Then cross the border for shopping and sight seeing in Mexico.

West Texas

Day One: Arrive in El Paso. Visit the downtown area and Chamizal National Monument. Dine in one of the popular restaurants along Cincinnati Street.

Day Two: Visit the Art Museum and the small galleries that display the work of regional artists. Treat yourself to a juicy steak at an area steakhouse.

Day Three: Take the trolley to Juarez, Mexico. Spend the day exploring areas of interest on the trolley route. Wind up with a shopping spree in the market area. Have dinner and drinks at Carlos n' Charlie's.

Day Four: Take a tour of the Spanish Missions and then the Tigua Reservation. Have dinner at the Tigua Casino.

Day Five: Drive to Franklin Mountains State Park. Take in the fresh air and amazing view from the nature trails. Visit the Wilderness museum. In the evening, take advantage of the many cultural events held in El Paso.

Extended Tour

Day Six: Drive to Fort Davis, making a stop at either Hueco Tanks State Park for some light hiking, or at Balmorhea State Park for a swim in the cool spring water.

Day Seven: Make an early trip to the preserved Fort Davis complex and museum. Then drive through the mountains to the McDonald Observatory for the tour of the telescopes. Participate in the solar observation held in the afternoon. Return to El Paso along the scenic mountain highway.

Doing The Old West

Day One: Arrive in Fort Worth; visit the Stockyards during the day. Get suited up in your finest cowboy hat and boots to go to Billy Bob's in the evening.

Day Two: Visit the downtown arts district. After touring the Kimbell Museum, visit the museums housing art that depicts the old west.

Day Three: Drive (or fly) to Abilene. Along the drive, stop at historic Fort Griffin, north of Abilene.

Day Four: Visit Abilene and Fort Phantom Hill.

Day Five: Continue south to San Angelo; stop at Buffalo Gap.

Extended Tour

Day Six: Visit San Angelo and Fort Concho, a major stop for stagecoach routes. Go to Miss Hattie's museum, an old west saloon.

Day Seven: Return along the open Texas highway to Fort Worth. Make a stop in Dublin to see the old Dr. Pepper bottling plant and museum.

The Republic of Texas Tour

Day One: Arrive in Houston. Visit Allen's Landing and the downtown historic area.

Day Two: Drive along Highway 290 to Brenham. Enjoy the quaint small town atmosphere. Visit the Blue Bell creamery.

Day Three: Spend the day at Washington-on-the-Brazos State Park. Take a side trip to Independence and Chappell Hill.

Day Four: Continue along Highway 290 to Austin. Tour the State Capitol, State Archives and Library, and the Governor's Mansion.

Day Five: Enjoy Austin.

Extended Tour

Day Six: Continue to San Antonio via Interstate Highway 35. Visit the Alamo. Spend the evening on the River Walk.

Day Seven: Tour the Missions or visit the Institute of Texan Cultures.

Day Eight: Spend the day doing what you skipped yesterday.

Day Nine: Drive to Columbus via Interstate Highway 10.

Day Ten: Continue on to Houston via Interstate Highway 10.

Seeing the Coastal Bend

Day One: Arrive in Corpus Christi. Visit the port of Corpus Christi and museum complex. Stroll along the waterfront, then dine at a seafood restaurant.

Day Two: Take a sailing tour of the Bay of Corpus Christi. Enjoy the laid-back nightlife of downtown Corpus Christi.

Day Three: Drive to Port Aransas; enjoy the best surf in the coastal bend and stay at a beachfront hotel or condo.

Day Four: Go deep sea fishing, diving, or just relax on the beach. Drive down the island to visit the National Seashore. Spend the night in Port Aransas.

Day Five: Take Highway 37 to Highway 77, and head south to Kingsville. Visit the King Ranch or enjoy Baffin Bay. Spend the night in Kingsville.

Extended Tour

Day Six: Have lunch at the King's Inn, then continue south to South Padre Island.

Day Seven and on: Enjoy the best beaches in Texas, and take time to visit Brownsville and Matamoros, Mexico. Return by car, or fly from Brownsville Airport.

Texas Wine & Beer Itinerary

Day One: Arrive in Austin. Visit the modern Celis Brewery and in the evening dine at the Bitter End brewpub.

Day Two: Take Highway 290 west to Fredericksburg, with a stop at Sister Creek Vineyards in Sisterdale. Dine and drink at Fredericksburg's Brewery.

Days Three and Four: Head south, taking Highways 16 to 39, then Highway 83 to Uvalde. Get on Highway 90 west to Del Rio. In Del Rio visit the oldest winery in the state, Val Verde Winery. Take an extra day to visit Ciudad Acuna, Mexico or Lake Amistad.

Days Five and Six: Take Highway 90 east, all the way to San Antonio. In San Antonio, visit the large Lone Star Brewery; have dinner at the Laboratory brewpub.

Extended Tour

Day Seven: Take Highway 90 east to Shiner, which is on Alternate Highway 90. Visit the Spoetzl Brewery, which is the second oldest brewery in the state. Rejoin Highway 90/Interstate Highway 10 and continue east. Make a stop at the Kreische Brewery State Historic Park, 17 miles west of Weimar on Farm Road 155. An immigrant from Saxony in the first half of the nineteenth century founded the Brewery, which now stands in ruins. Arrive in Houston.

Day Eight: Tour Houston and the Budweiser Brewery.

Day Nine: Fly back to Austin, or return via scenic Highway 290.

Visiting Towns Famous For Their Names!

Texas is full of interesting roadside attractions. But sometimes the attraction is all in the name. Texas is so big you can travel the world and never leave the state. You can make a brand new start of it in **New York, Texas** on Farm Road 607, about 13 miles from Lake Palestine.

Dublin, Texas has Dr. Pepper's oldest bottling plant. The town is 90 miles southeast of Waco, the birthplace of the Dr. Pepper soft drink.

Dallas could be in Europe judging from the towns around it. **Italy, Texas** is just east of Interstate Highway 35, about 45 miles south of Dallas. **Paris, Texas**, made famous by the movie of the same name, is in the northeastern corner of the state, about 75 miles from Dallas. **Athens, Texas**, one of the oldest settlements in the state, is a small east Texas town about 70 miles south of Dallas on Highway 175

Just 65 miles west of Houston, off Interstate Highway 10, is the hamlet of **Weimar, Texas**. You can visit one of the state's oldest breweries here. Nearby, **Egypt, Texas** is about 60 miles southwest of Houston, on Farm Road 102.

There is neither pomp nor circumstance in **London, Texas**, on Highway 377, about 130 miles northwest of San Antonio. Oddly enough, the replica of Stonehenge is not in London, but in nearby **Ingram**.

Of course, the only place everyone should want to go is **Utopia, Texas**, which is in the Hill Country. If nothing is to your liking visit **Nada, Texas**. *Nada* is the Spanish word for "nothing." The town is on State Highway 71, about 100 miles southwest of Austin.

⟩

Chapter 4

The varied and beautiful Texas landscape holds many wildlife habitats, ranging from western desert to southern tropical palm groves. Roughly 5000 species of fauna create diverse ecosystems in the state. Native animals include some 600 species of birds.

This natural kaleidoscope is composed of a number of smaller regions separated by geographical boundaries. In the north, sweeping prairies create a natural boundary to the Great Plains. Eastern Texas holds dense forests and thickets. Central Texas stands on a rocky plateau over the watery wealth of the Edwards Aquifer. West Texas holds both true desert areas and mountains. South Texas' coastal plains blend to expanses of beach-lined barrier islands along the Gulf of Mexico.

Often portrayed as a dry, desolate land, Texas actually has 15 major rivers. The river systems are concentrated in the eastern region and fall on diagonal lines from northwest to southeast. The Rio Grande, immortalized by songs both old and new, curves through mountain passes and forms the distinctive southern border of the state. The Red River has the longest run through Texas. Yet the Colorado River, which feeds the lakes of Central Texas, is the largest. Both Austin and San Antonio are built along rivers.

Over one million acres of lakes grace the state with their beauty. Many of these are man-made and provide miles of recreational activities. The largest lake, East Texas' **Sam Rayburn Reservoir**, has a surface area of over 113,000 acres. South Texas lakes, **Lake Amistad** in particular, offer exceptional sport fishing. **Lake LBJ** and **Lake Travis** in Central Texas are gorgeous boating areas.

True Desert Oasis

Even in the brutal desert lands of West Texas, nature provides a secret haven of cherished water. Luckily for travelers, the oasis is now a state park. The **San Solomon Springs** of **Balmorhea State Park** provide cool, crystal clear spring water all year round. SCUBA divers and snorkelers enjoy swimming here with the fish, even when the outdoor temperatures are bone chilling.

Land

The Woodlands

Moving north from Central Texas, or approaching from the plains of the north, the natural boundary of East Texas is unmistakable. Almost in an instant, landscape changes from scrappy brush into tall pine trees. The rich soil that supports the piney woodland accounts for the dramatic transition. Four national forests, covering a total of over 600,000 acres, thrive in this region:

• Angelina National Forest
• Davy Crockett National Forest
• Sabine National Forest
• Sam Houston National Forest

In these natural wonderlands you can explore ancient Native American mounds, canoe, hike and fish.

East Texas has the heaviest rainfall in the state, with yearly averages as high as 50 inches. This, combined with mineral-rich red clay topsoil, supports a great deal of agriculture including cotton and rice farming.

The dense piney woods support timber farms. Both oak and pine trees flourish throughout most of the area, with willows and mesquite appearing toward the coast. The swampland and cypress trees that characterize the **Big Thicket Preserve** are so dense that the land remained untouched until modern times when colonists moved into it.

The Hill Country

The rocky hills and steep river canyons of Central Texas had a fascinating history long before cowboys settled in and around campfires. During the age of dinosaurs much of Texas was covered by shallow sea; Central Texas was probably a coastal region. Today the dry creek beds and chalky hills are full of small, fossilized sea life.

The Hill Country offers other subterranean evidence of its colorful past. Beautiful caves brimming with crystal formations are found in **Sonora** and **New Braunfels**, as well as other cities. These wonderlands are open to the public for easy treks into prehistoric times.

The most accessible beauty of this region lies on its surface. Rough hills capped with stone ledges offer vantage points for watching striking sunsets. Tree-lined rivers, including the beautiful green **Guadalupe River**, offer cool escapes from hot summer days. These same rivers provided early settlers idyllic settings for hamlets. In the evenings the land, composed mostly of limestone and granite, quickly releases the day's heat, and a bright canopy of stars hangs overhead.

Outdoor enthusiasts take advantage of this magnificent environment year-round. Hikers and mountain-bikers find excellent terrain throughout the region. The lakes fill with jet skis and sailboats as well as SCUBA divers, while sun-worshippers line the shores most of the year.

The Panhandle Plains

The Panhandle region holds vast plains. Toward the west, grasslands become sparse as the terrain transforms into canyons and rock formations. The **Llano Estacado** plain covers most of the western part of the Texas Panhandle. Further east, rich blackland prairie soil supports livestock, cotton crops, and grapes for wine.

North Texas holds the very southern tip of the nation's **Great Plains**. It is a point of divergence, where not only the landscape changes, but so does the culture. Just south of the Panhandle, in cow towns such as **San Angelo** and **Abilene**, the old West and Texas frontier met.

The landscape is hardly uniform and anything but boring in the Panhandle. The nation's second largest canyon, **Palo Duro Canyon**, cuts through the center of this area. The most dramatic portion of the canyon is located near Abilene. Deep canyon walls run over 100 miles southward, where the canyon smoothes into the more rounded hills of **Cap Rock Canyon**.

The Desert

The deep, radiant sunsets of West Texas dissolve into starry, desert nights with clear midnight blue skies. West Texas contains the **Chihuahuan Desert**, the state's only true desert region. Cacti-covered land stretches for miles. Beautiful flowering trees and shrubs blossom for remarkable spring landscapes.

West Texas is also home to the state's mountainous region. The **Davis Mountains** bisect the desert, with some towns sitting on plateaus at heights over 3,000 feet above sea level. In the **Big Bend**, the desert meets the **Rio Grande** with an eruption of canyons. The mountains of Big Bend have extraordinary granite-faced peaks where only mountain lions can safely climb. In the higher elevations pine forests thrive. The Rio Grande snakes along the state's southern border. As Big Bend is almost all parkland, the flora and fauna are accessible to all.

El Paso is the westernmost city in the state, about 800 miles from both Houston and Los Angeles. It stands between the Rio Grande River and a mountain range, dramatically at a cultural crossroads. The city of **Juarez** bustles across the river in Mexico. Nearby, in the desert region just south of New Mexico, the Spanish established their first mission outposts over four centuries ago.

The Gulf Coast

The coastal plains of South Texas have become a thriving wetland habitat stretching along the Gulf of Mexico. **Padre Island**, a long barrier island, sits just off the Texas coast and offers hundreds of miles of untamed beach. On the eastern side you can enjoy the waves of the Gulf of Mexico; to the west you can relax on the calmer Intercoastal Waterway. A good deal of the land resembles simple grassland, so you would never guess that this area has the most diverse animal population in the state. Parts of South Texas are rather dry and receive as little as 16 inches of rain during the year. Closer to the coast, rainfall and humidity increase.

In South Texas, efforts are being made to preserve the unique tropical habitat of the region, which suffers from the potentially devastating effects of heavy tourism as well as occasional natural disasters. **Padre Island National Seashore** covers 130,000 acres. The park service has numerous nature trails and wildlife viewing areas and offers free maps to the public.

The southern tip of the state, the **Rio Grande Valley**, supports eco-systems unique in North America. A few of the last remaining sub-tropical forests on the continent are protected areas. Palm groves that resemble jungle habitat populated with wild distinctive olive trees characterize the region.

Wildlife

The most common wildlife in Texas would be considered exotic most anywhere else. The official state mammal, the **armadillo**, resembles a

Coastal Wildlife Refuge Areas

Two of the most fascinating natural preserves dedicated to preserving the delicate coastal environments are located in South Texas. Both are open to the public. The Audubon Society maintains a 45,000-acre tropical sanctuary, the **Laguna Atascosa National Wildlife Refuge**, *Farm Road 1847, Rio Hondo, Tel. 956/748-3608*, which offers educational programs year-round. The **Santa Ana National Wildlife Refuge**, *Farm Road 907, Alamo, Tel 956/787-3079*, preserves a rare palm tree grove. Thousands of acres of sub-tropical forest provide a home for many animals not seen elsewhere in the state.

dinosaur in miniature with its protective plates that cover its body. The famous **longhorn steer**, which is the mascot of The University of Texas, was imported from Spain as a cash crop for the dry ranchland of South Texas.

Wild animals inhabit all regions of the state. **Coyotes** prefer South Texas and **black bears** live in Big Bend. **Bobcats** still roam the East Texas forests. **Roadrunners** do indeed zip through West Texas, and love to scoot along the pavement. Far harder to spot are the elusive coyotes which roam during the evening. **Rattlesnakes** are found throughout the dry central and western regions, as are **scorpions** and **tarantulas**. The **opossum** (or simply "possums" to a Texan) live throughout the state.

Central Texas is on the migratory route of the **Mexican Freetail bat**. They fly through the state from March to November; in August you will see the greatest numbers. They live and breed in caves and also under the Congress Street Bridge in Austin, where they attract nightly crowds who watch their emergence at nightfall.

Monarch butterflies and **whooping cranes** make annual journeys through the state. Their migratory paths cross no cities so to get a good view of them you should visit a protected habitat. The Brazoria National Wildlife Refuge on the Coastal Bend harbors one of the nation's largest populations of **snow geese** during winter migration.

Texas makes a greater effort to protect endangered animals than it used to. In the West Texas mountains of Big Bend, **mountain lions** roam the rocky peaks. They have a sanctuary and breeding ground in the park. **Bison** (buffalo) now roam the river basins in the Panhandle. Once there were huge herds of these majestic creatures. Today they survive in small herds on nature preserves.

People
Native Americans

The true native Texans are the Native Americans who called Texas home over 10 millennia before the Spanish traversed the land in search of gold. During Paleolithic times, when the majority of the land was probably lusher with a milder climate, small hunting-gathering bands moved throughout the regions of Texas. They may have followed moving animals, but they probably relied on gathering what nature offered for their survival. Little is known about the culture of these peoples, save the small amount available as archaeological evidence.

In North Texas, archaeologists uncovered the remains of a 10,000 year-old buffalo kill. However, hunting large game is not a common characteristic of most ancient Native American evidence found in Texas.

The rugged territory of Seminole Canyon in the southwestern region of Texas, near the Rio Grande, holds over 300 cave paintings. Near Lake Amistad you can see ancient paintings at a cave site that was probably occupied for

13,000 years. Today the region is a desert; however over 10,000 years ago there was abundant foliage and small wildlife.

More ancient art exists in the west, near El Paso. The **Mescalaro Apaches** left a legacy of cave paintings at what is now Hueco Tanks State Park. Despite sharing the Apache name with more famous Native Americans who earned the reputation of being excellent warriors, the **Mescalaro Apaches** are not related to the later inhabitants.

In the forests of East Texas, unusual earth mounds provide a mysterious link to the past. The ceremonial mounds and artifacts in East Texas indicate the **Caddo** occupied the region as early as 1000 BC. Archaeological excavations at the Caddoan Mounds State Historical Park have yielded many artifacts including large ear spools that were worn like earrings, as well as ceremonial spears.

The Caddo were part of the Mississippi people of the southeastern part of North America. They enjoyed a peaceful, agriculture-based and highly developed culture. For unknown reasons, the civilization vanished in the twelfth century, although there are no signs of hostility or disaster, nor is there evidence of where they went. After the disappearance of the Caddo, the **Tonkawa** prospered in northern plains and eastern woodlands.

Native American Place Names in Texas

Wichita Falls and the Wichita River are named for the **Wichita** tribe that came to North Texas in the 1700s.

Comanche County, in East Texas, was a population center for the **Comanche** and **Creek** in the 1800s and 1900s.

Caddo Lake is named for the **Caddo** people who vanished from the region many centuries ago.

Seminole Canyon is near Eagle Pass, where some **Seminole** settled as others continued on to Mexico in the 1800s.

The most famous tribes are not the original inhabitants, but those who moved into Texas from other regions in North America. **Comanche**, portrayed as antagonists by many popular Western movies and novels, were native to the Great Plains. They moved into Texas territory as they were forced south by colonization.

The **Apache** once dominated the Great Plains of the United States, a region that includes the northernmost area of the Texas panhandle. Eventually the Comanche pushed the Apache out of this area. The **Lipan Apache** lived in the Central Texas region and had contact with the Spanish who colonized the state. They were both strong adversaries and — in fewer cases — allies of the Spanish. The Lipan Apache and Comanche were allies of Sam Houston in the fight for independence.

In South Texas, ancient history remains lost in speculation. South Texas coastal regions reportedly were inhabited by a tall, imposing people known as the **Karankawa**. Virtually none of their material history remains. Legends of cannibalism and cruelty linger in stories. Spanish explorers provided what little is known about their appearance and lifestyle.

African Americans

Texans of African American descent have played a major role in shaping the state. An African American was a member of the Spanish explorer Alonzo Alvarez de Pineda's expedition that mapped the state in the sixteenth century. Texas had a significant African American population before its entry to the United States. After the Civil War, freed slaves came to the state to serve at Army frontier forts. These regiments were dubbed the **Buffalo Soldiers**, a name that signifies their bravery and strength.

The **Seminoles**, who were displaced by colonization and driven from Florida, consisted of Native Americans and African Americans. In the mid-nineteenth century some African American Seminoles settled in Texas, while others continued to Mexico.

Europeans in Texas

The Spanish were the first Europeans to move into Texas. The missions and settlements they brought to this land became integral features of the landscape. The development of the **Camino Real**, a major route through Texas connecting eastern lands to the interior of Mexico, played an important role in forming population centers in the state. San Antonio was a meeting point along the Camino Real. The first settlements established by immigrants from the United States were placed in East Texas under Spanish authority.

Historically, South Texas was an indistinguishable continuation of the lands of northern Mexico. The large ranches of this area gave birth to the tradition of the cowboy. Mexican ranching methods were adapted to Texan needs. This area was the starting point of the cattle drives that pushed the growth of cities along the western frontier.

The **Latino** culture is an important part of Texas today. More than simply food, art, and architecture, Latinos contribute the deep roots of their collective identity. The rich and varied history of the state is composed to a large extent of Latino heritage. The vast majority of Latinos in Texas are **Chicanos**, who trace their lineage to Mexico.

The Mexican and Texan cultures remain so close that the national holidays and cultural celebrations of Mexico are celebrated in Texas. The **Sixteenth of September**, the commemoration of Mexico's independence from Spain, is celebrated throughout the state. Parties and festivities take place the preceding night. **Cinco de Mayo**, May Fifth, marks Mexico's liberation from French rule, when the emperor Maiximillian was ousted. This event is celebrated with festivals and parades during the day. Another cultural celebration is the **Dia de los Muertos**, or Day of the Dead, which occurs the day after Halloween. This is a time to commemorate ancestors and loved ones no longer with us. A parade marks the occasion, which has blended with All Souls' Day.

The sounds of Latino culture resonate with **Tejano music** played in the clubs and bars of Texas. The essence of this musical genre lies in the merging of German polka and traditional Spanish guitars. Small bands that play dance music, or **conjunto** music, are popular throughout central and south Texas. Freddy Fender popularized Tejano music nationwide in the 1970s. The tragic murder of pop singer Selena, a rising Tejano star, made national news in 1996. This is not to be confused with **Mariachi** music, a popular style of Mexican music with strong vocal harmony and traditional strumming guitars.

Other European cultures contribute to Texas. The mid-nineteenth century saw a wave of immigrants enter the state directly from Europe. For generations the inhabitants of many Central Texas towns spoke and published newspapers in languages such as German and Czech. Although it is now less common to find these foreign languages in use, the cultures are integral elements of the Texas persona. You can find strudel or German sausage as easily as a hamburger in towns like Fredericksburg. The legacy of the various groups lives in celebrations and museums that play active roles in many communities.

The largest number of nineteenth century immigrant families hailed from **Germany** and settled in Central Texas. They brought their native skills, food, and lifestyle. Traditions are kept alive by artisans who make fine furniture, practice the art of glass blowing, and continue other crafts.

In the northern part of Central Texas, **Czech** settlers established homesteads. Kolaches, sweet breakfast rolls, and Czech sausage are staples in the area. The town of **West** celebrates its Czech heritage with an annual festival. The town of **Panna Maria** in South Texas is the oldest **Polish** settlement in North America.

One example of the strength and determination of the European settlers is found in **Castroville**, a small town just outside of San Antonio. Here you will find the state's own piece of Alsace. The Alsace region of Europe is rich in the culture and tradition of Germany and France. Likewise, the Alsatian settlers who founded Castroville transplanted that Old World charm to Texas. Many of the historic buildings have the architecture of Germany blended with the style of old Texas. This unique combination of heritage remains a vibrant accent to the small community. Every year the town of Castroville remembers its founding and shares its traditions during the Saint Louis Day Celebration, held on the third Sunday of August. Music, food, and dancing let you enjoy the Alsatian culture and learn about the area's rich history.

Diverse European peoples have all contributed to the state. Immigrant families in the state represent every country in Europe. Scottish, Irish and Scandinavian immigrants came to Texas in particularly large numbers.

Texas in the Popular Consciousness

On the surface, it is easy to overlook the great diversity embodied in the reality of Texas. To a great extent, the world's image of Texas is formed by movies about Texans and in turn, the popular conception of a Texan is defined by the image of the cowboy. While they cannot present a complete picture, many of these iconic movies are a source of pride for those who call themselves Texan.

Perhaps the most well known portrayal of Texas and Texans occurs in the movie *Giant*, filmed in Marfa in 1955. Rock Hudson, James Dean, and Elizabeth Taylor starred in this Academy Award-winning epic of a family struggling to make the transition from frontier to modern day Texas. The roughhewn character Dean portrayed in his third and final movie role left a lasting impression of the rags-to-riches Texas oilman and his ways of excess – pointy boots, ten-gallon Stetsons and all. Dean's character in *Giant* was actually modeled on infamous wildcatter Glenn McCarthy, an Irish immigrant who struck it rich in oil. McCarthy spent an unheard of $25 million building Houston's Shamrock Hotel, which opened on St. Patrick's Day, 1949.

John Wayne played Davy Crockett in *The Alamo*, shot in Texas in 1959. In real life, Crockett was probably quite different than Wayne's character in appearance and personality. Certainly Crockett and the defenders of the Alamo were no less brave.

The film version of the outlaw life and bloody death of *Bonnie and Clyde* was shot outside Dallas in 1967. This classic stars Warren Beatty and Faye Dunaway. The gangsters fled thorough Texas before meeting a violent end amid a blaze of Texas Ranger gunfire.

More recently, the border towns have captivated the imagination of moviemakers. *El Mariachi*, the predecessor to *Desperado*, was shot in Ciudad Acuna, Mexico (just across the border from Del Rio). El Mariachi propelled writer/director/Austinite Robert Rodriguez to fame. *Lone Star*, an acclaimed 1994 release directed by John Sayles, may have had a fantastic story line but the setting and the characters were realistically plucked from the southwest Texas border.

Naturally no discussion of the Texas image would be complete without a nod to the television series *Dallas*. Millions of viewers followed the scandalous affairs of the wealthy (oil, of course!) Ewing family, and Texans who travel are still likely to encounter the question, "is Texas really like that?" The show was trashy, glamorous, campy fun and — fortunately — highly unrealistic.

Ever since there's been a Texas, its musicians have influenced music across genres and decades, and in return the Texas image has been influenced by its music. The music of Texas is a product of influences as diverse as the cultures of the state. Blind Lemon Jefferson, Huddie (Leadbelly) Ledbetter, and T-Bone Walker created the Texas blues in the clubs of Deep Ellum in 1920s Dallas. The Houston sound was born in the segregated Third, Fourth, Fifth, and Sixth wards where Sam (Lightnin) Hopkins and Bobby Blue Bland played and sang. Lubbock claims one of the pioneers of rock and roll, Buddy Holly, although the staid city elders disapproved of his raucous guitar music. Janis Joplin sang her blend of rock and blues in Austin before becoming an international celebrity. A native of Beaumont, Joplin attended the University of Texas before skyrocketing to fame.

Johnny Winter hails from sweltering South Texas. Guitarist Stevie Ray Vaughn brought the blues back to the forefront of the music scene about a decade ago. Vaughn's tragic death in a helicopter crash shook the music industry and the state. Another musician who died violently and prematurely was Selena, a Tejano superstar who hailed from Lake Jackson and achieved phenomenal popularity before her murder in Corpus Christi. Willie Nelson and Waylon Jennings, who made Luckenbach famous in the annals of country music, both hail from Texas. George Jones developed his brand of heartbreak song in East Texas. Lyle Lovett and his Big Band sound bridge the gap between jazz and country.

You will have no problem easing into Texan style. Texans are warm and welcoming hosts, and this is sure to be the only stereotype of Texans you will find to be completely true.

Texas, the Mother of all Capitals!

Austin, the state capital, is the seat of state government and also the home of The University of Texas. Many of the towns around the state have proclaimed themselves to be "capitals" in their own right. Austin modestly calls itself the **Live Music Capital of the World**.

In the Hill Country, you will find Bandera, the **Cowboy Capital of the World**. Stonewall, the birthplace of Lyndon Baines Johnson, is dubbed the **Peach Capital of the World**.

East Texas has food-related capitals. Jacksonville calls itself the **Tomato Capital of Texas**. Athens is proud to claim the title of **Black-eyed Pea Capital of the World**.

Temple, about 80 miles north of Austin, is the **Wildflower Capital of Texas**. Not to be outdone, Brenham, in east central Texas, is known as the **Bluebonnet Capital of the World**.

a short history

Chapter 5

At one time much of central Texas was submerged under the prehistoric ocean. If we could venture back about 100 million years, Texas would be a genuine Jurassic wonderland. From the late Triassic (about 200 million years ago) to the late Cretaceous (about 70 million years ago) dinosaurs roamed the lands of west, central and northern Texas.

Texas even has its own unique dinosaurs. Wandering the area with the better-known Tyrannosaurus was the Alamosaurus, a plant-eater who weighed about 30 tons. Alamosaurus was found near San Antonio, and was named after the state's most treasured monument, the Alamo. The Technosaurus was a tiny meat-eater that lived in North Texas. This dinosaur was discovered and named by researchers from Texas Tech University in Lubbock.

For much of its existence, Central Texas was probably a marshy, coastal land. A shallow sea covered what is today the Hill Country. West Texas presumably was covered with thick vegetation, hard to imagine when looking at the now cactus-covered desert. West Texas yields the greatest variety of fossil remains, but Central Texas has the greatest abundance. Weekend anthropologists can find the fossil remains of small sea creatures in most dry creek beds and rock faces in the Hill Country.

The first traces of human occupation date to sometime around the tenth millennium BCE. It is believed that people may have entered the territory of what is now Texas while migrating to South America. Many assumptions about their lifestyle come from the archaeological remains of a buffalo kill found in **Caprock Canyon**, near Lubbock. The site may date to 10,000 years ago.

Prehistoric civilizations in Texas carried on trade and lived as tribal communities as early as 8000 BCE, when skilled hunters dominated the vast plains to the north. The traces of the ancient past indicate the land offered an abundance of flora and fauna for ancient tribespeople. Yet for the most part the culture of the early Texans remains covered by mystery. Sparse archaeological remains leave the details of early societies unknown.

Even in ancient times a variety of cultures comprised the peoples of Texas. During the fourth millennium cave dwellers inhabited southwest Texas. The area was far more fertile and had a better water supply than today. The paintings they made on the walls of communal dwellings show artistic representation unlike any other in the world. Some of this cave art, which is believed to depict shamans and animals, can be visited.

A dramatically different culture thrived later in East Texas. The **Caddo**, related to the Mississippian culture, occupied the east Texas woods as early as 1000 BCE. They left their mark with ceremonial mounds that stand near Crockett, Texas. The Caddo were farmers and traders who had a rich material culture. Their civilization left the area for unknown reasons around 1100 AD.

The European Conquest

The lives of Native Americans in Texas proceeded unhindered by European interference until the Spanish conquest of Mexico in the seventeenth century. In 1519 the Spanish explorer Alonso Alvarez de Pineda sailed along the Texas coast and made the first known map of the region. When Spaniards set foot on Texan soil, they did so by accident.

In 1541 a shipwreck in the waters off Galveston left **Cabeza de Vaca** among the stranded crew. The men spent years as captives of the Karankawa of the Texas coast, a native tribe known for their strength and ferocity. In the end only four Spaniards survived. Cabeza de Vaca was among them and ventured on through south and west Texas for years.

The Spanish, thirsty for gold and riches, quickly pushed land exploration through Mexico, Texas, New Mexico, and Louisiana. **Francisco Coronado** traversed the Chihuahuan desert of West Texas seeking the fabled Seven Cities of Gold. He and his men did not find the cities and their fantasies of magical riches remained unfulfilled.

When the English first began to colonize Virginia, the Spanish had spent nearly a century mapping and exploring Mexico, Texas, and the American West. Despite early enthusiasm about the possibility of wealth in the New World, the Spanish found it difficult to live in Texas due to the harsh climate and long, difficult travel routes.

After conquering Tenochitlan (Mexico City), the Spanish concentrated on spreading their rule throughout central Mexico. They moved slowly into Texas, Louisiana, and the American West, all part of the Spanish/Mexican Empire.

The Spanish did not attempt to establish the first mission in Texas until 1619, some 162 years after Hernan Cortez defeated the Aztecs in Mexico. The first small settlement in East Texas quickly failed due to difficult conditions and isolation. Over 60 years later, in 1682, the first mission to endure was built, Corpus Christi de Isleta, near El Paso.

The Spanish explorers and merchants settled land grants in the fertile parts of Mexico, leaving the northern territories, including Texas, to the missionaries and their had ecclesiastical goals. Spanish missionaries worked in brutal environments, often in areas where the Native Americans were hostile toward outside influence. Mission life was extremely difficult; frequently missions had to be moved and reestablished in areas with better resources or a more acquiescent population. There are at least fifty mission sites in Texas, but only a handful of structures remain.

One of the main roads used during the Spanish and early Mexican times was known as *El Camino Real para los Texas*, The Royal Road to Texas. From 1690 to the mid-nineteenth century this road served as the main artery of commerce, communication, and migration for colonists. The Spanish developed the route along established trails used for generations by Native Americans.

The road stretched from Coahuila, Mexico to Louisiana, which was then called Los Ades. It passed through Saltillo, Mexico then broke into two branches - one going through Laredo, the other through Guerero. The branches met in San Antonio and continued through present-day Houston and East Texas. By the time the **San Antonio Valero Mission (the Alamo)** was founded, the route from Mexico City to Louisiana was well traveled. From the years 1691 to 1800 the Alamo was a central stopping point for travelers going to the small settlements of East Texas.

The Spanish were not the only ones curious about Texas. The French explorer **La Salle** sailed along the Texas coast and ventured into East Texas.

Driving El Camino Real Today

Much of the oldest part of **El Camino Real** can be traced by car today. Interstate Highway 35 from San Antonio to Austin was part of the earliest trail. A route known as the Camino Arriba, or High Road, was used from 1795 to 1900. The modern highway system could not improve on the basic trail that cuts across the state diagonally, and you can drive along much the same road as the early travelers used. From San Antonio, take Interstate Highway 35 to San Marcos, then head east on Highway 21. Just past Caldwell you can take the OSR, Old San Antonio Road, which is a scenic loop back to Highway 21. The last Texas town on Highway 21 is San Augustine.

A French settlement existed in South Texas, but the precise location is unknown. The French began to destabilize the Spanish stronghold on East Texas but despite pesky land disputes did little else.

In 1821 Mexico won independence from Spain. The Mexican government continued offering land grants as the Spanish had done. That same year Stephen F. Austin's father, **Moses Austin**, received a land grant from the Spanish government. Moses Austin died soon after receiving the grant, leaving his son Stephen to take responsibility. **Stephen F. Austin** went to Mexico City where with some difficulty he renegotiated his claim with the new government.

Independence & Statehood

The movement for an independent Texas grew in the settlements around the East Texas homestead of Stephen F. Austin. These settlers would be the founders of the republic and later the state of Texas.

Austin brought the first Anglo settlers into Texas; most were from Tennessee. They are known as the **Texas Original 300**. The families moved into territory settled by the Cherokee in modern Van Zandt County. One of the oldest towns is **La Grange**, founded in 1831. The first capital of the colony was called San Felipe de Austin, established in 1837.

The Mexican government believed the Austin settlement would secure the land of Mexico's northern frontier for the capital, Mexico City. Austin's

Famous Texans from Tennessee

Many of the original Anglo settlers in Texas came from Tennessee. They contributed their lives and legacies to the founding of the state.

Sam Houston was a politician from Tennessee when he came to Texas in the early nineteenth century. Houston led Texas forces fighting for independence from Mexico at the battle of San Jacinto. He then served two terms as President of the Republic of Texas. He became one of the first United States Senators from the State of Texas, and returned to serve as governor.

Jim Bowie was famous for the thick-bladed knife he carried which became known as the Bowie Knife. Bowie was a defender of the Alamo and died with William Barret Travis, leader of the Texan forces, and Davy Crockett.

Crockett, Texas is named for the legendary frontiersman **Davy Crockett**. Recent evidence indicates that Crockett may have survived the siege of the Alamo and been held prisoner by General Santa Anna. Crockett possibly would have undergone torture and almost certainly been killed.

colony also was a strategic stronghold against the threat of French interven-
tion in the area. What the Mexican government failed to realize was that the
settlers had leaders who were fiercely independent and politically ambitious.

Frontier life was very dangerous. The arrival of settlers aroused the
hostility of Native Americans as more and more of their territory was taken
over. Also, bandits roamed the lonely lands west of the Mississippi. The settlers
felt that Mexico did not provide adequate protection. Sam Houston requested
frontier police from Mexico City. When no action followed, the locals took up
arms to protect themselves against their enemies.

In 1822 Austin organized a defensive militia. Once the Republic of Texas
became a reality, this group officially declared itself the **Texas Rangers**. The
myth of the Texas Rangers as men who enforced their own brand of justice
by any means they saw fit is probably well founded. The Texas Rangers also
did much to protect families, uphold laws, and provide assistance to rural
settlements. The Rangers stepped in to fight outlaws that local lawmen could
not or would not confront. And there were plenty of outlaws to keep the
Rangers busy. *The Lone Ranger*, by Zane Grey, is said to be based loosely on
the Texas Rangers. Today the Texas Rangers are a state law enforcement
agency.

Other issues besides safety strained relations between the settlers and
Mexico. When the Mexican government declared that no more land grants
would be issued to North Americans, the leaders of Austin's colony were
incensed. Numerous small uprisings characterized the struggle on the frontier.
The unrest became an official armed rebellion in 1835 when the Mexican army
insisted that the residents of Gonzales, in south central Texas, return a cannon
given to them by Mexico. The people of Gonzales refused by raising a flag that
read "Come and Get It." Battle ensued and the slogan became another
catchphrase of Texas history.

The prominent men of the Austin Colony met to decide the fate of their
homes and families. In a small wooden house on the banks of the Brazos River,
the Declaration of Independence for the **Republic of Texas** was signed on
March 2, 1836. Revolution was underway.

The forces of **General Santa Anna** were already moving toward Texas
to squelch the small rebellion. The Mexican Army greatly outnumbered the
Texans. Moreover, Santa Anna was a distinguished military officer with
superior weapons and professional troops. It appeared the Mexican army
would easily reestablish its authority.

On the march north from Mexico, the Mexicans encountered armed
resistance at the **Alamo**. Although the defenders of the Alamo knew they
were outmatched ten-to-one, they valiantly decided to engage Santa Anna.
The 13-day siege remains the most remembered battle of the war.

Those who fought for independence called themselves Texian. They
vowed revenge for the massacre at the Alamo. When Sam Houston's militia

Texas History Timeline

1519: The Spanish crown claims territory which will one day become Texas
1718: Construction of the first missions in San Antonio begins.
1821: Mexico wins independence from the Spanish crown.
1822: Stephen F. Austin enters Texas with North American settlers.
1836: Texas declares independence from Mexico. Mexican forces enter Texas to crush the revolt.
1846: Texas is annexed to the United States; US-Mexico War ensues

engaged Santa Anna's army at **San Jacinto**, near Houston, the battle cry "Remember the Alamo" echoed. Houston emerged victorious and the Republic of Texas was born.

Mexico never recognized the Republic of Texas as a nation, although the United States and European nations did. The Republic of Texas even sent an ambassador to London. Still, in the eyes of the Mexican government, the land of Texas remained part of the Mexican territory of *Cohuila y Tejas*.

The frontier did not become quiet; fighting continued between Native Americans and settlers. Border disputes continued to erupt with Mexico as well. One noteworthy attempt at statehood was made by a group of ranchers in the Laredo area. They formed the Republic of the Rio Grande that existed from 1839-1841 and declared its capital to be Laredo.

As a nation Texas looked very different than its famous outline. Parts of Colorado, New Mexico and Oklahoma composed the northern and western borders. When Texas entered the United States as the 28th state in 1845 it relinquished these lands.

The annexation of Texas meant the United States took on war with Mexico. With the strength of the United States military, Texas was able to secure its border against Mexico. The **Treaty of Guadalupe Hidalgo** ended the war with Mexico and granted the United States new territory which included Texas. As westward expansion ignited the imagination of Americans, Texas grew in population.

The Civil War & Its Aftermath

Before serious integration into the national economic system could begin, the state found itself deeply involved in yet another bloody conflict. The Civil War greatly disrupted the advancement of Texas. The trauma of the Civil War caused intense moral dilemmas to arise. The Governor of Texas, **Sam Houston**, was firmly against joining the Confederate States, and the German settlers throughout the state, many newly arrived, did not want to fight for principles with which they disagreed. Under the government of Spain, slavery had not been common. During Spanish rule many African-Americans lived in Texas as free men. They played a major role in the settlement of the lands and before the year 1800 constituted as much as one-fourth of the population. Mexico made slavery illegal, although Anglo settlers did not necessarily recognize the laws of the Mexican government. On the other hand, many Texans had relocated from Tennessee and other southern states and had connections to the economic concerns of the Deep South. Geographically and culturally, Texas was much closer to the Confederate States.

Texas elected to join the Confederacy, after a great deal of heated debate and the resignation of Governor Sam Houston over the issue.

Texas was officially the last state to learn of the Union victory in the Civil War. Even after the Confederate Army surrendered in April of 1865, Texans remained unaware of the end of the war due to slow transportation and poor communication. When soldiers finally arrived in Texas on June 19, 1865, the news of freedom began to spread.

It was two years after the Emancipation Proclamation declared that all slaves became free citizens that the State of Texas declared this to be the law of the land. Every year this day, June 19th, known as **Juneteenth**, is an official holiday and is celebrated throughout the state.

Texas earned the dubious distinction of waging the last battle of the Civil War. Near Brownsville, at Palmito Ranch, on May 12 1865, Confederate forces defeated Union troops, although the South had fallen one month earlier. Union occupation of Texas followed the Civil War, although little fighting had occurred in the state.

How Texas Became a State

Some Texans will tell you they live in the only state that was not really annexed into the United States. The claim is based on a technicality of history. The Republic of Texas voted to join the United States before the annexation was official. Once Texas became a state, the United States military moved into the territory to quell the fighting with Mexico.

According to the history of Mexico, the **Republic of Texas** never did exist. The lands of Texas were a cause of turmoil, but never recognized as independent. Mexico offered Texas to the United States as a condition of the end of the war between Mexico and the United States.

Regardless of the legislative processes at play, ceremonies for the annexation of Texas took place in Austin, Texas in 1846, and the President of the Republic of Texas, Sam Houston, presided.

During Reconstruction, the Texas frontier was without organized national protection. The United States military sent newly formed cavalry divisions to defend settlers and travelers against possible attacks by Native Americans. Many of the enlisted men were African-Americans; the Native Americans called them **Buffalo Soldiers** in admiration of their strength.

The Buffalo Soldiers endured some of the harshest conditions in the United States. The heat and arid climate made life at the Texas forts nearly unbearable. Officers attempted to exercise control through rigid daily routines and severe punishments for those who deviated from regulations.

From 1867 to 1885 cavalry and infantry units of Buffalo Soldiers were stationed at Fort Davis in West Texas. The fort held 12 companies and was one of the largest of its kind. Before the railroad, Fort Davis secured the traveler's route to New Mexico. This fort saw some of the most brutal fighting with the Apache and Comanche in Texas. The many forts served a variety of purposes including protecting stagecoaches and moving mail.

The military played a major role in the development of the economy. The forts that sprang up in the new territory employed many men. Soldiers, clergy, medical staff and educators all contributed to the fort communities and many settled in Texas. Cities benefited from the security of having soldiers nearby. The era of frontier forts was important but short-lived. Rapid changes, including an influx of settlers, growth of the cattle industry and building of the railroad made the badlands of Texas safer. Most of the frontier forts closed by 1870.

Frontier Forts

The United States Army established forts throughout the west, including north and west Texas. A visit to a fort gives insight to the difficult lives and uncomfortable conditions the soldiers faced.

Fort Clark in Bracketville housed a regiment of Seminole soldiers.

Fort Davis, near El Paso, was a primary stronghold against hostile Apache and Commanche.

Two of the largest forts, **Fort Concho and Fort Stockton**, were homes for the Buffalo Soldiers.

Fort Griffin was a trade center for area settlers.

Frontier Life

With the end of Reconstruction, the rise of the cattle barons began. During the mid-nineteenth century, as beef became an increasingly valuable commodity to the United States, new breeds of cattle were introduced to Texas. The wide-open land gave ranching the opportunity to prosper. Cities like Fort Worth and Abilene sprang up as commercial centers.

The famous **Chisholm Trail**, the cowboy's highway, ran from South Texas through Fort Worth to Kansas City. Dusty cattle drives were grueling tests of endurance for cowboys; their lives were more difficult than romantic. Fledgling cities that grew at stopping points on the cattle drives were notoriously rough domains. The era of the cowboy passed quickly also. After only 12 years rail transportation eclipsed cattle drives.

The West was conquered by the iron horse. In 1883 the final stake was laid that connected the **Southern Pacific Railroad** from El Paso to San Antonio. This changed the face of Texas forever. For the first time the remote desert regions were accessible to American settlers. As Americans claimed more land English soon replaced Spanish as the common tongue of the region.

Texas was neither rich nor cosmopolitan at the turn of the century. It was a land of opportunity - at least for the opportunistic. The rough and tumble country was a haven for those who wanted to flee justice, strike out solo or start anew. At that time cities were seen as unfit for true gentlemen and ladies, and remote roads through the countryside offered little protection for residents or travelers. Outlaws took advantage of this.

Many wild men passed through Texas; most moved on to the boomtowns of the West. **Doc Holliday** began his life of crime in Dallas, leaving his dentistry practice behind. **Wild Bill Hickock** frequented the cowtown of Abilene. Still others stayed in Texas permanently, not by choice but by the firing of a gun.

John Wesley Hardin was both a family man and an outlaw. He moved between north and east Texas, and from time to time attempted to leave a life of crime. His reputation as a ruthless killer and inability to steer clear of trouble caught up with him in West Texas, where he was killed in 1895.

Although different tales tell conflicting stories, Hico claims to be the last home of and place where **Billy the Kid** died. Supposedly "the Kid" lived to the age of 90 and died of natural causes. This contradicts the stories of his flight to South America, but no one knows what version of history is true. The Billy the Kid Museum in Hico tells its own version of the outlaw's life.

The beginning of the twentieth century marked a difficult time for the state of Texas. The vast majority of people lived in the countryside and struggled as farmers. Still, Texans strove to pull their societies into the cultural forefront. A wave of construction swept through the state. Many courthouses were constructed at this time.

Some of the buildings were monumental in their design and materials. The most popular styles of the time, Renaissance Revival, Romanesque and French Second Empire, were European-influenced. Often the finest granite, limestone and native wood were used. Towns grew up around the courthouse squares, which became the center of social life in small towns.

Other monumental buildings include the Carnegie Libraries. Texas benefited greatly from the generosity of the Carnegie Foundation, which allocated funds to bring libraries to small communities. Thirty-four Carnegie

Majestic Courthouses of Texas

Many courthouses in Texas are exemplary Victorian buildings. **Lockhart**, the seat of Caldwell County, has a beautiful courthouse built in 1894 in the French Second Empire style. Tall, green-tiled towers and arched windows accent the limestone building.

The height of Victorian design in Texas is marked by the use of red brick and fanciful ornamental elements. The **Gonzales County courthouse**, built in 1894, has repetitive arches and columns of the Renaissance Revival architectural style. The courthouse is in the center of the town of Gonzales.

The **Erath County courthouse**, built in 1892, stands in Stephanville. Solid, square lines in heavy limestone blocks are offset by a red roof and red sandstone window frames. The large center clock tower dominates the city skyline.

Libraries were built around the turn of the century. Few of the Greek Revival buildings remain, and none are still used as libraries. Courthouses and libraries aside, most of Texas was anything but a peaceful haven of culture.

Technological changes brought further restructuring of the Texas economy. Riverboats, initially a vital method of transport and communication, disappeared as shipping and rail transportation gained a stronghold. Oil would fuel the new systems, but it took nearly twenty years for the industry to take shape.

Black Gold, Texas Tea

In the year 1901 the face of Texas changed forever, due to the unexpected discovery of a gusher in a salt dome formation outside of Beaumont, Texas. Mud, then gas, then thick black oil literally exploded out of the **Spindletop Oilfield**, sending six tons of drilling pipe ahead of it and creating a geyser over 100 feet high that took nine days to cap. The gushing Texas crude would usher in another phenomenon — the boomtown.

Communities based on quick money and hard labor sprang up across north and east Texas. Between January of 1901 (when Spindletop was tapped) and September of that year, Beaumont's population rose from 10,000 to 50,000. Workers flooded the towns hoping to earn quick money. A few impressive fortunes were made as well by people who could find oil by instinct. They were called **wildcatters**, and their abilities (not to mention their luck) were instrumental in shaping an industry that had yet to develop technological tools.

The companies that would become Texas oil giants were born at this time. The father of Howard Hughes made his first million producing parts for oilrigs.

Those who made the big money eagerly spent it. Stores that would grow into some of the nation's leading retailers, Neiman-Marcus and Sakowitz, opened during this era.

The economic contrasts in Texas were evident in the disparity between the wealthy and very poor, as well as in moral diversity. Even as boomtowns teemed with dance halls and saloons, the foundations of the **Bible Belt** were being laid. Small well-established towns had no use for decadence. Texans already had a history of temperance, and national Prohibition merely inflamed the controversy that already raged. The legacy of Prohibition remains to this day, as "dry" counties that restrict the sale of alcohol still exist.

Other changes were not the handiwork of man, but of nature. At the turn of the century **Galveston** was one of the largest cities in the state, with a population of about 50,000. The town, once a haven for pirates, retained its wild reputation into the twentieth century. Galveston overshadowed its sister city, Houston, and boasted the largest port on the Gulf of Mexico. In 1900 a fierce hurricane ripped through the town, destroying it almost entirely. Over 5000 people died and Galveston never regained its prominence.

Texas contributed soldiers and resources to World War I and a battleship proudly bore the state's name. **Battleship Texas**, docked outside Houston, is now a tourist attraction. It is not the only warship to be named after Texas. More recently a nuclear submarine was named after the city of Corpus Christi, which is the home of a naval air station. The name had to be changed when complaints about the implications of its Latin meaning (Body of Christ) were voiced.

The oil industry helped buoy Texas through the Great Depression. While the nation struggled though economic despair, Texas became the largest producer of oil in the country. Although the general population suffered through hard times, Texas became known as the land of oil barons. This added the tycoon, a new persona to the mythical figures of Texas.

Howard Hughes, a native of Houston, exemplifies the wealthy Texan stereotype. His father manufactured equipment for oil drilling, and began the fortune for which the more famous son would be known. Hobby Airport was first named Howard Hughes Airport, after he built the facility's first control tower in 1938. The name was changed because federal law denies government funding to an airport named for a living person.

The infamous gangsters **Bonnie and Clyde** briefly brought the wild west back to Texas when they spent over two years traversing the state as fugitives, with the Texas Rangers in pursuit. Bonnie Parker was born in Rowan, Texas and spent time in the Kemp, Texas jail. Their path went from Dallas to San Antonio, then through East Texas. With the Texas Rangers hot on their trail, the pair was gunned down just over the border in Louisiana in 1933.

Modern Texas

During World War II, Texas made yet another contribution of note. **Admiral Chester Nimitz** hailed from the small town of Fredericksburg. Today you can visit the boyhood home of Nimitz, and stroll through a museum that documents his life and monumental role in the War in the Pacific.

After the end of World War II, Texas benefited from the various governmental agencies that constructed bridges, highways and parks. Many of the lakes that now are enjoyed by thousands annually were constructed as part of these programs.

Along with the rest of the nation, Texas enjoyed the economic prosperity of the 1950s. As the Texas economy gained strength large cities like Dallas began to construct monumental buildings downtown. Small towns boomed as well. Many downtowns and main streets are lined with classic 1950s all-American buildings. The simple squared-off storefronts with large display windows are unmistakable. Department stores and drug stores sprang up to temper the last wilderness areas of the state.

Texas became a system of small cities, thus moving away from an economy dominated by rural farming communities. In many ways the state grew closer. Farm-to-market and Ranch-to-market Roads were replaced by major highway systems.

Texas struggled through the socially turbulent years of the 1960s, riding waves of civil and political unrest. The atmosphere was often tense, especially

The Scandalous State

Texas has had its share of infamy thorough tragedy and scandal. The most well known stories are often the darker tales. One of the most shocking events took place in August 1966, when a lone gunman atop the University of Texas tower opened fire on the campus. Seventeen people died and the shooter was killed by police. The tower recently reopened in September 1999.

The Branch Davidians put themselves and Waco on the map during a nearly two-month standoff with the United States Government. In August of 1993 the compound that housed the religious group burned to the ground. Ninety people died, including four government agents. Controversy surrounding this tragedy still rages today.

The Republic of Texas attempted to rise again when an obscure group claimed the right to this historic name and declared themselves an independent nation. In 1997, in the West Texas Davis Mountains, the trailer that was called an "embassy" was the scene of yet another standoff with government agents. In the end, the group was taken into custody.

in the larger cities of Dallas and Houston. The political leaders that rose to power during this time brought Texas into the forefront of national politics. At no time before this era were Texans able to wield as much power and influence in Washington.

John Tower was the first Republican from Texas to be elected senator since the time of Reconstruction. John Connally, the state Governor, would become well known as a passenger in the Presidential motorcade in Dallas in November 1963.

The day President Kennedy was assassinated in downtown Dallas drew all eyes to the Lone Star State. The event epitomized the chaotic times in the nation, and in Texas. Although not as engulfed in civil unrest as some of the neighbors in the Deep South, Texas fought turbulent currents of crisis.

The national leader who assumed the presidency, **Lyndon Baines Johnson**, was an example of Texan strength and determination. LBJ brought the image of the Texan to the stage of international politics. His no-nonsense style, smooth southern accent and obvious will once again defined the Texan persona. While governing the nation, LBJ remained prominent in the state political arena, with opinions and frequent visits. He stayed close to Texas, often traveling to his family ranch in Central Texas.

The need for faster means of communication and transportation made Texas a logical area for the growth of the technology industry. **Texas Instruments**, based in Dallas, was at the forefront of the development of semi-conductors and silicon chips. **NASA** began operations of its base in Houston. And the science and engineering departments of state universities gained prestige and endowments.

With the onslaught of efficient transportation and the development of air-conditioning systems for the mass market, Texas experienced unprecedented population growth. The 1970s were a boom time for the Texas economy. The oil industry kept the crude flowing at higher and higher prices. High tech, although in its infancy, was an important part of the Texas scene.

Texas experienced a building boom in the early 1980s, in part to keep up with the many new residents and businesses in the state, and in part to keep pace with the thriving economy. Skyscrapers had been part of the Dallas and Houston skylines for years, but now the modern age was upon us. And with it amazing post-modern architectural marvels shot up, above the skylines. Even smaller towns, such as Fort Worth, Austin and El Paso now could boast concrete and steel high-rises.

Investment money flowed so fast that nobody foresaw the impending bust. Suddenly construction halted, prices plummeted and many lost their jobs. Many bankruptcies ensued as the business economy tumbled. Savings and loans, entangled in their own scandals and teeming with defaulted investments, began to crumble. Real estate prices plummeted and many of the new office building stood nearly vacant.

The economic rumblings that shook Texas slowly spread across the nation. As the national economy faced hard times, Texas had already begun a recovery. The 1990's saw the influx of business and industry. A number of major corporations choose Dallas for the relocation of their headquarters. The low cost and high standard of living in Texas cities easily appealed to workers around the nation. Central Texas became a center of the high tech industry, and remains so today.

Now Texas is wading, with the rest of the nation, through the economic crisis caused by the collapse of the dotcom and tech stocks. Hard hit has been Austin, the home of many extinguished Internet start-up companies. Also suffering are the cities of Houston (home to Compaq) and Dallas. The collapse of energy giant Enron has far-reaching effects on its home base of Houston. The current President of the United States, Texan George W. Bush, survived a controversial election only to face the worst terrorist event ever to take place on American soil, the World Trade Center and Pentagon attacks of September 11, 2001. Nevertheless, the mood in Texas remains optimistic. The current crises, both economic and of confidence, are seen by most Texans as temporary hurdles on the road to bigger and better things.

Today Texas is truly a melting pot. The state has an abundance of big business and thriving small enterprises. With the second highest population in the United States, the state is home to people of all nationalities and backgrounds. The rich history is a fascinating collage of this dynamic and ever-changing state.

The State Symbols

Texas has many symbols that identify its unique land and heritage. These symbols are part of the pride for which Texans are famous.

The **Texas Lone Star flag**, with horizontal fields of red and white and a vertical blue field with a single, large star, served as the banner of the Republic of Texas before the state joined the union in 1845. Texans are deeply proud of their flag, and you will see it flown along highways, in front yards and just about anywhere there's a breeze.

Also of symbolic importance are the **Six Flags of Texas**, which reflect the varied history of the state. The flags serve as a timeline of the state's evolution from wild unsettled territory to modern state. Each stage of the state's development contributed to its cultural characteristics. You will see these flags flying side by side throughout the state.

The first to claim the land with a banner were the Spanish. The Spanish flag flew over Texas from 1519 to 1685 and 1690 to 1821. The deepest roots in the land are those of Hispanic culture. As the first explorers in the New World, the Spanish preceded the Dutch who settled New England. Over 100 years passed before missionaries began to settle the area.

The French made a brief and ill-fated attempt to settle the Texas coast. The French flag waved over Texas from 1685 to 1690. No French war in Texan territory was waged between the leaders and settlers. Eventually the French claim simply faded.

Once Mexico gained its independence from Spain the Mexican flag flew over the state from 1821 to 1836. For years the Germans and settlers of other European origin set up their homes and shops under the rule of Mexico. The influence of Mexico is still pronounced in south Texas, which was a center of frontier trade.

The Flag of the Republic of Texas, which flew from 1836 to 1845, developed into the present design. Texas made its way as an independent entity with its own legislature and presidents for nearly a decade. The idea of a fiercely independent Texan persona survives in Texas heritage and identity.

During the Civil War, from 1861 to 1865, the Flag of the Confederacy was officially flown. This is not the red banner with an "x" of stars, which was the war flag. Texas did not enter the Confederacy without turmoil. The State Governor at the time, Sam Houston, vehemently opposed the Confederacy, and resigned from office rather than govern a Confederate state.

The Flag of the United States, flown from 1845 to 1861 and 1865 to the present, is often unfurled next to the state flag.

Other Official Symbols

If you drive through Central Texas in the spring, you will understand why the **bluebonnet** is the state flower. The countryside becomes covered with these faintly aromatic blue blossoms, which belong to the lupine family.

The **pecan** is the state tree, and you will have no problem finding native pecan nuts to sample. East Texas has the greatest concentration of pecan trees in the state, and consequently the best pecan pie in the world. Many of the trees grow wild and reach heights of 100 feet.

Contrary to popular belief, the fire ant is not the state insect. The state legislature chose the **monarch butterfly** as Texas' official insect. Monarch butterflies have large gold and black wings. They are the only butterflies known to migrate. You may be lucky enough to see swarms of monarchs during the late fall in central and north Texas.

Since 1927, the State of Texas has claimed the **mockingbird** as the official state bird. The **Guadalupe Bass** is the official state fish and can be caught in the fast flowing rivers of Central Texas. The official stone is **topaz**.

Trace Your Texas Genealogy!

If you think you may be part of Texas history, you can easily find out more about your ancestry. Archives, museums and libraries throughout the state are at your disposal. With the assistance of historical societies, you can find the most effective place to conduct your research. Many visitors come to Texas to rediscover their roots, and many Texans find their family history far more exciting than they had imagined.

The Texas State Library and Archives, *1201 Brazos Street, Austin, Tel. 512/463-5455, Monday-Friday, 8am-5pm, Website: www.tsl.state.tx.us,* is a good starting point for research. Their online network is extensive and allows you to do a lot of research by computer. The site can link to research centers that provide documents that are difficult to find even at libraries, such as the Federal Register. You can search military rosters and county tax records, and other state records are available on CD-ROM or microfilm. They even offer a link to professional researchers. You can ask a question about Texas genealogy via email, *geninfo@tsl.state.tx.us.*

One of the most important research centers is **The Alamo Library**, which is part of the grounds of the Alamo. The library has extensive reserves that deal with the founding of Texas and the battles for independence. The library is open to the public. For more information about the facilities or to begin research contact The Daughters of the Republic of Texas Library, *P.O. Box 1401, San Antonio, Texas 78295-1401, Tel. 210/225-1071, Fax 210/212-8514, Website: www.drtl.org.*

More information on early settlers and their families is available at the **Sam Houston Regional Library & Research Center**, *Tel. 409/336-8821.* The library holds archives of southeast Texas including public records, manuscripts and newspapers. Research must be done in the facility, which is located about 40 miles north of Houston near Liberty.

The **Dallas Genealogical Society,** *P.O. Box 12446, Dallas, Texas 75225, Tel. 469/948-1106, Website: www.dallasgenealogy.org,* provides researchers with information and links to other sites on the web. Data is accessible through an index of counties; you can e-mail contacts in Texas counties directly through the web page. Links to government records offices are also provided.

Fayette Heritage Museum and Archives, *855 South Jefferson Street, La Grange. Tuesday to Friday 10am to 5pm, Saturday 10am to 1pm, Sunday 1pm to 5pm,* has information about the founding families of the East Texas area. Many of the settlers in the area were part of Stephen F. Austin's Original 300 who came from Tennessee. The archive collection is open to the public.

If you think that your ancestors may have immigrated to Texas or the United States via the port of Galveston, the **Texas Seaport Museum** in Galveston maintains the Galveston Immigrant Database. This computerized database includes names of passengers and members of their traveling parties, age, gender, occupation, country of origin, ship name, dates of departure and arrival, and destination in the United States. You can access the database from your own computer at *www.tsm-elissa.org/immigration-main.htm,* or you may use the computer terminals in the Texas Seaport Museum, *Pier 21, Number 8, Galveston, Texas 77550, Tel. 409/763-1877, Fax 409/763-3037.*

planning your trip

Chapter 6

Texas is a tourist-friendly destination. You can obtain a wealth of information before you even set foot on Texas soil. We'll try to point out some of the best resources for information as we give you what we consider our own essential travel tips.

When to Visit

Texas is not exactly celebrated for its mild climate, but with a bit of planning you can have a comfortable visit even in the heat of summer. In general, the best time to visit any region of Texas is either mid-spring or mid-fall, when temperatures are moderate. However, because Texans rely so heavily on air conditioning, you can expect a pleasant journey even in the middle of July.

Summers throughout the state are blazing hot, with the highest temperatures usually occurring in the Lower Rio Grande Valley and West Texas. Central and East Texas can be very humid, while the north and west are arid. Always pay close attention to the heat index, which is the temperature adjusted for other conditions, such as humidity and wind. When temperatures exceed 90 degrees Fahrenheit, the heat index can be substantially higher. A day with a temperature of 90 degrees can affect your body as though you were in 110-degree weather.

When you're outdoors in temperatures over 80 degrees Fahrenheit exercise extreme caution against sun exposure and dehydration. In temperatures over 90 degrees, beware of heat exhaustion and sunstroke. The best protection is a hat, umbrella or shade, and drinking a lot of water.

Winter does sweep through Texas. In the Panhandle, the temperatures regularly dip below freezing and snow and ice are not uncommon. Most of the rest of the state experiences only a few weeks of cold temperatures in the middle of winter. When severe winter weather such as ice or freezing rain does occur, businesses often close. Since Texans do not get a lot of practice driving on ice, the roads become very hazardous in cold weather. It's been known for entire cities to shut down when a severe winter storm hits. Icy roads in general cause many businesses (including restaurants) to choose to close temporarily.

The various regions each have unique weather phenomenon. The Gulf Coast stands in the center of "hurricane alley," and tropical storms are a threat from June through October. The north central part of the state gets the most tornadoes. The months between April and June are when tornadoes are most likely. Funnel clouds often develop in severe thunderstorms, and can occur in any month.

When thunderstorms develop they can be accompanied by flash floods, tornadoes, high winds and lightning. Spring and fall often bring dramatic fluctuations in the temperature and rainstorms often accompany these changes. While visiting coastal areas, be certain to check the weather advisories before entering the water, especially when sailing. Coastal conditions can change rapidly and without warning.

Despite the frequent storms, water shortages recur in Texas. Drought conditions and water rationing are common, especially in densely populated areas. Even during years with intense flooding, droughts may develop during the long, hot summers. All regions of the state are subject to droughts that sometimes last years, so water conservation is an ongoing concern to Texans. Increased chances of grass fires threaten the state during the summer.

What to Pack

Dallas and Houston are the places where dressing really counts. The people of these cities follow trends more closely and choose to dress up more often than other Texans. However, many Texans pride themselves in being relaxed and most parts of the state require casual attire only. You can always find places where coat and tie attire is appropriate. But if you are more comfortable in khakis or jeans, you will have no problem finding places to fit in the crowd.

When traveling in the summer months, a hat and sunscreen are essential for comfort and safety. Nothing will ruin fun more thoroughly than bad sunburn. Shoes that offer protection from the hot pavement of streets but are still lightweight will make your sightseeing easier. Most places are air conditioned, so you may want to carry a light sweater to protect against the chill of the indoors. Nights are generally cool and comfortable throughout the state.

In the spring and fall in most parts of Texas, carrying an umbrella or light raincoat is a good idea. Winter can be dramatic and unpredictable throughout the state. In the northern part of the state, including Dallas and especially in the Panhandle, the dead of winter can be very cold. Hat, gloves, and coat are often required from December through March. West Texas, with its clear skies, desert climate, and high altitudes also experiences cold winters. Regardless of the time of year call a regional tourist bureau before planning an outdoor camping trip to get details about protecting yourself against the elements.

The climate of the majority of the state is best described as unpredictable, so the best advice is to be prepared for anything. In the winter temperatures may drop 20 degree or more when a "blue norther," or true cold front, blows through. On the other hand even in December it is common to have very warm days. Then, seemingly without warning, a week or two of ice and freezing weather may appear.

Texas Tourism Information

Texans love to share their state and their hospitality. You'll often get the best travel tips by talking to local folks who can tell you their favorite spots. Doing a bit of pre-trip research never hurts, either, and it will whet your appetite for the trip ahead.

You can obtain a wealth of information from the **Texas Department of Transportation**, *Tel. 800/452-9292, Website: www.dot.state.tx.us.* They provide information on highways (including maps), aviation regulations and reports on road conditions. If you are planning a driving trip, check here to avoid construction delays, road closures, and detours.

Another source of current information that is especially useful when trying to decide what part of the state to visit is **TravelTex**, *P.O. Box 12728, Austin, Texas 78711, Tel. 800/888-8TEX, Fax 512/936-0450, Website: www.traveltex.com/high/home.asp*, sponsored by the Texas Department of Economic Development. The Website is excellent and thorough, with information on all regions, suggested routes, and printable coupons for discounts at hotels and attractions throughout the state. You can request a free enormous Travel Guide from TravelTex by writing, calling, or visiting the website.

Texas Highways Magazine, *Tel. 800/839-4997, or from outside the United States 850/683-1394, Website: www.texashighways.com*, is highly recommended for travelers who want to explore the smaller towns of Texas. Armchair travelers and natives with an interest in the state will enjoy the excellent articles and gorgeous photography. The magazine spotlights life in Texas, often providing pertinent information for off-the-beaten-path trips. Monthly issues offer calendars of events, articles about culture and life in Texas and breathtaking photos of the same.

Regional visitor's bureaus can be a great resource when planning your trip. They often will gladly send area maps, information about events and accommodations. You can also find out if the city you plan to visit will be crowded at a particular time of year. Once you arrive, drop by the office to get more information about attractions in and around the area.

- **Austin Convention & Visitor's Bureau**, *201 East 2nd Street, Austin. Tel. 512/474-5171, Toll free 800/926-ACVB, Fax: 512/474-5182, Website: www.austin360.com/acvb.*
- **Dallas Convention & Visitors Bureau**, *100 South Houston Street, Dallas. Tel. 214/571-1000, Toll free 800/232-5527, Fax 214/571-1008, Website: www.dallascvb.com.*
- **El Paso Convention & Visitors Bureau**, *1 Civic Center Plaza, El Paso. Tel. 915/534-0600, Toll free 800/351-0624, Fax 915/534-0686, Website: www.elpasocvb.com.*
- **Fort Worth Convention & Visitors Bureau**, *415 Throckmorton Street, Fort Worth. Tel. 817/336-8791, Toll free 800/433-5747, Fax 817/336-3282, Website: www.fortworth.com.*
- **Greater Houston Convention & Visitors Bureau**, *901 Bagby Street, Houston. Tel. 713/437-5200, Toll free 800/365-7575, Website: www.houston-guide.com.*
- **San Antonio Convention and Visitors Bureau**, *203 South St. Mary's Street, 2nd Floor, San Antonio. Tel. 210/270-6700, Toll free 800/447-3372, Fax 210/207-8782, Website: www.sanantoniocvb.com.*

Texas Travel Specialists

If you have an interest in visiting Mexico, **Sanborn's**, *2015 South Tenth Street, McAllen. Tel 800/395-8482, Fax 956/682-0016, Website: www.sanborns.com*, has an extensive offering of tours that make travel south of the border easy and inexpensive. Sanborn's has over 50 years of experience taking tourists to Mexico. The tours originate in various South Texas towns and last from a few days to weeks. Prices begin at $169 and destinations include nearby Monterrey, the beautiful Copper Canyon, Mexico City, Acapulco and Oaxaca. All tours are by motorcoach and designed for limited activity and maximum comfort.

Texpert Tours, run by "Texas Back Roads Scholar" Howie Richey, *Tel. 512/383-TXTX, Website: www.io.com/~zow*, offers tours to those who wish to get off the well-trodden path and learn the history, nature and ecology of Texas. The Texas Back Roads Scholar himself guides the tours. He has spent his life studying the state, its culture, and scenery. The span of tour topics is vast, from brewpub tours to hiking and camping expeditions. Each tour is a unique experience and can include your special interests.

For those of you who want to get up close and personal with West Texas wilderness, **Texas River Expeditions**, *P.O. Box 583, Terlingua, Texas 79852, Tel. 915/371-2633 or 800/839-7238, Website: www.texasriver.com*, offers river rafting and jeep tours of the Big Bend area. Trips range from half-day excursions to 7-day treks, and many include special features like wine tastings, bed and breakfast stays, and stargazing activities with McDonald Observatory staff.

Although their headquarters are not in Texas, **Outpost Wilderness Adventure**, *P. O. Box 7, Lake George, Colorado 80827, Tel. 210/238-4788, Fax 210/238-4348*, specializes in mountain climbing adventure trips. Rock climbing, alpine climbing and mountain bike treks are scheduled throughout the summer in Texas. Destinations include Hueco Tanks and Enchanted Rock for rock climbing. This tour company also takes groups through Mexico's Copper Canyon in the northern state of Chihuahua.

Crossing the Border

If you plan to cross into a border town for a short visit, you need to present a valid **passport** or **United States driver's license** at the customs points. Other documents you may use to identify yourself include a birth certificate or voter's registration card with valid photo identification. Naturalized citizens should present their naturalization papers, and permanent residents should carry the appropriate cards.

If you are driving into Mexico in your own car, you must have **proof of ownership** in the form of the car's title or registration in your name. You cannot drive someone else's car into Mexico. If you are driving a rental car, you must present the **rental contract**, and it must be in your name. You must also have **written permission** from the rental agency to take the rental car into Mexico.

Visitors are required to present a **passport** when staying in Mexico 72 hours or longer or traveling more than 26 miles from the border. Citizens of countries other than the United States and Mexico are required to present a passport to enter Mexico and to enter the United States.

Visitors that enter Mexico by plane will have to present a passport and fill out a **tourist card**. These cards are obtained at the airport or from your travel agent and allow you to stay up to 180 days without a visa. You must carry this card with your passport and present it upon leaving Mexico. Should you lose the card you may be detained at the airport and possibly fined. Travelers will also be charged a tourist tax at Mexican airports. This fee may be included in the price of the ticket.

Over fifty countries have consulate offices in Texas; most are located in Houston, and to a lesser extent in Dallas. These offices can answer specific questions about travel across international borders. Mexico has consulates in 13 Texas cities.

Flying to Texas

Texas is well stocked both internationally and domestically with air travel options. You can fly nonstop from Dallas or Houston to London, Paris, New

Foreign Consulates in Texas

Consulate General of Canada, *750 North St. Paul Street, Suite 1700, Dallas. Tel. 214/922-9806, Fax 214/922-9815, Email: dalastd@dfait-maeci.gc.ca*

Consulate General of Colombia, *5851 San Felipe, Suite 300, Houston. Tel. 713/527-8919, Fax 713/529-3395, Email: ConsulbiaH@aol.com*

French Consulate, *777 Post Oak Boulevard, Suite 600, Houston. Tel. 713/572-2799, Fax 713/572-2911, Email: info@consulfrance-houston.org*

Consulate-General of Japan, *1000 Louisiana Street, Suite 2300, Houston. Tel. 713/652-2977, Fax 713/651-7822, Email:*

Consulate General of the Federal Republic of Germany, *1330 Post Oak Boulevard, Suite 1850, Houston. Tel. 713/627-7770, Fax 713/627-0506, Email: info@germanconsulatehouston.org*

Consulate General of Mexico:
- *200 East Sixth Street, Suite 200, Austin. Tel. 512/478-2866, Fax 512/478-8008, Email: consulmx@onr.com*
- *8955 North Stemmons Freeway, Dallas. El. 214/252-9250, Fax 214/630-3511, Email: consulme@airmail.net*
- *910 East San Antonio Avenue, EL Paso. Tel. 915/533-8555, Fax: 915/532-7163, Email: pressepa@elp.rr.com*
- *4507 San Jacinto Street, Houston. Tel. 713/271-6800, Fax 713/271-3201, Email: cgdemex@pointecom.net*
- *127 Navarro Street, San Antonio. Tel. 210/227-1085, Fax: 210/227-1817, Email: cgmexsat@dcci.com*

Royal Thai Consulate General, *3232 McKinney Avenue, Suite 1400, Dallas. Tel. 214/740-1498, Fax 214/740-1499*

British Consulate-General, *Wells Fargo Plaza, 1000 Louisiana Street, Suite 1900, Houston. Tel. 713/659-6270, Fax 713/659-7094*

York, and Los Angeles. At the other end of the spectrum, Texas offers an extensive system of commuter air connections. Most airlines serve Texas and many major airlines have extensive routes or hubs in Texas.

Domestic Airlines

With its hub in Dallas, **American Airlines**, *Tel. 800/433-7300, www.aa.com*, offers extensive flights between Texas and other cities. American Eagle serves smaller cities in Texas.

Continental Airlines, *Tel.800/525-0280, www.continental.com*, uses Houston as its hub and offers many flights to Latin America as well as an extensive domestic network. Continental Express links smaller Texas destinations.

Dallas' Love Field was the birthplace of **Southwest Airlines**, *Tel. 800/435-9792, www.southwest.com*. Now the airline has flights connecting many Texas cities and most of the United States.

Other major airlines that serve Texas:

- **America West**, *Tel. 800/235-9292, www.americawest.com*
- **Delta Airlines**, *Tel. 800/221-1212, www.delta.com*
- **Northwest Airlines**, *Tel. 800/225-2525, www.nwa.com*
- **United Airlines**, *Tel. 800/241-6522, www.ual.com*
- **US Airways**, *Tel. 800/428-4322, www.usair.com*
- For travel in the western region of the United States, **Frontier Airlines**, *Tel. 800-432-1359, www.frontierairlines.com*, has flights to El Paso or Dallas/Fort Worth.

Foreign Airlines

Many foreign carriers connect Texas with the rest of the world. Both George Bush Intercontinental Airport in Houston and the Dallas/Fort Worth Airport offer direct flights to Europe and easy connections to Asia. You can fly nonstop to numerous cities in Mexico from Dallas, Houston, and San Antonio.

- **Aeromexico**, *Tel. 800/237-6639, www.aeromexico.com*, connects Mexico City and Cancun to San Antonio, Houston and Dallas. Check the Aeromexico website for promotional fares that can make travel to Mexico affordable and easy.
- **Air Canada**, *Tel. 800/247-2262, www.aircanada.ca*
- **Air France Group**, *Tel. 800/237-2747*, flies nonstop from Paris to Houston and Dallas.
- **British Airways**, *Tel. 800/247-9297, www.britishairways.com*, offers direct flights between London and Houston and Dallas.
- **KAL Korean Air**, *Tel. 800/438-5000, www.koreanair.com*
- **KLM Royal Dutch Airlines**, *Tel. 800/374-7747, www.klm.nl*, is in partnership with Northwest Airlines.
- **Lufthansa**, *Tel. 800/645-3880, www.lufthansa.de*

Weather Wise

You can find out up-to-the minute **weather information** no matter where you plan to land in Texas. Before you get on the plane you can check out the weather conditions at most Texas airports by going to The Weather Channel's online service at ***www.weather.com*** and typing in your destination.

Getting Around Texas

By Air

Texas has one of the busiest airport systems in the United States. The largest airports in the state are **Dallas/Fort Worth International** and **George Bush Intercontinental** in Houston. All major cites handle air traffic. From their airports, you can easily find car rental agencies, shuttle services and taxi stands.

Southwest Airlines got its start operating out of Love Field in Dallas. The airline quickly became popular as a hassle-free, no-frills way to get around the state. Southwest offers direct flights between major cities and package trips to major tourist destinations in Texas. For more information contact Southwest Airlines, *Tel. 800/435-9792.*

The larger airlines operate services to the far reaches of the state. **American Eagle**, *Tel. 800/433-7300*, and **Continental Express**, *Tel.800/525-0280*, are the commuter divisions of their parent airlines.

Conquest Airlines, *Tel. 800/722-0860*, serves some of the smaller metropolitan areas of Texas. With its home base in Austin, Conquest has direct flights between Austin and Abilene, San Angelo, Tyler, Beaumont, Corpus Christi and San Antonio. Laredo and McAllen are served through San Antonio. The best fares are offered for tickets purchased at least two weeks before travel.

By Train

One way to escape the monotony of the long deserted drive through west Texas is to travel by train. **Amtrak**, *Tel. 800/USA-RAIL (872-7245)*, *www.amtrak.com*, has one major line that cuts across the state along much the same route as Interstate Highway 10. The Sunset Limited is a transcontinental route that runs between Los Angeles and Miami. The train has reserved coach seats, First Class sleepers, a dining car, a lounge and recreational activities such as movies. Rail passes are sometimes offered, making train travel more affordable to those who have the time to do it.

Amtrak Vacations, *Tel. 800/321-8684*, let passengers expand their itineraries with travel packages and add-on hotel options that include San Antonio. Texas cities on this route, from east to west, are Houston, San Antonio, Del Rio, Sanderson, Alpine and El Paso. In the small cities of Sanderson and Alpine, accommodations are within walking distance of the train station. In the large cities, the stations are downtown, a short taxi ride from hotels or bed and breakfasts.

When traveling on the Amtrak Southwest Chief, which runs between Chicago and Los Angeles, you can connect to Amarillo via Albuquerque by **Greyhound Bus**. The Greyhound Station is one block from the Albuquerque Amtrak Station, *Tel. 505/247-2581.*

By Boat

Norwegian Cruise Lines, *Tel. 800/327-7030, www.ncl.com*, sails from Galveston to ports in Mexico and the Caribbean. **Carnival Cruises**, *Tel. 800/327-9501, www.carnival.com*, offers four- and five-day cruises from Galveston to the Yucatan Peninsula. **Royal Olympic Cruises**, *Tel. 800/872-6400, www.royalolympiccruises.com*, operates cruises to Central America and Mexico from the Port of Houston.

By Bus

Both express buses and regular routes serve the state of Texas. **Greyhound Bus Service**, *Tel. 800/231-2222, www.greyhound.com*, lets you sit back and enjoy the scenery of the state.

The **Gray Line/Kerrville Bus Company**, *Tel. 800/256-4723, www.kerrville-bus.com*, is one of the largest charter bus companies in the state. The Kerrville Bus Company offers tours throughout the state, some that include lodging and meals. Kerrville Bus Company also offers specialized services for groups. Their gateway cities include many outside the state of Texas.

By Car

At one time a Texan depended on a trusty horse—now Texans rely on horsepower. Not every Texan has a car, but at times it certainly appears as though they do. Texas, with its winding country roads and long highways, seems to have been designed with road trips in mind. The best way to see the most of the state is behind the wheel of a car.

The highway system in Texas is extensive with over 76,000 miles of roads. The quickest route between large cities often is on interstate highways. One word of caution: since trade to Mexico has increased, so has truck traffic on the interstates. The section of Interstate Highway 35 that runs from Laredo to Dallas has some of the heaviest truck traffic in the state.

The speed limit on Texas highways ranges from 55 to 70 miles per hour. Naturally some Texans choose to speed, but be warned, the police do an excellent job of catching speeding vehicles, especially since radar detectors are not legal in Texas. Also, each town sets the fines for speeding tickets and these can be extremely high. All drivers are required to carry proof of liability automobile insurance and present this to police officers if pulled over. If you do not have a current policy when renting a car be certain to add the coverage to the rental agreement.

If you plan to make a highway trip, rent a car large enough to allow you to feel comfortable and safe. Although convertibles are beautiful and romantic, during the summer months air conditioning will be your best friend. Keep in mind that unless you already know precisely where you plan to go, you will probably want the rental rate for unlimited mileage. Even if you stay in one large city, you may put a few hundred miles on a car in just a few days.

These are some of the national rental chains that provide service in Texas. Often you will receive the best rates and availability through the toll-free desk. The representative can place your rental at the most convenient branch office. Local car rental agencies are listed in each chapter.

•**Advantage**, *Tel. 800/777-5500, www.carrentals.com*
•**Alamo**, *Tel. 800/327-9633, www.alamo.com*
•**Avis**, *Tel. 800/831-2847, www.avis.com*
•**Budget**, *Tel. 800/527-0700, drivebudget.com*
•**Dollar**, *Tel. 800/800-4000, www.dollar.com*
•**Enterprise**, *Tel. 800/325-8007, www.enterprise.com*
•**Hertz**, *Tel. 800/654-3131, www.hertz.com*
•**National**, *Tel. 800-227-7368, www.nationalcar.com*
•**Thrifty**, *Tel. 800/367-2277, www.thrifty.com*

Should a car not be big enough to keep you in comfort on the road, you can rent a recreational vehicle. **American Dream Vacations**, *28,840 Interstate Highway 10 West, Boerne, Tel. 830/755-8883 or 800/970-7372, Web site: txrvrent.com, credit cards accepted*, has tent campers, travel trailers and motorhomes for rent by the day, week or month. Trailers range from $65 to $105 per day with discounted rates for long rentals.

Highway Travel

When you come to Texas you have over 75,000 miles of highways at your disposal. All the state asks is that you observe the laws, which include mandatory auto insurance and wearing of front seat belts.

The weather in Texas is known to change at the drop of a ten-gallon hat. Every region of the state has its own severe weather threats. The gulf coast receives hurricanes, north Texas has its share of tornadoes, flooding plagues central Texas, and west Texas is known for windstorms.

There is a saying in Texas: if you don't like the weather, wait ten minutes. For current highway conditions and latest information and travel advisories about highway construction, exit closings and weather, call the **State Department of Highways and Public Transportation**, *Tel. 800/452-9292*, or visit the Texas Department of Public Transportation's website, *www.dot.state.tx.us*.

Some of the most valuable resources for travelers are the **State Information Centers** found on major routes and by state borders. You can find free information about the entire state, including maps, tourist information and advice. Texas Travel Information Centers are found on the following highways:
•when arriving from the north on Interstate Highway 40, near Amarillo
•when arriving form the south, on Interstate Highway 35, near Laredo

•when arriving from the west, on Interstate Highway 10, near Anthony
•when arriving from the east, on Interstate Highway 10, near Orange

Two major Interstate Highways cross Texas. **Interstate Highway 10** runs east/west, through Houston and San Antonio to El Paso. Jacksonville, Florida and Los Angeles, California are at either end of Interstate Highway 10. Both Oklahoma and Mexico are connected to Texas by **Interstate Highway 35**. Running north to south, Dallas, Austin, San Antonio and Laredo lie on Interstate Highway 35. In San Antonio Interstate Highway 37 branches off to Corpus Christi and the Gulf Coast. Texas uses the highway and warning signs that are standard throughout the United States.

Rest areas are found throughout the state. Many people stop for a picnic, to walk around or to take a short nap. Some of these areas have historical markers and small park areas. Along large highways rest areas and vending machines may be available.

U.S. Highways in Texas
•**US 281** goes from North Dakota through San Antonio to McAllen, Texas.
•**US 90** begins in Jacksonville, Florida and continues through San Antonio.
•**US 87** runs from Raton, New Mexico through San Antonio and south to Port Lavaca, Texas.
•**US 181** connects San Antonio to Corpus Christi.
•**US 81** runs south from San Antonio to Laredo and continues through Nuevo Laredo, Mexico.

Texas Highway & Road Signs
RR: Ranch to Market Road
FM: Farm to Market Road
US: United States Highway
IH: Interstate Highway

Rural Roads
The older roads called **Farm-to-Market Roads** or **Ranch-to-Market Roads** connect small towns. Back roads often take you through the most scenic and interesting areas.

Since there are so many rural areas, the state has a few laws that apply to these settings specifically. When driving on a two-lane highway, you must yield to a car that wants to pass. When you enter a free-range area (marked by warning signs with animal icons) the animals have the right of way. At a livestock crossing, you must stop to let animals pass. Injuring or killing an animal in these protected areas carries a large fine.

Other driving habits are observed as courtesy. For example, when a car on a two-lane road wants to pass, the lead driver will pull as far onto the shoulder as possible to give the passing driver plenty of room. The most important of the many unwritten rules that Texans observe is a friendly wave in the rear-view mirror that is the standard "thanks" gesture.

You will find emergency phones along the major highways and in rest areas. When driving in rural areas, the State Highway Patrol assists drivers in trouble. You can call the **State Highway Department Hotline**, *Tel. 800/525-5555*, for roadside assistance.

The **American Automobile Association**, *Tel. 800/765-0766*, has 15 offices in Texas and offers 24-hour road service, *Tel. 800/222-4357*, for members.

By Ferry

Although you cannot take any major trips by ferry in Texas, if you have the opportunity to ride on a ferry, do it. The Port Aransas ferry crossing, just north of Corpus Christi, gives you the opportunity to see porpoises. You can ride a hand-pulled ferry across the Rio Grande. Other ferries include the crossing to Matagorda Island and the enjoyable ride from Galveston to the Bolivar Peninsula.

Traveling to Mexico

When taking an extended trip to Texas, remember that easy access to Mexico is one of the best bargains the state offers. The adventurous can embark on a train trip from Laredo (Nuevo Laredo, Mexico) or El Paso (Juarez, Mexico) into the interior of Mexico.

You can find bargain-priced all-inclusive package trips from major Texas cities. The best time for low fares is during the summer (from May to September) when travel to resorts slows down. The trips are advertised in the Sunday editions of *The Dallas Morning News* and *The Houston Chronicle*. Most travel agents can assist with trips to Mexico.

The easiest way to go to Mexico is to just walk across the border. The largest border cities are **Laredo** and **El Paso**. Naturally, bigger is not always better, and you may prefer the quaint atmosphere of the smaller border cities in the lower Rio Grande Valley or the villages across from West Texas.

The only document you need to cross the border by foot is a valid drivers' license or government issued photo identification card. Citizens of the United States may remain in Mexico for 72 hours without a special permit.

Driving in Mexico

Mexico uses kilometers to measure speed. A rule of thumb is that 60 miles per hour equals 100 kilometers per hour. Citizens of the United States are permitted to drive across the international bridges that connect border towns. The main traffic route is through Laredo on Interstate Highway 35. Brownsville and Hidalgo (near McAllen) are other major highway routes. In order to have an extended stay or drive into the interior of the country, you must have a special travel permit. Contact the Mexican Consulate to obtain forms and documents for your trip. It is best to have all your documents in order before you reach the border.

If you are not going to exceed the bounds of the Border Zone during your visit to Mexico, there are no special procedures you must perform. You may drive across the border without presenting any special documentation about vehicle ownership and insurance. You may travel freely within a fifteen-mile limit from the border crossing.

If you plan to go beyond the fifteen-mile limit, you are required to obtain a permit. You must present proof of vehicle ownership and United States automobile insurance. Once you cross the border into Mexico, your United States insurance policy probably does not provide coverage for accidents in Mexico. You can purchase temporary policies for Mexico. Contact your insurance company for advice concerning your specific situation. One of the oldest and largest traveler's insurance companies in Mexico is **Sanborn's U.S. Mexico Insurance Service**, *2212 Santa Ursula Street, Laredo, Tel. 210/722-0931.*

Customs Restrictions

Routine searches of vehicles and people are common at the border crossings. When driving to a border city in the United States, you may be required to stop at vehicle inspection point to answer questions about your trip. These immigration checkpoints are set up on most highways in Texas.

Tourists must obey certain restrictions on the items they bring back into the United States. Every 30 days, you may bring 100 cigars and 10 packages of cigarettes without paying a duty. Cuban cigars may not be brought back, and the minimum age to transport tobacco is 18 years.

Adults over the age of 21 years may bring one quart of alcohol, one case of beer (in 12 ounce bottles only), three gallons of wine without paying a duty. Beyond this limit you must pay a per item duty. Up to $400 of goods is duty-free. Produce, plants, and animals are not permitted.

Accommodations
Hotels & Motels

Texans enjoy luxury and style; this much is apparent in the beautiful hotels that grace the state. Dallas and Houston undoubtedly offer the most opulent hotels. From the urban resort of the Houstonian to Dallas' extravagant 1000-room Anatole, you can find exclusivity in a wide range of tastes.

Perhaps the most charming are the many historic hotels in Texas. Built during the 1920s, the Adolphus in Dallas, the Menger in San Antonio, and the Lancaster in Houston offer the highest standards the travel industry has to offer, and all in historic settings of taste and sophistication.

Each destination chapter will cover the best hotels individually. Some of these hotels are independent; while others are affiliated with the major chains we are all familiar with. Since it is impossible to include every hotel under each destination, listed below are the contact numbers for the largest hotel chains in Texas. We recommend the individual chapters if you are interested in the finest hotel experience in your chosen city, but if you're having trouble booking the hotel you want, try one of the numbers below. You may have to settle for an outlying location, but you're almost always guaranteed a quality stay with these experienced hoteliers.

The highways of Texas have a multitude of lodging options. Hotels tend to be grouped at interchanges of major highways. Quite a few of the accommodations are new and have high standards of service, providing excellent rooms at low rates. Such amenities as complimentary continental breakfast, fitness facilities and an indoor or outdoor pool are not uncommon. You should expect all rooms to have standard amenities such as cable television, phones, and non-smoking room options. Many hotels permit children to stay free with parents. Some offer playgrounds for children or areas for walking your pets.

Whether you elect to stay at a luxury inn or a chain motel, it's worth your time to check for discount rates. Take advantage of weekend specials, package deals, and Internet rates. Depending on your dates of travel, you can save significantly with off-peak rates. Just one example: At the enormous (and enormously popular) Adam's Mark in Dallas, peak rates range from $145 to $225. The off-peak rates plummet to $75-$189. Many hotels belong to "frequent lodger"-type clubs that allow you to earn points towards rewards, upgrades, and free stays. Finally, although we give you a range of rates for each hotel we list, keep in mind that rates fluctuate according to all sorts of circumstances, so please call ahead to confirm prices. You just may be pleasantly surprised!

Deluxe Lodgings
Try any of these high-end chains for deluxe accommodations:
- **Hilton**, *Tel. 800/916-2221*
- **Hyatt**, *Tel. 800/532-1496*
- **Omni**, *Tel. 800/843-6664 (THE OMNI)*
- **Sheraton**, *Tel. 800/325-3535*
- **Wyndham**, *Tel. 800/822-4200*

Moderate Lodgings
Best Western, *Tel. 800/528-1234*, has over 100 locations in Texas, in all large urban areas and many popular vacation spots. Many of the Best Westerns are new and some offer special amenities such as health and recreational facilities. The rates are usually reasonable and the standard of the rooms and

service very good. Perks like complimentary morning coffee and courtesy vans to airports make the hotels comfortable places when taking long trips.

The **Marriott Hotels** group includes lower priced hotel chains. **Courtyard Inn**, *Tel. 800/321-2211*, offers well-appointed motels, as does **Fairfield Inn**, *Tel. 800/228-2800*.

Holiday Inn, *Tel. 888/223-2323*, has four types of motels, ranging from resorts to the Holiday Inn Express, which are located on major highways.

Choice Hotels International, *Tel. 800/327-9155*, operates six hotel chains, including Clarion, Rodeway and Econo Lodge.

Other hotel chains that offer accommodations in Texas include:
- **Days Inn**, *Tel. 800/329-7466 (DAYS-INN)*
- **Hampton Inn**, *Tel. 800/426-7866 (HAMPTON)*
- **Howard Johnson** *Tel. 800/446-4656 (I-GO-HOJO)*
- **La Quinta Inn**, *Tel. 800/531-5900*
- **Ramada**, *Tel. 800/272-6232 (2-RAMADA)*
- **Quality Inn** *Tel. 800/228-5151*

Budget Lodgings
- **Motel 6**, *Tel. 800/466-8356*
- **Super 8**, *Tel. 800/800-8000*

Longer Stays
You can find hotels that are entire apartments or suites. These are excellent choices on long trips, when space and amenities such as a kitchen are desired. **Doubletree**, *Tel. 800/222-8733*, offers exceptional suites in luxuriously decorated buildings. **Embassy Suites**, *Tel. 800/362-2779*, also has large suites with kitchenettes or full kitchens. The **Marriott Residence Inn**, *Tel. 800/331-3131*, has apartment-style suites geared for long stays, as does **Homewood Suites**, *Tel. 800/225-5466*.

B&Bs
The bed and breakfast scene continues to expand in Texas, as residents and visitors alike discover the advantages of personalized service. All sorts of homes operate as bed and breakfasts and experiences can vary greatly, so do try to research your choice in advance.

From small towns to large cities, most areas now have some bed and breakfast (B&B) inns. Many are housed in historic homes or other buildings filled with antiques and an air of luxury. Others are simply run as guest rooms in modern houses. Still others sit in rural surroundings and offer you opportunities to hike, ride on horseback, or swim.

For many guests, the "breakfast" part of bed and breakfast is the highlight of their stay. Most breakfasts are homemade and you will usually have your choice of several items. Some inns offer elaborate weekend brunches, served on fine china. Often the proprietors are enthusiastic cooks, who can prepare dinner or picnic lunches for a fee. Most innkeepers are in town for a reason, and that reason is that they love the area. They can be a font of useful information, suggestions, and anecdotes.

Don't hesitate to discuss details of the arrangements with the proprietor when you make reservations. Many inns impose rules such as no children, no smoking, and so on. Minimum stays may be required at certain times of the year.

The bed and breakfast experience is always unique. Perhaps the most charming aspect of a stay at a bed and breakfast is the chance to learn firsthand about the history, legend, and quirky characteristics of the town you're in – things you'd never get at a chain motel.

Our favorite bed and breakfast resource is **HAT**, which stands for **Historic and Hospitality Accommodations of Texas**, *3353 Park Lane, Chappell Hill, Texas 77426, Tel. 800/428-0368, email: info@hat.org, Website: www.hat.org.* HAT imposes stringent requirements, which, if met, entitle a property to display the HAT logo. You may order a free copy of their *Great Stays of Texas* guidebook, or you may browse their properties online. HAT lists unhosted guesthouses as well as hosted B&Bs, and their membership includes a growing number of intimate luxury or "boutique" hotels. Another reservation service is **Bed and Breakfast Texas Style**, *Tel. 979/696-9222, Toll free 800/899-4538, Fax 979/696-9444, Website: www.bnbtexasstyle.com.* Established in 1982, this service works with over 100 B&Bs in 54 cities statewide. You can also browse Texas B&B inns online at *www.bbonline.com/tx* and at *www.bbchannel.com/usa/texas.*

Guest Ranches

Another way to experience Texas is at a guest ranch. Generally the stay is based on an all-inclusive package price. Depending on the time of year in which you visit, nightly entertainment, cookouts, or trips to local establishments for food and drink may be on the schedule. Some ranches offer golfing, swimming pools and other leisure activity that lets you leave the western theme behind.

You will even find genuine Texans at the guest ranches, vacationing in their own backyards. One town that is famous for operating cowboy theme ranches is **Bandera**, in central Texas.

Youth Hostels

Youth hostels offer rates far below the going market rate. You need not be a member to stay at most hostels, but members do get lower rates. The **El Paso** hostel, *Tel. 915/532-3661*, is in the historic Gardner hotel. It is a member of the Hostels of America. The **Austin** hostel, *Tel. 512/444-2294 or 800/725-2331*, is on lovely Town Lake, and offers exceptional budget accommodations. You can buy a one-year membership for Hostelling International there.

Elderhostel

Elderhostel programs, *Tel. 877/426-8056, 75 Federal Street, Boston, Massachusetts 02110-1941, www.elderhostel.org,* offer entertaining and educational travel opportunities for retired people. The nationwide organization has many regional programs in Texas that last from a few days to a few weeks. You can choose to stay with the group or attend classes only. Most programs are affiliated institutions of higher learning.

For example, the Southwest Texas State University in **San Marcos** hosts Elderhostel events at the beautiful Aquarena Center. The University owns an historic inn located on the San Marcos River near their research center. Courses offered include ecology of Aquarena Springs, golfing and literature of the southwest. Austin College holds a variety of classes at Lake Texoma, about 60 miles outside of **Dallas**, including the history of flight, southern mountain culture, and American folk music. You can study nature, astronomy or Texas folklore at the Davis Mountain Environmental Education Center in **West Texas**; some of these programs include extended trips to northern Mexico.

Park Systems

Texas has 125 State parks, many of which offer recreational facilities and camping areas. Some have screened shelters and cabins for rent. Camping facilities range from primitive campsites without water or electricity to historic inns. Campsites begin at $4 per night, those with full hook-ups cost from $10 to $16 per night. Cabins run from $35 to $75 per night, depending on the size and amenities. Each person over the age of 13 must pay a park entrance fee, from $1 to $5 per day. Some parks have special discounts and others waive the entrance fee.

You can call a central reservations number to check availability and reserve a spot at any of the state parks by calling the **Texas Parks and Wildlife Department**, *Tel. 800/792-1112.* They can provide information about facilities at each park.

Usually a deposit is required; parks may be booked-up weeks in advance, especially in the summer and over holiday weekends. Once you have made a reservation, a confirmation notice will be sent. The remainder the total amount will be due upon arrival at the park.

Some state parks offer rustic cabins that can accommodate up to six people. Other sites operate State Park Hotels, which can be exceptional values located in beautiful surroundings. One example of this is the 39-room **Indian Lodge**, *Tel. 915/426-3254, Rates: $60-85,* in the dramatic desert setting of the Franklin Mountains in West Texas.

In Castroville (15 miles west of San Antonio), the eight-room **Landmark Inn**, *Tel. 830/931-2133, Rates: $45-55,* is an historic building dating from the time Texas was still a Republic. The park grounds have trails, and guests can go fishing or canoeing on the river.

Chapter 7

Part of the pleasure of traveling through Texas is that even native Texans are often tourists in their own state. Texas is so vast, and the possibilities of recreation so exceptional, that on your travels you may meet Texans visiting their own back yards for the first time—so you need never be embarrassed to ask what may seem to be an obvious question.

Business Hours

Stores and shopping malls are generally open from 10am to 9pm. On Sunday, shopping malls open at noon. Many grocery and large general stores such as Wal-mart and K-mart are open twenty-four hours. Only in small towns might you have trouble finding an all-night pharmacy.

Breakfast is an important meal, especially Sunday brunch. Many restaurants have special breakfast hours. Texans generally do not eat late meals. Dinner is usually taken around 7pm.

Most grocery and convenience stores sell beer and wine. Hard liquor must be purchased in package stores. On Sundays hard liquor is not sold anywhere, and beer and wine are sold only after noon.

Cost of Living & Travel

Texas can be very economical compared to other domestic destinations. Texans expect to get as much as and even more than they pay for, and often they do. Even if you choose to dine at the finest restaurants in Dallas or Houston, you will find prices are significantly lower than in New York or San Francisco, and the quality of food and service can be just as high.

If you enjoy the great outdoors, Texas is a magnificent playground. Every city offers public parks, many with trails for walking. Municipal swimming pools, tennis courts and golf courses allow you constant access to sports facilities. The state and national park systems in Texas provide low cost access to the most spectacular resources of the state, its natural wonders.

Texans rely on their automobiles for long journeys and also everyday existence. Car rental and gas prices are reasonable even during the high travel season summer months. Gas costs are slightly higher in large cities and also in West Texas, especially around Big Bend.

Train travel is often overlooked as a mode of transportation because it is slow and expensive compared to driving. Making Texas a stop on an interstate train trip is a good idea. Amtrak stations are conveniently located to downtown areas in larger cities.

You can shorten long travel times by flying. Southwest Airlines made its start in Texas moving people across the state for reasonable fares; they and other smaller commuter airlines can get you almost anywhere in the state.

Getting Married Over the Border

Despite the romantic stories of hopping across the border to get married on a whim, the reality is that the process doesn't happen overnight. In order to get married in Mexico, you must secure the services of a lawyer and observe a waiting period. It is far easier to plan your wedding for the United States. The quickie Mexican divorce is more fiction than fact, too, in case you were wondering!

Holidays

Texas observes all national holidays and certain state holidays. State government offices may be closed on state holidays, but most businesses operate as usual. **Texas Independence Day** is commemorated on March 2, the date that the Republic of Texas declared independence from Mexico. The battle in which the troops of Sam Houston defeated Santa Anna is **San Jacinto Day**, celebrated on April 21. **Juneteenth**, or Emancipation Day, is June 19, the day that slaves were declared free. August 27 is the **birthday of Lyndon Baines Johnson**.

Health Issues

The greatest health threat in Texas is the heat. Whether you are in a humid or dry area, be careful about dehydration. When exerting yourself strenuously in the heat of summer, it can be necessary to drink up to one gallon of water per day, which is recommended for backcountry hikers in West Texas.

Many are drawn to the promise of sunny days in Texas. While the sun is one of the state's greatest attractions, care should be used to avoid overexposure. Daily use of sunscreen is advised.

In larger cities, pollution is a risk to air quality. Local television weather reports will alert you to days when the air is low quality. Advance notice of these conditions can help asthma and allergy sufferer to breathe more easily. Central Texas is the allergy belt of the state. In the spring, flowering plants and trees and molds often irritate allergy suffers. The fall brings cedar, elm, and ragweed pollen. Air quality reports on the news include information about air-borne allergens.

When trekking into the countryside, first seek information about possible threats from wild animals. Snakes live throughout the state, not just in the desert regions. Rattlesnakes, copperheads and water moccasins can inflict serious injury. In East Texas and along the coast, mosquitoes can be an annoyance. However there is not currently any major threat from mosquito-carried infectious diseases. The **Texas Department of Health**, *Tel. 888/484-8538*, can address specific concerns.

Money & Banking

Automated Teller Machines (**ATMs**) are located in many convenience stores, in tourist areas, and in shopping centers. The machines usually charge an access fee, and a screen providing the option to cancel the transaction alerts you to the amount of the fee. The use of debit cards at restaurants and grocery stores is becoming increasingly popular in Texas. Major banks in Texas include Chase Bank and Bank of America.

Western Union is now used primarily for wiring money instead of sending telegrams. You can find Western Union offices in most large grocery stores throughout the state.

Retiring in the Lone Star State

South Texas, especially the Lower Rio Grande Valley, West Texas, and the Hill Country are popular places for retirement and extended vacations. Every year the state becomes a temporary home to Winter Texans affectionately known as "Snow Birds"—retirees fleeing the harsh weather of northern climates. In some towns you may find more license plates from Canada than from Texas on recreational vehicles.

Many special offers are extended to Winter Texans, such as temporary country club memberships that may run as low as $33 per month with unlimited use of the club facilities.

Staying Out of Trouble

For the most part, Texas shares the same laws and restrictions as the rest of the United States. The legal drinking age is 21 years. According to law, all automobile drivers must have valid liability insurance. Passengers in the front seats must wear seat belts. On most parts of Interstate Highways and many

State Highways, the speed limit is 70 miles per hour. The speed limit is always posted. It is illegal to drink and drive in Texas. The legal blood alcohol level is below 0.1 percent. Texas does use breath tests to determine intoxication.

A few years ago, it became legal to carry a concealed weapon in Texas, provided that one has the proper permit. In anticipation of gun-toting patrons, establishments posted "no guns" symbols on the front doors of buildings and stores. However, very few Texans take advantage of the concealed weapon law. So just because you see the sign, for the most part there is no need to fear the presence of guns.

Taxes

Texas has the reputation as being a state with low, low tax rates. This is true if you live here — there is no state income tax. Visitors may find a different scenario. The **state sales tax is 6.25 percent**; local sales and use taxes cannot exceed two percent, making 8.25 percent the highest possible sales tax rate. Many cities charge hotel tax, which can add an extra three to five percent to a bill.

Time

Most of Texas is in the **Central Time Zone**, which is one hour behind the Eastern Time Zone. The very western region of the state, west of Van Horn and including El Paso, is in the Mountain Time Zone, which is two hours behind the Eastern Time Zone.

Chapter 8

The great outdoors is very accessible in Texas. Every city has a Parks and Recreation Department that operates public swimming pools, tennis courts, golf courses and park facilities. These are available at low cost and open during most of the year. The state park system manages camping facilities all over the state. Many parks have cabins, hiking trails, lakes with boat launches and day use facilities, such as picnic areas. The state park system offers informative guided walks and nature courses at some facilities. The national system is also well represented in the state. In West and East Texas, full park facilities are available. In the south, a number of national wildlife refuge areas can be visited during the day.

Eco-tourism is an emerging field of interest in Texas. The state's vast natural reserves are accessible through the State and National Park systems. As more people with less time wish to experience the state's natural beauty, eco-tourism will take hold. You can experience the best of each area of the state with **Texas Passport Adventures**. For a free catalog call: The Texas Parks and Wildlife Department, *Tel. 800/841-6547*. They work in cooperation with a number of tour companies to offer trips that respect and conserve nature. Some of the trips are educational, such as an artist's workshop in Big Bend or a nature photography workshop. Others, like trail rides, rock climbing, and mountain bike tours are hands-on adventures.

Biking

The rolling terrain of Central Texas is a favorite of cycling enthusiasts. The country roads and smaller highways run through spectacular scenery and offer challenging rides for even experienced cyclists. The **Texas Bicycle Coalition**, *www.biketexas.org*, provides information about cycling events throughout the state.

Every year on the second weekend in May, bicycle enthusiasts can join the **Rolling Hills Challenge**, a ride through East Texas sponsored by the Columbus Lions Club. The longest route is 100 miles; many participants choose shorter rides. For information, contact **the Columbus Convention and Visitor's Bureau**, *Tel. 409/732-8385, Fax 409/732-3022.*

Some cities have their own velocenters. The **Austin Veloway**, *4103 Slaughter Lane, Austin, Tel. 512/480-8921*, a 3.1-mile outdoor track near the Wildflower Research Center, is especially beautiful during the spring when wildflowers burst into bloom. The veloway is also popular with in-line skaters, and no joggers or motorized vehicles are allowed. The Houston Parks and Recreation Department operates the **Alkek Velodrome**, *19008 Saums Road in Cullen Park, Houston, Tel. 281/578-0858, Website: www.houstonalkekvelodrome.org*, built in 1986 for the Olympic Festival. This is the only velodrome in Texas, and one of only 20 in the entire United States. A monthly pass costs only $2. They have bicycles available for you to rent for $3 if you don't have your own.

Mountain Biking

There could be no better place for mountain biking than Texas.

Some of the state parks have trails designed specifically for mountain biking. **McKinney Falls State Park** near Austin offers both easy and challenging trails. Although primarily used by horse riders, the **Hill Country State Natural Area** in Bandera, Texas has 36 miles of trails, many of which can be used by mountain bikers.

In southwest Texas, **Seminole Canyon State Historical Park** on Highway 90 near Comstock has a six-mile mountain bike trail that includes a scenic overlook of the canyon. And the Dallas area has 100 acres of moderate to advanced trails at **Cedar Hill State Park**. In the woodlands of East Texas, **Tyler State Park** has an 8.5-mile trail for mountain bikes.

Birding

Bird watching, or birding as its serious devotees prefer to call it, is a pastime for many of the residents of the Texas shoreline. Texas birders are excited about the recent completion of the Great Texas Coastal Birding Trail. The trail links Beaumont to Brownsville with 500 miles of coastal trail marked with a special sign. There are

Along the northern coastline, **Galveston Bay** offers exceptional opportunities to observe many wetlands birds and animals. Nature preserves including **Anahuac National Wildlife Refuge, Galveston Island State Park** and the **Galveston Bay Prairie Preserve** are prime areas to watch birds and enjoy nature. The **Galveston Bay Foundation**, *Tel. 281/332-2281*, an organization dedicated to protecting and preserving the coastal region, offers guided tours and outings for kids and adults. The coastal bend is full of spots that birds love to frequent.

Mustang Island near Port Aransas has acres of undisturbed beach inhabited by coastal birds. Near Rockport, **Goose Island State Park** is yet another sanctuary. The **Aransas National Wildlife Refuge** is devoted to the preservation of birds and fauna, and is famous for its success with the endangered Whooping Crane. Further south, **Baffin Bay**, near Kingsville, has trails and quiet shores where you can view birds nesting.

The **Padre Island National Seashore**, with its miles of undisturbed beach, is a haven for shore birds. The national park service offers bus tours of bird habitats, and trails with observation areas are always open.

The **Texas Ornithological Society**, *Website: www.texasbirds.org*, organizes frequent field trips and publishes Texas Bird Magazine. Guided bird-watching tours are available from **Field Guides**, *9433 Bee Cave Road, Building 1 Suite 150, Tel. 512/263-7495 or 800/728-4953, Website: www.fieldguides.com*. Spring in South Texas and Texas Coast Migration Spectacle are just two of the many available itineraries.

Horseback Riding

When people imagine Texas, the images of oil wells and horses come to mind. Western trail riding is the common pastime here, although you can find English riding clubs in Houston and Dallas. The place that Texans go to ride horses is the central Texas Hill Country. The terrain can be flat or rugged, so the riding trails are exciting yet not perilous. Many ranches in the Hill Country rent horses by the day or hour. You can also get riding lessons or guided trips. The town of Bandera has a number of guest ranches that will get you saddled up.

Many Texas state parks maintain horse trails especially for equestrian activity. You may rent horses at the following state parks:
• **Caprock Canyons State Park**, *Quitaque, Tel. 806/455-1492*
• **Hill Country State Natural Area**, *Bandera, Tel. 830/796-4413*
• **Huntsville State Park**, *Huntsville, Tel. 936/295-5644*
• **Lake Livingston State Park**, *Livingston, 936/365-2201*
• **Palo Duro Canyon State Park**, *Canyon, 806/488-2227*

The camel cavalry did not prove to be a success in Texas, but llama trekking is here to stay. The climate of Texas is just the right combination of dry and hot to keep llamas happy. The **Jordan Ranch**, *Tel. 915/949-4757*, leads llama treks through San Angelo State Park. The llama carries your equipment and picnic lunch as you hike alongside.

Hiking

The state and national parks have extensive hiking trails of all levels of difficulty. The most challenging part of the state is found in **Big Bend**, which has many backcountry and mountain trails for expert hikers. You can read about this area and others ideal for hiking at the **Texas Hiking** website, *www.texashiking.com*.

You can get into the great outdoors while offering services to the community by participating in a volunteer vacation. The **American Hiking Society**, *1422 Fenwick Lane, Silver Spring, Maryland 20910, Tel. 301/565-6704, Fax 301/565-6714, Website: www.americanhiking.org*, has trips for those who want to volunteer to work on construction and maintenance of hiking trails. Participants usually work in a national park and must provide their own camping equipment. In the past, Big Bend has been one of the parks in which volunteers have been placed.

Hunting & Fishing

Hunting

The great outdoors beckons hunters to every region of Texas. State regulations require permit for seasonal hunting. Fall is the season that Texans take to the hills and hunting leases to bag their game for the winter. The dove season begins at the start of September in the southern coastal plains region. Quail are hunted from November to the end of February. Deer season begins in November. Exact dates of seasons vary by county, method of hunting and, of course, game.

In general, the year for sportsmen begins on September 1—this is the beginning of the annual hunting and fishing seasons. Before you load the rifles and put on camouflage, the proper licenses and permits must be purchased. Also, all hunters 17 years of age or older must complete the mandatory Hunter Education Course.

The *Outdoor Annual* publication provides detailed information about hunting and fishing. It is available at no cost. You can write to the **Texas Parks and Wildlife Department**, *4200 Smith School Road, Austin, Texas 78744, or call them at Tel. 800/792-1112 (General Information) Monday-Friday 9am-5pm; Tel. 800/895-4248(Licenses and Permit information); and Tel. 800/792-1112(Scientific and Education Permits)*.

Hunting licenses vary in price from $6 to $250 depending on residence status of the applicant and the type of game hunted. Exotic game, fur animals are two examples of fauna requiring special permits. In addition to the general permit, certain game such as turkey and migratory birds (including duck) require a special stamp. Those who hunt with archery equipment or muzzle-loading weapons need special stamps.

You can enjoy hunting on your own on leased land, or you can go on a real life safari. Texas has big game ranches that breed animals especially for hunters with exotic tastes. For more information about these opportunities, contact the **Exotic Wildlife Association**, *Ingram, Texas, Tel. 830/367-4997*.

Fishing

Fishing requires a general license and special tags for specific types of fish. All fish and shellfish are restricted by gear and area regulations. You may purchase fishing licenses at any of the 3000 locations where the permits are sold in Texas, or by phone with a credit card from the **Texas Parks and Wildlife Department**, *Tel. 800/895-4248.*

The coastal waters of the Gulf of Mexico teem with shrimp, blue crab, and a variety of sport fish. During every day of the year, at least three or more fish are at peak season in the Gulf. Redfish, black drum and croaker are some of the more popular varieties.

Freshwater offers excellent fishing year-round as well. Some varieties such as catfish, striped bass and crappie are plentiful nearly all year. Fly-fishing is a popular pastime on the **Guadalupe River**. Since 1933, **Pico Outdoor Company**, *Kerrville, Texas, Tel. 830/895-4348 or 800/256-5873,* has been the Hill Country expert on fly-fishing. The company makes equipment, offers lessons and guides tours. Saltwater fly-fishing is less popular although more challenging. The coastal tides and larger equipment add to the challenge. The only day of the year when you do not need a special permit for sport fishing is June 1.

Poaching is a serious violation of law and seriously threatens the safety of sportsman and wildlife. The **Texas Parks and Wildlife Department** operates a 24-hour hotline to report poachers, *Tel. 800/792-GAME or 713/649-0708 (in Houston), or 512/389-4848 (in Austin).*

◦ Hook, Line & Sinker

To introduce yourself and your kids to the sport of fishing, go to the **Texas Freshwater Fisheries Center**, *550 Flat Creek Road, Athens, Tel. 903/676-BASS, Website: www.tpwd.state.tx.us/fish/infish.* The center has a casting pond where you can catch catfish and trout. All gear is provided free of charge. The fishery grounds include a hatchery, nature preserve and giant aquariums.

Running

Just as nearly everywhere else, Texas is full of runners. Almost every city has parks with busy running trails. The cities that do not are so small that you will see running enthusiasts jogging down the Main Street. Some of the larger hotels offer indoor jogging tracks so you can avoid the Texas heat.

In the Houston area, **Huntsville State Park**, *Park Road 40, Huntsville, Tel. 409/295-5644,* hosts a marathon that is anything but the usual long-distance run. The annual **Texas Trail Endurance Run** is known as an ultra-marathon, and athletes from around the world participate. Runners must cross 20 miles of rough trails. A number of events lead up to the race and celebrate its completion.

Spectator Sports

Texas has world-class sports events for spectators. The **Dallas Cowboys**, *Tel. 214/556-9900*, may be the most famous football team in the world. At least they are no longer the only NFL team in the state, as the expansion team the **Houston Texans**, *Tel. 713/336-7700* brought football back to Houston in 2002.

Texas boasts two excellent baseball teams—the National League Central division champs, the **Houston Astros**, *Tel. 713/799-9600*, who play in Astros Field, and the American League West division champs, the **Texas Rangers**, *Tel. 817/273-5222*, based at The Ballpark in Arlington, near Dallas.

No town could be more proud of a basketball team than San Antonio is of its NBA National Champions, the **San Antonio Spurs**, *Tel. 210/554-7700*. The Alamodome in the center of the city is the Spurs' home. A nre arena will be completed in time for the 2003 NBA season. The **Dallas Mavericks**, *Tel. 214/748-1808*, play in Reunion Arena. You can catch the **Houston Rockets**, *Tel. 713/627-3865*, at home in the Compaq Center, which they share with perennial WNBA world champions, the **Houston Comets**.

Texas has universities with excellent athletic facilities and teams: **The University of Texas** in Austin, **Texas A&M** in College Station, and **Texas Tech** in Lubbock are but a few of the schools that field a variety of the best collegiate teams in the country. Football, basketball, baseball and volleyball fans will appreciate the quality and action of college sports in the state.

Ice Hockey is no longer a novelty in Texas. The state has only one NHL team, but they have become a powerhouse, playing in the Stanley Cup finals in 2001. The **Dallas Stars**, *Tel. 214/868-2890*, skate in Reunion Arena in Irving.

Water Sports

All along the Texas coast, water sports await you. In Galveston, Corpus Christi and South Padre Island, surf shops offer equipment rental for wind surfing and sailing. Just off the shore near Cole Park in Corpus Christi you will find one of the best windsurfing spots around. On the beach itself you will probably find sailboats for rent, either as equipment or part of a tour.

The warm waters of the Gulf of Mexico offer excellent diving. You can take long shallow dives off the coast, or go deep into the bays to descend on the living communities of the oilrig platforms. Entire ecosystems full of fish, crabs, starfish and anemones take over the legs of the rig. You can see sharks and rays in the deeper Gulf waters.

Chapter 9

Texas is an excellent place for family travel. Most hotels and motels have recreation areas with swimming pools and some have game rooms or outdoor play areas for kids. Some hotels offer baby sitting services and many have cribs available for guests.

Traveling with kids doesn't necessarily cost much more than leaving them behind, either. You can easily find accommodations that allow children to stay in their parents room at no extra charge. Many casual restaurants have special children's menus and some have play areas for kids. Watch for restaurants offering free dinners for children when they accompany parents.

The main health concern for kids is the same as for adults: the sun. Kids should always wear sunscreen, a hat and drink plenty of water. Watch your kids carefully for overexposure and overexertion exacerbated by heat. Give them enough "time outs" to keep them cool.

Texas & Kids

You can find tours that focus on families and include destinations with kid-oriented activities. There are a few major theme parks in the state, which are always popular with children. **Six Flags Over Texas** has parks in Dallas/ Fort Worth, Houston and San Antonio, which also has a **Sea World Park**. New Braunfels is the home of the wildly popular water park, **Schlitterbahn**, *305 West Austin Street, New Braunfels, Tel. 830/625-2351, Website: www.schlitterbahn.com*. Miles of chutes, a surf machine, and the incredible aquatic roller coaster known as the Master Blaster make for an entire day of fun.

Beaches, lakes and hiking trails are always fun for the entire family. National and state parks often offer special activities for kids. The **Texas Department of Parks and Wildlife** offers a variety of programs for all ages. For example, kids can learn about conservation and its challenges and rewards when they become park rangers for a day. **Junior Ranger Camps** are half-day programs for kids ages 6 to 12. Visit the website, *www.tpwd.state.tx.us*, for more information about fun, educational activities and events for kids.

Visiting archaeological sites provides the opportunity to mix education and fun. Numerous excavations are part of the state park system and have educational displays that offer information. Taking your kids to these parks is a great way to visit the outdoors and learn about history at the same time.

In the North Texas plains, where herds of buffalo still graze, the remains of a 10,000-year-old buffalo kill can be visited. **Hueco Tanks State Park** has trails leading to ancient cave paintings made by Native Americans.

The rugged territory of **Seminole Canyon** in the southwestern region of Texas, near the Rio Grande, has over 300 cave paintings. One of the easiest to view is a panorama painting at a cave site that was probably occupied for at least 13,000 years. Park rangers take visitors to the paintings twice per day.

Archaeological excavations at the **Caddoan Mounds State Historical Park** in East Texas have yielded many artifacts including large ear spools that were worn similar to earrings and ceremonial spears. These mysterious mounds are unique to Texas.

The ancient plains culture is preserved at the **Lubbock Lake Landmark State Historical Park**, which has a 20-acre excavation and an excellent museum.

Museums document the rich cultures of Native Americans. One of the most worthwhile museums in the state is the **Wilderness Museum**, *2000 Transmountain Road, El Paso, Tel. 915/755-4332, Tuesday to Sunday, 9am to 5pm*. Indoor/outdoor exhibits include trails leading to displays of daily life in Texas before European colonization. The nature trail stretches for one mile and has recreations of various houses including a pit house, a partially underground structure with a twig roof, and a pueblo, an early agricultural settlement. Archaeological sites of Mexico and the United States southwest are brought into context with maps, artifacts and historic descriptions. Paintings depict the daily life of the tribes of West Texas. Visitors gain valuable insight to the petroglyphs, painted pottery and material culture of the area's first inhabitants. Admission is free.

Visitors to Brenham can take the short, scenic trip to see the seat of the independence movement of the Texas pioneers at **Washington-on the Brazos State Park**, *Box 305, Washington, Texas, Tel. 409/878-2214*. The park has an excellent museum and the scenic drive makes you feel as if you are stepping back through time. The 154-acre park has reconstructed homes of the pioneers of the Republic of Texas. A small wood cabin, Independence

Hall, was the place where the Texas Declaration of Independence from Mexico was signed.

The **Star of the Republic Museum**, also in the park, provides a thorough overview of the road to independence and later statehood for Texas. This excellent collection has reproductions of photographs and portraits as well as artifacts from the Republic of Texas days. Many of the famous men for whom Texas counties were named are profiled here, as are other leaders of the Independence movement.

You and your kids can trek into the future at the **Museum of Science and History**, *1501 Montgomery Street, Fort Worth, Tel. 817/732-1631, Monday to Friday 9am to 5pm, Saturday and Sunday 9am to 9pm, Admission adult $5, child $3.* Learning is fun in this high-tech center located in the city arts district. The hands-on exhibits allow children to dig like an archaeologist, experience the galaxy in the planetarium and take fun and educational workshops. The museum's **Omni Theater**, *Tel. 817/732-1631*, shows movies from 10:30am to 11:30pm; daily schedules vary.

The **Children's Museum of Houston**, *1500 Binz Street, Houston, Tel. 713/522-1138, Website: www.cmhouston.org*, sports a riotously colorful, playful exterior that hints at the fun to be had within. Free Family Nights are offered every Thursday from 5pm-8pm. Among the permanent exhibits are an outdoors eco-station and the KID-TV studio, where children can explore video equipment and production.

In Austin, a city seemingly designed for children, you can spend entire days enjoying the great outdoors. Adults and kids alike fill Austin's largest playground, **Zilker Park**. There are over 400 acres of jogging trails from Town Lake through Zilker Park. Playing fields are used for soccer and Frisbee games nearly all year long. The outdoor Zilker Hillside Theater offers free summer performances. **Barton Springs**, *Tel. 512/476-9044*, a large, natural spring-fed pool is open year-round. The forever 68-degree water feels as good in the winter as the summer.

During the summer, Austin Circle of Theaters sponsors **Playfest**, which includes local and touring groups in performances designed especially for children. The festival runs for ten weeks in the spring and summer months. Performances include puppetry, storytelling, and theatrical productions.

Perhaps the most exciting event for children is the **Houston Livestock Show and Rodeo**, held annually in February. The festivities go on for weeks, and with such kid-friendly attractions as a circus, a Wild West show, a petting zoo, a mechanical-bull riding arena, and a Lil' Rustlers Rodeo, you're not likely to end up with bored youngsters on your hands while you're still rarin' to go. For more on this most Texan of events, see *Sports & Recreation* in the Houston section.

Major events

Chapter 10

In every season, throughout the regions of the state, Texans gather to celebrate the customs that make Texas unique. In many of these gatherings, entire communities welcome visitors to share their food, pastimes, and warmth.

Rodeo season kicks off the year in grand style. Rodeos aren't just about men riding bulls—they have many accompanying festivities including parades, live music, and lots of down-home cooking. The bigger rodeos can last for weeks. Spring celebrations generally focus on traditional fun like Mardi Gras, while the summer winds down with harvest festivals. The fall offers many opportunities to buy homespun gifts at autumn market days.

January

The small town of Mission, in the Rio Grande Valley, celebrates its vital citrus harvest each year in late January. At the **Texas Citrus Fiesta**, *Tel. 956/585-9724*, you can eat your fill of ruby red grapefruit and luscious oranges in their juicy natural state or made into imaginative recipes. The festivities culminate in a parade of inventive floats and costumes created entirely of citrus fruit.

The **Southwestern International Livestock Show & Rodeo** in El Paso, *Tel. 915/532-1401*, is a genuinely western event, drawing participants from Arizona and New Mexico. This rodeo is the final step in a cowboy's preparation for the National Rodeo held in Las Vegas. The rodeo features an old-fashioned cattle drive on the Rio Grande flood plain, a chili cook-off and a livestock auction.

February

One of the oldest festivals in the state, **Brownsville**

Charro Days, *Tel. 956/542-4545*, offers four days of Latino culture. Music fills the air, and dancers perform regional Mexican dances. Exceptional Tex-Mex cooking is plentiful in both Brownsville and just across the border in Matamoros, Mexico. Since 1938 the Charro Days week has united cultures beginning on the last Thursday of February.

The **Houston Livestock Show and Rodeo**, *Tel. 713/791-9000, www.hlsr.com*, held at the end of February and beginning of March, is the largest rodeo in the state. All tastes are catered to at this enormous gathering, from glitzy weekend cowboys to genuine bull riders. Famous country and western stars headline the musical line-up.

Mardi Gras in Texas

Texas has its very own version of **Mardi Gras** revelry along the Gulf Coast. **Galveston** celebrates with festivities, *Website: www.mardigrasgalveston.com*, scheduled over two weekends. Over 200,000 people participate in the seven Mardi Gras parades. Further south on the Texas coast, **Port Arthur** hosts a smaller, more family-oriented celebration, *Website: www.portarthur.com/mardigras*, over a four-day period.

March

The **Texas Cowboy Poetry Gathering**, *Tel 915/837-8191, Website: www.cowboypoetry.org*, extols the expressive side of the Wild West. Sul Ross University in the city of Alpine hosts the event on the first weekend in March. Poetry and music are celebrated as well as all aspects of cowboy life, including clothes, crafts and food.

Austin's **South-by-Southwest Conference** (SXSW), *www.sxsw.com*, was once simply a music festival. Independent bands from all over played clubs throughout the city, hoping to be signed by one of the many talent scouts who came to listen. In recent years SXSW has grown into an international conference that hosts separate film and multi-media events, but the music is still the focus. Fans and music industry types flood the city to partake of what has become one of the most important national arts conferences in the nation.

The Celtic life is not forgotten in the Lone Star State. For nearly 20 years the **North Texas Irish Festival**, *www.ntif.org*, has offered folk dancing, educational displays, food and drink. Over 20,000 people enjoy seven stages of entertainment including Celtic music competition. The festival is held at Fair Park in Dallas.

The **Easter Fires Pageant**, *Tel. 830/997-2359, Website: www.gillespiefair.com/easterfires/easterfires.htm*, mixes tradition and modern fun during Easter weekend in Fredericksburg. The origin of the celebration remains a mystery—possibly rooted in Old World Easter ritual—and offers egg hunts, story telling and much more for everyone.

April

The arrival of Spanish colonists passing thorough West Texas four hundred years ago is celebrated with the **First Thanksgiving** in El Paso. The events spotlight the rich Spanish culture including the costumes at time of the colonists. The event is featured on an informative website that highlights the missions, *missiontrail.elp.rr.com*.

For over 100 years, San Antonio has celebrated Texas heritage with **Fiesta San Antonio**, *Tel. 210/227-5191, www.fiesta-sa.org*. The event spans ten days and includes everything from a gala ball to weekend musical performances. This is one of the most popular and eagerly anticipated celebrations in the state.

For one long weekend in mid-April, the **MAIN ST. Fort Worth Arts Festival**, *Tel.817/336-2727, Website: www.msfwaf.org*, takes over downtown Fort Worth. The center of the city is closed for pedestrian-only traffic and food and arts booths take over the streets.

The **Houston International Festival**, *Tel. 800/541-1719, www.hif.org*, celebrates world cultures during the last half of April. Each year the festival chooses a focus; in 1999 it was South Africa, in 2002 it was France. Food, dance, music and art fill twenty blocks of downtown Houston for 10 days. Many of the events are educational and designed to help children appreciate other cultures. Bands from around the world and local talent keep adults entertained.

May

The beautiful grounds of the Laguna Gloria Art Museum in Austin are the setting for the **Austin Fine Arts Festival**, *Tel. 512/458-6073, Website: www.austinfineartsfestival.org*, a celebration of the arts in Texas. The event includes a juried fine arts exhibit, food from top local restaurants, and hands-on art activities for the young and the young at heart.

Everyone can participate in the **Cinco de Mayo** celebration at Austin's Fiesta Gardens, *Tel. 512/867-1999, Website: www.austin-cincodemayo.com*. Tejano and conjunto musicians perform and a variety of traditional Tex-Mex food is available. There is a Little Cinco for children (no admission price) with arts and crafts activities and games.

The **Kerrville Folk Festival** starts on the last weekend of May. The celebration attracts some of the best folk musicians in the nation and consequently a big group of folk fans. Three compact discs have been produced from past festivals. Still, there is nothing comparable to hearing the music under the night sky. Many camp out at the ranch where the festival is held to enjoy the outdoors and take in the most music possible. You can purchase tickets in advance by contacting the festival organizers, *Tel. 830/257-3600, www.kerrville-music.com.*

On the last Friday of May, come rain or come shine, fiddlers from all over converge on Athens in East Texas for the **Old Fiddler's Reunion**, *Tel. 903.675-5181, Website: www.athenscc.org/fiddlers.html.* This informal gathering is free, and many activities are intended to encourage kids to participate in music.

June

The day of Juneteenth commemorates the Emancipation Proclamation in Texas. The **Juneteenth Freedom Festival**, *Tel. 713/284-8350*, is an all day celebration of music held on June 19 at the Miller Outdoor Theater in Houston. San Antonio, Dallas, Austin, and many other cities and towns have Juneteenth events as well – check with the Convention & Visitors Bureau at each location to see what is on tap this year.

It takes a stadium to hold the **Scottish Festival and Highland Games**, *Fax 817/478-4489, Website: www.texasscottishfestival.com*, in early June. The festivities are held in Arlington at The University of Texas in Arlington. The Highland Games are genuine tests of strength and endurance. There is a lot of Scottish food and drink, as well as bagpipe bands and other cultural performances. Over 60,000 people turn out to learn some Gaelic, watch the falconry demonstrations, and just have fun.

Rodeo competitions, a cattle drive through the town, and a chuck wagon round up are featured at the **Cowboy Roundup USA**, *Tel. 806/374-1497*, in Amarillo. The events continue for five days and include music and good old-fashioned bar-be-cue.

The El Paso/Juarez **International Mariachi Festival**, *Tel. 915/566-4066*, aims at uniting cultures while spotlighting the foremost Mariachi bands from Mexico. The festival includes food and drink and is held on the last weekend of June.

July

Lots of real Texans celebrate Independence Day on July 4th at **Willie Nelson's Family Picnic**, *Website: www.willienelson.com*, a roaming festival that takes place in different cities (and sometimes even different months). Many excellent country music acts perform; of course, Willie Nelson is the featured act. The 2001 Picnic was held in August at The Woodlands in northwest Houston.

For over 100 years the **West of the Pecos Rodeo** has been the major event of West Texas summers. Many of the competitors are from the area. The four-day event features a parade and is held near Big Bend at the Buck Johnson Arena, *Highways 17 and 20, Big Bend Country, Tel. 800/588-2855.*

The **Clute Mosquito Festival**, *Tel. 979/265-8392*, makes light of those nasty pests that plague southern life. Such eccentricities as a mosquito calling contest and special events for senior citizens and young children make this small-town party good family fun.

August

All the cultures of Texas history come together at the **Texas Folklife Festival**, *Tel. 210/458-2225*, held at San Antonio's Institute of Texas Cultures. Folk costumes, dancing, music and traditional dishes create so much fun kids might forget they are learning about history.

The **National Championship Barbecue Cookoff** in Meridian, *Tel. 254/435-6113, www.bbq.htcomp.net*, is no ordinary competition. Chefs from across the nation compete for over $17,000 in prize money. The cooking competition is invitation only and includes categories such as "professional" and "celebrity." There's also a fish fry for those who aren't fond of meat and a carnival to entertain the kids.

September

The skies of the north Dallas suburb of Plano fill with color during the **Plano Balloon Festival**, *Website: www.planoballoonfest.org*, in mid-September. More than an amazing show of ballooning, children's activities and musical performances are featured.

The most famous celebration in the state is the **Texas State Fair**, *Tel. 214/565-9931, www.statefair.com*. The fair is a giant carnival-style event held in Dallas' Fair Park at the end of September and early October. The state fair has its share of esoteric events, like the Pygmy & Nigerian Goat Show. Most activities are all-American favorites, like the chili cook-off and the annual collegiate football game between rivals Oklahoma and The University of Texas.

October

Since 1933 Tyler has held the **Rose Parade and Festival**, *www.tylertexas.com/rosefest*. This is a small town experience complete with beauty pageant and ceremonies. The center of attention is the Tyler Rose Queen who enjoys a coronation ceremony and gala ball held in her honor. The culmination is the rose parade that draws the entire town to watch.

Fredericksburg, a town with German roots, brings **Oktoberfest**, *Tel. 866/839-3378, Website: www.oktoberfestinfbg.com*, to Texas. The event is held on the town square with three stages for German music. Food and drink are plentiful. Artisans offer the many arts and crafts they make from local materials.

One of the best times of the year in Texas is the fall when you can enjoy the outdoors without the heat of summer. The **Autumn Trail Rides Festival** in Winnsboro, *Tel. 903/342-3666*, is a great way to appreciate Texan culture. The entire schedule covers four weekends and includes a rodeo and a golf tournament. During one weekend riders saddle up to accompany wagons on an old fashioned trail ride. Other activities include contest riflery, a barn dance and a swap meet.

November

The German heritage of Central Texas is the theme of the New Braunfels' **Wurstfest**, *Tel. 800/221-4369, Website: http://www.wurstfest.com*. The sponsors are proud of the polka and waltz bands that headline. For the more serious, the local museums open for German heritage exhibitions. Walking tours of the historic section of town give participants a glimpse into the lifestyle of settlers.

December

Cities and towns with Hispanic roots all over Texas celebrate Christmas with candlelit Christmas parades called **Las Posadas.** They are all beautiful to watch, but the one in San Antonio is probably the largest and most impressive. The San Antonio Conservation Society, *Tel. 210/224-6163*, oversees the procession led by children, and everyone is invited to La Villita afterwards for hot chocolate and festivities.

Outdoor Musicals

Texans love to celebrate their history in the great outdoors. Summer musicals bring the past to life while giving the audience a bit of culture and a bit of nature. Even during the hottest summer, the evenings are cool and comfortable.

The frontier days of the west is portrayed in the **Fort Griffin Fandangle**, *Albany, Tel. 917/762-3642*. The musical is entertaining and teaches a good deal about history. Do not miss the pre-performance barbecue dinner, served picnic-style on the front steps of the Albany Courthouse. The town of Albany participates in this amateur musical interpretation of the westward push of the American frontier. The show has been produced every year since 1938, except during World War II.

God's Country, *Rio Blanco Heritage Foundation, Tel. 806/675-2906*, is an amateur musical is performed in Blanco Canyon. The beautiful setting is about as close to God's country as you can get on earth. Thousands have seen the musical in the ten years that it has been presented. Blanco Canyon is 11 miles north of Crosbytown, off FM 651.

Keepers of the Legend, *Muleshoe Heritage Center, Tel. 806/272-4405*, combines drama and music to tell the story of family life on the Texas frontier. The musical is performed for one week only in early July and is sponsored by. All seven performances begin at 8:30pm and admission is $10.

Texas! at *Palo Duro State Park, Amarillo* has drawn tens of thousands of visitors to the canyons of Palo Duro for over 30 years. The large amphitheater seats 1700 spectators under the clear night sky of north Texas. Performances are held each night at 8:30pm from June through August. Tickets often sell out far in advance, so it's best to make plans before the performance day.

Food Fesyivals

Harvests are not reserved for the fall. April brings the **Poteet Strawberry Festival**, *Tel. 830/742-8144*. Poteet strawberries are so good that it takes three days of concerts, kids entertainment and some rodeo events to celebrate them. Many camp out to fully enjoy every day.

Every September on the second Saturday of the month, the culture and food of Czech immigrants is celebrated at the **Kolache Festival**. The state championship bake-off of kolaches is held in Caldwell, the Kolache Capital of Texas. If you are not eligible to enter either the amateur or professional categories, consider taking a kolache baking class. Until you try one of the many varieties of kolache-poppy seed, apricot or sausage, for example-you are missing a culinary delight.

On Columbus Day the town of Columbus hosts **Columbus Day Fall Fest**. This has nothing to do with the discovery of the New World. Actually it's a celebration of the Old World, Germany to be precise. The day is full of cooking contests for the best sausage, sauerkraut and strudel. Local music played with German rhythm continues into the evening. Columbus is on Highway 71, west of Austin. Cooking festivals featuring strudel and sauerkraut highlight the event.

If you are not a big fan of black-eye peas, you haven't been to the **Black-eyed Pea Fall Harvest** *Athens, Tel. 800/755-7878*. Besides many variations of peas, a carnival provides entertainment. The warmth of local Texas comes through this family event held on the first weekend in October.

In the cold of November winter heats up with the **Terlingua Chili Cook-Off**. This small town near Big Bend ignites the taste buds with standard recipes and new renditions of the Texas-bred cowboy food. The event promises to be the largest Chili competition in the world.

Every Fourth of July the **Brisket Cook-Off** *Junction, Tel. 800/397-3916*, brings out the best barbecue cooks and hungriest locals. The three-day event includes live music and picnic games on ten acres of beautiful Hill Country.

Chapter 11

food & drink

All over the state, mealtime offers a chance for gustatory adventure. Texan pride certainly extends to the culinary arts, and whether you eat a simple hamburger or an innovative southwestern creation, you should expect an excellent meal. Texas is in an ideal location to absorb and recreate a number of southern cooking traditions, including Deep South home cooking, Cajun and Creole cuisine, and the fiery foods of the Southwest.

The cuisine of Texas is as varied as the cultures that formed the traditions of cooking. You will discover a world of flavors in the different regions of the state. Central Texas is replete with the food brought by Germans and Slavs who settled in the region during the nineteenth century. German and polish sausage is still ground fresh in the kitchens of many Central Texas restaurants. New Braunfels has a number of places that serve traditional German food. A multitude of small bakeries produces pastry and bread that rival the European variety. Take a break in West or Castroville to sample the bakery fare.

A more recent wave of immigration has bestowed unexpected flavors on the Texas. Vietnamese cuisine is found throughout most of the state, especially in Houston, Dallas and Austin. Almost every great cuisine of the world is well represented in Texas, including French, Italian, Mediterranean, Middle Eastern, and all types of Asian. In many small restaurants you will find exceptional ethnic cooking.

Of course, traditional Texan cooking draws on traditions found closer to home. Inventive chefs have favored southwestern flavors for nearly a decade now. Using a variety of chiles and other native ingredients, and borrow-

Hotter Than Hot!

It sounds crazy to have a chile festival in the middle of summer, but really its quite logical. When you eat spicy food, the theory goes, the pores on your skin open, causing you to cool off.

The **Texas Fiery Foods Show**, *Tel. 512/244-7378, Website: www.texasfieryfoods.com*, is held at the end of August in Austin's Palmer Auditorium. The event draws chile lovers from all over, as well as chefs and growers eager to talk shop.

Just as your taste buds cool down, the **Austin Chronicle Hot Sauce Festival**, *Tel. 512/454-5766*, takes place. Intrepid hot sauce enthusiasts with tongues of asbestos and stomachs of steel wander through Waterloo Park, sampling hundreds of concoctions with heat indices ranging from pleasantly warm to nuclear. The best hot sauce winners are crowned at the end of the day.

ing blue corn and smoked sauces from New Mexico, Texan chefs create a new breed of food. Even more daring are the dishes with Asian ingredients such as rice noodles, ginger or wasabi paste. The results are tempting and seldom disappointing.

Tex-Mex

Naturally Texas is heavily influenced by traditional Mexican cuisine. Tex-Mex, a cooking style originating in Texas, is the type of food most outsiders assume Texans eat all the time. It is similar to Mexican cuisine, which draws upon Spanish recipes and incorporates the food of the native peoples of Mexico. Genuine Mexican food is not as prevalent as Tex-Mex—in fact, at one time you would have had better luck finding haute French cuisine than authentic interior Mexican food. That's beginning to change, as Texan palates grow ever more sophisticated. Sometimes, though, nothing will do but a plate of good ol' comforting Tex-Mex.

Certainly tortillas and salsa are staples of the Texan diet, however the popular flour tortillas and mild smoke-flavored sauces are recent creations. You will find that authentic Tex-Mex relies on corn tortillas, not flour, and black beans, not the more popular pinto beans. The continual evolution of Tex-Mex gives the food its appeal and provides healthier menu choices. For example refried beans are high in fat. Choosing boiled black beans cuts the fat out of the dish.

Fajitas are an excellent way to get a taste of many of the flavors of Tex-Mex food. A small skillet of beef, chicken, shrimp or vegetables is brought to your table with side orders of guacamole, cheese, fresh vegetables and a few salsas. Simply pile these in any combination on tortillas and enjoy.

Salsas come in varying strengths from mild to palate singeing. The spiciness generally depends on the peppers used in the recipe. Jalapenos can be eaten whole, while serranos are smaller and far hotter.

Salsa verde, green sauce made from tart tomatillos with jalapenos, is generally mildest; orange sauce made with habanero peppers is the spiciest. Chipotle, a smoked jalapeno often used in southwestern dishes, is made into a thick, delicious salsa. The rather mild poblano pepper is stuffed with corn or cheese, then breaded and deep-fried to make chiles rellenos. Chile peppers are not to be confused with bowls of chili, which gets its flavor from ground red peppers. Real chili is made with meat (chile con carne), never beans.

One sauce that tastes far better than it sounds is mole (mo-lay). This dark brown sauce used on chicken or pork uses the unlikely ingredient cocoa as the source of its flavor. The taste is anything but chocolate, and it is fantastically dark and subtle.

Tamales are steamed masa (corn meal) cakes wrapped in cornhusks. They may be filled with a tasty meat mixture, usually pork, which is traditional, or contain cheese, beans or chopped vegetables, which is a vegetarian twist. In Mexico tamales are food of the indigenous people and depending on the region can be wrapped in banana leaves or cornhusks. Tamales are eaten especially at Christmas time; they take so long to make that "tamale season" is a big event. To eat a tamale, simply untie and peel the corn husk and eat the tamale with a fork. Another, less common way of preparing masa are gorditas, griddle fried cakes topped with beans and cheese.

Mexico supplies Texas kitchens with fresh, exotic produce. Avocado, mango, papaya and peppers are but a sampling of the array of Mexican

Basic Tex-Mex Vocabulary

Migas: scrambled eggs with pieces of crispy corn tortillas mixed in

Chorizo: spicy sausage

Chalupas: crispy corn tortillas served flat with beans and salad on top

Gorditas: thick corn tortillas topped with beans and cheese

Mole: succulent cocoa-based sauce for chicken

Menudo: tripe Soup, allegedly a hangover cure

Empanadas: sweet or savory filled pastry

Tamales: meat filling wrapped in corn meal wrapped in husks and steamed delicacies available in many supermarkets. Jicama is a root with a fresh, crisp taste resembling a large turnip and is eaten raw in salads. Nopal cactus leaves are pickled or stewed and said to have medicinal powers. The prickly pear fruit can be eaten raw or made into preserves—sometimes you can even find prickly pear ice cream!

Southern Cooking, Texas-Style

On the opposite end of the spectrum of spice is true southern cooking, an art that has been cultivated in Texas for generations. You won't find many low-fat or even vaguely healthy dishes in this repertoire, but the fantastic taste is worth every indulgence. The centerpiece of a meal is often chicken-fried steak. The pure variety, most easily found in small West Texas diners, is a real cut of steak, breaded, deep-fried and covered with homemade cream gravy. Other versions use ground beef, chicken breast (yes, that would be chicken fried chicken) and very rarely a vegetarian patty.

Southern cooking has its share of vegetables including okra (usually served in tomato sauce), succotash (a mixture of corn and lima beans or sweet peppers), and cole slaw to name a few. Cornbread or buttermilk biscuits are essential to most southern meals. The finishing touch is a hearty slice of pecan pie, the stickier the better.

You might be among the many who think that breakfast is the best meal of the day for fans of southern cooking. Fluffy biscuits, sausage patties and eggs accompany that Southern favorite, grits. This white grainy cereal is hominy that has been hulled, stripped, bleached, ground and finally boiled. Grits are eaten with butter, salt and pepper or honey. Most people either love 'em or hate 'em—with grits there seems to be no in-between.

Barbecue

Barbecue—the word and the cooking method—may have its origins in the cooking of the indigenous people of the Americas. In Texas you can sink your teeth into two types of barbecue. The first is prepared in the style of the American South, which focuses on pork and rich, sweet sauce. The second style, more prevalent in Texas, is the dry, smoked meat that relies on wood chips for flavor. Sauces are tangy and served on the side. The coup de grace of Texas barbecue is brisket, usually served in slices.

Steak & Game

The art of raising cattle is a refined one in Texas. Native meat from the larger ranches is sought after. Many of the best restaurants serve regional steak. You can dine at internationally known restaurants such as Morton's of Chicago in San Antonio and Houston. For variety, you cannot beat the exotic flavors of game meat, which Texas chefs love to serve.

Texas game runs the gamut from the common sustenance of frontier life like squirrel or rabbit-which is now basically found only in the tall tales of grandparents-to exotic ostrich and other ranch raised animals. Much of the game served in restaurants is imported from the far reaches of the globe. In southwestern Texas, a variety of game is raised on ranches which cater to safari-style hunters. Lone Star hunters usually bring home deer (venison), dove or quail. If you are lucky enough to be invited to a private cook-out you may have a chance to sample some Texan game.

Chain Restaurants

You are never far from a good meal in Texas. Some of the nation's most successful chain restaurants got their start in the Lone Star State. **Chili's** and

The Best Barbecue in Small-Town Texas

No greater controversy can arise than who serves the best barbecue. And in most every city and town you can find the local heroes of the art of smoked meat. The following humble suggestions are guaranteed to at least please your palate and satiate your hunger. Restaurants like Angelo's, Otto's, and Sonny Bryan's are the heavy hitters and can be found in the big cities. But for those of you who would drive 100 miles for authentic pit-smoked meat, here are a couple of small-town favorites. Whoever your favorite purveyor turns out to be, there is no more authentically Texan experience than visiting an out-of-the way barbecue spot.

Two great places to try include:

COOPER'S OLD TIME PIT BAR-B-Q, *604 West Young Street, Llano. Tel. 915/247-5713. Credit cards accepted.*

In a state as big as Texas, it could take a lifetime to find the very best barbecue restaurant. Luckily, everyone has his or her own favorite spot, which is proclaimed the very best. And time and again Cooper's receives this honor. It is easy to see why. The small town of Llano practically survives on hunters who know their meat. Cooper's caters to this crowd, and they are loyal fans.

JOE COTTEN'S BARBECUE, *Highway 77 South, Robstown. Tel. 512/767-9973.*

The least pretentious and most famous barbecue restaurant in South Texas serves its food on butcher paper. The atmosphere is pure Texas. The waiters will bring you all the barbecue you can eat, and then ask if you want more. This is the delectable mesquite-smoked variety of meat, served with Cotten's own tangy sauce.

Fuddruckers both originated in San Antonio, as did **Taco Cabana**. **Luby's** still has its corporate headquarters in the Alamo City.

Schlotzsky's has their flagship cafe in Austin, complete with a gourmet bakery. And at **U. R. Cooks**, you not only pick the steak you will eat, but you may grill it yourself also. **Zuzu**, a Dallas based chain, is somewhere between a restaurant and fast food. The three specialty salsas and the freshest produce are the trademarks.

Many the state's most loved restaurants are state-wide. The casual atmosphere of **Landry's** lets you imagine you are eating right at the docks. Landry's is best known for its shrimp specialties. Steak, chicken and pasta are also served.

Hardly a Texas city is untouched by the crazy waitstaff, party atmosphere and good food at **Joe's Crabshack**. Every type of crab you can imagine is served at Joe's. The bucket in the center of your picnic table is for the crab shells, and you will get another bucket if you order bottled beer. The fun, informality of Joe's Crab Shack, entertains as you eat. You cannot miss the big "eat at Joe's" signs throughout the state.

The Pappas family restaurants maintain gourmet standards. **Pappadeaux** specializes in Louisiana-style seafood, serving creamy crawfish etoufee, huge bowls of gumbo and generous po'boy sandwiches. **Pappasito's** offers upscale Tex-Mex food.

Le Madeleine, the French bakery from Dallas, serves the same rich and delicious treats in its Houston and Austin locations. A comfortable French-Country setting, great salads, rich individual quiches, breakfast sandwiches (including authentic Croque Monsieur) and wine tastings are the features of La Madeleine.

Mail Order Food From Texas

You don't even have to visit to taste the spice of Texas. The miracle of mail order puts the food within your reach anytime.

The **El Paso Chile Company**, *909 Texas Avenue, El Paso, Texas, Tel. 915/ 544-3434*, sells salsa, sauces and just about anything else you can put a pepper in!

The name says it all: **For Delicious Tamales**, *1330 Culebra Road, San Antonio, Texas 78201, Tel 210/735-0275 or 800/TAMALE-1*. One dozen tamales costs about $18 with shipping.

The **Salt Lick Barbecue**, *5446 Highway 290 West, Suite 103, Austin 78735, Tel. 800/690-1433, Fax 512/892-6237*, which made Driftwood famous, delivers Texas holiday meals to your door. Among the choices are Angus brisket or whole smoked turkeys. Certain meat can be marinated in the signature habanero pepper sauce. Naturally, you can get the famous Salt Lick Sauce with your feast.

Home Grown

Naturally not all the cattle in Texas become barbecue. A select few live on the state's dairies. The **Blue Bell Creamery**, *Farm Road 577, Brenham, Tel. 409/830-2197 or 800/327-8135*, is internationally famous for its delicious ice cream. The genuine Texas flavors, like the peach ice cream, are near and dear to the hearts and stomachs of all Texans.

In South Texas, the **Promised Land Dairy**, *Highway 181, Floresville, Tel. 210/393-7182*, churns out fresh, all-natural, gourmet-quality dairy products. They package the milk the old-fashioned way in glass bottles and sell flavors like chocolate, mocha and cherry. Promised Land boasts the largest herd of Jersey cows in the state.

Produce

Cooks love the sweet onions grown in south Texas. The rich but mild flavor, devoid of bite, accents soups and steaks alike. The onions have been farmed in this region since the late 1800's. Over fifty years of breeding give the Texas sweet onions their excellent quality.

Central Texas has a multitude of peach orchards, and the freshest are sold in roadside stands. Peach ice cream and preserves are often available.

The state tree is the pecan, which is native to the eastern region. Southeastern Texas produces an abundance of pecans. You will find front yards littered with pecans in the fall. The pralines, a sugary pecan candy from Louisiana, is a specialty of the region, and of course so is pecan pie. Seguin claims the title of Home of the World's Largest Pecan.

The citrus of South Texas is unsurpassed in quality. The Rio Grande Valley grows sweet ruby red grapefruit and oranges. In the late winter months you will find an abundance of Texas citrus in grocery stores, and produce stands throughout South Texas sell the freshest, most succulent fruit you will find.

Agriculture is a way of life for much of the state. Unique festivities have become annual celebrations of the harvest. In January, Mission, in the Rio Grande Valley, is the site of the **Texas Citrus Festival**. This celebration of fruit culminates in a parade that features entire floats made from citrus-peel, leaves and seeds. Just south of San Antonio, the small town of Poteet welcomes the spring with the **April Strawberry Festival**. Every September the tomato harvest is celebrated at the **Jacksonville Tomatofest**, which features the Miss Tomato Pageant.

A rather recent addition to the state's agriculture, herb farms are flourishing throughout the state. Fresh locally grown herbs can be found in many of the better supermarkets. And excellent restaurants in all regions of the state, in big cities and small towns alike, use these plants.

It seems ironic that in a state with recurring droughts, rice cultivation would flourish. Yet just south of Houston, rice fields produce year round. The most famous of the Texas-grown varieties is Texmati, a long-grained rice with superb flavor.

Hard Liquor

Over 20 percent of the counties in Texas are "dry," meaning you cannot buy liquor within county lines. Restaurants get around the law by offering membership to their own "clubs." A membership card may cost a few dollars, and will allow you to drink liquor with your meal.

Texas has no local spirit that it can claim as its own. Tequila is as close to a native drink as you will find. The only real tequila is made in Mexico from the agave cactus. If you decide to drink like a Texan, knowing the local rituals will add to the fun. Tequila is served in a small shot with coarse salt and lime on the side. The drinker licks the part of the hand between the first finger and thumb and makes a fist, then pushes it into the salt, so the salt sticks. Then the shot is consumed as quickly as possible. Lick the salt and bite the lime to kill the taste. Makes you wonder why people drink the stuff at all!

Beer

Small Texas breweries produce some excellent beer. Connoisseurs will enjoy visiting the local breweries, many of which are run by brew masters who earned their chops in the Old Country.

The undisputed granddaddy and all-time favorite of locally brewed beers is Shiner Bock. Shiner beer is made at the **Spoetzl Brewery**, *www.shiner.com*, in South Texas. Dark, rich Shiner Bock is the favorite variety, but newer, lighter beers like Hefeweizen are gaining in popularity. Spoetzl opened its doors in 1909 and is one of the oldest small breweries in the state.

Brewpubs became legal in the state in 1993. High quality house beer is produced at many. You will find brewpubs in all the major cities, and many of the smaller towns popular with tourists.

Wine

The hot, arid lands of Texas are excellent ground for growing grapes. There are wineries all over the state, each with varying degrees of quality and craftsmanship. You will find a select few that produce their own grapes and follow traditional aging methods for all their vintages. Some of the best wine comes from the northern wineries in the Lubbock area. **Llano Estacado** is known for producing exceptional varieties – they currently make 18.

At the state's largest winery, **Ste. Genevieve**, winemaking is truly a science. The winery works in cooperation with the University of Texas to research irrigation techniques, grape varieties and fermentation. They produce 1.5 million gallons of wine, which is sold nationwide. Their white wines are their best.

Some of the smaller wineries are the most interesting to visit. Many produce extremely select vintages made in the European tradition. Attention to detail and care shines through in the end product at **Grape Creek Vineyards**, in Central Texas. The barrel-aged white wine is extraordinary. A modern winery and gift shop stands on the small vineyard. The owners are often in the shop and offer personal insight to the making of their award-winning wine.

Other wineries overflow with history. **Val Verde Winery** in Del Rio is such a place. The winery was founded in the 1880s and is still run by descendants of the family that emigrated from Italy. The walls are lined with photos of the generations of wine-makers. The gift shop and storage area are in an original stone building which stays surprisingly cool with little need of air-conditioning. This is one of the few places that produced liquor during Prohibition, when their wine was made for the Church. Production is limited to 5000 cases per year and is not sold retail. The port wine is famous and should not be missed.

There are (as of this writing) 41 wineries in Texas. Below are some of our favorites – for information on all of the wineries, upcoming events, and maps, visit the Texas Wine Trails website at *www.texaswinetrails.com*.

North Texas

PHEASANT RIDGE WINERY, *Route 3, Lubbock. Tel. 806/746-6033, Website: www.pheasantridgewinery.com. Tours Friday and Saturday 10am-5pm, Sunday noon-5pm*

CAP-ROCK WINERY, *Route 6, Lubbock. Tel. 806/863-2704, Website: www.caprockwinery.com. Visitors Center open Monday-Saturday 10am-5pm, Sunday noon-5pm.*

LLANO ESTACADO WINERY, *PO Box 3487, Lubbock. Tel. 806/745-2285, Website: llanowine.com. Open Monday-Saturday 10am-5pm, Sunday noon-5pm (last tour at 4pm daily).*

Central Texas

BECKER VINEYARDS, *Jenschke Lane off Highway 290, Stonewall. Tel. 830/644-2681, Website: www.beckervineyards.com. Tours and tasting Monday to Saturday 10am to 5pm; Sunday noon to 5pm.*

SISTER CREEK VINEYARDS, *FM 1376, Sisterdale, Tel. 830/324-6704, Website: www.sistercreekvineyards.com. Open daily, noon to 5pm.*

GRAPE CREEK VINEYARDS, *Highway 290, Stonewall. Tel. 830/644-2710. Tours and tasting Monday to Sunday noon to 5pm.*

South/West Texas

STE. GENEVIEVE, *Fort Stockton. Tel. 915/395-2417. Tastings and tours available Wednesday-Saturday; call Fort Stockton Chamber of Commerce, Tel. 915/336-2264, for appointment.*

VAL VERDE WINERY, *100 Qualia Drive, Del Rio. Tel. 830/775-9714. Open Monday-Saturday 9am to 5pm.*

How Texas Saved the Wine Industry

Things were looking grim for European wines in the 1800s. By 1840, France had lost almost 80 percent of its vines to a parasitical fungus. The rootstock that was imported from the United States in 1868 to shore up the diminishing vineyards brought yet another problem, a nasty little plant louse that resulted in the destruction of yet another 60 million acres of European vines.

Enter Thomas Volney Munson, an Illinois nurseryman who had moved to Denison, Texas for the climate. Munson developed an expertise in American grapes, in particular the hardy wild Texas varieties. Munson sent some of his hybrid Texas rootstock to France, and *voila* – the vines prospered, and Munson was awarded the French Legion of Honor. The grafting of Texas rootstock to French vines actually continues to this very day, so in a sense there's a little taste of Texas in every glass of wine.

Chapter 12

THE HOUSTONIAN, *111 North Post Oak Lane, Houston. Tel. 713/680-2626 or 800/231-2759, Fax 713/680-2992, Website: www.houstonian.com. 289 Rooms, 8 Suites. Rates: $155-$595.*

Although located in the center of urban Houston, the Houstonian manages to create the atmosphere of a serene country retreat. Part country club, part spa, this hotel resort combines luxury accommodations with proximity to the business and shopping centers of Houston. The gorgeously manicured eighteen-acre grounds are a pleasure to stroll. The Houstonian is also recognized as a Green Hotel for its conservation and recycling practices.

The rooms have been recently renovated, and each is traditionally furnished with understated elegance. The suites are large and comfortable enough to be a home away from home. You can keep the drapes over the floor-to-ceiling windows open, as the oaks and pines provide both privacy and scenic beauty. Amenities at the Houstonian include complimentary Towncar service to the Galleria, 24-hour room service, cordless phones, and plush robes. Meander down the woodland path to the world-class spa, where you can receive a poolside massage or the latest European skin treatment.

The Houstonian Club is a nationally recognized health and fitness center. All guests at the Houstonian Hotel receive a temporary membership that allows them to play tennis, racquetball, paddleball, or use the rock climbing wall and three pools. The Houstonian Golf Course is not on the Houstonian grounds and the greens fees are steep. If you are primarily interested in a golf vacation, you may find that you prefer the Four Seasons in Irving or Barton Creek Resort in Austin.

Olivette, the hotel restaurant, serves haute Mediterranean cuisine meals in a warm setting. The Manor House, a stately old home on the grounds, used to be President George H. Bush's Houston residence. Now it serves American regional cuisine in a secluded lodge-like atmosphere. The tranquility of the location and feeling of privacy enhance the dining experience. The Manor House serves luncheon only – evenings are reserved for events and dinner parties. The Center Court Café, located in the Houstonian Club, provides light, nutritious meals for health-conscious patrons.

HYATT REGENCY HILL COUNTRY RESORT, *9800 Resort Drive, San Antonio. Tel. 210/647-1234, Fax 210/681-9681, Toll free 800/223-1234, Website: sanantonio.hyatt.com/sanhc. 500 Rooms, 58 Suites. Rates: $250-425; Suites $315-1700. Credit cards accepted.*

The invigorating atmosphere and recreational possibilities of the Texas Hill Country is all yours at this inviting resort. Only 20 minutes from downtown San Antonio and the River Walk and practically next door to Sea World, this is the place for families with children. In fact, the resort caters to children, with daily activities scheduled for kids between 3 and 12 at an onsite day camp. This allows parents ample opportunity to golf, luxuriate at the spa, or simply relax by the pool.

Built on the site of a historic ranch, the Hill Country Resort makes use of native materials such as limestone and granite. Hill Country architecture (albeit on a grand scale) gives the place a rustic feel despite its size. And make no mistake — this place is huge. The resort sprawls over 200 acres, 4 acres alone devoted to a water park with a man made river and beach.

The accommodation is comfortable and countrified. Some of the rooms can feel a bit small and, quite frankly, institutional, although the suites are quite nice. But guests don't come here to seclude themselves in opulent rooms — the real attraction here is the great outdoors. Try to get a room with a balcony or a porch. All of the standard amenities you would expect are included, as well as a few bonuses like free washers and dryers.

The rolling hills west of San Antonio are the backdrop for the pool and eighteen-hole golf course (rated one of the best courses in the United States by *Golf Magazine*). For those who want true escape, the day spa offers facials, massage and salon services such as manicures and haircuts. There is also a quiet "adults only" pool.

The best dining at the resort is found at Antlers Lodge, which serves dinner only on Tuesdays through Saturdays, reservations recommended. The Lodge features Texas regional cuisine with a contemporary touch. Mesquite-smoked prime rib and cedar plank barbecue salmon are both delicious. There are myriad other dining choices scattered throughout the resort serving breakfast, casual lunches, and cocktails.

INDIAN LODGE, *Davis Mountains State Park, Park Road 3, Fort Davis. Tel. 915/426-3254, Website: www.tpwd.state.tx.us/park/indian. 32 Rooms, 7 Suites. Rates: $65-100. Credit cards accepted.*

This adobe hideaway is the perfect retreat for nature lovers. Built in the 1930s by the CCC, with thick walls in a rambling Pueblo style, the hotel has outdoor patios with striking views of the mountains. Each room is charmingly furnished; many rooms have hand made rustic furniture that dates from the original construction. And the feeling of the old west remains in the decoration throughout. The secluded Davis Mountains offer miles of serene hiking trails. An outdoor pool and adjoining recreational room give the lodge areas for socializing. The rooms have modern amenities such as telephones, televisions and central heat and air conditioning. The Black Bear Restaurant serves breakfast, lunch and dinner meals, or you can drive into nearby Fort Davis for a meal at the Hotel Limpia.

There is a renovation going on at the time of this writing, and space will be limited through November 2002.

LAKE AUSTIN SPA RESORT, *1705 South Quinlan Park Road, Austin. Tel. 512/372-7300, Toll free 800/847-5637, Website: www.lakeaustin.com. 40 Guestrooms. Rates: $1280-4050 depending upon package selection. Credit cards accepted.*

This lovely, luxurious yet unpretentious spa nestles on the shores of Lake Austin, some 20 miles from downtown Austin. A $17 million-dollar renovation completed in 2001 has turned the property into a world-class spa. Named a Top Ten spa by Conde Nast and one of the Top 50 Best Kept Secrets in the World by *Travel & Leisure magazine*, Lake Austin Spa has definitely arrived among the elite resorts.

The rooms and common areas are decorated with casual elegance, the emphasis being on comfort. The floors are made of smooth saltillo tile, the fabrics are natural cotton, and sunlight streams in the windows. All of the rooms feature private patios, and the premiere rooms offer added amenities such as fireplaces, lake views, outdoor private hot tubs, and more.

The staff to guest ratio is three to one, yet the service is unobtrusive and expert, not fussy or overwhelming. You won't even think about whether the food served is low fat or health-conscious (it is) as you eat in the lakeside dining room. Much of the produce used in the eclectic menu is picked from the organic garden on the premises. Of course, health-consciousness does not stop at diet – Lake Austin Spa offers an impressive array of services ranging from hydrotherapy to kayaking. Nightly room rates are available, as are rates for accommodation and meals only, but where's the fun in that? If you stay here, go all out and treat yourself.

THE MANSION ON TURTLE CREEK, *2821 Turtle Creek Boulevard. Dallas. Tel. 214/559-2100, Fax 214/528-4187, Toll free reservations 800/442-3408 (in Texas), 800/527-5432 (outside Texas), Website www.mansiononturtlecreek.com. 126 Rooms, 15 Suites. Rates: $325-2400. Credit cards accepted.*

This is simply a stunning hotel. Texas cotton baron Sheppard W. King built the Italian-Renaissance style mansion in 1925. Since opening as a luxury hotel in 1981, the Mansion on Turtle Creek has hosted every living president as well as Queen Elizabeth II of England. The hotel has been ranked one of the worlds best by numerous publications, and receives five stars, five diamonds, and five-dollar signs by any rating system you'll find.

Turtle Creek runs through one of the most exclusive neighborhoods in Dallas, and the Mansion enjoys a residential aura. Don't be too intimidated by the prices—you'll occasionally find seasonal special rates as low as $150.

Service is impeccable, with over two staff members per guest. You will be greeted with fresh flowers in your room, and crystal decanters will hold your bath amenities. The rooms are elegantly decorated with antiques and original art. The outdoor swimming pool is heated for year-round swimming. Complimentary limousine service is available within a five-mile radius.

The hotel's restaurant is justly famous as the home of innovative Southwestern cuisine.

MESSINA HOF WINERY AND RESORT, *4545 Old Reliance Road, Bryan. Tel. 979/778-9463, Fax 979/778-1729, Website: www.messinahof.com. 10 Rooms. Rates: $150-250. Credit cards accepted.*

Messina Hof used to be a boutique winery with one cozy bed and breakfast room over the visitor's center. Now it is an intimate inn along the lines of a grand European estate. The bed and breakfast rooms are housed in a handsome brick building known as the Villa, and an innkeeper remains on site 24 hours to ensure your every need is attended to.

Old timers may wistfully remember the days when the one room at Messina Hof offered only a bed, but it's hard not to appreciate the telephone, DirecTV, coffee maker, and fresh flowers provided in each room today. There is a common living room where guests can mingle by the fireplace or watch the big screen television. There is also a utility room with a washer and dryer, and you can arrange spa treatments such as massage and facials in advance.

Each room has a private bath and a patio or balcony overlooking the Messina Hof estate and vineyards. The rooms are uniquely furnished with European antiques meant to reflect the room's name – the Romeo and Juliet, the Thomas Jefferson, and so forth. The Lancelot and Guinevere room is my favorite, with its hand-carved 17th Century bed, stained glass windows, and whirlpool tub.

The Vintage House restaurant serves gourmet lunches and dinners. Your breakfast is provided in a European buffet. The Messina Hof Winery began producing wine 15 years ago and has an annual bottling of 100,000 gallons. The winery sits on 45 acres of lush east Texas land. A stay here is for the true wine lover; breakfast features wine jelly, and port wine chocolates.

VILLA DEL RIO BED AND BREAKFAST, *123 Hudson Drive, Del Rio. Tel. 210/768-1100, Toll free 800/995-1887, Website: www.villadelrio.com. 3 Rooms, 1 Cottage. Rates $85-$195. Credit cards accepted.*

The true charm and beauty of South Texas is found at Villa Del Rio. This elegant and artistic home is nestled in the city's oldest neighborhood

The design and interior epitomize the traditions of the inhabitants of the settlers. The house is built in the Mexican style with porches lining the exterior, stucco walls. The bright, tile floors were shipped from Italy, and the wide beamed ceiling is Mediterranean cypress wood. The interior is a beautiful blend of original antiques and modern renovation. A series of small murals line the main rooms; the previous owner, Mrs. Foster, painted these. The house holds a treasure chest of such art, which the proprietor is happy to show.

The rooms are large and artfully decorated. The largest suite, the Judge's French Door Suite, has a large private bath and sun porch. The three upstairs rooms have queen size- beds. The Peacock room has a private balcony and separate sun porch and private bathroom.

You can spend hours of tranquility relaxing under the large shade trees on the two-acre yard. Allow ample time in your day to relax and savor the atmosphere of this historic house, which was built in 1887. Afternoon tea and breakfast features homemade bread and fresh juice.

central texas

Chapter 13

Here lies the ghost of Texas past, in the gentle countryside of Washington-on-the-Brazos, Chappell Hill, and Round Top. Here also you will find the presence of Texas future, as Austin continues to grow and nurture the next generation of silicone pirates and biotech wizards.

Austin

It's easy to visit and fall in love with **Austin**—the big question is why ever leave? For many that have come to this jewel on the Colorado River, the answer is simple: just stay. The city consistently makes the top ten lists of the best places to live in the US. Growth in the high tech industry, excellent institutions of higher education, and the beautiful environment of the nearby Hill Country contribute to the city's popularity.

This was not always the case. In the days when the Republic of Texas was a fledgling nation, some of the leaders wanted to move the capital to east Texas. Austin was chosen as the seat of government because it stood between the eastern settlements and the open ranges of west Texas. The dingy town, then named Waterloo, had dirt streets and few supporters outside the area. During a conflict with Mexico, word spread that the capital would be transferred east. A group of Austinites secretly hid the state archives so the government could not officially leave.

Today the city combines the best of urban life and nature. The area's explosive growth, though, has impaired the very quality of life that attracted many of its inhabitants. No longer is Austin the laid-back secluded hamlet it once was. The Austin Metropolitan Area (which includes five counties) has increased from a population of just over one-half million in 1980 to over one million in 1998. Austin itself has almost 650,000 residents.

Nevertheless, Austin is still considered paradise by most of its residents, old and new. The true quality of life in Austin cannot be measured by statistics. The city's casual atmosphere, lively music scene and abundance of good food keep Austinites happy. The city has a well-deserved reputation as a haven for environmentalists, and many parks grace the landscape.

Austin calls itself the "live music capital of the world," and in keeping with this, hosts music festivals geared to attract the world's attention. The largest such event is the **South-by-Southwest** (more commonly known as **SXSW**, *www.sxsw.com*) festival. For one week, practically every live music venue in town is packed with bands from all over the world. Producers and talent scouts fill the audience, and musicians hope for the fabled "big break." SXSW is held in mid-March. A film festival and a multi-media conference are part of the SXSW schedule.

If you enjoy street fairs, don't miss the **Old Pecan Street Spring Arts Festival** in May and the **Old Pecan Street Fall Arts Festival** in September. Both events take place on East Sixth Street (once named—you guessed it— Pecan Street) and feature hundreds of arts & crafts booths spotlighting local artisans, musical stages, and children's activities. The infamous **O. Henry Pun-Off** takes place during the Spring festival—spread a blanket out behind O. Henry's house (now a museum) and groan along as the punsters duel it out beneath the oaks. You can get information about both festivals by calling *512/ 441-9015*.

Austin is home to many writers and devoted readers. Each November, Austin celebrates its love of literature with a gala devoted to the written word, the **Texas Book Festival**. Readings, panel discussions, sales and exhibit tents, author signings, and a children's corner occupy the grounds of the State Capitol for a full weekend. For a schedule of activities, contact *Tel. 512/477-4055, Website: www.austin360.com/texasbookfestival, Email: bookfest@onr.com*.

Arrivals & Departures
By Air
The brand new **Austin-Bergstrom International Airport** (opened in late June 1999) is in southeast Austin, just off Highway 71 East at *3600 Presidential Boulevard, Tel. 512/530-ABIA, www.ci.austin.tx.us/austinairport*. The airport features local concessions and restaurants, a stage where local musical acts perform, and an outdoor family viewing area located near the east runway.

A **taxi** to downtown from the airport costs about $18. The cost to the Arboretum area in northwest Austin is about $30. The taxi pick-up is right outside the baggage claim area. **Capital Metro Buses** (Route 100/Bergstrom

Limited and Route 46/Bergstrom) serve the airport, and the bus stop is just in front of the Barbara Jordan Passenger Terminal. The bus connects the airport to downtown, UT, and South Austin, where you can transfer to other routes. For more information about city bus service call Capital Metro, *Tel. 512/474-1200 or 800/474-1201.*

The **Super Shuttle Service**, *Tel. 512/258-3826 or 800/258-3826, www.supershuttle.com,* provides shuttle service from the airport to Austin and nearby communities. You can book reservations online. A ride to downtown Austin costs $9. The reservation desk at the airport is located in the baggage claim area. In addition, many hotels provide their own shuttle services, so be sure to check with them when you make reservations.

By Bus & Train

Amtrak operates infrequent rail service through Austin. The route runs from San Antonio to Chicago and includes stops in Fort Worth and Dallas. The Amtrak Station, *215 North Lamar, Tel. 800/USA-RAIL, www.amtrak.com,* is about one mile west of the downtown area.

The **Greyhound Bus** Station, *916 East Koenig Lane, Tel. 512/458-4463,* is located near the intersection of Interstate Highway 35 and Ranch Road 2222 (Koenig Lane), near Highland Mall.

By Car

If you are driving in from the north or south (Dallas or San Antonio), you will be coming in on Interstate Highway 35. Interstate Highway 35 is congested and badly designed, but fairly direct. Exiting Interstate Highway 35 anywhere from Cesar Chavez Street (also known as First Street) to 15th Street and heading west puts you squarely downtown. If you are arriving from the east (Houston), you have your choice of Highway 71, which runs past Bergstrom Airport and intersects with Interstate Highway 35 in South Austin, or Highway 290, which intersects Interstate Highway 35 in the northeastern section of town. Coming from the west, you'll likely arrive on Highway 290, which you can take over to Interstate Highway 35 or exit sooner onto the MoPac Expressway, depending on where your destination is.

Orientation

MoPac Expressway (Loop 1) runs between Highway 71 in the south and Highway 183 in the north. It's called the Mopac Expressway because it runs parallel to the Missouri-Pacific (Mopac) Railroad. The main roads for east-west access between Mopac and Interstate Highway 35 are 38th Street and Sixth Street. The University of Texas campus is bordered on the south by Martin Luther King Jr. Street (MLK Street), on the north by 26th Street, on the west by Guadalupe, also known as "the Drag," and on the east by I-35.

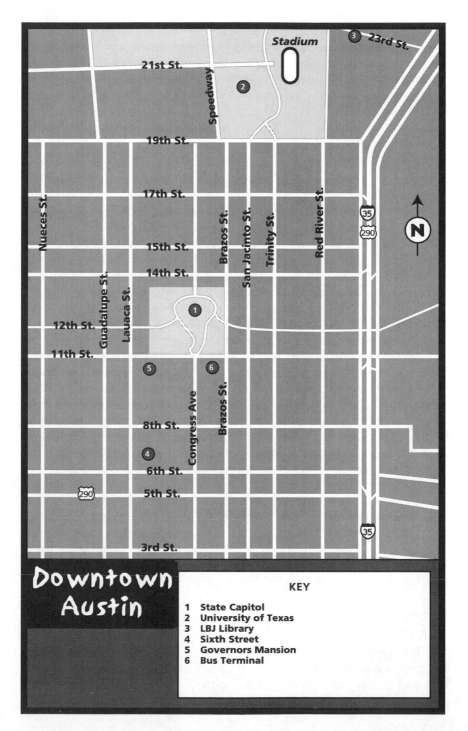

Downtown Austin

KEY

1 State Capitol
2 University of Texas
3 LBJ Library
4 Sixth Street
5 Governors Mansion
6 Bus Terminal

Finding an address in central Austin is easy if you remember that numbering from east to west refers to Congress Avenue, and from north to south refers to Town Lake. For example, an address in the 700 block of a north/south street will be seven blocks north or south of Town Lake, while an address in the 400 block of an east/west street will be four blocks east or west of Congress Avenue.

Getting Around Town

The **Capital Metro** public transportation system in Austin provides easy access by bus to the central business district, the Capitol and the University of Texas. Regular adult fare is 50 cents one way (carry exact fare, as drivers do not make change). Transfers are free. Senior citizens, the mobility-impaired, and children under six accompanied by an adult ride free. In keeping with Austin's constant efforts to combat pollution, all bus rides are free on Ozone Action Days. Green trolley-style buses called 'Dillos run special centralized routes and are always free. You can get information about the routes and schedules, as well as discounted books of 20 or more tickets, by visiting the Downtown Customer Information Center at *106 E. 8th Street, Tel. 512/474-1200 or 800/474-1201, www.capmetro.austin.tx.us.*

You can take a romantic horse-drawn carriage ride through central Austin with **Die Gelbe Rose Carriage Tours**, *Tel. 512/477-8824, www.angelfire.com/biz/DieGelbeRoseCarriage*. The owner of the company uses draft horses, mostly handsome Clydesdales, who are big and strong enough to handle carriage work. The carriages will take walk-up rides and one is stationed by the downtown Radisson at the corner of Cesar Chavez and Congress Avenue until 11 pm nightly. On weekends there are carriages stationed along Sixth Street at the corners of San Jacinto, Trinity, and Neches until midnight. Tours cost $80 an hour, and you can choose from standard routes such as Town Lake, The Capitol or Sixth Street.

Even better than riding around the lake is taking a boat ride on Town Lake. The **Lone Star River Boat**, *Tel. 512/327-1388, Website: lonestar.austin.citysearch.com*, offers one and one-half hour cruises from March through October. Boats leave for afternoon, sunset and evening cruises; times depend on the season. Adult fare is $9; children $6. The dock is located on the south side of the lake, on the trail between the Congress Avenue and South First Street Bridges.

Where to Stay
CENTRAL

The central area is bordered by Interstate Highway 35 to the east, MoPac (or Loop 1) to the west, Town Lake to the south, and Koenig Lane to the north. This part of town includes the State Capitol Complex and the University of Texas.

Expensive

THE DRISKILL, *604 Brazos Street. Tel. 512/474-5911, Fax 512/474-2214, Toll free reservations 800/252-9367, Website: www.driskillhotel.com. 178 Rooms. Rates $165-245, Suites $200-1500. Major credit cards accepted.*

The Driskill combines opulence and historic charm in the heart of downtown Austin. Built in the 1880s by a cattle baron, it has been designated a Historic Hotel of America by the National Trust for Historic Preservation. The Richardsonian Romanesque design was acclaimed as the most elegant in the southwest when the hotel opened. For the past couple of years, the Driskill has undergone a massive 26 million-dollar renovation, and has reclaimed its title of "Grande Dame" among Texas hotels.

Guest accommodations range from small but elegant rooms to massive suites. The furnishings are Victorian, with modern amenities such as data port phones, cable, and 24-hour room service. The rooms shine with black granite vanities and there is a D entwined in the headboard of each iron bedstead. There's more good news—the Driskill has a ghost. Legend has it that a jilted bride who killed herself still haunts the fifth floor. Claudia "Lady Bird" Taylor had her first date with another Texan by the name of Lyndon Johnson here at the Driskill in 1934—they met for coffee. Hear these and many other fascinating historical anecdotes on a walking tour of the hotel (check with the concierge).

Even if you don't stay here, be sure to stop by and gape at the ornate exterior with its arches, gables, gargoyles and shorthorn cattle carved into the façade. The lobby bar is decorated in grand western fashion, with large paintings of important Austinites from the turn-of-the century. The imposing entrance glitters with original marble columns and a large stairway leading to the ballrooms.

The Driskill Grill & Bar is slowly but surely reclaiming a spot among Austin's elite restaurants. Salads and seafood are particularly savory. The room is a perfect place to linger over coffee and conversation, with its beautiful Victorian pressed-tin ceiling and gleaming wood. The Grill also offers a daily breakfast buffet from 6:30-11 am, as well as an enticing Sunday Brunch.

Located on the corner of Brazos and Sixth Streets, the Driskill is within walking distance of the State Capitol, the Warehouse District and Congress Avenue. The hotel has recently added an onsite fitness center with free weights and cardiovascular machines. For five dollars a visit, guests can use the World Gym facilities across the street.

THE FOUR SEASONS, *98 San Jacinto Boulevard. Tel. 512/478-4500, Fax 512/477-0704, Toll free reservations 800/332-3232, Website: www.fourseasons.com/locations/Austin/index.html. 292 rooms. Rates: $195-875. Major credit cards accepted.*

The Four Seasons dukes it out with the Driskill and the Stephen F. Austin for the title of Austin's premier hotel. Everything about the calmly expert service whispers, "we know what we're doing." The beautiful building stands on manicured grounds adjoining Town Lake, with the bar and dining room overlooking the lakeside patio. The hotel is built in the style of a large villa, with an airy lobby handsomely decorated in a contemporary Texana theme. In the lobby lounge, sandstone, wood, leather, and glowing lamps set the tone.

The Café at the Four Seasons may not be the best dining experience in Austin anymore, but that is due to Austin's growing sophistication and the emergence of excellent local restaurants rather than to any decline in quality at the Café. Dinner in the beautiful dining room or out on one of the serene patios is still a wonderful treat, and makes for great people watching. The Sunday brunch remains celebrated for its decadence.

Each of the 292 rooms is elegantly furnished with the same low-key luxury, but rooms with a view of the river cost more, and they're worth it. The hotel offers large suites with king-size beds and two bathrooms. The usual Four Seasons attention to detail prevails here, with down pillows, bathrobes, twice-daily housekeeping and 24-hour room service provided. The Four Seasons is within walking distance of the Austin Convention Center. Runners take note: the Four Seasons sits right against the ten mile jogging trail which encircles Town Lake. The onsite fitness facilities are excellent, as is the lovely pool.

INTER-CONTINENTAL STEPHEN F AUSTIN, *701 Congress Avenue, Austin. Tel. 512/457-8800, Fax 512/457-8896, Toll free 800/327-0200, Website: www.austin.interconti.com. 189 Rooms, 21 Suites. Rates: $199-675, lower rates available on weekends. Credit cards accepted.*

This handsome old hotel, built in 1924, sits about as close to the heart of Austin as you can get, right on Congress Avenue at Seventh Street, five blocks from the Capitol Building and mere steps from the entertainment districts. Vacant and unused for many years, the Stephen F Austin reopened in 2000 after a 30 million dollar renovation and immediately set about the business of vying with the Driskill for the title of Best Atmospheric Hotel in Town.

The lobby and other public spaces are elegant – not in an ornate breathtaking manner like the Driskill, but in a powerful and grounded sense. The rooms are more spacious than the Driskill's (although smaller than the Four Seasons) and serene; the custom furniture has clean lines and the color scheme whispers in earth tones. Amenities include marble baths, high-speed Internet connections with on-site technology assistance, bathrobes, and down duvets. There is a Business Center and A Fitness Center in the hotel itself.

The Stephen F bar restaurant is reminiscent of an old-fashioned private club, where you can easily imagine politicians, cattle barons and assorted wheeler-dealers sinking into their giant leather wingchairs while puffing on cigars. Nowadays the crowd is more likely to attract entertainment industry types and the titans of tech. The bar terrace overlooks Congress Avenue, offering a view of the Capitol building, and Seventh Street. The menu here is clubby as well – tequila selections, wines by the glass, cigars, and upscale appetizers. It's a popular pre-theater or concert stop for the fashionable crowd, and you'll see more suits and expensive jewelry than you expect in Austin. For breakfast and lunch, Café Julien offers a well-stocked buffet, and room service is available 24 hours a day. The newly arrived Star Canyon restaurant occupies space in the Stephen F's building. For more information, see *Where to Eat*.

THE OMNI DOWNTOWN, *700 San Jacinto Boulevard. Tel. 512/476-7000, Fax 512/320-5882, Toll free reservations 800/843-6664, Website: www.omnihotels.com. 375 rooms. Rates: $179-209 during the week, call for weekend rates. Major credit cards accepted.*

The chic, sleek Omni is built around a twenty-story atrium that connects it to the Austin Centre building. Glass elevators and an all-glass exterior characterize this glitzy hotel that was built during the boom-economy of the early 1980s. The outdoor heated pool is located on the roof, and recreational facilities include a fitness room and spa. The hotel's restaurant, Ancho's, serves southwestern and "New Texas" cuisine. A second Omni Hotel, the **Omni Austin Hotel at Southpark**, *4140 Governors Row, Tel. 512/448-2222*, is located about ten minutes south of downtown.

Moderate

HABITAT SUITES, *500 Highland Mall Boulevard. Tel. 512/467-6000, Fax 512/467-6000, Toll free reservations 800/535-4663, Website: www.habitatsuites.com. 96 Rooms. Rates: $104-167, weekend rates available. Children 12 and under free. Credit cards accepted.*

This hotel operates on an environmentally friendly basis, and sits in a landscape of herb gardens despite its rather urban location right next to Highland Mall. All rooms in this hotel are suites, with fully equipped kitchens and either one or two bedrooms. This is an ideal accommodation for a family or for those who want the feel of a home instead of a hotel. Although a bit farther away from the center of action, Habitat Suites is fairly close to the University of Texas, 15 minutes from downtown, and next to Interstate Highway 35 and U. S. Highway 290. A full-course hot buffet breakfast and evening hors d'ouerves are included in the price of the rooms. This hotel is certainly one of the better values in town.

DOUBLETREE CLUB AUSTIN/UNIVERSITY AREA, *1617 Interstate Highway 35 North at MLK exit. Tel. 512/479-4000, Fax 512/479-6400, Toll free reservations 888/444-CLUB, Website: www.doubletree.com. 152 Rooms. Rates: $89-114. Credit cards accepted.*

This most recently built Doubletree Hotel is ideally located near the University of Texas and the State Capitol. You can easily walk to Memorial Stadium and other campus areas from here. The pleasant, spacious rooms have coffee makers and phone lines with data ports for computer hook-up. The hotel offers business services, informal dining and a complete fitness center with outdoor pool. Doubletree also operates a Guest Suites location in central Austin and a Doubletree Hotel on North Interstate Highway 35.

BROOK HOUSE BED & BREAKFAST, *609 West 33rd Street. Tel. 512/ 459-0534, Fax 512/459-4821, Website: www.governorsinnaustin.com/ 3.5.html. 6 Rooms. Rates: $75-119. Credit cards accepted.*

Located close to the University of Texas, the Brook House was built in 1922 and has an elegant grey and white exterior. Three of the rooms are in the main house. The Loer Carriage Room has a private deck under shade trees; the Cottage is a secluded suite with a kitchen and its own yard. A full breakfast is served daily, and on cool days a fire in the dining room provides warmth. From Interstate Highway 35, take the 38 1/2 Street exit west. At Guadalupe Street, turn south to 33rd Street.

BRAVA HOUSE, *1108 Blanco Street. Tel 512/478-5034, Toll free 800/ 545-8200, Website: www.bravahouse.com. Rates: $85-99. Credit cards accepted.*

This charming little house used to be part of what was known as the Southard House B&B. Built in the 1880s, the Victorian exterior beckons cheerfully. The inn offers 4 spacious suites named after influential and inspiring Texas women. Floor-to-ceiling windows allow light, filtered by the trees outside, to stream in and warm the atmosphere. Each suite has its own private entrance and bathroom, and the Babe Didrickson Suite is completely handicapped accessible. The Barbara Jordan Suite has a kitchenette, fireplace, and an antique claw-footed tub in which to luxuriate. The location is very central and all modern amenities are offered, including cable television, irons and ironing boards, telephones, and hair dryers. From Interstate Highway 35, take 10th Street west. Turn south on Blanco.

Inexpensive

SUPER 8 CENTRAL, *1201 Interstate Highway 35 North. Tel. 512/472-8331, Fax 512/476-6610, Toll free reservations 800/800-8000, Website: www.super8.com. 60 Rooms. Rates: $45-85. Credit cards accepted.*

This budget motel was renovated in 1996, and offers great convenience for the price. You're just across the freeway from the State Capitol Complex. You get microwaves, refrigerators, and there's even an outdoor pool. There's no charge to use the parking lot, and free parking is not to be sneezed at in this part of town.

SOUTH

This area includes everything south of the Colorado River, also known as Town Lake. Down here you will find Zilker Park, the Travis Heights neighborhood, and the Wildflower Center.

Expensive

THE HYATT REGENCY, *208 Barton Springs Road. Tel. 512/477-1234, Fax 512/480-2069, Toll free reservations 800/233-1234, Website: www.hyatt.com/usa/austin/hotels. 447 Rooms, 18 Suites. Rates: $175-360. Credit cards accepted.*

This seventeen-story high-rise hotel has comfortable rooms decorated with a Southwestern flair. It's got a laid-back feel, and is a favorite among visiting football alums and their rival visitors from out of town. The best part of a stay at the Hyatt is on the outside—the Hyatt sits right on the south shore of Town Lake. You can take full advantage of the Town Lake jogging trail with the hotel's mountain bikes for guest use. The hotel has a pool, large indoor atrium, and workout facilities. Clean up after your workout with the complimentary laundry facilities on the ninth floor.

From the Branchwater Lounge, you have a romantic view of the sparkling Austin nighttime skyline. The bar stays open until 2am, and offers Tex-Mex appetizers to go with your Margaritas and Mexican Martinis. The LaVista restaurant overlooks the atrium and offers serviceable food, with fajitas the best item on the menu. The hotel is located just on the south side of the Congress Avenue Bridge.

Moderate

THE SUMMIT HOUSE BED & BREAKFAST, *1204 Summit Street. Tel. 512/445-5304, Website: summit.home.texas.net. 5 Rooms. Rates: $69-99. Visa and MasterCard accepted.*

The tranquil Summit House sits on a hill amid large trees. The location provides a true neighborhood oasis in Austin, not far from the hustle of downtown. The Baby Bear Room is a good value, but be aware that it does not have its own bathroom. The Blue Room offers more privacy, with its own bathroom and other amenities such as a coffeemaker and a private cactus garden. Every day at this gay-friendly inn begin with a home-style breakfast and fresh-baked bread. Massages and reflexology sessions are available, and friendly pets are welcome, too.

AUSTIN MOTEL, *1220 South Congress Avenue. Tel. 512/441-1157, Website: austinmotel.com. 39 Rooms, 2 Suites. Rates: $60-133. Credit cards accepted.*

This funky relic of the 1930's has been renovated into one of Austin's favorite stopovers. The retro neon sign outside proclaims, "so close yet so far out," and the emphasis on far-out cool carries on throughout the hotel. The rooms vary in size, are simple and comfortable, and each one is individually decorated. The precious vintage swimming pool is the shape and size of a kidney bean. El Sol y La Luna, the restaurant attached to the motel, serves excellent Mexican food in the laid-back style for which Austin is famous (see *Where to Eat*). Clientele ranges from grown up baby boomers to the young and the pierced. A caveat – I recommended this hotel to some friends, and promptly upon their arrival the toilet overflowed. No one was sent to clean up the mess for hours, and the cleanup was cursory at best. In other words, service here has been wanting in the past. Reserve your room well in advance, as the hotel is often booked up. The Austin Motel is located on revitalized South Congress, across the street from the happening Continental Club.

Inexpensive

AUSTIN INTERNATIONAL YOUTH HOSTEL, *2200 South Lakeshore Boulevard. Tel. 512/444-2294, Toll free 800/725-2331, Website: www.hi-austin.org. 39 beds. Rates: $16 for members, $19 for nonmembers. Visa/MC accepted.*

The Austin Youth Hostel is open to people of all ages. The large lakeside hostel is right on the Hike and Bike Trail and has a complete kitchen and common area. Rooms have multiple beds, but are smaller than dormitory-style facilities. A "family room" that sleeps four is available for a minimum of $33. The friendly staff can offer information about experiencing the best of Austin. Plenty of free parking is available and you can purchase travel books or an International Youth Hostel (IYH) membership at the front desk.

NORTH

This is the high-tech corridor, where all the newcomers chasing the dotcom rainbow flocked during the nineties. Retail areas, condos, and secluded wealthy neighborhoods characterize this part of town.

Expensive

RENAISSANCE AUSTIN HOTEL, *9721 Arboretum Boulevard. Tel. 512/343-2626, Fax 512/346-7945, Toll free reservations 800/468-3571, Website: www.renaissancehotels.com/AUSSH. 478 Rooms, 16 Suites. Rates: $135-1,500. Credit cards accepted.*

The Renaissance Hotel is the cornerstone of Austin's toniest shopping area, the Arboretum. The liberal use of marble and brass would overwhelm if not for a large atrium, which lightens the atmosphere somewhat. Although the Renaissance is Austin's largest hotel, service remains excellent, with an emphasis on attention to detail. This is a good place to stay with children, as there are walking trails and a little lake nearby, as well as the famous reclining cow sculptures that I've never seen without a garland of kids about their necks and on their backs.

The guest rooms are spacious and decorated in a faintly Asian theme, with silk wallpaper and lacquered chests. The hotel has a full gym and indoor and outdoor pools. Of the three dining facilities, the Trattoria Grande is the best, and an excellent restaurant in its own right. Specializing in the cuisine of northern Italy, it is open for lunch and dinner. The hotel has its own Euro-style nightclub, Tangerines, where both guests and locals dance the night away.

Moderate

HOMEWOOD SUITES HOTEL, *10925 Stonelake Boulevard. Tel. 512/ 349-9966, Toll free reservations 800/CALL-HOM, Website: http:// www.homewoodsuitesaustin.com. Rates: $109-179.*

Spacious residential-style suites, a large outside pool, and plenty of parking make guests feel that they are staying in a home, not a hotel. Guests enjoy a free continental breakfast, evening snacks, and exercise facilities. The Homewood Suites Hotel is in the heart of Austin's suburban growth area, about 15 miles north of downtown. Many high-tech companies and a lot of shopping centers make this part of town popular for young professionals. From Mopac Expressway, exit Braker Lane. The hotel is on the west side of the expressway.

THE CHEQUERED SHADE, *2530 Pearce Road. Tel. 512/346-8318. Rates: $75-85. Credit cards accepted.*

This bed and breakfast is on Lake Austin, just a short distance from Emma Long Park. The two story stone house offers one suite upstairs. To reach the house from Interstate Highway 35 or Mopac expressway, take Highway 290/ Ranch Road 2222 west. After you pass Loop 360 take a left at City Park Road, which leads to Emma Long Park. Turn down Pearce Road.

Inexpensive

RED ROOF INN, *8219 North Interstate Highway 35. Tel. 512/835-2200, Fax 512/339-9043, Toll free reservations 800/THE-ROOF, Website: www.redroof.com. Rooms. Rates: $43-50. Major credit cards accepted.*

This unassuming motel chain offers a great value for this part of town, where budget accommodations are growing scarce due to the technology explosion. The rooms are downright huge for the price, and you are about a ten-minute drive from downtown. Only drawback—the traffic on Interstate 35 can be horrendous. There is another Red Roof Inn on Interstate 35 south of town, at the Ben White Boulevard exit.

SPAS & RESORTS

BARTON CREEK RESORT, *Barton Club Drive. Toll free reservations 800/ 336-6158, Website: www.bartoncreek.com. 147 Rooms. Rates: $210-780. Credit cards accepted. Spa and golf packages are available, as are Sunday night discounts. Located west of town, take Bee Caves Road to Barton Creek Boulevard and follow signs.*

Barton Creek Resort claims to embody the quiet elegance of an Alpine chateaux. Perhaps—but it does so on a lavish Texas scale. There are three, count them, three championship golf courses, designed by Tom Fazio, Arnold

Palmer, and native son Ben Crenshaw. The European Spa and fitness center, tennis complex with lighted courts, and breathtakingly scenic location on Austin's treasured Barton Creek complete the setting.

The rooms are commodious, and the views are restful. There are two dining options at the resort, a casual clubhouse-style grill and a formal dining room. A 47 million dollar expansion is underway, adding a fourth golf course, a mind-boggling resort pool, and over 150 new guestrooms. The place is very popular for corporate retreats, and, needless to say, is considered a golfer's paradise.

LAKE AUSTIN SPA RESORT, *1705 South Quinlan Park Road, Austin. Tel. 512/372-7300, Toll free 800/847-5637, Website: www.lakeaustin.com. 40 Guestrooms. Rates: $1280-4050 depending upon package selection. Credit cards accepted.*

This lovely, luxurious yet unpretentious spa nestles on the shores of Lake Austin, some 20 miles from downtown Austin. A $17 million-dollar renovation completed in 2001 has turned the property into a world-class spa. Named a Top Ten spa by Conde Nast and one of the Top 50 Best Kept Secrets in the World by *Travel & Leisure magazine*, Lake Austin Spa has definitely arrived among the elite resorts.

The rooms and common areas are decorated with casual elegance, the emphasis being on comfort. The floors are made of smooth saltillo tile, the fabrics are natural cotton, and sunlight streams in the windows. All of the rooms feature private patios, and the premiere rooms offer added amenities such as fireplaces, lake views, outdoor private hot tubs, and more.

The staff to guest ratio is three to one, yet the service is unobtrusive and expert, not fussy or overwhelming. You won't even think about whether the food served is low fat or health-conscious (it is) as you eat in the lakeside dining room. Much of the produce used in the eclectic menu is picked from the organic garden on the premises. Of course, health-consciousness does not stop at diet – Lake Austin Spa offers an impressive array of services ranging from hydrotherapy to kayaking. Nightly room rates are available, as are rates for accommodation and meals only, but where's the fun in that? If you stay here, go all out and treat yourself.

LAKE TRAVIS BED & BREAKFAST, *4446 Eck Lane. Tel. 512/266-9490, Toll free reservations 888/764-LTBB, Website: www.laketravisbb.com. 4 Rooms. Rates: $145-195. Credit cards may be used to guarantee reservations, but cash or check is preferred upon check-in.*

This is not your typical bed & breakfast—it's more like a miniature resort. The comfortable modern home on Lake Travis has a lovely pool and hot tub on one of the many decks overlooking the lake. There's a comfortable yet hedonistic lakehouse feel to the place, with marvelous vistas of water and green hills. And yes, the sun sets over the lake. The emphasis is on romance at this secluded residence—you can order breakfast to have in bed or on your own private deck. You may never actually want to leave the grounds—there's a private boat dock, a home theater with a 5-foot screen, fitness equipment and an on-site massage therapist. A minimum stay of two nights is required, three nights on holiday weekends. The B&B is for adult guests only, and the grounds are smoke-free.

AROUND THE REGION

DABNEY HOUSE, *701 Autumn Lane, Dripping Springs. Tel. 512/894-0161. Rates: $75.*

Two lovely rooms are available at the Dabney House; both have private bath. The homey decoration lets you feel as though you are visiting family. The Cottage Garden Suite is a second floor apartment behind the house. The suite has a kitchenette and patio. Dripping Springs is located about 25 miles from Austin. The rustic town has quaint shops. From Austin go West of Highway 71/290. Head south on County Road 190 for tow miles, then east on County Road 220. for about 3 Miles. Take a left of County Road 191 and look for the mailbox labeled Dabney. The Dabney House does not accept credit cards.

ST. CHARLES SQUARE BED & BREAKFAST, *8 Chisholm Trail, Round Rock. Tel. 512/244-6850, Website: www.lnstar.com/mall/stcharles/index.html. 3 Rooms. Rates: $70-110. Credit cards accepted.*

The St. Charles Inn began its raucous history in 1850 along a stagecoach route that later became the Chisholm Trail. The outlaw Sam Bass once spent some time here, under far less pleasant circumstances than you will. He was brought to the inn to recover after a shoot-out with the Texas Rangers in 1878, but his wounds proved fatal. The present owners bought and restored the place in 1966. The Carriage House suite has its own private entrance, as well as antiques and a claw-foot tub. In the Main House, two guestrooms are decorated in Old West and Victorian fashion. The St. Charles is on both the National and Texas Historic Registers.

Where to Eat
CENTRAL
Expensive

JEFFREY'S, *1204 West Lynn. Tel. 512/477-5584. Credit cards accepted.*

Many consider Jeffrey's the best restaurant in Austin. The menu changes daily, and is always full of exotic gourmet dishes. Appetizers such as crispy Oysters on Yucca Root Chips and Habanero Honey Aioli or Crab Cakes with Mango Relish and Yellow Pepper Sauce are but a prelude. The entrees include meat such as elk loin or veal ossobuco; duck and pheasant are regularly featured. Monday to Thursday, 6pm to 10pm; Friday and Saturday, 6pm to 10:30pm. Reservations recommended.

SULLIVAN'S, *300 Colorado. Tel. 512/495-6504. Credit cards accepted.*
In Texas, the land of cattle, it is difficult to stand apart as a steakhouse. Sullivan's distinguishes itself both with its food and decor. The sophisticated piano bar attracts a full house on weekend nights. The restaurant has a warm, refined atmosphere and exemplary wait staff. The steaks here are the best you will find in central Texas. The 12-ounce Filet Mignon is cooked to perfection and the house specialty is the mammoth 20 ounce Kansas City Strip. Every entree is served with a large wedge of iceberg lettuce covered in Sullivan's own creamy bleu cheese dressing. Side dishes are served family style, in generous portions. The creamed spinach and horseradish-mashed potatoes stand out as the biggest crowd pleasers.

CASTLE HILL CAFE, *1101 West 5th Street. Tel. 512/476-0728. Credit cards accepted.*
Castle Hill Cafe is one of the best-kept dining secrets in Austin. The restaurants reputation is based on the marvelous sauces- from the very mild white sauce used on seafood pasta to the fiery habenero pepper sauce served on meat-which are original creations. The menu changes weekly and reflects an eclectic mix of world cuisine such as chutneys, oriental noodle dishes and Middle Eastern side dishes. The Tuscany-style lasagna made with cream and tomato sauces is a vegetarian feast. With only 30 tables, the warm atmosphere and artistic decoration is a pleasure for the senses. The upstairs room is used for private parties. The excellent wine is offered at reasonable prices. Top your meal off with the chocolate mousse-a chocolate fantasy.
Expect at least an hour wait on weekends; reservations are not taken. Monday to Friday 11am to 2:30pm and 6pm to 10pm; Saturday 6pm to 10pm; closed Sunday.

MEZZALUNA, *310 Colorado Street. Tel. 512/472-6770. Credit cards accepted.*
Mezzaluna has been a favorite of Austinites since it first opened. Many of the regulars crowd the bar for a few hours before settling down to a late Saturday night dinner. The menu selection changes according to the season, with heavy cream pasta sauces featured in the winter and lighter vegetable sauces in the summer. The wood-fired oven in the middle of the dining room cranks out superb pizzas all night. Lunch specials are featured on weekdays. Monday to Thursday, 11:30am to 10:30pm; Friday 11:30am to 11pm. Saturday 5pm to 11pm; Sunday 6pm to 10pm.

STAR CANYON, *701 Congress Avenue. Tel. 512/391-1550, Fax 512/391-1554, Website: www.starcanyon.com. Reservations highly recommended. Credit cards accepted.*
People may grumble that Star Canyon has become a franchise, they'll either love or hate the over-the-top Nuevo Western atmosphere, but there's one thing they can't argue about – Star Canyon still serves incredibly good food. Located in the refurbished Stephen F Austin hotel, this branch of the

granddaddy of Southwestern cuisine has attracted a steady stream of pilgrims eager to sample the legendary fare. You won't be disappointed if you try the Enchilada of the Day for lunch or the Bone-in Ribeye for dinner. Whatever the time of day, finish off with a slice of Heaven and Hell Cake, the famous chocolate dessert.

Moderate

BITTER END BISTRO AND BREWERY, *311 Colorado Street. Tel. 512/ 478-2337. Credit cards accepted.*

This was one of the first brew-pubs to open in Austin, and one of the first restaurants to bravely move into the warehouse district. The risks paid off, as Bitter End is one of the most popular night spots in the city. The bar, which overlooks the dining tables and is a smoking area, becomes crowded in the evening, although there is usually no wait for a table in the dining area.

The fried calamari is a platter large enough for three people to share. The grilled vegetables vary in quality from day to day; the polenta and portabella mushroom is usually very tasty. After 10:30pm you can still order appetizers and wood-fired oven pizza. The pasta dishes are generally good, and the salad Nicoise is a true version of the French, with a generous amount of olives and pickled vegetables. The lamb is generally good. Monday to Friday, 11:30am to 1am Saturday and Sunday, 5 to 2am. (full menu served until 10:30pm).

Bitter End is in the warehouse building at the corner of 3rd and Colorado. You can valet park across the street. B Side Bar is connected to Bitter End, but may require you to pay a cover charge, even if you dined in the restaurant.

HYDE PARK BAR AND GRILL, *4206 Duval Street. Tel. 512/458-3168. Credit cards accepted.*

A meal at Hyde Park is not complete without an order of the batter-dipped fries. One full serving is enough for four hungry folks. The cafe, in a cozy, remodeled house, has the classic neighborhood feeling of Austin's Hyde Park. The salads are fresh and generous. Hamburgers are served in numerous styles, including a very good vegetarian burger. The restaurant has daily soup specials and fresh, steamed seasonal vegetables. Sunday brunch features eggs benedict and french toast. Local art lines the walls, and is both an exhibit of talent and a gallery of works for sale. Monday to Sunday, 11am to midnight.

Z TEJAS, *1110 West 6th Street. Tel. 512/478-5355. Credit cards accepted.*

This is one of Austin's most enjoyable dining experiences. The airy atmosphere of Z Tejas resembles a large patio. The food integrates foreign flavors into the south's own taste. The Voodoo Tuna is a blackened Tuna fillet served with soy mustard sauce. The Grilled Ribeye is served with chipotle pepper sauce. Breakfast served every day, starting at 7:30am. Monday to Thursday, 7am to 10pm; Friday 7am to midnight; Saturday, 8am to midnight; Sunday 8am to 10pm.

GILLIGAN'S, *407 Colorado Street. Tel. 512/474-7474. Credit cards accepted.*

The amusing island decor is a prelude to the tangy southwestern touches on the menu. A large variety of fresh fish fillets prepared with sassy sauces is the trademark of Gilligan's. In the evening, live piano music rings through the restaurant. Monday to Thursday 11:15am to 10pm; Friday 11:15am to 11:30pm; Saturday, 5-11pm; Sunday 5:30 to 9:30pm.

IRONWORKS BAR-B-QUE, *100 Red River. Tel. 512/478-4855. Credit cards accepted.*

The shack that houses this barbecue restaurant was an old iron works in the days before Austin was but a town. Fans of "the Works" will swear this is the best barbecue in the galaxy. The meat and chicken are mesquite smoked to perfection. The tangy sauce is excellent. You can sit at a picnic table inside or on the patio overlooking Waller Creek.

MANUEL'S, *301 Congress Avenue. Tel. 512/472-7555. Credit cards accepted.*

Manuel's brings the sophisticated taste of Mexico to Austin.

The fresh, full spinach salad or Sopa de Elote, creamy corn soup begins the meal. Specialties of the house include Lomo de Puerco, grille pork tenderloin medallions with sesame and pumpkin seed sauce, or Enchiladas de Jaiba, stuffed with fresh crab and tomatillo sauce. The drink list is eclectic as well, with drinks like the Tatooed Canary, a spicy mango and tequila shot, and the watermelon margarita. From 4pm to 7pm every day, half price appetizers and drinks are offered. On Sunday you can have brunch while listening to live Jazz music. Monday to Thursday and Sunday, 11am to 10:30pm; Saturday and Sunday, 11am to 11pm.

Inexpensive

LAS MANITAS AVENUE CAFE, *211 Congress Avenue. Tel. 512/472-9357. Credit cards accepted.*

Las Manitas serves simple dishes with the authentic flair of the food of interior Mexico. This is a good place to hunt down dishes like Huevos Motulenos, which are standard fare in Mexico. The sauces here have the punch of Mexican peppers, like ancho and chipotle. The aguas frescas, sweet fresh fruit drinks, are excellent. The art over the booths changes often and adds to the Mexican flavor of the restaurant.

Las Manitas is a favorite informal spot and does get crowded, especially around noon on the weekend. There's never a wait if you sit at the bar. And if you're solo, you can take the opportunity to catch up on the news in the latest local periodicals (which are found on the shelves at the front of the restaurant). Or, if you prefer fresh air, walk straight through the kitchen to the back patio. Las Manitas is open for breakfast and lunch only. The weekday lunch specials are a favorite of the downtown business crowd. The outdoor patio is a favorite of the weekend brunch crowd.

MANGIA CHICAGO STUFFED PIZZA, *3500 Guadalupe Street, and 2401 Lake Austin Boulevard. Tel. 512/469-7677. Credit cards accepted.*

Don't be put off by the dinosaur on wheels in the parking lot. That's just the Mangia signature delivery vehicle. You will get a true pizza pie at Mangia. The Chicago-style thin-crust slices are overstuffed with toppings, sauce and cheese. Lunch specials of lasagna or pizza with salad for around $5. One slice makes a meal.

STUBBS, *801 Red River Street. Tel. 512/480-8341. Credit cards accepted.*

The first barbecue joint opened by Stubbs was a small stand that sold home smoked meat and the sauce that won the reputation as Austin's best. Now the operation works on a grand scale. Stubb passed away some years ago, leaving his name and secret recipes behind. The barbecue is still excellent southern-style food, without the neighborhood atmosphere. Side dishes are good, try the onion rings which are heavy on the grease and light on the batter. The restaurant strives to be as much a music venue as a food establishment. On most nights a band will play the inside or outside stage, occasionally without a cover charge. The shows outside have the atmosphere of a party, while the inside is a less desirable venue because the space is simply too small to do justice to amplified music.

The happy hour is a favorite of Austinites; free music shows and discounted beer are the highlights. If you want to take home some of Stubb's secret recipes, go ahead-the sauce and spices are sold under their own label.

TRUDY'S TEXAS STAR, *409 West 30th Street. Tel. 512/477-2935. Credit cards accepted.*

The patio at the West 30th Street location is a great spot for taking in a summer happy hour. Trudy's makes a great frozen margarita which can put out the fire of the red and green salsa that comes with the baskets of tortilla chips. Fresh, delicious non-greasy renditions of your favorite Tex-Mex dishes-including some vegetarian selections-are served. Monday to Thursday, 7am to midnight, Friday to Sunday, 8am to 2am. Credit cards accepted.

WATERLOO ICE HOUSE, *600 North Lamar. Tel. 512/472-5400. Credit cards accepted.*

This is a wholesome alternative to fast food. Place your order at the counter and seat yourself. Good hamburgers, fresh salads and delicious creamy corn soup are the house specialties. On Friday and Saturday nights local bands provide music. Monday to Saturday 7am to 11pm. Sunday 8am to 10pm.

HUT'S HAMBURGERS, *807 West 6th Street. Tel. 512/472-0693. Credit cards accepted.*

It would be hard to convince an Austinite that a better hamburger could be found anywhere other than Hut's. Even the vegetarian burgers are excellent. Weekly two-for-one specials offer a great bargain for the budget-conscious traveler. Once you step inside the campy little establishment, go all out and indulge in the giant onion rings.

NORTH
Expensive
FONDA SAN MIGUEL, *2330 West Loop Boulevard. Tel. 512/459-4121. Credit cards accepted.*

The lush garden atmosphere and rich colors replicate a Mexican hacienda. The finest food of interior Mexico is served at Fonda San Miguel. Quail and fresh seafood highlight the menu. The excellent sauces are true to genuine Mexican traditions. The quesidillas stuffed with flowers from squash plant should not be missed. Happy hour drink specials are offered in the patio bar. Every Sunday a large buffet brunch is served. Take Lamar Street North and turn west onto West Loop Boulevard. The restaurant is located in a residential area. Monday to Thursday, 5:30pm to 9:30pm; Saturday 5:30pm to 10pm; Sunday 11am to 2pm and 5:30pm to 9:30pm. Credit cards accepted.

Moderate
HOUSTON'S, *2408 West Anderson Lane. Tel. 512/451-7333. Credit cards accepted.*

This is the original Houston's, and operated independently from the restaurants with the same name and theme in other cities. The food meets or surpasses the other locations. Large, fresh salads, steaks and fish grilled to perfection and delicious sides such as couscous and creamed spinach are the mainstay of the short menu. Houston's is known for its exceptional standard of service

THREADGILL'S, *6414 North Lamar Street. Tel. 512/451-5440. Visa/MC accepted.*

Threadgill's has been around long enough to establish itself as an Austin legend. Janis Joplin sang at Threadgill's when she was an undergraduate at the University of Texas. Today most come for the decadent home cooking. The chicken-fried steak is a masterpiece of crunchy breading and thick gravy. The cornbread is moist and sweet. Although Threadgill's is known for the hearty vegetable side-dishes, these can be a bit of a disappointment. The corn and spinach taste as if they're fresh from a can. So skip the greens and head straight to Threadgill's homemade pies, they're a taste of true Texas home cooking. Threadgill's is on the west side of Lamar Street. Monday to Sunday 11am to 10pm.

SOUTH
Moderate

EL GALLO, *2910 South Congress Avenue. Tel. 512/444-6696. Credit cards accepted.*

For over a generation El Gallo has served homey tasting Tex-Mex to south Austin and especially the students of Saint Edward's University, located across the street. The food here is authentic Tex-Mex, which means you should expect pinto beans, corn tortillas and specialties such as cabrito (goat meat) fajitas. The salsa has a bite to it, which makes the margaritas all the better. Prices are low and the atmosphere is great. Mariachis play on weekend nights

GUERO'S TACO BAR, *1412 South Congress Avenue. Tel 512/447-7688. Credit cards accepted.*

Guero's is an informal and enjoyable dining experience. For nearly ten years this restaurant has been a favorite, for both food and drinks. Guero's is in an historical building which was once the Central Feed & Seed Store. Now Ausitnites come to feed themselves, instead of buying groceries or animal feed.

The restaurant is reminiscent of a border-town cafe. Reproductions of old photographs of the Mexican frontier (and those brave enough to live there) cover the walls. A guitar player makes the rounds, taking requests and tips from dinner guests. And, of course, a photographer, instant camera in hand, is eager to record your evening. As you sit under the tall, rough sandstone walls, senses are filled with the aromas of the open kitchen: fresh tortillas, sauces and sizzling meat.

Before you order a meal, turn to the best part of the menu—the very back—that lists the margaritas. The margaritas are made with fresh lime juice and hand-shaken at the bar. You can choose specifically which type of tequila (from Cuervo Gold to Patron Silver) best suits your taste.

Guero's is on Congress Avenue, about one-half mile south of the Congress Avenue bridge that crosses Town Lake. Monday to Friday 7am to 10pm; Saturday to Sunday, 8am to 10pm.

Inexpensive

MAGNOLIA CAFE, *1920 Congress Avenue. Tel. 512/445-0000. Credit cards accepted.*

You do not really know Austin until you have eaten at Magnolia Cafe, preferably in the wee hours of the morning. Slackers gravitate to weekend brunch; sometimes the wait is over an hour for a table. Late night study sessions are a great reason to indulge in the pancakes that are the trademark of Magnolia Cafe. If you can't decide what to eat, the menu features well-known locals espousing their favorite dishes. Monday to Sunday open 24 hours per day.

EL SOL Y LA LUNA, *1224 South Congress Avenue.*

This small restaurant attached to the Austin Motel reflects the eclectic nature of south Austin. The whimsical interior offers an insight to the food, which is Tex-Mex cooking with the flair of interior Mexican cuisine. El Sol y La Luna reproduces Mexican dishes, such as tacos al pastor, which is simply grilled meat in a soft corn tortilla. The caldo de pollo, Mexican chicken soup, is delicious and also a meal in itself. You can choose from a full array of breakfast at any time. The weekday lunch specials often feature vegetarian food.

WEST

CARLOS 'N CHARLIE'S, *5973 Hi Line Road. Tel. 512/266-1685.*

The famous party filled Carlos 'n Charlie's has made its way form the heart of Mexico to Austin's own Lake Travis. Somewhere along the way the great Mexican food became Tex-Mex, and the margaritas lost the fresh, tart lime. Still, sitting on the lake makes up in atmosphere for the food, which doesn't rate much better than average. Live music on weekend evenings is featured. The best way to reach Carlos 'n Charlie's is by boat. If you're confined to the road, take

COUNTY LINE, *5204 Ranch Road 2222. Tel. 512/346-3664.*

The County Line is on an inlet of Lake Austin. From the patio you can have a beautiful view of the rolling hills surrounding Bull Creek. The restaurant is famous for giant servings of family-style barbecue dishes. Steaks and seafood are available, but the ribs are reputed to be unbeatable. There's not much for vegetarians here, especially when the kitchen runs out of baked potatoes. Open daily 11:30am to 2pm and 5pm to 10pm.

THE OASIS, *6550 Comanche Trail. Tel. 512/266-2441. Credit cards accepted.*

The Oasis has 28 rambling decks that cover a hillside overlooking Lake Travis. This is a standard stop for a visitor to Austin. Drop by to catch the sunset over Lake Travis. On long summer evenings, you can spend a few hours out here waiting with a few hundred other patrons for the last rays of light. Particularly beautiful nights warrant a gentle round of applause.

The menu includes appetizers and sandwiches. This is not the place to have your evening meal-just the prelude to it. To get to the Oasis, from MOPAC Expressway, take Ranch Road 2222 west. Continue past Loop 360 and the road becomes Bullick Hollow. Turn left onto Oasis Bluff and follow this to the Oasis. Monday to Thursday and Sunday 11am to midnight; Friday and Saturday 11am to midnight

Outside Austin

THE SALT LICK, *Ranch Road 1826, Driftwood. Tel. 512/858-4959.*

Sawdust floors, picnic tables, and the best barbecue around-the Salt Lick is has the stuff that legends are made of. The barbecue served is the traditional southern style, heavy on the sauce and nice, juicy meat. On Sunday, the specialty is ribs. You can bring your own bottle of beer or wine. Wednesday to Sunday noon to 10pm; closed Monday to Tuesday.

GUMBO'S, *14735 Bratton Lane, Round Rock. Tel. 512/251-1606. Credit cards accepted.*

On a weekend night you may have to wait an hour for a table. Although the restaurant does not appear to be anything special from the outside-it's housed in a suburban shopping center-its worth the wait. This is real New Orleans Cajun-style cooking. The generous bowls of thick and spicy gumbo are practically a meal in themselves. The etoufee is the hearty tomato-based version, and one serving is enough to feed two people. You may want to sample the delicious bread pudding, but unless you are careful you may be too full to down another bite by the end of the meal. Even the coffee is served in a big, bowl-sized cup.

LA MARGARITA, *1402 North Interstate Highway 35, Round Rock. Credit cards accepted.*

Take a step back in time to the mid-1900s when you enter La Margarita. The Tex-Mex standards, like enchiladas and fajitas are served with plenty of fresh vegetables. The Margaritas are so good that an after-work crowd fills the restaurant nearly every night. Tel. 512/388-1103. Monday to Thursday and Sunday, 11am to 10pm; Friday and Saturday 11am to 11pm.

CAFÉ CULTURE

Austin has a coffee cult to rival those found in Seattle and San Francisco. Each coffeehouse has its own personality and regular clientele. There's probably no better way to take the city's pulse than to enjoy a morning cup or an afternoon jolt in one of these cafes.

MOZART's COFFEE ROASTERS & LAKEFRONT CAFÉ, *3825 Lake Austin Boulevard. Tel. 512/477-2900.*

The atmosphere is the thing at Cafe Mozart, which sits right on the water. This is a less expensive way to enjoy the atmosphere of Lake Austin's trendy entertainment and restaurant district. A variety of coffee drinks, pastries and desserts are offered. Jazz bands are featured on weekend nights; during the summer the bands play on the outside deck.

DOLCE VITA GELATO & ESPRESSO BAR, *4222 Duval Street. Tel. 512/ 323-2286. Credit cards accepted.*

This cafe is next to Hyde Park Bar and Grille. The gelato and sorbetto are made on the premises. Technical lingo aside, this is the best ice cream in the city. Coffee and an array of unusual spirits are offered. Other tempting and rich European-style desserts such as creme brulee are offered.

BOULDIN CREEK COFFEE HOUSE & CAFÉ, *1501 South First Street, Tel. 512/416-1601.*

Formerly the High Time Tea Bar, this coffee house carries on the delightful tradition of South Austin eccentricity. Settle in on a cozy old sofa and play a board game or sit outside in the sun and sip a latte. Local bands and artists perform and exhibit here, and the atmosphere is often that of a laid-back neighborhood block party. This is a great, lazy, read-the-morning-paper kind of place.

RUTA MAYA COFFEE HOUSE, *218 W. Fourth Street, Tel. 512/472-9637.*

This is THE quintessential Austin coffeehouse. Slackers and yuppies mingle affably, watching the next big folk band strut their stuff at one of the open mike nights or sitting outside on the raised concrete sidewalk. An adjoining tobacco shop offers imported cigarettes and cigars. No matter what time of day or night it is, this Warehouse District spot is always an ideal spot for people watching.

SPIDER HOUSE, *2908 Fruth Street. Tel. 512/480-9562.*

Spider House is always a contender in the "Favorite Hangout" stakes, no small honor in Austin. The staff spins their favorite CDs, University of Texas students get wired and study, and in the evenings the beverage of choice switches from coffee to Fat Tire Beer. An eclectic menu provides nourishment, so you can stay and watch the parade all day and night.

TEXPRESSO, *718 Congress Avenue, Tel. 512/477-3275 and 2700 West Anderson Lane #409, Tel. 512/467-9898. Credit cards accepted.*

Texpresso claims to have "the best coffee in the Lone Star State." Actually they should lay claim to the best cheesecake, which is flown in from Los Angeles. The owners fine-tuned their coffee serving skills on the glitzy Rodeo Drive in Beverly Hills, California. Their photo collection of celebrities smiling and sipping coffee lines the walls of the cafes. They still have the cheesecake shipped from California. Although it's hard for a Texan to admit a preference for anything Californian, the deserts at Texpresso are phenomenal. The north location, on West Anderson Lane, is across from the Village Cinema, a theater that shows excellent films, both domestic and foreign.

Seeing the Sights

The brand new **Bob Bullock Texas State History Museum**, *at the corner of Martin Luther King, Jr. Boulevard and North Congress Avenue, Tel. 512/936-8746, Website: www.thestoryoftexas.com*, does an admirable job of telling the story of Texas in an exciting multimedia presentation. The museum combines three floors of exhibits in a strikingly designed building with an IMAX theater and the Spirit of Texas theater to illustrate the themes of Land, Opportunity, and Identity. The museum is open Monday-Saturday from 9am-6pm and Sunday from noon-6pm.

In the center of Austin stands the **State Capitol**, taller than the US Capitol Building in Washington, DC. The impressive pink granite structure took over four years to build and the job was done in exchange for the land that would become the 3-million acre XIT Ranch. You can tour the Senate and House Chambers from Monday to Friday 9am to 5pm and Saturday 10am to 5pm. Guided tours are free to the public; for information or special arrangements call the Visitors Center, *Tel. 512/463-0063*. When the legislature is in session you can view the action during the morning hours.

Housed in the General Land Office built in 1856, the **Capitol Complex Visitors Center**, *112 East 11th Street, Tel. 512/305-8400*, is located on the southeast corner of the Capitol Grounds. The Center has a small display about the building and recent renovation of the Capitol and a short movie which gives the historical account of the founding of the state capitol.

The **Governor's Mansion**, *1010 Colorado Street, Tel. 512/463-5518, open weekdays 10-11:40 am only*, is a Greek Revival-style mansion dating from 1856. In 1861, Governor Sam Houston crossed the street from this house and stood on a platform to deliver a passionate speech begging his fellow Texans not to secede from the Union. He did not succeed. Part of the lower floor is open to the public on weekdays and tours are free. This is the official residence for the governor and family.

You will have no doubt that Texas was indeed a nation when you visit the only foreign diplomatic residence in the Republic of Texas. In 1839, the French king commissioned the **French Legation**, *802 San Marcos Street, Website: www.french-legation.mus.tx.us*. You can take a tour of the museum and house from Tuesday to Sunday, 1pm to 4:30pm. The home looks much as it may have when it stood overlooking vast empty land and a young capital. The landscaping reflects the southern charm of the architecture. To reach the French Legation, travel east on 7th Street. Turn north on San Marcos Street, which is east of Interstate Highway 35.

The **Republic of Texas Museum**, *510 Highway 183, Tel. 512/339-1997, Monday to Friday 10am to 4pm. Admission $2 adults, .50 students*, is a proud remembrance of the days of true independence on the frontier. The museum is operated by the Daughters of the Republic of Texas, an organization of descendants of the founding fathers of the Republic of Texas and their families. The exhibits include documents and memorabilia. From Interstate Highway 35, go west on Highway 183; the Museum is close to the intersection on the north side of the highway.

The **Lyndon Baines Johnson Library and Museum**, *2313 Red River Street, Tel. 512/916-5136, Website: www.lbjlib.utexas.edu, open daily 9am to 5pm*, is one of two presidential libraries in Texas. There are only ten presidential libraries administered by the National Archives and Records Administration in the entire nation. The large travertine building stands on the University of Texas campus near the LBJ graduate school of Public Affairs. The Library houses forty-five million pages of historical documents, including the recently released transcripts of LBJ's telephone conversations on Kennedy's assassination, campaigning for President, and the crisis in the Congo. Museum exhibits display memorabilia from the presidency and traveling exhibitions related to American History. Use of the museum and library are free to the public. From Interstate Highway 35, exit 26th Street and take the loop under the highway. Turn south onto Red River. Free visitor parking is available in the university lots. The **Visitor's Center for the University of Texas** is located in the low-rise building close to the parking lot. The main areas of the campus are quite far away, however.

The **Austin Museum of Art**, *823 Congress Avenue, Tel. 512/458-8191, Tuesday to Saturday 10am to 9pm; Sunday 1pm to 5pm, Admission: adults $2, children $1*, is housed in a temporary location. Exhibits featuring contemporary artists change frequently. The aim of the museum is to bring international art to the local audience. On Thursdays the museum remains open until 9pm and does not charge admission.

The **Laguna Gloria Museum**, *3809 West 35th Street, Tel. 512/458-8191*, highlights artists of prominence in the southwest. The museum grounds on the shore of Lake Austin boast modern sculpture and walking trails. During the first weekend of May the museum hosts Fiesta, a celebration of children and art.

The **Austin Children's Museum**, *201 Colorado Street, Tel. 512/472-2499, Website: www.austinkids.org*, is underwritten by Dell Computers.

Austin's largest playground, **Zilker Park**, covers 400 acres. Jogging trails from Town Lake run through Zilker Park, and the many fields are used for soccer and Frisbee games nearly all year. **Barton Springs**, *Tel. 512/476-9044*, a large, natural spring fed pool, is open year-round. Nearby, **Zilker Hillside Theater** hosts free summer performances. The **Austin Area Garden Center** spotlights plants native to the region. The botanical gardens include a tour of dinosaur tracks unearthed at the site. Adjoining Zilker Park is the **Umlauf Sculpture Garden**, *605 Robert E. Lee Road, 512/445-5582. 10 am to 4:30pm W-F, 1-4:30pm Sat.-Sun*. To get to Zilker Park, from central Austin take Mopac Expressway south, exit Zilker Park. The park entrances are located on West Barton Springs Road.

For a breathtaking view of Lake Austin (which is actually a dammed portion of the Colorado River), drive over to **Mount Bonnell**. Park at the base of a series of steps carved into the hillside, which will take you to the peak overlooking west Austin. Mount Bonnell is a favorite romantic picnic spot—you'll always find lovebirds cooing as the sun sets over the picturesque hills of Westlake.

Austin has the one and only **National Wildflower Research Center**, *4801 La Crosse Avenue, Tel. 512/292-4100*. Most of the facility is devoted to cultivation and research of native plants. The main building has informative displays about local wildflowers, and you may walk around the seasonal growing beds. The facility sponsors classes throughout the year. Across the street the veloway is an ideal track for in-line skating and bicycle riding. The National Wildlife Research Center is located off Mopac Expressway South.

Moonlight Towers

If you spend any amount of time strolling about the older neighborhoods of Austin, you will spot curious but strangely graceful towers of metal scattered about the city. Their purpose becomes apparent at night, when the lamps at the top of the 165-foot-tall "moon towers," as the locals call them, shed a soft ethereal light over the streets of Austin. This beloved and peculiar lighting system has been in continuous operation in Austin since 1895. Nineteen of the original 31 structures remain and have recently been restored, the only tower lighting system still intact in the United States. You can see Moonlight Towers downtown at the corners of Guadalupe and 9th Streets, 12th and Blanco Streets, and 11th and Trinity.

Nightlife & Entertainment

The **Austin Symphony**, *1101 Red River Street, Tel. 512/476-6064*, performs at the beautiful Symphony Square outdoor auditorium and at various indoor concert facilities. Guest musicians of international stature are featured during the season. The city receives its dose of opera from the **Austin Lyric Opera**, *1111 West Sixth Street, Suite B-320, Tel. 512/472-5992*, which stages its spectacles at the Bass Concert Hall on the University of Texas campus. Also performing at Bass Hall, the **Ballet Austin**, 3004 Guadalupe Street, Tel. 476-2163, presents both premiere and classic ballets. The **University of Texas Performing Arts Center**, *Tel. 512/471-1444, Website: www.utpac.org*, a complex of six theatres on the UT campus, hosts these Austin companies and traveling shows throughout the year. The enormous drum-shaped **University of Texas Frank Erwin Center**, *1701 Red River Street at Martin Luther King, Jr. Boulevard, Tel. 512/471-7744, Box office 512/477-6060*, hosts large events and concerts.

You can buy full and half priced tickets to local theater productions and some touring performances at **Austix**, *located inside Cheapo, 914 North Lamar, Tel. 512/454-TIXS (for full-price tickets), 512/454-HALF (for half-price tickets), Wednesday to Saturday 11:30am-3pm, 3:30pm-6:30pm, Sunday to Tuesday closed; cash and checks only*. Half-price tickets are available only on the day of performance, and must be purchased in person (full-price tickets may be purchased in advance). Sunday performance tickets must be purchased on Saturday. These tickets are offered at the discretion of the producers of each performance, so there are no advance schedules available for upcoming events. Availability of tickets for weekend performances is announced each Wednesday. Credit cards are not accepted.

The Austin Circle of Theaters sponsors **Playfest**, *Dougherty Arts Center, 1100 Barton Springs Road, Austin, Texas. Tel. 512/454-TIXS*, a festival of performance for children. The fun lasts for nearly a month in the summer, and includes puppet theater, artistic performances and theater productions. Tickets are $4.50 for all ages; most performances run from Tuesday-Saturday at 10am and 3pm on weekends.

Central Austin

THE TAVERN, *922 West 12th Street. Tel. 512/474-7494. Monday to Sunday, 11am to 2am. Credit cards accepted.*

Outside the neon sign reads "air-conditioned." And it's true. The tavern offers a taste of college life, with pitchers of cold beer, greasy burgers and fries. The university crowd has filled this bar for over 60 years. You will find yourself in a cheering section when the Longhorns play ball. Upstairs are the pool tables and smoking section.

TEXAS CHILI PARLOR, *1409 Lavaca Street. Tel. 512/472-2828. Credit cards accepted.*

The bravest souls who venture into the Texas Chili Parlor order a bowl of XXX Chili. The "X" designates the spice factor: one "X" is merely mild, which means you may need a very cold beer to cut the sting; "XX," or medium is strong stuff. The "XXX" will light a fire in your mouth. This is the real thing, filled with meat and no beans. Vegetarians should stick to the Tex-Mex dishes.

The Texas Chili Parlor is close to the state government offices and the University of Texas. It is a friendly saloon with good drinks and a smoking section. Happy hour specials draw a local clientele and offer a good excuse to avoid the rush hour traffic that clogs the streets downtown. Monday to Wednesday, 11am to midnight; Thursday to Saturday, 11am to 2am; Sunday, noon to midnight.

THE DOG & DUCK, *406 West 17th Street. Tel. 512/479-0958. Credit cards accepted.*

The venerable Dog & Duck, or the Bark n' Quack as it's known to some, has a fiercely loyal clientele who swear

The Bats of Austin

Most of the year, at sunset you will see crowds lining the Congress Avenue Bridge over Town Lake waiting for the bats to appear. On summer nights, just after dark, hundreds of thousands of Mexican Freetail bats emerge in clouds. Austin is part of their migration which in the Austin area begins in the spring and ends in November. During August you have the chance to see the greatest number of bats. You can watch the bats from the Town Lake aboard Capital Cruises, at the Hyatt Regency on Town Lake, *Tel. 512/480-9264*. The boat leaves 15 minutes before sunset; fare $8 adult, $5 child.

that it's the best British-style pub in Austin. It's certainly one of the older, and one of the first to serve authentic pub grub. Bask in the noisy, smoky atmosphere inside or sit outside at one of the long tables under the trees.

Sixth Street

Sixth Street fancies itself a Bourbon Street in miniature. Most people who visit Austin believe that Sixth Street is the center of Austin's nightlife. The blocks between Congress Avenue and Interstate Highway 35 are filled with bars, music and dancing. The historic buildings give the area character. The street even has its own website: *www.6st.com*. When locals talk about "going down to Sixth Street," they usually mean they'll cruise the whole area, including neighboring Fifth and Seventh Streets.

PARADISE CAFÉ, *401 Sixth Street. Tel. 512/476-5667. Credit cards accepted.*

The Paradise Café feels like a neighborhood hangout. The casual renovation of an historic building provides an excellent atmosphere for relaxed drinks or a simple meal. The young crowd at Paradise represents the mature side of college life. Generally a low-key and crowded bar on the weekends, this is a good spot to either begin or round off your evening. Light food such as sandwiches, salads and pasta is served from lunchtime (11:30am) until 1am.

WYLIE'S BAR AND GRILL, *400 East Sixth Street. Tel. 512/472-3712. Credit cards accepted.*

Wylie's is a classic 6th Street bar-packed with college students on weekend nights. This bar still retains enough dignity to attract professionals as well. In an environment that is used to places coming and going almost overnight, Wylie's has stood the test of time. The space often fills to standing room only, even on the patio. During the day food is served.

ESTHER'S POOL, *525 East Sixth Street. Tel. 512/320-0553. Credit cards accepted.*

Some of the best and brightest actors and comedians perform at Esther's, painted to resemble a large swimming pool. Two shows on Friday and Saturday night poke political satire and slapstick comedy at local politicians. Even if you are not up on the latest local news, you will get a big laugh from the Esther's performers.

STUBB'S, *801 Red River Street, Tel. 512/480-8341. Credit cards accepted.*

Stubb's is the home of the Gospel Brunch, every Sunday. A groaning buffet where you can eat everything you want of breakfast or lunch while the gospel group on stage offers praise. In the Waller Creek Amphitheater you can catch a range of national acts ranging from Merle Haggard to Public Enemy. Willie (that's Willie Nelson, but everyone knows who you mean when you say "Willie") has been known to make an appearance or two as well.

Warehouse District

THE ALAMO DRAFTHOUSE CINEMA, *Colorado Street. Tel. 512/476-1320.*

Yet another unique Austin experience. It's a movie theater! It's a restaurant! It's a movie theater *and* it's a restaurant! Where else but in Austin could you order a sudsy pint to wash down your hotwings while you watch a new release? The Alamo Drafthouse also presents classic silent movies, documentaries, and the occasional spaghetti western.

B-SIDE, *300 Colorado Street. Tel. 512/478-2337. Credit cards accepted.*

Generally this small bar attached to the Bitter End restaurant features local jazz musicians. Some nights, however, homegrown celebrities such as Will Sexton take the stage. The beer on tap is the same as those featured in the Bitter End brewpub. Their trademark bitter beer has a strong aftertaste and full body; the softer EZ Wheat beer is complimented by a slice of lemon and is a very satisfying brew on a hot summer night. A full selection from the bar is also available. This is a comfortably trendy spot with a reasonably-sized crowd.

CEDAR STREET COURTYARD, *208 West Fourth Street. Tel. 512/495-9669. Credit cards accepted.*

Jazz music bounces off the stone walls surrounding Cedar Street's outdoor stage. The bar specializes in redefining the martini; the Cedar Street Martinis mix tequila, Cointreau, and Cabernet Sauvignon-and the taste is extraordinary. The cigar room just inside the bar on the right sells only the best stogies.

FADÓ, 214 West Fourth Street. Tel. 512/457-0172. Credit cards accepted.

This lively Irish pub is a self-described walk through Irish Pub history. Four different traditional pub designs have been combined to create cozy conversation nooks, rowdy gathering areas, and welcoming spots for socializing. Live Gaelic music is a specialty here, as is authentic Irish pub food.

SPEAKEASY, *412 Congress Avenue. Tel. 512/476-8017. Credit cards accepted.*

Indeed, the crowd is *tres chic*; and as long as cigars are in vogue, Speakeasy will lead the local bar scene. The entrance is through the alley behind the building on Congress Avenue. This bar has the dark wood paneling and crystal chandeliers that so compliment beautiful people drinking martinis. Lounge music featured on the weekends. Dance lessons are given on Tuesday nights at 8pm. If you can learn in a crowd of about 50 novices, you may have a shot at success with the jitterbug.

RUTA MAYA, *218 West Fourth Street. Tel. 512/472-9637 Credit cards accepted.*

The coffeehouse is named for the route that connects the ancient Maya cities of Central and Meso America. Ruta Maya imports its coffee beans from the Maya region and roasts the beans in Austin. Ruta Maya has successfully done what few cafes can claim, merged an alcohol-free environment with the night scene. Bands play almost every night, alternating with spoken word performances and the ever-popular open-mike sessions. If the music is too loud, you can hang out with the slackers on the sidewalk in front of Ruta Maya and watch the crowds shuffle by. Bulletin board monitors the latest web-site chatter about revolutionary conflicts in Mexico. The tobacco shop sells cigarettes and cigars.

South Austin

BROKEN SPOKE, *3201 South Lamar Boulevard. Tel. 512/442-6189, Website: www.lone-star.net/bspoke.*

Owner James M. White gets up on stage every night to remind audiences that his dance hall "ain't fancy, but it's damn sure country!" Willie Nelson played here back when he still had a crew cut, and bands like Alvin Crow fiddle away in the Bob Wills tradition to this very day. The dance floor is covered in sawdust, the parking lot is unpaved, and the chicken-fried steak is mouth-watering.

THE CONTINENTAL CLUB, *1315 South Congress Avenue. Tel. 512/441-2444, Website: www.continentalclub.com/Austin.html.*

The Continental Club had a lot to do with the renaissance of South Congress Avenue. The no-frills music-first attitude drew crowds who stayed to make this neighborhood one of the most vibrant and eclectic in the state. Playboy named The Continental Club one of the best bars in the country. This is where Toni Price plays each Wednesday for "Hippie Hour."

THE SAXON PUB, *1320 South Lamar Boulevard, Tel. 512/448-2552, Website: www.thesaxonpub.com.*

If you'd like to know what Austin was like back in the day, before broadband and Lexus convertibles and infotainment television, then this is the place to be. A giant knight in armor stands forbiddingly outside the modest exterior, but on the inside this veteran live music venue is funky, relaxed, and dedicated to Austin artists.

Sports & Recreation

The best outdoor trails in the Austin area are along the **Barton Creek Greenbelt**. Hikers, mountain bikers, cross-country runners and even leisurely walkers flock to the greenbelt. Do not despair if the serenity of the preserve is threatened by hoards of nature seekers; the crowds thin out by the time you hit the interior trails. **Running** enthusiasts, be sure to check out this invaluable website: *www.webrag.com/runningcentraltx/index.html.*

There are a number of access points for the greenbelt, and a variety of paths you can take once on it. You can pick up a map at most local bookstores or just go to one of the trail heads and follow the signs. The easiest access is from **Zilker Park** (park by Barton Springs Pool).

The young, mobile population of Austin is crazy about **mountain biking**. There are a number of excellent trails ranging in difficulty from beginner to very advanced. **Emma Long Park** lets bikers enjoy Lake Travis from atop two wheels. The short trail loop is entirely over difficult terrain. This is also a **moto-cross loop**. From Austin, take Farm Road 2222 west. Just past the intersection with Loop 360, take the first road north; a sign will point the way to the city road that leads to the park.

Sailing on Lake Travis is perhaps the best way to see the beauty of the Hill Country. You can charter or rent a sailboat from **Sail Aweigh Charters**, *Tel. 512/250-8141*. Hourly rates for a boat and captain range from $35 to $55 for up to six adults. Customized cruises and sailing lessons can be arranged.

Town Lake, in the center of Austin, is one of the few places in the southwest where you can go **sculling**. The **Texas Rowing Club**, *Tel. 512/328-7180*, located off the Hike and Bike Trail on Town Lake, offers lessons that begin at $55 per hour. The boats are located on the north side of the lake on the trail between the First Street and Lamar Street Bridges.

Spectator Sports

Get out your burnt orange sweatshirt and support Big XII Conference champions **The University of Texas Longhorns**, *Tel. 512/471-3333 or 800/982-BEVO*. The football season runs September to December; the baseball season runs from February through May. And both women's and men's Longhorn basketball is exceptional.

Excursions & Day Trips

Why not take a train to nowhere? The **Hill Country Flyer**, *Tel. 512/477-8468*, is a steam train which travels along rails laid in 1881. The train starts in the Austin suburb of Cedar Park. The 33-mile trip to Liberty Hill takes two and one-half hours; the train runs once per day on weekends. Departure from Cedar Park is at 10am, and departure from Liberty Hill is at 3pm. Occasionally the **Twilight Flyer** makes evening runs.

The pretty town of **Bastrop** lies about 30 miles east of Austin on Highway 71. Perhaps the most interesting thing about the town is the story behind its name. Bastrop was named for Philip H. Nering Boegel, a tall and charming military adventurer and raconteur who fled the threat of imprisonment in Holland and christened himself the "Baron" de Bastrop. He curried favor with the Spanish government and received a land grant that he later sold to Aaron Burr.

The charming pocket-sized historical district provides some pleasant shops as well as the **Bastrop County Historical Museum**, *702 Main Street, Monday to Friday 12 to 4pm, Saturday and Sunday 1 to 5pm,* situated on the Colorado River. Bastrop is also the seat of Bastrop County. The stuccoed,

A Beautiful Detour Through the Lost Pines

From Bastrop you can take one of the most scenic drives in this part of the state. This byway through the woods links two state parks, both of which offer ample charms to tempt the passerby into a detour. To start, follow Highway 21 east from Bastrop until you get to **Bastrop State Park.** There is a $3 entrance fee to the park, which offers a golf course, a small lake with fishing, nature trails, and extremely popular cabins. The Civilian Conservation Corps built the handsome facilities. From Bastrop State Park, take Park Road 1C, and follow it for 13 winding miles to **Buescher State Park.**

Almost immediately you are plunged into an evergreen forest where soft brown piles of fallen needles line the narrow paved road. These are the Lost Pines, so called because they are isolated from their cousins to the east. Roll down the windows. Often bird song and the wind sighing in the loblollies are your only companions on this road. If you're lucky enough to have the time, bike it. Whatever the time of year, it's a lovely meditative drive.

Once you get to Buescher State Park, which features more fine CCC depression-era buildings as well as fishing and hiking, you can rejoin Highway 71 and drive west to Austin or east to La Grange.

squat, friendly-looking **Bastrop County Courthouse**, *807 Pine Street,* shares a square with an elegant old County Jail building.

Practical Information

The **American Automobile Association (AAA)**, *3005 South Lamar Boulevard, Suite D113, Tel. 512/444-4757*, offers maps and directions to everyone (for free if you are a member, otherwise there is a modest charge).

The excellent **Austin Visitor Center**, *201 East 2nd Street, Tel. 512/478-0098*, is located downtown near the Convention Center. Many free publications are available here, including self-guided walking tours of historical areas of town.

Waco

Waco is named for the Native Americans who lived in the area at the time of the Spanish Conquest. Agriculture has always played a major role in the city of Waco. The historic downtown area is the product of the cattle boom days, when the Chisholm Trail blazed through Waco.

Baylor University is located in Waco. The Baylor mascot, a baby black bear, lives in a park at Baylor University. Actually there are three bears, one year apart in age, which live together on the stream. The Baylor Bears are always cubs; when they reach adulthood they are given to wildlife preserves.

Arrivals & Departures

The **Waco municipal airport** is 10 miles from the center of the city. American Eagle and Continental Airlines serve Waco.

Orientation

Downtown Waco is just west of Interstate Highway 35. Baylor University is located on the east side of Interstate Highway 35. Waco Transit Service operates the city buses, *Tel. 254/753-0113.*

Where to Stay

THE BRAZOS HOUSE BED AND BREAKFAST, *1316 Washington Avenue. Tel. 254/754-3565, Toll free 800/729-7313, Website: www.thebrazoshouse.com. 4 Rooms. Rates: $75-90. Credit cards accepted.*

This 113-year-old house was used as a law office until the current owners purchased and renovated it in 1997. Now it serves as the prettiest accommodation in Waco. The 200,000 bricks of the house are made from Brazos River clay, and the walls are three bricks thick both inside and out. Every morning guests are treated to a full breakfast in the downstairs dining room.

COURTYARD BY MARRIOTT WACO, *101 Washington Avenue. Tel. 254/752-8686, Toll free reservations 800/321-2211. 147 Rooms, 6 Suites. Rates: $79-129. Credit cards accepted.*

Staying in downtown Waco is a pleasant switch from the anonymous highway orientation of the most modern part of the city. The central business area has a number of turn-of-the-century high-rise office buildings that exemplify the boomtown era. The Courtyard is attractive, the rooms are comfortable, and service is quite good. The inn has a fitness center, whirlpool, and outdoor pool. The hotel is at the corner of University Parks Drive and Washington Avenue.

HAMPTON INN, *4259 North Interstate Highway 35, Lacy Lakeview. Tel. 254/412-1999, Toll free reservations 800/HAMPTON. 119 Rooms. Rates: $76-150. Credit cards accepted.*

The Hampton Inn just south of Waco is new and offers amenities that appeal to business travelers. A hospitality room can be provided for groups of 18 or more and there is a business center with fax and copy machines. Rooms have microwave ovens, coffee makers and hair dryers. Some rooms have a spa bath. From Interstate Highway 35, exit Lakeshore Drive. The inn is on the west side of the highway.

FAIRFIELD INN, *5805 North Woodway Drive, Woodway. Tel. 254/776-7821. 64 Rooms, 8 Suites. Rates $60-90. Credit cards accepted.*

The Fairfield Inn is a comfortable and convenient place to stay while in the Waco area. Amenities include an indoor pool. All rooms receive continental breakfast. The inn is about five miles southwest of the city center. From Interstate Highway 35, take the Loop 340/Highway 6 exit. Travel north to Waco Drive, also called Highway 84. The inn is at the intersection of Highways 84 and 6.

Where to Eat

THE ELITE CAFE, *2132 South Valley Mills Drive at IH-35 on the Circle. Tel. 254/754-4941. Credit cards accepted.*

For over 50 years, the Elite Cafe has been catering to the residents of Waco and those just passing though. Elvis ate here once, while he was stationed at nearby Fort Hood. This is a pleasant place to stop for coffee break or a full meal. The Elite Cafe is just what its name says, an upscale diner that serves both healthy and downright decadent food. The cafe is known for its generous chicken fried steaks. And, naturally, the shakes are great. Soups and salads are among the lighter menu items.

Seeing the Sights

The first fort of the Texas Rangers was constructed in Waco. Today the **Texas Rangers Museum**, *University Parks Drive, Tel. 254/750-8631, open daily 9am to 5pm, admission $3.50 adult, $1.50 child*, documents the history of this famous police force. Displays chronicle the history of the Texas Rangers and shed light on the dangerous life on the Texas frontier. The museum sits on 35 acres and wagon tours of the grounds are conducted daily.

To the west of Interstate Highway 35, at University Parks Drive and 4th Street, you will find a **suspension bridge** built in 1870. According to local lore this very bridge was used as a model for the much larger Brooklyn Bridge.

Waco is the birthplace of the Dr. Pepper soft drink, and the **Dr. Pepper Museum**, *300 South 5th Street, Tel. 254/757-1024, Monday to Saturday 10am to 4pm and Sunday noon to 4pm, admission $3.50 adult, $1.50 students*, pays homage to the tasty concoction. The drink was invented in 1885 at a local soda fountain which stood at Austin Avenue and 4th Street. The popularity of it quickly grew, and by 1906 the drink was being bottled for distribution. Dr. Pepper has not been produced in Waco since 1922, but a bottling plant still runs nearby (see Excursions & Day Trips). The museum features memorabilia and an old-fashioned soda fountain that serves Dr. Pepper.

Excursions & Day Trips

The oldest Dr. Pepper bottling plant, operating since 1891, is in Dublin, 94 miles west of Waco. The **Dr. Pepper Bottling Company**, *Highway 377, Dublin, Tel. 817/445-3466, Monday to Friday 8am to 5pm*, jumps into action every Tuesday, when the bottling is done. Visitors are welcome to tour the small factory and museum. You can buy the Dr. Pepper produced here, which is made according to the original specifications with pure cane sugar. From Waco, take Highway 6 west. Dublin and the Bottling Company are located at the intersection of Highways 6 and 377.

Practical Information

The **Waco Chamber of Commerce**, *University Parks Drive, Tel. 254/752-6551 or 800/WACO-FUN*, provides tourist information.

A **hotline** lists upcoming special events in Waco, *Tel. 254/752-9226*.

La Grange

Yes, this is *that* **La Grange**, the one in the song by ZZTop. La Grange was once famous for being the home of the most notorious brothel in Texas. The Chicken Ranch, the institution upon which the play and movie *The Best Little Whorehouse in Texas* is based, burned down years ago, so don't go expecting to see red lights. What is left of La Grange is a lovely small town, the seat of pastoral Fayette County, both historically and architecturally rich.

La Grange has a strong German and Czech heritage, and its settlers fought and died in the struggle for Texas Independence. The town was settled in 1831 along the ancient buffalo and Indian trail that the Spaniards later called **La Bahia Trail**. The founder of the town, Colonel John Henry Moore, later commanded the force that fired the first shot of the Texas Revolution.

Arrivals & Departures

La Grange is 88 miles east of Austin, at the intersection of Highways 77 and 71.

Where to Stay

BRENDAN MANOR, *345 East Travis Street. Tel. Toll free 866/658-1100, Website: www.brendanmanor.com. 5 Rooms. Rates $175-95.*

Housed in the historic Bradshaw/Killough home, Brendan Manor brings long-needed quality accommodations to La Grange. The original structure was built in the 1840s, and in true Victorian style boasts ornate stairways, intricately carved fixtures, and gleaming rich wood. The Sarah Ellen Room has become a favorite, with its king-sized sleigh bed and Jacuzzi corner tub for two in the private bath. A freshly prepared breakfast is included in the room rates.

Where to Eat

Since the Bon-Ton closed there aren't any sit-down restaurants of note in La Grange, but stop by **Weikel's Store and Bakery,** *2247 West State Highway 71, Tel. 979/968-9413,* and load up on kolaches and pigs-in-the-blanket. Weikel's has become so indispensable to its fans that it has started up an online store, *www.weikels.com,* where you can get your Czech pastry fix delivered to your doorstep.

Seeing the Sights

The beautiful **County Courthouse**, *Business Highway 71 between Main and Washington Streets,* was built in 1891 of limestone, and each side of the building is unique. The architecture is Richardsonian Romanesque (another building built in the same style is the Driskill Hotel in Austin). The **Saint James Episcopal Church**, *156 Monroe Street,* built in 1885, is an old-world delight with its bright paint and wooden shingles.

The **N. W. Faison Home and Museum**, *822 South Jefferson Street,* was the home of a survivor of the Dawson Massacre (more on that under Monument Hill, below) and contains original furnishings and art from the 1870s. Across the way, you'll find the **Fayette Heritage Museum and Archives & Public Library**, *855 South Jefferson Street, Tuesday to Friday 10am to 5pm; Saturday 10am to 1pm, Sunday 1pm to 5pm,* which has information about the founding families of the area. Displays also feature local artwork.

Not to be missed is the **Kreische Brewery State Historical Park and Monument Hill**, *414 State Loop Spur 92, Tel. 979/968-5658.* This breathtakingly scenic site, located on a bluff overlooking the Colorado River, is a testimony to both the pioneering spirit and the bravery of those who fought for Texas Independence. In 1848, the remains of Texan volunteers who had died fighting Mexico in the battle of Salado Creek, as well as those killed during the Mier Expedition were given a military burial here. Soon after, H.L. Kreische, an immigrant stonemason from Germany, purchased the land and decided to become a brewer. In the 1860s, he built the three-story commercial brewery and family home entirely from the stone and resources of the land. By the late 1870s, Kreische's "Bluff Beer" brewery was the third largest in the state.

In the park now there is a 48-foot tall monument honoring the dead, as well as the remains of the brewery and the remarkably preserved Kreische house. The park is open daily from 8am to 5pm. Entrance fee $2; children 12 and under free. Guided tours of the brewery are offered every Saturday and Sunday at 2 and 3:30pm; tours of the house are held on the first Sunday of the month at 1:30 and 3:00pm. Take Highway 77 south of La Grange for one mile. Turn right onto Spur 92 and go west. Signs lead to the park.

Excursions & Day Trips

One of the most fascinating aspects of Texas is the plethora of cultures that settled the state and retain their roots. Among the many groups of European immigrants to arrive in Texas were the Wends, Slavic people who lived in eastern Germany. Wends began arriving in 1849 and settled in east-central Texas. They brought the culture and traditions of Lusatia to a land grant, which later became Serbin, Texas. The Wendish culture is celebrated at the **Texas Wendish Heritage Museum**, *Farm Road 2239, Serbin. Tel. 979/ 366-2441, Sunday to Friday 1pm to 5pm, admission $1 adults, free to children under 14 years old.* From Highway 71, exit Farm Road 2104, which is between Bastrop and La Grange. Travel north on farm Road 2104 to Farm Road 2239. Head east to Serbin.

Practical Information

The **La Grange Chamber of Commerce and Visitor's Center**, *171 South Main Street, Tel. 979/968-5756, 800/LaGrange,* is now housed in the impressive 115-year-old county jail.

Round Top/Winedale

A world-class fine arts center lies hidden in the gently rolling countryside north of La Grange. The communities of Round Top and Winedale offer Shakespeare, concerts, superior bed & breakfasts, antique shopping, and historical charm. As the hometown slogan of Round Top has it, "who would have thought a town of 81 could offer the world so much to do?"

Arrivals & Departures

To get to Round Top and Winedale from Austin, drive east on Texas Highway 71 to La Grange. In La Grange, go north (to your left) on State Highway 159 and drive about 7 miles to Round Top. To get there from Houston, take Highway 290 West. At the town of Carmine, turn left onto Highway 458 and follow the fork to the right to Round Top.

Where to Stay & Eat

HEART OF MY HEART RANCH, *Florida Chapel Road, Round Top, Tel. 979/249-3172, Fax 979/249-3193, Toll free reservations 800/327-1242, Website: www.heartofmyheartranch.com. 12 Rooms. Rates: $145-250, call about winter rates.*

This bed and breakfast is actually a collection of houses and cottages. The Main House is a lovely Victorian-style lakeside residence with roomy wrap-around porches. All of the rooms are furnished with antiques. The breakfast buffet is served on the big wrap-around porch. Orchards, flower and herb gardens, and burros will delight children and adults alike. There is a swimming pool with a Jacuzzi and a playground for children. In-room VCRs and a complimentary video library offer you further entertainment options if you can resist fishing and rowing about on the lake.

Three rooms are available in the Main House—of these the prettiest is the Bluebonnet Room, light and airy. The Frontier House, a charming fachwerk structure, contains five other rooms. There is a carriage house with two rooms that can be connected, a self-contained cottage, and a log cabin, as well. Each room has a distinctive atmosphere, some have fireplaces, and all are comfortable.

BRIARFIELD AT ROUND TOP, *219 FM 954. Tel. 979/249-3973, Toll free 800/472-1134, Website: www.briarfieldatroundtop.com, 7 Rooms. Rates: $95-115. MasterCard, Visa, Discover, and personal checks accepted.*

Two renovated farmhouses have been transformed into one delightful bed and breakfast on the Briarfield property. The Giddings House, built in the 1880s, has five bedrooms, each with a private entrance and bath. Rocking chairs line the three porches where you can sit and listen to the rain on the tin roof if the weather cooperates. The Paige House has a blue ceiling, believed by early settlers to resemble the sky enough to confuse barn swallows and mud wasps who might otherwise nest there. There are two rooms in the Paige House, again with their own entrances and bathrooms.

The rooms are uniquely furnished with antiques such as four-poster beds, folk art, and vintage prints. There are five acres of landscaped grounds to explore as well as a bulb garden, an herb garden, and a southwest garden featuring native plants. You can have your breakfast delivered hot to your room or porch if you wish, or join other guests in the Gathering Room.

ROYERS ROUND TOP CAFÉ, *Route 237 on the Square. Tel. 877/866-PIES (7437), Website: www.royersroundtopcafe.com. No reservations, but you can call ahead on the day of your visit and put your name on a waiting list.*

This 38-seat café is owned and operated by Bud and Karen Royer and their extended family. It's an exuberant, eclectic place, known far and wide for its ambience and food, and it has the long lines to prove it. The menu specializes in what the Royers call "sophisticated comfort food." If you're wondering what the initials OMG next to some of the entrees mean, they stand for "Oh my God." Among the OMG choices are the Black Angus filet, the Grilled Salmon, and the Shrimp-Stuffed Grilled Quail. The real star here, though, is pie. Pecan pie is a must – this could possibly be the best pecan pie in Texas. If you just can't bear to decide, get the Pie Sampler Plate with four different slices and split it amongst your table.

Seeing the Sights

The **Winedale Historical Center**, *Tel. 979/278-3530, www.cah.utexas.edu/divisions/Winedale.html*, a division of The University of Texas Center for American History, serves both as an exhibit and a stage. Its 225 acres contain historical buildings from the nineteenth century, a decorative arts collection, a conference center, and even some wildlife habitat demonstrations. The highlight of the Winedale calendar is the annual **Shakespeare at Winedale** festival, *www.shakespeare-winedale.org*, when University of Texas students of many disciplines offer cutting-edge interpretations of Shakespeare's works. Reservations for this immensely popular event are recommended well in advance.

Round Top is also home to **Festival Hill**, *Tel. 979/249-3129, www.festivalhill.org*, an amazing cultural gem that attracts thousands of music lovers every weekend. The grounds are open year-round to the public. From April to August of each year a series of weekend concerts is given. After the concerts, a complimentary tour of the facility is offered. Old classic movies are shown too! The outstanding event of the year is the yearly International Festival, bringing the best classical musicians in the world and throngs of music lovers to the premises.

Henkel Square, *Thursday to Sunday, 12 to 5pm, entrance fee $3.25*, is a collection of historic buildings from all over Central Texas. You can wander through old homes, churches, and barns that belonged to early settlers.

If you arrive or leave on 237 south, you will pass **St. Martin's**, the world's smallest Catholic Church. Stop and look into the tiny structure (it is open all the time, and there are Sunday services). There are two rows of simple pews, and the altar is covered with offerings and hand-scribbled noted of praise and thanks from passersby.

Nightlife & Entertainment

It is a tradition among Texans to drive into the area for a weekend of Shakespeare, music, and plain relaxing. If you wish to join them, make your reservations in advance.

Practical Information

The **Round Top Chamber of Commerce** website, *www.roundtop.org*, is well organized and features some lovely local photography to boot.

Brenham

The rolling hills and picturesque farmland of **Brenham** were part of the first land grants given to the founders of Texas by the Mexican government. German and European settlers who cleared the land for cattle carved the personality of the area out. Today this part of Texas is unlike any other. The green hills, manicured dairy farms and white fences seem far removed from the cowboy image of Texas.

Most visitors to Brenham stop in as a retreat from the city life of Houston or Dallas. The old downtown is undergoing a revitalization, which includes the opening of a number of antique and gift shops and a mural project depicting the city's life and history.

Arrivals & Departures

Brenham is located between Houston (to the east) and Austin (to the west) on US Highway 290.

Where to Stay

ANT STREET INN, *107 West Commerce Street. Tel. 979/836-7393, Toll free 800/805-2600, Website: www.antstreetinn.com. 14 Rooms. Rates: $105 to $235. Credit cards accepted.*

This may be the only inn in Texas that has an antique elevator as the centerpiece of one of its guest rooms. You will not be able to go anywhere in the elevator – it's merely a conversation piece in the already fascinating Ant Street Inn. The inn, built in 1900, stands in the heart of reborn downtown Brenham. It has been exquisitely restored and expertly refurbished. The 14 rooms have decorations reminiscent of the year of its construction and private baths. The bar offers occasional nightlife in sleepy Brenham. Innkeeper Pam Traylor used to work with Southern Living Magazine's Cooking School, and it shows in the artfully arranged breakfast that greets each guest in the morning. This is a no-smoking, pet-free establishment, and children must be over the age of 12.

THE BRENHAM HOUSE, *705 Clinton. Tel. 979/830-0477, Toll free 800/259-8367. Rates: $75 to $80. Credit cards accepted.*

The Brenham House gives visitors the flavor of old Brenham. It is in the center of the historic town, so you can take an evening stroll through the city, or walk to the museums. The four rooms are lovingly furnished with antiques and homey accents. As you relax in one of the libraries or the sun porch, you can make friends with one of the cats.

HEARTLAND COUNTRY INN, *Route 2 Box 146. Tel. 979/836-1864, Toll free 800/871-1864, Website: www.heartlandcountryinn.com. 14 Rooms. Rates start at $80.*

This large home dates from the early 1900's and has 14 guest rooms. One pastime that guests enjoy is having picnic lunches on the 158 acres of beautiful land that surrounds the farmhouse. To reach the Heartland Country Inn, take County Road 68 from Brenham for 10 miles.

NUECES CANYON BED AND BREAKFAST, *9501 Highway 290 West. Tel. 979/289-5600, Toll free 800/925-5058, Website: www.nuecescanyon.com. 11 Rooms. Rates $75-90. Credit cards accepted.*

The Nueces Canyon Bed and Breakfast has 11 guest rooms on a working ranch that sits on 135 acres of land. Every day begins with a hearty country breakfast. There is plenty to do right on the ranch-horseback riding and hiking trails and fishing can fill your days. Special events include hayrides and western-style cookouts. The inn is ideal for group events and special arrangements can be made for group activities and rates.

THE SCHUERENBERG HOUSE, *503 West Alamo. Tel. 979/830-7054, Toll free 800/321-6234. Rates: $85-120. Credit cards accepted.*

This beautiful home was held in the family of the original landowners for four generations. The home has been renovated into a modern guesthouse, but the grandeur of the Victorian era building remains intact. Throughout the house, Schuerenberg family furnishings add the authentic accents that make a stay in this historic landmark much like a night in a museum.

SECRETS BED & BREAKFAST, *405 Pecan Street. Tel. 979/836-4117. Rates: $65-85.*

The Victorian theme of Secrets is carried through the decor and antique shop. There are only three bedrooms, each with special touches such as hand-made quilts. Breakfast is included in the room price. The house is six blocks from downtown Brenham.

Motels

PREFERENCE INN, *201 Loop 290 East. Tel. 979/830-1110, Fax 979/830-0826. Rates: $45-60. Credit cards accepted.*

This older 99-room hotel on Highway 290 has an outdoor pool and small restaurant. The simple rooms have standard amenities such as television and telephone.

RAMADA LIMITED, *2217 South Market Street. Tel. 979/836-1300, Toll free 800/272-6232. Rates: $50-65. Credit cards accepted.*

The newer Ramamda has large rooms with comfortable modern decor. The motel facilities include an outdoor pool, gym, and safety deposit boxes at the front desk.

Where to Eat

FLUFF TOP ROLL RESTAURANT, *210 East Alamo Street. Tel. 979/836-9411.*

The restaurant is named for their trademark light and fluffy Lucas rolls. The rolls have made Fluff Top locally famous, but out-of-towners enjoy stopping in for a full serving of the small town atmosphere, as well as the home-style cooking. The rolls come out of the oven all day and accompany homemade lunch. The restaurant is open daily until 2pm.

MUST BE HEAVEN, *107 West Alamo Street. Tel. 979/830-8536. Credit cards accepted.*

This re-creation of an old-time soda shop will be heaven for anyone with a sweet tooth. It's hard to not start lunch with the dessert selection of homemade pies, hand-dipped Blue Bell ice cream and freshly baked cookies and cakes. The restaurant has two rooms. You walk into the ice cream parlor. The larger dining room has a cafeteria-style sandwich shop that offers everything from grilled chicken breast sandwiches to peanut butter and jelly served on homemade bread. The type of quiche changes daily. Must Be Heaven is open Monday to Saturday from 8am to 5pm.

Seeing the Sights

The most famous thing about Brenham is not its history, but the **Blue Bell Creamery**, *Farm Road 577, Tel. 979/830-2197 or 800/327-8135*. The Blue Bell company bills itself as a local creamery which captures the flavor of simple country goodness in its product. Indeed, many Texans will confirm that Blue Bell is the best ice cream around. The operation is large-scale and modern, although the scenery is quaint and rural. The creamery conducts 45-minute tours during the week (Monday to Friday at 10am, 11am, 1pm, 1:30pm, 2pm, and 2:30); reservations are required for groups of 15 or more; during March and April reservations are necessary for all tours. The admission fee is $2 for adults and $1.50 for children over 6 years old. After the tour, participants receive a complimentary sample of ice cream.

The **Blue Bell Creamery Country Store** is open from 9am to 3pm on Saturday, although the creamery is closed for tours on Saturday. The creamery is located on FM 577. From Highway 290, take 577 north. The creamery is on the east side of the road; look for the signs.

The history of Brenham is preserved in the **Brenham Heritage Museum**, *105 South Market Street, Tel. 979/830-8445, Wednesday 1pm to 4pm, Thursday to Saturday 10am to 4pm, closed Sunday and Monday*, which houses exhibits showing life in the heart of Texas farming country. The museum's centerpiece is an early steam-powered fire engine, restored to mint condition. The museum building was constructed as a post office in 1915, and since that time has remained in constant use. Donations are accepted as admission charge

For an even keener insight into life in this historic part of Texas, contact the **Heritage Society of Washington County**, *Box 1123, Tel. 979/836-1690*, to arrange a tour of the historic homes that are not open to the general public.

Shopping

The **Antique Rose Emporium**, *9300 Lueckemeyer Road, Tel. 979/836-5548, Fax 979/836-7236, Monday to Saturday 9am to 6pm; Sunday 11am to 5:30pm*, is a unique shop that specializes in the small-blossomed wild rose bushes. This particular type of rose was commonly used in elegant gardens of the late nineteenth century. Today the flowers are somewhat of a rarity. The shop is in a beautiful Victorian house in the farming area north of Brenham.

From Highway 290 in Brenham, travel east on Highway 105, then go north on Highway 50 for about nine miles.

Excursions & Day Trips

Set in the rural hills near Brenham, you can visit the **Pleasant Hill Winery**, *Farm Road 345 and Salem Road, Tel. 713/350-3685 or 979/830-VINE, Website: pleasanthillwinery.com*. The close attention given to the winemaking process at Pleasant Hill is evident, as the vintages are excellent. The public is invited to take free tours of the wine cellar and estate grounds and to enjoy a wine tasting. Harvest weekends take place in July and August, and the crushing and pressing usually takes place on Saturdays.

Visitors to Brenham can take the short, scenic trip to see the seat of the independence movement of the Texas pioneers at **Washington-on the Brazos State Park**, *Farm Road 1155, Box 305, Washington, Tel. 936/878-2214*. The park has an excellent museum and the scenic drive makes you feel as if you are stepping back through time. The 154-acre park has reconstructed homes of the pioneers of the state of Texas. A small wood cabin, Independence Hall, was the place where the Texas Declaration of Independence from Mexico was signed. The **Star of the Republic Museum** provides a thorough overview of the road to independence and later statehood for Texas. This excellent collection has reproductions of photographs and portraits as well as artifacts from the period of the Republic of Texas. Many of the famous men for whom Texas counties are named are profiled here, as are the leaders of the Republic of Texas. On the drive to the park you can see some of the estate homes of the first settlers of Texas, which are private residences to this day.

Most visitors who come to the **Monastery of Saint Clare**, *Highway 105, Tel. 979/836-9652, Website: www.monasteryminiaturehorses.com*, do not make the pilgrimage for religious reasons, but to see the miniature horses. The Franciscan nuns raise miniature horses that stand only 15" tall. The horses and arts and crafts produced by the sisters are for sale to the public. You can take a self-guided tour of the horse farm; from April through June you may arrange a guided tour. The horse farm is open daily from 2pm to 4pm. From U. S. Highway 290 near Brenham, take Highway 105 north for ten miles. There is no admission charge, but the sisters greatly appreciate donations to the monastery.

Practical Information

For tourist and local event information, contact the **Washington County Convention and Visitors Bureau**, *314 South Austin Street, Tel. 979/836-3695, Website: www.brenhamtx.org*.

Independence

This is one of the oldest towns in the state, founded in 1823 as Coles Settlement. Thirteen years later, when Texans declared their independence from Mexico, they met in log cabins in the piney woods along the Brazos River. Thus the town of **Independence** earned its name.

Sam Houston chose this as the site of his homestead when he settled the area as a land grant from Mexico. The 300 families who colonized this land were led by Texas founding fathers, including William B. Travis and Stephen F. Austin. Many of the adventurous individuals who were drawn to Texas came from the southern United States. The few homes from the early period of statehood exhibit the charm and stateliness of the American south.

Today, the town is a tiny community of less than 150 people.

Arrivals & Departures

From Austin, take Highway 290 east. At Brenham, take Highway 105 north and travel five miles. Turn north onto Ranch Road 50 and continue nine miles. Independence is at the intersection of Ranch Roads 50 and 390.

Where to Stay

CAPTAIN TACITUS T. CLAY'S HOUSE, *Route 5, Box 149, Tel. 979/836-1916. 4 Rooms, 3 with private bath. Rates: $50-90.*

The farmhouse was built in 1852 and remains true to that period. The gracious home sits on rolling acreage and miniature horses romp in the back pasture. Wine and cheese in the afternoon and home cooked breakfast the following morning are included. The farm is on FM 390.

Seeing the Sights

Independence was important in the founding of the Baptist religion in Texas. The **Independence Baptist Church** is the oldest Baptist congregation in the state, active since 1839. The historical center next to the church holds artifacts of Baptist history.

This town is the site of the founding of Baylor University, then Baylor College, which moved to Waco in 1887. Only a few pieces of the walls and parts of the foundation of Baylor College buildings remain in **Old Baylor Park**, *Farm Road 390, one-half mile west of town*. The park has serene rolling hills and picnic tables. The historic home which is the birth place of the founder of Baylor University, John Coles, stands on the park and may be visited by making an appointment with the **Washington County Convention and Visitors Bureau**, *314 South Austin Street, Brenham, Tel. 979/836-3695.*

Chappell Hill & Burton

The first stagecoach line that blazed its way through Texas stopped in the small town of **Chappell Hill**. Today Chappell Hill is considered one of the prettiest small towns in Texas—in fact, the entire downtown area has been designated of historical importance.

If you have never had the opportunity to see a genuine tractor pull, do not miss the **Burton Cotton Gin Festival**. The country festivities commence on a Friday in mid-April and include goat milking, goose plucking, and a pie-eating contest. Indoor activities are held in one of the few remaining working cotton gins in the nation. The three-day celebration features plenty of regional music and dance, such as zydeco, polka and country. For more information contact the festival directly, *Tel. 979/289-3378, Website: www.cottonginmuseum.org.*

Arrivals & Departures

Chappell Hill is on Highway 290, between Houston and Austin. From Highway 290, take the Ranch Road 1155 exit. This scenic road continues past Chappell Hill and Burton to Washington-on-the-Brazos (see Excursions & Day Trips under Brenham, above).

Where to Stay & Eat

THE BROWNING PLANTATION, *Route 1 Box 8, Chappell Hill. Tel. 979/836-6144, Toll free 888/912-6144, Website: www.browningplantation.com. 4 Rooms. Rates: $85.*

The elegant Browning Plantation is listed in the National Register of Historic Places. It is a three-story Greek Revival mansion surrounded by verandas and southern charm. Four spacious guest rooms occupy the second floor, replete with 12-foot ceilings and large windows. Guests can relax under the shade trees or in the pool. Breakfast is served in the formal dining room.

THE STAGECOACH INN, *Main and Chestnut Streets, Chappell Hill. Tel. 979/830-8861, Website: www.thestagecoachinn.com. Rates: $90.*

The stately elegance of the Stagecoach Inn offers a trip through time to the mid-eighteenth century. The architecture is accented with Greek-revival touches, and the furnishings are of museum quality. This is unusual for Texas, which has few landmarks from pre-Victorian times. The inn includes a separate guesthouse and sits on five acres of manicured grounds. The significance of the Stagecoach Inn is noted by its inclusion in the National Register of Historic Places.

THE KNITTEL HOMESTEAD, *520 Main Street, Burton. Tel. 979/289-5102, Fax 979/836-1056. Rates: $75-85.*

The Victorian home is located in the center of Burton, at the corner of Main and Washington Streets. A full breakfast is included with your stay, and arrangements can be made for dinner or special meals. The common area, the home's sitting room, has a television and VCR. The owner serves an adult-only clientele and does not accept credit cards.

THE LONG POINT INN, *Route 1 Box 86-A, Burton. Tel. 979/289-3171, Toll free 877/989-3171, Website: www.longpointinn.com. 3 Rooms. Rates: $80-130. Credit cards accepted but cash or personal check preferred.*

The Long Point Inn is a modern building modeled after an old world chalet on a working cattle ranch. The pastoral setting offers ample opportunity for relaxation. Three guest rooms, two with private baths, are available in the main house. A separate log cabin with a native stone bathroom and several beds is available as well. The inn is a lovely retreat, and is especially recommended to travelers who enjoy indulging in a hearty breakfast – the one served at the Long Point Inn features fresh fruit and juices, local German sausage, homemade breads, and more. Children under six stay for free, and children of any age will be delighted by the six ponds stocked with fish.

Seeing the Sights

The **Museum of Chappell Hill**, *Church Street, Wednesday to Saturday 10am to 4pm; Sunday 1pm to 4pm*, traces the history of the formation of Texas and shows the contributions Polish immigrants made to the state. The museum building was one of the first women's colleges in Texas; unfortunately the school is no longer in operation.

Bryan/College Station

Bryan and neighboring College Station are the cities that grew up around Texas A&M University. The two cities merge around the university and are indistinguishable from each other. The University began as an agricultural institute and the home of the Corps of Cadets.

The weekend following Thanksgiving marks the most important football game of the season, when the Texas Aggies face their archrival the University of Texas Longhorns. To prepare for the game, a large bonfire was traditionally held at the university. In 1999, the enormous pile of logs collapsed as students worked upon it, killing 12 students and injuring 27 others. Since the bonfire tragedy, the status of this most cherished ritual has been in limbo. As of now, no future bonfires are planned.

Arrivals & Departures

Bryan/College Station is located on Highways 6 and 21. From Austin take Highway 290 east, then Highway 21 north. From Houston, take Highway 290 west and Highway 6 north.

Where to Stay

LA QUINTA INN, *607 Texas Avenue, College Station. Tel. 979/696-7777 or 800/531-5900, Fax 979/696-0531. 176 Rooms. Rates: $65 to $85. Credit cards accepted.*

The La Quinta is a comfortable hotel located near the main entrance of the university. Each room receives a complimentary breakfast of pastries, fruit and juice. The hotel has an outdoor pool and offers shuttle service to guests. Children under the age of 18 stay free with parents.

VINEYARD COURT HOTEL, *216 Dominik, College Station. Tel. 979/693-1220, Fax 979/764-1250. Rates: $60. Credit cards accepted.*

This establishment offers apartment-style accommodation near the university. Many families and faculty use this as temporary housing while relocating in the area, so there is a professional atmosphere. Each suite of rooms has a full kitchen. Business services such as fax and copy machines are available for guest use. The hotel is located near a university shuttle bus stop, so you can easily visit the university area. Recreational areas include an outdoor pool and yard.

MESSINA HOF WINERY AND RESORT, *4545 Old Reliance Road, Bryan. Tel. 979/778-9463, Fax 979/778-1729, Website: www.messinahof.com. 10 Rooms. Rates: $150-250. Credit cards accepted.*

Messina Hof used to be a boutique winery with one cozy bed and breakfast room over the visitor's center. Now it is an intimate inn along the lines of a grand European estate. The bed and breakfast rooms are housed in a handsome brick building known as the Villa, and an innkeeper remains on site 24 hours to ensure your every need is attended to.

Old timers may wistfully remember the days when the one room at Messina Hof offered only a bed, but it's hard not to appreciate the telephone, DirecTV, coffee maker, and fresh flowers provided in each room today. There is a common living room where guests can mingle by the fireplace or watch the big screen television. There is also a utility room with a washer and dryer, and you can arrange spa treatments such as massage and facials in advance.

Each room has a private bath and a patio or balcony overlooking the Messina Hof estate and vineyards. The rooms are uniquely furnished with European antiques meant to reflect the room's name – the Romeo and Juliet, the Thomas Jefferson, and so forth. The Lancelot and Guinevere room is my favorite, with its hand-carved 17th Century bed, stained glass windows, and whirlpool tub.

The Vintage House restaurant serves gourmet lunches and dinners. Your breakfast is provided in a European buffet. The Messina Hof Winery began producing wine 15 years ago and has an annual bottling of 100,000 gallons. The winery sits on 45 acres of lush east Texas land. A stay here is for the true wine lover; breakfast features wine jelly, and port wine chocolates.

Where to Eat

CAFE ECCELL, *101 Church Avenue, College Station. Tel. 979/846-7908. Credit cards accepted.*

The casual atmosphere at Cafe Eccell reflects the easy-going nature of this university town. The restaurant is located in the building that used to be the city hall. The interior is now refreshingly modern. The menu includes individual pizzas, grilled meat and fish. The pizza is cooked in a wood burning oven until the crust is crisp yet tender. The grilled selections have the full flavor of mesquite smoke. The prices are reasonable. On weekends, from 8am to 2pm, Cafe Eccell features a brunch menu.

Seeing the Sights

Texas A&M University, *Rudder Hall Visitor's Center, College Station, Tel. 979/845-5851*, has been in operation since 1876. It is famous for the elite Corps of Cadets, which now constitutes a small portion of the student body. The university's enrollment tops 42,000. The excellent teaching facilities are highlighted by museums on campus. During the academic year you can watch excellent collegiate sports.

When you arrive at the university, enter through the main entrance on Texas Avenue. Take the road that veers left, Lubbock Street. This will take you to the Rudder Complex and a public parking garage on Houston Street.

On campus you will find the **George Bush Presidential Library and Museum**, *100 George Bush Drive West, Tel. 979/260-9552*. The museum encompasses United States History since World War II, with a focus on major world events during the Bush Sr. presidency.

A taste of old world charm is found near Aggieland. The family that founded the **Messina Hof Wine Cellars**, *4545 Old Reliance Road, Bryan, Tel. 979/778-9463, Fax 979/778-1729*, traces its roots back through six generations of wine-makers from Italy. Messina Hof began producing wine 15 years ago and has an annual bottling of 100,000 gallons. The 45 acres of grounds is the tranquil setting for festivities that celebrate wine, including a grape stomping competition. The winery offers tours Monday to Friday 1pm; Saturday 11am, 12:30pm, 2:30pm and 4pm; and Sunday 12:30 and 2:30pm. There is no charge for the tour, but reservations are necessary.

Nightlife & Entertainment

THE DIXIE CHICKEN, *307 University Drive, College Station. Tel. 979/ 846-2322.*

For years, the casual western atmosphere and pitchers of beer has made the Dixie Chicken the place for some collegiate country-style fun. The place is usually packed with university students. The dance floor is full of country buffs, from novice to expert. So don't be shy; get up and dance.

Excursions & Day Trips

The town of **Anderson** stands on land that was once on a Native American trail. The Spanish also journeyed through the area, and part of El Camino Real, the old Spanish Royal Way, went through Anderson.

One of the first postmasters in Texas, Henry Fanthorp, built his home here in 1834. The house soon became an important stop on the road for travelers traversing the state and is known as the **Fanthorp Inn**, *Main Street, Anderson, Tel. 979/873-2633*. Today the inn is a state historic site, and visitors can tour the rooms where Sam Houston and Stonewall Jackson are said to have stayed. You can relive the past on the second Saturday of each month, with a ride in a stagecoach. The stagecoach rides are from 1pm to 4pm in the afternoon. Anderson is located on Highway 90.

Practical Information

To explore Bryan/College Station online visit their website at *www.b-cs.com*.

Caldwell

The old buildings that line Main Street downtown are reminiscent of the idealistic simplicity of small town life in the first half of this century. Unfortunately, many of the businesses are now closed. **Caldwell** pays homage to the Czechs who settled the area, many of whose families still call Caldwell home.

Caldwell proudly calls itself the **Kolache Capital of Texas**. Kolaches are sweet pastries, and the variety baked in Texas is actually better than the authentic Czech version. The town is a quiet repose for those who enjoy getting out of the big cities and getting to know the locals.

Caldwell remembers its Czech heritage every September with the **Kolache Festival**. The baker who produces the most delicious kolache takes home the $100 state championship award. The best part is that everyone can sample the entries. The festival offers more than just food. Polka, folk and country bands provide entertainment all day. Classes teach traditional Czech arts and crafts as well as kolache baking. Antiques and art from the region are on display and on sale.

Arrivals & Departures

Caldwell is on Highway 21 at the intersection of Highway 36, about 25 miles south of Bryan.

Where to Stay

CALDWELL MOTEL, *1819 Highway 21. Tel. 979/567-4000 or 567-9293. Rates: $35-45. Credit cards accepted.*

The 48-room motel offers rooms with kitchenettes and extra-large beds. All rooms have standard amenities such as telephone and cable television. The restaurant is open all day. Discounted rates for long stays.

SURREY INN, *403 Highway 21. Tel. 979/567-3221. Rates: $40. Credit cards accepted.*

The Surrey Inn is a comfortable roadside stop when traveling through Texas. The inn has a homey feeling and rooms are neat and comfortable. You can enjoy the outdoor pool or the fishing pond, which is on the grounds. The Surrey Inn is at the intersection of Highways 36 and 21. The Surrey Inn restaurant serves home cooked meals, a salad bar and offers daily lunch specials.

Where to Eat

CRAZY HORSE BBQ & STEAKHOUSE, *Highway 36. Tel. 979/567-7722.*

All the meat is prepared fresh, from the cutting to the smoking. Even the sausage is made fresh. If you prefer your meat cooked quickly, try the steaks, which are grilled as you order. Homemade side dishes include potato salad and cole slaw. Daily specials are featured at lunch and dinner. Monday to Thursday 10am to 8pm, Friday and Saturday 10am to 9pm.

KOLACHE CAPITAL BAKE SHOP, *Highway 21. Tel. 979/567-3474.*

This bakery claims the grand prize as having the best professionally baked kolaches in the state, as decided by the Kolache Festival judges. The sandwiches are served on fresh bread and stacked tall. Baked potatoes and soup round out the lunch menu.

Seeing the Sights

The **Burleson County Czech Heritage Museum**, *212-A West Buck Street, Tel. 979/567-3218, Fax 979/567-0818*, exhibits everyday items of Czech settlers in Texas. Much of the tiny museum educates people about the Czech culture. A display of woodcarving and musical instruments from Moravia provides an interesting glance at a part of the world that at first seems far removed from Texas. The museum is upstairs in the Chamber of Commerce building.

The small Victorian home of Thomas Kraitchar, Jr. is open to the public by appointment. The area historical society restored **Kraitchar House**, *corner of Buck and Porter Streets*, to represent the Victorian era in Texas. To schedule a tour of the Kraitchar House call the Caldwell Chamber of Commerce, *Tel. 979/567-3218.*

A unique opportunity awaits those with an interest in small-scale self-sufficient farming. The **Purple Gate Farm**, *Ranch Road 5, Box 88E, Tel. 979/567-9824*, relies on wild vegetation, solar power and water conservation to provide a sustainable environment for the family farm. Native plants are used for decoration and as a learning tool about the uses of wild fauna. Private tours of the farm may be arranged by appointment.

Practical Information

Tourist information is provided by the **Caldwell Chamber of Commerce**, *212-A West Buck Street, Tel. 979/567-3218, Fax 979/567-0818*.

Chapter 14

hill country

The Texas Hill Country is a land of granite and limestone softened by water and wildflowers. This part of the state is a favorite for vacationers, retirees, artists, and outdoor enthusiasts. The cultural landscape is rich here, as well. German and European immigrants settled many of the towns in the Hill Country. The picturesque architecture of Fredericksburg and Comfort bears witness to the love these people had for fine craftsmanship. In particular, watch for buildings constructed with a technique known as Fachwerk—an eye-pleasing combination of hewn timbers and limestone or adobe.

San Marcos

The city of **San Marcos** is known for its stately homes, the mammoth springs that give rise to the San Marcos River, and for Lyndon Baines Johnson's alma mater, **Southwest Texas State University**. The university has a student population of over 21,000, which gives this town of 42,000 much of its personality.

Before the area was colonized in the mid-nineteenth century, Native Americans had inhabited the fertile riverbanks as early as 12,000 years ago. The cool springs and river access made San Marcos a desirable retreat for settlers and travelers in the nineteenth century. Today the city is an escape for Austinites seeking a little fun. The San Marcos River stays a perfect 72 degrees, making it a year-round sports attraction. City parks line the river, offering beautiful spots for picnics and recreation.

On the first weekend of May you can get a rare glimpse into the historic homes of San Marcos when they are open to the public for the **Tours of Distinction**. On the first weekend of April you can see the sky fill with color at the **Bluebonnet Kite Festival**, *Tel. 512/392-2900*. Just as the heat of summer is beginning to subside, the **Chilympiad**, *Tel. 512/396-5400, Website: www.chilympiad.org*, ignites taste buds. The chili cook-off is held in mid-September and is one of the largest events of its kind.

Arrivals & Departures
San Marcos is on Interstate Highway 35, about 40 miles south of Austin. Highways 21, 80 and 123 from the east meet in San Marcos. When departing, if you are heading south to **New Braunfels**, an alternative to congested Interstate Highway 35 is Hunter Road (Farm Road 2439). This road follows the Union Pacific Railroad tracks south through Gruene to New Braunfels.

Getting Around
San Marcos Transit (SMT), *Tel. 512/353-4768, Website: ci.san-marcos.tx.us/Transportation.htm*, runs trolley-style buses that serve all the tourist destinations and the outlet malls, Southwest Texas State University and the parks along the river. The main transfer point is located at San Antonio and LBJ Streets. Regular one-way adult fare is $.50, children under five ride free.

The **Greyhound Bus Station**, *338 South Guadalupe Street, Tel. 512/ 392-4649*, is open seven days a week. The **Amtrak Texas Eagle** makes a stop in San Marcos at this same station.

Where to Stay
CRYSTAL RIVER INN, *326 West Hopkins. Tel. 512/396-3739, Toll free 888/396-3739, Website: www.crystalriverinn.com. 13 Rooms. Rates: $50-150. Credit cards accepted.*

This gracious bed and breakfast establishment is one of the best-run inns in Texas. The main house, a large Victorian home, was constructed in 1883. The two-story columns and verandahs give the house an old southern air. Two other buildings, the Young House and the Rock House, are a part of the inn complex. The rooms are sumptuous, each exquisitely furnished and offering special touches like claw-foot tubs, fireplaces, and canopied beds. You can walk through the surrounding quiet streets and see the town practically as it may have been at the turn of the century. Special packages such as murder mystery weekends, gourmet picnics, and wildflower expeditions are also available.

HONEY MOON COTTAGE, *951 Aquarena Springs Drive. Tel. 512/245-7583. Rates: $75 on weeknights, $90 on weekends. Credit cards accepted.*

The old Aquarena Inn was closed to the public in 2001, and has been turned into office and exhibit space for the Texas Rivers Center. One last overnight accommodation still exists at Aquarena Center, however – a small cottage with a kitchenette, dining table, Queen bed, and cable television. It's bare bones, but you can't beat the location on the crystal blue water of the San Marcos Springs. Step out your door and swans and sunning turtles greet you.

HOLIDAY INN EXPRESS, *108 Interstate Highway 35 North. Tel. 512/ 754-6621, Fax 512/754-6946, Toll free 800/HOLIDAY. 106 Rooms, 25 Suites. Rates: $69-119. Credit cards accepted.*

The Holiday Inn Express includes a breakfast buffet and free local calls in all the rooms. The rooms are very basic, but spacious and comfortable. Cable television and fax/modem phone lines are some of the perks. Recreational facilities include an outdoor pool and hot tub.

PECAN PARK RV PARK, *175 Squirrel Run. Tel. 512/396-0070, Website: www.pecanpark.com. 81 Sites. Rates: $20 night, $100 week.*

It's almost worth buying an RV just so you can stay at Pecan Park. Nestled in a grove of giant shady pecan trees one the banks of the San Marcos River, this tranquil spot will leave you refreshed and relaxed. You can go canoeing and tubing in the river, or just sit and watch the turtles and the birds. Basic cable runs to each site, and there are laundry facilities, showers, and an indoor pool available.

Nearby

FORGET-ME-NOT RIVER INN, *310 Main Street, Martindale. Tel. 512/ 357-6385. Rates: $60-100. Credit cards accepted.*

The Victorian house, built in 1899, has unique architectural features. The center room is a round tower. The grounds run right to the banks of the San Marcos River, and are surrounded by wooded land. Each of the three rooms is decorated in a theme, such as the Russian Ivy room or the Irish Rose room. A separate three-bedroom cottage can accommodate an entire family. For a romantic touch, you can request breakfast in bed instead of dining with other guests in the music room. The house is about five miles from San Marcos, in the center of Martindale, one of the towns where the movie *A Perfect World* was filmed. From San Marcos, take Highway 80 southeast to Martindale.

Where to Eat

PALMER'S, *216 West Moore Street at Hutchison. Tel. 512/353-3500, Website: www.palmerstexas.com. Credit cards accepted. Open daily 11am-10pm, 11pm on Fridays and Saturdays.*

This is the most upscale restaurant in San Marcos, but you'll be welcome in shorts if you don't feel like dressing up. There's something inexplicably hospitable in a Texas hill country way about this place. The old house has been opened up, but still has a cozy den-like feeling. Outside is a large courtyard, lush with plants and trees. Sit outside by the fountain in the shade, if weather permits (it usually does). The extensive menu covers pastas, salads, steaks, and burgers at lunch. The chicken dishes and vegetables are particularly wonderful. The flauta appetizer is big enough to serve as lunch all by itself, and the southern corn fritters served with honey are as good as dessert.

CAFÉ DE CORTE, *127 East Hopkins. Tel. 512/396-2221.*

This is a delightful place to satisfy a yen for Tex-Mex while watching the activity on the Square through the windows. The menu offers sandwiches, soups and salads, but everyone seems to order off the breakfast menu. It's available all day, and nothing beats a plateful of migas or breakfast tacos and a bottomless cup of coffee while you read the local paper. In the back of the restaurant is TopCat's Billiards, a congenial place to shoot a little pool.

THE BLUE PEARL JUICE AND JAVA BAR, *129 East Hopkins, Tel. 512/396-1689. Closed Sunday.*

An airy relaxing spot on the Square, ideal for slow sipping beneath the pressed tin ceilings. All your favorite coffee concoctions, Italian syrups, a view of the Courthouse and the Square—what more could you ask for on a sleepy Texas morning?

CENTERPOINT STATION, *3946 Interstate Highway 35 South. Tel. 512/392-1103, Fax 392-1108. Credit cards accepted.*

Located right across the Interstate from the outlet malls, Centerpoint Station is a collection of small buildings that have been joined together to form a restaurant and antiques emporium. The food is simple and homey, mostly burgers and sandwiches, but the real standout is the selection of malts, shakes, and other ice cream treats made with Blue Bell ice cream. If you wander about the premises you will find a great collection of antique signs and merchandising, as well as the usual gifts and postcards.

Seeing the Sights

The **Calaboose African-American History Museum**, *200 Martin Luther King, Jr. Drive, Tel. 512/393-8421*, was the first Hays County Jail. After 1880, it became an annex that housed only black prisoners. The original brick structure was enlarged in the 1940s, and served as the USO center for black World War II servicemen. Now the Calaboose is a historical museum detailing the African-American heritage of San Marcos and Texas. The museum is open by appointment, and closed on Mondays.

The graceful gabled Old Main Building of Southwest Texas State University sits on a hill to the west of downtown. On campus, **The Southwestern Writers Collection and Witliff Gallery**, *Seventh floor of the Alkek Library, Tel. 512/245-2313, Website: www.library.swt.edu/swwc/wg/index.html*, showcases the art and literature of the Southwest and Mexico. Included in the collection are the creations, personal papers, and archives of Texas writers and artists such as J. Frank Dobie, Sam Shepard, Willie Nelson, and Selena. The exhibits are free to the public.

San Marcos is the seat of Hays County, and the **Hays County Court-house**, built in 1909, sits in the middle of the Courthouse Square. Just off the Square you will find the historic homes on **Blevins Street** a lovely atmosphere for a stroll or Sunday Drive. If you would like to take a guided tour, hop on the **Living History Trolley Tour**, *departing from the Tanger Outler Center Visitor Center at 2pm on the first Saturday of each month, Tel. 512/396-3739.* The tours are led by guides posing as General and Mrs. Edward Burleson, the founders of San Marcos, and cost $3 per person.

The **Charles S. Cock House**, *400 East Hopkins Street at C. M. Allen Parkway*, has been turned into a museum. This pretty little stone house built in 1867 was the first San Marcos building to be entered in the National Register of Historic Places. It is furnished inside with antique Texas primitive furniture, and every Friday the public is invited for lunch in the Cottage Kitchen from 11am to 1pm. The food is home-cooked by volunteers, and proceeds from the popular luncheons go towards further preservation and beautification efforts. If you would like information on the Friday luncheons and guided or self-guided tours of the historic buildings of San Marcos, contact the **Heritage Association of San Marcos**, *Tel. 512/393-3735, Website: www.sanmarcos.net/ HeritageAssociationofSanMarcos.*

Formerly an amusement park, **Aquarena Center**, on *Aquarena Springs Drive, Tel. 512/396-8900, Website: www.aquarenacenter.com*, now belongs to Southwest Texas State University, and is an educational center that teaches guests about the rich flora and fauna native to the San Marcos River. The grounds are a delightful mix of disintegrating resort attractions that have been left as is or transformed into educational exhibits. The Endangered Species Exhibit gives you a personal look at creatures you will find nowhere else in the world. The glass bottom boat tours of the river are the main attraction. You can see straight through the crystal clear water of the San Marcos River, and practically enter the underwater world.

The **Merriman Cabin**, the oldest surviving home in San Marcos, has been moved here. It served as clinic, operating room, and residence for Dr. Eli T. Merriman, a Yale grad who was one of the first Anglo settlers of San Marcos as well as its postmaster and doctor. From Interstate Highway 35, take the Aquarena Springs exit and follow the signs about one-half mile to Aquarena.

Mix a dribbling of science with an amusement park and you come up with **Wonder World**, *Highway 80, Tel. 512/392-3760 or 800/782-7653, extension 228, Website: www.wonderworldpark.com, Open daily 9am to 6pm.* The main attraction is Wonder Cave, which has crystal rock formations and fossils. Wonder Cave became the first commercially operated cave in the state around 1900, when tours were led by candlelight. It was sold in 1916 for $50 and a grey horse. Above ground, you can climb the steps of the really tall (110 feet) observation tower that overlooks the petting zoo. The park is great for small children who will get a kick out of the "anti-gravity house" and miniature train rides. The Wonder Cave is interesting in itself, but pales in comparison to the Caverns of Sonora and Longhorn Caverns, and the admission price of $15.95 for adults ($11.95 for children age 4-11, 3 and under admitted free) may cause you to blanch.

Nightlife & Entertainment

During the summer, the **River Pub & Grill**, *701 Cheatham Street, Tel. 512/353-3747, Website: www.riverpubandgrill.com*, features live music on their front lawn overlooking the San Marcos River. Popular local acts perform in the open air, and it's free.

Being a college town, San Marcos has a number of pubs and music venues that jump through the night. Pick up an issue of The Chautauquan, available all over town free of charge, to find out about special events and bands. Some of the more popular nightspots are:

• **Cafe on the Square & Brew Pub**, *126 North LBJ Street, Tel. 512/353-9289*
• **Gordo's Bar & Grill**, *120 East San Antonio Street, Tel. 512/392-1874*
• **Nephew's**, *100 North Guadalupe Street, Tel. 512/558-2337*
• **Triple Crown**, *206 North Edward Gary, Tel. 512/396-2236*

Sports & Recreation

The truly adventuresome can jump out of a plane with **Sky Dive San Marcos**, *Tel. 512/488-2214*. They can plan dives for all skill levels, from advanced to novice.

To enjoy the fun of river sports, you can visit either of two canoe and rafting rental shops. Both the **TG Canoe Livery**, *Tel. 512/353-3946*, and **Spencer Canoes**, *Tel. 512/357-6113*, are located on Highway 80, just southeast of the Blanco River. From Interstate Highway 35, take exit 205. If you would like to go for a leisurely drift on the crystalline waters of the San Marcos River, pick up a tube at the **San Marcos Lions Club Tube Rental** in the City Park. It only costs $4 to rent a tube for the entire day, and the proceeds go to charity.

Birdwatchers will find diverse and fruitful habitats to explore in the San Marcos area. In addition to being on the major migratory flyway, San Marcos is home for many wintering species. You can pick up a guide to the top ten favorite sites of local birders at either of the Visitors' Centers (see Practical Information), or you can plan ahead by looking online at *www.centurytel.net/birding*.

Shopping

You can actually spend days shopping in San Marcos. The **Prime Outlets** and **Tanger Outlet Center** together create the largest outlet shopping complex in Texas. The outlet centers are on the east side of Interstate Highway

35; take exit 200. Outlets include the usual designers, as well as Nike, J. Crew, housewares, shoes—even a bible outlet store. Shop seven days a week, Monday to Saturday 10am to 9pm, Sunday 11am to 6pm.

For something a bit more unique, not to mention personal, take a look inside **Light Impressions Candle Art**, *in Aquarena Center (see Seeing the Sights), Tel. 512/392-3001.* This is not your typical "candle shop" found in malls and shopping centers—these people are artists. Ooh and aah over exquisitely charming and intricate wax tableaus created in the Victorian Wax Sculpting tradition. The owners have been commissioned to create hanging candles intended as gifts for no less an icon than Lady Bird Johnson. We mortals can special order our own candles personalized with names, messages, or particular colors and motifs.

Excursions & Day Trips

Thirty miles west of San Marcos, on Highway 473 you will find a small, white Catholic Church built in 1889. The modest house of worship does not have a name. The structure and interior were constructed from materials that had to be transported at least 30 miles over the unsettled Texas hills. The original interior remains intact, but the church is usually closed. It stands as a testimony to the resilience and determination of Texas settlers.

Visitors are welcome at the **Holy Archangel Greek Orthodox Monastery**, which is found at the end of a winding single-lane country road off of Highway 473. The ranch-style buildings have a single bell tower in the Greek style. The countryside is beautiful and the quiet manicured grounds provide a refuge for religious contemplation. Visiting hours are during daylight and religious services. The dress code should be respectfully observed. Women should wear skirts that fall below the knee (pants and shorts are not permitted), and should wear a scarf or veil. Men should wear long pants and shirts with long sleeves.

Practical Information

The **San Marcos Convention & Visitors Bureau**, *202 North CM Allen Parkway, Tel. 512/393-5900 or 888/200-5620*, is open Monday-Friday, 8:30am-5pm. Another Tourist Information center is located right off Interstate Highway 35, at Exit 200. The municipal home page is at *ci.san-marcos.tx.us*. The Chamber of Commerce website is at *www.sanmarcostexas.com*.

Wimberley

Not long ago, this was the place you went to get away from it all—literally. Out here you are surrounded by nothing but the Hill Country environment of river, rock, and tree. **Wimberley** began to attract attention in the 1980s as a healthful place to live for those with severe allergies to chemicals, synthetics, or just plain urban aggravation. Before this modest fame, it was a vacation destination only for the lucky few that already knew it existed. All of that is beginning to change.

Wimberley is now a sizable artisan community, and developments of vacation homes are growing as fast as the hardy little juniper trees that blanket the area. While not as large as its sister Bed and Breakfast towns of Fredericksburg and New Braunfels, gone are the days when you could just "drop in" to Wimberley for the weekend without reservations. **Market Days**, held on the first Saturday of every month from April through December, are wildly popular, meaning you should book far in advance.

Arrivals & Departures

To get to Wimberley from San Marcos, take Ranch Road 12 and follow it for 16 scenic miles. From Austin, take Highway 290 west to Dripping Springs and then turn south on Ranch Road 12.

Where to Stay

There are over 100 places to stay in the Blanco River area. The following accommodation services can make reservations to your specifications:

- **All Wimberley Lodging Reservation Service**, Tel. 800/460-3909, Website: www.texashillcountrylodging.com.
- **Hill Country Accommodations**, Tel. 800/926-5028, Website: www.texasvacation.com.

BLAIR HOUSE, 100 Spoke Hill Road. Tel. 512/847-1111, Fax 512/847-8820, Toll free 877/549-5450, Website: www.blairhouseinn.com. 9 Rooms. Rates: $15-275. Credit cards accepted.

For a complete soul-satisfying lodging and dining experience, Blair House is the destination in Wimberley. This nationally acclaimed inn offers beautiful rooms, each uniquely furnished with an elegant touch that manages to remain light. The commodious house sits on 85 acres of land about a mile and a half from the center of town. Southern Living magazine recently proclaimed breakfast at the Blair House to be "the best in Texas." In the evening your sweet tooth will be delighted with homemade desserts. Saturday evening dinner is a pull-out-all-the-stops five-course affair. If the food inspires dreams of culinary greatness, you can take one of the classes offered at the on-site cooking school.

SINGING CYPRESS GARDENS, 400 Mill Race Lane. Tel. 512/847-9344, Toll free reservations 800/827-1913, Website: www.scgardens.com. 14 Rooms. Rates: $50-150. Credit cards accepted.

This enchanting bed and breakfast is within walking distance of Wimberley Square but feels miles away. The house lies on 3 custom-landscaped acres in a veritable Green Mansion of ancient cypress trees, ferns, and gardens. There are several self-contained suites including kitchen facilities, and a separate building called The Carriage House which contains 8 more units with amenities like fireplaces and and whirlpool baths. Explore the large greenhouse, a replica of the one at Kew Gardens, or just sit and watch the mesmerizing clear waters of the creek.

MOUNTAIN VIEW LODGE, *10600 Ranch Road 12. Tel. 512/847-2992. Rates: $65-80. Credit cards accepted.*

This simple, country hotel is a quaint no-frills alternative to staying in a local bed and breakfast. The solitude and beautiful vistas from the hotel make up for the lack of decorative flair on the interior. Continental breakfast is included. Take Ranch Road 12 south for three miles.

7-A RANCH RESORT AND PIONEER TOWN, *333 Wayside Drive. Tel. 512/847-2517, Website: www.7aranchresort.com. 30 Cabins. Rates: $53-86. Credit cards accepted.*

There is a virtual community of weekend outdoor enthusiasts at the 7-A ranch. You can rent an entire lodge that will hold up to 40 people. Contact the ranch for more information about large groups. This also a great place to stay with children, as the old west village of Pioneer Town gives them plenty to explore. Swimming in the creek or hiking along the nature trails is another good way to pass the time at the 7-A Ranch.

Where to Eat

CYPRESS CREEK CAFÉ, *on the Village Square. Tel. 512/847-2515. Credit cards accepted. Tuesday to Thursday 7:30am to 9:30pm, Sunday 7:30am to 3pm, closed Mondays.*

The cafe serves light fare including vegetarian items and all day breakfast. Try the lip-smacking Banana Nut-Buttermilk Pancakes. The bar in the back becomes lively on weekend nights.

LOOKOUT MOUNTAIN, *5300 Mount Sharp Road. Tel. 512/847-5010. Reservations essential. Open February through November, Saturday lunch 11:30am-2pm, Thursday, Friday, Saturday Sunset Dinners.*

This unique dining experience is for people who want to connect with each other and the Hill Country, all while eating a delicious meal in a glass-walled dining room with a breathtaking view. The Lookout Mountain café serves sunset dinners by reservation only. Diners receive a choice of several mouth-watering entrees, one of them always a vegetarian meal, or gourmet sandwich platters. The pesto tuna served on a baguette is especially toothsome, and you can eat inside or out while watching the one of the spectacular sunsets the Hill Country is famous for.

Lookout Mountain is the second highest in Hays County. Dining customers won't want to miss the "Learn About Our Land" tour given three hours before dinner begins. The tour consists of about an hour and 20 minutes of easy walking with owner Joe Day, who imparts historic and ecological information all while pointing out wildlife and native plants. The Nature Art Gallery and Gift Shop on the premises features local artists.

JITTERS ESPRESSO STOP, *Wimberley North Shopping Center, Tel. 512/ 847-6101. Open M-F 6am-5pm, Sat. 7am-5pm, Sun. 7am-12noon.*

You can duck in here to revive yourself after a day of shopping. Coffee drinks and tasty snacks are served.

Seeing the Sights

The biggest influx of tourists to Wimberley is during **Market Days**, *every first Saturday of the month, April-December, at the Lion's Field and Park, on Ranch Road 2325 about half a mile from its junction with Ranch Road 12.* There are usually close to 500 booths selling antiques, collectibles, handicrafts, custom clothing, jewelry, flowers, and just about anything else you can imagine. There is no admission charge, although there is a fee for parking. The Wimberley Lions Club donates proceeds from Market Days to charitable groups and organizations.

If you don't happen to be in town for Market Days, you can still browse the antique shops and art galleries clustered about the Square downtown.

A mixing of craftsman and artist describes the resident glassblower at **Wimberley Glass Works**, *Spoke Hill Road, Tel. 512/847-9348 Website: www.wgw.com, Friday Saturday, Sunday and Monday noon to 5pm and by appointment.* Age-old glass blowing techniques coupled with creative designs produce a show and a work of art. You can watch unique pieces being blown while a guide tells you about the history and technique of glass blowing. From Wimberley, take Ranch Road 12 south about one and one-half miles. The sign points the way to the Glass Works entrance behind a church. During the summer Wimberley Glass Works opens at 10am.

A marvelous blend of Japanese tradition and Texas resources results in the **Central Texas Bonsai Exhibit**, *Jade Gardens, 12404 Ranch Road 12, Tel. 512/847-2514.* The charming display is devoted to trees native to Central and South Texas that have been trained in the ancient art of Bonsai. There is a gift shop, and admission is free.

The Wimberley locals hang out atop **Lookout Mountain**, *Ranch Road 2325 (Mount Sharp Road) at Woodcreek.* The limestone cliff stands 1200 feet high, but getting to the summit is easy. A path of steps leads you there with no mountain climbing gear necessary.

Nightlife & Entertainment

CYPRESS CREEK CAFE, *on the Square. Tel. 512/847-2515. Credit cards accepted.*

After dinner at the Cypress Creek Café, you can linger to take in some live music. There's a full bar in the back, where you can drink and dance to the tunes of local jazz bands on Thursday, Friday and Saturday nights.

Excursions & Day Trips

One of the most scenic drives in the state is a stretch of curving country road called the **Devil's Backbone**. Take Ranch Road 12 south out of Wimberley for about 4.5 miles. At Ranch Road 32, turn right and head west— you're on the Devil's Backbone. The Balcones Fault Line created the ridge on which you drive. Gorgeous vistas are revealed at every twist and turn for nearly 20 miles, until you arrive in Blanco. About three miles after the junction of Ranch Roads 12 and 32 there is a scenic overlook that gives a perfect photo opportunity.

During the afternoon or evening, stop by the **Devil's Backbone Tavern**, *401 FM 32, Tel. 830/964-2544* about 5 miles west of San Marcos. This old-time diner and watering hole will give you a chance to meet some local folk.

Practical Information

The **Wimberley Visitors' Center and Chamber of Commerce**, *1400 Ranch Road 12, Tel. 512/847-2201, Website: www.wimberley.org, open Monday-Saturday 9am-4pm, Sunday 1 pm-4pm*, offers information about recreational activities and accommodations along the Blanco River. Be sure to linger over the herb garden next to the front porch—you are encouraged to touch and smell the plants.

Fax service and **Western Union** services are available at **Welcome to Wimberley**, *next to the Brookshire Bros. Food Store, Tel. 512/847-3601, open Monday-Thursday 10am-7pm, Friday-Saturday 10am-8pm, closed Sundays*. While you're there you can rent a movie, too.

New Braunfels

Prince Carl Solms of Germany, who purchased the land for German settlers during the days of the Republic of Texas, named the city of New Braunfels. The German heritage remains strong in the town; food, language, and architecture stand out as the most obvious signs of the past. The entire small community of **Gruene** has been designated a historical area, and lies within New Braunfels city limits.

During the summer, Texans seeking the refreshing waters of the Comal and Guadalupe Rivers flood the area. Local industry including mills on the Comal River, farming, and ranching have sustained New Braunfels over the decades. Today tourism is one of the city's largest industries.

You can have the best time at **Wurstfest**, *www.wurstfest.com*. While that pun is hardly new, this German celebration never grows old for locals and visitors alike. You will encounter lots of sausage, accordions, and a general carnival atmosphere. A ten-kilometer run is part of the festivities that take place in the first week of November. The event is held at the Wursthalle, which is on Landa Park Drive, just north of the city square.

Arrivals & Departures

New Braunfels is on Interstate Highway 35, between Austin and San Antonio. The city is only 45 miles south of Austin and 30 miles north of San Antonio. National chain restaurants and hotels are located along the highway.

Orientation

From Interstate Highway 35, take the Seguin Street exit. Head west along Seguin Street to reach the town square.

Where to Stay

HOTEL FAUST, *240 South Seguin Street. Tel. 830/625-7791, Fax 620-1530, Website: www.fausthotel.com. 62 Rooms, 1 Suite. Rates: $69-225. Credit cards accepted.*

The Faust is by far the most historical, cozy, and interesting hotel in the area. The legendary ghost sightings come to life when you look at the old pictures of the former owners hanging in the halls. The Faust opened in 1929 mere weeks before the giant stock crash on Black Friday, and must have been the largest hotel by far in the city. The interior is furnished in period decor and an antique car stands in the entry foyer. The hotel has been renovated, but certain original fixtures such as the tile bathrooms and large bathtubs have been left to add character to the rooms. Each room has a phone, television and ceiling fan. A complimentary continental breakfast is offered seven days a week. Travelers and locals alike frequent the hotel bar.

KUEBLER-WALDRIP HAUS, *1620 Hueco Springs Loop. Tel. 830/625-8300, Toll free 800/299-8372, Website: www.cruising-america.com/kuebler-waldrip. 9 Rooms. Rates: $115-230. Credit cards accepted.*

You can wander around real frontier buildings on the 40-plus acres of grounds. The main house, built in 1847, is an extraordinary example of hand construction in the German style. The area's children used the 1863 Danville Schoolhouse for years. The name Kuebler-Waldrip does not hint about the origins of the land's first owners, who were French. The house has been lovingly maintained and restored over the years. The farm-style decorations are true to the central Texas lifestyle, which has the rugged flair of a ranch tempered by the grace of country decoration.

Each of the rooms has a private bath and includes a large homemade country candlelight breakfast. A separate five-room cottage with two queens and one twin bed is also available for rent. Special amenities include spa baths, kitchens and business facilities. Ask about off-season midweek rates.

PRINCE SOLMS INN, *295 East San Antonio Street. Tel. 830/625-9196, Toll free 800/625-9169, Website: www.princesolmsinn.com. 9 Rooms, 2 Suites. Rates: 75-150. Credit cards accepted.*

The beautiful two-story Prince Solms Inn is as historic as its namesake, the founder of New Braunfels. For over 145 years the hotel has given travelers a cushy haven in the city. The beautiful antique and modern furnishings reflect the elegant character of the German architecture of 1898, when the house was built. Behind the house a lush courtyard provides a garden setting for relaxation and reading. The inn is home to a romantic bar, Giovani's Cellar, which also serves a limited menu. Room service is provided by Giovani's Restaurant. You can arrange special events here, including Mystery Weekends, where guests solve a mystery played out by actors. From the main plaza, take San Antonio Street east; the inn is on the corner of Market and San Antonio.

RIVERSIDE HAVEN BED & BREAKFAST, *1491 Edwards Boulevard. Tel. 830/625-5823. 4 Rooms. Rates: $95-125. Credit cards accepted.*

The large white house, with two levels of porches, overlooks the Guadalupe River. The four guestrooms have river views and homey decor. The largest, The Room with a View, sleeps four. This is the perfect place to stay if you want to enjoy the fun of the Guadalupe River and return home to a lovely accommodation. The owners make every effort to ensure you have an enjoyable stay. Two canoes are available to guests, or you can launch your own tube and float down the river with the stream of summer sun-worshippers. The European breakfast is served in a breakfast room with a view of the river. Riverside Haven is only one-half mile from the restaurants and fun of Gruene. From Interstate Highway 35 north of New Braunfels, take Farm Road 306 west to Hunter Road. When the road stops at the Gruene Dance Hall, bear right onto Gruene Road. Take the first right after the bridge on Ervenberg Road and follow this to the end. Turn right on Edwards Boulevard.

THE WHITE HOUSE, *217 Mittman Circle. Tel. 830/629-9354. Rates: $65-105. Credit cards accepted.*

The White House gives you southern hospitality and personal service, with rates far lower than most inns and hotels. The White House is one of the first bed and breakfasts to be established in the area and has operated for over a decade. With only three guestrooms, you will be able to enjoy the peace and quiet of the hill country nights while relaxing on the outdoor patio. The contemporary Spanish-style house has a small pond and acreage for nature walks. The breakfast, served in the garden room, is a hearty assortment of fresh fruit and juice, homemade pancakes or waffles and sausage.

GRUENE MANSION, *1275 Gruene Road. Tel. 830/629-2641, Website: www.gruenemansioninn.com. 30 Units. Rates: $125-1210. Credit cards accepted.*

The Gruene Mansion is a large exuberant Victorian home that is a bed and breakfast. The beautiful rooms provide an elegant place for repose when visiting Gruene. Each room has a private entrance, private bathroom, and its own porch. The Gruene Dance Hall is just a few steps away. A large deck overlooks the hill country. To get to Gruene, from Interstate Highway 35, exit Highway 337 and travel west. At Gruene Loop Road go north, this will lead you to Gruene.

THE STAGECOACH STOP BED AND BREAKFAST, *5441 FM 1102. Tel. 830/620-9453, Toll free 800/201-2912, Website: www.texasguides.com/stagecoachstop.html. Rates: $85-140. Credit cards accepted.*

Just north of Gruene on the Old Hunter Road, you have the opportunity to sleep in the same cabins used by travelers on this stagecoach route in the 1800s. Unlike those who went before, however, you will be surrounded by every modern luxury, including clawfoot tubs, early Texas antique-furnished rooms, and gourmet breakfasts. Although this small painstakingly restored Fachwerk house and Log Pen cabin was a stagecoach stop and not an inn, travelers would sojourn here several times a year when the river was high or conditions were too dangerous to continue their journeys. The proprietress goes out of her way to make you feel at home—she knows wonderful stories about the region, and even designed the beautiful gardens of herbs, antique roses, and native plants. Children are welcome.

RODEWAY INN, *1209 Interstate Highway 35 East. Tel. 830/629-6991, Fax 830/629-0754, Toll free 800/967-1168. 130 Rooms. Rates: $45-100. Credit cards accepted.*

The Rodeway Inn offers comfortable standard chain-motel rooms. Continental breakfast is included and laundry facilities on the premises are available for guest use. The inn is located at the intersection of Interstate Highway 35 and Highway 46.

Where to Eat

HUISACHE GRILL, *303 D East San Antonio Street. Tel. 830/620-9001. Credit cards accepted.*

The Huisache (pronounced "wee-satch") Grill is a gem of a restaurant. The casual yet elegant atmosphere reflects the nature of the food-easy going and original. The menu items could be described as American or German cuisine, but that would not give credit to the accents, such as cilantro sauce, jalapeno butter and mint salsa. The Vegetarian Feast is a plate of the season's freshest veggies grilled to perfection. The flavors used fill the senses. For example, Chicken Del Rio has roasted red pepper sauce and comes with a side of garlic spinach. Lighter fare includes sandwiches and appetizers. The 3030 Salmon Salad is salade Nicoise with a twist, salmon instead of tuna. Entrees are reasonably priced, and wine and beer are served.

THE GRISTMILL, *1287 Gruene Road. Tel. 830/625-0684. Credit cards accepted.*

This is one of the more unique places in the area to eat. The restaurant is built in the ruins of a nineteenth century cotton gin. Fans and breezes from the nearby river cool the outdoor seating. The food and atmosphere is informal, making the Gristmill a family tradition for vacationers after a long, hot day of tubing on the Guadalupe River. All the salsas are homemade; the best is the tomatillo sauce, made with avocados and green Mexican tomatoes and served with corn chips. Entrees range from grilled chicken to Texas T-bone steak. The hamburgers are a sure bet, and a good deal. The fries are round-cut and a delicious indulgence.

NEW BRAUNFELS SMOKEHOUSE, *Corner of Highway 46 and Interstate Highway 35. Tel. 830/625-2416, Website: www.nbsmokehouse.com. Credit cards accepted.*

This local favorite has become a virtual industry, with a burgeoning mail order business and a store in San Antonio. However, the original restaurant still stands where it always has, and carnivores all over the Hill Country still flock in to sample bratwurst, applewurst and yes, even jalapeno wurst. If sausage doesn't interest you, the restaurant also serves country favorites such as chicken and dumplings, smoked pork chops, and barbecue.

Seeing the Sights

The local historical society preserves a small corner of the past at **Conservation Plaza**, *1300 Church Drive, Tel. 830/629-2943, Tuesday to Friday 10am to 3pm, Saturday and Sunday 2pm to 5pm*. This cluster of restored frontier buildings includes a barbershop, a cabinetry workshop and schoolhouse. Some of the historical homes were moved from the surrounding countryside. The oldest structure, the Baetge House, dates from 1852. This is the largest collection of *fachwerk* buildings in the world. A lovely collection of antique roses enhances the beauty of the grounds.

To catch a glimpse of what may have gone into the old structures, visit the **Museum of Handmade Furniture**, *1370 Church Hill Drive, Tel. 830/629-6504, Website: www.nbheritagevillage.com, open daily 1pm to 4pm, admission $5 adults, closed December and January*. The collection showcases Texas Biedermeier furniture crafted by local German cabinetmakers between 1845 and 1880. You can walk into the cabinetmakers' workshop to see the tools and techniques used by the furniture craftsmen. From Interstate Highway 35, take exit 189 and travel north on Loop 337. Church Hill Drive intersects with Loop 337.

To complete your tour of German settlement history, venture to the **Sophienburg Museum**, *401 West Coll Street, Tel. 830/629-1900, Website: www.nbtx.com/sophienburg, Monday to Saturday 10am to 5pm, Sunday 1pm to 5pm*. The exhibits include the personal possessions of Prince Solms of Germany, who founded the town.

Fans of Texas and German music, writing, and art will enjoy the **New Braunfels Museum of Art & Music**, *199 Main Plaza, Tel 830/625-5636 or*

800/456-4866, Website: www.nbtx.com/nbma, open Monday to Saturday 10am to 5pm, Sunday noon to 5pm. There are permanent exhibits as well as rotating exhibits on topics such as Cowboy Poetry and Legends of Texas Music. A gift shop on the premises offers interesting decorative items and musical instruments. This building used to be the Hummel Museum.

The oldest landmark in the area is **Natural Bridge Caverns**, *26495 Natural Bridge Caverns Road, Tel. 210/651-6101, Website: www.naturalbridgecaverns.com,* which is 140 million years old. Guided tours take you through the many "rooms" of crystal stalactites and stalagmites. It takes 120 minutes to make your way through these caverns. At the Mining Sluice, kids can pan for gemstones and minerals and keep what they find. The caverns open at 9am daily and tours leave every 30 minutes. Admission for adults is $12, $7 for children. From Interstate Highway 35, exit Farm Road 3009 and travel west.

Up on the surface of the earth you can visit the **Natural Bridge Wildlife Ranch**, *26515 Natural Bridge Caverns Road, Tel. 830/438-7400, Website: www.nbwildliferanchtx.com, open daily 9am to 5pm,* a 200-acre safari-style park. Drive along paved paths to see the ranch, which was turned into a wildlife park for endangered species. Among the animals is a pair of Southern White Rhinoceros. There is also a petting zoo with llamas and goats.

Nightlife & Entertainment

When in New Braunfels for the evening, head over to Gruene. Even if you are not a country music fan, you will have a ball at the **Gruene Hall**. *1281 Gruene Road, Tel. 830/629-5077, Website: gruenehall.com.* The restored town of Gruene is actually part of New Braunfels. The old buildings and Gruene Hall stood vacant for decades. An artful renovation turned the city into a popular destination for vacationers. The many antique and crafts shops in Gruene are only a fraction of the attraction. In fact, you can do everything in Gruene that you can in New Braunfels.

Gruene Hall calls itself the oldest dance hall in Texas, and there's no doubt that the high-caliber music offered here keeps toes tapping. The second Sunday of every month is reserved for a rousing Gospel Brunch.

Sports & Recreation

Tubing is the national sport of the **Guadalupe River**. Occasionally the river has real rapids for kayaking. But most of the summer the water is a highway of people floating along in giant inner tubes. They bring along beer-filled coolers on more inner tubes. You can rent an inner tube from the concessionaires on the river. Usually the tube rental is for the entire day, and you can take the company's shuttle bus back to the starting point. If you have a choice go ahead and get a tube with a bottom—the extra cost will be well worth it when you bottom out in the shallow rocky segments of the river.

For man-made water fun, try the giant German-theme water park, **Schlitterbahn**, *305 West Austin Street, Tel. 830/625-2351*, which stands on the banks of the Guadalupe River. Many giant curly waterslides, a wave pool and a small, contained segment of the river for tubing are parts of the attraction.

During the spring and fall parts of the river become rapids. You can rent canoes at **Whitewater Sports**, *11860 Farm Road 306, Tel 830/964-3800*. The outfitters will allow you to canoe from three to six and a half hours, then arrange a shuttle to bring you back to the store. From interstate Highway 35, take the Farm Road 306/Canyon Lake Exit. Go west to the store. Canoe rental costs about $35 for two people.

The **Ole Mill Stream** claims to offer the longest segment for floating on the river. The charge for a tube is $5; admission is $2 if you bring your own tube. The picnic tables at the park must be rented, but most people snack on the river then head over to nearby Gruene for dinner. From Interstate Highway, exit New Braunfels (#187) and go west on South Seguin Street. Landa Street is a fork in the road that veers to the left.

Right in the center of New Braunfels you will find one of the nicest public parks anywhere, **Landa Park**, *110 Golf Course Drive, Tel 830/608-2160*. There are a variety of outdoor activities for all interests. The park has an Olympic-size spring-fed swimming pool, 18-hole golf course (green fees $12-16), and an area for tubing. You can take a walking tour of the grounds with a park ranger, or rent a picnic table for the afternoon.

Golf Enthusiasts will enjoy **Sundance Golf Course**, *2294 Common Street, Tel. 830/629-3817*. The 18-hole par-58 course has a driving range and offers lessons. Greens fees range from $7-12; golf carts available for $6-8. From Interstate Highway 35, take Exit 189 and go west on Loop 337. Common Street is about one mile from the highway.

Texans who love tennis often spend a few weeks at the **John Newcombe Tennis Ranch**, *Highway 46 (P. O. Box 310469), Tel. 800/444-6204*. The training camp has taught children and adults for over 20 years. Adult packages are from two to five days. The children's and junior's programs run throughout

---

Volksmarsch

If you happen to be in New Braunfels during the first week of January, you will find the water of the Guadalupe is far too cold for a swim. But you can still get into the local outdoors by participating in the annual **Volksmarsch**. This is an eleven-kilometer walk through the scenic hill country to benefit charity. For more information about the upcoming walk, contact the **New Braunfels Marsch-und-Wandergruppe**, *PO Box 310778, New Braunfels, Texas 78131-0778*.

the summer. Special arrangements can be made for visitors who want to use the courts during the day or arrange overnight stays without lessons.

Shopping

The **New Braunfels Factory Stores**, *651 Interstate Highway 35 North, Tel. 5830/620-6806 or 888/SHOP-333*, was one of the first outlet malls to be built in the state. You can avoid the mobs that clog the larger mall in San Marcos by stopping here instead. From Interstate Highway 35, take Exit 188; the mall is on the west side of the highway.

Excursions & Day Trips

Situated between San Antonio and New Braunfels, **Canyon Lake** provides a refreshing change from the more crowded lakes of central Texas. The lake is well known by fishing enthusiasts as a haven for different varieties of bass. The state parks of New Braunfels provide easy access to both Canyon Lake and the Guadalupe River. The largest of the public parks in this area, Canyon Park offers over 180 acres equipped with sites for both tent camping and primitive camping. The park has a convenience store and toilet facilities. Day visitors may use the picnic shelters and boat ramp. Boat rental is available. From Interstate Highway 35 take Ranch Road 306 west about 8 miles then follow signs to the campground entrance.

Practical Information

For tourist information contact the **New Braunfels Chamber of Commerce**, *Tel 800/572-2626, Website: www.nbcham.org.*

Comfort

This little community resembles a frontier town out of an Old West movie, and the many antique stores in **Comfort** allow visitors to take home a bit of yesteryear. The center of town has over 100 historical buildings and a proud history. In 1854, German settlers who admired the picturesque scenery and fresh water offered by the Guadalupe River founded the town.

The Civil War erupted in miniature in Comfort, when a group of representatives from the town attempted to flee to Mexico in order to fight against slavery and the Confederate cause. The **Treue der Union** monument commemorates the site where fighting erupted between the Union sympathizers and Confederate soldiers.

Spend Your Holidays In Comfort

Traditional holiday celebrations in a small community make memorable times. The townspeople are welcoming to visitors who want to participate in holiday activities. Comfort sponsors **Volksmarsch**, a 10-kilometer walk and Easter egg hunt on the Saturday before Easter. You can register the day of the walk and there is no fee for participation.

On July Fourth the **Independence Day Parade** down Main Street kicks off a day of celebration. Food, entertainment and country dancing last all day and into the evening in Comfort Park.

Halloween is occasion for the fall Volksmarsch, with costumed participants and a bike route. And the year draws to a sentimental close with a **candlelight Christmas celebration** on the first Saturday of December. In the afternoon tours of historic homes decorated for Christmas run until 5pm, then the streets alight with candles and merriment.

For more information about holiday celebrations contact the **Comfort Chamber of Commerce**, *Tel. 830/995-3131.*

Arrivals & Departures

You can reach Comfort from Fredericksburg to the north along Highway 87. From San Antonio, travel west on Interstate Highway 10, which crosses Comfort from southeast to northwest. Comfort is a half-hour drive from San Antonio.

Orientation

Unlike most towns, Comfort usually sleeps during the week and awakens on weekends. If you pass through during most weekdays, you may find the shops and streets deserted. Highway 27 runs west along the Guadalupe River and Ranch Road 473 continues east.

Where to Stay

COMFORT COMMON, *717 High Street. Tel: 830/995-3030, Website: www.comfortcommon.com. 5 Rooms, 2 Suites, Cottages. Rates: $70-110. Credit cards accepted.*

Originally the Ingenhuett-Faust Hotel, the Comfort Common was constructed in 1880 and renovated recently. The old hotel remains true to its Victorian character, with antiques throughout. A large part of the ground floor is an antique shop. The bed and breakfast portion of the building provides a mix of endearingly odd-shaped rooms, all with private baths. A separate cottage has a single bedroom and a kitchen. One block away is a Victorian cottage called Storyville with a bedroom, sitting room, and the optional use of a kitchen and dining room. Storyville is beautifully decorated in a white-on-white color scheme. The hotel is in the historic downtown area.

LOVETT'S LANDING, *PO Box 391. Tel: 830/995-2836, Fax 830/995-2839. Rates: $125. Credit cards accepted.*

The small country house with a single attic window has two rooms for guests, each with a private bath and kitchen. The home has a unique barn that has been converted into a guesthouse that sleeps eight comfortably. The quaint surroundings and antique furnishings allow you to feel that you are far from modern cities and times. The house is on the Guadalupe River, and guests can swim, fish or go boating. This retreat is a good alternative to staying in neighboring Kerrville, which is a larger tourist destination. Guests who stay a full week (seven nights) receive one night free.

From Interstate Highway 10 west of San Antonio, take exit 523 and travel south. Just past Cypress Creek Bridge, take a left on Hermann Son's Road. This will lead you to the bed and breakfast.

MEYER BED AND BREAKFAST, *845 High Street. Tel. 830/995-2304, Toll free 888/995-6100, Website: www.meyerbedandbreakfast.com. 9 Suites. Rates: $79-99.*

The Meyer family built the stone buildings of this bed and breakfast. The earliest building was a stagecoach stop in the last half of the nineteenth century. Later the hotel building accommodated travelers arriving by train. The Meyer Bed and Breakfast is part of the historic downtown of Comfort. The six buildings overlook limpid Cypress Creek. Each suite has been uniquely furnished with antiques and all have a private bath, cable television, and air conditioning. Breakfast is served in an airy dining room built in 1887. The lovely grounds contain a fishpond, fountain, summer kitchen, and pool.

Where to Eat

ARLENE'S CAFE, *426 7th Street. Tel. 830/995-3330. Thursday to Sunday 11am to 4pm.*

Arlene's served home-cooked meals without the heaviness of most country recipes. The staples of this cafe, soup and salad, are a refreshing break from the chicken-fried-everything of most central and west Texas diners.

MIMI'S CAFÉ AND DELI, *814 High Street. Tel. 830/995-3470. Tuesday to Friday 11am to 2pm, Friday 6pm-8:30pm, Saturday 11am-3pm, closed Sunday.*

Mimi's Cafe on High Street highlights the downtown area. Even if you are not hungry enough to fill up on a meal, stop in for a slice of pie. Every Friday night is steak night.

CYPRESS CREEK INN, *408 Highway 27 at the Cypress Creek Bridge. Tel. 830/995-3977, Tuesday-Saturday 11:30am-2:30pm and 5:30pm-8:30pm, Sunday 11:30am-2:30pm, closed Mondays.*

This old fashioned cafe, around since the early 1950s, serves up hearty helpings of beef and pork prepared like a Texas grandma would make. The cafe is right on Cypress Creek and is the oldest operating restaurant in Comfort. The food is inexpensive and only cash is accepted.

Shopping

The shopping in Comfort is more for entertainment value than serious antique browsing. Many of the stores are run in very old buildings and have eclectic merchandise. **Turkey Ridge Trading Company**, Highway 27, Tel 830/995-4265, is a large store with western-style furniture, knickknacks and memorabilia. The nearby **Hospice Thrift Store** is in a small stone house, which has the distinctive crossbeam construction of traditional German villages. Across the street, the **Whistle Stop Tea Room** provides a quaint and quiet setting for an afternoon tea break.

Excursions & Day Trips
SISTERDALE

A visit to the **Sister Creek Winery**, *FM 1376, Sisterdale, Tel. 830/324-6704 or 324-6682; open daily noon to 5pm*, gives you two experiences. The first is an historic journey. The winery of Sister Creek Vineyards is housed in a cotton gin dating from the 1890s. You walk in the front entrance, right into the renovated old gin.

The second is an exploration of wine. The winery was founded in 1988 and cultivates vines that originated in France. The trouble taken to use traditional aging techniques pays off in rich, aromatic reds and smooth whites. Only a few varieties are produced in very limited quantities each year. To reach Sister Creek Winery, from Interstate Highway 10, turn north onto FM 1376 at Boerne. The winery is about 12 miles from the interstate, just south of Luckenbach.

BOERNE

Boerne (pronounced Bur-nee) was settled over 140 years ago by German immigrants. To get there from Comfort, take Highway 87/Interstate Highway 10 east. There is good antiquing to be had up and down the Main Street in Boerne, but the real attractions around these parts are made by nature, not man.

The rugged beauty of the hill country around Boerne makes the area a favorite for lovers of the outdoors. The **Guadalupe River State Park**, *Tel. 830/438-2656*, has over 159 camper sites all with water and half with electricity hook-ups. The excellent facilities at this park include showers, rest rooms and a convenience store. You can fill your days with trail hiking, canoeing and picnicking. From Boerne, take Highway 46 east, and proceed eight miles to the park road.

Practical Information

Tourist information is available at the **Chamber of Commerce and Community Center**, *700 High Street, Tel. 830/995-3131, Friday and Saturday 12:30pm to 4:30pm*, located at the corner of 7th and High Street. The quaint building dates from 1907.

Bandera

Bandera has a long, interesting history. Two years after Polish immigrants founded the town in 1852, a group of Mormons established a colony. One of the oldest Catholic churches in the state, Saint Stanislaus, was built by the Polish settlers in 1876. The cattle drives of pre-railroad Texas stopped in Bandera and ingrained ranching into the lifestyle. Now urban cowboys have taken over and Bandera dubs itself the "Cowboy Capital of the World." Most of the wrangling is done on dude ranches.

Tourists that stay in Bandera usually visit all-inclusive vacation ranches. Activities during the day, such as trail rides and sports, as well as meals and entertainment in the evenings are taken care of by the ranch.

Arrivals & Departures

Bandera is on Highway 16, south of Kerrville and west of San Antonio.

Where to Stay & Eat

DIXIE DUDE RANCH, *PO Box 548, Ranch Road 1077. Tel. 830/796-4481, Toll free 800/375-YALL, Website: www.dixieduderanch.com. 20 units. Rates: $95-115. Credit cards accepted.*

This oldest of dude ranches in an area famous for dude ranches has it all. As the folks at the Dixie are quick to point out, however, this is not just a guest ranch – the Dixie is a working stock-ranch founded in 1901. Activities include horseback riding, swimming, hayrides, and more. You can even arrange to go on an overnight trail ride and camp under the stars.

Accommodations range from cabins to two-story bunkhouses, and there are family-style rooms available. Rates include three meals a day, two horseback rides daily, and all other ranch activities. Children under two stay free, while children between the ages of two and 12 pay $30-50 a night. There is a two-night minimum stay, increasing to three nights from June through August.

RUNNING-R RANCH, *9059 Bandera Creek Road. Tel. 830/796-3984, Fax 796-8189, Website: www.rrranch.com. Rates: $85-110 per night. Credit cards accepted.*

The 230-acre ranch feels even larger because it stands next to the beautiful woodlands of a state park. Every guest at the Running R Ranch gets two hours of horseback riding per day included with the room. Guides lead trail rides through the Hill Country Natural Area and point out wildlife, birds, and plants. You can brush up your western riding skills with special lessons from an experienced, trophy-winning trainer. There are four cabins that can sleep four people and one lodge house that can sleep six. The cabins are finished off with rustic interiors and knotty pine furniture. Room rates also include breakfast and lunch. Children two and under stay free, while the rates for children between the ages of 3 and 12 range from $40-50. A minimum two-night stay is required.

Nightlife & Entertainment

During the summer Bandera holds a rodeo every weekend. The grande finale of the season is the **Cowboy Capital PRCA Rodeo Week** on Memorial Day Weekend. You can attend the bull bustin' and barn dances and golf tournament held in conjunction with the rodeo. Rodeo admission is $10 for adults and $6 for children.

Sports & Recreation

A piece of central Texas for everyone to enjoy is the **Hill Country State Natural Area** a few miles southwest of Bandera. Formerly a ranch, the over 5000 acres of rough land is now a nature preserve. Thirty-six miles of trails traverse streams, rocky hills and canyons. The area is open for primitive camping, hiking and swimming. To get to the Hill Country Sate Natural Area, take Farm Road 1077 from Bandera.

The **Lost Maples State Natural Area**, *Ranch Road 187, Vanderpool, Tel. 830/389-8900*, is a 2000-acre preserve open for camping, hiking and fishing. Not only are the maple trees here unique in the state, rare birds live in the park. Golden-cheeked warblers can be seen during certain times of the year. A visit to Lost Maples in early autumn lets you take in bright fall foliage, which is unusual in the southwest. Lost Maples has campsites with water and electricity, as well as primitive camping areas. The park's interesting exhibits provide information about the flora and fauna unique in this area. From San Antonio, take Highway 16 north Medina, and then continue west on Highway 337 to Vanderpool. Ranch Road 187 meets Highway 337 in Vanderpool.

Vanderpool sits close to the **Edwards Plateau**, and offers some of the best countryside in the area. Continue north on Highway 337 to enjoy one of the loveliest scenic drives in the Hill Country.

Practical Information

The **Bandera Convention and Visitors Bureau**, *PO Box 171, Bandera, 78003, Tel 830/796-3045 or 800/364-3833, Website: www.tourtexas.com/bandera/bandera.html*, can provide information and advance tickets for the rodeo.

Kerrville

Kerrville is large for a Hill Country town. It's the seat of Kerr County, and though the official town population is 18,000, an estimated 20,000 more live in the surrounding area, which is noted for its rough beauty and crisp, clear evenings.

Early settlers came to this region in the mid-1800s. They were attracted to the lovely countryside and headwaters of the Guadalupe River. Kerr County was created by an act signed in the Texas legislature in 1856. The small community began to blossom when an active grist and sawmill was established on the river. Now Kerrville is a diverse and bustling place favored by retirees and young professionals alike, described by the Wall Street Journal as one of the wealthiest small towns in America.

One of the most enjoyable events in Texas is the **Kerrville Folk Festival**, *Tel. 800/435-8249*, which takes place each year during the last week of May and first week of June. The outdoor festival lasts 18 days. Many favorite local musicians as well as artists from around the world take the stage, and families enjoy the hot days that mark the onset of summer. The evening shows take place under a brilliant canopy of stars and the cool night air.

Kerrville is a center of folk art and crafts. Seasonal celebrations allow local artists to offer their wares as the community comes together. The **Easter Hill Country Bike Tour** and **Easter Festival & Chili Classic**, *Tel. 830/792-3535*, are great reasons to get out and enjoy spring. If the bike tour through the Hill Country does not tire you out, participate in the 5K run. The festival features all-American events such as a washer pitching tournament, a 4x4 bedpost derby, armadillo races, and, of course, a chili cook-off.

Every Memorial Day weekend, Schreiner College hosts the **Texas State Arts and Crafts Fair**, *Tel. 830/869-5711, Website: www.tacef.org*. The event began in 1971 and has been designated the "official state arts and crafts fair" by the Texas Legislature. Two hundred artisans from around the state are chosen to exhibit and sell their crafts. Paintings, jewelry, stained glass and sculpture are among the works on display. To reach Schreiner College Fairgrounds, take Interstate Highway 10 or Highway 27 east to Kerrville. Signs will lead you to the Schreiner College Fairgrounds. Shuttles provide transportation from the parking to the fair. Admission is $6 for adults and $1 for children under 12 years old.

Festivals in Kerrville

Hill Country Junior Livestock Show – Mid-January
Easter Bike Tour and Festival – Easter weekend
Kerrville Folk Festival – Last week of May
Texas State Arts and Crafts Fair – Memorial Day Weekend
Kerrville Wine & Music Festival – Labor Day Weekend
Kerr County Fair – Mid-October

Arrivals & Departures

Kerrville is located at the intersection of Highways 16 and 27, two miles south of Interstate Highway 10.

Orientation

Kerrville is 66 miles northwest of San Antonio and roughly two hours from Austin.

Where to Stay

INN OF THE HILLS RIVER RESORT, *1001 Junction Highway. Tel. 830/895-5000, Fax 830/895-6091, Toll free 800/292-5690, Website: www.innofthehills.com. 228 Rooms. Rates: $65-165. Credit cards accepted.*

This hotel aims to provide a resort atmosphere at a reasonable price. Despite the title of resort, the rooms here are your basic mid-range hotel accommodations, and vary from budget quality to more luxurious apartment-style suites. The grounds are lovely, with several outdoor pools, including one with a view of the Guadalupe River. Guests also receive free access to the adjacent Family Sports Center, a recreational complex with two indoor pools, a volleyball court, dry sauna and a gym. Annemarie's Alpine Lodge Restaurant serves enormous buffets of varying kinds for lunch and dinner. For more formal dining, The Riverview Restaurant is open for dinner only, Tuesday through Saturday. The Inn Pub features live music and country dancing six nights a week, Monday through Saturday.

This is also the home of the Texas Heritage Music Museum, an enjoyable exhibit of music memorabilia and a great place to pick up CDs or cassettes of Texas musicians for someone else's or your own music collection.

THE Y.O. RANCH RESORT HOTEL & CONFERENCE CENTER, *2033 Sidney Baker Street. Tel. 830/257-4440, Fax 830/896-8189, Toll free 800/292-2800. 200 Rooms. Rates: $89-119. Credit cards accepted.*

This is not the famous Y.O. Ranch (see Day Trips & Excursions), but this popular hotel is named after it. The hotel is now owned and operated by Gal-

Tex Hotel Corporation. The lobby resembles a ranch-house trophy room, with enough exotic game animals to fill a zoo. The hotel restaurant, the Sam Houston Dining Room, is a casual bar and grill decorated in a San Francisco Gold Rush theme.

The rooms are modern and have complete amenities such as television and telephones. Some suites have their own stone fireplaces. The western-theme furnishings were specially made for the hotel. If you're traveling with children, you'll love the Family Suites—special rooms with separate split-wood "forts" with bunk beds, Nintendo games, and free movies.

There are plenty of recreational facilities at the hotel, including an outdoor pool, tennis courts, and children's play area. Golf and horseback riding can be arranged at the front desk.

THE PAINTED HORSE RANCH AND BED & BREAKFAST, *1904 Bear Creek Road. Tel. and Fax 830/367-4738, Toll free 888/813-6238, Website: www.thepaintedhorsebb.com. 1 Cottage. Call for rates.*

It's not just a marketing ploy – this cottage truly is on a working ranch. Bud and Sandy Bonner raise painted horses and live on the same property in a separate house. The cottage is a secluded western-style rock house with a wrap-around porch and sits on Bear Creek. There are two bedrooms, a bathroom, living room, and kitchen. Continental breakfast is left out in the main house for guests to enjoy at their leisure. Walk about and look for native and exotic deer, admire the horses and the orchard, or just sit on the porch and listen to the birds.

TARNISHED SPUR BED & BREAKFAST, *1120 Spur 100. Tel. 830/896-8802, Fax 830/792-4292, Toll free 800/362-7095, Website: www.horseadventure.com. 1 House. Rates: $125.*

It's wonderful to have your own house in the Hill Country, but that doesn't even begin to describe the pleasure of a stay at the Tarnished Spur. This bed & breakfast is on the Leon Harrel Ranch, home of Leon Harrell's Old West Adventure, one of the most exciting western vacation destinations in the state.

The house has three bedrooms and two bathrooms, as well as a private full kitchen and pet kennels. It is comfortably decorated and even comes with satellite television – not that you'll be watching it. All around you are acres of gorgeous Hill Country, training stables, and beautiful horses of all kinds. Leon Harrel is something of a legend in his field, which is the riding and training of cutting horses. He and his staff offer training clinics for the expert rider and the beginner alike. For more on the Old West Adventure, see *Sports & Recreation*.

Where to Eat

THE CYPRESS GRILL, *2124 Sidney Baker. Tel. 830/257-7171. Credit cards accepted. Tuesday-Saturday 7am-2pm and 5pm-9pm, Sunday 7am-2:30pm. Reservations recommended.*

"Comfort food with an attitude," states the menu, and let's hope that attitude never adjusts. The food here is beautifully presented, as in the house-cured salmon starter – a generous plate of tempting pink salmon criss-crossed with white and green sauces, garnished with tobika caviar, and crisp seeded bread fanned behind. Nightly dinner specials might consist of chile crusted shrimp or a tender veal chop on a bed of mashed potatoes. Dessert selections include a rich bread pudding in a warm rum sauce and a piquant cactus pear sorbet.

PATRICK'S LODGE RESTAURANT & BAR, *2190 Junction Highway. Tel. 830/895-4111. Monday-Friday 11am-2pm, Dinner Monday-Saturday beginning at 5pm. Credit cards accepted.*

Chef Patrick Peralt trained in France and has over 30 years under the toque, and since 1994 Kerrville has enjoyed his expertise. Lunch is presented as an attractive buffet, or you can order from a menu of entrees, sandwiches, and salads. Dinner is when Peralt demonstrates his flair for preparing game such as quail and venison. A well-chosen wine list features local wines, and there is a full bar as well. The dining room overlooks verdant Goat Creek.

THE LAKEHOUSE, *1655 Junction Highway. Tel. 830/895-3188. Credit cards accepted.*

This family restaurant offers home-cooked favorites like fried catfish and chicken fried steak in a casual dining room with wonderful river views. You may dine in, drive through, or carry out every day from 11am until 8pm. There are riverside picnic tables out behind the restaurant.

Seeing the Sights

For a look back through history, visit the **Hill Country Museum**, *226 Earl Garrett Street, Tel. 830/896-8633*. The museum is housed in the handsome Romanesque home of Kerrville's most important founding father, Captain Charles Schreiner. The antiques and period decor provide a glimpse into the genteel life enjoyed by the privileged settlers of the region. The museum is located near the City Park on the Guadalupe River. Earl Garrett Street is just off Highway 27, south of Sidney Baker Street.

One of Kerrville's unique attractions is the **Cowboy Artists of America Museum**, *1550 Bandera Highway, Tel. 830/896-2553, Website: www.caamuseum.com. Open Monday to Saturday 9am-5pm; Sunday 1pm-5pm, closed Mondays Labor Day to Memorial Day, admission $5 adults, $1 children*. This is one of the few museums devoted exclusively to art that portrays both the old and contemporary west. Some of the country's finest Western painters and sculptors have had their works displayed here. The collection includes permanent and rotating works by artists such as James Boren, Robert Duncan, Melvin Wheeler and others. The museum has its own library dedicated to the study of the genre of Western painting.

Nightlife & Entertainment

During the summer months, the Hill Country Arts Foundation sponsors evening outdoor theater performances at the **Point Theater**. The outdoor amphitheater seats 700 and sits right on the banks of the beautiful Guadalupe River in nearby Ingram, Texas. During the winter, performances move to the indoor stage. For information about current and upcoming performances, contact the **Hill Country Arts Foundation**, *Tel. 830/367-5122, Website: www.hcaf.com*.

If you're lucky enough to be in the area on a summer Saturday night, run over to **Crider's**, *Highway 39, Hunt, Tel. 830/238-4441*, for the weekly rodeo and dance. Bring the kids, too – there's a calf scramble especially for children. Crider's is the real deal, a honky-tonk and roping arena where the locals go to kick loose. The rodeo starts at eight and the music starts at nine and lasts until one in the morning.

Sports & Recreation

Photographers and nature lovers will delight in the **Kerrville Camera Safari** through the *Wilson Haley Ranch, at Interstate Highway 10 and Highway 16 (exit 508), Tel. 830/792-3600*. The drive-through wildlife ranch is open from 9am to dusk daily, and admission is $6 for adults, $4 for children. Exotic animals from addax to zebra roam the grounds, with a few Texas longhorn cattle thrown in for good measure.

The Colorado River is one of the best areas for **fly-fishing** in the state. If you have never experienced the lure of this sport, a visit to Kerrville would be a great time to give it a try. Lessons, equipment and guides are available from **Pico Outdoor Company**, *Tel. 830/895-4348 or 800/256-5873*.

The Harrel Family Ranch, *1120 Spur 100, Tel. 830/896-8802, Fax 830/896-1820, Toll free 800/362-7095, Website: www.leonharrel.com*, is no ordinary dude ranch. World Champion and Hall of Fame Cowboy Leon Harrel provides **horsemanship training, cattle roundups, trail rides and cowboy cookouts** to those yearning for a taste of western life. The ranch teams up at times with the Y.O. Hotel (see *Where to Stay*) to offer special packages.

The **H.E. Butt Municipal Tennis Center**, *Sidney Baker Drive, Tel. 830/257-4982*, has six lighted hard courts that are open to the public. Court fee is $2 per person. The tennis courts and pro shop are open from Monday to Thursday, 9am to 5pm; Friday and Saturday 9am to 5pm and Sunday 1pm to 5pm. To reserve a court or get information about tennis lessons, call the pro shop.

Kerrville has a fine municipal golf course, located near the center of the city and close to most hotels. The **Scott Schreiner Municipal Golf Course**, *Country Club Road, Tel. 830/257-4982*, features 18 holes of rolling greens. The facilities include a pro shop, putting green, showers and locker room. The course is open daily from 7am until dusk. Greens fees range from $8.50 to $11.50.

The **Kerrville-Schreiner State Park**, *2385 Bandera Highway, Tel. 830/257-5392*, offers 500 acres along the Guadalupe River for camping, fishing, swimming, and hiking. To get there, take Highway 173 to the south edge of the city.

Excursions & Day Trips

Although a granite marker is all that is left to commemorate the site, Kerrville is the home of the only United States Military camel "cavalry." Camels were brought to **Camp Verde** as an experiment in 1856. The mission for the camel corps was to serve as transportation and to aid in moving supplies long distances over rough terrain. The camel is a slow and nearly untrainable beast, which may be why the experiment failed, even before the onset of the Civil War. The site of Camp Verde is one mile west of Texas 173, on Camp Verde Road. There is a roadside park on the bank of Verde creek where you can cool your toes, and an old-fashioned general store and post office where you can wet your whistle.

Drive out west on Highway to the little town of Ingram. **"Old" Ingram** is all that is left of the original town following a devastating flood in 1936. It is now a charming collection of art galleries, antique shops, and boutiques. From here, the road grows even more scenic, hugging the banks of the Guadalupe River as it continues past the little town of **Hunt** with its wonderful general store and dozens of summer camps nestled in the hills. Continuing west on Highway 39 is a truly curious sight—an almost full-scale replica of Stonehenge! **Stonehenge II**, as it is called, is on FM 1340, two miles west of Hunt.

The **Y.O. Ranch**, *Mountain Home, Tel. 830/644-3222, toll free 800/967-2624, Website: www.yoranch.com*, is about 32 miles from Kerrville, off Highway 41. This legendary ranch belonged to Captain Schreiner (see Hill Country Museum under Seeing the Sights, above) and is still managed by his family today. Once encompassing 600,000 acres, the ranch is now smaller, but still one of the most amazing of its kind. The 40,000-acre Y.O. is home to North America's largest collection of exotic wild animals. Hunting, photography, and tours are available year-round. Tours at 10am, 1pm, and 4 pm daily. If you decide you'd like to stay, lodging is provided in 1880s-era old west cabins.

Practical Information

The **Kerrville Visitors' Center**, *2108 Sidney Baker, Tel. 830/792-3535, toll free 800/221-7958, Website: www.ktc.net/kerrcvb*, is open seven days a week, Monday-Friday 8:30-5, Saturday 9-3, and Sunday 10-3.

Fredericksburg

The town of **Fredericksburg** was founded by a group of German settlers from New Braunfels in 1846, and still retains a decidedly European ambiance. Famous for all things Deutsch, including the state's largest Oktoberfest, Fredericksburg is that most rare of Texas commodities, a town designed for pedestrians. Walking through the picturesque environs today, you could hardly guess that the town once marked the dangerous borderland between settlers and Native Americans.

Weekend travelers flood Fredericksburg and the surrounding hill country, so bed and breakfasts abound. Outdoor enthusiasts cannot get enough of **Enchanted Rock**, a large granite dome that was a sacred spot for Native Americans, and nearby lively **Pedernales Falls**. Those who have no desire to escape the trappings of civilization enjoy the specialized gift and antique shops in Fredericksburg. Many of the merchants in Fredericksburg are true crafts-people. The handicrafts offered are of high quality and represent a unique blend of interests. You can pick out a handcrafted guitar, toiletries made from locally grown herbs or wine from the area.

Arrivals & Departures

Highway 290, which passes through Austin to the east, turns into Main Street in Fredericksburg.

Orientation

Main Street runs through the center of the old town, a prosperous area full of shops and restaurants. The streets that surround Main Street to the north and south have charming old houses and are pleasant for an afternoon stroll. The town square is on Main Street, just east of the merchant center. This is where you will find the visitor information center and town museum.

The Easter Fires of Fredericksburg

One of the more unique celebrations in the area is the **Easter Fires**. Every Easter hillside fires light up the horizon. The tradition has been part of the Easter holiday as long as locals can recall. A few different explanations of the ritual persist. The hillside fires may be a carry on of the old European Easter fires. The fires are set to chase bad spirits away from the cites and are known as "witch burning." Another oral tradition asserts that when the pioneer children saw fires on distant hills, the adults told them that the Easter Bunny was boiling eggs. Actually the fires were Cherokee camps.

Where to Stay

If you plan to visit on a holiday weekend you may find using a reservation service is the easiest way to get a room, since they have a variety of options and can save you the time and trouble of calling many inns. Many of these offices serve other towns in the Hill Country as well:

- **Bed and Breakfast of Fredericksburg**, *619 West Main Street, Tel. 830/ 997-4712, Toll free 877/396-9240, Website: www.bandbfbg.com*
- **Be My Guest**, *110 North Milam Street, Tel. 830/997-7227, Toll free 800/ 364-8555*
- **Gastehaus Schmidt Reservation Service**, *231 West Main Street, Tel. 830/ 997-5612, Toll free 866/427-8374, Website: www.fbglodging.com*
- **First Class Bed & Breakfast Reservation Service**, *Fax 830/997-0040, Toll free 888/991-6749, Website: www.fredericksburg-lodging.com*

GILES MANOR, *110 North Bowie Street. Tel. 830/990-9970. Rates: $70-100. Credit cards accepted.*

Giles Manor has two separate bed and breakfasts on the premises. Alfred's is a log cabin dating from the 1870s that has been made into a cozy hide-away. The Granary is the building that was once the smoke house for the manor. Both accommodations are inviting and have romantic accents, such as fireplaces. They cannot help but pale in comparison, though, to the elegant main house, a two-story limestone home built in the 1870s.

DELFORGE PLACE, *710 Ettie Street. Tel. 830/997-6212, Toll free 800/ 997-0462, Website: www.delforgeplace.com. Rates: $105-120. Credit cards accepted.*

At the Delforge Place the rooms are decorated using four different themes – Victorian, turn-of-the-century American, German, and European Emigration. The original house, built in 1898 as a one-room Sunday Haus, was moved to its present site in 1975. The house maintains an authentic Victorian atmosphere, with perhaps its most striking feature being exquisite beveled, stained, and etched-glass windows. Breakfast is marvelous, and different every morning, served either in the charming dining room with its calligraphied walls or outside on the rock patio.

FREDERICKSBURG BED & BREW, *243 East Main Street. Tel. 830/997-1646, Fax 830/997-8026, Website: www.yourbrewery.com. 12 Rooms. Rates: $89. Credit cards accepted.*

Upstairs at this bustling brewpub you will find an unexpected bed and breakfast, pleasantly furnished. Part of the charm of staying here is the convenience of being on Main Street, where the town's shops and restaurants are located. If you do not want to join the fun downstairs, you can have a sampling of the beer, which is brewed on-site, sent to your room.

MAGNOLIA HOUSE, *101 East Hackberry Street. Tel. 830/997-0306, Fax Fax 830/997-0766, Toll free 800/880-4374. Rates $95-140. Credit cards accepted.*

Located in a quiet residential neighborhood just a few blocks from Main Street, the Magnolia House epitomizes the classic architecture of small-town Texas. The house was built in 1923, and is now designated a Texas Historic Landmark. The large front porch is a relaxing place for morning and evening alike. Each of the six rooms in the Magnolia House is lovingly furnished with antiques and a unique theme. The romantic Bluebonnet Room has a private entrance and wood-burning fireplace. The large bathroom has an antique tub. All rooms include a homemade breakfast buffet.

Where to Eat

FREDERICKSBURG BREWING COMPANY, *245 East Main Street. Tel. 830/997-1646. Credit cards accepted.*

You can't miss the brewpub; it is one of the largest storefronts on Main Street. Copper tanks line the walls of the dining room. You can ask for a sample of the current featured beer or buy a sample tray that gives a substantial taste of each. The beer is of excellent quality, and the bar is a good place to spend a few hours in the evening if you desire some social interaction.

The food here is good; grilled chicken, burgers and pasta dishes are made with enough flavor and spice to accompany the beer well. Rock climbers making the trek home from a long day at Enchanted Rock often fill the pub on Friday and Saturday nights. They usually head for the back room, which is filled with picnic tables.

THE NEST RESTAURANT, *607 South Washington Street. Tel. 830/990-8383, Website: www.thenestrestaurantfredericksburg.com. Dinner only, Mondays through Thursdays starting at 5:30pm. Reservations recommended. Credit cards accepted.*

This casually elegant little restaurant is tucked inside a charming house, where Chef-owner John Wilkinson conjures up wonderful sophisticated Continental cuisine. Steak and seafood are given culinary refinement, and every entrée comes with an organic field green salad with delicious house vinaigrette. Desserts range from the spectacular (profiteroles) to the delicate (lavender ice cream with spiced red wine sauce).

NAVAJO GRILLE, *209 East Main Street. Tel. 830/990-8289. Credit cards accepted.*

Southwest flavors enliven the food of the Navajo grille. The sophisticated, modern atmosphere brings a new aspect to dining in traditionally German Fredericksburg. The food comes alive with piquant spices and the taste of the grill. Grilled rack of lamb, fresh fish, and steak with crawfish remoulade are examples of the always-changing nightly specials. The cornbread is mouth-watering.

Outside Fredericksburg

HILLTOP CAFE, *10661 North Highway 87. Tel. 830/997-8922, Website: www.hilltopcafe.com.*

Something of a hill country legend, this former filling station now fuels stomachs, not gas tanks. The menu is an eclectic combination of Greek and Cajun fare. The little place is packed on the weekends, especially in the summer. Reservations are essential. Take Highway 87 north from Fredericksburg for 10 miles to reach Hilltop Cafe.

Seeing the Sights

Growing and using herbs is a tradition that has been raised to an art form at the **Fredericksburg Herb Farm**, *402 Whitney Street, Tel. 830/997-8615*. Over fourteen acres are cultivated in lovely patterned gardens. Guests can tour the grounds and learn about growing and utilizing the small crops.

Barbecue Road Trip!

COOPER'S OLD TIME PIT BAR-B-Q, *604 West Young Street, Llano. Tel. 915/247-5713. Credit cards accepted.*

Eating barbecue is practically a hobby for many Texans. And driving one hundred miles to chow down at your favorite restaurant is not out of the question. Cooper's brisket is smoked for nearly a full day in giant barbecue pits. It comes out plain and simple-no fancy spices or oil-and perfect. The servings are generous and the meat has an unbeatable flavor. Not a few barbecue connoisseurs anoint this the best barbecue in the state.

Cooper's is located just west of Llano on Highway 29, which is also called Young Street. From Fredericksburg, take Highway 16 north about 40 miles.

The herbs are made into a variety of products from candles to toiletries to edible infusions. The selection of essential oils is extensive and of the highest quality. The shop offers a selection of books to turn the novice into a masterful herb gardener. The herb farm is on the western outskirts of Fredericksburg. From Main Street (Highway 290), head west out of the town. Go south on Whitney Street. The Fredericksburg Herb Farm has a bed and breakfast and a tearoom. The Tea Room is open for lunch and dinner seven days per week. Try the homemade soup, which proves that homegrown fresh herbs make the meal.

History buffs will enjoy the **Vereins Kirche Museum**, *100 Main Street*, which is a replica of the city's first public building. The museum represents the melding of European and Texas cultures and shows the transition between tradition and innovation in its unusual design. The wooden, octagonal structure holds a small collection of personal artifacts from the pioneers who settled Fredericksburg. The distinctive white structure stands on Market Square.

The famous admiral of World War II, Chester Nimitz, was born and raised in Fredericksburg. The **Admiral Nimitz Historical Center**, *304 East Main Street, Tel. 830/997-4379, open daily 8am to 5pm*, provides an historical overview of the man and of World War II in general. The outdoor exhibit includes armament from the World War II era, and a park is dedicated to presidents who served in the war. The museum building, called the Nimitz Hotel, was built in the mid-nineteenth century.

You enter a land of miniatures when you step into the **Bauer Toy Museum**, *233 East Main Street, Wednesday to Monday 10am to 5pm*. The collection is really aimed more at adult collectors than children. Many of the toys are rare antiques, and the exhibits are strictly "hands-off."

Nightlife & Entertainment

FREDERICKSBURG BREWING COMPANY, *245 East Main Street. Tel. 830/997-1646.*

The large Fredericksburg Brewing Company stays open late serving the beer brewed on the premises. The variety and flavor are excellent. You are likely to meet other weekend visitors among the friendly clientele, as the bar becomes lively in the evening.

LINCOLN STREET WINE MARKET, *111 South Lincoln Street. Tel. 830/997-8463, Toll free 888/395-1069, Website: www.lincolnst.com. Credit cards accepted. Sunday-Monday 1pm-9pm, Tuesday-Thursday 10am-9ish, Friday-Saturday 10am-late.*

A good friend and I once spent an entire day camped out comfortably in this little bar, sipping wines suggested by the knowledgeable staff, talking, laughing, reading, nibbling on cheese and bread. That's the sort of place this is. All of the many wines from around the world here are available by the glass.

Sports & Recreation

The best rock climbing in Central Texas is at the base of **Enchanted Rock**, *Ranch Road 965, Tel. 915/247-3903*, which is a huge granite dome formation that reaches a height of 500 feet. Climbers and rappellers stay in the rocky cliffs at the base of Enchanted Rock. Walking though these trails on a Saturday afternoon is like entering a land of giant spiders-rappellers glide down from all around, and climbers scale up rock-face at each turn.

Campsites are available at Enchanted Rock; during most times of the year reservations are necessary. If you plan to visit the park, arriving in the early morning hours may save you the hassle of waiting for admission. Often the park fills to capacity, and you may find a line of cars waiting to get in. From Fredericksburg, go west on Main Street (Highway 290). Turn north onto Ranch Road 965, which intersects with Main just west of the center of town. You will see the awesome granite hill long before you complete the 18 miles to the park entrance.

Shopping

You could easily devote an entire day of shopping to Main Street alone. Dozens of stores line the quaint downtown street, selling everything from homemade fudge to handmade furniture.

A genuine five-and-dime in a small town is a true find. So go ahead and spend some time strolling the aisles of **Dooley's**, *131 East Main Street*. If none of the toys, trinkets or toiletries appeal to you, check out the post cards at the cashiers stands; they are the cheapest in town.

One of the most unusual and captivating shops is the **Hill Country Music Store**, *151 East Main Street*, where exquisite handcrafted dulcimers are sold. Dulcimers are small stringed instruments that resemble mandolins. The Hill Country Dulcimer Factory has produced dulcimers and other stringed instruments for generations.

Design and decorating devotees make a beeline for the Homestead stores as soon as they get to Fredericksburg. Even if you can't afford the hefty prices attached to the antiques and custom furnishings sold by this group of six stores, it's fun to browse through them. Each store has its own personality. The original store, **Homestead Downtown**, *223 East Main Street*, has as its theme the American cottage. Overstuffed furniture, beautiful wrought iron beds, French quilts and incredible fabrics envelop you as soon as you enter. You can get a list of the other five stores here, as well as addresses and directions.

Excursions & Day Trips

This is peach country and the roadside is dotted with stands selling fresh peaches and peach ice cream in the late summer. The place that has won the hearts and stomachs of many locals is **Das Peach Haus**. The fresh peach ice cream remains unsurpassed. From the center of Fredericksburg take Highway 87 south. You will also find many similar places along Highway 290.

In the early spring, wildflowers blanket the countryside in white, blue, red and yellow. The most spectacular stretch of road to see the beauty of this natural phenomenon is the **Willow City Loop**. The road, Farm-to-Market 1323, twists and turns for about 20 miles until it ends just north of Johnson City, each section aglow with flowers. Many Sunday drivers flood the area and there is no parking anywhere on the loop, so expect a good deal of traffic. If you can go on a weekday you may have some tranquillity. Take Highway 16 north out of Fredericksburg—you will find the marked turn off for FM 1323 before you reach Enchanted Rock. The only establishment on the loop is Harry's. The address is inexact, but you cannot miss it.

The only establishment on the Loop, **Harry's On the Loop, Willow City**, *830/685-3553*, is a backcountry road stop that has prospered with the influx of tourists. Harry's is really just a shack; but since it's the only shack within about twenty miles, it has a captive patronage. Harry's sells canned drinks, bags of snack chips and barbecue sandwiches. You can buy brisket by the pound or the plate. The staff seems to be resentful of the tourists that crowd the small diner, but the clientele is usually friendly and you may strike up a few conversations.

LUCKENBACH

Over 20 years ago the song "Luckenbach, Texas" filled the nation's airwaves. Waylon Jennings and Willie Nelson made the town a country myth. You can visit the genuine article, which is just south of Fredericksburg and has a population of only 25 by the official count. Luckenbach consists of a handful of buildings and a parking area, except on July Fourth weekend, for that is when Willie Nelson holds his annual picnic and Luckenbach overflows with partying fans. It's worth the trip to Luckenbach, just to say that you have been there.

The small back roads that lead to Luckenbach are not well marked. From Highway 290 east of Fredericksburg, take Farm Road 1376 south and continue for four miles.

Tourist information and a map of historic sites are available at the **Chamber of Commerce**, *106 North Adams Street, Tel. 830/997-6523, Monday to Friday 8am to 5pm, Saturday 9am to 5pm, closed Sunday.*

Where to Stay

THE LUCKENBACH INN, *County Road 13. Tel. 830/997-2205, Fax 830/ 997-1115, Toll free 800/997-1124. Rates: $95-125. Credit cards accepted.*

The ranch house is located in the rural outskirts of Fredericksburg. The lovely home sits high atop a hill, isolated from the nearest highway or town.

Johnson City

The grandfather of the nation's 36th president, Lyndon Baines Johnson, founded **Johnson City**. Johnson was raised on the ranch in Johnson City although he was born in nearby Stonewall. President Johnson so well represented the strength and stature of the Texan persona, that to native Texans he is simply "LBJ."

Arrivals & Departures

Johnson City is on Highway 290, about 50 miles east of Austin. Highway 281 connects the city to the north and south.

Where to Stay

CRIDER'S MOTEL, *Highways 290 and 281. Tel. 830/868-7163.*

A night at Crider's takes you back in time to the 1950s. Every front door of the motel is painted a different color, as are the metal lawn chairs on the porches. Each room has a small kitchenette and homey furnishings. This is a cute and comfy place to bunk for the night.

Camping

The **Lyndon Baines Johnson State Park**, *Highway 290, Stonewall, Tel. 830/644-2252 or for reservations 512/389-8900*, has campsites, recreational areas and nature trails. The park is 15 miles east of Johnson City on Highway 290.

Camp at the **Pedernales Falls State Park**, *Ranch Road 3232, Johnson City, Tel. 830/868-7304 or for reservations 512/389-8900*, to enjoy the natural beauty of the hill country. The park has 69 sites with hook-ups and primitive camping areas. The many underground springs near Pedernales Falls allows the lush trees and seasonal foliage to thrive.

Where to Eat

THE FEED MILL CAFE, *103 West Main (Highway 290). Tel. 830/868-7771 or 868-7299.*

The funky Feed Mill is a big piece of "living art" in the center of Johnson City. Fried green tomatoes and chicken fried steak sandwiches are Texas sized and will fill up the hungriest cowboy. For an unusual and delicious twist to a Texas classic, order the grilled cilantro catfish. Do not pass up the chance to start your meal with a big plate of fried green tomatoes. Beer, wine and margaritas accompany the food.

Seeing the Sights

The modest childhood home of the nation's 36th president, Lyndon Baines Johnson, is part of the **Lyndon Baines Johnson National Historical Park**, *Tel. 830/644-2252*, which includes two separate sites in central Texas. The museum complex is located in Stonewall on the **LBJ Ranch**, where Johnson was born. The **LBJ Boyhood Home** is in Johnson City. Both parks receive over 180,000 visitors annually.

The main entrance to the park and the museum complex is in **Stonewall**. Stonewall is 15 miles east of Johnson City on Highway 290. From this point you can take a bus tour of the ranch (admission $2 adults, free for children under 12 years) and visit the Sauer-Beckman living History Farm. Each year the park celebrates President Johnson's birthday by offering free tours of the ranch. A small ceremony is held in the morning and light refreshments are offered to guests all afternoon.

Lyndon Baines Johnson National Historic Park in **Johnson City** has a visitor center, the home in which Johnson grew up and an exhibit which describes the Johnson Settlement family life. The park is open daily from

8:45am to 5pm. There is no admission charge to walk through the exhibits. A shuttle bus runs from the National Park Visitor Center in Stonewall to the park in Johnson City. The Visitor's Center is open daily from 8:45am to 5pm.

Just east of Johnson City is the **Pedernales Falls State Park**, *Ranch Road 3232, Tel. 830/868-7304 or for reservations 512/389-8900*. The waterfalls are really gentle cascades of the Pedernales River as it slopes through the Hill Country. The water ranges from a trickle to rushing rapids depending on the rainfall of the season. The park has campsites, swimming and fishing areas and a 7.5 mile nature trail.

Nightlife & Entertainment

Old Crofts Mill, which produced feed, cotton and flour was hand built over 115 years ago. Modern artistic vision transformed the mill into an eccentric shopping center. Now called the **Feed Mill**, *103 West Main (Highway 290), Tel. 830/868-7771 or 868-7299*, it includes a theater that occasionally holds plays or poetry readings. The Theater is located in the rough stone cellar of the Feed Mill Mall. You sit under cross-timbers in the cool cave-like atmosphere. The Feed Mill Cafe has live country music performances on the weekends. Out back you will find an antique carousel that really works and a petting zoo.

Shopping

Johnson City has a number of unique shops that sell gift items. You can stroll through the stores at the **Feed Mill** like Enchanted Olive, which sells gourmet olive oil and food. Or walk along the old streets through shops brimming with kitschy memorabilia.

Excursions & Day Trips

The dry climate has proven excellent for vineyards and the production of wine. Most of the local wineries grow their own grapes. The operations are small enough to keep the vintner's fine art at a level that produces consistently excellent table wines.

A trip to the **Becker Vineyards**, *Jenschke Lane, Stonewall, Tel. 830/644-2681, Fax 644-2773*, is well worth the stop. A visit to this idyllic rural corner of Texas lets you imagine the area as it may have looked when first settled. The winery operates out of a nineteenth century home, made from the local stone. The small winery produces 5000 cases per year and is particularly known for its white varieties. You can take a tour and sample the wine on a walk-in basis. Stonewall is about 3 miles west of Johnson City on Highway 290.

BLANCO

The sleepy hamlet of **Blanco** is a favorite spot for day trips from Austin or San Antonio. This town was usurped as the county seat of Blanco County by Johnson City in 1891. The town square used to be the seat of local government and is now virtually frozen in time. Today the tourists that trickle through town on weekends appreciate the antique shops on the town square and the beautiful courthouse.

If you are serious about finding unique antiques, try the **Olde Blanco Auction Company**, *318 4th Street*, just a few blocks off the town square. The large, un-air conditioned warehouse is a cross between a great country garage sale and antique mart, with seemingly acres of memorabilia, glassware and furniture. On the third Saturday of the month at 6pm, the Old Blanco Auction Company practices what it does best, auctions. This is in conjunction with **Olde Blanco Market Day**, when the town itself becomes a marketplace. Market Days are held from April to November, the third Saturday of each month.

After a long day of shopping, stop by the **Blanco Bowling Club Café**, which serves diner food such as fries and burgers. But don't eat and run—in the back of the cafe is a small bowling ally. The German-style lanes have ninepins. **Pecan Street Bakery** on the town square attracts the weekend city escapees by serving brunch into the afternoon on weekends.

MARBLE FALLS & BURNET

North of Johnson City on Highway 281 lies an area of recreational lakes and charming towns. Your first stop is in Marble Falls, at a state treasure known as the **Bluebonnet Café**, *211 Highway 281, Tel. 512/693-2444*. You will find the drive worthwhile, just to have breakfast at the Bluebonnet Cafe. While the crowds press into nearby Austin restaurants for brunch, enduring long waits, you can be in a genuine diner instead. For over 50 years the Bluebonnet has served the best Texas breakfasts you can find. If you don't fill up on the pancakes, have a slice of homemade pie. Lunch and dinner are equally good, with favorites like chicken-fried steak done up to perfection. The Bluebonnet is at the intersection of Highways 71 and 281. Monday to Thursday, 6am to 8pm; Friday and Saturday 6am to 9pm; Sunday 6am to 1:45pm. Cash only.

In Burnet, you'll have a choice of exploring underground or on the water. No matter how hot the weather gets, **Longhorn Cavern**, *Ranch Road 2 Box 23, Tel. 512/756-4680 or 756-6976 (recorded tour information)*, remains a cool 64 degrees. Visiting the caves allows a look into the spectacular geology of central Texas. The guided tour leads through 1.25 miles of underground rock formations. On the outside you can walk along two miles of easy trails that cover but a fraction of the 600-acre park. Tours of the cavern begin daily at 10am. From Burnet, take Highway 281 west. The Longhorn Cavern State Park is on Park Road 4.

The **Vanishing Texas River Cruise**, *Tel. 512/756-6986*, is a good way to see the bio-diversity of the lakes of Central Texas. The cruise takes two and one-half hours and sails all year. You will see small waterfalls, lovely rock cliffs and the flora and fauna of the Hill Country. At the right time of year, you will also be treated to the gorgeous spectacle of bald eagles fishing, nesting, and flying. The cruises run Wednesday, Saturday and Sunday at 11am. During the summer, schedule increases to Wednesday to Sunday. From Burnet, take Highway 29 west for three miles, then head north on Ranch Road 2341 for 14 miles. Call ahead for current schedules and fares.

The **Chamber of Commerce**, *406 Highway 290, Tel. 830/868-7684*, offers general information and a map that shows historical buildings in the city.

Junction

The city of Junction thrives on the local hunters that pour into town in the spring and fall. Turkey is probably the most popular game in the area; deer, javelina, and exotic game fill the local ranches.

Junction's only unusual monument is a tall Christmas-Tree-shaped sculpture made of deer antlers called the **Deer Korn Tree**. It stands in a tiny park in front of the Kimbell Processing Company on Main Street. The Women's Professional Business Club donated the Deer Korn Tree to the city.

Barbecue lovers head to Junction on July 4th for the annual **Brisket Cook-Off**, *2341 North Main, Tel. 800/397-3916*. The three-day event includes live music, picnics, and games on ten acres of beautiful Hill Country. The best brisket brings home a $1500 purse. The best part is that everyone can sample the cooking. To reach the Brisket Cook-Off, take Exit 456 from Interstate Highway 10. The cook-off is near the intersection of North Main and Interstate Highway 10.

Arrivals & Departures

Junction is located about 120 miles northwest of San Antonio on Interstate Highway 10, which is also Highways 290 and 83 at that spot. Take Exit 456 or Exit 457 to get into town.

Where to Stay

DAYS INN, *111 Martinez Street, Tel 915/446-3730, Fax 915/446-3730, Toll free 800/329-7466. 50 Rooms. Rates: $55-65. Credit cards accepted.*

The motel stands on a bluff overlooking the countryside, offering rooms with spectacular vistas. The hotel has an outdoor pool and areas for walking your pet. The building is rather new, so the rooms still have a crisp feel. Continental breakfast included with each room. This is probably the most comfortable hotel in the city. The Days Inn is located just off Interstate Highway 10; take Exit 457.

LA VISTA MOTEL, *2040 Main Street, Tel. 915/446-2191. Rates: $45. Credit cards accepted.*

Reasonably comfortable older motel, popular with the hunting crowd. The small hotel is quaint, but musty. Those with an appreciation for neon signs and 1950s roadside architecture may enjoy the La Vista.

SLUMBER INN, *2343 North Main Street, Tel. 915/446-4588. Rates: $45. Credit cards accepted.*

This is the newest of the hotels in Junction. The rooms are large and immaculate with modern furnishings. The Slumber Inn offers by far the best deal in the area. The hotel is located close to Interstate Highway 10, behind the Dairy Queen on Main Street, and it is difficult·to see the inn when approaching from either direction.

SUN VALLEY MOTEL, *1161 Main Street, Tel. 915/446-2505. Rates $40-68. Credit cards accepted.*

The large neon sign marks the center of Main Street. This hotel has a swimming pool and the rooms are decent, but the weekly and monthly rates attract a clientele who are not your typical campers or travelers.

Camping

KOA, *2145 North Main Street, Tel. 915/446-3138.*

The KOA campground is located on the banks of the Guadalupe River, less than one-half mile from Interstate Highway 10. Fishing and swimming in the river let you beat the heat. The campground has electrical hook-ups at each site. If you left your RV at home, the campground has three small but cozy cabins.

Where to Eat

ISAAC'S, *1606 Main Street, Tel. 915/446-4202. Credit cards accepted.*

The neon sign outside of Isaac's lets you know that this is an old-fashioned establishment. Isaac's is a down-home diner overflowing with friendly atmosphere and good food. The onion rings, with their flaky almost sweet batter, could pass for gourmet food. Sirloin steaks are carefully prepared; the chicken fried steak is more than a meal. Dinners come with salad and French fries or a baked potato. The menu includes sandwiches, a small salad bar and delicious home-made pie. Open daily 6 am to 10pm.

COME 'N GIT IT, *2341 Main Street, Tel. 915/446-4357, Fax 915/446-4476. Credit cards accepted.*

The breakfast at Come 'n' Git It will definitely fill you up. The Sombreros are giant breakfast tacos that require a knife and fork. The largest overflows with 5 items (try eggs, sausage, cheese, hash-browns and bell peppers as stuffing) and costs a pittance. The grits and biscuits are good, but my favorite is the Apple Jacks, flapjacks topped with fried apples. The lunch and dinner selections are no less satisfying. The salad bar is fresh and well stocked. With a twist on the traditional southern, the menu includes an array of fried food such as spicy chicken wings, batter-fried whole onion, and chicken fried chicken breast. Open daily 6 am to 11pm.

Sports & Recreation

Hunting leases are available for all types of land and accommodations throughout the area. Some have cabins on the property, others are only rough land. The **Kimball County Chamber of Commerce**, *402 Main Street, Tel. 915/446-3190*, publishes a list of hunting leases and also posts it outside the office.

Excursions & Day Trips
ROCKSPRINGS

The seat of Edwards County is **Rocksprings**, a sleepy town settled in 1889. The area served as rest stop for weary travelers in the last century. The rock spring that is the town's namesake provided a flow of fresh water.

The entire town is little more than the courthouse and surrounding town square. The courthouse is a late Victorian building. The town square is lined with simple white stucco establishments, at least half of which are now closed. The **Mohair Weekly Bookstore**, *Monday to Friday 8:30am to noon; 1pm to 5pm*, in the Mohair Weekly Building sells field guides and books about local history and lore. **Mary's Cafe & Bar**, *Monday to Saturday 10am to 1am*, serves inexpensive diner food.

Organized hunting trips are offered by **Helwig Hunting Services**, *P.O Box 483, Rocksprings, 78880, Tel. 830/683-5104*. Package hunting trips cost roughly $350 per person for two days. Hunting expeditions for exotic animals are a specialty of this service agency.

If you'd like to stay, try:

MESA MOTEL, *PO Box 1043, Rocksprings. Tel. 830/683-3241. Rates: $32-40.*

This small stone motel has 12 old but clean rooms. As the only place in town to bunk for the night, the rates seem reasonable. The hotel is family-run. The motel is two blocks from the town square on Highway 377.

Going west on Interstate Highway 10 will bring you to the town of Sonora, a former trading post that is now in ranch country. The **Caverns of Sonora**, *Ranch Road 1989, Tel. 915/387-3105 or 387-6507, open daily 9am to 5pm*, offer breathtaking crystal formations. You can walk through one and one-half miles of gorgeous natural artwork. The caves are always a comfortable 70 degrees, and tours leave throughout the day. Camping facilities are available on the park grounds. During the summer the **Covered Wagon Dinner Theater** provides nightly entertainment.

Chapter 15

The Texas frontier meets the west in the **Panhandle** region. The vast plains were traversed by cattle drives that changed the face of the state. **Palo Duro Canyon** is the second largest canyon in the United States, and it is here that the legends of cowboys live most vividly. You can take part in a chuck wagon meal, watch a herd of buffalo graze, or attend a rodeo. That famous American artery of literature and song, **Route 66**, dips through the Texas Panhandle.

Lubbock

Lubbock was once a twin city. The two settlements of Old Lubbock and Monterrey were combined to create Lubbock in 1890. The city stands near low, rolling plains, which mark the beginning of the Permian Basin geological region to the south. When rail service arrived in Lubbock, it became an agricultural marketing center, earning the nickname "Hub of the South Plains." Recent history distinguishes Lubbock from other Texas cattle towns—this is the birthplace of rock n' roll legend Buddy Holly. The city is also the home of **Texas Tech University** and has an active cultural life.

Arrivals & Departures

Highway 87 divides Lubbock on a north-south axis. Highway 62 runs from northeast to southwest and is crossed by Highway 84, which runs northwest to southeast. **Lubbock International Airport**, *5401 North Martin Luther King Jr. Boulevard, Tel. 806/775-2036, Website: www.flylia.com*, is just to the east of Interstate Highway 27, north of the city.

Orientation

Lubbock is 318 miles west of Dallas/Fort Worth, 345 miles east-northeast of El Paso, and nearly halfway between San Antonio (to the southeast) and Denver, Colorado (to the northwest).

The streets in central Lubbock make a nearly perfect grid, along with the county line adjoining the city. Loop 289 completely encircles Lubbock. Texas Tech University and the Museum district are in the northwest region of the city.

Getting Around Town

A metropolitan bus system, *Tel. 806/767-2380*, serves the city of Lubbock.

Where to Stay

ASHMORE INN & SUITES, *4019 South Loop 289. Tel. 806/785-0060, Fax 806/785-6001, Toll free 800/785-0061. 100 Rooms, 16 Suites. Rates: $65-74. Credit cards accepted.*

The Ashmore Inn offers an agreeable motel setting. The rooms are large, with ample sitting areas. Each room has a microwave and refrigerator as well. Continental breakfast is offered each morning at no cost to guests. A pretty courtyard contains a heated swimming pool.

KOKO INN, *5201 Avenue Q. Tel. and fax 806/747-2591, Toll free 800/782-3254. Rates: $40-85. Credit cards accepted.*

There is no better description of this motel than "cute." The Koko Inn is a family-owned full-service hotel with an air of tropical kitsch. The indoor atrium is packed with greenery, and the little indoor heated pool is adorable. The décor isn't exactly subtle – pink carpeting and pink walls – but the rooms are cheerful and comfortable. Amenities include cable television, free local calls, and free morning coffee. There is a full-service restaurant on the premises.

LA QUINTA, *4115 Brownfield Highway. Tel. 806/792-0065, Toll free 800/531-5900. Rates: $65-74. Credit cards accepted.*

The six-story hotel is in the vicinity of Texas Tech University and the Medical Center. The modern building is constructed around an atrium lounge. Continental breakfast is complimentary. The hotel has an outdoor pool. La Quinta is located On Highway 82, just south of Highway 62. Free shuttle service to the airport is available. La Quinta also has a location on Avenue Q, near the civic center.

FOUR POINTS BY SHERATON, *505 Avenue Q. Tel. 806/747-0171, Fax 806/747-9243, Toll free 800/925-3535. 145 Rooms. Rates: $79-89. Credit cards accepted.*

The Sheraton Four Points is geared towards business travelers. The hotel is located in the city center. The hotel has computer data ports on phones and ample space for meetings in the conference rooms. The rooms are comfortable and modern with data ports, coffee makers, and all other basic amenities. An indoor pool and a lounge offer leisure time activities.

WOODROW HOUSE BED & BREAKFAST, *2629 19th Street (at the corner of Boston Avenue across from Texas Tech University). Tel. 806/793-3330, Toll free 800/687-5236, Website: www.woodrowhouse.com. 8 Rooms. Rates: $85-155. Credit cards accepted; cash or checks preferred.*

Woodrow House, built specifically in 1995 to be a bed & breakfast, is the first structure to occupy this corner of land. Owners and hosts David and Dawn Fleming dreamed of building Woodrow House for years, and the care and thought they poured into it is evident.

There are eight rooms in the house itself, all with private bath, and a restored caboose complete with bedroom, futon, and kitchenette. Every room is impeccably decorated with antiques and family heirlooms according to the theme suggested by the room's name. Some of the rooms are the Fifties Room, the Equestrian Room, and Granny's Attic. Rates include a full breakfast in the dining room with its grand Sheraton banquet table. The kitchen is open for guests to grab snacks, juice, and homemade cookies.

Where to Eat

GABRIEL'S, *8201 Quaker Avenue. Tel. 806/794-5444. Credit cards accepted.*

Gabriel's is usually packed in the evenings. As one of the most popular restaurants in the city, it sometimes struggles to keep up with its demanding (and hungry) clientele. The menu takes regular Italian dishes, such as lasagna, and brings them up-to-date; the chef uses the best ingredients, rich cheeses, imported vinegar, and the freshest fish. The wine list offers a variety to suit every palate. Reservations are highly recommended, especially on weekends.

GRAPEVINE CAFE, *2407 19th Street. Tel. 806/774-8246. Credit cards accepted.*

You could easily pass by the Grapevine and not look twice. Visitors do not often find this small, unassuming eatery. The refreshing menu offers light fare for lunch, like generous salads, fresh soup and crepes. Dinner has a more extensive selection. The pasta dishes are very satisfying, and the combination of ingredients is the focus of the taste, not the sauce. The desserts are excellent. The cafe is open until 11pm nightly.

LA CUMBRE, *2610 Salem Avenue (in the Cactus Alley Courtyard Mall). Tel. 806/792-5006. Monday-Saturday 11am-2pm and 5pm-9pm, closed Sunday.*

This Mexican restaurant has been pleasing palates since 1968. In addition to Tex-Mex favorites the restaurant also provides live music on weekend nights.

LALA'S, *1110 Broadway Street. Tel. 806/747-2334. Credit cards accepted. Monday-Saturday 11am-3pm, closed Sunday.*

The time to eat at Lala's is when you wake up really hungry, yearning for a hot plate of huevos rancheros. The eggs and omelets come with a big side of crispy potatoes. You can order breakfast until the restaurant closes in the afternoon. The walls teem with photographs, prints, and oil paintings, and the air teems with lively chatter.

Seeing the Sights

You may be surprised by how many famous entertainers hail from the dusty plains of Texas. The **Walk of Fame**, *8th Street and Avenue Q*, contains bronze plaques in honor of Roy Orbison, Tanya Tucker, and Waylon Jennings, among many others. The centerpiece of the walk is a giant bronze statue of the most revered Lubbock native, Charles Hardin "Buddy" Holly.

The park that surrounds **Lubbock Lake Landmark**, *2401 Landmark Lane, Tel. 806/742-1116, open Tuesday through Saturday 9am-5pm, Sunday 1pm-5pm, admission free*, holds archaeological remnants that date from the Paleoindian era. This is the only known site in North America that contains deposits relating to cultures that existed on the Southern Plains 12,000 years ago. Extraordinary fossil evidence records fauna unique to the region. The ongoing dig has yielded artifacts from a hunt that may be 10,000 years old. You can take a guided tour of the excavation site while the dig is in progress. Self-guided tours are also available. The park's museum explains the significance of the finds and our understanding of the prehistory of the region. The park is north of the city at Loop 289 and Highway 84.

Texas Tech University, *400 Indiana Avenue, Tel. 806/742-2490, Tuesday to Saturday 10am to 4pm, admission free*, has archives that cover every field from art history to science. The **Texas Tech Library**, *Tel. 806/472-3758*, has the nation's second largest archive of documents dealing with the Vietnam War. **The Museum of Texas Tech University**, *Fourth Street and Indiana Avenue, Tel. 830/742-2490, Website: www.ttu.edu/~museum, Tuesday to Saturday 10am-5pm, Sunday 1pm-5pm, closed Mondays*, houses almost 2 million objects related to the arts, humanities, and sciences. The museum also encompasses a planetarium and a sculpture garden.

One of the largest and most acclaimed wineries in the state is the **Llano Estacado Winery**, *Highway 84, Tel. 806/745/2258, Fax 806/748-1674. Open daily noon to 4:30pm*. Llano Estacado produces 12 varieties and 75,000 cases annually. Wine tasting is conducted at the modern visitors building.

One of the most absorbing attractions in the area for children and adults alike is the **National Ranching Heritage Center**, *3121 Fourth Street, Tel. 806/742-0498, Website: www.ttu.edu/RanchingHeritageCenter*. This outdoor museum is dedicated to preserving the legacy of ranching, pioneer life, and the development of livestock. More than 35 authentic buildings dating from the late 1780s through the 1930s are collected here. Tours are mostly self-guided, and admission is free. Ranch dances are held throughout the summer and into early fall.

Nightlife & Entertainment

The **Depot District**, *at 19th Street and Avenue Q*, is the center of nightlife and live music in Lubbock. You can find a variety of distractions in this trendy area, from live rock music to country western dancing. Lubbock's own microbrewery, **Hub City Brewery**, is located here. This historic warehouse area is popular with the Texas Tech crowd.

Excursions & Day Trips

The buffalo roam at **Caprock Canyon State Park**, *Ranch Road 1065, P. O. Box 204, Quitaque. Tel. 806/455-1492 or 800/792-1112*. The park hosts occasional safari-style tours to view buffalo herds and other wildlife. Visitors can marvel at the excavation of a 10,000 year old Native American buffalo kill. Another unusual site is an abandoned railroad tunnel, one of the few in the nation. The park also has herds of Pronghorn Antelope and many other types of wildlife. Over 13,000 acres and 24 miles of hiking trails and paths for mountain bikes await the adventurous at Caprock Canyons. The land rises high above the riverbeds and is the backdrop for beautiful sunsets.

At **Big C's Trading Post** you can rent canoes and paddle-boats to use on small **Lake Theo**. Facilities include campsites, both primitive and with hook-ups, and a small lodge. From Lubbock, take Interstate Highway 27 north to Tulia, then Highway 86 east past Silverton to the park.

In the winter, migratory sandhill cranes flock to the **Muleshoe National Wildlife Refuge**, *Highway 214, Muleshoe, Tel. 806/946-3341*. As many as 100,000 cranes nest in the tall grasses along the lake. You can follow motor routes or hiking trails through the refuge. Regardless of the season in which you visit, you should catch a glimpse of birds. Over 280 species inhabit the area during the year. From Lubbock, take Highway 84 north. At Muleshoe, go south on Highway 214. When you reach the park entrance, you will have to drive about two miles on a rugged road to reach the refuge headquarters.

Practical Information

The **Lubbock Convention & Visitors Bureau**, *1301 Broadway, Suite 200, Tel. 806/747-5232 or 800/692-4035, Website: www.lubbocklegends.com*, has information about attractions in the area.

Amarillo

You can get your kicks just outside of Amarillo on the old Route 66! From the Cadillac Ranch to the Quarter Horse Museum, Amarillo is a good stop wherever you're headed.

Arrivals & Departures

Amarillo is in the center of the Texas Panhandle, at the crossroads of Interstate Highway 40, which runs east to west, and Highway 87, which runs north to south.

The **Amarillo International Airport**, *10801 Airport Boulevard*, is on the west side of the city. American, Delta and Southwest have service to and from Amarillo. From Interstate Highway 40, exit Airport Boulevard. Taxi service is available from the airport.

Getting Around Town

The **Amarillo City Transit**, *Tel. 806/342-9144*, provides public bus service for the city.

Taxi companies in Amarillo include:
- **Bob's Taxi Service**, *Tel. 806/373-1171*
- **Royal Cab**, *Tel. 806/376-4276*
- **Yellow Cab**, *Tel. 806/374-5242*

Where to Stay

ADABERRY INN, *6818 Plum Creek Drive. Tel. 806/352-0022, Fax 806/356-0248. Rates: $125-200. Credit cards accepted.*

Constructed and opened in 1997, the Adaberry Inn was built to be a bed and breakfast for the businessperson. The rooms here combine luxurious appointments with high technology. This is where Oprah Winfrey stayed when she came down to defend herself in a libel case brought by the beef industry.

Adaberry Inn provides king-sized beds, private balconies, voice-mail messaging, data port telephones, a fireplace, whirlpool, and even a theater with reclining seats. There is a gourmet kitchen, basketball court, and a workout room as well.

AMBASSADOR HOTEL, *3100 Interstate Highway 40 West. Tel. 806/358-6161, Fax 806/358-9869, Toll free 800/537-8483. 256 Rooms. Rates: $94-149. Credit cards accepted.*

This is Amarillo's finest large hotel. The 10-story building towers over every other building in the vicinity. The interior atrium garden twinkles with lights and the service here is definitely a notch above any other hotel in town.

The spacious rooms are pleasantly decorated with plush carpet and floral fabrics. Amenities include complimentary transport to and from the airport, in-room coffee makers, an indoor heated pool and whirlpool, and fitness center.

PARKVIEW HOUSE BED & BREAKFAST, *1311 South Jefferson Street. Tel. 806/373-9494, Fax 806/373-3166. Rates: $75-135. Credit cards accepted.*

This Victorian home is located near central Amarillo, and is the home of the former Mayor. The home later became a hotel, then a boarding house.

Renovated to reflect the charm of the early 1900's, Parkview House has special touches such as antiques from the area and stained glass windows. Some rooms have private baths, or you can elect to share a bath for a lower room rate. The Victorian Rose Suite offers the most romantic decor and has an antique tub in the bath. A separate cottage with a kitchen and hot tub access is available for rental. From Interstate Highway 40, exit Jefferson Street and proceed north to 14th Street.

Where to Eat

BIG TEXAN STEAK RANCH, *7701 Interstate Highway 40 East. Tel. 806/ 372-6000, Website: www.bigtexan.com. Credit cards accepted.*

This is the place to come for a good old-fashioned meat-and-potatoes meal. The steaks here are big enough to suit the most ravenous appetite you could imagine. The steak that put this restaurant on the map is the famous 72-ouncer. In fact, if you can finish the steak, you don't have to pay for it! There are smaller and tenderer steaks to be had, however, especially the Big Texas Filet. The restaurant occasionally features entertainment.

OHMS, *619 Tyler Street. Tel. 806/373-7476. Credit cards accepted.*

This art gallery and restaurant combination has the best of both. The atmosphere is upbeat and trendy. The recipes take chances, bringing together Asian influences, like pungent ginger, and Tex-Mex selections. The menu covers all the bases including Italian, Cajun and a bit of standard Texas fare. The very casual restaurant does not have a wait staff, but instead you serve your self from the cafeteria-like line. OHMS is a good place to enjoy a cup of coffee and take in the surroundings.

Seeing the Sights

One of the oddest works of monumental art is the **Cadillac Ranch**, a row of ten vintage Cadillacs standing in the ground headlong. The Cadillac Ranch is west of Amarillo on Interstate Highway 40.

Art of a more mainstream nature can be found in the city. The **Amarillo Art Musuem**, *Amarillo College, 2200 Van Buren Street, Tel. 806/371-5050, Tuesday to Friday 10am to 5pm, Saturday and Sunday 1pm to 5pm*, features art by the students and faculty of Amarillo College, and also offers exhibits of interest by national artists.

The **American Quarter Horse Heritage Center and Museum**, *Quarter Horse Drive at Interstate Highway 40, Tel. 806/376-5181*, is devoted entirely to the plucky breed favored by Western riders all over the US. The history of the Quarter Horse is shown through museum exhibits. The facility includes a research library and rotating exhibits.

The **Amarillo Zoo**, *Thompson Park, Highway 287, Tel. 806/381-7911*, is a natural preserve for animals that are native to the state and in need of protection. You can watch a herd of buffalo graze. The petting area is the main attraction at the zoo.

Nightlife & Entertainment

The **Amarillo Symphony**, *1000 Polk Street, Tel. 806/376-8782*, began filling the city with classical music in 1927. The symphony performs in the **Civic Center**, *Tel. 806/359-5941*, located at 3rd Street and Buchanan. Guest musicians and touring concerts are also hosted in this venue.

For a good pint in a fun atmosphere, try **The Brewpub**, *3705 Oleson, Tel. 806/353-2622, credit cards accepted.* This unpretentious bar with a strong showing of regulars serves its own brew on tap. Special beers are regularly featured and pub food is served. The lively atmosphere is often the place to be on weekend nights.

Excursions & Day Trips

Native Americans used distinctively colored flint from this region for thousands of years. The **Alibates Flint Quarries National Monument**, *Highway 136, Fritch, Tel. 806/857-3151*, gives you an up-close look at this mineral, so indispensable to the development of early man. You can take guided tours during the summer at 10 am and 2pm. During other months, tours can be made by reservation. The quarry mounds are located at the end of a one-mile trail that includes a number of stone steps. It takes about two hours to complete the tour. The park is about 40 miles north of Amarillo. Take the Lake Meredith Recreational Area exit then follow the signs to the ranger station. From Amarillo, take Highway 136 north; signs clearly mark the monument.

Lake Meredith, *Highway 136, Fritch, Tel 806/857-3151*, is a popular area for boating enthusiasts. Primitive campsites are free of charge. From Amarillo, take Highway 136 north; the lake is 30 miles north of Amarillo.

Route 66 has been overshadowed by Interstate Highway 40. But the old route, in parts a ghost highway, still covers nearly 180 miles, running straight across the panhandle from east to west. Most diners and businesses long ago moved to more traveled territory. Nevertheless, a trip along Route 66 appeals to the truly nostalgic. The one stronghold for travelers is the **Old Route 66 Musuem**, *Old Route 66, Kingsley, Tel. 806/779-2225*, that features barbed wire as the mainstay of the collection. The museum has on display over 450 types of barbed wire and the machines that made the fencing. Also, artifacts and memorabilia from the glory days of Texas Route 66 are throughout the museum. There is no admission charge.

How Barbed Wire Changed the West

Barbed wire changed the face of Texas, especially in the Panhandle. Before its invention in 1874, cattle and cowboys roamed free. Ranchers ended this by stringing up cheap and effective barbed wire. Millions of acres of land became impenetrable, thanks to the fencing that was invented in Illinois, not Texas. With their land and cattle secure, the ranchers provided fodder for the railroad industry, which soon connected Texas to the larger markets in the east.

By the way, Texans pronounce it "bob wahr."

Practical Information

American Automobile Association (AAA), *2607 North Wolfin Village, Tel. 806/354-8288*, provides maps and traveling tips to its members free of charge.

The **Amarillo Visitor Center**, *7703 East Interstate Highway 40, Tel. 800/894-9103*, offers information about the panhandle region.

Canyon

Canyon originally served as the headquarters for an enormous ranch. Now the home of **West Texas State A&M University**, Canyon also serves as the gateway to the isolated beauty of **Palo Duro Canyon**.

Arrivals & Departures

Canyon is 15 miles south of Amarillo on Interstate Highway 27.

Where to Stay & Eat

HUDSPETH HOUSE BED & BREAKFAST, *1905 Fourth Avenue. Tel. 806/655-9800, Toll free 800/655-9809, Website: www.hudspethinn.com, 7 Rooms. Rates $85-150. Credit cards accepted.*

Right on the downtown square sits the historic Hudspeth House, built in 1909 from a Sears and Roebuck Catalog kit. Although that may sound like the punch line to a joke, it was no laughing matter – kit homes were all the rage back then, and this one cost a princely $2500 and contains 8000 square feet. Today Todd and Andrea Stevens run Hudspeth House as a bed and breakfast, providing charming antique-filled rooms and a gracious atmosphere to travelers hoping to stay somewhere more personal than a motel. They will put together a custom weekend package for you centered upon a picnic trip to

Palo Duro Canyon, for example, or a romantic theme with champagne glasses and bath baskets.

Each room is unique and has a different layout – some with shower only, others with private baths and claw foot tubs. The Empire and Collegiate Rooms are refreshingly unfussy and have handsome color schemes in blue, if you're looking for a more "masculine" room. Smoking is allowed only on the porch. Children over 12 are welcome, and there is no accommodation for pets.

Seeing the Sights

A worthwhile stop is the **Panhandle-Plains Historical Museum**, *West Texas State University, Canyon, Monday to Friday 9am to 5pm, Sunday noon to 6pm*. As you walk in, note the decoration of cattle brands. The museum pays tribute to the cultures of north Texas. Displays show the archaeological findings from Native American sites. A recreation of a chuck wagon gives insight as to how cowboys actually lived. And the petroleum wing shows the beginnings of the technology of the oil industry. The museum building is an unusual mix of art deco design and native limestone. The structure dates from 1933. Mural-sized paintings depict the history of the Panhandle area.

Twenty-five miles from Amarillo and twelve miles east of Canyon stands one of the great natural wonders of the Plains—**Palo Duro Canyon State Park**. Not many people know about this "other" Grand Canyon, the second largest in the US. Eight miles across at its widest, Palo Duro's spectacular spires and pinnacles reward the traveler who strays from the beaten path. The Red River carved this fantasia, and the canyon is now one of the state's largest parks at 15,103 acres. There are 28 miles of hiking, biking, and horse trails. At **Goodnight Riding Stables**, *Tel. 806/488-2231*, at the bottom of the canyon you can rent bicycles or take a guided horseback tour.

Do be sure to bring lots of water, as there are few facilities. If you would like to stay overnight, there are primitive and improved **campsites** available. For a real treat, try to reserve one of the two stone cabins that teeter on the canyon rim. The views, as you might expect, are spectacular. **Cabins** are $65, reservations *Tel. 512/389-8900* (note that this is not a local number).

To get to Palo Duro Canyon State Park from Amarillo, take Interstate Highway 27 south, then Texas Highway 217 8 miles east to the Park Road. Entrance fee $3, children under 12 free.

San Angelo

The name San Angelo conjures up images of dusty cattle drives and burnt orange sunsets. As the cattle industry settled into ranching, San Angelo became a hub of the wool trade. **San Angelo State University** is a major contributor to the cultural life of the city.

The Wild West lives on in San Angelo. You can visit a preserved house of ill repute over a saloon, then venture to the frontier stronghold **Fort Concho**, which provides a lasting reminder of how the west, and San Angelo, was conquered.

Every September 16th, San Angelo hosts a **Fiestas Patrias de Diez y Seis de Septiembre** celebration. This date commemorates the beginning of an uprising in 1810 that eventually resulted in Mexico's independence from Spain. The celebration is held on the grounds of El Paseo de Santa Angela and includes a historical pageant, music, folk dances, and an assortment of delicious food.

Arrivals & Departures

San Angelo is at the crossroads of Highways 67, 87 and 277, which meet in the center of town. To the south stands Twin Buttes Reservoir; the North Concho River flows into the OC Fisher Reservoir to the northwest.

Orientation

Old Ballinger Highway is the business branch of Highway 67 that cuts through town from the northeast to the southwest. Highway 87, which passes over OC Fisher Reservoir in the north, makes a diagonal cross with Highway 67. Highway 87 and Bryant Street are the same road.

Getting Around Town

San Angelo Public Transportation, *Tel. 915/655-9952*, operates bus service in the city.

Where to Stay

HINKLE HOUSE, *19 South Park Street. Tel. 915/653-1931. 3 Rooms. Rates: $75-85. Credit cards accepted.*

The Hinkle house was built in 1921 and retains the charm of the architecture of the Roaring Twenties. Hardwood floors run throughout the house and porches let you enjoy the outdoors. There are only three guest rooms in Hinkle House, so you pretty much have the entire house to yourself. Breakfast is prepared each morning, and guests may choose from menu selections. The Garden Room is decorated with a floral motif. French doors lead to the private patio. The Concho Room is full of antiques. The home is located west of downtown, off Beauregread Street.

INN OF THE CONCHOS, *2021 North Bryant Street. Tel. 915/658-2811, Fax 915/653-7560, Toll free 800/621-6041, Website: www.inn-of-the-conchos.com. 125 Rooms. Rates: $49-59. Credit cards accepted.*

This is an old fashioned motel. A recent renovation has restored some of the shine and added amenities such as cable television. You will have a clean and comfortable room for a very reasonable rate here. The inn has a certain charm to it simply because it is not affiliated with a large chain. Crossroads restaurant provides buffet means and steak dinners, while the Crossroads Club provides a quiet place to have a beer.

HOLIDAY INN CONVENTION CENTER, *441 Rio Concho Drive. Tel. 915/ 658-2828, Toll free 800/465-4329. 148 Rooms. Rates: $79-87. Credit cards accepted.*

The Holiday Inn is the second largest motel in the city (the La Quinta Conference Center is the first) and offers the nicest facilities. The fitness center includes an indoor pool, spa and gym. The hotel is located in the heart of the city and is within walking distance of city sights.

BEST WESTERN INN OF THE WEST, *415 West Beauregard Street. Tel. 915/653-2995, Toll free 800/582-9668. 75 Rooms. Rates: $45-60. Credit cards accepted.*

The Best Western is a good standard motel close to the city center. The fitness facilities include a gym and indoor pool. There are a restaurant and lounge on the premises.

Where to Eat

OLD TIME PIT BAR-B-QUE, *1805 South Bryant Boulevard. Tel. 915/655-2771. Credit cards accepted.*

This simple barbecue house serves the best brisket any cowboy could expect to sink his teeth into. Simply load up your plate at the counter and sit down at one of the picnic tables to enjoy your meal. The potato salad is creamy and slightly sweet.

MEJOR QUE NADA, *1911 South Bryant Boulevard. Tel. 915/655-3553.* Credit cards accepted.

The name translates to "better than nothing," but false modesty aside this is the best place in town to get your Tex-Mex fix. The most popular dish is the fajitas, delivered sizzling to your table with all the necessary condiments. There is also a huge selection of steaks prepared every way imaginable, including Tampico style, Ranchero, and of course, chicken-fried. There are a few selections for the health-conscious – no-guilt fajitas, grilled chicken with steamed vegetables, and comforting caldo soup.

Seeing the Sights

The town of San Angelo grew up around a military base in the late nineteenth century. To understand the hardships and lifestyle of the Texas frontier, visit **Fort Concho**, *213 Avenue D, Tel. 915/657-4441, Tuesday to Saturday 10am to 5pm, Sunday 1pm to 5pm, closed Monday; admission, adult $1.50, student $1.* This is one of the most interesting and extensively preserved sites remaining from the days of the old west. Besides preserved buildings, the fort has two museums. The **Danner Museum of Telephony** has early telephones on display, tracing the development of communication. The **Robert Wood Johnson Museum of Frontier Medicine** shows the cutting edge of frontier medical care. Admission to both museums is included in park admission.

After discovering the hardships faced by the soldiers of Fort Concho, you can see the illicit pleasures they had at their disposal. The saloon and "business" quarters of the ladies of the evening is now **Miss Hattie's Museum**, *18 East Concho, Tel. 915/655-1166, Tuesday to Saturday 9:30am to 4pm, closed Sunday and Monday, admission*. Miss Hattie's operated for nearly a century. The rooms remain with original decoration.

The 7000-acre **San Angelo State Park**, *Farm Road 2288, Tel. 915/949-4757*, brings you closer not only to nature but history also. The park stands on the shore of the OC Fisher Reservoir. The ancient remains of dinosaurs were found here, and this is one of the few areas where you can see Native American petroglyphs. You can reach the park by taking Farm Road 2288 from either Highway 67 or 87; follow the signs to the state park.

Excursions & Day Trips

Fort McKavett, *FM 854, Menard, Tel. 915/396-2358, Wednesday to Sunday 8am to 5pm*, was constructed on the San Saba River in 1852 as a post against the Natives Americans who were hostile to settlers. The fort was under construction for four years, and then abandoned only three years later when troops moved north. In 1869 the fort reopened, and the 24th Infantry of Buffalo Soldiers were stationed there.

Today you can visit the reconstruction of the fort. Replicas of frontier buildings, including military barracks, a post office and school are open to the public. From San Angelo, take Highway 87 east (about 45 miles) to Highway 83. Head south on 83 to Menard. From the town of Menard, take U. S. Highway 190 south to Farm-to-Market Road 854. Signs will show the entrance to Fort McKavett.

Practical Information

The **San Angelo Convention & Visitors Bureau**, *500 Concho Drive, Tel. 915/653-1206 or 800/375-1206*, can provide information about events and destinations in the region.

Abilene

Abilene stands alone on the plains, between the urbanity of Dallas and Fort Worth and the beginnings of the desert in West Texas. Abilene is a center of higher education; Abilene Christian University, Hardin-Simmons University and McMurray University are located in the city. The wide-open plains of this region made Abilene a hub of the cattle trade in the late 1800s. Although oil played a minor role in the shaping of this city, Abilene has always taken its character from the lore of the cowboys.

In September, the glory days of cattle driving come back to life in Abilene. The **Western Heritage Classic**, *held at the Taylor County Expo Center, 1700 Highway 36, Tel. 915/677-4376*, revisits the lifestyle of working the range. Of course a rodeo is held, but the event runs for ten days and is far more than just roping and riding. Vittles are served up at the Championship Chuck Wagon Cook-off. The melodious lyrics of Cowboy Poets are celebrated. And the entire event winds up with the Rhinestone Gala. Arts, crafts, and food are for sale every day.

Aviation buffs will enjoy the **Southwest Regional EAA Fly-In**, *Abilene Regional Airport, Website: www.swrfi.org*, which is held during the fourth weekend of September. Airplanes of all types, from vintage models to experimental craft, can be seen both on the ground and in the air. The Fly-In moved to this location from Kerrville in 1998. There is no admission charge for this event.

Arrivals & Departures

Interstate Highway 20 crosses Abilene from east to west. Highway 87 runs north to south through the city.

Getting Around Town

The **Abilene Transit Authority**, *Tel. 915/676-6403*, which operates the bus service, provides public transportation.

Where to Stay

BJ'S PRAIRIE HOUSE BED & BREAKFAST, *508 Mulberry Street. Tel. 915/675-5855, Toll free 800/673-5855. 4 Rooms. Rates: $75-85. Credit cards accepted.*

BJ's Prairie House bed and breakfast is located close to the center of town. Built in 1902, the quaint two-story home is a pleasure to visit. The house offers four guest rooms with the optimistic names of Love, Joy, Peace, and Patience. Two of the rooms have private baths and all guests have use of the downstairs living area. A country-style breakfast is served.

KIVA INN HOTEL, *5403 South First Street. Tel. 915/695-2150, Fax 915/698-6742, Toll free 800/592-4466. 181 Rooms. Rates: $51-179. Credit cards accepted.*

The Kiva Inn has conference center facilities including meting rooms. Both a lounge and full service restaurant are located on the premises. A pool enclosed in an atrium with a fitness center provides recreational opportunities. The inn has a game room with ping-pong tables and other diversions. The simple rooms are adequately comfortable.

HOLIDAY INN EXPRESS, *1802 East Interstate Highway 20. Tel. 915/ 675-9800, Fax 915/673-8240, Toll free 800/465-4329. 65 Rooms. Rates: $79-94. Credit cards accepted.*

This new hotel has an outdoor pool and is located near attractions and public transportation. Continental breakfast is included with every room. This is a convenient place to stay for those who are taking a highway trip.

Where to Eat

BETTY ROSE'S LITTLE BRISKET, *2402 South 7th Street. Tel. 915/673-5809.*

Years ago, if you filled up at Betty Rose's you would have been putting gas in your car. The restaurant is a former filling station. The retro roadside attraction atmosphere adds to the experience of eating truly good barbecue. The brisket is the specialty of the house. Side dishes include macaroni and potato salad. The beans are good, but the desserts are better. They do not take credit cards, but the meals rarely cost more than $7.

Seeing the Sights

In 1851, a fort was established to protect the town from hostile attacks. Today **Fort Phantom Hill** is a ghost fort, with an eerie, deserted character. Three buildings remain intact and many lie in ruins on the hilltop preserve. The fort was deserted only three years after being built, in part due to the difficult conditions in the deserted, dry area. The fort stands on private property and is open to the public. There are no facilities or museum buildings at the site. From Interstate Highway 20 in Abilene, take Farm Road 600 north and continue for 14 miles. The fort overlooks a lake that shares its name.

Abilene has a respectable arts community housed in the interesting **Grace Museum Center**, *102 Cypress Street, Tel. 915/673-4587*. The historic Grace Hotel, circa 1909, was the premier accommodations establishment in the area when it was built. A section of the hotel has been restored for viewing. The **Abilene Fine Arts Museum**, *Tuesday to Friday 9am to 5pm and Saturday and Sunday 1pm to 5pm, closed Monday*, displays regularly changing exhibits of work by local artists and of interest to the community. Children will get a kick from the whimsical world of discovery at the **Abilene Children's Museum**, also housed in the Grace Museum Complex.

Hardin-Simmons University, which is in central Abilene, has an arts area open to the public. The **Frost Visual Arts Center**, *Hardin-Simmons University, 2200 Hickory Street, Tel. 915/677-7281*, highlights the work of students, faculty and renowned artists.

Air travel has been of primary importance since its beginnings, perhaps because Abilene is far from the nearest city, or maybe because the Texas skies are clear and bright in this region. The **Dyess Air Force Base**, *Tel. 915/696-2863*, has been in operation since just after World War II. The base has a collection of vintage and modern aircraft, which can be viewed by the public through an arranged tour. The tours are free, but you must call in advance. Dyess Air Force Base is located west of the city. From the business loop of Interstate Highway 20 West, take Loop 312 south to the base entrance.

The Abilene Municipal Airport has a collection of World War II fighter planes. **The Phantom Squadron**, *Abilene Municipal Airport, Hanger 2, Saturday and Sunday noon to 5pm*, can be viewed on weekend afternoons only. From Interstate Highway 20, take Highway 322 south to the Abilene Municipal Airport.

Nightlife & Entertainment

The historic **Paramount Theater**, *310 North Willis Street, Tel. 915/676-9602*, presents classic films and theatrical and musical performances. The beautiful theater has been renovated, and the building itself is a piece of art.

Sports & Recreation

The Tonkawa Native Americans once inhabited attractive **Abilene State Park**, *121 Park Road 32, Tuscola, Tel. 915/572-3204*. The park has a long and complex history as a cattle ranch, a stop on the Western Cattle Trail, and finally as a natural preserve. Rolling hills, large pecan trees and streams characterize the landscape. Lake Abilene is only a half-mile away. The park has hiking trails and wildlife observation spots, many picnic sites and a swimming pool. Camping facilities include over 90 campsites, from tent areas to full hook-ups facilities. From Abilene or Interstate Highway 20, take Farm Road 89 south for sixteen miles, and then look for the signs indicating the park road.

Excursions & Day Trips

You can gain insight to the real old west at the **Fort Griffin State Historical Park**, *Route 1, Box 125, Albany, Tel. 915/762-3592, Fax 915/ 762-2492*. Some of the original frontier buildings of Fort Griffin remain standing. Reconstructed buildings and a visitors center provide a complete picture of life in this trading outpost. In some ways this was a rougher settlement than others of the western region of Texas. Gunfights were a leading cause of death here in the late nineteenth century. Members of a history club reenact Civil War battles twice a year. The park arranges trail rides throughout the year. Fort Griffin is north of Abilene on Highway 283. Take highway 351 north from Abilene. At Albany go north on Highway 283 and continue for 15 miles.

A mix of authentic frontier building and new tourist attractions is found at **Buffalo Gap**, *Tel. 915/572-3365*. An old courthouse and jail and log cabins are among the nearly 20 old buildings. A doctor's office, barbershop and print shop, are modern reconstructions. The plain white chapel is one of the oldest houses of worship in the region. To get to Buffalo Gap from Abilene or Interstate Highway 20, take Farm Road 89 south. It is about 15 miles south of Abilene.

Practical Information

The Abilene Convention & Visitors Bureau, *1101 North First Street, Tel. 915/675-2556, Toll free 800/727-7704, Website: www.abilene.com*, provides information about area attractions, dining, and entertainment.

north texas

Chapter 16

Geologically speaking, much of North Texas is part of the Blackland Prairie. Rich soil made cotton farming in this area lucrative. These days, the vast and glittering urban centers of **Dallas** and **Fort Worth**, collectively known as the **Metroplex**, dominate the physical and cultural landscape. There's more to the area, though, than skyscrapers and museums. Man-made lakes surround the Metroplex, and small towns provide world-class antiquing.

Dallas

The first Anglo-American settler built a single log cabin here in 1841. Two years later, the town consisted of *two* log cabins. Growth has picked up considerably in **Dallas** since. Today, the Big D is the face of big business in Texas. It is the nation's leading banking center, third in terms of million dollar companies—a city of corporate headquarters and the largest wholesale trade market complex in the world. Lest you think Dallas is all about money, the urban arts district is one of the largest in the U.S.

A conglomerate of smaller cities surrounds urban Dallas, each city with a distinct personality. **Plano**, directly north of Dallas, is known as an affluent suburban area. **Mesquite**, to the east of Dallas, has a western appeal and holds a rodeo year-round. **Irving**, on the west side, is the home of the Las Colinas development, an upscale planned business area. These are only a few of the over twenty "cities" that comprise the Dallas area. Still, Dallas has a definite heart, a nerve center with some of the best food, entertainment, shopping, and culture in the nation.

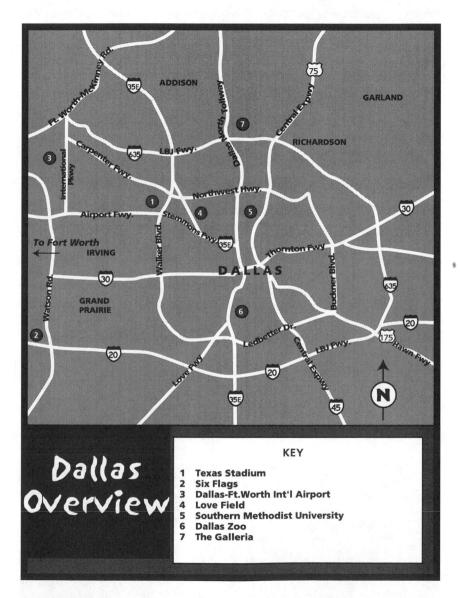

KEY

1 Texas Stadium
2 Six Flags
3 Dallas-Ft.Worth Int'l Airport
4 Love Field
5 Southern Methodist University
6 Dallas Zoo
7 The Galleria

Dallas Overview

The biggest party in town takes place each fall, and the whole world is invited. For 24 days in late September and early October, the **State Fair of Texas** attracts over three million visitors to Fair Park. There are the traditional fair exhibits, Broadway musicals, and a huge midway featuring the Texas Star — the largest Ferris wheel in the Western Hemisphere. Presiding over the festivities is oft-photographed Big Tex, the famous 50-foot cowboy with a goofy grin on his face.

The **West End Taste of Dallas**, *Tel. 214/665-9533, Website: www.tasteofdallas.org*, is a giant outdoor culinary extravaganza held in the West End Historic District in the middle of July. You can sample the many flavors of Texan cooking as well as international dishes. Admission is free.

Arrivals & Departures
DFW

The **Dallas-Fort Worth International Airport** (Airport Code **DFW**), *Tel. 972/574-6000, Website: www.dfwairport.com*, is located between the two cites and is practically a city in itself. In 2000, DFW ranked third among the world's airports in daily arrivals and departures. Each day roughly 2500 flights connect DFW to the rest of the world. The airport covers some 29.8 square miles in area, has seven runways and three control towers.

The airport has four passenger terminals (A, B, C, and E). As you drive up the main entrance on International Parkway, large signs post the current gate information for departing flights. The upper-level roadway allows arriving passenger pick-up. Passenger drop-off and ticket counters and baggage checking for departing passengers are located near the upper-level terminal entrance. Taxicab service is available at designated upper-level curbside exits; other ground transportation such as buses and shuttles is on the lower level. Baggage carousels in each terminal are just outside the secured areas.

Taxicab fares from DFW to downtown Dallas average about $38. Fares to downtown Fort Worth run approximately $43.

Helpful Numbers for DFW

The **DFW Main Number**, *Tel. 972/574-8888*, offers a menu covering airport information, customs, and ground transportation.

Lost and Found can be reached at *Tel. 972/574-0172* or *toll free 866/DIAL DFW*.

The **DFW Airport Assistance Center**, *Tel. 972/574-4420*, can help passengers needing special attention. Foreign language information and assistance in arrangements for the handicapped are handled through this office.

A number of shuttle services serve the Dallas area. Two of these are **Super Shuttle**, *729 East Dallas Road, Grapevine, Tel. 817/329-2001, Website: www.supershuttle.com/htm/cities/dfw.htm*, which offers door to airport service at any time; and **Classic Shuttle**, *3615 Ross Avenue, Dallas, Tel. 214/ 841-1900*. For limousine service, try **American Limos and Transportation**, *Tel. 972/256-0546, Fax 972/255-3818, Toll free 877/604-5466, Website: www.americanlimos.net*. If you don't want all the bells and whistles of a limousine but you'd like something more than a rental car, call **ExecuCar**, *Tel. 888/473-9227*. This subsidiary of Super Shuttle offers late model luxury sedans with business-clad drivers.

All of the rental car facilities at DFW are housed in the **Rental Car Center**, which is located near the south entrance of the airport. To get to the Car Rental Center from the passenger terminals, follow the rental car signs through the terminal to the designated pick-up spot. The provided shuttle is free and departs every five minutes during peak travel hours from the lower level of each terminal. At the 200-acre Rental Car Center you can choose from ten national companies (see Chapter 6, *Getting Around*, for contact details).

Other Airports

The smaller **Love Field**, *8008 Cedar Springs Street, Tel. 214/670-6080*, is only seven miles from downtown Dallas. **Southwest Airlines**, *Tel. 214/263-1717*, is based at Love Field. American Airlines, Continental Express, and Delta also schedule flights to and from Love Field.

Helicopter traffic is handled at the **Dallas Heliport**, *801 South Lamar Street, Tel. 214/670-4338*. The heliport has a waiting area and parking lot.

Train & Bus Stations

The **Amtrak Station**, *400 South Houston Street, Tel. 214/653-1101 or 800/872-7245*, is located in the southern part of downtown. Amtrak operates one route through Dallas that connects San Antonio to Chicago three times per week.

The **Greyhound Bus Station**, *205 South Lamar Street, Tel. 214/655-7082 or 800/231-2222*, is located downtown at the intersection of Lamar and Commerce Streets. The **Kerrville Bus Company**, *701 East Davis Street, Grand Prairie, Tel. 214/263-0294*, operates regular routes as well as tours throughout the state.

Orientation

Dallas is a merging point for many major roads. The highway system in Dallas can be confusing, even to those who have lived in the area for a while. Interstate Highway 35 runs through Dallas from north to south. This is the east branch of the interstate, which splits south of the city; the western branch runs through Fort Worth.

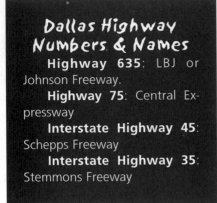

Dallas Highway Numbers & Names

Highway 635: LBJ or Johnson Freeway.

Highway 75: Central Expressway

Interstate Highway 45: Schepps Freeway

Interstate Highway 35: Stemmons Freeway

Interstate Highway 20 approaches Dallas from the east and skirts the city to the south; it continues west to Fort Worth. Interstate Highway 30 cuts east-west through central Dallas and also through Fort Worth. Highway 635 loops around the northern and eastern sections of the city. In the south, Highway 635 merges into Interstate Highway 20. Highway 75 runs north-south through the city center. Loop 12 makes a circle of the central area. The Dallas North Tollway runs from Interstate Highway 35, just west of downtown, to North Dallas.

Getting Around Town

The **Dallas Area Rapid Transit (DART)**, *Tel. 214/979-1111, Website: www.dart.org*, serves the Dallas area with bus, trolley and rail service. The light rail system operates daily from 5:00am to roughly midnight. One-way adult fare for bus and rail service is $1, and a day pass is available for $2. Fares increase by a dollar if you travel between more than one zone. This really is the best way to travel around central Dallas. The light rail system is new, clean, and easy to use, with stops close to all the major downtown attractions.

The **McKinney Avenue Trolley**, *Tel. 214/855-0006, Website: www.mata.org*, is a restored antique transportation trolley that connects the Dallas Museum of Art with the restaurant area of McKinney Street. The cars date from the early 1900's and were used until the 1950's. Today the line is a reminder of yesteryear and an enjoyable way to get around congested downtown streets. The trolleys run seven days a week from 10am to 10pm. One way adult fare is $1.50, and a day pass is $3. McKinney Avenue is located just west of Interstate Highway 35 in the downtown area. You can begin your trolley trip at the Dallas Museum of Art (the St. Paul Terminal), where there is ample parking.

The standard fare for taxi rides in Dallas is $1.50 for the first quarter mile and 30¢ for each following quarter mile. A charge of $1 is assessed for each additional person, with a maximum charge of $3. You might want to call one of the following companies if you need a taxi:
• **Allied Taxi**, *Tel. 214/654-4444*
• **Terminal Taxi**, *Tel. 214/350-4555*
• **West End Cab**, *Tel. 214/902-7000*
• **Yellow Cab**, *214/426-6262 or 800/749-9422*

Where to Stay
DOWNTOWN

Dallas is made up of dozens of smaller neighborhoods, communities, and incorporated towns. For purposes of this section, Downtown means the business and arts districts, including Deep Ellum, Market Center, and the West End.

Expensive

ADAM'S MARK DALLAS, *400 North Olive Street. Tel. 214/922-8000, Fax 214/922-0308, Toll free reservations 800/444-2326, Website: www.adamsmark.com/dallas. 1,842 Rooms. Rates $145-225. Credit cards accepted.*

Located in the downtown Arts and Financial District, this absolutely huge hotel (38 floors) has so many amenities and facilities you might never leave the building. Game room, health club, flower shop, two cafes, an elegant restaurant on the top floor, a sports bar, a nightclub, and of course the obligatory indoor and outdoor pools. Have they left anything out? Oh, and the hotel sits right on the DART Light Rail at the Pearl Street stop, so you won't even need your car.

Unless you can spring for the Presidential Suite, the rooms are rather ordinary. The bedspreads are somewhat institutional, the furnishings are uninspired, and the artwork is far from original. People don't stay at the Adam's Mark if they want an intimate luxury experience, however. They stay here if they need a lot of meeting room, convenience, business amenities, and comfort. Where the Adam's Mark shines is in its public spaces. The lobby delights visitors with its Texas-sized bronze statue of a bucking bronco shedding a cowboy from its back.

This hotel is kid-friendly, and is a good choice if you're traveling with your children and looking for accommodations downtown. The Chaparral Club, high atop the city on the 38th floor, was recently named one of "The Best New Restaurants of 1999" by *D Magazine*. Once a private club, it is now open for all to enjoy. The city views are marvelous. For more on the Chaparral Club, see *Where to Eat*.

THE ADOLPHUS, *1321 Commerce Street (between Field and Akard Streets, Akard Station on DART Light Rail). Tel. 214/742-8200, Fax 214/651-3561, Toll free reservations 800/221-9083, Website: www.hoteladolphus.com. 432 Rooms, 20 Suites. Rates: $230-2000. Credit cards accepted.*

The Adolphus is the Grande Dame among Dallas hotels. Its founder, beer baron Adolphus Busch, made Dallas a second home, and decided in 1912 to build the most splendid hotel money could buy. The lobby living room resembles the reception room of a fine English castle, with its lavish art collection and 17th century Flemish tapestry. Even the façade of the building is beautiful.

The rooms are elegantly furnished in the English Country style so favored by the doyennes of fashion in the late fifties. Fittingly enough, Queen Elizabeth II stayed here on her official state visit in 1991. Suites offer such luxuries as floor-to-ceiling windows or grand terraces overlooking the city. The hotel is a short walk from the downtown Neiman Marcus department store and the West End entertainment district. There is a fitness room on the 15th floor, but no pool.

A three-course English Tea is served each day in the lobby living room from 3pm-5pm. Dinner at the French Room is an absolute must, whether you're staying here or not. It is one of the most romantic places in the state, let alone the city. For more, see *Where to Eat*.

FAIRMONT HOTEL, *1717 North Akard Street. Tel. 214/720-2020, Fax 214/720-5269, Toll free reservations 800/527-4727, Website: www.fairmont.com. 550 Rooms, 51 Suites. Rates: $150-350. Credit cards accepted.*

Attention to detail has placed the Fairmont among the finer hotels in the city since it opened over thirty years ago. The hotel is located in the heart of downtown Dallas, within walking distance of many of the city's best attractions. The luxury suites in the north and south tower have fantastic views.

A renovation completed in 1998 has brought the Fairmont up to par with any other luxury hotel in the city. The décor is described as classic Italian style, but the feel of the rooms is decidedly modern. Marble bathrooms, down pillows and comforters, and plush towels and robes are standard amenities for every room. If you can stand to leave your delightful bed, there is an Olympic-size swimming pool outside on the terrace.

The Pyramid is recognized as one of Dallas' best restaurants. Elegant decor combines smartly with the equally elegant menu choices. Romantic setting, courteous service and live music make this an excellent choice for honeymoon or anniversary dinners.

MAGNOLIA HOTEL, *1401 Commerce Street. Tel. 214/915-6500, Fax 214/253-0053, Toll free 888/915-1110. 200 Rooms, 130 Suites. Rates: $120-599. Credit cards accepted.*

Back in 1922, the Magnolia Petroleum Company built itself a beautiful 29-story building designed by eccentric British architect Sir Alfred Blossom. Dallas' first true skyscraper, the Magnolia Building was also the tallest building south of Washington D.C. Eventually Magnolia Petroleum became Mobil Oil, and the famous insignia of Pegasus was mounted atop the building to become the most recognizable landmark on the skyline. Generations of children would scan the horizon eagerly for the "flying red horse."

The building was almost lost, but has been rescued and turned into a lovely and urbane downtown hotel of character. Pegasus glows again, and what's more, the hotel underneath him earns its own wings. The Magnolia Hotel is geared for the business traveler, but anyone who enjoys a tailored retro-modern atmosphere will appreciate it as well. The $42 million restoration was conducted with integrity and provides every modern convenience without sacrificing the flavor of history.

Amenities in each room include a refrigerator, coffee maker, hairdryer, cable television and Nintendo, an iron and ironing board, two phones, and a business desk. Rates include a breakfast buffet and a nightly cocktail reception. Weekend rates and discounts for extended stays are available.

HOTEL ST. GERMAIN, *2516 Maple Avenue. Tel. 214/871-2516, Fax 214/871-0740, Website: www.hotelstgermain.com. 7 Suites. Rates: $290-650. Credit cards accepted.*

Publication after publication has awarded top honors to this jewel nestled close to the McKinney Avenue area. Proprietor Claire Heymann remodeled this historic 1909 house into an exclusive intimate inn with such elegance and attention to detail you will wonder if you haven't been transported somehow to 19th century France. Each suite contains a canopied feather bed, wood-burning fireplace, Jacuzzi or soaking tub, and sumptuous furnishings.

Naturally, a Continental breakfast is included in the price, and the butler will be happy to serve you wherever you'd like — in your suite, in the courtyard, or even in the dining room. The hotel chef prepares a five-course dinner on Tuesday through Saturday nights, served by candlelight on fine Limoges antique china. Dinner reservations are necessary, and the price is fixed.

LE MERIDIEN DALLAS, *650 North Pearl Street. Tel. 214/855-1703, Fax 214/953-1931, Toll free 800/543-4300, Website: www.lemeridien-dallas.com. 407 Rooms, 19 Suites. Rates: $279-650. Credit cards accepted.*

There is a definite Gallic aura about this hotel, even though it looks like any other large urban American hotel from the outside. Air France started this chain of hotels to give their pilots the sort of accommodation they were accustomed to. Either the Le Meridien scope has expanded, or legions of Air France pilots lead pampered lives.

Le Meridien is convenient to the Arts District and DART, but my fondness for this hotel springs from what it's like on the inside. The 15-story atrium lifts the whole atmosphere into something light and sparkling. The rooms envelop you in privacy and soundproofed comfort. The color scheme is cream-based with burgundy or jade accents, and the view – either of the atrium and its skating rink or the Dallas skyline – is guaranteed to be excellent.

The hotel restaurant is called 650 North, and it is excellent. Located at the lobby level, it serves breakfast, lunch, and dinner with an emphasis on New American cuisine. A semi-private dining room lined with wine bottles in mahogany racks would make a warm setting for a group meal.

Moderate

AMELIA'S PLACE BED & BREAKFAST, *1775 Young Street. Tel. 214/ 651-1775, Fax 214/761-9475, Toll free 888/651-1775, Website: home.flash.net/~ameliaj. 6 Rooms, 1 Suite. Rates: $95-115. Credit cards accepted.*

It's unusual to find a bed and breakfast in downtown Dallas, but Amelia's would have an atmosphere all its own no matter where it was. Amelia describes herself as a feminist from Louisiana and the best cook in three parishes. This inn is housed in one of the only remaining apartment buildings from the 1920s. The warehouse-style loft is spacious and airy. Each room is

---

Dallas's Intimate, Historic Hotels

THE MELROSE, *3015 Oak Lawn Avenue. Tel. 214/521-5151, Fax 521-9306, Toll free reservations 800/635-7673, Website: www.melrosehotel.com/dallas/home.html. 184 Rooms, 21 Suites. Rates: $138-300. Credit cards accepted.*

The historic Melrose dates from the roaring 'twenties. The flagship hotel of the Melrose Group, this uptown inn is an intimate size by Dallas standards and has undergone a recent renovation that thoroughly updated the amenities while retaining that elegant old house feeling. The rooms are sleek in mahogany and jewel tones, the baths are marble, and the robes are long and soft. The Library is a sophisticated piano bar that attracts the Bright Young Things of Dallas, who chatter over ice-cold classic martinis. The Landmark Restaurant serves excellent and innovative cuisine with French and Asian touches.

THE STONELEIGH, *2927 Maple Street. Tel. 214/871-7111, Fax 214/871-9397, Toll free reservations 800/255-9299, Website: www.stoneleighhotel.com. 153 Rooms, 9 Suites. Rates: $148-250, Suites $250-375. Credit cards accepted.*

There is something ineffably sweet about the old brick Stoneleigh and its cheerful sign that belies the luxury within. The historic building was constructed in 1923 and the decor lovingly recreates the era. The rooms reflect the character of a time past, when one settled into a place, not merely passed through. The atmosphere of the hotel is gracious rather than grand. The National Trust has named the Stoneleigh one of the Historic Hotels of America for Historic Preservation. A recent $1.6 million renovation created the Celebrity Level rooms with 18th century English mahogany furnishings and granite bathroom counters. Many of the suites have parlor areas. The hotel offers an outdoor pool and an excellent restaurant, Seville. The Lion's Den Lounge recreates the intimacy of an English pub, and serves lunch as well as libations.

named and decorated after Dallas women of color who have made outstanding contributions to the city. Rates include a large home-cooked breakfast. No children or pets, but anything else goes. As Amelia herself says: "Welcome: People of Any Color, Unmarried Couples, Same-sex Couples, Smokers. Amelia's Place is inappropriate for pets, children, snobs, bigots, and fanatics."

AMERISUITES DALLAS WEST END, *1907 North Lamar Street. Tel. 214/ 999-0500, Fax 214/999-0501, Toll free reservations 800/833-1516, Website: www.amerisuites.com. 149 Suites. Rates: $80-200. Credit cards accepted.*

If you are looking for affordable comfort in the downtown area and some room to sprawl out, this is your spot. Every room in this hotel is a suite, with a microwave, refrigerator, and wet bar in addition to the usual amenities. The Amerisuites West End sits less than a block away from the West End Entertainment Area, one block from the Arts District, and three blocks from the J.F.K. exhibit. Guests are given a free breakfast buffet, and there is a pool and fitness center available as well.

COURTYARD BY MARRIOTT MARKET CENTER, *2150 Market Center Boulevard at Stemmons Freeway. Tel. 214/653-1166, Fax 214/693-1892, Toll free reservations 800/321-2211. 184 Rooms. Rates: $95-179. Credit cards accepted.*

This chain hotel next to Market Center caters to the business traveler, and that means lower weekend rates. Be sure to check for them (a good rule of thumb for any hotel in Dallas). Amenities include indoor and outdoor swimming pools, a hotel restaurant, high speed internet access. Marriott operates another Courtyard at 2823 Stemmons Trail, off of the North Stemmons Freeway

HYATT REGENCY DALLAS, *300 Reunion Boulevard. Tel. 214/651-1234, Fax 214/651-0018, Toll free reservations 800/233-1234, Website: www.dallas.hyatt.com. 940 Rooms. Rates: $175-750.*

The bright glass Hyatt has been a part of the Dallas skyline since 1978. Located downtown right next to the giant bauble of Reunion Tower, the hotel is most notable for its size, thirty stories with a 65 million dollar expansion to the hotel that opened in 2000. The feeling of this hotel is somewhat impersonal, possibly due to the modern decor or the fact that many large groups choose this location. Reunion Tower is part of the hotel complex; the tower restaurant overlooks the entire city. The hotel has extensive fitness facilities, including a large pool, track and gym. An underground tunnel connects the hotel to historic Union Station.

RAMADA PLAZA, *1101 South Akard Street. Tel. 214/421-1083, Fax 214/428-6827, Toll free reservations 800/527-7606. 238 Rooms. Rates: $80-99. Credit cards accepted.*

This hotel underwent a complete renovation about four years ago. Many small comforts were added, such as hair dryers and coffee makers in each room. Each of the spacious rooms has a balcony that overlooks Dallas. A modern gym and indoor pool are available. When you stay at the Ramada, you receive complimentary parking and shuttle service to the airport or anywhere within a five-mile radius of the hotel. The Ramada is located close to the convention center and the West End entertainment district.

Inexpensive

BEST WESTERN MARKET CENTER, *2023 North Market Center Boulevard at Stemmons Freeway. Tel. 214/741-9000, Toll free reservations 800/ 275-7419. 98 Rooms. Rates: $65-150. Credit cards accepted.*

This motel has a lot of amenities for the budget-conscious traveler, including in-room hair dryers and an outdoor pool with hot tub. A complimentary continental breakfast is included for the price of the room. Children under 16 stay free in the same room.

UPTOWN

Uptown covers areas immediately north of downtown, including Crescent Court, the Oak Lawn neighborhood, and the towns of University Park and Highland Park.

Expensive

HOTEL CRESCENT COURT, *400 Crescent Court. Tel. 214/871-3200, Fax 214/871-3272, Toll free 800/654-6541, Website: www.crescentcourt.com. 178 Rooms, 40 Suites. Rates: $230-1800. Credit cards accepted.*

Like its famous sister the Mansion on Turtle Creek, Hotel Crescent Court places a premium on service and elegance. The hotel is part of the Crescent Complex, a ten-acre limestone development of shops and offices. Philip Johnson and John Burgee designed the palatial French-style building modeled on the Royal Crescent in Bath, England. The Great Hall lobby continues the French theme in lavish style with Louis XV furnishings, Louis XIV tapestries, and numerous works of art and statuary.

This is rock-star lodging — when you stay here, you're a celebrity. The Rosewood Group owns this European-style luxury hotel. The spacious rooms reflect the emphasis on comfort and the decor exudes distinction. The suites offer the plushest accommodations in Dallas, with features such as hardwood floors, spiral staircases, sound systems and, of course, exquisite furnishings. There is a spa and fitness center and an outdoor heated pool at the hotel.

The Beau Nash, the hotel's restaurant, offers excellent dining in a comfortable setting, and is a popular spot for drinks and live jazz. A more casual café, the Crescent Gourmet, provides light breakfast and lunch selections. Some of the finer shops in Dallas are located in the shopping center surrounding the courtyard of the hotel. The Crescent is located close to the excellent restaurants on Routh Street and the McKinney Avenue Trolley.

THE MANSION ON TURTLE CREEK, *2821 Turtle Creek Boulevard. Tel. 214/ 559-2100, Fax 214/528-4187, Toll free reservations 800/442-3408 (in Texas), 800/527-5432 (outside Texas), Website: www.mansiononturtlecreek.com. 126 Rooms, 15 Suites. Rates: $325-2400. Credit cards accepted.*

This is simply a stunning hotel. Texas cotton baron Sheppard W. King built the Italian-Renaissance style mansion in 1925. Since opening as a luxury hotel in 1981, the Mansion on Turtle Creek has hosted every living president as well as Queen Elizabeth II of England. The hotel has been ranked one of the worlds best by numerous publications, and receives five stars, five diamonds, and five-dollar signs by any rating system you'll find.

Turtle Creek runs through one of the most exclusive neighborhoods in Dallas, and the Mansion enjoys a residential aura. Don't be too intimidated by the prices—you'll occasionally find seasonal special rates as low as $200.

Service is impeccable, with more than two staff members per guest. You will be greeted with fresh flowers in your room, and crystal decanters will hold your bath amenities. The rooms are elegantly decorated with antiques and original art. The outdoor swimming pool is heated for year-round swimming. Complimentary limousine service is available within a five-mile radius. The hotel's restaurant is justly celebrated as the home of innovative Southwestern cuisine (see *Where to Eat* for more information).

WYNDHAM ANATOLE HOTEL, *2201 Stemmons Freeway. Tel. 214/ 748-1200, Fax 214/761-7242, Toll free reservations 800/WYNDHAM, Website: www.wyndham.com. 1,749 Rooms. Rates: $149-235. Credit cards accepted.*

The mammoth glass and steel Anatole Hotel is an entire complex unto itself. The grandiose scale seems appropriate for the bigger-than-life character of metropolitan Dallas. More than seventeen hundred rooms sprawl over 27 floors. The indoor atriums are so large and manicured that you feel as though you are actually outdoors. The hotel has all the recreational facilities you could need—an indoor pool, tennis courts and a complete fitness center—and each is of the finest quality.

The hotel could almost double as a museum – the in-house collection includes 10 Picassos, precious urns, and a Louis XIV bronze sculpture. Two pieces of the Berlin Wall adorn the enclosed park and jogging trail. By contrast, the rooms are standard and almost pedestrian, although the views are wonderful. The hotel's formal restaurant, the Nana, has recently undergone a renovation, and offers topnotch dining with panoramic views. The more casual Terrace Café is open 24 hours.

Moderate

CROWNE PLAZA, *7050 Stemmons Freeway. Tel. 214/630-5800, Fax 214/ 630-9486, Toll free 800/227-6963, Website: www.sixcontinentshotels.com. 352 Rooms, 2 Suites. Rates: $89-169. Credit cards accepted.*

This hotel looks and feels like it should be more expensive than it is, making it an excellent value for this part of town. Each room features a full-sized work desk, cable television, a Nintendo center, hair dryer, coffee maker, iron, and ironing boards. There is an indoor pool and spa, a well as a fitness center with satellite TV and fresh fruit to reward the healthy. The Bristol Bar & Grill serves full breakfast, lunch buffet, and traditional dinner fare.

WILSON WORLD, *2325 North Stemmons Freeway. Tel. 214/630-3330, Fax 214/689-0420, Toll free 800/WILSONS, Website: www.wilsonhotels.com. 200 Rooms, 40 Suites. Rates: $89-119. Credit cards accepted.*

Another good value in the Market Center area, Wilson World is a well-equipped homey sort of hotel, with a Southwestern theme. Every room has a microwave, refrigerator, and sitting area with a leather armchair and love seat, in addition to all the standard amenities such as hair dryers and cable television. To reach the hotel from Interstate 35 East, take the Wycliff Avenue exit.

Inexpensive

CLASSIC MOTOR INN, *9229 Carpenter Freeway. Tel. 214/631-6633 or 800/662-7437, Fax 214/631-6616. 134 Rooms. Rates: $50-65. Credit cards accepted.*

This motel recently underwent a complete renovation. The simple rooms have brass beds and sparse furnishings. A complimentary continental breakfast is served every morning in the dining room. The hotel has a small fitness room and a pool. The Classic Motor Inn is ideal for those on a budget who do not want to stay at a large chain hotel.

DAYS INN CENTRAL, *4150 North Central Expressway. Tel. 214/827-6080 or 800/325-2525, Fax 214/827-0208. Rates: $47-70. Credit cards accepted.*

This location is just a few miles up Central Expressway from downtown Dallas. The hotel is convenient for those who want a location near the cultural sights and have a car to get around town. Children under the age of 12 stay free with parents. The hotel offers an outdoor pool and free continental breakfast.

NORTH

North Dallas encompasses Inwood, the Galleria area, and Addison.

Expensive

THE GUEST LODGE AT COOPER AEROBICS CENTER, *12230 Preston Road. Tel. 972/386-0306, Fax 972/386-2942, Toll free 800/444-5187, Website: www.cooperaerobics.com. 62 Rooms, 12 Suites. Rates: $155-280. Credit cards accepted.*

Ever since Dr. Kenneth Cooper published his famous book *Aerobics* in 1968, the name "Cooper" has been associated with health and fitness. But luxury? Absolutely. On the grounds of the Cooper Aerobics Center lies a handsome Southern colonial estate, where guests receive world-class service and accommodation while simultaneously enjoying access to perhaps the most famous fitness center in the world.

The Center and Guest Lodge occupy 30 acres of lushly landscaped park like grounds. The Guest Lodge is a full service hotel with conference and meeting facilities, complimentary continental breakfast, and spacious guest rooms. The atmosphere is serene and somewhat staid, but not stuffy. Most rooms have French doors that open onto private balconies. There are two restaurants, Tyler's for casual dining and The Colonnade for elegant healthy meals.

The Cooper Fitness Center consists of a one-mile outdoor jogging trail that winds through the country club setting, a heated outdoor lap pool, and state-of-the-art exercise facilities, including classes in everything from Tai Chi to Pilates. The Spa offers skin care, massage therapy, marine and mud body wraps, and salon treatments. The Guest Lodge offers several Getaway packages in which spa, fitness center, lodging, and fitness clinics can be combined.

WESTIN GALLERIA, *13340 Dallas Parkway. Tel. 972/934-9494, Fax 972/851-2869 Toll free reservations 800/228-3000. 431 Rooms, 9 Suites. Rates: $209-300. Credit cards accepted.*

The Westin is part of the large Galleria complex that includes a shopping mall and office tower. The hotel soars 21 stories above the "city of glass" it serves to survey the surrounding north Dallas neighborhoods. You are located in the middle of all that epitomizes Dallas – money, glamour, and excess.

All rooms have Internet access, hair dryers, irons and ironing boards, coffee makers, and mini-bars. Some of the rooms have that most rare of big-city amenities, a balcony. Two restaurants cater to your dining needs, the upscale Huntington and the more casual Options Lounge. Recreational facilities include a heated outdoor pool and rooftop jogging track. Even if overpowering consumerism is not your bag, the best of Dallas refinement is reflected in the sleek decor and attentive staff of the Westin.

WESTIN-SHERATON PARK CENTRAL HOTEL, *12720 Merit Drive at Coit Road. Tel. 972/385-3000, Fax 972/991-4557, Toll free reservations 800/228-3000. 545 Rooms, 22 Suites. Rates: $160-300. Credit cards accepted.*

Just minutes from the shopping centers of NorthPark and the Galleria, a stay here will leave impulse buyers in heaven. Complimentary Westin vans operate within a five-mile radius. Fitness room and outdoor pool.

Laurels, the hotel restaurant, has one of the best wine lists in town. Wines are classified by body and flavor rather than region, which makes it easy to pick out the perfect complement to your meal.

Until recently, this hotel was known as the Sheraton Park Central. When Westin and Sheraton consolidated, this hotel took the Westin name, and another smaller hotel close by became (confusingly enough) the Sheraton Park Central.

Moderate

COURTYARD ON THE TRAIL BED & BREAKFAST, *8045 Forest Trail. Tel. 214/553-9700, Fax 214/553-9700, Toll free reservations 800/484-6260 PIN# 0465, Website www.bbonline.com/tx/courtyard. 3 Rooms, 1 Suite. Rates: $125-170. Credit cards accepted.*

This two-story stucco home overlooks White Rock Lake, Dallas' only urban park with a lake. A stay here allows you to remove yourself from the rest of the world. The spacious accommodations have luxurious marble baths. The ceilings are painted blue with happy white clouds for you to gaze at as you lay back in your extra large bathtub. A pool in a garden setting is yours to enjoy. Both bedrooms have French doors that open to the courtyard. The décor is fresh and elegant, not at all stuffy. This is a place you can sprawl out in. Rates include a full breakfast and cable television. From Loop 635 north, take the Skillman Exit. Head south on Skillman to Kingsley, then turn left on to Kingsley. Follow this to White Rock Trail, turn right and proceed to Forest Trail.

DOUBLETREE HOTEL AT CAMPBELL CENTER, *8250 North Central Expressway. Tel. 214/691-8700, Fax 214/706-0186, Toll free 800/222-TREE, Website: www.doubletree.com. 300 Rooms, 21 Suites. Rates: $80-270. Credit cards accepted.*

This 21-story hotel tower provides upscale urban ambience and excellent service to its guests, as well as the two chocolate chip cookies Doubletree visitors have grown to love. The rooms have floor to ceiling windows – ask for a room with a view of downtown Dallas for the best nighttime scenery. Every room is packed with amenities such as coffeemakers, hair dryers, Sony Playstations, two telephones with voice mail and data ports, and more. There is currently no pool, but there is a fitness center, and the Princeton Grill restaurant earns high marks for its above average food. Parking is free.

HILTON DALLAS PARKWAY, *4801 LBJ Freeway. Tel. 972/661-3600, Fax 972/385-3156, Toll free 800/774-1500, Website: www.hilton.com. 266 Rooms, 34 Suites. Rates: $83-130. Credit cards accepted.*

From the outside it looks rather plain, but the Hilton Parkway was completely renovated in September 2001 and the rooms are now fresh and modern. Amenities such as a large armoire, work desk with ergonomic chair, lamps equipped with data ports, three phones per room, and premium television complement each room.

The lobby area sports a two-story atrium, and recreational features include an indoor/outdoor heated pool, sauna, Jacuzzi, and fitness center. Cottonwood's, the hotel restaurant, provides breakfast, lunch, and dinner, with a buffet from 11am-2pm Monday through Friday. Cottonwood's Bar is open for lunch and dinner and serves an appetizer menu. You'll be just minutes away from the Galleria.

HOTEL INTER-CONTINENTAL DALLAS, *15201 Dallas Parkway, Addison. Tel. 972/386-6000 or 800/426-3135, Fax 972/404-1848, Website www.interconti.com/usa/dallas/hotel_dalic.html. 498 Rooms, 31 Suites. Rates: $100-205. Credit cards accepted.*

The elegant Inter-Continental rivals other Dallas luxury hotels by maintaining the standard of service of grand European hotels. The Galleria-area hotel has a nightclub, complete gym, indoor pool and tennis courts. Until recently, this hotel was named the Grand Kempinski, called affectionately by the locals "the Kempi." Kempi's Nightclub, on the premises, pays homage to the hotel's lineage with a popular bar scene and contemporary music. Sunday brunch is quite popular here.

Inexpensive

TERRA COTTA INN, *6101 LBJ Freeway. Tel. 927/387-2525, Fax 927/387-3784, Toll free 800/533-3591, Website: www.terracottainn.com. 98 Rooms. Rates $63-129. Credit cards accepted.*

This Spanish-style hotel is a real find. It has character and charm, good location, and you can't beat the price. The wrought iron front doors hint at the eclectic charm inside. There are fountains from San Miguel de Allende splashing softly amidst the tropical foliage, an outdoor swimming pool, free newspapers, a complimentary continental breakfast including kolaches, burritos, fresh fruit, and all sorts of touches you wouldn't expect from a budget hotel. The rooms feature Mexican antiques and oriental rugs.

SOUTH & WEST DALLAS

South and West Dallas include the neighborhood of Oak Cliff and the town of Irving.

Expensive

THE FOUR SEASONS RESORT & CLUB, *4150 North McArthur Boulevard, Irving. Tel. 972/717-0700, Fax 972/717-2550, Toll free reservations 800/332-3442, Website www.fourseasons.com/dallas. 357 Rooms, 12 Suites. Rates: $295-415. Credit cards accepted.*

The Four Seasons is a favorite getaway spot for locals as well as travelers. If your pocketbook allows, treat yourself to this marvelous Las Colinas resort that combines world-class sporting activities with the legendary Four Seasons attention to detail and luxury.

There are three outdoor and one indoor swimming pools, a spa and beauty salon, and several excellent restaurants. Bring your golf shoes—a superb 18-hole golf course and golf school occupies much of the beautiful 400-acre grounds. The championship course hosts the PGA Byron Nelson Classic each May. Serene rooms and public spaces complete the tranquil Four Seasons experience.

Fifty of the guest rooms are grouped in split-level villas overlooking the 18th green and the Resort pool. Each Villa Room has its own private indoor garden court with vaulted ceilings and skylights. Other rooms and suites are located throughout the main building, with Deluxe Rooms occupying the corners. The rooms are richly appointed and maintain a resort feeling with jewel-tone colors and half-moon balconies. All rooms are supplied with robes, slippers, twice-daily housekeeping services, private stocked bars and refrigerator, and a host of other luxuries.

There are three restaurants on the premises: Racquets for casual fare, Café on the Green for quiet dining in an elegant atmosphere, and Byron's in the Sports Club overlooking the fairway. Several lounges provide drinks, music, pub-like atmosphere, billiards, and televised sports. The outdoor Resort pool undulates free form through a gorgeously landscaped deck.

It would be a crime to stay here without indulging yourself in the world-class European-style spa. Choose from Swedish massage, body wraps, salt rubs, aromatherapy, reflexology, Kniepp therapy baths, and every other imaginable treatment for the body and soul. In-room massages are also available, as are salon services such as cutting, coloring, and styling hair. The professionally-managed child care center will give you both the free time and the peace of mind you need to relax completely away from the kids for a few hours.

OMNI MANDALAY HOTEL AT LAS COLINAS, *221 East Las Colinas Boulevard, Irving. Tel. 972/556-0800, Fax 972/556-0729, Toll free reservations 800/THE OMNI, Website www.omnihotels.com. 421 Rooms, 96 Suites. Rates: $150-285. Credit cards accepted.*

Only 15 minutes east of DFW Airport and beautifully situated on the shores of Lake Carolyn, the Omni Mandalay is favored by touring rock stars and professional athletes. The handsome 27-story hotel is designed around a Burmese theme. Rare Asian treasures caress the eyes, and even the resident swans are exotic. King Mindon and King Thiban are black swans with their own regal pagoda where their loyal subjects may watch their feedings.

Rooms feature views of either the lake and Las Colinas canals or the downtown Dallas skyline. The fully equipped fitness and exercise facilities are more than adequate, but if you're feeling timid, try the Get Fit Kits available at the front desk. You get a floor mat, dumbbells, and elastic workout bands to take back to your room where you can shape those thighs in private. A heated lakeside swimming pool, manicured jogging trail, and children's play area offer outdoor diversion.

Services include an in-house masseuse, 24-hour guest room dining, and twice-daily housekeeping. Three restaurants and a cozy Internet café fulfill your dining and wining desires. Spa Atelier, a full-service Aveda concept salon, is located adjacent to the hotel.

Near the Airports

There are literally dozens of chain hotels ranging from luxury to budget that specialize in catering to the passengers who are passing through one of Dallas' busy airports. Here are a few that we recommend:

Love Field

CLARION SUITES, *2363 Stemmons Trail (off Interstate 35 East). Tel. 214/350-2300, 214/350-5144, Toll free 800/4-CHOICE. 96 Suites. Rates $74-155. Credit cards accepted.*

RADISSON HOTEL DALLAS, *1893 West Mockingbird. Tel. 214/634-8850, Fax 214/630-8143, Toll free 800/333-3333. 305 Rooms. Rates: $58-129. Credit cards accepted.*

DFW Airport

DALLAS/FORT WORTH MARRIOTT, *8440 Freeport Parkway, Irving. Tel. 972/929-880, Fax 972/929-6501, Toll free 800/228-9290. 491 Rooms, 7 Suites. Rates: $89-199. Credit cards accepted.*

HARVEY SUITES, *4550 West John Carpenter Freeway, Irving. Tel. 972/929-4500, Fax 972/929-0733, Toll free 800/922-9222. 64 Suites. Rates $89-129.*

HILTON DFW LAKES, *1800 Highway 26 East, Grapevine. Tel. 817/481-8444, Fax 817/481-3160, Toll free 800/774-1500. 395 Rooms, 9 Suites. Rates: $89-150. Credit cards accepted.*

Where to Eat
DOWNTOWN
Expensive

THE CHAPARRAL CLUB, *at the Adam's Mark Hotel, 400 North Olive Street. Tel. 214/777-6539. Reservations essential. Credit cards accepted.*

Dallasites of old remember when the Chaparral Club was a swanky private dining room, perched atop the tallest skyscraper west of the Mississippi when the Southland Life Building opened in 1959. The members-only club swaggered through the Sixties and Seventies, declined through the Eighties, and finally closed in 1995. A few years later the Adam's Mark Hotel chain purchased the Southland Life Building and brought the Chaparral Club back to life.

Now open to the public, the Chaparral Club serves delicious Southwest-tinged fusion cuisine at the top of the world again. The vistas from the 38th floor are unimpeded, and the deco décor is wisely understated the better to showcase the glittering city backdrop. Dance combos play while the romantically inclined dance, and the comparison to New York City's Rainbow Room becomes irresistible.

Service is naturally impeccable, the wine list is excellent, and the food is delicious. Eclectic entrees might include sugarcane-cured pork tenderloin or veal loin with wild mushroom gnocchi. The restaurant serves dinner only, and is closed on Sundays and Mondays.

DAKOTA'S, *550 North Akard Street. Tel. 214/740-4001. Reservations recommended. Credit cards accepted.*

Dakota's is a downtown classic offering chic New American cuisine in an elegant setting. The bread that starts your meal comes warm from the oven. The environment is solid and elegant but unpretentious, and straightforward good food keeps patrons returning. Much of the food is grilled or smoked over mesquite wood that eliminates the need for fancy sauces or spices.

This is a popular spot for lunch with the power broker set, and it makes an ideal pre-theater dinner setting. Every evening the "twilight menu" offers a set three-course meal at an excellent price until 6pm. The restaurant is located below street level (you ride an elevator from the street).

THE FRENCH ROOM, *at the Adolphus Hotel, 1321 Commerce Street. Tel. 214/742-8200. Reservations essential. Credit cards accepted.*

The food is great, but more about that later. The most impressive thing about the French Room is the atmosphere. The gorgeous dining room drips with Baroque décor. It's opulent, it's romantic, it's dining on a grand scale. Cherubs on the ceiling smile down on blissful diners—if you're going to pop the question, this is the place in Dallas to do it.

The menu is indeed French, as the name implies, but this is not your grandmother's French restaurant. No pallid stuck-in-the-fifties American cum Continental cuisine here, no sir. This is lighter cuisine, more global in nature, influenced by flavor and style over tradition. One welcome tradition that has been maintained, however, is the sorbet served as a palate-cleanser between courses. Try the six-course chef's menu with matching wines ($90 or $125), or order from the menu. As in many European restaurants, you pay by the course. The sublime seared foie gras is a perennial favorite, and the vintage chocolate cake has to be tasted to be believed. The French Room serves only dinner and is closed on Sundays and Mondays. Try to make your reservations as far in advance as you possibly can.

GREEN ROOM, *2715 Elm Street. Tel. 214/748-7666. Reservations recommended. Credit cards accepted.*

This hip Deep Ellum spot bills itself as the only "four-star rock and roll restaurant in America." Thanks to live alternative music offerings, a cooler than cool bar scene, and most importantly the talent of chef Marc Cassel, the Green Room delivers. For the passive-aggressive gourmet, this restaurant offers a "Feed Me" four-course dinner, in which the chef selects your meal. Most listed choices reflect the chef's penchant for Asian flavorings. The succulent black mussels pan roasted with ginger are outstanding. Nothing is out of Cassel's reach, from Gulf shrimp and roasted shallot salad to braised rabbit with breakfast radishes.

This is the best dining to be found in Deep Ellum. The din can be somewhat overwhelming; so don't make plans for an intimate quiet meal. If you don't have reservations, expect a wait, but you can always hang out in the bar and celebrity-spot until you get a table.

Moderate

GUTHRIE'S HISTORICAL AMERICAN RESTAURANT, *400 South Ervay Street. Tel. 214/760-7900. Monday-Tuesday 11am-6pm, Wednesday-Thursday 11am-10pm, Friday 11am-10:30pm, Saturday 5:30-10:30pm, closed Sundays. Credit cards accepted.*

Lucky you – owner-chef William Guthrie, who developed his chops at such upscale places as St. Germain, offers delicious eclectic food at more than reasonable prices, and all you have to do is show up. There's an unexpected but delicious mix of cuisines in the Guthrie menu. Friday night draws a crowd for the all-you-can-eat fish fry. If you're in the mood for German food, try the pork schnitzel. If it's Italian you crave, go for the spinach-ricotta ravioli with walnut cream sauce. Daily lunch "blue plate" specials are popular with City Hall employees and other downtown types.

MONICA'S ACA Y ALLA, *2914 Main Street at Malcolm X Boulevard. Tel. 214/748-7140. No reservations. Credit cards accepted.*

Monica's Aca y Alla provides Deep Ellum's best salsa-salsa combination – that is, the hot sauce and the dance. For lunch the place is hopping with devoted diners who appreciate the imaginative Nuevo-Mex cuisine and the affordable prices. After closing for the afternoon, the restaurant opens again for dinner in a party atmosphere, with live music on weekends. Try Mexican lasagne or pumpkin ravioli, and have a margarita to wash it down.

Inexpensive

SAMMY'S, *2126 Leonard Street at Maple Avenue. Tel. 214/880-9064. Monday-Saturday 11am-3pm, closed Sundays. Credit cards accepted.*

Sammy's is a family-run barbecue joint dishing out mouth-watering ribs, tender brisket, and spicy hot links. The sides are something special here – baked potato casserole should be illegal, and the light, fried okra will convert even the most hard-core veggie-phobe.

UPTOWN

Uptown restaurants include areas immediately north and west of downtown as well as the neighborhood known as Lower Greenville, or "Restaurant Row."

Expensive

ABACUS, *4511 McKinney Avenue. Tel. 214/559-3111, Website: www.abacus-restaurant.com. Reservations essential. Monday-Thursday 6pm-10pm, Friday-Saturday 6pm-11pm, bar opens at 5pm, bar and restaurant closed Sundays. Reservations essential on weekends. Credit cards accepted.*

If you asked a master chef or a food critic where they would like to have dinner in Dallas, chances are the answer would be this sleek award-winning restaurant. Since opening in 1999, Abacus has garnered every accolade the dining industry has to offer. Chef Kent Rathbun blends Mediterranean, Southwest, Asian, and Creole influences to arrive at his own distinct style.

Meals begin with a selection of artisan breads, and continue with exquisitely prepared and presented dishes that will leave you nourished body and soul. One signature dish is lobster-scallion "shooters" with red chile-coconut sake. Another is the flash-seared foie gras with a duck confit crepe. You can order "small plates" or "big plates" here, and there is a nine-course chef's selection that is well worth trying.

The interior design of the restaurant is as rich and intriguing as the cuisine. Lush saturated color, custom lighting, abstract art – all combine to produce a vibrant but somehow tranquil atmosphere. The open theater kitchen makes for fascinating viewing, but if you'd like to get even closer you can reserve the Chef's Table in front of the kitchen counter.

ADELMO'S RISTORANTE, *4537 Cole Avenue at Knox Street. Tel. 214/559-0325. Reservations recommended. Closed Sundays. Credit cards accepted.*

Owner Adelmo Banchetti runs this cozy bistro serving imaginative Mediterranean cuisine. The restaurant occupies a two-story house – seating is a bit on the close side, so you might think twice before bringing small children. The food is fabulous, and the blackboard specials are reliably wonderful. Favorites are the huge veal chop, osso bucco, and the beef tartare. Try to get an upstairs table, where the atmosphere is gregarious and lively for lunch, romantic for dinner.

JAVIER'S, *4912 Cole Street. Tel. 214/521-4211. Reservations recommended. Credit cards accepted.*

Dark, heavy Caribbean decor reminiscent of Colonial Mexico matches the cuisine. Offerings range from Interior classics to tasty seafood as well as wild game. Javier's is well known for serving generous portions of excellent food. This is definitely not Tex-Mex but true Mexico City-style food, sophisticated and edgy.

The undeniable favorites from the menu are Barra de Navidad (shrimp in a diablo sauce of coffee, orange juice, tomato, and spices) and Filete Cantinflas (beef tenderloin stuffed with Chihuahuan cheese and spiced butter, toped with a mulate sauce and sliced avocado). Thin hot chips come before your meal accompanied by two warm sauced (we prefer the green tomatilla sauce).

This is a popular neighborhood eatery, and is almost always crowded; do be sure to call ahead for reservations.

THE MANSION ON TURTLE CREEK, *2821 Turtle Creek. Tel. 214/526-2121. Credit cards accepted. Reservations essential, jackets required.*

Elaborately carved fireplaces, stained glass windows, marble underfoot and inlaid wood ceilings overhead create an assured and elegant atmosphere. As the finest and possibly only truly world-class restaurant in Dallas, this is the place for beautiful people who eat beautiful food. The Mansion became famous for daring Southwestern cuisine and awe-inspiring prices.

What gives the cuisine such a sterling reputation is the amazing juxtaposition of tastes and textures that create something fresh and agreeable. Those in the know always order the warm lobster taco with yellow tomato salsa as an appetizer. Duck crepes and venison fajitas are examples of the innovative extras. The menu is continually refreshed and reinvented. Chef Dean Fearing was named by *Food & Wine* magazine as one of America's Top 10 Young Chefs. The four-course Tasting Menu offered for $90 gives you an excellent opportunity to marvel at his expertise from appetizer through dessert.

Lunch is served Monday to Saturday from 11:30am to 2:00pm, dinner on Sunday through Wednesday from 6:00pm to 10:00pm, with the hours extended to 10:30pm on Thursdays through Saturdays. Sunday brunch is served from 11am to 2:30pm.

STAR CANYON, *3102 Oak Lawn Avenue. Tel. 214/744-3287. Reservations essential on weekends. Credit cards accepted.*

Perhaps the most famous restaurant in Texas, Star Canyon is internationally recognized for serving the best Southwestern cuisine in the world. The big question now is whether, without star chef Stephen Pyles, Star Canyon continues to shine. The answer, devotees will be relieved to know, is an unqualified yes.

For now Star Canyon remains atop Dallas' dining scene. The menu continues to evolve without sacrificing traditional favorites, and the transfer of the restaurant to corporate hands does not seem to have tarnished its quality. Chef Matthew Dunn carries the torch for New Texas fare in admirable style. Even the simplest sounding of entrees sings. Old favorites like the bone-in cowboy ribeye with red-chili onion rings, tamale tart with roast garlic custard and Gulf coast crabmeat, and the signature Heaven and Hell cake remain on the menu to greet returning diners like old friends.

The décor flaunts its Texas heritage unabashedly. Branded into the ceiling are the names of Texas towns like Muleshoe and Deaf Smith and Dime Box. The televisions in the bar area play nothing but old westerns. Although the restaurant is still packed on weekends, it's now possible to walk in on a weeknight and get a table without making reservations in advance. Of course, it's always safer to call ahead just in case. Smoking is allowed in the bar area only, and there is no pipe or cigar smoking anywhere in the restaurant.

Moderate

CAFE IZMIR, *3711 Greenville Avenue. Tel. 214/826-7788. Reservations recommended. Credit cards accepted.*

The true star of the Greenville scene is this unique Middle Eastern café opened in 1996 by the brothers Ali and Beau Nazary. Meals are served family-style. One by one platters of richly flavored Mediterranean influenced food are brought to your table. All you have to decide on is what to drink with your meal. The stuffed dolmas are pungent and very tasty. The grilled vegetables and lamb are extraordinary. All meals include smooth and garlicky hummas and buttered saffron rice.

If a full meal isn't in your plans, nibble on tapas alongside a bottle of European table wine from the excellent menu. Tuesdays are "customer appreciation" nights, when all tapas are $2 and you can order wine by the bottle for $12.

DADDY JACK'S, *1916 Greenville. Tel. 214/826-4910. MasterCard and Visa accepted.*

When Daddy Jack's opened it appeared to be just a "chowder house" on restaurant row. Don't be fooled by the casual atmosphere. The excellent seafood does in fact include chowder, as well as other New England -style seafood dished. Lobster is the big draw here, and for $10.95 on weekdays you can experience "Lobster Madness" – that is, you can order cull lobsters (those missing a claw) at bargain basement prices. The reputation of this small place has grown exponentially and it is truly a Dallas favorite. Daily specials highlight the freshest seafood. This is the original Daddy Jack's. The second Dallas location is downtown in Deep Ellum, *2723 Elm Street, Tel. 214/653-3949.*

DREAM CAFE, *2800 Routh Street. Tel. 214/954-0486. Credit cards accepted.*

The fanciful decoration is a prelude to the dreamy food. Expect a wait, especially for weekend brunch, as the health-conscious but delicious cuisine is in high demand. Try the Eggs Oscar, a variation on eggs Benedict made with crabmeat and a decadent dill-hollandaise sauce. So much of the food is downright healthy; you can enjoy eating something that is good for you. The salads are full of flavor, such as the Thai Noodle Salad with shrimp and corn cakes over a bed of field greens and soba noodles with a spicy peanut dressing. The most popular meal of the day here is breakfast. Granola, pancakes, French toast, omelettes, all freshly made. The bakery always has specialty bread, such as apricot walnut sourdough. Go ahead – get a whole loaf. Dream Cafe is in the Quadrangle Building. This is an extremely kid-friendly restaurant, so bring the whole family.

KATHLEEN'S ART CAFE, *4424 Lovers Lane. Tel. 214/691-2355. Credit cards accepted.*

Named after the art that lines its walls, this tiny bistro-style restaurant with periodically changing menus offers eclectic fare, not dissimilar to the mismatched furniture. Somehow it works; everything including the food comes together in a pleasant, cozy environment. The pasta specialties are always very good. Brunch is served on Saturday from 8am to 4pm, and on Sunday from 8am to 3pm. Sunday night is half-priced entrée night.

MARIANO'S MEXICAN CUISINE, *5500 Greenville Avenue. Tel. 214/ 691-3888. Credit cards accepted.*

What makes this restaurant unique is that it claims to be the original home of the frozen margarita. It shares this claim with a few other restaurants in Texas, but no other restaurant has a shrine to frozen drink machines as you enter. If you're looking for something with a little more pizzazz than cheese enchiladas, Mariano's has a lively menu of Tex-Mex variations at very reasonable prices. The poblano al carbon with chicken is tender and tasty without being overwhelmingly spicy. (Mariano's is in the Old Town Shopping Center; also located downtown, *1402 Main Street, Tel. 214/742-2521.*)

MATTITO'S CAFE MEXICANO, *3011 Routh Street. Tel. 214/922-8835. Credit cards accepted.*

"Little Matt's" is an offshoot of the famous Matt's El Rancho in Austin. Mattito's offers upscale Tex-Mex specialties, including fabulous chile rellenos, to an appreciative local crowd. The food is fresh, and the excellent lunch specials always draw a crowd. The big margaritas are a happy-hour favorite. Mattito's boasts a tequila bar that sells every legally available variety.

SAM'S CAFE, *100 Crescent Court. Tel. 214/855-2233. Credit cards accepted.*

The airy, comfortable atmosphere of this restaurant reflects the entire dining experience to come. Sam's serves Southwestern food that bursts with flavor. The creamy chipotle cheese that is served with fresh bread sticks is good enough for a meal in itself. But don't stop there – order one of the four types of quesadillas stuffed with grilled vegetables and meat. The simple pasta dishes are consistently good, and vegetarians will enjoy the grilled portabella sandwich. The restaurant is located in the Crescent Building.

Inexpensive

CAFE BRAZIL, *6420 North Central Expressway. Tel. 214/691-7791. Open 24 hours. Credit cards accepted.*

Coffee brings people to Cafe Brazil. They typically offer about eight of their special house blends at a time, in large comforting mugs that you can refill as often as you want. The Breakfast Blend is rich and aromatic, and their flavored coffees are daring and fun. It's the food though, that keeps people coming back. Veggie empanadas (a heavy Brazilian pastry pocket), with grilled potatoes in rosemary cream sauce and your choice of eggs will keep you satisfied all day. Café Brazil also offers sumptuous build-your-own crepes and a variety of tantalizing soups and sandwiches. This University Park branch is the oldest extant location (the original Lakewood location burned in 1993), and attracts scores of hungry SMU students in search of a pick-me-up on those late study nights.

There are currently five other locations:

- **Café Brazil in Carrollton**, *2610 North Josey Lane, Carrollton, Tel. 972/242-8228*
- **Café Brazil Lakewood**, *2221 Abrams Road, Tel. 214/826-9522*
- **Café Brazil Deep Ellum**, *2815 Elm Street, Tel. 214/747-8725*
- **Café Brazil in Richardson**, *2071 North Central Expressway, Richardson, Tel. 972/783-9011*
- **Café Brazil Cedar Springs**, *3847 Cedar Springs Road, Tel. 214/461-8762*

CAMPISI'S EGYPTIAN RESTAURANT, *5610 East Mockingbird Lane. Tel. 214/827-0355. Credit cards accepted.*

Revered by Dallasites as having the best pizza in town, this restaurant also boasts a fine menu of traditional Italian food - if you're not in the mood for pizza, try the decadent lasagna. What really stands out about Campisi's, though, is the atmosphere. Darkly lit, with old red booths and ancient juke boxes at each table, it's clear this place hasn't changed much in over 50 years in Dallas. At a circular booth in the back of the restaurant you can see a large portrait of the original owners - Frank and Joe Campisi - now both deceased. Ask for a table in the back room so you can soak up the photo gallery of Frank and Joe with such brat pack-era luminaries as Frank Sinatra and Sammy Davis, Jr. As for the name, a former tenant left a sign out in front of the building that read "Egyptian Restaurant."

EL FENIX, *1601 McKinney Ave. Tel. 214/747-1121. Credit cards accepted.*

This venerable Tex-Mex chain established in 1918 has stood the test of time in the turbulent world of Dallas restaurants. The menu, which was inventive fifty years ago, offers the standard Tex-Mex fare that everyone enjoys. Corn tortillas are the standard for enchiladas and the cheese tacos are terrific. Lunch specials are delivered to your table in five minutes or less. The downtown location is just north of the West End off Field Street. Fifteen locations in the Dallas/Fort Worth Metroplex ensure that Dallasites are never far away from El Fenix's beloved picante hot sauce and "secret recipe" corn chips.

MAI'S RESTAURANT, *4812 Bryan Street at Fitzhugh. Tel. 214/826-9887. Credit cards accepted.*

Mai Pham operated the second Vietnamese restaurant in Dallas in the space next door to the current location. Though she sold this restaurant years ago, it still bears her name, although some locals in the know say that the magic has gone. Many dishes are variations on the cuisine of central Vietnam, the most flavorful of the country.

The soups are meals in themselves and for about $5 per bowl, they're one of the best deals in Dallas. Mai's version of the classic Vietnamese spicy chicken soup (bun ga hue) is full of noodles and the broth has a deep flavor and marvelous aroma. The house specialties are seafood dishes, such as char-broiled shrimp wrapped in sugar cane or sautéed catfish in a clay pot. Vegetarians have a variety of choices from soup to curry. Lunch specials are served from 11am to 3pm on weekdays.

The best way to begin your meal is with an appetizer of summer rolls, soft rice paper filled with salad and served with peanut sauce. And don't forget a cup of the genuine and potently sweet Vietnamese coffee.

Mai's restaurant is located about 1.5 miles east of Central Expressway (Highway 75). Exit Fitzhugh and travel east about 1.3 miles. Take a right on Bryan Street and you will find Mai's just south of the intersection of Fitzhugh and Bryan Streets.

SONNY BRYAN'S SMOKEHOUSE, *2202 Inwood Road at Harry Hines Boulevard. Tel. 214/357-7520. M-F 10am-4pm, Sat 10am-3pm, Sun 11am-2pm. Credit cards accepted.*

Dallas businessmen and women arrive early and sit on their cars to eat, because Sonny Bryan's has no chairs save a few school desks inside, and when the food's gone the smokehouse stand closes for the day. But for those who yearn to have tangy sauce dribbling down their chin as they devour chopped beef sandwiches, there is no substitute for Sonny's magical combination of mesquite smoke and zesty marinade. In fact the humble smokehouse stand has such an ardent following, it finally had to accept its destiny and become a proper restaurant in other locations all over town. For the true Sonny's Experience, however, the original location is the only one that counts.

SOUTH & WEST DALLAS
Expensive
COOL RIVER CAFÉ, *1045 Hidden Ridge Road, Irving. Tel. 972/871-8881. Open Monday-Thursday 11am-11pm, Saturday and Sunday 5pm-11pm. Reservations recommended. Credit cards accepted.*

This enormous concept restaurant seats 1,000 diners and covers a whopping 23,000 square feet. Fortunately the dining room has been divided into smaller areas, so it is possible to have an intimate dinner here. A manmade river flows outside, and if there's a wait you can cool your heels in the bar/pool room, or sample the wares in the Cognac and Cigar Lounge.

The meat is what you want to order here. Everything else is quite good, but it is as a steakhouse that Cool River has made its name. Try any of the steaks or the Prime Rib, and save room for the signature dessert Diablo Helado, a combination of Bailey's Irish ice cream and chocolate Belgian waffles. The secret ingredient is a tinge of habanero pepper.

Moderate

GLORIA'S RESTAURANT, *600 West Davis at Llewellyn Street. Tel. 214/ 948-3672. Open daily 11am-10pm. Reservations recommended. Credit cards accepted.*

At Gloria's there is a small selection of Tex-Mex favorites, and they're very well prepared, but the star attraction here is the Salvadoran food. Pork, black beans, and plantains serve as the backbone of Salvadoran cuisine, and Gloria's way with them has proved so popular that there are now three Dallas locations. This is the original, and funkiest, of the three.

Try the national dish of El Salvador, *papusas*, corn tortillas stuffed with pork and cheese. Get a side of fried yuca (rather like potato) or some plaintains to go with, and you're set. Don't pass up on dessert here – the milk flan is justly celebrated.

LA CALLE DOCE, *415 West Twelfth Street. Tel. 214/941-4304. No reservations accepted. Open M-F 11am-9:30pm, Sat 11am-10:30pm, Sun 11am-9pm. Credit cards accepted.*

La Calle Doce (Spanish for "12th Street"), in an unassuming blue house, is a haven for those longing for Veracruz-style seafood. When La Calle Doce opened in 1981, Mexican-style fresh seafood was a novelty. They have since raised it to an art form. Before you begin your Mexican coastal meal, remember the margaritas. The frozen margaritas are so smooth they taste almost creamy and are served in glasses so large that one will last the entire meal.

Seafood specials come with a cup of fish soup that has delicate broth and flaky white fish. Another excellent soup is the Caldo Xochitl, the house version of the chicken soup made in the southern Mexico state of Oaxaca. The main dishes suit appetites for very rich, chile relleno de mariscos, a mild poblano pepper stuffed with shrimp, scallops, octopus and fish and blanketed with thick, white cheese sauce. Shrimp Veracruzana is an mixture of large shrimp, bell peppers and black olives in light tomato sauce and gentle spices, served with rice. On weekends you can indulge in paella, seafood chicken and pork prepared in the special Spanish style with rice.

For those who do not love seafood, there is an entire section on the menu devoted to meat dishes and a few vegetarian choices. The flan, or Mexican custard, is deliciously authentic. A small breakfast menu of egg dishes is served from 11am to 2:30pm daily.

Another La Calle Doce has opened in East Dallas at *1925 Skillman Avenue, Tel. 214/824-9900.*

Inexpensive

GENNIE'S BISHOP GRILL, *321 North Bishop at Eighth Street, Tel. 214/ 946-1752. Open M-F 11am-2pm. No reservations. Cash only.*

Where do you go in Dallas for home cooking – real home cooking, not that "New Texas" fancy grub? To Gennie's Bishop Grill, that's where. This Oak Cliff establishment is only open for weekday lunch, which doesn't stop the hordes of faithful who flock here for chicken-fried steak, towering fluffy yeast rolls, and peanut butter pie. The sign over the counter reads, "We cook for Texans, not for Frenchmen."

NORTH

For purposes of this section, North Dallas listings cover Addison, Garland, Carrollton, and other locations lying north of Highway 635 (The LBJ Freeway).

Moderate

BAVARIAN GRILL, *221 West Parker Road, Plano. Tel. 972/881-0705. Credit cards accepted. Reservations recommended for large groups.*

Central Texas isn't the only place you can find good German food in this state. The authentic German cuisine here is truly outstanding, with seasonal entrees and old favorites to explore. There is an extensive selection of German beer to accompany your sauerbraten and bratwurst, and to add to the biergarten atmosphere there is live German music on the weekends.

Inexpensive

BARBEC'S, *8949 Garland Road. Tel. 214/321-5597. No reservations. Cash only.*

In a sea of cookie-cutter look-a-like diners, Barbec's stands alone as a Dallas original. Breakfasts are traditional, quick, and cheap with the best beer biscuits in the entire world. Lunch and dinner specials vary but offer a standard and consistent fare of old-fashioned Southern home cooking. If you're looking for breakfast on the weekend, expect a brief wait, but rest easy in the knowledge that you'll be offered one of their fabulous biscuits to make the time go by easier.

Seeing the Sights
DOWNTOWN (BUSINESS & ARTS DISTRICT)

Downtown Dallas is a curious place. It is full of architectural marvels and public art, but the area isn't an indispensable aspect of Dallas life. Most residents of Dallas live far away from downtown, and many who live in Dallas never even venture into the downtown area. Downtown Dallas has its rewards, however, and a day spent exploring this angular place of glass and steel will leave you with a new appreciation for the beating heart underneath the imposing façade.

Start with a bird's-eye view of downtown Dallas by taking the elevator to the top of **Reunion Tower**, *300 Reunion Boulevard*. This endearing sparkly geodesic dome atop its 50-story tower is the most recognizable object on the Dallas skyline. The observation deck provides a 360-degree view. You're on the far west side of downtown, so look east to get a view of the rest of the city stretching out below you. To your west you can see the Fort Worth skyline. The dome is covered with a web of hundreds of lights, and after dark a computer system creates nightly light shows. A rotating restaurant and bar operated by the adjoining Hyatt Regency share this space. Admission to the observation deck is $2 or free with a receipt from the restaurant.

A Walk Through Dallas History

From Reunion Tower, walk through the tunnel to **Union Station**. This restored 1916 Beaux-Arts railroad terminal houses the AMTRAK facilities and also serves as a stop on the DART light-rail line. Take the DART train to the West End station to continue your downtown tour.

From the West End DART station it's just a short walk to the spot that is the first place many people still associate with Dallas, **Dealey Plaza**, *Elm, Main, and Commerce Streets at Houston Street*. A historical marker on Houston Street marks the spot where Kennedy was assassinated. It is not uncommon to see people standing here with tears in their eyes — many people still remember exactly where they were when they heard President Kennedy had been shot. It's an emotional pilgrimage to a spot that represents the loss of a nation's innocence.

Across Houston Street from Dealey Plaza is the **Kennedy Memorial Plaza**. The centerpiece of the plaza is Philip Johnson's 50-foot square memorial cenotaph, inside of which is a slab of black stone inscribed simply, "John Fitzgerald Kennedy." Granite markers on opposite ends of the plaza explain, "It is not a memorial to the pain and sorrow of death, but stands as a permanent tribute to the joy and excitement of one man's life."

The official collection that records for history the assassination of President John F. Kennedy is **The Sixth Floor Museum**, *inside the former Texas School Book Depository, 411 Elm Street, Tel. 214/653-6666, open daily from 9am-6pm, admission $4*. Dedicated to the slain President, it contains more than 400 photographs as well as videos and other artifacts and displays. If you look up at the building from the street you will notice that a window on the sixth floor is open. This is believed to be the place from which the fatal bullets were fired.

The controversial **Conspiracy Museum**, *110 South Market Street, Tel. 214/741-3040, open daily 10am to 6pm, admission $7 adults, $3 children*, stands a few blocks south and east of the former Texas School Book Depository. The Conspiracy Museum capitalizes on Dallas' unfortunate notoriety following the assassination, and through its text-intensive exhibits attempts to link assassinations of the twentieth centuries. You can purchase hard-to-find books about presidential assassinations and other alleged government cover-ups here.

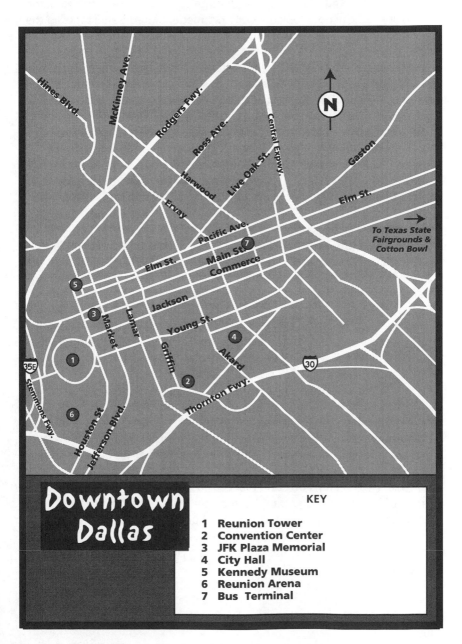

Downtown Dallas

KEY

1 Reunion Tower
2 Convention Center
3 JFK Plaza Memorial
4 City Hall
5 Kennedy Museum
6 Reunion Arena
7 Bus Terminal

About a block west, the original Dallas County Courthouse, known popularly as **Old Red**, still stands at the intersection of Main and Houston Streets. It's an ominous-looking building made of red sandstone in the Romanesque Revival style – gaze up at the gargoyles gaurding the eaves. Old Red is currently being transformed into the Museum of Dallas History.

Back up towards the Sixth Floor Museum, north of Kennedy Memorial Plaza at Main and Record Streets and surrounded by skyscrapers, the reconstructed **John Neely Bryan Cabin** reminds everyone that even the biggest cities have humble beginnings. A tiny log cabin like this one served as Bryan's home and trading post in the 1840s. Imagining the solitary wooden house standing on empty plains is nearly impossible.

If you would like to see one of the original 23 copies of the United States Declaration of Independence, visit the **J. Erik Jonsson Central Library**, *1515 Young Street*. The document, printed on July 4, 1776, is on the seventh floor.

Architecture & Public Art

The **Dallas City Hall**, *1500 Marilla Street at Akard*, is a fitting place to begin a tour of Dallas architecture, not only because it is the center of city government, but because it is the building most likely to stick in your memory. It is an inverted pyramid designed by renowned architect I. M. Pei in 1978, set on a seven-acre site that includes a large reflecting pool. Henry Moore designed a 16-foot high 24-foot wide sculpture especially for the site entitled "The Dallas Piece." Children particularly enjoy this building, as it looks as though it is upside down and standing close to it easily conjures up an exciting sense that the whole thing is about to fall over!

I. M. Pei has left his mark all over downtown Dallas. Up in the Arts District, his **Morton H. Meyerson Symphony Center**, *2301 Flora Street, Tel. 214/670-3600*, appears to warp and undulate before your eyes. You may tour the building on selected Mondays, Wednesdays, Fridays and Saturdays at 1pm, but call in advance to make sure performances or rehearsals do not interfere with the tour schedule.

A third Pei building, **Fountain Place**, *1445 Ross Avenue*, is a geometrical mixture of triangles and rectangles that seems to change from different vantage points. The blue-green glass of the building is beautifully reflected in the six-acre water garden covering the plaza.

Another watery refuge, this one designed by Philip Johnson, is **Thanksgiving Square** – an island of tranquility in the center of the city. The waterfall and serene landscaping give people a place to pause and meditate on the good in life. A non-denominational chapel with a modern spiral shape stands in the park. Akard, Bryan, Pacific and Ervay Streets form the corners of the park.

Philip Johnson also designed the **Bank One Center**, *1717 Main Street*, a 60-story building that occupies an entire city block. The tower that rises from the base of the building forms a cross, with a glass vault capping each arm. The glass that forms these barrel vaults extends down the center sections of the building in a shimmering curtain reflecting cloud and sky.

One of the most distinctive buildings on the Dallas skyline is the 1987 **Chase Bank Tower**, *once the Texas Commerce Tower, 2200 Ross Avenue*, with its six-story "keyhole" near the top of the structure. The design seems to be an act of whimsy, but is actually an intentional engineering device to reduce the wind load on the 55-story building.

The tallest building in Dallas is the 72-story **Bank of America Plaza**, *901 Main Street*. You'll have no trouble spotting this building at night, either – it's the one outlined in green neon lights.

Downtown Dallas isn't just about modern buildings, however. There are also many fine examples of design from the early 20th century in all their rococo glory. **The Adolphus Hotel**, *1321 Commerce Street*, was built the year the Titanic sank (in 1912), and in many ways the hotel still reflects that era of doomed luxury. There are Flemish tapestries and antiques all about the lobby.

The **Davis Building**, *1309 Main Street*, is a Classic Revival building constructed in 1925 to house Republic Bank. The four-story cupola atop one side of the building was added to make the building taller than a competitor's bank building. In 1931 an identical 20-story addition was erected, but without a cupola on top, giving the building an asymmetrical façade.

Back towards City Hall, between the Convention Center and the Pioneer Cemetery, **Pioneer Plaza** is a refreshing place to stop and relax. If you have children with you, let them run about and explore the three bronze cowboys driving the 40 bronze longhorn steers weighing 1,000 pounds each through the park. Each longhorn even carries a brand on its left hip. The plaza is landscaped with native plants and a flowing stream through a natural setting.

Museums

The **Old City Park Museum**, *1717 Gano Street, Tel. 214/421-5141, Admission $6, open Tuesday-Saturday 10am-4pm, Sunday noon-4pm, closed Monday*, preserves life in turn-of-the-century Dallas through various examples of historical architecture relevant to Dallas culture. This was originally Dallas' first city park, and now it contains 37 restored historic homes and buildings on 13 acres. Structures include an old bank building, an ante-bellum mansion, and the oldest of the buildings, two 1840s log cabins. Volunteers give guided tours, and there are usually artisans and craftspeople on hand to demonstrate such necessary talents as candle making, printing, and weaving.

At the **Dallas Museum of Art**, *1717 Harwood Street, Tel. 214/922-1200, Website: www.dm-art.org*, the permanent collection includes masterworks of art by Matisse, Monet, and Rodin. Since opening in 1903 the museum has amassed a collection of significant art from many cultures and periods of time. The extensive pre-Columbian wing displays rare and amazing artifacts and art by the Native Americans of Meso- and South America. Picasso, Bracque, Mondrian, and many others represent the 20th century with their revolutionary modernism. Excellent traveling exhibits routinely visit. Admission is free except for special exhibits. The two restaurants on the premises, the Seventeen Seventeen Restaurant and the Atrium Café, serve excellent food.

FAIR PARK AREA
Some of the nation's best examples of monumental art deco architecture are found east of downtown Dallas. **Fair Park**, *1300 Robert B. Cullum at Grand Avenue, Tel. 214/670-8400*, was named a National Historic Landmark because of the grandiose deco buildings, but it is best known as the home of the State Fair of Texas. This complex houses 8 museums, the Music Hall, the Cotton Bowl, an IMAX theater, even a restaurant open year round. Fair Park also frequently hosts local cultural festivals. Take the kids to **Science Place**, an interactive museum that fosters a hands-on approach to science. Other museums on the premises include the **Age of Steam Railroad Museum**, and the **Dallas World Aquarium**; all are open year round. There is a flea market held at Fair Park once a month.

A large collection of African art is on display at the **African-American Museum**, *3536 Grand Avenue, Tel. 214/565-9026, Tuesday to Thursday and Sunday noon to 5pm, Friday noon to 9pm Saturday 10am to 5pm*. The museum is in Fair Park. The exhibits provide a fascinating perspective on the richness of the African-American heritage.

The **Vietnam Memorial**, *3809 Grand Avenue*, designed by Richard Matrix in 1989, also stands in Fair Park. It honors the 3,271 Texans killed in the Vietnam Conflict, as well as the 156 Texans still missing in action. Their names are engraved upon native Texas granite slabs that stand alongside a granite-lined pool.

NORTH DALLAS
The **Freedman's Cemetery**, *2470 Five Mile Parkway, Tel. 214/333-0983*, is pre-Civil War African-American cemetery that has been preserved as a state and local historical landmark. The new Freedman's Memorial is now open just east of the cemetary. The statuary inside the entrance gate arches is particularly moving.

The **Dallas Memorial Center for the Holocaust**, *7900 Northaven Road, Tel. 214/750-4654, open daily 10am to 4pm*, is an archive of the experiences of the survivors of the Holocaust. The museum exhibits documents, photos and artifacts from the Holocaust. The large archive includes a library of books and videos. The center is open year-round and free to the public.

A piece of genuine living history is found in the **Wilson Blocks Historic District** on Swiss Avenue. The boulevard is lined with painstakingly restored Prairie-style late Victorian homes. Most were converted into apartments during World War II and have been returned to their original glory through the efforts of individuals reclaiming the turn-of-the-century neighborhood. The Swiss Avenue Historic District is about three miles northeast of downtown Dallas. From Interstate Highway 30 exit at Munger and drive north about one mile to Swiss Avenue.

Crowds turn out en masse to see the "Spring Blooms" at the **Dallas Arboretum and Botanical Garden**, *8525 Garland Road, Tel. 214/670-6374*. The gardens have seasonal floral exhibits for year round enjoyment. This scenic spot is often chosen for celebrations. You can spend hours enjoying the 66 acres of cultivation. The Arboretum frequently offers seminars in various horticultural techniques.

A wide ranging variety of mostly fighter planes expertly restored to their original condition is housed at the **Cavanaugh Flight Museum**, *4572 Claire Chennault, Addison Airport, Tel. 214/380-8800*. The collection includes several WW1 era fighters as well as a number of intimidatingly modern aircraft. A must see for aviation buffs.

South & West

Kids will love the **Dallas Zoo**, *621 East Clarendon, Tel. 214/946-5154, Open daily 9am-5pm, Admission $3 adult, $1.50 child*. The Wilds of Africa monorail exhibit is the best part of the zoo, with its nature trail and a gorilla conservation center. Other more standard exhibits feature over 2,000 animals. The zoo has been undergoing extensive renovation for several years and promises more extensive and habitat-like conditions. A new addition is the giant 67-foot tall giraffe statue, visible from the Interstate. From downtown, take Interstate Highway 35-E south, exit Marsalis Street; follow the signs.

Nightlife & Entertainment

The **Dallas Opera**, *3102 Oak Lawn Street, Suite 450, Tel. 214/443-1000*, offers five performances in a season. The performances feature talent of international acclaim. The venue is the **Morton H. Meyerson Symphony Center**, *2301 Flora Street, Tel. 214/670-3600, see above for more*, a modern masterpiece with flowing lines designed by I. M. Pei. The center is the latest gem in Dallas' cultural arts crown.

The venue for many summer concerts is the **Starplex**, *1818 First Avenue at Fair Park, Tel. 214/373-8000, www.starplex.com*. It defines, for the time being at least, the easternmost border of Fair Park. The large outdoor amphitheater hosts such big-ticket acts as B.B. King, LL Cool J, and Van Halen. Bring an umbrella if it looks like rain, because you can't go back to your car once you enter the grounds.

The **Majestic Theater**, *1925 Elm Street, Tel. 214/880-0137*, is a fabulous vintage venue for theater and music, charmingly evoking the spirit of 1920s

Texas with its murals. Originally vaudeville acts played the Majestic. Today you can see touring performances on the restored stage.

Dallas has a wealth of nightlife in several different areas of concentration about town. The Greenville Avenue venues have been around longest. Lower Greenville offers many restaurants and casual bars in a neighborhood setting. The **West End Marketplace**, *603 Munger Avenue, Tel. 214/748-4801*, is a shopping and entertainment development located in what was once deserted warehouse buildings. Many restaurants and distractions from movies to bars guarantee the family will have something fun to do at the West End. From Highway 75, exit McKinney Avenue and go east.

During prohibition, **Deep Ellum** was a jazz, blues, and speakeasy neighborhood before it entered a decline. For decades the area was nearly abandoned. Today, Deep Ellum has blossomed into an entire district filled with fine local restaurants and the best live music in the city. Over sixty clubs, restaurants and interesting shops are packed into this roughly nine block area. You can easily visit a number of clubs in one night, as the streets are filled with "club hoppers." As more buildings offering loft apartments open, the traffic and congestion become worse. This remains the place to be for a night on the town. The area is bordered by Elm Street on the north, Canton Street on the south, and Hall Street on the east. Deep Ellum is located just north of Interstate Highway 30 and east of Highway 75, to the east of downtown.

NIGHTCLUBS
Greenville Avenue
• **Dreams Club**, *7035 Greenville Avenue, Tel. 214/368-4981*. Jazz.
• **Eden 2000**, *5500 Greenville Avenue, Tel. 214/361-9517*. Dance.
• **Muddy Waters**, *1518 Greenville Avenue, Tel. 214/823-1518*. Blues.
• **Poor Richard's Pub**, *1924 Greenville Avenue, Tel. 214/821-9891*. Eclectic.
• **Royal Rack Reggae Club**, *1906 Greenville Avenue, Tel. 214/824-9733*. Caribbean.
• **Terelli's**, *2815 Greenville Avenue, Tel. 214/827-3993*. Jazz.

Deep Ellum
• **Blind Lemon**, *2895 Main Street, Tel. 214/939-0202*. Dance.
• **Blue Cat Blues**, *2617 Commerce Street, Tel. 214/744-2287*. Blues.
• **Club Dada**, *2720 Elm Street, Tel. 214/744-3232*. Eclectic.
• **Dread-n-Irie**, *2897 Commerce Street, Tel. 214/742-4743*. Caribbean.
• **Trees**, *2709 Elm Street, Tel. 214/748-5009*. Eclectic.

SAMBUCA JAZZ CAFÉ, *2618 Elm Street. Tel. 214/744-0820 credit cards accepted.*

In an area of town where restaurants and clubs shoot across the sky and burn out as quickly as meteorites, Sambuca has enjoyed a lasting success. This

Deep Ellum nightspot and supper club is the premiere jazz venue in town. Jazz acts of local and national interest play every night of the week. Although music is the focus, the Mediterranean food is quite good in its own right. If you're coming for dinner, get here before the music starts at eight, when conversation becomes difficult.

Sambuca has expanded to a north Dallas location at *15207 Addison Road, Addison. Tel. 972/385-8455.*

UPTOWN

SIPANGO, *4513 Travis Street. Tel. 214/522-2411. Credit cards accepted.*

This darkly lit, crowded nightspot draws a mostly thirty-something crowd, but all ages will feel comfortable here. Although the restaurant serves the ubiquitous "New American" cuisine with above average panache, the real scene here is the crowded bar. Live music, hand-rolled cigars, and a weekend nightclub in the Rio Room attract a flashy crowd.

Sports & Recreation
Golf

Dallas has long been a center for golf. For over seventy years the **Cedar Crest Golf Course**, 1800 Southerland, *Tel. 214/670-7615, Fax 670-7641*, has been a challenging test of skill. The rolling hills and tall trees make a beautiful setting for the 18-hole par 71 course. You can rent clubs, take lessons, and practice on the putting green here. Cedar Crest is located south of the city, off Interstate Highway 35.

One of the most difficult private courses in the area is open to the public. The **Sleepy Hollow Country Club**, *4747 South Loop 12, Tel. 214/371-3430, 371-5466*, has one 18-hole, par 71 course that non-members may use. The club facilities include a restaurant, locker room, driving range and putting green.

Tennis

The **Hyatt Bear Creek Golf and Racquet Club**, *West Airfield Drive, Arlington, Tel. 972-615-6882, Fax 453-6410*, is an excellent public facility. The club offers two golf courses with bent grass greens. Of the seven tennis courts, three are indoor; ten racquetball courts are available. The Hyatt Bear Creek Club is located near Dallas/Fort Worth International Airport.

Biking

Bicycling, jogging and walking enthusiasts will enjoy **White Rock Lake**, off Loop 12 east, which has over 11 miles of trails and lovely scenery.

Spectator Sports

Dallas is full of sports excitement. The renowned **Dallas Cowboys** meet head-to-head with other NFL teams at **Texas Stadium**, *2401 East Airport Highway, Irving, Tel. 972/556-2500*. The season runs from September through December.

The excitement of professional basketball is brought home by the **Dallas Mavericks** at Reunion Arena, *777 Sports Street, Tel. 214/748-1808*. You can see them play from November through April.

And the all-American sport, baseball, is played by the **Texas Rangers** at the Ballpark in Arlington, *1000 Ballpark Way, Arlington, Tel. 817/273-5100*. The Rangers play in the American League.

Dallas is proud to have the only major league professional hockey team in the state, the **Dallas Stars**, *901 Main Street, Tel. 214/GO-STARS*.

Even polo is represented in Dallas. The **Dallas Dragons**, *5210 McKinney Avenue, Suite 280, Tel. 214/979-0849*, play every Sunday in the spring and summer. Occasional Saturday matches are held in the fall. The home games are held at the Polo Range in Red Oak, about 20 miles from the city. From downtown Dallas go south on Interstate Highway 35. Take the Ovilla exit and travel east.

There is almost always a rodeo in Dallas. The **Mesquite Rodeo**, *1818 Rodeo Drive, Mesquite, Tel. 214/285-8777 or 800/833-9339*, is held Friday and Saturday nights from April through September. You can see all the real live action of bull riding, roping and barrel racing. A barbecue buffet is offered and the kids will enjoy the petting zoo. From Loop 635 East, take Exit 4 to Mesquite and follow the signs to the rodeo.

Shopping

The flagship store for **Neiman Marcus**, *1618 Main Street, Tel. 214/741-6911*, is located downtown. The building was constructed for the department store in 1914, and since then the elite of Dallas will not shop anywhere else.

The shopping area of the **Galleria**, *Loop 635 and Dallas North Tollway, Tel. 214/702-7100*, is but one piece of this amazing complex. A high-rise office tower and first class hotel are located here as well. You can easily spend at least an entire day shopping in this deluxe mall. The Galleria features over 200 stores including Nordstrom and Tiffany & Co.

North Park Mall, *Loop 12 and Central Expressway, 214/363-7441*, has 160 shops including Lord & Taylor, Neiman Marcus and Tiffany.

Excursions & Day Trips

Do not expect to find J. R. Ewing at the **Southfork Ranch**, *3700 Hogge Road, Parker, Tel. 214/442-7800*. The old farmhouse used for the television series draws tourists; unfortunately there is little of interest among the "Dallas memorabilia" that people pay to see. To get to the attraction, take Highway 75 north to the Parker Road exit, and then continue east, following the signs.

CANTON

On most days you might drive through **Canton** and barely notice the tiny town. But on the weekend preceding the first Monday of each month, the town of 3000 blossoms into a bargaining Mecca. Thousands flood the 100 acre flea market known as **Canton First Monday Trade Days**. You can find everything from antiques to livestock, and you are sure to take back vivid impressions of country life. The vendors cannot reserve spaces, so each month the entire market changes.

The first Monday tradition began in the 1870s, when stray horses were auctioned once per month. Despite the name, you will not find much of a market left on Monday; all trading is done on the weekend. Take Interstate 20 east about 63 miles; Canton is at the intersection of Interstate Highway 20 and Highway 64. Admission is free; parking $3.

Practical Information

The **American Automobile Association** has two offices in Dallas; the main one is at *4425 North Central Expressway, Tel. 214/526-7911; for 24-hour road service 214/528-7481.*

Bed and Breakfast Texas Style, *Tel. 214/298-8586 or 800/899-4538, Fax 214/298-7118*, can help you find the right accommodations for your stay in the area.

You can find out what's hot in Dallas through the **Dallas Events Hotline**, *Tel. 214/746-6679.*

Fort Worth

The name **Fort Worth** conjures up images of cattle drives and cowboys. The town actually *was* a fort before the cattle industry took over. Fort Worth stands in the shadow of the larger, more metropolitan Dallas. Yet the personality of the city gives perhaps a truer representation of the diverse nature of Texas overall. Traces of the old cow town are maintained and even celebrated in the midst of a thriving urban center. The city has a reputation for being a center of visual and performing arts. Five institutes of higher learning are based in Fort Worth.

The Fort Worth area celebrates its artistic heritage and cultural diversity with the **Main Street Arts Festival**. For one long weekend in mid-April, Main Street is closed for this pedestrian fair. Stages come alive with dance and musical performances, many of which highlight the contributions of different cultures to Fort Worth. The street is filled with booths where artisans sell their crafts. Exhibitions of fine art are featured and special activities for children both entertain and challenge their imaginations.

Arrivals & Departures

The **Dallas-Fort Worth International Airport (DFW)** is located between the two cities for which it is named. The clear skies over Arlington often look like a superhighway in the sky, especially at night with the frequent takeoffs and landings. For complete information on DFW, see Arrivals & Departures under Dallas.

Airport Van Service, *1000 East Weatherford Street, Tel. 817/334-0092*, provides transpiration from the airport to Fort Worth. One-way fare to or from the downtown area is $8.

The **Amtrak** route that serves Fort Worth originates in San Antonio, with a stop in Austin, and continues north to Chicago. The train station is located at *1501 Jones Street, Tel. 817/332-2931*.

Orientation

Interstate Highway 30 runs from Dallas to the central part of Fort Worth. Interstate Highway 20, which enters on the south side of the city, also runs east/west. Interstate Highway 35 West bisects the city on a north-south axis. This highway splits into two branches south of the Dallas-Fort Worth area. The east branch runs to Dallas.

The arts district is located on the western side of the city center. From Interstate Highway 30, take the University Exit north. To get to the Stockyards, exit Commerce and go north on Commerce to the complex.

Getting Around Town

The bus system in Fort Worth is called simply **"The T,"** *Tel. 817/870-6200*. Special routes cover areas of interest to visitors. The 73A and 73B bus travels between the downtown area and the Stockyards. The standard adult fare is $1. Private tours of city attractions are offered through **Gray Line**, *Tel. 817/429-7563*.

A number of taxi companies operate in Fort Worth. **Yellow Cab**, *Tel. 817/534-5555 or 800/749-0900*, serves the entire Dallas-Fort Worth area.

Where to Stay

Expensive

ASHTON HOTEL, *610 Main Street. Tel. 817/333-0100, Fax 817/332-0110, Website: www.slh.com/ashton. 39 Rooms, 6 Suites. Rates $207-750. Credit cards accepted.*

In April 2001, the historic old Floyd J. Homes Building reopened as Fort Worth's newest and most luxurious small hotel, The Ashton. The exterior remains of a piece with the heart of old Fort Worth, but inside modernity rules. A beautiful cubist-patterned carpet in the lobby combines with elegant furniture, dropped glass ceilings and subtle sophisticated lighting to create a unique mid-century Modernism atmosphere. The artwork features a fine collection of original Fort Worth Circle artists, a group of painters who worked from the 1930s to the 1960s to introduce elements of Modernism into art that also represented their Fort Worth heritage.

Every guest room features a king-sized bed draped in down comforters under crisp Frette Linens from Italy. The towels and bathrobes are also made by Frette, and the toiletries are Moulton Brown. Each room also offers custom furnishings in gorgeous woods of varying hue and grain, a sitting area, and an oversized bathroom with a pedestal sink and tub. Other rooms offer Jacuzzi tubs, DirecTV, and walk-in showers.

Needless to say, the Café Ashton is also setting new standards for dining in Fort Worth. See *Where to Eat* for more information on the outstanding menu. There is a fitness center on site with Universal Gym Equipment, treadmill, and free weights.

RADISSON PLAZA, *815 Main Street. Tel. 817/870-2100, Fax 817/335-3408, Toll free reservations 800/333-3333. 500 Rooms. Rates: $130-178. Credit cards accepted.*

The Radisson has over 500 rooms and is located in the downtown area. The hotel first opened in 1921 as the old Texas Hotel, Fort Worth's finest luxury hotel and only high-rise. This hotel is famous as the last place that President Kennedy stayed before his fateful trip to Dallas. The rooms are nondescript but pleasant, and the on-site restaurant is popular. Amenities include a heated outdoor pool on the rooftop and a fitness area. The hotel is within walking distance of the convention center and restaurants and bars.

THE RENAISSANCE WORTHINGTON HOTEL, *200 Main Street. Tel. 817/870-1000, Fax 817/335-3847, Toll free reservations 800/468-3571, Website www.worthingtonhotel.com. 504 Rooms, 44 Suites. Rates: $185-375. Credit cards accepted.*

The beautiful Worthington is one of the most elegant hotels in Fort Worth. Located in the heart of the city, right in the Sundance Square entertainment district, this modern twelve-story hotel is adjacent to the city convention center. The rooms are spacious and some have lovely views of the city. Relax in the piano bar or by the water garden. This is the only four star hotel in the area and strives to provide exemplary service. On the premises you will find two restaurants (the better of which is Reflections), a gym and outdoor pool.

THE SANFORD HOUSE, *506 North Center Street, Arlington. Tel. 817/861-2129, Fax 817/861-2030, Toll free reservations 877/205-4914, Website: thesanfordhouse.com, email: info@thesanfordhouse.com. 8 Guestrooms, 4*

Cottages. Rates: $125-150 for guestrooms, $200 for cottages. Credit cards accepted.

If you plan to explore Dallas and Fort Worth, Arlington makes an ideal home base. This pleasant bed and breakfast establishment, though neither historic nor old, is charming nonetheless. French Country appointed rooms surround you in solid comfort. Cottages feature fireplaces, king-sized beds, and leather sofas. The grounds are attractively landscaped with fountains, gazebos, and walled-in gardens. There is an outdoor pool, and a full breakfast is included in the rate.

STOCKYARDS HOTEL, *109 East Exchange Avenue. Tel. 817/625-6427, Toll free reservations 800/423-8471. 52 Rooms. Rates: $135-165. Credit cards accepted.*

You will get a taste of the Old West at the Stockyards Hotel, which is located on historic Exchange Street. The building was constructed as a hotel in the early 1900's and has hosted the famous and infamous, like the real Bonnie and Clyde gangster duo. You can simply mosey down the street for daytime entertainment or nightlife. The western theme decor is downright kitschy, with rooms styled like a Victorian parlor or Wild West abode. This hotel is a favorite of foreign tourists who want to get a full dose of cowboy atmosphere. There are a restaurant and bar on the premises.

Moderate

AZALEA PLANTATION BED AND BREAKFAST, *1400 Robinwood Street. Tel. 817/838-5882 or 800/687-3519. Rates: $89 to $110. Credit cards accepted.*

The Azalea Plantation is located north of downtown Fort Worth, still within a short drive from major attractions and entertainment. The lovely old home has four rooms for guests and two rooms which are used as a common area for visitors. The home is located on lovely property which has large trees and a secluded feeling. On weekends a full breakfast is served. Children under the age of six years may stay for no charge with parents.

BLOOMSBURY HOUSE, *2251 Lipscomb Street. Tel. 817/921-2383 or 888/652-7378. Rates: $99 to $110. Credit cards accepted.*

The home was built at the turn-of-the-century and is complete with a carriage house in the back. The three rooms in the main house have old-fashioned furnishings and offer a tranquil hide-away close to major attractions in the city. Guests enjoy a hearty breakfast in the morning and a light desert in the evening. You can dine in your room or on the bright patio downstairs.

MISS MOLLY'S HOTEL, *109 West Exchange Avenue. Tel. 817/626-1522 or 800/996-6559, Fax 817/625-2723. Rates: $95 to $170. Credit cards accepted.*

Miss Molly's is the most unusual place to stay in the city. In the good old days, this hotel was not exactly intended for overnight guests. The eight-room establishment was once a house of ill repute. The painted ladies have long since left, and today this is a cozy and unique luxury hotel. The decor is reminiscent of the past, with plenty of red fabric and Victorian style accents. Breakfast is included with your stay.

TEXAS WHITE HOUSE, *1417 English Avenue. Tel. 817/923-3597 or 800/279-6491, Fax 817/923-3597. Rates: $85 to $105. Credit cards accepted.*

This charming house has three guest rooms. Recreational facilities area located nearby, including a golf course. Adults only are welcomed to stay at this house.

Inexpensive

HOTEL TEXAS, *2415 Ellis Avenue. Tel. 817/624-2224 or 800/866-6660, Fax 817/624-7177. Rates: $49 to $109. Credit cards accepted.*

The Hotel Texas was built in 1921 as the luxury accommodation for the Stockyards business district. The two-story building is made of yellow brick. The twenty-one rooms have the old-time western feeling and are completely modernized. Children under the age of 18 stay free with parents.

THE PARKS CENTRAL, *1010 Houston Street. Tel. 817/336-2011 or 800/ 848-Park, Fax 817/336-0623. Rates: $50 to $85. Credit cards accepted.*

This motel has 121 rooms and is located close to the Convention Center. The hotel has an outdoor pool, but no other recreational facilities. Children may stay with parents at no additional charge.

REMINGTON HOTEL, *600 Commerce Street. Tel. 817/332-6900, Fax 877-5440. Rates: $49 to $120. Credit cards accepted.*

This 300 room hotel is near the center of town, and convenient for the various tourist area in the city. The modern rooms are comfortable. The hotel has a restaurant, lounge and fitness facilities on the premises.

Where to Eat

CAFÉ ASHTON, *610 Main Street in the Ashton Hotel. Tel. 817/332-0100. Credit cards Accepted. Reservations recommended.*

This New American restaurant helmed by young chef Diarmuid Murphy sets a new standard for fine dining in Fort Worth. Only open since 2001, the Café Ashton provides an atmosphere of upscale inventiveness in the elegant boutique Ashton Hotel. The décor is rich but serene in blonde wood and soft yellows with splashed of blue in the dropped glass ceiling. Your food comes dramatically arranged on plates for maximum visual impact, but the taste is what will really make you want to sing.

Breakfast here offers American traditional favorites such as pancakes and eggs, but you should take the opportunity to sample a Continental-style full breakfast and order fresh fish with fried potatoes. For lunch, try the beef stroganoff with herb oil over angel hair pasta. Standouts at dinner include venison and duck, as well as marvelous salads and appetizers.

CACHAREL, *2221 East Lamar Street, Arlington. Tel. 817/640-9981. Credit cards accepted.*

This is not just another French restaurant with the standard fare. The charm of provincial French cooking is found at Cacharel; but here it is permeated with the influence of Texas. The inventive recipes recreate traditional French dishes with American flare. Fresh fish from the Gulf, ostrich meat and tropical fruit, among other non-French ingredients, are used. The intimate dining room overlooks metropolitan Fort Worth. The set course meals are recommended. Each night the menu changes. From Fort Worth, travel east on Highway 30; take Highway 360 south and exit Lamar Boulevard.

CATTLEMEN'S STEAK HOUSE, *2458 North Main Street. Tel. 817/624-3945. Credit cards accepted.*

With all the fancy grilling and smoking that has overtaken current cooking trends in other cities, it is not easy to find a charcoal broiled steak—except at Cattlemen's, where that is the norm. You can also select from a variety of seafood or juicy ribs. The logical place for a steak house is right next to the stockyards, which is where you will find Cattlemen's.

JOE T. GARCIA'S, *2201 North Commerce Street. Tel. 817/626-4356.*

Dining at this restaurant is a tradition for most residents of Fort Worth, and part of the ritual is a very long wait. The Tex-Mex food tastes as though you were sitting down for dinner cooked in a family's kitchen. You could toss a coin to decide what to order-really you have but two choices, either enchiladas or fajitas. The dishes are equally popular and delicious. The enchiladas are made in the old-fashioned way, which means heavy on the oil. The margaritas complete the experience of a meal at Joe T. Garcia's. The prices are so low, that the restaurant accepts neither credit cards nor reservations. You can go around the corner to Joe T. Garcia's bakery for desert.

PARIS COFFEE SHOP, *700 West Magnolia Avenue. Tel. 817/335-2041. Credit cards accepted.*

This place is all coffee shop, and no Paris (unless, of course, we're talking about Paris, Texas). The food is southern cooking at its best. Nothing fancy, but the sort of plates you would get from your grandma's kitchen. Lunch is usually a meaty dish, like chicken-fried steak or meatloaf. Breakfast comes in huge portions, with plenty of eggs, sausage and (of course) grits. The corn bread arrives at the table hot, and the gravy has the full flavor that means it can be only homemade.

PULIDO'S, *2900 Pulido Street. 817/732-7571. Credit cards accepted.*

People from all around the Metroplex come to Pulido's. While the food is good, they often come for the music. On Friday nights Pulido's features a harp player from Veracruz, Mexico. He is the foremost musician in this particular style of music, and he has played Carnegie Hall among other notable venues. As you enjoy the tropical decor of the restaurant and absorb yourself in the harp melodies, do not forget to order. Among the selections are many combination platters, such as the Caballero Platter which comes with a 10-ounce sirloin, enchilada, beans and potatoes. The homemade tamales are exceptional. And for dessert you can get fluffy sopapillas, light puff pastry served with honey.

Seeing the Sights

There is no doubt that the **Stockyards**, *140 East Exchange Avenue, Tel. 817/624-4741*, are the primary attraction in the city. The many turn-of-the-century buildings were the center of life in Fort Worth at one time. Today the entire area is renovated for visitors. The area recreates the Old West, with shops, restaurants and entertainment. The **Stockyards Museum**, *131 Exchange Avenue, Tel. 817/624-4741*, shows the importance of the cattle industry during Texas in the early twentieth century. The exhibits reveal the economic and social impact of ranching.

Every Saturday evening, from April through September, a rodeo is held at the Stockyards. The cowboys are some of the finest professionals around and are sure to put on a good show. The stockyards are located north of Interstate Highway 30; take the Commerce Street exit. You can take a steam train, the **Tarantula**, *Tel. 817/625-7245 or 800/952-5717*, from the Stockyards to the Arts District.

Life in the early days of Fort Worth is reconstructed at the **Log Cabin Village**, *2250 University Drive, Tel. 817/926-5881*. You can walk through homes that are decked out as though the pioneers were still living in them. The arts district is north of this area, on University Drive.

The **Kimbell Art Museum**, *3333 Camp Bowie, Tel. 332-8451, Tuesday to Thursday and Saturday 10am to 5pm, Friday and Sunday noon to 5pm*, is often referred to as the finest art museum in Texas. The museum was based on a private collection and over the years has grown into one of the most comprehensive representations of art to be found anywhere. Much of the lighting is natural, allowing masterpieces to be seen in a unique manner. The museum hosts traveling exhibitions of international stature.

The work of current artists is displayed at the **Modern Art Museum**, *1309 Montgomery Street, Tuesday to Sunday noon to 5pm*. Exhibits change regularly. Educational programs add to the offerings of this museum.

The new **Museum of Science and History**, *1501 Montgomery Street, Tel. 817/732-1631, Monday to Friday 9am to 5pm, Saturday and Sunday 9am to 9pm, admission fee*, is a welcome high-tech learning center in the city arts district. The hands-on exhibits allow children to dig like an archaeologist, experience the galaxy in the planetarium and take fun and educational workshops. The museum's **Omni Theater**, *Tel. 817/732-1631*, shows movies from 10:30am to 11:30pm; daily schedules vary.

Sid Richardson made his fortune in Texas oil, but he left his mark by the many endowments he made. The **Sid Richardson Collection of Western Art**, *309 Main Street, Tel. 817/332-6554*, is one such gift. The museum highlights masterpieces that portray life in the American West. The collection breathes depth and passion into the lore of the cowboy.

The **Fort Worth Botanical Garden**, *3220 Botanic Drive, Tel. 817/332-2272*, has acres of outdoor gardens that replicate a variety of habitats. The conservatory offers a more formal look at fauna and presents educational programs. The Japanese Garden is a tranquil and meditative abode sculptured in the formal Japanese style.

The **Fort Worth Zoo**, *1989 Colonial Parkway, Tel. 817/871-7050, open daily 10am-5pm, admission fee*, represents the amazing bio-diversity of the planet. As home to over 5000 animal, the zoo provides habitats for reptiles, birds of prey, primates and a special area for Asian animals. The zoo has received kudos as one of the finest in the nation. From Interstate Highway 30, take the University Street exit south to Colonial Street.

Nightlife & Entertainment

The **Bass Performance Hall**, *525 Commerce Street, Tel. 817/212-4300*, opened in 1998 and provides a home for the **Fort Worth Symphony**, *Tel. 817/926-8831*, **Fort Worth Ballet**, *Tel. 817/763-0207*, and the **Fort Worth Opera**, *Tel. 817/731-0833*. The magnificent concert hall and theater opens directly onto Sundance Square, making it an integral and lively part of Fort Worth's night life.

According to legend, when Butch Cassidy and the Sundance Kid were hiding from the law, they came to Fort Worth. The town had a rough area known as Hell's Half Acre, which was the setting for debauchery cowboy-style. Times have indeed changed, and the convention center stands on what was once Hell's Half Acre. But to keep the memory of by-gone wild days intact, a small historic square bears the name of Butch Cassidy's partner. **Sundance Square** covers fourteen downtown blocks and is full of casual restaurants, bars and entertainment. The area is within Second and Fifth Streets, to the north and south, and Throckmorton and Commerce to the east and west.

To the west of Fort Worth you will find **Six Flags Over Texas**, *Tel. 817/2640-8900*, which is not a history lesson, but a grand Warner Brothers amusement park. This was the first of the parks in Texas, but continual additions keep the rides as loopy and frightening as technology allows. Like the twin cities of Dallas and Fort Worth, there are twin Six Flags. Hurricane Harbor is a giant water park, with the tallest water raft ride in the nation. From Fort Worth, take Highway 30 west, then Highway 360 south.

NIGHTCLUBS

Billy Bob's Texas, 2520 Rodeo Plaza, Tel. 817/624-7117, is the definition of "honky tonk." And this dance hall seems to be about as big as Texas; the dance floor alone is over 1500 square feet. If you want to be a cowboy-even just for one night-this is the place to go. The dance floor is full of people sporting cowboy hats and boot-cut jeans. The club is an institution in Fort Worth, and certainly the most famous country-western scene in the state. Billy Bob's is open every night. Live entertainment is featured some nights; there is always a cover charge.

Caravan of Dreams, *312 Houston Street, Tel. 817/877-3000*, is one of the Southwest's premier venues for live jazz music. The complex has a club which attracts music enthusiasts, and a theater that incorporates nature into its construction. The performing arts stage holds productions in the spring through the late summer. The Caravan of Dreams is part of the civic center and hosts excellent performances during the year.

Sports & Recreation

The finest animals in the state are found at the **Fort Worth Stock Show and Rodeo**, *Tel. 817/877-2400*, which is held at the end of January. The events span three weeks and include a rodeo, parade, and of course, livestock show. The **Will Rogers Memorial Center**, *3400 Burnett-Tandy Drive*, is the site of the celebration. The Center is west of the center of town; from Interstate Highway 30, take the Montgomery Street exit north.

The **Texas Rangers** thrill fans at *The Ball Park in Arlington, 817/273-5100*. The season begins in April and runs through September (October if the team is in the playoffs); games are held in the evening. You can tour the stadium for a behind-the-scenes perspective of the game. Also the **Legends of the Game Baseball Museum and Learning Center**, *Tel. 817/273-5099*, is on the complex grounds. From Interstate Highway 30, exit Collins Street south. The Ballpark is close to the highway.

NASCAR racing has become one of the most popular spectator sports in the United States. When it opened in 1997 the **Texas Motor Speedway**, *3601 Highway 113 at Interstate Highway 35, Tel. 817/215-8500*, brought this exciting sport to Texas. The track is an enormous one and a half mile oval, allowing important races to be run. The total estimated seating capacity of the Speedway is a mind-blowing 205,000.

Excursions & Day Trips

American Airlines chose the Dallas-Fort Worth area as its home base, and consequently the museum that chronicles American's history is located near DFW Airport. The **American Airlines C. R. Smith Museum**, 4106 Highway 360, Tel. 817/967-1560, Wednesday to Saturday, 10am to 6pm, Sunday noon to 5pm, Admission free, chronicles the history of commercial flight through this airline's perspective. From Highway 183, take Highway 360 south.

GLEN ROSE

Nature lovers will enjoy the wildlife at **Fossil Rim Wildlife Center**, *Highway 67, Glen Rose, Tel. 817/897-2960*, a preserve for living animals. Visitors drive along nine and one-half miles of trails through the homes of giraffes, large cats, zebras and an array of other animals. Prehistory is well represented at Fossil Rim; guests can walk along nature trails and hunt for fossils. Fossil Rim is an educational facility. The 3000-acre preserve is home to nearly 1000 species of exotic animals, some of which are rare. Part of the preservation attempts includes breeding endangered species such as the white rhino. Taking a guided tour will acquaint you with the science behind managing the preserve. The cozy lodge provides a luxurious vacation in the country. The more adventurous can take an African-style tent safari. The only shots fired on the safari will be with a camera, though. From Fort Worth, take Loop 820 south, exit Highway 67 and go south to Glen Rose. Fossil Rim is three miles south of Glen Rose on Highway 67.

The **Dinosaur Valley Park**, *Farm Road 205, Glen Rose, Tel. 806/897-4588*, is named for the fossilized dinosaur footprints found there. You can view some of the tracks at the park's museum. The exhibits provide information about the geography of the area in the age of the dinosaurs. The park offers primitive campsites and some with hook-ups. Six miles of hiking trails lead through the interesting river landscape. You can swim in the Brazos River. From Fort Worth, take Highway 67 south to Glen Rose. Head west on Farm Road 205. Dinosaur Valley is on Park Road 59, four miles from Highway 67.

Practical Information

- **American Automobile Association (AAA)**, *5431 South Hulen Street, Tel. 817/370-3000*
- **Fort Worth Convention and Visitors Bureau**, *415 East Street, Tel. 817/336-8791 or 800/433-5747*
- **Arts Council of Fort Worth**, *Tel. 817/870-2564*. Provides information about performing arts events in the city.
- **Stockyards Visitor Center**, *130 East Exchange Street, Tel. 817/626-7921*

Athens

This unassuming town created the staple food of the all-American hamburger. Every September the city commemorates the inventor, Fletcher Davis, with a Hamburger Cook-off and Trade Fair.

Arrivals & Departures

From Dallas, take Interstate Highway 45 south for about 55 miles to Corsicana. In Corsicana, take Highway 31 east another 37 miles to Athens. This stretch of Highway 31 is a scenic little part of the Texas Lakes Trail.

Where to Stay

DUNSAVAGE FARMS, *6044 FM 804, Tel. 903/675-4193, Website: www.virtualcities.com/ons/tx/d/txdc801.htm. 3 Rooms. Rates: $90-100.*

A peaceful retreat in the woods east of Athens awaits you at this Bed and Breakfast establishment. The bright red house sits on a hill overlooking a small lake. Rooms contain king or queen-sized beds and private baths. A hearty gourmet breakfast will tempt you out of bed early, and guests are entitled to use the nearby Cain Center fitness facility.

CARRIAGE HOUSE, *Hickory Hill Farm, Route 2 box 2153. Tel. 903/677-3939 or 800/808-BEDS. Rates: $90-120. Credit cards accepted.*

Hickory Hill Farm is only three miles from Athens, but it seems to be an eternity away from any city. Rolling hills and a rustic setting provide a perfect get-away. The carriage house of the old farm has been remade into three guest rooms. The rooms are furnished with antiques and each has a private bath. The upstairs is actually a private suite. All rooms include breakfast and a snack in the afternoon. From downtown Athens, take Highway 19 south for three miles. Turn west on Farm-to-Market Road 753. Travel about two and one-half miles; the farm is on the north side of the road

Seeing the Sights

The **Texas Freshwater Fisheries Center**, *5550 Flat Creek Road, Tel. 903/676-BASS, Fax 903/676-FISH, Open daily 10am to 5pm, Admission $4 adults; $3 seniors; $2 children*, lets you into the world of game fish. The Texas Parks and Wildlife Department runs the complex that includes the Edwin L. Cox visitors center, pond and reservoir, and casting pond. The wetlands and alligator pond give you a glimpse of the fearsome American alligator, an east Texas native. During the dive show, the theater turns into a 26,000-gallon dive tank, and the diver answers audience questions. If learning about the fish makes you want to eat one, you can get casting lessons and catch fish in the casting pond. Scientific research is conducted at the fish hatchery, which is open for tours.

Tyler

Tyler is the "Rose Capital of the U.S.A." due to the prominence of its rose-growing industry. The centerpiece of the city is the nation's largest public rose garden. Tyler is best known for its annual **Rose Festival**, which has been held for over 65 years. This old-fashioned remnant of southern culture is part floral celebration and part pageantry. Tyler became a city in 1848, and grew when the railroad became the main artery of transportation through the area. Today Tyler is a small town with a big tradition of rose growing.

The **Annual Texas Rose Festival** is held in mid-October. The highlight of the five-day event is the Rose Festival Parade, which takes place near downtown. Stadium seats require a ticket ($5 admission), and spectators can stand along the closed parade route ($3 admission). Numerous other events such as square dances, a car show, and informative lectures about roses are open to the general public. The coronation of the Rose Queen is the main event for Tyler locals. An entire year of preparation culminates in the fanciful Coronation performance (tickets $20 or $25), where area debutantes dressed in giant hoop-skirted ball gowns.

For more information or an order form for tickets, contact the **Texas Rose Festival Association**, *PO Box 8224, Tyler, Texas 75711, Fax 903/597-3031.* Tours of the **Tyler Nursery** are by reservation only (no admission charge). To arrange a tour, contact the Convention and Visitors Bureau, *Tel. 903/592-1661, ext. 229.*

Arrivals & Departures

Air traffic in Tyler uses **Ponds Field Airport**, which is about seven miles west of the city on Highway 64. Tyler is south of Interstate Highway 20. Take Highway 69 south from Interstate Highway 20 to reach Tyler.

Orientation

Highway 69 bisects the city from north to south; Loop 323 circles the city. Highway 110, which is in the southeast corner of Tyler, is also called Troupe Highway.

Where to Stay

ROSEVINE INN BED AND BREAKFAST, *415 South Vine Avenue. Tel. 903/592-2221, Fax 592-5522, Website: www.rosevineinn.com. 5 Rooms, 2 Suites. Rates: $79 to $150. Credit cards accepted.*

The Rosevine Inn is a two story brick home located a few blocks from downtown. The neighborhood is a good area for long, quiet strolls. Although the house itself is not very old, the antique furnishings provide a quaint atmosphere. The rooms are large with warm decor. You can enjoy the perks of staying in a modern home, such as the hot tub and sauna and private baths for each room. Guests receive complimentary refreshments and a full breakfast.

WOLDERT-SPENCE MANOR, *611 West Woldert Street. Tel. 800/965-3378 or 903/533-9057, Fax 903/531-0293, Website: www.woldert-spence.com. Rates: $90 to $125. Credit cards accepted.*

The family members that built the house were prominent landholders in

Texas when it was an independent republic. The home was constructed in 1859 and no doubt was a landmark in its time. The single-story home close to downtown has beautiful antiques throughout and stained-glass windows in many of its rooms. Large shade trees adorn the property. Guests can relax in the large yard or outdoor hot tub.

BED OF ROSES COUNTRY INN, *Highway 69 North. Tel. 800/265-7673, Fax 903/882-3597. Rates: $55 to $65. Credit cards accepted.*

This home, built in 1953, has three guest rooms with a shared bathroom. Each room has a telephone. The quaint furnishings reflect the character of the area.

HAMPTON INN, *3130 Troupe Highway. Tel. 903/596-7752, Fax 903/596-7765. Rates: $63 to $89.*

Rooms have amenities such as microwave ovens, small refrigerators and hair dryers. Some rooms have spa bathtubs. From Interstate Highway 20, exit Highway 69 and go south to Loop 323. Take 323 south to the Troupe (Highway 110) exit. Take Troupe Highway north for about five miles.

LA QUINTA INN, *1601 West Southwest Loop 323. Tel. 903/561-2223, Fax 903/581-5708. Rates: $59 to $66. Credit cards accepted.*

This comfortable motel offers free continental breakfast to its guests. Children under the age of 18 stay free with their parents. The La Quinta is located on the southwest part of Loop 323. From Interstate Highway 20, take Highway 69 south to Loop 323. Travel south on 323, exit Old Jacksonville Road.

RESIDENCE INN, *3303 Troup Highway. Tel. 903/595-5188 or 800/331-3131, Fax 903/595-5719. Rates: $69 to $89. Credit cards accepted.*

Studio style rooms have kitchen and living areas. The Residence Inn has fitness facilities that include a heated pool and spa. Pets may stay in rooms for an extra charge. Complimentary breakfast provided. A free shuttle service to the airport is provided. From Interstate Highway 20, exit Highway 69. Travel south to Loop 323, then go east to Highway 110. This inn is 17 miles from the airport and four miles from the city center.

Where to Eat

BERNARD CASE'S, *7701 South Broadway. Tel. 903/581-0744. Credit cards accepted.*

This restaurant is a few miles from the center of the city, but you will feel as though you are eating in Louisiana. A combination of delicate French sauces and the true zeal of Cajun cooking make the meals exceptional. Seafood is the house specialty, and steak and chicken are also on the menu.

Seeing the Sights

The hallmark of Tyler, roses, are grown to abundance in the **Tyler Municipal Rose Garden**, *1900 West Front Street, Tel. 903/531-1370, Open* *daily 8am to 5pm.* The garden covers 22 acres and has the latest and some of the most unusual rose bushes in the 500 varieties grown here. A museum dedicated to the Annual Rose Festival is on the garden grounds.

The former Carnegie Library is now the **Carnegie History Center**, *125 College Street, Tuesday to Sunday 1pm to 5pm*, has a good collection of pieces of daily life from the time of the Republic of Texas. Exhibits focus on life in Texas during the Civil War. The museum is free to the public.

An interesting glimpse into the past is revealed at the **Goodman Museum**, *624 North Broadway, Wednesday to Sunday 1pm to 5pm*. The Musuem is in a Grecian Revival home built in 1859. The stately manor holds a very extensive collection of furniture and medical instruments from the years before the Civil War.

Sports & Recreation

The **Tyler State Park**, *789 Park Road 16, Tel. 903/597-5338*, allows guests to enjoy the beautiful nature of the Piney Woods area. Wooded hiking trails and an 8.5-mile mountain bike trail take visitors into the serene wilderness. Swimming and fishing are permitted on the park's small lake. Campsites with full hookups and picnic areas are available. From Tyler, travel north on Farm Road 14. The park is two miles north of Interstate Highway 20.

Practical Information

You can learn more about Tyler by contacting the **Convention and Visitor's Bureau**, *P. O. Box 390, Tyler, Texas 75710. Tel. 903/592-1661 or 800/235-5712.*

Jefferson

Jefferson grew quickly from a frontier village of log cabins into a town of elegant homes belonging to wealthy merchant families. In the late 1800's, when Jefferson refused a railroad in order to concentrate on the already established steamboat business, the town could not have realized that it was freezing itself out of the chance to become a big, prosperous city. But all's well that ends well, and today the town is a time capsule of prosperous Victorian-era Texas.

Jefferson is full of historic homes, many of which are bed and breakfast establishments. The city offers tours of these historic sites or you can take a self-guided tour. Most homes charge admission fees, but walking or driving past and admiring the ornate exteriors is free.

Christmas in Northeast Texas & Louisiana

Texans are not known as sentimental folk, but venture to northeast Texas during the Christmas season and you'll find old-time country celebrations. Marshall, famous for its Christmas light decorations that include a courthouse illuminated with five million lights, is only part of the month-long seasonal celebration. Jefferson offers a more traditional candlelight trail of the city's historic homes. Jacksonville has an Old-fashioned Christmas with a parade, sing-a-long and boat parade on Lake Jacksonville during the second week of December.

Cross the border to Shreveport, Louisiana for Lights On Line, a five-mile light show on Line Avenue. The American Rose Center in Shreveport has a show of light sculptures. Bossier, Louisiana strings lights along the Barksdale Air Force Base water tower and hosts an annual Christmas parade. On the first Saturday in December, Natchitoches, Louisiana holds its Christmas Festival that includes a parade, fireworks and lights.

Marshall is on Interstate Highway 20. Jefferson is just north of Marshall, on United States Highway 59. Shreveport and Bossier City Louisiana are east of Marshall on Interstate Highway 20. Natchitoches is south on Interstate Highway 49, which crosses Interstate Highway 20.

Arrivals & Departures

Jefferson is located at the crossroads of Highway 59, which runs north/south, and Highway 49.

Getting Around Town

To catch a glimpse of the history of Jefferson the easy way, jump aboard one of the trolley-style buses that offer tours. The tours include all major places of interest and fill tourists in on the regional folklore. Tours leave at 11am, 1pm and 3pm daily from the **Historic Jefferson Tours Headquarters**, *222 East Austin Street, Tel. 903/665-1665.*

You can also take a one-hour narrated tour of Jefferson and the surrounding bayou with **Turning Basin Riverboat Tours**, *across the Polk Street Bridge from downtown, Tel. 903/665-2222.* Tours are given daily from April through October, and cost $6.50 for adults, $4 for children 12 and under.

Where to Stay

You can easily find a bed and breakfast by using the **Book-A-Bed-Ahead Reservation Service**, *P.O. Box 723, Jefferson, Texas 75657, Tel. 903/665-*

3956 or 800/486-2627, Fax 903/665-8551, which offers accommodation at 15 of the best historic inns in Jefferson. There is no charge for the service.

THE CAPTAIN'S CASTLE AND CARRIAGE HOUSE INN, *403 East Walker Street. Tel. 903/665-2330, Toll free 800/650-2230, Website: captainscastle.com. 7 Rooms. Rates: $100 to $120.*

The main house is built in the style of Tennessee Planters Architecture. Tall trees and manicured gardens highlight the beauty of the tall columned estate. The main house has three rooms, each furnished with period antiques. Adjacent to the house is the smaller carriage house, which has three guest rooms, each with a private bath. The private cottage has a fireplace and romantic sitting room. Guests awaken to fresh coffee and muffins in the morning. A full breakfast is served in the dining room.

JEFFERSON HOTEL, *124 West Austin Street. Tel. 903/665-2631, Fax 906/665-2222, Toll free 866/33-HOTEL, Website: historicjeffersonhotel.com. 25 Rooms. Rates: $60 to $125. Credit cards accepted.*

When this hotel first opened for business its guests were cotton bales-the building was a warehouse until 1900. When the railroad finally squelched the steamboat as a practical mode of shipping, the need for cotton warehouses consequently dried up. Tourism still played a role in Jefferson, so the Hotel Jefferson opened its doors. The modern, renovated Hotel Jefferson has a variety of room sizes, from those with a standard full bed to the luxurious master suite. Every one of the 25 rooms is different. Lamache's Italian Restaurant occupies the ground floor, serving lunch and dinner.

McKAY HOUSE BED & BREAKFAST, *306 East Delta Street. Tel. 903/ 665-7322, Fax 903/665-8551, Toll free 800/468-2627, Website: www.mckayhouse.com. 5 Rooms, 3 Suites. Rates: $89 to $169. Credit cards accepted.*

The McKay House has a sturdy front porch and a white picket fence, the perfect home away from home. Each of the four rooms and one suite in the main house has a private bath. Lady Bird Johnson's favorite room is the McKay Room, featuring a majestic four-poster bed and a coal-burning fireplace. The Sunday House, the cottage, has two suites each with its own bath and living areas. The home is decorated with furnishings from the late 1800s, and even the guests are clothed in their own set of Victorian nightclothes, complete with nightcap. A generous breakfast called "the Gentleman's breakfast" is served in the conservatory. Reservations are recommended.

Where to Eat

THE STILLWATER INN RESTAURANT, *203 East Broadway. Tel. 903/ 665-8415. Dinner served nightly except Sunday, from 6pm to closing. Credit cards accepted.*

This 1890s house contains a fine bed and breakfast inn, but the real star here is the cuisine. Given three stars in the Mobil Travel Guide, the Stillwater provides the best food in town in a lovely and intimate setting. The food is mostly familiar favorites like shrimp scampi, roasted pork tenderloin, New York strip, and rack of lamb. The wine list is extensive, and you can sip a glass of port after your meal.

Seeing the Sights

The **Twin Oaks Plantation**, *Farm Road 134, Tel. 903/665-3535, open Wednesday to Saturday 4 and 5pm*, is worth a visit simply because it is an uncommon type of house in Texas. The mansion represents more closely the life of Louisiana and the Deep South. Working plantations were not common in Texas, although there were slave-holding families. The Twin Oaks Plantation was a working farm. The home has original decor, with a notable collection of the European art fashionable in the south at the time. The Twin Oaks Plantation is open for tours only which are given at 4pm and 5pm. Special arrangements can be made for group tours.

The **Carnegie Library**, *301 Lafayette Street, Tuesday to Friday noon to 5pm, closed Monday, Saturday and Sunday*, has served the community since it was built in 1907. Displays about the history of the area are free to the public. The building itself is a living museum of the life, history and community of the area.

For a different take on the historic tour route, **Wagon Tours** depart across the street from the Jefferson Historical Society Museum. Mules pull the small wagons, so the pace is leisurely.

The best way to see big **Cypress Bayou** is by boat. Small tourist boats make trips daily. The boat dock is located under Polk Street Bridge on United States Highway 59, *Tel. 903/665-2222*. The tranquillity of the bayou envelops visitors. You can see some of the last remaining untouched bayou areas in Texas. Thick trees and calm glassy water is the backdrop for the 45-minute ride.

Practical Information

The staff at the **Marion County Chamber of Commerce**, *118 North Vale Street, Tel. 903/665-2672, Toll free 888/GO RELAX*, will be happy to fill you in on all the best bed and breakfast spots in town and arrange tours for you.

e a s t t e x a s

If you spend some time in this part of the state, your vacation photographs will confuse the folks back home. Instead of the expected images of endless dusty prairies with an arid blue sky stretching out overhead, they'll see pictures of lush forests, limpid bayous, and mysterious Indian mounds. The **Piney Woods** of East Texas cover an area the size of *all* of New England's forest areas combined. While **Houston** is the mass of sprawling urban energy you would expect, past its boundaries another, older Texas exists. Languorous and humid, sharing more ambiance with the Deep South than the Western frontier, East Texas is a place to pause...relax...and enjoy.

Houston

Houston is the fourth largest city in the United States, with a greater metropolitan population of 4.3 million. It traces its beginnings to the ambitions of two brothers, Augustus and John Allen. They arrived in the small settlement of what was then called Frottstown in 1836, and imagined it as a center of commerce and growth. They ran advertisements for "the town of Houston," and cajoled the state Congress into designating the town the capital of the new Republic of Texas. On January 1, 1837 the "town" was 12 residents and one log cabin – four months later 1,500 people and 100 houses had sprouted in the gumbo soil of Houston.

And so the story has continued even to the present day. Houston seems to grow in spurts, booming markets spurring explosions of development that inevitably collapse back into periods of tranquility, until the next big boom

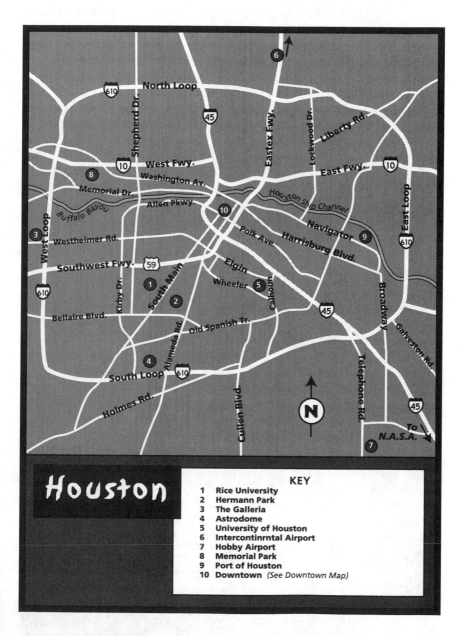

Houston

KEY

1 Rice University
2 Hermann Park
3 The Galleria
4 Astrodome
5 University of Houston
6 Intercontinrntal Airport
7 Hobby Airport
8 Memorial Park
9 Port of Houston
10 Downtown *(See Downtown Map)*

comes along. Houston has relied on waterway access for trade and growth since the days of its infancy. The brothers Allen envisioned huge ships steaming right up tiny Buffalo Bayou into the city. Today, the **Houston Ship Channel** remains one of the busiest waterways in the nation. Within the city's inner sanctum, however, the sound and fury of commerce gives way to quiet streets lined with mossy oaks, top-notch museums, and an exuberant, diverse community.

Sam Houston

Sam Houston did not actually spend much time in his namesake city. The state government abandoned the town of Houston for the more temperate climes of Austin in 1839. Something of Sam Houston's tempestuous nature must have rubbed off on the fledgling city, however, for it remains as rambunctious as the man it honors.

Samuel Houston, born in 1793 on a plantation in Virginia, ran away from home as a teenager to live with the Cherokee. He stayed with them for three years, earning the Indian name Colonneh, or "the Raven." For the rest of his life, Houston maintained great respect and sympathy for Native Americans.

During the War of 1812, Houston became a favorite of General Andrew Jackson. After practicing law and embarking upon a successful political career in Tennessee, eventually becoming governor of that state, something happened. What it was, nobody can say for certain, but Houston's eleven-week-old marriage and political office both ended abruptly, and he joined the Cherokee again in a self-imposed exile. After a second marriage (under Cherokee law, his first marriage still on the books) and a scrape with a United States representative, Houston sought yet another new beginning – in Mexican Texas.

Did Houston go to Texas with the idea of forming an independent nation, did he go as an agent for U.S. interests, or was he simply hoping to make a fortune on land speculation? In the end, the answer doesn't matter, for he did all three. His role in the battle for independence with Mexico and his emphatic defeat of Santa Anna's troops at San Jacinto made Houston's name synonymous with Texas.

After Texas joined the United States, Sam Houston went on to become a United States senator, then governor of the State of Texas. Opposed to Texas joining the Confederacy, Houston lost that battle and resigned the office of governor in 1861. He moved to Huntsville, north of Houston, where he lived for his remaining years with his third wife and their eight children.

Market Square was the meeting place of merchants and the site of local government buildings throughout the nineteenth century. This area fell into economic depression, and then was used as a parking lot. Market Square is once again a center of commerce, albeit of another type. Restaurants and bars surround Market Square Park, which offers a striking view of the downtown skyscrapers.

During the nineteenth century, the city was a rugged place, and women were not permitted downtown. So when the wealthy merchants built their homes, they went to what was then the outskirts of town. East Texas cotton farmers made downtown Houston their center of commerce. The **Houston Cotton Exchange** on Travis Street, built in 1884, shows that cotton was indeed king when it came to the Houston economy.

Houston remained in the shadow of neighboring Galveston, which had a larger port and thriving economy at the turn-of-the century. Galveston rivaled New Orleans in importance as a shipping center until the hurricane of 1900 devastated the coast. That fierce storm washed the city away, and permanently diminished its importance as a commercial center. Trade quickly shifted to Houston.

Houston's biggest boom came courtesy of oil. The **Port of Houston** looms amid many smaller port cities, making the area an artery for the oil trade. Much of the city took shape in the 1970s and early 1980s; the unbridled glitz of that era gives the high-dollar gloss to Houston's facade. The image of the urban cowboy, though fading, remains evident in pockets of the city.

You can step into cowboy boots of your own at the largest rodeo in the world - which is, of course, held in Houston. The annual winter event has grown in size every year since its founding in 1932. The **Houston Livestock Show and Rodeo** starts in mid-February and lasts until Texas Independence Day on March 2nd. Houstonians and visitors alike attend festivities like the annual Trail Ride, a Rodeo 10K Run, and the Rodeo Parade. For more information on the rodeo, see *Sports & Recreation* below.

Arrivals & Depatures
By Plane

Houston has two major airports. **George Bush Intercontinental Airport** (airline code IAH), *Website www.houstonairportsystem.org/ iah_default.htm,* renamed in honor of the elder Bush president who calls Houston home, is the 11th busiest airport in the nation. Bush Intercontinental has four terminals with a total of 89 gates. An underground train connects terminals A, B, C, The Mickey Leland International Terminal, and the Marriott Hotel, which is on the airport grounds. IAH serves as the hub for Houston-headquartered Continental Airlines.

Many area hotels and motels run courtesy vans to Bush Intercontinental Airport for their guests. Public METRO buses stop at the south side of Terminal

C. Routes 101 and 102 serve Bush Intercontinental, and the fare for either is $1.50.

Each terminal has a passenger pick-up area for taxicabs. Fares to Houston range from $33.50 to the north sections of the city to $73.50 to NASA. Four passengers can ride for the price of one, so if you can share a cab you'll save some money. Be aware that IAH is about 23 miles north of downtown, and give yourself ample time to get there.

Inexpensive shuttle service to the airport and central Houston is provided by **Express Shuttle USA**, *950 McCarty Road, Tel. 713/523-8888, Toll free 888/COACH USA, Website: www.coachusa.com/houston/index.cfm?mode=shuttle_resi*. The shuttles serve downtown, the Medical Center, the Reliant Stadium, the Galleria, Greenway Plaza and Westside. Special shuttles connect Bush Intercontinental to Hobby Airport. Fares range from $20-24 one-way. Children under 12 are charged $6.

Galveston Limousine Service, *Tel. 409/744-5466, Toll free 800/640-4826, Website www.galvestonlimousineservice.com,* serves Galveston and the Bay Area. Fares range from $25-30 for a one-way ride to League City, Texas City, NASA, or Galveston.

William P. Hobby Airport (Airline code HOU), named for a former state governor, handles domestic flights to over 60 cities and is used by eight airlines, including Southwest, American, and Delta. As they do for IAH, many hotels have courtesy vans for guests arriving and departing from Hobby Airport. If you are planning on staying in downtown Houston and the airfares to either airport are roughly the same, try to get a flight to Hobby. It's smaller and much closer to the center of town. To get to Hobby Airport, take the Gulf Freeway (Interstate Highway 45) south from Loop 610.

Taxi Rates & Airports in Houston

Whenever you take a taxicab to or from a Houston airport, be sure to ask what the flat rate is in advance. All taxi fares to and from the airports in Houston are required to adhere to a flat zone rate. Taxicabs are also required to keep a list of the zone rates posted where passengers can see it. Fares are regulated by the City of Houston, and are among the least expensive in the country for a city of this size. However, this leads to an unfortunate tendency for some unscrupulous drivers to overcharge. A local news investigation in 1998 found that 80 percent of the cab drivers they tested charged the more expensive meter rate rather than the flat rate.

Additional charge-per-load fees are included in the flat rates, but tips are not. If your driver has delivered you successfully to your destination in a courteous and efficient manner, it is customary to tip about 15 percent of the fare, with an additional $.50-1.00 per large bag.

Express Shuttle USA, *950 McCarty Road, Tel. 713/523-8888, Toll free 888/COACH USA, Website www.coachusa.com/houston/index.cfm?mode=shuttle_resi*, charges between $14-24 for one-way shuttle service. The shuttles serve downtown, the Medical Center, the Reliant Stadium, the Galleria, Greenway Plaza, and Westside. Children under 12 are charged $6.

Galveston Limousine Service, *Tel. 409/744-5466, Toll free 800/640-4826, Website www.galvestonlimousineservice.com*, serves Galveston and the Bay Area. Fares range from $18-25 for a one-way ride to League City, Texas City, NASA, or Galveston.

Taxicabs have a passenger pick-up station just out the doors by the lower level baggage claim. Taxi rates to different areas in Houston range from $18.50 (downtown) to $53.50 (north Houston). The city METRO bus service has a bus stop on the same level, outside the baggage claim area.

Both airports have car rental desks and all major national car rental agencies serve Houston.

By Bus & Train

The **Greyhound Bus Terminal**, *2121 Main Street, Tel. 800/231-2222 or 713/759-6565* is near the business district.

The **Amtrak Station**, *902 Washington Avenue, Tel. 800/USA-RAIL (872-7245)*, is located downtown. From Interstate Highway 10, exit Smith Street, take Franklin Street to Bagby and continue to Washington.

Houston is on the Amtrak Sunset Limited route, which travels between Los Angeles and Miami. From Houston the Sunset Limited goes to San Antonio, Del Rio, Sanderson, Alpine and El Paso. Passengers going to Dallas transfer to the Amtrak Throughway Bus.

Cruise Ships

Houston is a port for **Royal Olympic Cruises**, *Tel. 800/872-6400, Website www.royalolympiccruises.com*, which offers a 12-day Panama Canal cruise, as well as cruises to Cozumel, Mexico and Ocho Rios, Jamaica.

Other cruise lines such as Norwegian Cruise Line and Carnival include Houston in their itineraries, but the schedules are constantly changing. For up-to-date information on cruises from Houston and Galveston, contact **The Texas Cruise Company**, *P.O. Box 1502, Crosby, Texas 77532, Tel. 281/328-3504, Toll free 800/955-1665, Website: www.cruisecompany.net*.

Orientation

Loop 610 encircles the central part of Houston. Another loop, the Sam Houston Parkway (or Beltway 8) makes a larger concentric circle around the whole Greater Houston area. Unlike Dallas, which is a conglomeration of small cities, Houston is more cohesive. There are various incorporated cities and

Houston Highway's Changing Names!

When you get directions for highway driving in Houston, the name of the highway may not match the name on the map. Each highway in Houston has a given name that lets you know more specifically which way you're heading.

Katy Freeway: Interstate Highway 10 west of downtown

East-Tex Freeway: Interstate Highway 10 east of downtown

Gulf Freeway: Interstate Highway 45 south of downtown

Southwest Freeway: Highway 59

North (South, East, West) Loop: Loop 610

Beltway 8: Sam Houston Tollway

districts and bedroom communities, but they feel (once you get "inside the Loop," as locals call the part of town inside Loop 610) all of a piece. All highways lead to the city center, which has three main commercial areas – downtown, Greenway Plaza, and the Galleria.

Interstate Highway 10 cuts through the city's northern half from east to west. The western part of Interstate Highway 10 is called the Katy Freeway, and the eastern section is known as the East-Tex Freeway. Interstate Highway 45 continues north to Dallas and south to Galveston. The southern part of Interstate Highway 45, which leads to the Gulf of Mexico, is known as the Gulf Freeway.

The historic district to the north and the theater district to the east border the business center of downtown Houston. The Museum District, just south of downtown near Rice University, is home to the major art museums, many cafes, and lovely tree-lined residential areas. Montrose Street and Westheimer Road are popular areas for shopping and nightlife.

Getting Around Town

Taxicabs charge $3.00 for the first mile, and $1.50 for each additional mile; a $1 surcharge is added to all rides from 8pm to 6am. The rates are not high, but fares can add up for the long distances involved in Houston driving. There is no additional charge for up to four passengers. Some recommended cab companies include:

• **American Liberty Cab**, *Tel. 713/999-1096*
• **Fiesta Cab**, *Tel. 713/236-9400*
• **United Cab**, *Tel. 713/699-8040*
• **Yellow Cab**, *Tel. 713/224-4445*

All the major national car rental agencies have offices in Houston; most have more than one. A few of the local companies that rent automobiles and trucks are:

• **Bay Area Auto & Truck Rental**, *2800 Gulf Freeway, Tel. 281/337-1529*
• **PV Car & Truck Rental**, *1201 Crawford Street, Tel. 800/ASK-PVPV*
• **Hillcroft Ford**, *6445 Southwest Freeway, Tel. 281/588-5000*

Private limousines are plentiful in Houston and can be arranged through a hotel or travel agent. **Action Limousines**, *6104 Windswept Lane, Tel. 713/ 781-5466, Toll free 800/736-3546, Website: www.actionlimo.com,* was named operator of the year by *Chauffeur and Limousine Magazine.* The company maintains a 24-hour service line and an immaculate fleet of sedans and luxury vehicles.

Houston has an extensive public bus system, the **METRO**, *Tel. 713/635- 4000, Website: www.hou-metro.harris.tx.us,* which reaches all parts of the metropolitan area. High Occupancy Vehicle (HOV) lanes on the highways allow the buses to stay on schedule. During the week, buses run on 20-minute intervals, and during rush hour this increases to every 10 minutes. In the evenings, service cuts back to 20-minute intervals. On Saturdays the buses come every 20 minutes all day; on Sundays every 30 minutes. Fare is $1 for adults and $.25 for children. A Day Pass allows unlimited transfers for 24 hours and costs $2. You may also purchase 7, 30, and 365-day passes at discounted prices. The route that serves most areas that visitors will want to go is the 15 Fulton/Hiram Clarke. This route runs from the downtown business district through the Medical Center to Reliant Park. One transfer will take you to the Galleria area. Twenty-two hotels are on this route.

In addition to regular city buses, Houston METRO also operates a small fleet of free trolleys that make over 100 downtown stops. The trolleys run about every seven minutes along color-coded routes. Houston METRO is also developing a light-rail system scheduled to begin operation in 2004.

Tours

You can take a variety of tours of Houston and the surrounding cities. Those who enjoy walking can check out historic districts and other attractions with **Discover Houston Tours**, *Visitors Center at 901 Bagby Street, Tel. 713/ 222-9255.* Walking tours are scheduled daily and can be customized for groups with special interests. One of the most popular routes is a tour of downtown Houston's labyrinth of tunnels beneath the skyscrapers.

For an offbeat experience, get to know the ghosts of Houston with **High Spirits**, *2121 Allen Parkway, Tel. 713224-2868.* You'll visit the haunted places of the city by both van and foot. The tours run about three hours and cost $34.95 per person.

Gray Line Tours, *950 McCarty Drive, Tel. 800/334-4441,* offers bus tours of the NASA Space Center and downtown Houston for $45 and $25, respectively.

Excursion tours designed to fit interests of a small or large group can be arranged through **Star Shuttle & Charter**, *Tel. 713/540-6700 or 800/341-6000*. The multilingual guides speak Spanish, French, German or Japanese and offer different modes of transportation from motor coach to limousine.

Where to Stay
DOWNTOWN
Downtown Houston refers to the business district inside Loop 610 (the area smack in the middle of town with all the skyscrapers), and the neighborhoods immediately surrounding it.

Expensive
THE DOUBLETREE AT ALLEN CENTER, *400 Dallas Street. Tel. 713/759-0202, Fax 713/759-1166, Toll free reservations 800/222-TREE, Website: www.doubletree.com. 350 Rooms, 6 Suites. Rates: $139-675. Credit cards accepted.*

The 20-story building, circa 1979, is a textbook example of the penchant for reflective glass that seized developers and came to characterize the style of the 80s. This is an extremely convenient location for anyone who wants to concentrate on downtown business or entertainment. You are within walking distance of the George R. Brown convention center, the theater district, and Enron Field. The rooms are attractive, and offer good views of either the surrounding city or the courtyard.

For casual dining try the Brasserie. The Lobby Lounge, open until 1am, is a good place for nightcaps. Neither restaurant is anything special, but there is no shortage of memorable dining and/or nightspots in the surrounding area.

There is no hotel pool. Valet parking here is pricey – $17 a day. Standard rooms include phone with data port and voice mail, hair dryer, handheld shower, coffee maker, cable TV, and 24-hour housekeeping. You also get two of the famous Doubletree chocolate chip cookies upon check-in.

FOUR SEASONS HOTEL, *1300 Lamar Street. Tel. 713/650-1300, Fax 713/652-6220, Toll free reservations 800/332-3442, Website: www.fourseasons.com/houston. 404 Rooms, 7 Suites. Rates: $215-370. Credit cards accepted.*

The lovely Four Seasons Hotel is a mere three blocks from the George R. Brown Convention Center and provides every amenity guests have come to expect of this prestigious chain of luxury hotels. The rooms shimmer with traditional décor in warm color schemes; the ambience is residential despite the size of the hotel. Bathrooms are positively cavernous, and come equipped with the requisite lush terrycloth bathrobes. For the best views, get a Deluxe Room. These rooms occupy corner spots and have floor-to-ceiling windows overlooking the city.

After a workout in the fitness center, guests can indulge in European spa treatments. The imposing Houston skyline is visible from the rooftop pool. The top floor takes elegance to the highest level with VIP suites that offer security and stunning views. Service is unobtrusive but attentive, delivered by an expert staff. One of my favorite things about this hotel is that the lap pool, Jacuzzi, and spa facilities are open around the clock. Sometimes the performers who favor this luxurious hotel slip in for a late-night soak and a relaxing sauna.

The venerated DeVille Restaurant and Terrace Café have been closed, but weep not as the spaces have been combined into a contemporary Italian-American restaurant called Quattro. Accolades are already pouring in for the new dining room, reviewed in *Where to Eat*, below.

HYATT REGENCY, *1200 Louisiana Street. Tel. 713/654-1234, Fax 713/951-0934. Toll free reservations 888/591-1234, Website: www.hyatt.com/usa/houston/hotels. 977 Rooms, 30 Suites. Rates: $205-280. Credit cards accepted.*

Houston's largest hotel is also one of its best. The Hyatt feels even larger than it is because of the generous open spaces in the handsome lobby and public rooms. The atrium soars 30 stories high. The Hyatt Regency houses the revolving Spindletop Restaurant, offering a complete 360-degree view of the city skyline. Two other restaurants and a bar at the lobby level provide casual dining alternatives.

This hotel's New Years' Eve festivities are among the most popular in the city. Bands play, champagne flows, and at midnight thousands of balloons fall from the top of the atrium upon the revelers.

The Hyatt makes getting around Houston easy – the hotel is on the downtown tunnel network and has shuttle service to the airports and Galleria. A complimentary shuttle runs to the Galleria shopping district. Hyatt Regency has another hotel near Bush Intercontinental Airport.

THE LANCASTER, *701 Texas Avenue. Tel. 713/228-9500, Fax 713/223-4528, Toll free reservations 800/231-0336, Website: www.lancaster.com/hotel. 93 Rooms, 9 Suites. Rates: $250-850. Credit cards accepted.*

The Lancaster, an easy walk from both the business and theater districts, is one of Houston's only true luxury hotels after the European style. The homey interior provides a serene respite from Houston's hectic pace. The hotel's decor is reminiscent of an English country manor. Many of the antiques pre-date the building itself, which was built in the 1920s. Fresh flowers accent the romantic rooms, which have modern amenities including compact disc players and speakerphones. Excellent personal service includes an on-site fitness facility, valet, and lush terry cloth robes.

Theatergoers enjoy after-performance cocktails at the Bistro Lancaster. Chef Tommy Child specializes in what he calls "Gulf Coast Cooking," a homey but innovative cuisine that spotlights the freshest locally available seafood and

B&Bs in The Heights

The Heights is a historic neighborhood of beautiful historic homes and tree lined streets. Although the area is close to downtown, the faded elegance of Houston's first subdivision provides an escape from the concrete-and-steel city lifestyle. The Heights is just west of Interstate Highway 45, between Loop 610 and Katy Freeway (Interstate Highway 10).

ANGEL ARBOR BED & BREAKFAST INN, *848 Heights Boulevard. Tel. 713/868-4654, Fax 713/861-3189, Toll free reservations 800/722-8788, Website: www.angelarbor.com. 4 Rooms, 1 Suite. Rates: $95-125. Credit cards accepted.*

This red brick Georgian-style house is a City of Houston historical landmark, and a favorite B&B getaway for locals as well as tourists. Breakfast is lavish, and the rooms are heavenly (pun intended, as each room is named after an angel). Afternoon tea is sometimes offered in the sunroom. Clancy, the resident Basset hound, welcomes guests and asks for tummy rubs. One of the most popular activities at the Angel Arbor is the Murder Mystery Dinner Party. Each participant assumes a role and helps solve an original mystery set in the roaring 20s or another bygone era. The inn is in the Heights, an historic neighborhood ideal for walking tours and antiques shopping.

SARA'S BED & BREAKFAST INN, *941 Heights Boulevard. Tel. 713/868-1130 or 800/593-1130, Fax 713/868-3284, Website: www.saras.com. 8 Rooms, 4 Suites. Rates: $70-150. Credit cards accepted.*

Sara's Bed & Breakfast occupies one of the grand historic Queen Anne-style houses on Heights Boulevard. This popular inn has a garden room that provides a charming setting for the wonderful full breakfasts. The Balcony Suite can accommodate four people and has adjoining bedrooms, each with its own bath, plus living and dining areas. All of the other rooms are named and furnished after Texas towns. There is a large wraparound porch for sitting and daydreaming.

WEBBER HOUSE, *1101 Heights Boulevard. Tel/Fax 713/864-9472. Rates: $75-110. Credit cards accepted.*

Like Sara's, this is another of the historic Heights Boulevard homes so popular for weddings, retreats, and parties. Each of the four rooms is furnished in a different theme that compliments the Victorian home. The Attic Hideaway is a private, romantic guest suite with an antique claw foot tub.

produce. Breakfast, lunch and dinner are served, and reservations are recommended at all times.

Only eight blocks from Enron Field, the Lancaster offers a package certain to please the oddest of couples – pre-purchased ballpark tickets and $175 entitle you to a deluxe room, baseball-themed welcome amenities, and limo service to Enron Field. Play ball, indeed.

Moderate

BRAESWOOD HOTEL AND CONVENTION CENTER, *2100 South Braeswood at Greenbriar. Tel. 713/797-7000, Fax 713/799-8362, Toll free 800/722-1368. 331 Rooms. Rates:*

Located west of downtown near the Medical Center and Astrodome, the Braeswood Hotel is popular for family reunions and conventions, although it will suit your vacation and travel needs just as well. This large hotel complex is made up of seven buildings interspersed with breezy tropical courtyards. A Jr. Olympic sized Texas-shaped pool provides kitschy appeal and relief from the summer sun. The Garden Terrace is a full-service restaurant, and room service is available. The hotel runs a free 24-hour shuttle to Medical Center and plenty of parking.

HOLIDAY INN ASTRODOME, *8111 Kirby Drive. Tel. 713/790-1900, Fax 713/799-8574. 235 Rooms. Rates: $89-150.*

The Astrodome may not be the home of the Astros anymore, but Reliant Park, the new home of the NFL Houston Texans is right next-door, and there are plenty of other area attractions that make this an excellent lodging choice. It's not just convenience that makes the Holiday Inn Astrodome attractive – the rooms are big and airy, the amenities are extensive, and the outdoor pool surrounded by hibiscus is charming.

MUSEUM DISTRICT, MEDICAL CENTER, & WEST UNIVERSITY AREA

Just to the south and west of downtown lie these lovely neighborhoods shaded by giant live oaks. Greenway Plaza, towering next to Highway 59, is this area's business district, and is also known as Houston's "second" downtown.

Expensive

LA COLOMBE D'OR, *3410 Montrose Boulevard. Tel. 713/524-7999, Fax 713/524-8923, Website: www.lacolombedor.com. 6 Suites. $200-575. Credit cards accepted.*

Possibly the most sought-after vacation address in Houston, this intimate boutique hotel has only six suites. Originally built in 1923 as the home of the founder of the Humble Oil Company, the building was bought and restored in 1979. Each suite is exquisitely decorated in with antiques from different eras, and has its own private dining room, marble bath, and king size bed. The overwhelming theme is European elegance and you may rest assured the staff will attend to your every need. The French restaurant in the hotel has an impeccable reputation. The Grand Salon is a Regency-era French ballroom that was transported in its entirety to Houston.

PARK PLAZA WARWICK HOTEL, *5701 Main Street. Tel. 713/526-1991, Fax 713/526-0359, Toll free reservations 800/, Website: www.warwickhotelhouston.com. 308 Rooms, 74 Suites. Rates: $169-500. Credit cards accepted.*

The Warwick is one of the city's grand old hotels. The 12-story hotel was built in 1925 and underwent a complete renovation in 1999. So close to the Museum of Fine Arts that you can easily walk over, the hotel is also near Rice University and Hermann Park. The rooms are traditionally furnished with handsome furniture in rich fabrics. The views from the rooms are fabulous, whether you are facing the glittering downtown of skyline or the verdant acres of Hermann Park.

Separate saunas for men and women and an outdoor pool complement the fitness room. Golfers will be pleased to find that the Hermann Park Golf Course is just a short walk away. The Hunt Room serves dinner only in a clubby, intimate setting. The rooftop Sunday brunch is justifiably celebrated.

Moderate

HILTON HOUSTON PLAZA, *6633 Travis Street. Tel. 713/313-4000, Fax 713/313-4660, Toll free reservations 800/445-8667, Website: www.hilton.com. 181 Rooms. Rates: $119-200. Credit cards accepted.*

Hilton's version of a boutique hotel is located 4 miles south of downtown and sits within convenient access of the museum district, Rice University, and the Medical Center area. The 10-floor hotel is well equipped for business travelers, with computer connections and voice mail in each room. Art lovers shouldn't overlook this little charmer either – it makes a perfect base for exploration of the museums and shops of the area.

The hotel stands on manicured grounds that have an outdoor pool and jogging track for guests. Courtesy transportation provided to major attractions within three miles of the hotel. Other Hilton Locations include the University of Houston, Hobby Airport and West Houston. Complimentary hors d'ouevres are served in the lounge during early evening.

PATRICIAN BED AND BREAKFAST INN, *1200 Southmore Boulevard. Tel. 713/523-114, Fax 713/523-0790, Toll free 80/533-5797, Website: www.texasbnb.com. 4 Rooms, 2 Suites. Rates $80-150. Credit cards accepted.*

On a shady boulevard close to Rice University and the Museum District, the Patrician offers a stately welcome. The Colonial Revival mansion was built in 1919 and has been restored with a sensitive hand. The guest rooms are on the second and third floors, while the first floor consists of the parlor, dining room, and other public areas, beautifully painted in sanguine tones of roses, pinks, and reds. All of the rooms have private baths (some with two-person whirlpool tubs) and modern amenities such as data port telephones and work areas. You may enjoy your breakfast in the dining room or the solarium – you'll be served with fresh fruits and juices, home-baked bread, and aromatic coffee.

RENAISSANCE HOTEL, *6 Greenway Plaza East. Tel 713/629-1200, Fax 713/629-4706, Toll free reservations 800/468-3571, Website: www.renaissancehotels.com. 379 Rooms, 9 Suites. Rates: $99-209. Credit cards accepted.*

The high-rise Renaissance Hotel is part of the Greenway Plaza business complex and it's all business in the best sense of the word. Service is efficient and gracious. Even the lobby of white marble and brushed steel feels more like a luxury corporate office building than a hotel. Bistro 59 specializes in seafood but serves three meals a day, and sits in a lofty atrium-like setting with a view of the manicured greenery outside. There is an outdoor pool, and guests may use the Houston City Club's facilities or the on-site fitness center. As this is a 20-story tower, many of the rooms have spectacular views. This is a very convenient place to stay if you are in town for a concert or sports event at Compaq Center. The hotel shuttle offers complimentary rides within a three-mile radius and to the Galleria.

Inexpensive

HOUSTON INTERNATIONAL HOSTEL, *5302 Crawford Street at Oakdale. Tel. 713/523-1009, Fax 713/526-8618. 30 beds in dormitory-style rooms. Rates: $13. No credit cards.*

This pleasant two-story house in the Museum District has a number of flags flying outside, the better to welcome the students and travelers from all over the world who stay here. There's a big front porch and picnic table under the trees where you can sit and visit with the other residents. Dormitory-style rooms contain about six beds apiece. Hostel members pay a lower rate for accommodations, and you can buy memberships at the hostel.

LA QUINTA INN, *4015 Southwest Freeway. Tel. 713/623-4750, Fax 713/963-0599, Toll free reservations 800/531-5900. 128 Rooms. Rates: $57-73. Credit cards accepted.*

La Quinta offers a no-frills approach to accommodations. Children under the age of 18 stay here free. A light breakfast is included with your stay. Houston has 17 La Quinta Inns spread throughout the urban area. To find the one closest to the attractions you want to be near, call the toll free number above.

RIVER OAKS, GALLERIA AREA & UPTOWN

River Oaks is the most exclusive of Houston's residential areas. Mansions both stately and nouveau line its streets. Further west, just outside the 610 Loop, you'll find the Galleria shopping and business district. The main streets here are Post Oak Boulevard and Westheimer Road.

Expensive

HOTEL DEREK, *2525 West Loop South. Tel. 713/961-3000, Fax 713/297-4392, Website: www.hotelderek.com. 341 Rooms, 10 Suites, 16 Studios. Rates: $155-875. Credit cards accepted.*

Hotel Derek opened in 2001, taking over the unremarkable Red Lion inn and transforming it into Houston's first ultra-hip Euro-cool boutique hotel. The hotel is stylishly designed and outfitted in clean lines and a sophisticated palette accented with bursts of color. The rooms are both restful and energizing with their crisp linens, duvets in pinstriped covers, and bathrooms in corian, glass, and porcelain.

There is an outdoor pool with outrageously sleek upholstered deck chairs, an excellent gym, and a day spa where you can indulge in a full range of treatments. The restaurant, named Ling and Javier, serves breakfast, lunch, and dinner. It's a trendy spot and an excellent place for people watching, but the Cuban-Chinese fusion cuisine can be a little too clever for its own good. Come here for drinks and appetizers and enjoy the scene, but save your dinner expense account for a safer bet.

THE HOUSTONIAN, *111 North Post Oak Lane. Tel. 713/680-2626 or 800/231-2759, Fax 713/680-2992, Website: www.houstonian.com. 289 Rooms, 8 Suites. Rates: $155-595. Credit cards accepted.*

Although located in the center of urban Houston, the Houstonian manages to create the atmosphere of a serene country retreat. Part country club, part spa, this hotel resort combines luxury accommodations with proximity to the business and shopping centers of Houston. The gorgeously manicured eighteen-acre grounds are a pleasure to stroll. The Houstonian is also recognized as a Green Hotel for its conservation and recycling practices.

The rooms have been recently renovated, and each is traditionally furnished with understated elegance. The suites are large and comfortable enough to be a home away from home. You can keep the drapes over the floor-to-ceiling windows open, as the oaks and pines provide both privacy and scenic beauty. Amenities at the Houstonian include complimentary Towncar service to the Galleria, 24-hour room service, cordless phones, and plush robes. Meander down the woodland path to the world-class spa, where you can receive a poolside massage or the latest European skin treatment.

The Houstonian Club is a nationally recognized health and fitness center. All guests at the Houstonian Hotel receive a temporary membership that allows them to play tennis, racquetball, paddleball, or use the rock climbing wall and three pools. The Houstonian Golf Course is not on the Houstonian grounds and the greens fees are steep. If you are primarily interested in a golf vacation, you may find that you prefer the Four Seasons in Irving or Barton Creek Resort in Austin.

Olivette, the hotel restaurant, serves haute Mediterranean cuisine meals in a warm setting. The Manor House, a stately old home on the grounds, used to be President George H. Bush's Houston residence. Now it serves American regional cuisine in a secluded lodge-like atmosphere. The tranquility of the location and feeling of privacy enhance the dining experience. The Manor House serves luncheon only – evenings are reserved for events and dinner parties. The Center Court Café, located in the Houstonian Club, provides light, nutritious meals for health-conscious patrons.

INTER-CONTINENTAL HOUSTON, *2222 West Loop South. Tel. 713/ 627-7600, Fax 713/961-5575, Toll free 888/567-8725, Website: www.interconti.com. 485 Rooms, 21 Suites. Rates: $199-279. Credit cards accepted.*

This high-rise is conveniently located on Loop 610, near the Galleria area. At one time a Crowne Plaza, this hotel is currently undergoing an extensive renovation, and will open in April 2002 as the Inter-Continental Houston. The Inter-Continental chain has an excellent global reputation for superior service. In-room amenities will include marble baths with telephone, refrigerated mini-bars, bathrobes, CD player alarm clocks, and more. There will also be an outdoor swimming pool, a restaurant, and a fully-equipped fitness center.

THE ST. REGIS HOTEL, *1919 Briar Oaks Lane. Tel. 713/840-7600, Fax 713/840-8036, Toll free , Website: www.starwood.com/stregis. 180 Rooms, 52 Suites. Rates: $155-350. Credit cards accepted.*

This lovely hotel nestled among the leafy streets of River Oaks is the former Ritz-Carlton. As the St. Regis it still provides the elegant accommodation for which this address has long been noted. Although at 12 stories the hotel is by far the tallest building in the neighborhood, it manages to feel like a small, intimate establishment. Polished mahogany, ornate fixtures, and rich fabrics exude an old-world formality. The rooms are simply beautiful, not as over-whelmingly grand as the lobby and other public areas, but sumptuous nonetheless, with plenty of room (500 square feet) to spread out in. You don't just get fresh flowers in your room at the St. Regis – you get orchids.

There is 24-hour room service and concierge service, and several excellent dining facilities. The Astor Court is open for Sunday brunch only and features an impressive array of culinary selections. Afternoon tea is a delightful ritual here. The hotel offers a small fitness center and an outdoor pool. Valet parking is mandatory for guests with cars. One caveat – there are train tracks nearby. If you're easily awakened by noise, ask for a room facing away from the tracks.

Inexpensive

MARRIOTT FAIRFIELD INN, *3131 West Loop South. Tel. 713/961-1690, Fax 713/627-8434, Toll free reservations 800/228-1690. 107 Rooms. Rates: $59-75. Credit cards accepted.*

This motel-style inn has an outdoor pool and does not charge for continental breakfast or local calls. The Galleria is mere steps away, Greenway Plaza another two miles, and you are six miles from downtown. There is no

Houston Area Resorts

THE WOODLANDS RESORT & CONFERENCE CENTER, *2301 North Millbend Drive, The Woodlands. Tel. 281/367-1100, Fax 281/ 364-6299, Toll free 800/533-3052 (in Texas) or 800/433-2624 (outside Texas), Website: www.woodlandsresort.com. Rates begin at $125. Credit cards accepted.*

The tall pines of the Woodlands provide a beautiful backdrop for the Woodlands Resort. The Woodlands is a planned city just north of Houston. Most attractive to visitors are the privacy, recreational facilities, and access to nature. The numerous golf courses include the Tournament Players Course, which hosts the Houston Open. Nature trails stretch throughout the Woodlands and are open to joggers and bicycles. Add to the mix a world-class Tennis Complex, spa and fitness center, four restaurants, and the new Forest Oasis Waterscape with its double-helix slide, white sand beach, and diving "cliffs," and you will be hard-pressed to find a reason to leave the grounds.

DEL LAGO RESORT, *600 Del Lago Boulevard, Montgomery. Tel. 936/582-6100, Toll free 800/DEL-LAGO, Website: www.dellago.com. Rates: $115-160. Credit cards accepted.*

The manicured grounds of the Del Lago Resort let you enjoy the more active aspects of a vacation, such as golf, boating and tennis—but you can still opt for mere relaxation in a private villa. The resort is self-contained and has a restaurant, lounge business center and children's center. The main building is a high-rise hotel. For those who desire more privacy, cottages on the golf course and villas on the waterfront are available. Lake Conroe is a freshwater lake perfect for water skiing and fishing.

The resort is 65 miles north of central Houston. Take interstate Highway 45 north to Highway 105. Travel east on Highway 105 to Walden Road. Turn onto Walden Road; this will lead you to the resort.

SOUTH SHORE HARBOUR RESORT, *2500 South Shore Boulevard, League City. Tel. 281/334-1000, Fax 281/334-1157, Toll free 800/ 442-5005, Website: www.sshr.com. Rates: $110-170. Credit cards accepted.*

League City is about halfway between central Houston and Galveston Island, on Clear Lake. The South Shore Resort has large rooms with ultra-modern decoration. The more traditional style of the Paradise Reef and Harbour Club provide atmosphere for intimate dinners and romantic evenings. Many rooms have lake views. There is an enormous fitness center with an indoor jogging track, lap pool, and raquetball courts.

restaurant in the Fairfield, but the adjacent Courtyard Hotel welcomes Fairfield guests to eat at their restaurant. The Fairfield Inn is located between Westheimer Road and Richmond Street on the east side of West Loop (610) near the Galleria.

NORTH

North of Houston lies the town of Spring, as well as Bush Intercontinental Airport.

Expensive

HOTEL SOFITEL, *425 North Sam Houston Parkway East. Tel. 281/445-9000, Fax 281/445-0629, Website: www.sofitel.com. 334 Rooms, 2 Suites. Rates: $ 129-199.*

The French Sofitel chain has only one hotel in Texas, and this is it. Only ten minutes from Bush Intercontinental, this European hotel cossets its guests with Continental flair and expert service from the moment they arrive. The eight-story atrium and 92-foot mural set a grand stage, and the rest of the hotel does not disappoint. Twice-daily maid service is just one of the perks you'll experience, along with the fresh-cut rose that greets you and the baguette presented to you upon check out.

The rooms are spotless and decorated in French Country fashion with European period pieces. Outside is a beautiful swimming pool; inside is a cushy fitness center. The food served at the hotel's two restaurants and in-house pastry shop is very French, and very good. The hotel offers free shuttle service to and from Intercontinental Airport. Pets are allowed (with a deposit) and children under 12 stay for no charge.

Moderate

HYATT REGENCY HOUSTON AIRPORT, *15747 John F. Kennedy Boulevard. Tel. 281/987-1234, Fax 281/590-8461, Toll free 888/591-1234, Website: www.houstonairport.hyatt.com. 314 Rooms, 11 Suites. Rates: $80-175.*

Although mere minutes away from one of the busiest airports in the world, the Hyatt utilizes a courtyard setting and tall pines to create an inviting atmosphere. The lobby is decorated in solid comforting Arts & Crafts style, and the rooms are expansive. Each room features a large work area with a comfortable leather chair. There is an outdoor free-form pool (unheated, alas), an outdoor whirlpool, and a fitness center. Oakley's Restaurant serves American cuisine. Catch the big game on the big screen at Derricks Saloon, and have a plate of Tex-Mex while you're at it.

LEXINGTON HOTEL SUITES, *16410 Interstate Highway 45 North. Tel. 281/821-1000, Toll free reservations 800/53-SUITES. 247 Suites. Rates: $80-120. Credit cards accepted.*

Lexington Suites provides the amenities of a hotel, such as dry cleaning service and daily complimentary breakfast served in the atrium. Business rooms and services cater to corporate travelers. One or two bedroom suites include kitchens and comfortable living areas. Special rates for long-term rates are offered. The hotel is only three miles from the town of Spring with its antique stores and shopping. To reach Lexington Suites travel 11 miles north from Bush Intercontinental Airport on Interstate Highway 45.

Inexpensive

RAMADA LIMITED, *15350 J. F. K. Boulevard. Tel. 281/442-1830, Fax 281/987-8023, Toll free reservations 800/2-RAMADA. 126 Rooms. Rates: $65-75. Credit cards accepted.*

The Ramada Inn is located close to the Houston Bush Intercontinental Airport. Facilities include an exercise room and outdoor pool. All rooms use electric key locks for added safety. Guests can take the Ramada shuttle service to the airport or nearby Greenspoint Mall. J. F. K. Boulevard runs from the airport to Beltway 8 (Sam Houston Parkway). The Ramada is on the east side of this intersection. Ramada has five locations including hotels near the Galleria and the Astrodome.

WEST

West Houston includes the upscale Memorial neighborhood and Spring Branch.

Expensive

ADAM'S MARK HOUSTON, *2900 Briarpark Drive at Westheimer. Tel. 713/978-7400, Fax 713/735-2727, Toll free reservations 800/444-2326, Website: www.adamsmark.com. 604 Rooms. Rates: $100-225. Credit cards accepted.*

The glitz that makes Houston famous is the hallmark of Adam's Mark. The interior style is neo-art deco on a grand scale. In the atrium lobby, glass elevators soar above tall stained glass lights that dominate the lobby bar. The hotel restaurant serves "contemporary regional fare with a distinctively Southern flair." There is also a Sunday Champagne Jazz Brunch from 10:30 am until 2 pm. Fitness facilities include an indoor/outdoor heated pool, whirlpool, and private putting green. Located in the Westchase Business District, just off Beltway 8, the hotel is a 35-minute drive from both Intercontinental and Hobby Airports. From the Sam Houston Tollway, exit Westheimer Road.

HILTON HOUSTON WESTCHASE, *9999 Westheimer Road. Tel. 713/974-1000, Fax 713/974-6866, Toll free 800/774-1500, Website: www.hilton.com. 298 Rooms, 38 Suites. Rates $75-188.*

From the outside, this hotel looks like another glass-fronted office building in the Westchase office park, but inside the casually elegant lobby makes you feel instantly at home. A sunny atrium lounge invites guests to linger over newspapers and coffee, ensconced in soft armchairs and cozy sofas. The hotel lies about 20 miles from downtown Houston.

Guest rooms feature floor-to-ceiling windows and deluxe pillowtop mattresses. The work desks provide high-speed Internet hookups. Deluxe rooms in the top four floors, or "towers", of the hotel take service to an even higher level, with complimentary hors d'oeuvres and breakfast, electric massage chairs, and complimentary business center. The grounds are landscaped with pretty gardens and an outdoor pool. The Rio Ranch Restaurant, open for breakfast, lunch, and dinner, affects a Hill Country lodge atmosphere, with deer horn chandeliers and a large limestone fireplace.

MARRIOTT WESTSIDE, *13210 Interstate Highway 10. Tel. 713/558-8338, Fax 713/558-4028, Toll free reservations 800/228-9290. Rates: $124. Credit cards accepted.*

This 400 room sprawling glass and steel hotel is west of downtown. The grounds resemble a first-class office building; a manicured lawn and water fountains complement the indoor gardens. The lobby garden has plenty of fresh air, with full-size trees and a large water pool. The hotel has 26 meeting rooms ranging in size from a capacity of 1500 to 15. A large outdoor pool and lighted tennis courts let guests unwind outside. The hotel restaurant features Sunday brunch with live Dixieland music. Marriott has hotels at the Medical Center, Bush Intercontinental Airport, Greenspoint (north) and the Galleria.

THE BAY AREA

The cities that surround the bay east of Houston are known as the Bay Area. Many who are just passing through Houston proper choose to stay in the Bay Area to avoid the urban congestion of the city.

HOLIDAY INN, *300 South Highway 146, Baytown. Tel 281/427-7481. Rates: $45-70. Credit cards accepted.*

This hotel was recently renovated and offers comfortable rooms with standard amenities such as cable television and room service. The location is good for those who want easy access to attractions in the south of Houston, while avoiding staying in the center of the metropolitan area. When traveling from Houston, take Interstate Highway 10 to Baytown, Exit Highway 146 (Alexander Drive) and travel south about 10 miles; the Holiday Inn is on the west side of the highway. Baytown is located east of Houston on Interstate Highway 10.

MARRIOTT RESIDENCE INN, *525 Bay Area Boulevard, Houston. Tel. 281/486-2424 or 800/331-3131. Rates: $89-125. Credit cards accepted.*

This hotel has the feel of an apartment community. Rate incentives are offered for long-term stays. Some rooms have fireplaces, kitchenettes, and ceiling fans. Larger suites include two bedrooms and living areas.

TEXAS CITY FAIRFIELD INN, *10700 East Lowry, Texas City. Tel. 409/ 986-3866 or 800/228-2800. Rates: $68-75. Credit cards accepted.*

A stay at the Fairfield Inn includes continental breakfast. The hotel has an indoor pool. From Interstate Highway 45, exit Lowry Expressway. The hotel is at this intersection. Suites are available for a nominal extra charge.

Camping

SOUTH MAIN RV PARK, *10100 South Main. Tel. 713/667-0120, Fax 713/668-7343, Toll free reservations 800/626-Park, Website: www.smrvpark.com. Daily $17; weekly $100. Credit cards accepted.*

Got an RV? Want to stay in downtown Houston? No pr0oblem. This large recreational vehicle park has 72 spaces with electricity and full hook-ups, including telephone. This is more a residential community than a vacation spot. The location on South Main allows easy access to the downtown business area and museum district. Special monthly rates are available and change by season.

Where to Eat
DOWNTOWN
Expensive

BRENNAN'S, *3300 Smith Street. Tel. 713/522-9711, Website: www.brennanshouston.com. Monday-Saturday 11:30am-1:30pm, Sunday 10am-2pm, 5:45-10pm daily. Credit cards accepted. Reservations essential.*

Chef Alex Brennan-Martin was trained at the Commander's Palace in New Orleans, and for over 30 years now, Brennan's has been Houston's own sophisticated Creole legacy. Southern hospitality is no cliché here – it's a palpable ingredient to this restaurant's success. Executive Chef Carl Walker knows many of his devoted customers by name.

This is one of Houston's favorite "special occasion" restaurants. Every table is lovely, but for the best ambience, try to sit close to the beautiful courtyard. Must-try dishes include the famous turtle soup, Louisiana pecan-crusted fish, and the legendary white chocolate bread pudding for dessert. The New Orleans jazz brunch is delicious fun.

DAMIAN'S CUCINA ITALIANA, *3011 Smith. Tel 713/522-0439, Website: www.damians.com. Credit cards accepted. Reservations recommended.*

This is the self-proclaimed granddaddy of Italian cuisine in Houston, still a beloved institution and a prom night favorite. A special treat is the Chef's Table tucked away in a corner of the kitchen, where Chefs Napoleon Palacios and Tommy Leman will guide you through six memorable courses for $65 per person (excluding wine, tax, and gratuity).

Valet service is complementary and there is even an air-conditioned bus shuttle for guests who are planning to attend the theater but don't want to run the parking gauntlet. Although jackets and ties are not required, you'll probably feel more comfortable if you dress for dinner.

MAXIM'S, *3755 Richmond Avenue. Tel. 713/877-8899. Credit cards accepted.*

This intimate French restaurant glows with the warmth of European elegance. Seafood, steak and pasta are traditionally prepared and served. In the evening the piano bar adds to the lavish ambience. The wine cellar holds vintages that were bottled before the opening of Maxim's in 1950. Maxim's is located in the Greenway Plaza area near the Compaq Center.

Moderate

GOODE COMPANY, *5109 Kirby Drive. Tel. 713/522-2530. Credit cards accepted.*

Goode Company calls its food "Texas barbecue," and no words could better describe the selection, which ranges from duck to Czech sausage. In addition to exemplary beef brisket, you will find turkey breast or jalapeno sausage—not your usual barbecue fare. The choice can be difficult, so the combo dinner is a sure winner. The Jambalya Texana is the best and spiciest side dish. Vegetarians need not feel left out; loaded baked potatoes, baked beans, and coleslaw are filling in themselves. The restaurant is located two blocks south of Highway 59.

MIYAKO JAPANESE RESTAURANT & SUSHI BAR, *6345 Kirby Drive. Tel. 713/520-9797. Credit cards accepted.*

The freshest, most expertly prepared sushi and sashimi around. Every weekday the sushi happy hour offers discounts on tasty sushi morsels. Tempura specialties and beef are also made. Lunch specials are featured on weekdays. All locations feature a brunch buffet every Sunday from noon to 3pm. *Other restaurants at 6345 Westheimer Road, Tel. 781-6300 and 910 Travis Street (in the Bank One Building), Tel. 752-2888.*

PATRENELLA, *813 Jackson Hill Street. Tel. 713/863-8233. Credit cards accepted.*

This cozy Italian restaurant is one of the best-kept secrets in Houston. It is located in an offbeat neighborhood. The place is so popular that the waiting crowd must spill out onto the patio. Once you are seated, take your time to enjoy the splendid food. Each night a variety of specials are featured, but for me the standard red sauce is unbeatable. The pasta is prepared in the kitchen; the gnocchi is exceptional. Wine by the bottle is very affordable.

THAI PEPPER, *2049 West Alabama. Tel. 713/520-8225. Credit cards accepted.*

Inside Thai Pepper, the elegant, modern atmosphere sets the stage for great food. The extensive menu offers a wide variety of authentic Thai dishes, heavy on the spices and sweet sauces that distinguish the cuisine. The Clay Pot chicken comes over crystal rice noodles with rich aromatic undertones. The

Pad Thai is made with red sauce, and is a dark, sweet version of the traditional dish. Seafood is the specialty of the house. The Royal seafood is a succulent mixture of shrimp, scallops, and crawfish with light garlic sauce. If you are lucky, the Cashew Crab—Alaskan King crab with cashew nuts and straw mushrooms— will be in season. The food is prepared according to your preference of spiciness; MSG is never used.

Inexpensive

BIBA'S GREEK RESTAURANT, *607 West Gray Street. Tel. 713/523-0425. Credit cards accepted.*

No matter what hour you crave a gyro or Greek salad, Biba's on West Gray will fill your stomach. This location is open around the clock. The blue awnings tell you that the Mediterranean influence remains strong. The stuffed dolmas are not to be missed. Weekday happy hour includes a buffet of Greek food.

BUFFALO GRILLE, *3116 Bissonnet. Tel. 713/661-3663. Credit cards accepted.*

Known for its huge breakfasts, Buffalo Grille offers a great casual meal at any time of the day. The pancakes are exceptional. The menu offers a variety of light fare. The Buffalo Grille is open Monday to Friday 7am to 2pm; Saturday and Sunday 8am to 2pm.

FRESH MARKET CAFE, *6560 Fannin Suite 120. Tel. 713/ 799-9211. Credit cards accepted.*

The Fresh Market has a bounty of healthy food in a deli-style restaurant. All the menu items, down to the sauces are prepared from scratch and made with healthy eating in mind. Stop in for a guiltless snack. The fixings-cheese, sprouts, and the like-come separately from the sandwich, so each person can suit their own taste. The Healthy Hero is an all-time favorite, with marinated vegetables and mozzarella cheese. The Chocolate Fix is non-fat chocolate frozen yogurt topped with chocolate sauce and bits of brownie.

KIM SON, *7531 Westheimer Road. Tel 713/783-0054. Credit cards accepted.*

Kim Son is probably the most successful Vietnamese restaurant in the state. The restaurant takes traditional Vietnamese food and transforms it into modern cuisine. The hot pot dishes of Vietnam are made with the succulent mix of spices that cannot be duplicated by any other cuisine. Brave new combinations, such as Vietnamese Fajitas, actually come together in a delicious way. *Other locations include 2001 Jefferson, Tel. 222-2461, and 8200 Wilcrest, Tel. 498-7841.*

RIVER OAKS
Expensive

ANTHONY'S, *4007 Westheimer Road in the Highland Village Shopping Center. Tel. 713/961-0552. Reservations recommended. Open Mon 11:30am-*

10pm, Tue-Fri 11:30am-11pm, Sat 5:30pm-11pm. Closed Sundays. Credit cards accepted.

This posh restaurant with its striking Neo-Classical décor is a favorite for business lunches and expense account dinners. Famed Houston restaurateur Tony Vallone opened this bolder, more eclectic cousin to his original Tony's, and well-heeled Houstonians instantly swept the new arrival to their bosoms.

The menu changes daily, which makes recommending an individual dish difficult, but in general try the seafood or shellfish entrees. The tiramisu here is a perennial finalist in various "Best Dessert" polls.

RIVER OAKS GRILL, *2630 Westheimer. Tel. 713/520-1738. Credit cards accepted.*

This restaurant has an up-beat and airy atmosphere where you will hear the clamor of the crowd. The extraordinary food is focused on steak. Filet mignon, Veal Parlante, veal on wilted spinach with white wine sauce, and grilled quail are good selections. The focus is also on lobster, a refreshing choice in an area where it is difficult to find. The lobster bisque is a perfectly smooth soup. The Lobster Capellini, made with brandy cream sauce, is sinfully delicious. For a particularly good side dish, try the baby artichokes, prepared with red pepper and basil. You can choose from a very good selection of wine.

GALLERIA/POST OAK AREA
Expensive

AMÉRICAS, *1800 Post Oak Boulevard. Tel. 713/961-1492. Reservations required. Open Mon-Thu 11am-10pm, Fri 11:30am-11pm, Sat 5:30pm-11pm. Closed Sundays. Credit cards accepted.*

Notice that the phone number contains a date that every American schoolchild learns by heart? "In 1492, Columbus sailed the ocean blue..." It's a sly tribute to the South American theme of this restaurant, where the food is served in a fantastical atmosphere that almost borders on the bizarre. The restaurant was designed and handcrafted by Jordan Mozer – the décor is truly difficult to describe except in abstract artistic terms. There is a suspended dining area, fixtures and hardware that refer to Mayan and Aztec architecture, and nary a straight line in the house.

All of this is not to take away from the excellent fare here, which reflects the exuberance of the surroundings. Each meal begins with complimentary crisp-fried plantains served with a chimichurri sauce. Satisfying entrees like signature beef Churrasco, house-smoked rack of lamb and grilled seafood come with imaginatively prepared vegetables. You must leave room for the *tres leches* cake, cake soaked in three kinds of milk – the Américas version is the best I have ever had. If you don't have time for dinner but you'd like to see the place, go to the bar for wine and tapas.

HARRY'S AMERICAN BAR & RESTAURANT, *1717 Post Oak Boulevard. Tel. 713/622-0022. Credit cards accepted.*

Hemingway could have dined here-the dark wood decor and elements of by-gone eras transport you to another time. The food is far from standard— Welsh rarebit and lamb chops are two dishes which are succulently prepared. Italian fare is well represented with pasta dishes. Enjoy the rich flavors of European inspired cuisine while piano music fill the air during weekend evenings. Open Monday to Friday 11am to 11pm; Friday and Saturday 11am to midnight.

ROTISSERIE FOR BEEF AND BIRD, *2200 Wilcrest. 713/977-9524. Credit cards accepted.*

The Rotisserie specializes in serving feasts of wild game. You step inside to the warmth of an American colonial home. For special occasions guest can dine in the wine cellar, surrounded by vintage reserves. Seafood and Maine lobster highlight the non-meat menu choices. During the week, the restaurant is open for lunch from 11:30am to 2:30pm and dinner 6pm to 10:30pm; only dinner is served on Saturday; closed Sunday.

Moderate

HUNAN, *1800 Post Oak Boulevard. Tel. 713/965-0808. Credit cards accepted.*

The exotic cuisine of Hunan China is prepared to perfection at Hunan. The classic dishes that you already know are prepared with the zest and flare of fine dining. Elegantly understated atmosphere is the hallmark of this restaurant, which has been open since 1976 and remains one of the best in Houston. Hunan is located in the Pavilion shopping center, in the Galleria area.

JIMMY G'S, *3009 Post Oak Boulevard. Tel. 713/629-5380. Credit cards accepted.*

It's hard to find a good Houston restaurant that can limit itself to only two locations. Jimmy G's is just that; despite its success, it has managed to limit itself to a size that permits the quality of the seafood to remain constant. This is a necessary stop for seafood lovers who want a real taste of the Gulf of Mexico. The food and spices of the coasts of Louisiana and Texas combine for spicy Cajun creations. Fresh seafood from the Texas Gulf is prepared with sassy Cajun recipes The stuffed red snapper is excellent. Start the meal with a crawfish saute—the easiest, and once you taste it, only way to eat these critters-or a creamy crabmeat au gratin. *Other location at 307 Sam Houston Parkway, Tel. 713/931-7654.*

THE STABLES, *3734 Westheimer Road. Tel. 713/621-0833. Credit cards accepted.*

Although the name of this restaurant does not conjure up the most inviting images for dining, The Stables is a lovely restaurant that strives for perfection. At times the ambiance goes overboard, and the atmosphere can be described as snooty. *The second location is at 7325 South Main, Tel. 713/795-5900.*

MONTROSE & MUSEUM DISTRICT
Expensive

ARIES RESTAURANT, *4315 Montrose Boulevard. Tel. 713/526-4404, Fax 713/526-8725, Website: www.ariesrestaurant.com. Credit cards accepted. Open Monday-Thursday 5:30pm-9:30pm, Friday-Saturday 5:30pm-10:30pm, closed Sunday.*

The husband-and-wife team of Scott and Annika Tycer (both Aries, natch) has created a lovely, lively oasis of New American Cuisine in a space that manages to balance contemporary with cozy. Esquire Magazine named Aries one of the Ten Best New Restaurants of 2001, and has developed a reputation for serving fresh, seasonal cuisine to warm a foodie's heart.

The menu highlights seasonal and rare ingredients. Recent standouts were a Hudson Valley Foie Gras appetizer with pistachio date bread and orange gastric, and salmon from British Columbia with Savoy cabbage, dill, and citrus glaze. If you simply can't decide, try the Chef's Tasting Menu.

OUTSIDE THE LOOP

59 DINER, *3801 Farnham. Tel. 713/523-2333. Credit cards accepted.*

This is a genuine diner, complete with daily Blue Plate Specials. The down-home comfort food includes chicken potpie, homemade meatloaf and beef liver & onions. The menu also includes burgers, sandwiches and deluxe plates, like chicken fried chicken. The side dishes feature daily vegetables and standards like cornbread dressing and baked sweet potatoes.

BRENNER'S, *10911 Katy Freeway. Tel. 713/465-2901. Credit cards accepted.*

It's like being out on a ranch at this cozy restaurant. Brenner's has been a favorite of Houstonians since it opened in 1936. Texas meat and potatoes fare fills the menu. All the sauces are made from family recipes.

CIMARRON, *3000 North Loop. Tel. 713/688-0100. Credit cards accepted.*

The menu borrows heavily from the tastes of the southwest and is decorated with West Texas images. The food is of an exceptional standard, with specialties such as fresh Gulf shrimp over filet mignon or pasta primavera. Cimarron is in the Houston Medallion Shopping Center, at the intersection of Loop 610 and Highway 290.

GUADALAJARA MEXICAN GRILLE & BAR, *Towne & Country Village, Katy Freeway. Tel. 713/461-5300. Credit cards accepted.*

Texas-style Mexican food is prepared a step above the usual standards at the Guadalajara Bar & Grille. The standards, like beef fajitas, chicken enchiladas and carne asada are made with the freshest vegetables and authentic Mexican spices. Quail grilled over mesquite chips is a house specialty. Happy hour specials featured from 3pm to 7pm on weekdays.

KELLY'S DEL FRISCO STEAKHOUSE, *14641 Gladebrook Drive. 713/ 893-3339. Credit cards accepted.*

Many find this to be one of the best steakhouses anywhere. Steak and lobster highlight the traditional selections on the menu. After your meal, relax in Resa's Piano Bar. From Interstate Highway 45 North, exit Farm Road 1960 and travel west. Gladebrook intersects with Farm Road 1960.

OLD HEIDELBERG INN, *1810 Fountainview. Tel. 713/781-3581, Fax 713/781-3350. Credit cards accepted.*

For over 20 years the Old Heidelberg Inn has served traditional German food in a European atmosphere. Good selections include such European delicacies as fried Camembert, vichyssoise, and veal schnitzel "Heidelberg style." The goulash soup tastes like it was made in Budapest. There is little for the vegetarian here. Open Monday to Saturday 11:30am to 2am.

TASTE OF TEXAS, *10505 Katy Freeway. Tel. 713/932-6901. Credit cards accepted.*

This is what you might imagine a Texas steakhouse a la theme park might look like. The restaurant is large and filled with Texas-style decor. You can handpick the steak you want to have prepared for your dinner. The menu itself is reminiscent of a tourist attraction and is available in 12 languages. Nonetheless, the steaks are good and the food is guaranteed to fill you up.

Seeing the Sights

You can walk through Texas history by visiting Houston's historic downtown parks. Modern Houston's history began at **Allen's Landing Park**, *1001 Commerce Street*, where the Allen brothers first set foot on Texas soil. The city hall once stood on Market Square. The square, which was once the heart of the commercial district, became a parking lot. In 1976 revitalization began, and today the area is a renovated historic district.

Another center of historic Houston is the **Sam Houston Park**, *1000 Bagby, Tel. 713/655-1912, Monday to Saturday 10am to 4pm; Sunday 1pm to 5pm*. Plan to spend a few hours to really take in all the history that is documented by the 19-acre museum complex and park in the city center. The indoor and outdoor exhibits recreate over 150 years in Houston through seven restored residences of prominent residents and a museum. The earliest example of life in Houston is the **Old Place**, a rendering of the first colonial houses constructed in 1826, while Texas was part of Mexico. Tours of the homes are conducted until 3pm each day. The **Museum of Texas History** has temporary and permanent exhibits about the history of Texas from the time of the sixteenth century Spanish colonial explorers to the present. Finish your trek through time at the museum's tearoom, a cafe located in a reconstructed nineteenth century store.

Houston is a modern marvel as well as an historic one. The famous Houston skyline is one of the most familiar in the world, a virtual museum of monumental architecture. The downtown business district has the greatest concentration of skyscrapers. Among the most notable is **Pennzoil Place**, *700 Milam*, a large, split building with a glass pyramid entrance. Pennzoil Place and neighboring postmodern **Nations Bank** (formerly Republic Bank), *700 Louisiana Street*, which has large-scale elements of traditional European design and soars to 56 stories, were both designed by the famous architect Philip Johnson.

A network of **pedestrian tunnels** connects Houston's skyscrapers, historic district and theater district. The tunnels were designed primarily for business people who need to comfortably and safely walk through the business district. During the sweltering summer months, walking underground is preferable to the baking in the daytime sun, which seems to be magnified by the glass and steel buildings. The main network of tunnels runs roughly north to south, and much of it resembles a shopping mall. Numerous small shops and eateries line the central junctions. Some segments of the tunnels connect small groups of buildings that are not part of the main tunnel system.

The **Houston Chronicle Building**, *801 Texas Avenue*, is the only entrance in the historic district that connects to the main tunnel system. The **Alley Theater**, *615 Texas Avenue*, and its parking garage are a good starting

Williams Tower

The skyscraper most deserving a visit in Houston is not found downtown. The **Williams Tower**, *2800 Post Oak Boulevard*, is the world's largest building in a suburban area. Of course a Houstonian will tell you that the Williams Tower is not in a suburb at all, but in Houston's "second downtown," the Galleria area. Although the name of the building has changed, to most Houstonians it remains (and always will) the Transco Tower. The Tower is located at Post Oak Road and West Alabama Street, near Loop 610 West.

The design of the building is as ominously futuristic as its name; this is another masterpiece by Philip Johnson. The tall, shiny, dark Willimas Tower reaches straight into the sky to over 50 stories. The Wall of Water is a large semi-circular water fountain standing on the Williams grounds. You can walk through the neo-Romanesque facade into a thundering waterfall.

point to enter the tunnels from the theater district. The large Allen Center Garage, *3 Allen Center, Polk Street*, has a tunnel entrance.

The Four Seasons Hotel and the Hyatt Regency Hotel have entrances to the tunnel system. The Doubletree Hotel and the Lancaster Hotel are both across the street to entrances to the tunnel system.

Houston is known to offer some the finest medical care in the world. The sprawling complex of the **Texas Medical Center**, *1155 Holcombe, Tel. 713/790-1136*, is sometimes called "Houston's Third Downtown." And the buildings do make their own mark on the Houston skyline. Research, treatment and education are conducted in the 100 buildings of the Medical Center. Many patients seeking specialized care for cancer and heart disease make Houston their first choice. You can arrange a tour of the facilities by contacting the medical center; people with all interests are welcome.

The Museum District

The Museum District is just south of downtown Houston where Montrose Boulevard and Main Street intersect at the Mecom Fountain. Hermann Park is located on Hermann Drive, which also intersects with the Mecom Fountain traffic circle.

The **Museum of Fine Arts**, *1101 Bissonnet, Tel. 713/639-7300, closed Monday, Tuesday to Saturday 10am to 5pm; Sunday 12:15pm to 6pm, admission $3 adults, $1.50 children, students and seniors*, is the centerpiece of the Arts district. Major exhibits from around the world are shown in the large gallery space. The permanent collection features paintings and sculpture from Europe, Africa and Oceania. Touring exhibits of international fame regularly grace the halls of the main gallery. Cafe Express, the museum's in house cafe, offers light lunches and snacks. This is the most convenient place in the area to get food while touring the exhibits.

The museum hosts a lunchtime series called "Drop-in Tours," held Tuesday to Friday at noon. Every Thursday, admission to the permanent collection is free and the museum stays open until 9pm. Admission for traveling expositions varies; on Thursday, a discounted rate is offered. The museum is located at the corner of Bissonnet and Main Street. Parking in the lot across the street from the main entrance is free.

The museum's art school, the **Glassell School of Art**, *5101 Montrose Boulevard, Tel. 713/639-7500*, has temporary exhibitions and educational programs. Frequent lectures for adults and workshops for children are conducted throughout the year. Most are free or have a nominal admission. The museum sponsors on-going art films, *Tel. 713/639-7515*, which are shown on Friday evenings and weekends.

The freshly renovated **Contemporary Arts Museum**, *5216 Montrose Boulevard, Tel. 713/526-6749, Fax 713/526-6749, Tuesday to Saturday 10am to 5pm, free admission*, hosts unusual and thought-provoking exhibitions which change frequently. Just down the street from the art museums is the **Lillie Hugh and Roy Cullen Sculpture Garden**, *Bissonnet at Montrose, 9am to 5pm*. This is a refreshing place to appreciate fine art outdoors.

Houston has its own museum dedicated to kids, and creative learning is the element that puts fun into the **Children's Museum**, *1500 Binz Street, Tel. 713/522-1138, Tuesday to Saturday 9am to 5pm, Sunday noon to 5pm, closed Monday, admission $5 adults and children*. A variety of topics from science and technology to health are covered with inventive exhibits that allow hands-on activity. Children from the ages of 6 to 12 years will find the material to their liking. The museum is 6 blocks southwest of the Museum of Fine Arts. A trip to the **Museum of Health and Medical Science**, *1515 Hermann Drive, Tel. 713/521-1515, Tuesday to Saturday 9am to 5pm; Sunday noon to 5pm*, is good for your body and mind. Interactive exhibits teach you about the way a body works and is put together. The museum is full of

The Jung Center

During his lifetime, Carl G. Jung made some of the most important contributions to the field of analytical psychology. In 1954 two students of Jung opened the **C. G. Jung Educational Center**, *5200 Montrose Boulevard, Tel. 713/524-8253*. The center serves the community primarily as an educational facility. During the year numerous short courses are offered, and frequent lectures are held. Dance, art and writing are taught on an ongoing basis. Some of the programs are offered free to the public. The bookstore offers an array of hard-to-find books that deal with spirituality and psychology, among other topics.

For thirty years the center's annual conference has drawn academics, professionals and students from around the globe. The three-day conference is held in July and features lectures and workshops.

health and nutrition information. Even the snack bar and the gift shop sell treats that are good for you. Children's programs sponsored by the museum include films and artistic programs.

The chilling photographs of the Holocaust are perhaps the most vivid memories to take away from the **Holocaust Museum**, *5401 Caroline Street, Tel. 713/942-8000, Fax 713/942-7953*, but the entire experience leaves an emotional impression. Although the subject matter may be difficult to confront, the power of remembering tribulations of the past can be an important tool for learning. The exhibits strive to reach into the hearts and minds of visitors, providing not only the historical account but also the human side of the Holocaust. The Memorial Room allows you to rest and consider the powerful information that the museum delivers. Movies, research facilities and teaching programs are part of the museum's outreach program.

Hermann Park

The most popular attraction in Hermann Park is the zoo, more formally known as the **Houston Zoological Gardens**, *1513 North MacGregor Street, Tel. 713/525-3300, open daily 10am to 6pm, Admission $2.50 adults, $2 seniors, $.50 children.* The zoo takes up 55 acres of Hermann Park. The large grounds provide a variety of habitats for the over 3500 animals at the zoo.

Natural history from the age of the dinosaurs throughout our time of space exploration is chronicled in the **Museum of Natural History**, *One Hermann Circle Drive, Tel. 713/639-4629, Admission $3.50 adult, $2 children.* Three stories of live butterflies are a larger-than life exhibit. The planetarium and IMAX theater have daily shows that bring the vastness of the universe within reach.

Outside the Museum District

The private collection of John and Dominique Menil is one of the most extraordinary assemblages of art you will see in Texas. **The Menil Collection**, *1515 Sul Ross Street, Tel 713/525-9400, Wednesday to Sunday 11am to 7pm, closed Monday and Tuesday*, offers an extensive assortment of art spanning the breadth of time from the age of Byzantium to the post-modern era. Works by modern masters grace the walls. Art and artifacts from all over the world are on display; of particular interest is the collection of African art. The Menil Collection is behind the University of St. Thomas. From Interstate Highway 59, exit Montrose and go north to Sul Ross Street.

Next door to the Menil Collection stands the **Rothko Chapel**, *3000 Yupon Street, Tel. 713/524-9839, open daily 10am to 6pm*, a non-denominational religious sanctuary designed by abstract expressionist painter Mark Rothko. The simplicity and unity of his painting is reflected in the architectural design, which unifies spiritual experience by allowing visitors to meditate in a temple devoid of religious imagery.

The decor is sparse, but the furnishings are undeniably Gothic in the **American Funeral Service Museum**, *415 Barren Springs Drive, 713/876-3063, Monday to Saturday 10am to 4pm; Sunday noon to 4pm, Admission $5 adults, $3 children.* This is one of the more unusual collections you will find anywhere. Among the exhibits are a collection of caskets from the time of the Civil War, a group of hearse sleighs and a replica of Abraham Lincoln's coffin. The museum is north of downtown. From Interstate Highway 45, take the Airtex Exit, travel west. Turn north onto Ella Boulevard; Barren Springs is the first intersection.

In a city as hot as Houston, it seems appropriate that there would be a fire museum. The **Houston Fire Museum**, *2403 Milam, Tel. 713/524-2526,*

Tuesday to Saturday 10am to 4pm, features displays on Houston firefighting. The first firefighters were the volunteer residents of Houston who were organized by the city founder Augustus Allen. They are remembered as the Bucket Brigade because buckets were their tools of fire fighting. Exhibits include the city's oldest fire fighting wagons, and trace the history of firemen up to the modern day.

Part of the Museum of Fine Arts is the former resident of prominent Texan, Ima Hogg. She was the daughter of the state's first governor to be born in Texas. For her entire life she collected American antiques, and that collection remains in her home, **Bayou Bend Collection and Gardens**, *1 Westcott Street, Tel. 713/639-7750, closed Monday, open Tuesday to Friday 10am to 2:45pm, Saturday 10am to 5pm, Sunday 1pm to 5pm, admission $10 adults, $5 children*. The gardens are open Tuesday to Saturday 10am to 5pm, Sunday 1pm to 5pm. Bayou Bend is one of the most extensive collections of its type open to the public. You will gain a rare glimpse into the life one of the most powerful families in Texas at the turn-of-the-century. The grandeur of the home is matched by the elegant manicured gardens. The collection is free to families with small children on the third Sunday of each month.

The **Port of Houston**, *7300 Clinton Drive, Gate 8, Wharf 7, Tel. 713/670-2614*, is one of the largest in the world. See the ships from the observation deck or take a free sightseeing cruise. The ninety minute trip is sponsored by the port authority and you must make reservations at least two months in advance to get a seat. The Port of Houston is accessible from Loop 610 east.

Clear Lake Area

Clear Lake is the closest body of water to central Houston, and therefore popular for boating, wind-surfing and sunbathing. The area is the home of NASA, which has been an important part of Houston for decades. The **Space Center Houston**, *1601 NASA Road 1, Houston, Tel. 713/244-2100 or 800/972-0369, Monday to Friday, 10am to 5pm, Saturday and Sunday 7pm*, brings to earth the marvels of man's encounters with outer space. A visit to the Space Center takes at least four hours to appreciate the many films and exhibits. The Space Center has an extensive collection of space suits, the Apollo 17 module, and the Saturn V rocket, among others. But there is far more than museum-style exhibits.

The interactive displays let you experience the feeling of repairing a satellite in space and landing a space shuttle. Movies explore the far reaches of space and the question of man's destiny in space. The Space Center is an amazing trek to where we have been and will go in our universe. From Memorial Day to Labor Day the Space Center has extended hours, daily 9am to 7pm. To get to NASA from Houston, take Interstate Highway 45 (Gulf Freeway) south to the Space Center/NASA Exit. The clearly marked signs lead you to the center.

You can visit the **Budweiser Brewery**, *755 Gellhorn, Tel. 713/670-1695*. The brewery is open year-round and there is no admission charge. A tour will take you through the entire process of brewing beer. From central Houston, take Interstate Highway 10 east to Gellhorn.

Nightlife & Entertainment

Astroworld, *Loop 610 South, Tel. 713/799-8404*, is one of the Six Flag amusement parks featuring Warner Brothers characters Bugs Bunny and Batman. This is the largest theme park in Texas and its newest ride, the Dungeon Drop, plummets 237 feet. Of the 34 rides, nearly one-third are twisting, spiraling roller coasters that can keep you occupied all day. Or you can take a water break at **Waterworld** next door. In the summertime Waterworld features stunt shows and even more rides. The parks are open almost every weekend through the year and during the weekdays in summer.

Even though Houston has no professional football team (for the time being)) and the Houston Astros left the poor old **Astrodome** behind, it is still a tourist site in itself. Reaching a height of 18 stories, the Astrodome is a feat of modern engineering and design and was billed the Eighth Wonder of the World when it was built in the 1960s. Tours are held each day at 11am 1pm and 3pm. To reach the Astrodome, take Loop 610 south to Kirby Drive; you can't miss the giant dome.

Houston has a vibrant and active arts scenes. Both the **Houston Grande Opera** and **Houston Ballet** perform regular seasons in the **Wortham Center**, *510 Preston Boulevard, Tel. 713/237-1439*. This amazing modern theater complex is part of the Houston Civic Center. You can purchase tickets at the Ticket Center, *550 Prairie Street*. The world-class performances of the **Houston Symphony** are held at the **Jesse H. Jones Hall**, *615 Louisiana Street, Tel. 713/222-3415*.

You can enjoy the arts and culture of Houston in the heart of Hermann Park. The **Miller Outdoor Theater**, *Hermann Park, Concert Drive, Tel. 713/ 520-3290*, hosts evening performances and daytime festivals. The symphony, ballet and theater companies perform here throughout the year. General admission is free; you may purchase tickets for reserved seating. Children's shows are held on many weekend mornings from March to October. Some of the recent performances include Ambassadors International Ballet Folklorico, the Houston Grand Opera and the Houston Youth Symphony.

For nearly two decades the annual festivals at the Miller Outdoor Theater draws huge crowds and the best talent in the country. In March, the Sounds and Dance of Puerto Rico brings the color and festivity of the island to Houston. The Pan African Cultural Festival, a celebration of African-American heritage, is held for three days at the end of May and includes one evening performance. A Freedom Festival and Blues Festival celebrates Juneteenth on June 19, the day slavery ended in Texas. In mid-October, Asian food, martial arts exhibition performances, music and dance, fill the day for the Asian-American Festival.

Houston's first professional dramatic company, the **Alley Theater**, *615 Texas Avenue, Tel. 713/228-8421*, holds performances during the week, on an on-going basis. The **Ensemble Theater**, *3535 Main Street, Tel. 713/520-0055*, is Houston's African-American professional theater. For 20 years this company has produced the highest quality plays. In addition to the regular season, youth programs and community outreach projects are held during the year.

Bars & Clubs

THE FABULOUS SATELLITE LOUNGE, *3616 Washington Avenue, Tel. 713/869-2665.*

The live music here *is* fabulous. Jazz and swing tunes set the stage for the martini-and-cigar crowd. The bands that play here often are not well-known, but they are usually very good. Occasionally the dance floor is hopping.

THE HOUSTON BREWERY, *6224 Richmond Avenue, Tel. 713/953-0101. Credit cards accepted.*

This is Houston's largest brew pub. The large dining room serves food during the day and evening. The bar area has a somewhat more cozy feeling. The best way to enjoy the pub is to bring your own crowd of beer lovers. Each day a different stout, bitter or ale is featured in the special. The beer is exceptional.

LA CARAFE, *813 Congress Avenue, Tel. 713/229-9399.*

The downtown area in Houston, long deserted in the evening, is once again becoming the place for going out. La Carafe is unquestionably the bar with the most personality in Houston-possibly in the entire state. The dark, cozy narrow room remains untouched by time, and takes you back to the days of the Old West. The bar overlooks Market Square. From the tall bar windows you can see the skyscrapers of downtown. La Carafe serves beer on tap and wine by the bottle.

SOLERO, *910 Prairie Street, Tel. 713/227-2265. Credit cards accepted.*

Solero stands in a fabulous antique building amid the skyscrapers of downtown Houston. This bar serves tapas all day, and many come here for dinner. It is easy to spend hours over the delicious small servings of marinated mushrooms, Spanish tortilla and Manchego cheese with apples. You can also try not-so-Spanish selections such as Tempura vegetable medley or grilled chorizo with sausage. The tapas can be ordered in small or large servings. The crowd, mostly young and beautiful, throw back martinis and wine by the bottle late into the evening.

For a night on the town, you can join trendy Houstonites at the **Richmond Avenue District**. This area, which runs from the 5600 to the 6500 block of

The Houston International Festival

The **Houston International Festival** celebrates world cultures during the last half of April. The main events focus on music and art and are held on the last two weekends of April. During the week, free outdoor concerts are held downtown during the lunch hour. On the weekends twenty blocks of downtown are taken over by the festival. Food, dance, music and art from just about every culture you can imagine are here. For more information, contact the offices of the Houston International Festival, *1221 Lamar, Suite 715, Houston, Tel. 713-654-8808, Fax 654-1719.*

Richmond Avenue, has many bars, restaurants and night clubs. Pedestrians crowd the sidewalks and establishments.

Sports & Recreation
The Houston Livestock Show & Rodeo

The **Houston Livestock Show and Rodeo**, *Reliant Center, Reliant Stadium, and various venues about town, Tel. 713/791-9000, Website: www.rodeohouston.com, tickets available online at ticketmaster.com, by Tel. 713/629-3700, major credit cards accepted*, takes place in mid-February. The Trail Ride and Rodeo Parade are the big events, along with nightly concerts by big name country and western acts.

The **Trail Ride** is a unique event that takes days to complete. It's actually many trail rides, all of them converging in Houston's Memorial Park to participate in the traditional **Rodeo Parade** through downtown Houston. Over 6,000 riders, some from nearly 400 miles away, descend with their horses, covered wagons, and western gear for a grand rodeo kick-off celebration.

Also on opening weekend, the **World's Championship Bar-B-Que Contest** gets underway. The event started as a friendly little competition in 1973, and now draws over 300 competing teams and 175,000 hungry fans. The proceeds from your $6 admission ticket to this colossal-sized picnic go to charity, and you may redeem your stub for a free chopped brisket sandwich, beans, and cole slaw.

The **RodeoHouston** is the richest regular-season rodeo in the world, with only the National Finals in Las Vegas offering a bigger purse. The prizes equal over three-quarters of a million dollars, and each event features only the top sixty-four cowboys and cowgirls in their field. The crème de la crème compete in bareback bronco riding, steer wrestling, barrel racing, calf roping, and many other events. Country music performances and fireworks wind down every night's events.

And don't miss the **Livestock Show** that gives ranchers a chance to exhibit their best stock and you a chance to gawk at the prizewinners. The auctions are fascinating to watch, and will give you a whole new perspective on farming and ranching. Who knows, you might see a celebrities bidding on champion livestock for their own ranches – the 2001 Grand Champion Steer was purchased for $600,000 by wrestler Stone Cold Steve Austin!

Enjoying Nature

The environmental surroundings of Houston provide an abundance of natural beauty. A variety of plants from tropical palm trees to evergreen pines thrive in Houston's hot, humid climate. You can enjoy the flora almost all-year round at any of the area's nature preserves and gardens. The **Houston Arboretum and Nature Center**, *4501 Woodway, Tel. 713/681-8433, open daily 8:30am to 6pm*, has five miles of trails for easy hikes and self-guided tours. The **Discovery Room**, *open daily 10am to 4pm*, in the Nature Center is an educational facility that provides resources for children's groups to have a hands-on learning experience in nature. Classes about native flora and fauna take place throughout the year.

For a more formal approach to the outdoors, visit the **Houston Garden Center**, *1500 Hermann Drive, Tel. 713/529-3960*. The garden areas include flowerbeds, rose gardens, a sculpture garden and Chinese-style pavilion. **Hermann Park**, *6001 Fanin Street, Tel. 713/522-8490*, is the home of the **Japanese Garden**, *Tel 713/520-3283, open daily 10am to 6pm, Admission $1.50 adults, 1.00 seniors, .25 children*, which is a tranquil place for a casual stroll and some contemplation. The garden was designed by famous landscape architect, Ken Nakajima.

Kids have a place of their own at Hermann Park. The **Playground For All Children** is a large recreational area with challenging and enjoyable outdoor activities.

Biking enthusiasts will enjoy the **Alek Velodrome** *in Cullen Park, 19,008 Saums Drive, Tel. 281/578-0858*. This is a full Olympic-size arena and is open to the public for training. Hours of the velodrome vary by season: from March to October, Tuesday to Thursday 5pm to 9pm, Saturday to Sunday 4pm to 8pm; from November to February, Monday, Wednesday and Friday 5pm to 9pm, Saturday and Sunday 2pm to 6pm.

The Houston Parks Department operates the **Memorial Fitness Center**, *6402 Arnot, Tel. 713/802-1662*, which has aerobic classes, weight training facilities and a swimming pool that are open to the public.

Tennis

Houston has a number of public tennis courts:
- **Homer L. Ford Center**, *5225 Calhoun, Tel. 713/747-5466*
- **Memorial Tennis Center**, *6000 Memorial Loop Drive, Tel. 713/861-3765*
- **Le Clear Tennis Center**, *9506 Gessner, Tel. 713/772-0296*

Golf

Golf is a very popular recreational activity in Houston, in part because of the excellent weather year-round. Municipal golf courses offer easy access to the game for a nominal greens fee. Public courses have seasonal hours.
- **Hermann Golf Course**, *6201 Golf Drive, Tel. 713/526-0077*
- **Melrose Golf Course**, *401 East Canino Road, Tel 281/847-1214*
- **Memorial Golf Course**, *6001 Memorial Loop Drive, Tel. 713/862-4033*
- **Wortham Golf Course**, *7000 Capital, Houston, Tel. 713/921-3227*

Spectator Sports

The **Houston Aeros** are the city's professional hockey team that plays in the International Hockey League (IHL). They are one of ten teams in the western conference and play national teams from San Antonio, Chicago, Las Vegas and the Canadian team the Manitoba Moose. Games are held at the Summit, which seats over 15,000 spectators. The season runs October through March.

Trying to follow the status of Houston's professional sports temas the last few years could leave your head spinning. The **Houston Astros**, perennial National League divisional champs, used to play baseball in the Astrodome until they moved to their new field, Astros Park. Astros Park is an interim name, mind you, as disgraced energy corporation Enron's name was stripped from the ballpark following its spectacular collapse. In any case, you'll find the Astros in their state-of-the-art field with its retractable roof downtown – who knows what the field will be named by the time you read this!

NFL football is no less confusing. Houston used to be home to the Houston Oilers, who moved to Tennessee and became the Titans. For a few years Houston languished without a pro football team until they were awarded a new franchise. The **Houston Texans** will begin playing in the fall of 2002, but they will not be playing on the hallowed old Astrodome. They will be playing in their brand new **Reliant Stadium**, which has been constructed right next to the Astrodome.

Finally, Houston has the NBA **Houston Rockets** who play at Compaq Center (formerly the Summit). Another excellent basketball team plays at Compaq, the **Houston Comets**. This is the WNBA team that won the first four championships of women's professional basketball.

Horse races are held in the spring and summer at the **Sam Houston Race Track**, *Sam Houston Tollway, Tel. 281/807-7223*. Class 1 thoroughbred races are run in the late summer, from July to September.

Shopping

The **Galleria**, *5075 Westheimer Road, Tel. 713/621-1907*, is Houston's premier shopping mall, with Marshall Field's, Lord & Taylor and Neiman Marcus as the major stores. The Galleria has three phases and some 300 merchants: the Galleria I, on the east, home to the Westin Oaks Hotel, Galleria II, the central area which has a high-rise office building and Galleria III, on the west side. The Galleria has an ice skating rink. An express parking entrance is located at Post Oak Boulevard and Westheimer Road, or valet park at Neiman Marcus or one of the Westin hotels.

The entire area along Post Oak Boulevard just south of Loop 610, known as the Galleria area, has upscale shops and fine restaurants.

The Heights

The charming old streets of the Heights are lined with Victorian homes that now hold antique shops, gift stores and cafes. You can spend at least an afternoon here browsing through the art and artifacts. One of the largest stores is **Antiques on Nineteenth**, *345 West 19th Street, Tel. 713/869-5030*, which has over 5000 square feet of furniture and memorabilia. **The Heights Station**, *121 Heights Boulevard, Tel. 713/868-3175*, is a conglomeration of 15 small stores that sell small antiques, glassware and collectibles. Those with high-end collections may find something at **Chippendale, Eastlake, Louis & Phyfe**, *250 West 19th Street, Tel. 713/862-3035*. The art stores in the area have off-beat collections that are usual even for the southwest. **Yubo's Ethnic & Folkart Gallery**, *1012 Yale, Tel. 713/862-3239*, sells handmade crafts from the far reaches of Mexico and South America.

The Heights is located just north of downtown, in the nine blocks west of Interstate Highway 45, between Loop 610 to the north and Katy Freeway to the south.

Old Town Spring

If you desire the surrounding of a small town, venture to **Old Town Spring**, just north of Houston on Interstate Highway 45. The renovated shopping district has 150 small shops in antique homes. Many of the arts and crafts are hand-made by the shop owners themselves. Spring was once a small town isolated from Houston. Now it has become a suburb and a fashionable area for young professionals to call home. To get to Spring, take Interstate Highway 45 North to the Spring Cypress exit (70-A). Go east one mile.

Bay Area

Naturally a city the size of Houston has bargain hunters, and they shop at the **Lone Star State Factory Stores**, *Interstate Highway 45, LaMarque, Tel. 409/938-3333*. This outlet center advertises that its prices are from 30 to 70 percent below retail. The stores include national clothing, kitchenware, china and shoe stores. From Houston, take Interstate Highway 45 south to exit 13. The outlet center is open seven days a week.

Excursions & Day Trips

The final battle in the Texas war for independence was fought at San Jacinto. The battleground at San Jacinto is both a State and National Monument. The **San Jacinto Monument**, *3523 Highway 134, La Porte, Tel. 713/479-2431 or 479-2411, open daily 10am to 5:30pm*, stands 489 feet tall and marks the final military victory of Sam Houston's Texas forces over the Mexican Army of General Santa Anna. The bottom floor houses a visitor's center and provides elevator access to the observation deck on the top. A thirty-five minute film describes the military victory and its impact upon the histories of Texas, Mexico and the United States.

The **San Jacinto State Historical Park**, *3523 Highway 134, La Porte, Tel. 713/479-2431 or 479-2411*, covers 1,000 acres of coastal plains. The park offers areas for fishing and bird watching. Picnic facilities have shelters. The battlefield has a trail of markers that describe the event. You can visit an important part of twentieth century history at the San Jacinto State Historical Park. The World War I **Battleship Texas**, *Wednesday to Sunday 10am to 5pm*, is open to the public. The ship served in both World Wars.

To reach the park, take Loop 610 east to Highway 225. Travel east on 225, then exit Highway 134 and travel north.

LIBERTY

Liberty is one of the few towns in Texas that was once a Spanish settlement that was not a mission. In the eighteenth century a small Spanish military post stood here. After the decline of the steamboat industry, Liberty ceased to maintain its economic importance. Today the town is remembered at the one-time home of Sam Houston, who practiced law here.

Liberty is about 50 miles east of Houston on US Highway 90. Beaumont lies about 60 miles east of Liberty on the same highway. Many notable historic monuments are north of the town. The Liberty Chamber of Commerce, *1915 Trinity Street, Tel. 409/336-5736*, offers tourist information.

The **Geraldine D. Humphreys Cultural Center**, *1710 Sam Houston Street, Tel. 409/336-8901, open Monday to Thursday 9am to 6pm, Friday 1pm to 5pm, Saturday 10am to 4pm*, located in the historic downtown, sponsors plays and houses a small museum.

Liberty's Bell

When the founding families of Texas planted their roots, they aspired to reproduce the idealism and independence of the American Colonies. Town names such as Liberty, Lexington and William Penn are hardly coincidence. In Liberty, the town took their homage to the American colonists one step further – they commissioned their own **Liberty Bell**. The bell was made by the same British foundry that produced the Liberty Bell in Philadelphia, Pennsylvania. The bell stands next to the Humphreys Cultural Center, in the center of town. The Texas version is in working order, and on special occasions you can hear freedom ring in Liberty, Texas.

Texas history buffs will love the **Sam Houston Regional Library and Research Center**, *Texas Highway 146, Liberty, Tel. 409/336-8821*, which is part of the Texas State Library system. Part of the research collection is on display in the museum. The early development of Texas is shown through some of the earliest display, such as written accounts of the first Anglo settlers in the region. Sam Houston's life and achievements are the focus of a section of displays. Two historic nineteenth century homes stand on the library grounds and are open to the public. From Houston, take Highway east to Liberty. Turn north on Highway 146 and travel two miles. Signs clearly indicate the entrance.

Practical Information

The **American Automobile Association (AAA)**, *3000 Southwest Freeway, Tel 713/524-1851; for 24 hour road service 713/521-0211*, provides information and assistance for AAA members.

American Express has six travel service locations in Houston, three of which have mail service for card holders. The most centrally located office, American Express Travel Services, *5015 Westheimer Road, 713/626-5740*, can assist with travel arrangements.

A number of international carriers have offices in Houston:
- **Air France**, *500 Dallas Street, Suite 2850, Tel. 713/654-3600*
- **Aeromexico**, *4900 Woodway, Suite 750, Tel. 713/939-0077*
- **American Airlines**, *5858 Westheimer Road, Suite 207, Tel. 281/878-0005*
- **Aviateca Guatemalan Airways**, *5821 Southwest Freeway, Suite 100, 713/665-3090*
- **British Airways**, *10700 North Freeway, Suite 900, Tel. 281/878-2700*
- **Continental Airlines**, *George Bush Intercontinental Airport, P. O. Box 4607, Tel. 800/525-0280*

- **Delta Airlines**, *340 North Sam Houston Tollway, Suite 216, 800/221-1212*
- **KLM Royal Dutch Airlines**, *One Allen Center, Suite 2810, 713/658-9741*
- **Lufthansa German Airlines**, *1221 Lamar Street, Suite 1313, Tel. 800/ 645-3880*
- **TACA Costa Rican Airlines**, *5821 Southwest, Suite 100, 713/665-3090*
- **United Airlines**, *George Bush Intercontinental Airport, P. O. Box 60909, Tel. 281/230-8100*

You can find out anything you may need to know about all aspects of visiting or living in Houston from the **Greater Houston Convention and Visitors Bureau**, *801 Congress, Tel. 713/227-3100 or 800/4-HOUSTON, Monday to Friday 8:30am to 5pm*. The bureau sells tee shirts, coffee mugs and other gifts emblazoned with the "Houston Proud" slogan. And you are only a phone call away from what is happening in Houston, thanks to the **Downtown Events Hotline**, *Tel. 713/654-8900*.

Columbus

Columbus claims the distinction of being the oldest surveyed and platted Anglo-American settlement in Texas. The legendary Indian village of Montezuma used to occupy the area.

Columbus has a rich history and played an important part in the Texas Revolution. It was settled by some of Stephen F. Austin's Original 300 Families in 1821. Sam Houston burned it to the ground in March of 1836 as he retreated from Santa Anna's forces to San Jacinto. The flight of all the settlers before the armies became known as the Runaway Scrape, but by 1837 Columbus was rising from the ashes. Now this little town flourishes in a genteel country atmosphere, with a focus on historic buildings and homes.

The layout is classic small-town Texas—a handsome old courthouse stands smack in the middle of town with a square surrounding it. The barbershop with its candy-striped pole sits next to the meat market on Milam Street. Nearby stands the Stafford Opera House, which also houses the visitor's bureau.

Each May, Columbus holds the **Live Oak Festival** featuring German food and music on the Courthouse Square, a parade, an arts & crafts show, a historic homes tour, a fun run, a dominoes tournament, and more. For specific dates and additional information, contact the Columbus Convention & Visitors Bureau (see *Practical Information*, below).

Arrivals & Depatures

Columbus is located on the Colorado River, about 70 miles west of Houston at the junction of Interstate Highway 10 and State Highway 71.

Where to Stay

MAGNOLIA OAKS, *634 Spring Street. Tel. 979/732-2726, Fax 979/733-0872, Toll free 888/677-0593, Website: www.magnoliaoaks.com. $100-195. Credit cards accepted.*

This bed & breakfast is located in an historic house, with the historical marker in the front yard to prove it. It's a charming high-ceilinged Victorian confectionary of an inn, complete with magnolia trees, lacy gingerbread front porches, and stained-glass windows. There are four bedrooms in the main house, three with king-sized beds and two with fireplaces and Jacuzzi baths. There is also a German saltbox cottage on the property that contains three more bedrooms and is available for extended stays.

COLUMBUS INN, *2208 Highway 71 South. Tel. 409/732-5723, Fax 409/732-6084. 72 Rooms. $40-60. Credit cards accepted.*

This no-frills inn has clean rooms and plenty of parking. All rooms come with morning coffee and a newspaper. The two-room suites are spacious. The outdoor pool has a hot tub attached. From Interstate Highway 10 take exit 696.

HOLIDAY INN EXPRESS, *4321 Interstate Highway 10. Tel. 979/733-9300, Fax 979/732-2364, Toll free 800/465-4329. 67 Rooms. $69-150. Credit cards accepted.*

Located just off the Interstate, this is a pleasant and fairly new motel. There is an outdoor pool as well as a free continental breakfast, and pets are allowed.

Where to Eat

SCHOBEL'S RESTAURANT, *2020 Milam Street. Tel. 979/732-2385.*

This family-style restaurant is by far the most popular spot in town, where both locals and passersby load up on good old-fashioned favorites like the German Plate and homemade pie. There is a daily noon buffet.

JERRY MIKESKA'S BAR-B-Q, *Interstate Highway 10, exit 696. Tel. 979/732-3101.*

Just look for the round building and you'll be at Mikeska's. The atmosphere is decidedly on game, hunting, and livestock, the bar-b-q is quite good, and the Sunday buffet is popular.

Seeing the Sights

One of the nifty things about Columbus is that you can give yourself an in-depth historical driving tour simply by tuning your car radio to the specified AM radio frequency! Your starting place will be the **Stafford Opera House**, *425 Spring Street at Spur 52 (Milam Street)*, where you can pick up the driving tour maps and other materials, as well as take a look at the historic 1886 building where plays and concerts are still given. You may also take a self-guided walking tour featuring historic homes, antiques shopping, and eateries.

Columbus contains more than 70 historical markers, so consider these listings the mere tip of the iceberg. The first judicial court of the Republic of Texas was held under a tree on what are now the grounds of the **Colorado County Court House**, *Courthouse Square*, in 1837. The courthouse was not built until 1890, long after Texas was a state. Note the Masonic symbol engraved in the granite cornerstone. Visitors can step inside the District Court Room for a look at the green stained-glass ceiling. Outside the courthouse a tall castle-style tower stands on the southwest corner of the square. Now the **United Daughters of the Confederacy Museum**, this was the water tower for the city from 1883 to 1912. It took 400,000 hand-made bricks to build the tower's 32 inch-thick walls.

The **Alley Log Cabin Museum**, *1224 Bowie Street*, was built by one of Stephen Austin's colonists in 1836, just after the Runaway Scrape. It is a period furnished two-room log cabin, one of the last surviving structures that links Columbus to its distant past. In a small frame building behind the Alley Log Cabin is the **Antique Tool Museum**.

Nightlife & Entertainment

If you are a fan of country and western music the way it used to be, the **Columbus Opry**, *The Oaks Theater, 715 Walnut Street, Tel. 979/732-9210, Website: www.columbusopry.com*, is probably your idea of heaven. Every Saturday night a variety of performers gather to provide a family show of traditional and contemporary country and western, polka, bluegrass, and gospel music. The intrepid house musicians, The Texas Sagebrush Band, provide accompaniment.

Practical Information

The **Columbus Convention & Visitors Bureau**, *425 Spring Street in the Stafford Opera House, Tel. 979/732-5135, Fax 979/732-5881, Toll free 877/444-7339, Website: columbustexas.org*, has information about the productions at the Stafford House, maps of downtown, historical brochures and pamphlets, and wildflower trails and information.

If you would like someone else to provide the commentary, the **Magnolia Homes Tour Office**, *Tel. 409/732-5135*, offers guided tours of the city's historic sites and homesteads. The Magnolia office is located right next to the Stafford Opera House.

San Augustine

This city shares the name of a larger city in Florida for good reason. The first road to cross Texas was mapped out by the Spanish in the seventeenth century. El Camino Real, or The Royal Way, ran from Mexico City to San Augustine, Florida. Part of Highway 21 covers the same ground as the old Spanish Imperial route.

This small town stands in the heart of the Texas piney woods region. The landscape is characterized by rolling hills and tall evergreen trees. The winters are cold and crisp, with frequent morning frost. The summers are very hot and humid.

Arrivals & Depatures

San Augustine is located on Highway 96 near the Louisiana border. Highway 21 takes you directly into town.

Where to Stay

CAPTAIN E. E. DOWNS HOUSE, *301 East Main Street. Tel. 409/275-2289, Fax 409/275-3444. Rates: $45 to $75. Credit cards accepted.*

This Victorian home is in the center of town, just off the town square. Its five rooms are furnished with antiques that bring the historic character of the home to life. The lovely neighborhood provides ample opportunity for a stroll. The largest room, the master suite, is spacious and accommodating. A light breakfast is served in the morning.

THE WADE HOUSE, *128 East Columbia Street. Tel. 409/275-5489. Rates: $40 to $80. Credit cards accepted.*

The historic highlight of this relatively modern home is a large collection of hats. This home does not reflect the long history of the area. But the friendly atmosphere is inviting, and you will leave with a sense of really getting to know the small town. Three of the five guest rooms have private baths.

Seeing the Sights

In the early 1700's the Spanish established a mission in San Augustine. The **Mission Senora de los Dolores de los Ais**, or Dolores Mission, was the site of conflict between the French and Spanish, and was deserted by the late 1700s. Nothing remains of the Spanish settlement, although the site of the Dolores Mission is commemorated with an historical marker. To find the Mission grounds, walk four blocks south from the courthouse.

The most important historic home in town is the home of **Ezekiel W. Cullen** *at the corner of Congress and Market Streets, open Thursday to Sunday 1pm to 5pm; closed Monday to Wednesday,* which was built in 1839. Cullen was a judge, and the house is evidence of his wealth and political power. The Greek Revival structure has a full-sized ball room which takes up the entire top story.

The main attraction in the area is the beautiful national forest preserves. Eleven miles north of San Augustine, on Texas Highway 147, you will find the **Angelina National Forest**. The large **Sabine National Forest** is only five miles west of San Augustine on Farm-to-Market Road 353.

Practical Information

The **San Augustine Chamber of Commerce**, *West Columbia Street, open Monday to Friday 9am to 4pm*, provides area information.

Palestine

In Palestine, the annual **Dogwood Trails Heritage Festival** starts the spring with a celebration of the dogwood blossom season. Downtown Palestine hosts a carnival and theater productions. Square dances and a bicycle tour through the countryside get the community and visitors active. The festival takes place on the last two weekends of March and the first weekend of April.

Arrivals & Departures

Palestine is on Highway 287, which can be reached by Interstate Highway 45 from Dallas in the north or Houston in the south.

Where to Stay

SPIRIT INN, *921 North Sycamore Drive*, and **SPIRIT HOUSE**, *109 East Pine. Tel. 903/723-9565 or 800/224-0999. Rates: singles $45 to $65; doubles $65 to $85.*

The Spirit Inn and Spirit House are two historic homes about one block from each other that offer comfortable accommodations in the heart of one of Palestine's most historic neighborhoods. The Spirit Inn has four rooms, all with cable television; the Spirit House has three rooms and an outdoor courtyard with a hot tub. Both houses were constructed in the first part of the century and retain their historic charm. Children are welcome and a bassinet can be rented for infants. Weekend stays include a delicious country breakfast, usually served outdoors. From Highway 79, turn north onto Sycamore Street.

APPLE ANNIE'S, *1014 North Sycamore Street. Tel. 903/729-1789, Website: www.appleanniesbedandbreakfast.com. 2 Rooms. Rates: $75-100. Credit cards accepted.*

The beautiful Colonial-style home was built in 1912 and has been designated a historical landmark. The large gardens are lush with the Southern fragrance of magnolias, and alaze with the colors of azaleas and other seasonal flowers. There is one guest room in the main house and a separate cottage. Both come with a full home-cooked breakfast. No pets, children under 12, or smoking.

COUNTRY CHRISTMAS TREE FARM, *514 North Sycamore. Tel. 903/ 729-4836 or 729-2671, Fax 729-0322. Rates: $60-85. Credit cards accepted.*

Located in the historical district, this inn offers several options for accommodation. The Sunday House is a two-bedroom country-theme residence with kitchen and dining room. The Carriage House is a studio residence located above the garage. You can also make arrangements to stay at the rural tree farm. The modern house has four guest rooms, the bunkhouse has two rooms, and there are two private cottages. The farm is located miles from the nearest city; call for details.

DAYS INN, *1100 East Palestine Avenue. Tel. 903/729-3151 or 800/DAYS INN. Rates: $35 to $79.*

This is a better-than-average budget hotel with a fitness room, outdoor heated pool pool, tennis courts and ample parking areas. The Gazebo Restaurant serves food all day. The rooms include cable television and HBO. Palestine Avenue is Highway 79.

Camping

RED ROCK RANCH, *Route 8 Box 121. Tel. 903/723-1836. Camp sites $12 to $27.*

Red Rock Ranch is a small, private park and campground located just a few miles from Palestine. Facilities include a picnic area, bathrooms and showers. Entrance to the park is $3 per car. Rustic campsites are available, and priced according to the number of people camping. Call ahead to reserve a space and get directions to the campground.

Where to Eat

EILENBERGERS BAKERY, *512 North John Street. Tel . 903/729-2253. Credit cards accepted.*

The bakery is an institution in Palestine. Eilenbergers once supplied East Texas with baked bread. Today the bakery specializes in fruitcake and pastry. The tearoom is a cozy spot for a light snack and coffee. Here you will taste the flavor of baked goodies that make an East Texan feel at home.

RANCH HOUSE, *301 East Crawford. Tel. 903/723-8778. Credit cards accepted.*

The Ranch House is the family dining spot of choice for locals. The generous steaks, hearty side dishes and children's plates please everyone. The restaurant is known for their fresh salads.

OLD BOSTON SANDWICH SHOP, *119 West Main Street. Tel. 903/729-4099.*

This small shop makes fresh deli sandwiches and soup of the day. Stop in for ice cream and a soda when visiting the historic section of downtown.

Seeing the Sights

In the center of the city you will find the landmark buildings of Palestine's past. The **Anderson County Courthouse**, *Courthouse Square, Lacy Street*, was built in the neo-Classical style in 1914. The courthouse is located between Fannin and Dechard Streets. The beautiful **Carnegie Library**, *502 North Queen Street, Tel. 903/729-6066*, is now used as the Palestine Chamber of Commerce.

In 1851, Colonel Howard built his home in Palestine. **Howard House Museum**, *1011 North Perry Street, Tel. 903/584-3225*, has a collection of antiques from the mid-nineteenth century reflecting the lifestyle of the merchant class of East Texas. Visitors must schedule an appointment to visit the museum.

Local history is preserved in an exemplary fashion at the **Museum for East Texas Culture**, *400 Michaux Street, Tel. 903/723-1914*. The building was once the only high school in Palestine, then later served as the junior high school. The park surrounding the museum has picnic tables and tennis courts that are open to the public.

Shopping

Those who appreciate the work of artisans should take the time to find an out-of-the-way shop, **Old Farmhouse Pottery**, *Country Road 1805, Maydelle, Tel. 903/795-3779*. True to its name, the shop is indeed in a farmhouse dating from the 1930s. The resident artist, David Henly, is a master of hand-made pottery who makes functional stoneware and gallery-quality art. You can visit the studio from Thursday to Monday 1pm to 5pm or by appointment.

TO get there, travel east from Palestine on US Highway 84. Turn north onto County Road 1804, which turn into County Road 1805 after a half mile. The shop is on the east side of the road, about three-quarters of a mile from the highway.

Excursions & Day Trips

The **National Scientific Balloon Facility**, *Tel. 903/729-0271*, is open to the public. Tours of the facility are free, but you must call in advance to make arrangements. To reach the National Scientific Balloon Facility, take Highway 287 west for five miles.

Every September the tomato harvest is celebrated at the **Jacksonville Tomatofest**. The festivities include the Miss Tomato Pageant, barbecue cooking and hot sauce making contests and lots of games for kids. Jacksonville is at the intersection of US Highways 69, 79 and 175, about 25 miles northeast of Palestine.

Steam Trains

The years when the steam engines tamed the American frontier were the glory days of east Texas. The Palestine-Rusk Railroad was a working industrial line from 1896 to 1921. The **Texas State Railroad Historical Park** captures the by-gone railroad days with working tourist trains.

Today the Texas State Railroad operates locomotives that run between Palestine and Rusk from March to November. Eight antique locomotives make the 25-mile trip. The one-way journey takes one-and-one-half hours and passengers must return the same day. Trains leave both Rusk and Palestine at 11am and return to the city of origin at 1:30pm. Each station is reconstructed in the turn-of-the-century style and has a visitor's center, gift shop and restaurant. Round trip fare is $15 per adult and $9 per child. Evening trains run one evening in the spring and once in the summer. To make reservations, call the **Texas State Railroad**, *P. O. Box 39, Rusk, Tel. 800/442-8951 (in Texas), 903/683-2561 (outside Texas).*

Both train depots are surrounded by state parks offering picnic areas and playgrounds. The Rusk Park has camping sites and tennis courts. To reach the Palestine Station and State Park, from Loop 256 take Highway 84 and travel east 2 miles. The Rusk Station and State Park is on Highway 84, three miles west of downtown.

Texas' Only Native American Earth Mounds

The only Native American structures in the state are earthen mounds at the **Caddoan Mounds State Park**, Highway 21, Route 2 Box 85C, Alto, Tel 409/858-3218, open daily 10am to 6pm. The mounds were constructed just after the turn of the first millennium, and they have been studied by American archaeologists since 1919. A reconstructed Caddoan home and a museum are open to the public. Visitors can take a self-guided tour on a 3/4 mile trail. From Rusk, take Highway 21 south approximately ten miles.

Mission Tejas State Historical Park

To venture even farther back in history, visit a bit of the Spanish legacy in East Texas. The first Spanish mission built in Texas was not an adobe compound in West Texas, but a small log cabin in the East Texas woods built in 1690. Mission San Francisco de los Tejas no longer is standing, but a replica of what the building may have looked like commemorates the site at the **Mission Tejas State Historical Park**, *Route 2 Box 108, Grapeland, Tel. 409/ 687-2394.* The park has over three miles of hiking trails, picnic areas, a playground, campsites with full hookups and a fishing pond. From Crockett, travel north on Highway 21 for 22 miles.

Practical Information

The **Palestine Convention and Visitors Bureau**, *North Loop 256 at Highway 287/19, Tel. 903/723-3014, Toll free 800/659-3484, Website: www.visitpalestine.com*, provides literature and brochures, maps of the city, and a self-guided walking tour of downtown.

Rusk

The small town of **Rusk** is responsible for several "firsts" in the State of Texas. The town is named for Thomas Jefferson Rusk, one of the human cornerstones of the state and a leader of the independence movement. He signed the Texas Declaration of Independence and served as the Republic's Secretary of War. After Texas jointed the United States, Rusk became one of the first United States Senators to represent Texas.

Also among the famous who claim Rusk as their home is James Stephen "Jim" Hogg, the first native Texan to become governor of the state. (He may be even better known as the man who named his daughter Ima Hogg. The name was not meant as a joke—Ima was named after a heroine in a novel.) Jim Hogg State Park houses a scale replica of the dogtrot cabin where Hogg was born.

Arrivals & Departures

Rusk is on Highway 84, just east of Palestine.

Where to Stay

Rusk has a number of booking services for its numerous bed and breakfasts. **AAA Reservations**, *Tel. 800/299-1593*, and **Classic B&B Inns**, *Tel. 800/468-2627*, provide information and reservations.

Seeing the Sights

Rusk is a designated **Texas Main Street City**, devoted to the proposition that revitalization does not have to come at the expense of the historical structures that represent the town's heritage. Walk the historic square that surrounds the old courthouse and you'll see cafes, a post office, local dry goods stores—scenes from the American past.

One block east of the town square is **the Rusk Footbridge**, a replica of a footbridge built in 1861 for crossing the gentle valley it spans during rainy seasons. The 546-foot path is said to be the nation's longest footbridge, and runs through shady trees.

The **Thomas J. Rusk Hotel**, *105 East Sixth Street*, sits on the town square. Built in the 1920s, the 36-room hotel is not currently available to guests (hopefully that will change in the near future), but is kept intact with its antique furnishings, waiting for the day when it returns to service.

The **Rusk Post Office**, also on the town square, is remarkable for a mural inside painted by Bernard Baruch Zakheim, an immigrant from Poland who studied under Diego Rivera. "Agriculture and Industry" was painted in 1940 as part of a WPA project.

Practical Information

Most visitors to Rusk spend only a few hours in the city as a stop on the Texas State Railroad historic steam engine. For more information about the city, contact the **Rusk Chamber of Commerce**, *408 North Main Street, Rusk, Texas 75785, Tel. 903/683-2213, Website: www.rusktx.com.*

Chapter 18

If you are used to paying resort prices on the East or West Coast, you're in for a pleasant surprise. This is the "Third Coast," and not many know about the hundreds of miles of shoreline that it has to offer. Everyone knows about **Galveston**, that island of hurricane lore and Victorian gingerbread architecture so close to Houston, but only Texas natives seem to appreciate the charms of the rest of the coastline. From sleepy **Matagorda Bay** to wind-swept **South Padre Island**, the great coastal plain of Texas beckons travelers year-round.

High season on the Texas Gulf Coast runs from May through October. During March and April thousands of students on Spring Break descend on the coast and many hotels demand deposits to secure rooms, while rates can almost double. After that, it's possible to find excellent off-season special fares at many hotels and resorts, and you'll have the beaches and the trails to yourself.

Galveston

The first thing you need to know about **Galveston** is that you'll want to spend more than a day here. Even Texas natives driving down from nearby Houston for the fortieth time know enough to clear off a full weekend. Spend at least one day touring the city and another lolling on the beach. You could throw in a third day devoted just to eating seafood so fresh you'll want to slap it.

During the fin de siecle, Galveston was the largest city in Texas, the second wealthiest city in the United States, and the busiest port in the South. Cotton was King and Galveston not only harvested the cotton that grew in the rich coastal soil of the mainland, but shipped it all over the world. The Strand was the deal-making hub of the world's cotton trade. At the same time businessmen were adorning the city with mansions and palatial public buildings, it garnered a reputation as something of a "sin city," with gamblers, sailors, and clandestine lovers frequenting the many seaside hotels.

Abruptly and tragically, Galveston suffered a reversal of fortune that still ranks as the worst national disaster in U.S. history—the "Great Storm" of 1900. At least 6,000 people died in the fearful hurricane, fully two-thirds of the city's population. It took years (and a 10-mile seawall) for Galveston to resurrect itself, and it never again achieved the status of trade capital of America.

Today, Galveston still recalls its days of grandeur as the greatest port city on the Gulf of Mexico. Though it suffered a decline into tawdriness in the fifties and sixties, several loyal citizens and a devoted historical society have worked tirelessly to transform Galveston into a year-round tourist destination with something for everyone. They have succeeded—enjoy the fruits of their labor.

Each December, the wheels of time turn back to Victorian days for **Dickens on the Strand**, *held the first weekend in December, Tel. 409/765-7834. Website: www.dickensonthestrand.org*. Parades, costumed street vendors, roving entertainers, carolers, and even snow (until it melts!) create seasonal cheer under the gas streetlights of the Strand. Many festivalgoers don Victorian outfits for the occasion, which has grown so much in recent years it now garners national attention.

Galveston hosts the oldest, biggest and best **Mardi Gras**, *Tel. 888/425-4753, Website: www.mardigrasgalveston.com*, celebration in the state. The entire city turns out for the parades that mark Fat Tuesday. Beads and token coins fill the air as the Strand celebrates, and several stages provide live music from acts like BB King and Jonny Lang.

Arrivals & Depatures

Galveston is located on Interstate Highway 45, about 50 miles south of Houston.

Orientation

Past the bridges that connect the barrier island to the mainland, Interstate Highway 45 turns into Broadway, the main thoroughfare that bisects Galveston. Broadway dead-ends into Seawall Boulevard, which runs along the waterfront. Seawall Boulevard becomes Farm Road 3005 outside the city.

Getting Around Town

The **Galveston Island Trolley**, *Tel. 409/797-3900*, is a system of real antique trolleys that run from Seawall Boulevard to the Strand and to assorted major hotels. The main station is located at 21st Street and Seawall Boulevard.

You can catch the trolley approximately every 20 minutes at any given stop. The downtown route is free, while the Seawall route costs a mere $.60.

A grand old triple-decker paddle wheel boat takes tours of Offats Bayou and Galveston Bay. **The Colonel**, *One Hope Boulevard at Moody Gardens, Tel. 409/740-7797 or 888/740-7797*, runs both day and night. The evening cruises include dinner and dancing. You may also reserve one of the Colonel's private rooms, each with its own dance floor and bar, for parties and special occasions.

Where to Stay

HOTEL GALVEZ, *2024 Seawall Boulevard. Tel. 409/765-7721, Fax 409/ 765-5623, Toll free reservations 800/WYNDHAM, Website: www.galveston.com/accom/galvez.html. 228 Rooms, 7 Suites. Rates: $110-475. Credit cards accepted.*

The Galvez embodies Galveston for many people. You see it in photograph after photograph of Galveston's Gilded Era, and many servicemen were quartered here as they waited to be shipped off to their destination during World Wars I and II. Almost everyone who is familiar with Galveston has a story to tell about the Galvez. Built as a showcase of palatial luxury in 1911, the gild has worn off the lily only slightly, and the Galvez still has the power to dazzle. The beautiful loggia and the grand public rooms outshine anything else on the Golf Coast.

A recent renovation modernized every room, and made each one quite comfortable. The hotel is across from the beach, so you can hear the pounding of the surf from sea view windows. Bernardo's Restaurant offers a continental breakfast, lunch, and dinner, as well as champagne Sunday brunch. The Galvez has the best outdoor pool on the Seawall, filled with crystal blue water and surrounded by palm trees and flowering vines. There is a swim-up bar, Jacuzzi, and children's pool with its own little waterfall. Be warned that the atmosphere can run to the "beach party" scene on weekends. Naturally, that's what most people who come to the beach are looking for, but if you prefer more staid surroundings, consider staying at the Tremont in the Strand Historical District.

THE STACIA LEIGH BED & BREAKFAST, *Pier 22 at Harborside Drive. Tel. 409/750-8858, Website: www.stacia-leigh.com. 11 Rooms. Rates: $150-175. Credit cards accepted.*

This floating bed and breakfast is for the traveler who wants something completely out of the ordinary. Housed aboard the 120-foot schooner *Chryseis*, which belonged at one time to none other than Benito Mussolini, the Stacia Leigh is moored right next to the gorgeous tall ship Elissa. Imagine waking each morning in your gently rocking cabin, seagulls calling outside your porthole!

If the *Chryseis* looks familiar, you may have seen it in the movies (most famously *Chitty Chitty Bang Bang*.) It was purchased by the current owner in 1998 and completely renovated to provide eleven staterooms with such amenities as jacuzzi bathtubs. The rooms are small – this is a ship, after all – but the ambiance is refreshing and unique. Next to the ship is a 75-foot two-story observation deck with a hot tub, so you can sit outside and watch the busy harbor in complete luxury.

Breakfast is available every morning, and Megan, the onboard dog, is the picture of decorum. There are no televisions or telephones in the rooms. As the proprietor explained, the rooms were originally equipped with them, but they were removed at the guests' request! Each room is named after a significant World War II personage. You won't find a more historical or romantic place to stay than the Stacia Leigh.

THE TREMONT HOUSE, *2300 Ship Mechanics Row, Galveston. Tel. 409/ 763-0300, Fax 409/763-1539, Toll free reservations 800/874-2300, Website: www.galveston.com/thetremonthouse. 117 Rooms. Rates: $99-185. Credit cards accepted.*

The Tremont House offers the most sophisticated accommodations in town. The hotel is in the center of the historic downtown area, so you are only a short walk away from shopping, entertainment and dining. The feeling is seaside Victorian with a cosmopolitan flair. The elegant four-story atrium lobby features ironwork balconies, potted palm trees, and lacy birdcage elevators. The handsome mahogany Toujouse Bar occupies one corner of the atrium and provides a pleasant place to sip cocktails or read your morning newspaper.

Each room has period-style modernized rooms with hardwood floors. The linens are tailored and crisp, thankfully free of psuedo-Victorian floral overkill. The bathrooms glow in Italian hand-painted tile, and after your bath you can snuggle into a cozy towel fresh off your towel warmer. Although the hotel does not have its own swimming pool, guests have privileges at the Hotel Galvez' tropical outdoor pool and facilities. Guests also have membership privileges at the Galveston Country Club 18-hole golf course.

HARBOR HOUSE AT PIER 21, *28 Pier 21. Tel. 409/763-3321, Toll free 800/874-3721, Website: www.harborhousepier21.com. 42 Rooms, 3 Suites. Rates: $99-219. Credit cards accepted.*

This unique hotel used to be the warehouse terminal for an old steamship line. The result of its conversion into a hotel is a building with a trendy warehouse/loft feeling. Comfortable, contemporary rooms overlook Galveston Harbor and its busy docks. You may find yourself taking full advantage of your room's sitting area to watch the fascinating rhythm of the cargo and cruise ships arriving and setting sail. There are 9 boat slips adjacent to the hotel in case you prefer to arrive by sea. A complimentary continental breakfast is provided each morning for guests. Harbor House is the anchor of a large retail project and adjoins several wharf side restaurants. Like the Tremont, this hotel has no pool of its own, but guests are entitles to pool use and signing privileges at the Hotel Galvez. Check for special rates available Sunday through Thursday. Parking is available for $8 a day.

THE VICTORIAN CONDO-HOTEL, *6300 Seawall Boulevard. Tel. 409/ 740-3555, Fax 409/744-3801, Toll free reservations 800/231-6363, Website: www.galveston.com/victorian. 330 Suites. Rates: $89-229. Credit cards accepted.*

This large seaside condominium-style hotel allows you to practically set up temporary residence while visiting Galveston. The suites have small kitchens, living areas, and separate bedrooms with modern, simple furnishings. Recreational facilities include tennis courts, a children's play area and an outdoor heated pool. Every room has a private balcony overlooking the Gulf of Mexico.

MOODY GARDENS, *Seven Hope Boulevard. Tel. 409/741-8484, Toll free 888/388-8484, Website: www.moodygardens.com/hotel/index.html. 303 Rooms, 15 Suites. Rates: $150-275.*

Moody Gardens may not be on the Seawall or on the Strand, but it is one of the best places on the island to stay, and perhaps *the* place to stay when traveling with kids or on business. It took me a long time to come around to the charms of the place – I clung to the firm belief that the only place to stay in Galveston was either surf side or in the Historic District, and there was no in-between. What really turned me around was a stay at Moody Gardens Hotel with a young teenager. She was absolutely enchanted by the lobby with its huge pool of exotic carp, the aviary, the trendy little boutiques, and, of course, the adjoining attractions of the Moody Gardens Pyramids (see *Seeing the Sights* for more information).

The rooms are very spacious, tastefully decorated, and chock full of amenities. For the fitness buff, there is an indoor heated lap pool, outdoor jogging track, and fitness center with Cybex weight machines. Outside is a captivating pool with waterfalls and surrounded by tropical foliage. The Terace Restaurant is a casual dining establishment on the lobby level. On the ninth floor, Shearn's is a formal dining room serving dinner only. Reservations are recommended for Shearn's, which serves food that equals the best you can find elsewhere on the island.

A VICTORIAN BED & BREAKFAST INN, *511 Seventeenth Street. Tel. 409/ 762-3235, Website: www.vicbb.com. 3 Rooms, 3 Suites. Rates: $100-150.*

Those who stay at this bed and breakfast establishment can walk home from a day of shopping and dining on The Strand. The house, built in 1899, retains an air of opulence with its birds-eye maple woodwork, Belgian tile fireplaces, and sumptuous fabrics. There are three bedrooms upstairs that share a central hallway bath. The two suites have their own bathrooms, and the cottage has a full kitchen in addition. Mauney's Suite on the second floor is our favorite, with its private screened-in veranda. Five miniature bunnies call the garden home.

Beach House Rentals

Beach front, beach side, bungalow or maritime Tara, Galveston and the surrounding area abound in beach property rentals. It's a summertime tradition among Texans and visitors alike to find a dream cottage somewhere on the shore and stay for a week or so. If you are traveling with a large group or family, this is an ideal way to give everyone a place to stay together while offering everyone the flexibility to pursue his or her own interests. These are some agencies with listings of rental properties:

• **Cottage by the Beach Rentals**, *810 Avenue L, Galveston, TX 77550. Tel. 409/770-9332, Email: info@cottagebythebeach.com, Website: www.cottagebythebeach.com.*
• **Sand 'n Sea Pirates Beach**, *P.O. Box 5165, Galveston, TX 77554. Tel. 409/737-2556, Fax 409/737-5168, Toll free 800/880-2554, Website: www.sandnseapiratesbeach.com.*
• **Bay Reef Realty**, *12200 FM 3005, Galveston, TX 77554. Tel. 409/,737-2300, Fax 409/737-3755, Toll free 800/527-7333, Website: www.bayreef.com.*

Where to Eat

CLARY'S SEAFOOD RESTAURANT, *8509 Teichman Road. Tel. 409/740-0771. Tuesday-Friday 11:30am-2:30pm, Tuesday-Saturday 5pm-10pm, Sunday noon-9pm, closed Monday. Credit cards accepted. Reservations suggested.*

Clary's overlooks Offats Bayou rather than the Gulf of Mexico, but the view and the atmosphere are just as lovely as anything on the other side of the island. The fresh seafood here is prepared with a Creole touch, and the gumbo is rich and dark, New Orleans style. The stuffed flounder is superb, and the Saralynn B. Platter is a divine combination of baked shrimp, grilled oysters, and butter lump crab. Scenes from the movie *Evening Star* were filmed in Clary's elegant dining room.

GAIDO'S, *3800 Seawall Boulevard. Tel. 409/762-9625. Sunday-Thursday noon-8:30pm, Friday and Saturday noon-9:30pm. Credit cards accepted. No reservations.*

If you can only have one dinner out in Galveston, this is the place to have it. Gaido's is a Galveston institution, from the 12-foot, 650-pound blue crab glaring down from the roof to the delicious fresh Gulf seafood that it serves to thousands of grateful patrons daily. The Gaido family has owned and operated the restaurant since 1911.

If you are looking for avant-garde New American cuisine, you won't find it here. The emphasis is on tradition and ritual – Gaido's has remained relatively unchanged since the nineteen fifties, and its devotees wouldn't have it any other way. The main dining room possesses the most ambiance. If you're lucky, you'll nab a window table overlooking the sea wall and the waves just before sunset. When crab is in season, consider yourself blessed by the seafood gods. The crab at Gaido's is prepared in a number of ways, using family recipes and sauces. Flounder and red snapper are always excellent, too. The only thing lacking is a better selection of wines to do justice to the marvelous seafood.

Gaido's never takes reservations, and you can count on a wait on the weekends, but believe it or not, it's pretty painless as waits go. With a gift shop, a big outdoor waiting station with a great view of the seawall, and a funky cocktail lounge featuring Kewpie Gaido's crystal collection, you won't run out of distractions. There's a statue of a child feeding the seagulls in the lobby, and bags of bread for the birds are placed under the statue for customers to take with them.

HILL'S PIER 19 RESTAURANT & FISH MARKET, *Pier 19, 20th Street at Harborside Drive. Tel. 409/763-7087. Credit cards accepted.*

Down on the wharf, Hill's serves super-fresh seafood in a casual atmosphere with a great view across the busy harbor. The original fish market adjacent to the restaurant has been here since 1932. From your table you can survey the Mosquito Fleet, the fishing and shrimping boats that come to Pier 19 to unload their daily catch. Service can be slack during off hours. My favorite item here is the delectable oyster Po-Boy. The variety shrimp platter will put crustacean lovers on cloud nine. This is a good place for kids and family-style dining.

THE PHOENIX BAKERY & COFFEE HOUSE, *23_ Ship's Mechanic Row, in the Washington Hotel Building. Tel. 409/763-3764.*

Located just across the street from the Tremont Hotel, this Strand area coffeehouse has a cheerful courtyard/garden setting. If you prefer, you can linger over your morning paper and genuine New Orleans-style beignets in the bright Victorian white interior. Breakfast, pastries, and dessert selections are served as well as soups and sandwiches for lunch.

RUDY & PACO, *2028 Postoffice Street. Tel. 409/762-3696. Monday-Friday 11am-2:30pm and 5:30pm-10pm, Saturday 5:30pm-11pm, closed Sunday. Credit cards accepted.*

Next door to the 1894 Grand Opera House, this downtown restaurant has been welcomed into the elite company of Galveston's favorite restaurants – no mean feat when customers are as seafood-savvy as they are here. Restaurateur Francisco Vargas (Paco) is originally from Nicaragua, and high-lights his native cuisine in a delicious blend with grilled seafood and steaks. End your meal with the marvelous Tres Leches Cake for dessert.

Seeing the Sights
Historic Homes & Architectural Grandeur

One of the highlights of any trip to Galveston is a tour of the grand old houses of the **Silk Stocking, Lost Bayou, Strand, and East End Historical Districts**. As a child I loved the beach, of course, but begged my parents to drive down Broadway first, where my siblings and I would gape at the mansions and palaces, picking out our favorite ones and arguing over which one was the best.

On Broadway, the main street that runs from the east side of the island to the west, still stand huge palatial residences that managed to withstand the Great Storm. Your first stop on any architectural tour of Galveston should be **Ashton Villa**, *Tel. 409/762-3933, 2328 Broadway*, the first of the great Broadway mansions and the home of the **Heritage Visitors Center**, *Website: www.galvestonhistory.org*, where you can pick up brochures, maps, and guides. Looking at the elegant redbrick Italianate mansion today, it's hard to believe it was slated for demolition in the early 1970s. An hour-long tour of the structure is offered that includes a fascinating multimedia presentation on the history and society of Victorian-era Galveston.

Nearby **Bishop's Palace**, *1402 Broadway*, took seven years to build and cost an estimated quarter of a million dollars – an astonishing sum on 1886, the year of its completion. This was the only residence in Texas named to the American Institute of Architecture's list of the hundred most architecturally significant buildings in the United States. You can take hourly tours of this ornate granite and limestone palace, which is now owned by the Catholic Galveston Diocese.

Nicholas Clayton, the architect behind Bishop's Palace, also designed the dramatic red granite Ashbel Smith Building, better known as **Old Red**, *310 University Boulevard, Tel. 409/772-2618*. With its ornate columns and ornamentation, Old Red exemplifies neo-Renaissance design in Victorian architecture in Texas. Old Red is the oldest medical school building west of the Mississippi, and still houses The University of Texas Medical Branch.

There are literally dozens of other historic sites to explore in Galveston, concentrated in pockets throughout the city. The Galveston Historical Foundation gives the **Historic Homes Tour**, *Tel. 409/765-7834, Website: http://www.galvestonhistory.org/ec-hht2002.htm*, annually during the first two weekends of May. This eagerly anticipated event allows participants to explore eight privately owned homes not otherwise open to the public in addition to free or reduced admission to the accessible structures like Ashton Villa.

Museums & Exhibits

The classic tall ship *Elissa* is berthed at Pier 21, at the **Texas Seaport Museum**, *Tel. 409/763-1877, Website: www.tsm-elissa.org, open 10 a.m. to 5 p.m. daily*. You can walk aboard the magnificent vessel, a product of the age when wind still powered the ships at sea. There is an admission charge that also includes entry to the museum and access to a computerized immigration database. In late March through early April, the *Elissa* goes out on sailing trials—it's a great thrill to watch her depart or return under sail.

Even if you are not the multi-media type, don't miss a viewing of the 30-minute documentary **The Great Storm** at the *Pier 21 Theater, Tel. 409/765-7834*. Historic photographs, voiceovers reading eyewitness accounts, and other techniques create a gripping depiction of the fatal hurricane that leveled Galveston a century ago. Among those who responded to the great tragedy was Clara Barton, who said of the terrible destruction, "no exaggeration was possible." You can get a ticket for the presentation alone or as part of the Texas Seaport Museum package.

The sprawling grounds of **Moody Gardens**, *1 Hope Boulevard, Tel. 800/582-4673, open daily 10am to 6pm, Friday and Saturday until 9pm*, are definitely worth a visit. Towering glass pyramids house three separate attractions. The **Rainforest Pyramid** is a vast tropical environment for fauna from Asia and South America. Birds fly freely, enormous fish inhabit ponds, and colorful snakes hang from tree branches inches above your head. You can visit a bat cave to get a rare look at these creatures up close. Try to be there for one of the two daily butterfly releases, at 11am and 2pm.

The **Aquarium Pyramid** is just that—a series of enormous tanks and habitats for water life of all kinds, from sharks to otters to seals. There are touch tanks where the curious can stroke rays and starfish. If the aquariums leave you with the urge to get wet, visit the white sands and blue freshwater laggons of Palm Beach. Kids love the Yellow Submarine and its water guns, periscope, and Octopus Slide. The **Discovery Museum Pyramid** contains revolving exhibits and the IMAX theaters. You can purchase a one or two day pass to save money on admission if you plan to visit more than one attraction. When you've finished with the gardens, you can dine at one of several excellent restaurants in the vast hotel.

The Ferry

At the east end of Galveston is a commuter ferry over to Bolivar Peninsula, which connects This is also your best chance to see dolphins in the area. Look for them trailing in the ferry's wake, feeding and playing

Nightlife & Entertainment

Frankly, the ideal night in Galveston for most people consists of hitting a seafood restaurant, stuffing themselves to the gills, walking along the seawall in a vain attempt to relieve the feeling that they are going to pop and stumbling home so they can put aloe on their sunburn, get up early, and do it all over again. In other words, this isn't an all-night kind of town. However, there are convivial places to hoist an evening glass and a burgeoning arts scene as well.

Modern and classical musical performances are held at the opulent and magnificently intimate **Grand 1894 Opera House**, *2020 Postoffice Street,*

Tel. 409/765-1894 or 713/480-1894, www.thegrand.com. Recent performers have included Mandy Patinkin and Johnny Mathis.

Neighborhood Pubs & Bars

YAGA'S CAFE, *2314 Strand. Tel. 409/762-6676, Website: www.galveston.com/yaga.*

Bands play in this eclectic café every weekend, where an additional attraction is the no smoking policy. This is one of the few late nightspots in downtown Glaveston. Just outside the building is a giant chess set on the square.

THE STRAND BREWERY, *23rd Street. Tel. 409/763-4500. Credit cards accepted.*

This microbrewery prepares four specialty beers made in the German style. The brewery is in middle of the lively Strand area. From the rooftop deck you can look over the city or harbor. The delicious food includes selections like hamburgers, individual pizzas and pasta. Try the artichoke ravioli served in cream sauce. Open Sunday to Thursday 11am to 10pm. On weekends, the Strand Brewery has live music and stays open until 2am.

WOODY'S COASTAL CANTINA, *1726 Seawall Boulevard. Tel. 409/763-1616. Open daily noon-2am. MasterCard and Visa accepted.*

Over on the Seawall side of the island, Woody's anchors the beach bar scene. The wooden open-air building faces the Gulf, the better to catch the cooling breezes. A full bar, large selection of beer and pool table keep the place lively.

Sports & Recreation

Galveston Island offers 32 miles of beach to explore, from the Seawall out to the West End with its colonies of beach houses perched on the shore. These are not white sand beaches next to sparkling clear water – some visitors to Galveston beaches are put off by the murky-looking water and dark wet sand. The water and the sand are not dirty, but chock-full of sea life, from plankton to seaweed.

Along the **Seawall**, the hottest scene is up above the water. The Seawall has become a public space to stroll, skate, bike, and walk, similar to the boardwalks along the Atlantic coast. Across the boulevard from the "world's longest continuous sidewalk," you can rent a bicycle at one of the many hotels and souvenir shops. The most popular beach in this area is **Stewart Beach**, which offers a pavilion and amusement park.

Wide-open beaches perfect for fishing, surfing, and swimming beckon visitors to **Galveston Island State Park**, *14901 Farm Road 3005, Tel. 409/737-1112.* Flounder, redfish and drum are some of the fish native to these waters. There are covered picnic tables with grills, 150 campsites with complete hook-ups and four miles of easy hiking trails. The park is six miles south of Galveston on Seawall Boulevard (Farm Road 3005).

Shopping

The commercial center of historic Galveston is the street known as the **Strand**. Both Strand and Mechanic Streets are designated National Historic Landmarks. Many restaurants, art galleries, and shops line the Strand, which has been restored to its Victorian grandeur.

For many visitors the one can't-miss shopping stop on their list is **Colonel Bubbie's Strand Surplus Senter**, *2202 Strand, Tel. 409/762-7397*, the biggest, finest, liveliest authentic military surplus store you'll ever visit. Vintage and current issue military uniforms and accessories for just about every nation in the world (except Switzerland) are crammed into this sprawling warehouse, where people wind and squeeze through the aisles in a daze of sensory overload. Want a United States Navy issue blue Melton wool pea coat? This is your place. How about some Bay of Pigs leftover M-1 Carbine cotton canvas mag pouches? Tinned rations from World War II? Russian Army brown fur *Ushankas*? Nowhere but Colonel Bubbie's. If you're not a military buff and a companion has dragged you in, entertain yourself by wandering through the store and seeing how many of the ultra-relaxed napping store cats you can find.

Excursions & Day Trips

Angleton, south of Galveston on Highway 35, is a small town that provides some excellent wildlife viewing opportunities. The **Brazoria National Wildlife Refuge**, *1212 North Velasco Street, Angleton, Tel. 409/849-6062*, has one of the nation's largest populations of snow geese during winter migration. A six-mile hiking trail offers a self-guided tour of the refuge and a chance to see some of the over 200 types of birds that inhabit it.

Brazoria County Museum, *100 East Cedar Street, Angleton, Tel. 409/849-5711 extension 1208, open Tuesday to Friday, 9am to 5pm, Saturday 9am to 3pm, Sunday 1pm to 4pm*, is housed in the historic county courthouse built in 1897. The centerpiece of the museum is an exhibit about Stephen F. Austin's colony, which was one of the original settlements in Texas. Native American history of the region is the focus of other exhibits.

The protected land of the **Big Thicket**, *Farm Road 420, Kountz, Tel. 409/246-2337*, is a short drive from Beaumont. Much of east Texas was covered in swampy woodlands so dense that even the Native Americans of the region left places unexplored. Development has cleared much of these lands; what remains is 96,000 acres that spreads into 12 counties.

Village Creek State Park, *Lumberton, Tel. 409/755-7322*, offers camping, hiking and bird watching areas. This small but lush park offers easy access to the Big Thicket. The Village Creek is a quiet waterway, perfect for an easy-going canoe ride. Canoes are available for rental on the creek.

To get to the Big Thicket and Village Creek from Galveston, take Interstate Highway 45 north. Continue on Highway 146 north to Interstate Highway 10; travel east. From Beaumont, take Highway 96 north. For Big Thicket, from Highway 96 north continue on Highway 287 north. Farm Road 420 is about 20 miles from the turn-off.

Practical Information

You can obtain maps, trolley tickets, historic home tours and information about recreational activities at one of the two locations of the **Galveston Visitors Center**, *2428 Seawall Boulevard and 2215 Strand, Tel. 409/763-4311, Toll free 888/425-4753, open daily 8:30am to 5pm.*

Helpful websites are *www.galvestonhistory.org* and *www.galveston.com.*

Corpus Christi

The Texas coast has awe-inspiring natural beauty. The cultures of Mexico and Texas draw tourists to **Corpus Christi** all year. You can pack a variety of vacations in one trip. Downtown meets the Corpus Christi Bay at the marina, which is filled with sailboats and shrimp boats. One of the best windsurfing launches in the area is just down Ocean Drive, at Oleander Point, overlooking Coal Park. The gorgeous natural beaches of **North Padre Island** are only a few miles from Corpus Christi's upscale restaurants and museums.

The citywide celebration, **Buccaneer Days**, is part carnival, part debutante ball. The parade features the season's debutantes in sparkling gowns. The summer closes with **Bayfest**, a weekend celebration held along the bayfront at the end of September. A regatta and street festival are the highlights.

Arrivals & Depatures

The **Corpus Christi International Airport**, *1000 International Drive, www.ci.corpus-christi.tx.us/services/airport*, is located in the northwest part of the city. Take Interstate Highway 37 north and look for the airport exit.

Orientation

Interstate Highway 37 from San Antonio is the main route to Corpus Christi. The highway ends at Shoreline Boulevard, which turns into Ocean Drive and runs along the Corpus Christi Bay. The Harbor Bridge connects downtown to Corpus Christi Beach, where you will find a number of tourist attractions.

Getting Around Town

The "B," *Tel. 361/883-2287*, as the city buses in Corpus Christi call themselves, serve all areas of the city. You can also shuttle under the Harbor Bridge on the Water Taxi, which connects the Convention Center and nearby museums with the State Aquarium on Corpus Christi Beach. The Corpus Christi Shuttle connects the attractions on the land. You may ride the shuttle free when you purchase a tip on the Water Taxi. These services operate during the summer only, from Memorial Day until Labor Day. Round trip fare is $2.

Taxi companies in Corpus Christi include:
- **City Cab**, *Tel. 361/881-TAXI*
- **Liberty Taxi**, *Tel. 361/882-7654 or 749-5589 (in Port Aransas)*
- **Yellow Checker Cab**, *Tel. 361/884-3211 or 800/944-4983*

Where to Stay

Expensive

OCEAN HOUSE, *3275 Ocean Drive. Tel. 361/882-9500, Website: www.oceansuites.com. 5 Suites. Rates: $155-495. Children over 10 by special request only. Credit cards accepted.*

This elegant contemporary house sits on an exclusive residential street right across from the seawall. Some rooms have skyline views and others have bay views in this sophisticated bed and breakfast. All rooms are fully furnished suites, tastefully decorated with minimum bric-a-brac but maximum luxury.

This is a romantic getaway, and definitely not your run-of-the-mill casual beach house. In fact, this place reminds me of nothing so much as a swinging bachelor's idea of the perfect pad! There's a wine cellar in the main house, a steamy sauna, balconies, decks, and a lovely pool. Private entrances allow you to decide just how much you want to interact with your fellow travelers. From Interstate 37, take the Shoreline Boulevard exit and head south. Shoreline Boulevard turns into Ocean Drive after you leave the downtown area.

OMNI CORPUS CHRISTI HOTEL-BAYFRONT TOWER, *900 North Shoreline Boulevard. Tel. 361/887-1600, Fax 361/883-8084, Toll free reservations 800/the-omni, Website: www.omnihotel.com. 475 Rooms. Rates: $140-200. Credit cards accepted.*

This high rise overlooks the marina on the Corpus Christi Bay. Just as when it was built in the early 1980s, the hotel offers the premier accommodations in the area. The heated rooftop pool has a striking view of the marina. You can walk to downtown restaurants and bars in the evening. During the day you can stroll to the marina to rent a boat or go deep-sea fishing. Recreational facilities include a gym, outdoor pool and racquetball courts.

OMNI CORPUS CHRISTI HOTEL-MARINA TOWER, *707 North Shoreline Boulevard. Tel. 361/882-1700, Fax 361/882-3113, Toll free reservations 800/the-omni, Website: www.omnihotel.com. 343 Rooms. Rates: $135-200. Credit cards accepted.*

This Omni is an older and slightly smaller building than its sister hotel, the Omni Bayfront. The difference in rates is minimal considering the facilities at the Omni Marina are less than adequate for a hotel in this price range. You will have no doubt that the luster has worn off this hotel; spend the extra few dollars and treat yourself to the Omni Bayfront next door.

Moderate

HOLIDAY INN-EMERALD BEACH, *1102 South Shoreline Boulevard. Tel. 361/883-5731, Fax 361/883-9079, Toll free reservations 800/465-4329. Rates: $91-139. Credit cards accepted.*

This is the only downtown hotel actually on the waterfront. Although the hotel has added its own 600-foot manmade beach, the bay is used primarily for sailing. The long low-rise hotel has an indoor pool and gym. The adjoining lounge tries to shed the hotel cocktail bar image. This is a convenient location for visitors who plan to drive to their recreational destinations.

BAY BREEZE BED & BREAKFAST, *201 Louisiana Parkway. Tel 361/882-4123, Toll free reservations 877/882-4123, Website: www.baybreezebb.com. Rates: $65-95.*

Built in 1936, the Bay Breeze is located in one of the well-established residential areas in the city. Only a few blocks from the bay and two miles from downtown, the location is excellent if you would like to feel as though you actually reside in the city. The Tree House, the largest of the four rooms, has a view of the bay and a patio. Each room has a private bath.

RAMADA INN BAYFRONT, *601 North Water Street. Tel. 361/882-8100, Fax 361/888-6540, Toll free reservations 800/688-0334. Rates: $65-89. Credit cards accepted.*

The Ramada Inn is not on the water and can offer no views of the marina, but considering that the price is significantly lower than other downtown hotels the view is a small sacrifice. The rooms are spacious and comfortable; downtown restaurants and the marina is just a short walk from the hotel. The Ramada is an excellent choice for families, because children under the age of 17 years stay at no charge with parents. Corpus Christi has a second Ramada Inn located near the airport.

Inexpensive

BEST WESTERN SANDY SHORES, *3200 Surfside Boulevard. Tel. 361/883-7456, Fax 361/883-1437, Tll free reservations 800/528-1234. Rates: $59-149. Credit cards accepted.*

You can have a lovely view of downtown without staying in the center of the city if you choose Corpus Christi Beach. The coarse sand and bay water is not inviting to swimmers, so most do not come to this area for the beach. Just across the Harbor Bridge from downtown, the Sandy Shores is within walking distance from the Lexington Battleship and the Texas State Aquarium

BEST WESTERN CORPUS CHRISTI INN, *2838 South Padre Island Drive. Tel 361/854-0005, Fax 361/854-2642, Toll free reservations 800/445-9463. Rates: $45-71. Credit cards accepted.*

This hotel stands on the highway that leads to Padre Island. The location is convenient for travelers who want to be near shopping centers and restaurants. The hotel has an outdoor pool and can make arrangements for golfing.

North Padre Island

If you desire an active night-life, stay in the city center, but for moonlight strolls on the beach, stay on North Padre Island. The evenings on the island are quiet, with the sound of the surf the only distraction. The island is about 15 miles from downtown Corpus Christi.

SURFSIDE CONDOMINIUMS, *15005 Windward Drive. Tel. 361/949-8128, Toll free reservations 800/548-4585. Rates: $110. Credit cards accepted.*

Just 100 yards from the ocean, the Surfside Condominiums have kitchens and the conveniences of home such as televisions and stereo systems. If you use only one of the two bedrooms, lower rates apply. The facilities include an outdoor pool and laundry room. Children under the age of six stay for free.

PORT ROYAL OCEAN RESORT, *6317 State Highway 361, Port Aransas. Tel. 361/749-5011, Fax 361/749-6399, Toll free reservations 800/242-1034. Rates: $150-225. Credit cards accepted.*

Port Royal is a favorite vacation spot of tourists and natives alike. The condominium resort sits quite a distance from the crowds and traffic congestion of the public beaches near Corpus Christi. And it is also a drive from the town of Port Aransas; you really can get away from it all at Port Royal. Each condominium offers the comforts of home. The building is built courtyard-style around and outdoor pool and has tennis courts on the side yard. The pool is a short walk from the surf, so you can enjoy the best of fresh and salt water. One and two bedroom units are available. Rates change by season.

Camping

Corpus Christi and Padre Island are popular destinations for campers. There are many private campgrounds in the area, most are located in Flour Bluff, between the mainland and Padre Island. The camping facilities at Mustang Island are excellent and allow campers to stay right on the beach. Some campers choose to set up camp for overnight stays right on the beach, usually near the sand dunes. This can be difficult due to lack of facilities and high winds that can knock over a tent or disrupt a campsite.

COLONIA DEL REY RV PARK, *1717 Waldron Road, Corpus Christi. Tel. 361/937-2435 or 800/580-2435. Credit cards accepted.*

The campground, which is a Good Sam Park, sits on 12 acres and has large shade trees to offer a break from the summer heat. Camper hook-ups have electricity and propane can be delivered. Amenities such as a swimming pool, air-conditioned laundry room and shower facilities will make traveling feel more like being home. Classes and special events are held in the recreation hall during the winter months. To reach Colonia Del Rey, when entering Corpus Christi on Interstate Highway 37, exit Highway 358. Continue on 358 for about 9 miles, then exit Waldron Road and take a right. You will find the park on the left about one-half mile from the highway.

Where to Eat

WATER STREET OYSTER BAR AND SEAFOOD COMPANY, *309 North Water Street. Tel 361/881-9448. Credit cards accepted.*

If you have only one meal in Corpus Christi, take it at Water Street Oyster Bar or its sister restaurant, Water Street Seafood Company. The Cajun-influenced seafood specialties are the finest in town. The large airy dining room in the oyster bar is a feast for the eyes, with its open kitchen and kitschy two-story mural of Botticelli's *Venus*.

Every day the fresh fish specials are listed on the blackboard. You can order your fish grilled over mesquite, sauteed, or, for those with a taste for the robust, blackened. The wait-staff can offer suggestions on the best preparation to bring out the flavor of each fish. The gumbo is thick, full of seafood and probably the best in Texas. The Caldo Xochitl, a soup with aromatic chicken stock, captures the true subtlety of Mexican cuisine. Chicken Rockefeller and beef tenderloin are alternatives to seafood. A good selection of wine and a full bar are available.

OLD MEXICO, *3329 Leopard Street. Tel. 361/883-6461. Credit cards accepted.*

This is what a real Tex-Mex restaurant should be, unpretentious and straightforward food. You will have no problem with the amount of spice; since the plain rice-and-beans cooking relies on you adding the salsa yourself. Corn tortillas are the basis of the food here, but you can order the more trendy flour variety. And the food stands the test of time. The traditional south Texas style has remained consistent over the decades and has won a strong local following. An average meal costs under $10.

JOE COTTEN'S BARBECUE, *Highway 77 South, Robstown. Tel. 361/ 767-9973.*

It's a twenty-mile drive from Corpus Christi to Joe Cotten's in Robstown. But a barbecue lover would be willing to walk-the food is that good. The atmosphere may surpass the cuisine, though. You sit at a wooden table in the restaurant that resembles a Texas dance hall. A waiter takes your order and puts down a strip of butcher paper. Once your food arrives there is no limit to the number of "seconds" you can have, but most fill up after the first helping. This restaurant has served the best barbecue in south Texas for over fifty years, and includes the Bush family among its distinguished clientele. Only cash is accepted.

Seeing the Sights

Corpus Christi's museums stand in Bayfront Arts and Science Park, next to the city convention center, just under the Harbor Bridge. You can spend a few hours in this area taking in the history, culture and nature of the coastal bend. Nearby Heritage Park, which is adjacent to the Bayfront Arts and Science Park, has restored historic homes, which are open to the public.

Corpus Christi Museum of Science & History, *1900 Chaparral, Tel. 361/883-2862, open Monday to Saturday 10am to 5pm, Sunday noon to 5pm, Admission $8 adult, $4 children under the age of 12*, traces the natural history of the area from prehistoric times to the present. Special exhibits geared especially for younger children include the touch tables and wharf play area. Part of the museum features an exhibit devoted to the significance of the 1492 voyage of Christopher Columbus. Outside you can visit replicas of the Columbus ships, the Nina, Pinta and Santa Maria. The boats found a permanent home in the Corpus Christi Harbor soon after they visited during the 500th anniversary of his first voyage to the North America. You can come aboard the **Columbus Ships**, which are surprisingly small, and see how the crew lived. Admission to the ships is included with museum entrance.

The **South Texas Institute for the Arts**, *1902 North Shoreline Boulevard, Tel. 361/884-3844, www.stia.org, Tuesday to Saturday 10am to 5pm, Sunday 1pm to 5pm, closed Monday, admission $3 adult, $1 children*, overlooks the bay. The building, designed by Philip Johnson, is a work of art in itself. Exhibits change regularly and focus on art of national interest. Kids who want to get their hands active with art can visit the **Art Center**, *100 Shoreline Boulevard, Tel. 361/884-6404, admission free*. This innovative approach to children and the arts lets kids create their way to artistic expression.

Across the Harbor Bridge, **The Texas State Aquarium**, *Corpus Christi Beach, Tel. 361/881-1200, www.txstateaq.org, Monday to Saturday 9am to 5pm, Sunday 10am to 5pm, admission $8 adults, $5.75 children*, places the depths of the Gulf of Mexico before your eyes. The most dramatic exhibit shows the marine life that inhabits an oilrig. You can walk right up to the walls of aquariums, as though you were swimming through the legs of the rig.

The **U.S.S. Lexington**, an aircraft carrier that served in World War II, stands on Corpus Christi Beach and is open to tourists, *Tel. 800/LADY-LEX, www.usslexington.com, admission $8 adults, $4 children*. You can see the engineering room, living quarters and walk on the deck. Since there is neither heat nor air-conditioning, you'll get an inkling of the adverse conditions faced by the sailors aboard the Lady Lex—especially if you tour the boat in summertime!

Nightlife & Entertainment

BUCKETS, *227 North Water Street. Tel. 361/883-7776.*

Sports bar, pool hall, live music venue-all these describe Buckets-under one large roof. The younger crowd of the coastal bend fills this casual downtown hang-out, downing table top mini-kegs of beer and socializing. If your tan is not up to par, you may be spotted as a tourist.

YUCATAN, *208 North Water Street. Tel 361/888-6800.*

This large, party place features live music on weekend nights. The casual beach bum atmosphere was an instant hit in the city, and Yucatan's is the right mix of club and bar to keep the crowds coming back.

EXECUTIVE SURF CLUB, *309 North Water Street. Tel. 361/884-7873.*

Surfboards are tables, and the atmosphere is definitely island inspired. This small bar in the Water Street Shopping Center serves beer and fried food. Live music is featured on the weekends.

Sports & Recreation

Birdwatching is a popular pastime for many residents of the Coastal Bend. The **Padre Island National Seashore**, with its miles of undisturbed beach, is a haven for water birds, notably whooping cranes and kingfishers. Guided birdwatching tours are available from **Bird Song Natural History Adventures**, *3525 Bluebonnet, Tel. 361/882-7232.* Tours range from half-day to extended trips for groups or individuals.

There are enough dive areas around Corpus Christi to keep the avid diver underwater for years. **Copeland's**, *4041 South Padre Island Drive, Tel. 361/854-1135*, offers day dives from $45 or overnight trips from $99. Another reputable dive shop, **See Sea Divers**, *4012 Weber Road, Tel. 361/853-DIVE*, offers a full range of services including equipment rental, dive trips and deep sea fishing charters.

Boating in the Corpus Christi Bay is an excellent way to enjoy the beauty of the coastline and refreshing water. You can rent sailboats by the day or week at the **Corpus Christi International School of Sailing**, *Cooper's Alley L-Head, Tel. 361/881-8503, Fax 881-8504.* Prices range roughly as follows: $210 to $230 per day or $1000 to $1300 per week. The fleet of six boats includes a 38-foot sloop, each of which is available for rental throughout the year. You can also charter a boat for a four-hour cruise around Corpus Christi Bay.

The **Captain Clark**, *People's Street T-head, Tel. 361/884-4369*, docked at the city marina, offers three bay fishing trips per day during the summer. The 65-foot double-deck tourist boat has a lounge and snack bar; equipment rental is available. The Captain Clark is docked at the city marina, across from downtown.

From Port Aransas, you can embark on the area's best deep-sea fishing expeditions. **Deep Sea Headquarters**, *Ferry Landing, Port Aransas, Tel. 361/*

749-5597, has three boats which can hold up to 100 people for half or full day expeditions.

The **Greyhound Race Track**, *5302 Leopard Street, Tel. 361/289-9333 or 800/580-RACE*, has a club house and a grandstand. If the live dogs are not enough, you can bet on six other racetracks shown on monitors. From Interstate Highway 37, take the Navigation Boulevard exit.

Golf

The city's main municipal course, **Gabe Lozano Sr. Golf Course**, *4401 Old Brownsville Road, Tel. 361/883-3696, open daily*, offers excellent no-frills facilities for golf. Two standard courses, an 18 hole and a nine hole course, are features at this municipal park. Fees for the 9 hole course range from $4.75 to $7.25; fees for the 18 hole course range from $6.50 to $11, depending on the day of play. The grounds have a pro-shop and snack bar. Golf carts are available for rental. If you don't like the sun, try the lighted driving range for evening practice.

The **Pharaoh Country Club**, *7111 Pharaoh Drive, Tel. 361/991-1490*, opens its golf facilities to the public for a fee of $25 per person on weekdays and $35 per person on weekends and holidays. Golf cart rental is included in the greens fee. The course is located in the Pharaoh Valley neighborhood, close to Oso Bay. You may arrange monthly membership to the course, which ranges in price from $150 to $300 per person.

To reach the Pharaoh Country Club, take Ocean Drive east (away from downtown) to Ennis Joslin Street. Turn onto Ennis Joslin Street, which begins at Ocean Drive, and go about 1.5 miles to Pharaoh Drive. Take Pharaoh Drive to the club entrance.

South Texas Golf

Golf is one of the most popular sports in south Texas. Many of the winter Texans take advantage of the mild climate to play golf in every season. Many of the private clubs have reasonable greens fees, and some offer temporary memberships. The following clubs are located in small towns on the coastal bend:

Alice Country Club, *Country Club Road, Alice. Tel. 361/664-3723. Open Tuesday to Sunday. Fees $10 for weekday play; $15 for weekend play.* Temporary memberships available and include use of all club facilities. The club is located near Highway 44.

North Shore Country Club, *801 East Broadway, Portland. Tel. 361/643-1546 or 643-2798. Open Tuesday to Sunday; closed Monday. Greens fees $45 to $55 per person, including cart.*

Rockport Country Club, *101 Champions Drive, Rockport. Tel. 361/729-4182 Open Tuesday to Sunday. Greens fees $40 to $50 per person, including golf cart.*

The **Oso Beach Golf Course**, *5601 South Alameda, Tel (361) 991-5351, open daily*, is close to Oso Bay, in a pleasant residential area. The facilities include a pro-shop and a restaurant. The 18-hole regulation course is spotted with palm trees and traps of fine, white sand. Fees range from $9 to $11, depending on the day of play. Special rates available for junior and senior players. Golf cart rental runs from $10.13 to $14.79, including tax.

You can play a full 18 holes on the Island at the **Padre Island Country Club**, *14353 Commodore Drive, Tel. 361/949-8006, open Tuesday to Sunday, closed Monday, except during February and March*. The only country club on Padre Island offers a pro-shop and club facilities. The club is not near the Gulf of Mexico, but sits amid a cozy neighborhood of beach-houses and canals for small boats. Greens fees range from $36 to $46 and includes the use of a golf cart.

Excursions & Day Trips

The beautiful, and in some places wild, **Padre Island National Seashore**, *www.nps.gov/pais*, is part of a chain of barrier islands along the Texas Gulf Coast. Covering over 130,000 acres, the island offers visitors nature trails, camp sites and a variety of educational programs.

Padre Island is just east of Corpus Christi. Take South Padre Island Drive through Flour Bluff. After you cross the Intracoastal Waterway you will see the Padre Island National Seashore Offices, which can provide information about access roads to the beach.

The south end of the island has the most pristine beaches. The National Park at **Malaquite Beach** offers 47 campsites and swimming areas. To reach Malaquite Beach, take Highway 22 south along the Island. The road ends at the Visitor Center, which has picnic areas and showers. The national seashore extends sixty miles south of this beach, but is accessible only by four wheel drive vehicle. The drive along the water takes at least a few hours. Primitive campsites are located at Yarborough Pass, 15 miles south of Malaquite Beach.

Mustang Island State Park has camping facilities with full hook-ups. The beach has its own access road and public showers for the use of park guests. A section of the beach reserved for swimming has a bath house and concession facility. To get to Mustang Island State Park, take a left at the first stoplight, heading north on Highway 361 (Park Road 53). This highway continues to Port Aransas about 26 miles north. At **Port Aransas** you can take the free ferry boat across the bay to **Aransas Pass**. Get out of your car to enjoy the sea breezes and to spot porpoises. Highway 361 continues west to Highway 181; take Highway 181 south to get back to Corpus Christi.

Practical Information

The **Corpus Christi Visitors Center** is located downtown at *1823 North Chapparral Street, Tel. 361/561-2000, Toll free 800/766-2322*. Another location is just off Interstate Highway 37 at Exit 16. The **Corpus Christi Convention and Visitors Bureau**, *1201 North Shoreline Boulevard*, is located in the center of town.

You may also visit the **Padre Island Information Center**, *14252 South Padre Island Drive, Tel. 361/949-8743*. Information is available online at *www.cctexas.org, and corpuschristi-tx-cvb.org*.

The **Padre Island National Seashore Offices**, *9405 South Padre Island Drive, Tel. 361/949-8713, Fax 361/949-9951*, can provide information about events and nature classes.

You can book a stay at a bed and breakfast, hotel or motel through **Sand Dollar Hospitality**, *Tel. 361/853-1222 or 800/528-7782*.

Kingsville

Probably more people have heard of the **King Ranch** than of **Kingsville**. With good reason-it's larger than the state of Rhode Island and one of the most important working ranches in the world. In the mid-nineteenth century a sea captain named Richard King came to the area. He pioneered ranching in Texas and built a legacy that has endured over 130 years. Visitors come to see the King Ranch and enjoy **Baffin Bay**, a large inlet of the Gulf of Mexico.

The Christmas season is celebrated with **La Posada de Kingsville**, a traditional candlelight procession through town. The events begin during the last weekend of November and start with a parade, and a five-kilometer run/walk through downtown and two days of festivities in the park featuring arts events, markets and caroling. The Posada procession itself takes place on the weekend before Christmas. For the complete schedule contact La Posada de Kingsville, *Tel. 512/592-8516 or 800/333-5032*.

Arrivals & Departures

The main route to Kingsville is Highway 77, which runs through Corpus Christi from the north.

Where to Stay

B-BAR-B RANCH INN, *Route 1 Box 457. Tel 512/296-3331, Fax 296-3337. Rates: $75 to $100. Credit cards accepted.*

The adult-only guest ranch has eight rooms, each outfitted in western style. The ranch offers activities such as hay rides, hunting, fishing and cookouts. You can observe life on a real working ranch, or simply lounge at the outdoor pool. A full country breakfast is prepared every day. Call for special activities or group arrangements.

BEST WESTERN KINGSVILLE INN, *2402 East King Avenue. Tel. 512/ 595-5656 or 800/528-1234, Fax 512/595-5000. Rates: $45 to $51. Credit cards accepted.*

The Best Western is located on the highway. This hotel has an outdoor pool and spa. There is no charge for children under the age of six years. Laundry facilities are on the premises.

Where to Eat

THE KING'S INN, *Farm Road 628 at Loyola Beach. Tel. 512/297-5265.*

At first glance you may not believe the sign on the small wooden building that proclaims "World Famous King's Inn." But do not pass it by. The thick guest book attests with rave reviews from around the world that the King's Inn serves exceptional seafood.

The restaurant opened in the 1940s, and still serves basically the same seafood specialties. The meal comes family-style, so all you have to do is sit down and look hungry. Fresh crab and shrimp are featured daily, with chicken or steak for the less nautically inclined. Choose your main dish, and the sides are brought to your table in large servings. You can eat like a king for less than $15 per person.

From Kingsville, take Highway 77 south. Turn east on Farm Road 628 and travel eight miles to Loyola Beach.

Elderhostel Classes

Learning never stops with the **Texas A&M Kingsville Elderhostel Program**, *Tel. 512/595-2111*. During the winter, short courses are offered in subjects ranging from bird watching to a variety of more traditional classroom subjects. The courses usually run for one week.

Seeing the Sights

At the **King Ranch**, you can visit the site where the first cowboys set up camp on what would become the 825,000-acre ranch. The ranch is so large it straddles four counties. Tours of the grounds are conducted daily. Start your visit at **The King Ranch Visitor Center**, *Highway 141, Tel. 512/592-8055, open Monday to Saturday 10am to 3pm, Sunday 1pm to 4pm*, where you can watch an orientation movie and begin a guided tour.

The **King Ranch Museum**, *405 North Sixth Street, Tel. 512/595-1881, Monday to Saturday 10am to 2pm, Sunday 1pm to 5pm*, is not on the ranch, but in downtown Kingsville. The museum displays antiques from the ranch and feature photographs depicting ranch life in the 1940s.

The natural history of the area is preserved at the **Conner Museum**, *Texas A&M University Campus, Tel. 512/595-2819, open Monday to Saturday 9am to 5pm, admission free*. The main halls are dedicated to the ecology of south Texas. Temporary exhibits about science change about 10 times per year. The trophy room displays enough hunting trophies to fill a wildlife refuge.

Sports & Recreation

Nearby Baffin Bay gives you the opportunity to enjoy the coast on the calm waters of a large bay. The area is famous as a sportsman's paradise. Migratory birds flock to Baffin Bay throughout the year. Excellent salt water fishing, either from one of the many piers in the area or by boat, is readily available. However, if activity is not your desire, simply relax and enjoy the tranquil water.

Golf

The main golf course in Kingsville is the **L. E. Ramey Municipal Golf Course**, *Highway 77 South, Tel 512/592-1101 or 800/879-7263, open daily*. During the winter months, the course holds weekly tournaments for senior citizens. Tournament play begins Wednesday mornings at 9am. The facilities include 18 hole course and driving range, as well as a pro-shop and snack bar. Greens fee range from $6.75 to $8.25; golf cart rental from $10 to $15. Memberships are available by the month, and allow unlimited play. Individual monthly membership dues are $50, and only $80 for an entire family.

During the fall football season you can watch the **Texas A&M Javalinas** play home games at Texas A&M Kingsville, *Tel. 512/595-2111*.

Shopping

There is no finer place to buy western riding accessories than the **King Ranch Saddle Shop**, *201 East Kleberg Street, Tel. 512/595-5761 or 800/282-KING*. You will find many local crafts for sale along with the famous King Ranch purses and backpacks

Practical Information

The **Kingsville Visitor Center**, *101 North 3rd Street, Box 1562, Tel. 800/333-5032*, has information about the King Ranch and the city.

South Padre Island

The gorgeous beaches of **South Padre Island** are unmatched in Texas. Miles of dunes and surf are reserved as park areas. Public beaches prohibit driving on the sand, leaving the waterfront unsullied by auto pollution.

The wildlife of South Padre Island is as extraordinary as the beaches. Dolphins and sea turtles swim along the coast; migrating birds nest in the wetlands. Scuba enthusiasts can take dive trips into shark territory or float along side manta rays. A number of Spanish shipwrecks off the coast provide an historical backdrop for dives, or you can venture through a modern undersea community of sea-life on the oilrigs in the Gulf.

If you do choose to venture to the state's most radiant beaches, beware the spring break crowds. During the month of March, the Island becomes inundated with college revelry. They come from all over the nation and cause traffic and beach congestion. Hotels charge bolstered rates and add-on room charges. At motels you may find your rooms without towels and the front desk without service. The best months to visit the beach are May and September, when the summer weather is in full swing and crowds are minimal.

Be certain to book reservations well in advance; weekends and holidays often sell out months ahead.

Arrivals & Departures

From Highway 77, take Highway 100 west; this leads straight to Port Isabel and the Queen Isabella Bridge.

Grey Line Tours, *Tel. 956/761-4343*, operates shuttle service from the Brownsville Airport to South Padre Island. The tour company also has buses that run to the border or gives tours of Matamoros, Mexico.

Orientation

South Padre Island is at the southern end of the long, thin barrier island chain that runs along the Texas Gulf Coast. The Queen Isabella Causeway connects the Island to Port Isabel on the mainland. The concentration of hotels and restaurants covers about five miles on the island's southern tip. Padre Boulevard runs through the center of the island; Gulf Boulevard is the major north-south street connecting the beachfront condominiums on the Gulf side and runs parallel to Padre Boulevard.

Getting Around Town

Shuttles run along Padre and Gulf Boulevards, stopping at the major hotels and restaurants.

Where to Stay

Daily, weekly and monthly rental of beach houses cam be arranged through **South Padre Beach Houses, Inc.**, *5009 Padre Boulevard, South Padre Island, Tel. 956/76-6554 or 800/377-3262*. Weekly rates range from $450 to $1375. This is an ideal way to stay if you plan an extended visit or will be traveling with a few people.

SHERATON FIESTA, *310 South Padre Island Boulevard. Tel. 956/761-6551, 800/325-3535, Fax. 791-6570. Rates: $109 to $290. Credit cards accepted.*

The twelve-story Sheraton is the premier resort hotel on the Island. Tile floors and a poolside cabana let you indulge in the south-of-the -border atmosphere. The excellent food ensures that you never have to leave the hotel. But if you do choose to venture out, recreational activities from parasailing to fishing can be arranged at the front desk. The gym overlooks the Gulf of Mexico and the pool offers an expanse of crystal blue water.

RADISSON RESORT, *500 Padre Boulevard. Tel. 956/761-6511 or 800/333-3333. Rates: $95 to $350. Credit cards accepted.*

The recreational facilities include sand volleyball courts, sea-side tennis courts, two lovely pools and outdoor shuffleboard. The 182 rooms are furnished in crisp, tropical colors and have excellent views of the Gulf of Mexico. Two restaurants on the beach and the bar at the pool provide food and entertainment. Special weekly rate offered during certain times of the year. The hotel has two bedroom condominiums, which comfortably sleep four adults.

BROWN PELICAN INN, *207 W. Aries, South Padre Island. Tel. 956/761-2722, Website: www.brownpelican.com. 8 Rooms. Rates: $90-115 during peak season, $73-95 during off peak season. Credit cards accepted.*

This big Cape Cod-style bed and breakfast sits right on the shoreline. Laguna Atascosa is the most popular room, and it is one of the only two that have a tub and shower combination. The other rooms have showers only. Covered porches overlook the bay. This is a place to escape the telephone and the TV (and there aren't any in the rooms). Listen to the calling of seabirds, and instead of prime time television watch the sun set over Laguna Madre. Children over 12 are welcome.

HOLIDAY INN SUNSPREE RESORT, *100 South Padre Boulevard. Tel. 956/761-5401 or 800/531-7405, Fax 956/761-1560. Rates: $69 to $160.*

The Holiday Inn, designed as a fun-filled resort, is right on the beach. The hotel has complete recreational facilities including a gym, outdoor pool and planned activities. Children stay free with their parents, so this is a good choice for family travel.

RAMADA LIMITED, *4109 Padre Boulevard. Tel. 956/761-4097 or 800/2-RAMADA. Rates: $65 to $180. Credit cards accepted.*

This budget conscious accommodation is in the center of the island, but far from the beach. If you want only a room with no frills, the Ramada delivers. The hotel is new and the large rooms each have a small refrigerator and hair dryer.

Where to Eat

BLACKBEARD'S, *103 East Saturn Street, Port Isabel. Tel. 956/761-2962. Credit cards accepted.*

You will have to travel back across the Queen Isabella Bridge to eat at one of the most frequented seafood restaurants on the coast. Blackbeard's serves most of its dishes - shrimp, crab, and fish - batter-dipped and fried. The food is refreshingly without frills; no spicy sauces, no unusual combinations. All the food is catch-of-the day fresh, and a full meal is reasonably priced.

SCAMPI'S, *206 West Aries, Port Isabel. Tel. 956/761-1755. Credit cards accepted.*

When it's time to indulge in upscale seafood, south Texans come to Scampi's. Naturally the shrimp dishes are all specialties of the house. Fresh fish fillets and sauces with both European and Mexican influence highlight the daily selections.

AMBERJACK'S, *209 West Amberjack Street, South Padre Island. Tel. 956/761-6500. Credit cards accepted.*

The restaurant is located on the calm bay waters near the Queen Isabella Bridge. For casual seafood made in gourmet fashion, this restaurant remains unsurpassed. The layered Crab and Shrimp Enchiladas in tomatillo sauce is an exquisite mix of flavors. The sautéed amberjack, the signature dish, is served with fresh mango creme sauce. This restaurant sets the standard for excellent seafood on the Island. Plan to come back a few times to explore why. Steak, chicken and sandwiches also served. Amberjack's is a favorite local hangout with live music on weekends.

PADRE ISLAND BREWING COMPANY, *3400 Padre Boulevard, South Padre Island. 956/761-9585. Credit cards accepted.*

The only brewpub on the Island serves excellent food to accompany the fresh beer. The restaurant offers six kinds of hamburger. Pizza can be traditional or racy, with toppings that include grilled quail, Gorgonzola cheese or shrimp. Dinner, served from 5pm to 10pm, features eclectic entrees. The Crab Stuffed Chilies Rellenos are served in tomato sauce made with amber ale. The Grilled Swordfish has a deliciously tangy marinade of ginger and cilantro. The Beer Batter Shrimp is a sure winner for less exotic palates.

Seeing the Sights

The beach is the reason to visit Padre Island, and you will be surrounded by it. From the Isabella Bridge, turn north onto Padre Boulevard and continue past the hotels. The next ten miles are beaches with access roads.

There is a great deal to learn from the natural wonderland of the coastal bend. The **South Padre Island Aquarium**, *2305 Laguna Boulevard, South Padre Island, Tel. 956/761-7067, open daily 10am to 10pm*, allows you to enter the underwater world without getting wet. A more personal look is offered by **Sea Turtle Inc.**, *5805 Gulf Boulevard, South Padre Island, Tel. 956/761-2544*, which is run by a lady who has devoted her life to saving the sea turtle. Periodic lectures and presentations about the sea turtle are given; call for the current schedule.

Nightlife & Entertainment

PADRE ISLAND BREWING COMPANY, *3400 Padre Boulevard, South Padre Island. 956/761-9585. Credit cards accepted.*

The beer selection will not disappoint even the true brew connoisseur. From the refreshing Padre Island Pale Ale to the Longboard Lager, the tastes and subtleties of the beer are excellent. You will enjoy spending some time at the long bar overlooking the dining room, where you are sure to meet locals and vacationers alike.

BLUE RAY'S, *100 Padre Boulevard, South Padre Island Tel. 956/761-7297.*

This unique clothing/Harley Davidson Motorcycle shop has a restaurant that serves light gourmet meals. Lunch specials such as blackened red snapper sandwich or white cheese steak sandwich with mushrooms will enliven your tastebuds. The pride of the kitchen is the pizza, which is made with split flatbread instead of traditional crust. During the evening entertainment is featured.

Sports & Recreation

The water off South Padre Island is rich in red snapper, kingfish, wahoo and marlin. **Jim's Pier**, *209 West Whiting, South Padre Island. Tel. 956/761-2865, Fax 761-4911*, has cruises to suit most every taste in fishing. Deep Sea fishing trips take you 50 miles into the Gulf and last all day. Less intense half-day bay fishing trips start at only $15 per person. Private charters can be arranged.

Scuba divers should not pass up the opportunity to jump into the warm, inviting waters off South Padre Island. Just a boat ride away, you can dive along the warm coast or venture to an oilrig, which offers vertical ocean communities. **American Diving**, *1807 Padre Boulevard, South Padre Island, Tel. 956/761-2030, Fax 956/761-6039*, conducts specialized dives, teaches certification courses and has dolphin watch cruises.

The **Island Equestrian Center**, *Tel. 956/761-4677 or 800/761-4677*, provides horses for riding on the beach by the hour and can arrange hayrides or cookouts.

For a bird's-eye view of the Island, jump out of plane with **SPI Divers**, *Tel. 956/761-6026 or 233-9430*. Novice skydivers are welcome; SPI Divers specializes in tandem jumps. Each jump requires special arrangements, so call for more information. **Parrot Eyes**, *6101 Padre Island Boulevard, South Padre Island. Tel. 956/761-9457 or 761-7619*, rents small and large boats, water ski equipment and offers parasailing.

Excursions & Day Trips

Matamoros, the Mexican border city across the Rio Grande from Brownsville, is a short drive from South Padre Island. See the Excursions section under Brownsville, below.

Practical Information

The **South Padre Island Convention and Tourist Bureau**, *600 Padre Boulevard, South Padre Island, Tel. 800/SOPADRE*, offers information about the area.

Brownsville

The city of **Brownsville**, resting at the southern tip of Texas, has a long and remarkable history. The area may have been one of the first parts of Texas explored by Cabeza de Vaca, who traveled up the Rio Grande in the sixteenth century. The town was established in 1846, when General Zachary Taylor constructed a military fort at the site in order to establish a claim to the land. Mexico considered this act an invasion of Mexican soil, attacked the fort, and the United States declared war on Mexico. The Treaty of Guadalupe Hidalgo, signed in 1848, established the Rio Grande as the boundary between the United States and Mexico (as well as granting to the United States the future states of California, Arizona, New Mexico, and Nevada, thus expanding U.S. territory from the Atlantic to the Pacific).

Like El Paso and Juarez today, Brownsville shares a very fluid border with its neighbor across the Rio Grande, Matamoros, Mexico. Many of the residents of Brownsville live here for its proximity to the recreational areas of South Texas and the year-round mild climate. Tourists flock into the area to visit Matamoros and South Padre Island. Whatever brings you to this furthest flung arm of Texas, take some time to slow down and appreciate the vibrant culture and warmth that the city has to offer. If you are visiting during the last week of February, don't miss the colorful **Charro Days Fiesta**, a celebration of the Mexican cowboy spirit.

Arrivals & Departures

Brownsville is located at the southern end of Highway 77. Highway 83 joins Highway 77 from the west and leads into Brownsville. Highway 281 runs along the Rio Grande to the west until Pharr; this highway connects to San Antonio in the north.

The **Brownsville/South Padre Island International Airport**, *700 Minnesota Avenue, Tel. 956/542-4373, Website: www.flybrownsville.com*, is slightly east of the city and is served by Continental Airlines. **Gray Line Tours**,

Tel. 956/761-4343, Toll free 800/321-8720, operates shuttle service from the airport to Brownsville and South Padre Island.

Orientation

Highways 77 and 83 combine to become the major north/south thoroughfare through Brownsville. The highways end at International Boulevard, which leads to the border with Mexico. Highway 4, also called Boca Chica Boulevard, cuts east/west across the city and ends at Boca Chica Beach on the west.

The new Veterans International Bridge connects Highways 77 and 83 to Matamoros, Mexico. The bridge is located east of the center of town and provides a direct driving route between Texas and Mexico.

Getting Around Town

The easiest way to get around town and see the sights is with the **Historic Brownsville Trolley Tours**, *Tel. 956/546-3721 or 800/626-2639*. The Brownsville Convention & Visitors Bureau operates the trolleys; routes include the "Port of Brownsville" and "Historic Sites in Brownsville" tours. Adult fare is $6, children is $3. Reservations should be made at least one day in advance.

Bus service in Brownsville starts at 6am and ends at 7pm. Fares are $.75. To obtain information about city bus routes, contact the **Brownsville Urban System**, *700 South Iowa Street, Tel. 956/548-6050*.

Where to Stay

FOUR POINTS HOTEL BY SHERATON, *3777 North Expressway (Highway 77). Tel. 956/547-1500, Fax 956/547-1550, Toll free 888/625-5144, Website: www.fourpoints.com/brownsville. 141 Rooms. Rates: $69-129. Credit cards accepted.*

This is one of the newer hotels in Brownsville, located north of the city. Handsomely landscaped grounds with tropical and native plants surround the Spanish-style building and outdoor pool. The rooms are modest but spacious, decorated with Southwestern touches, and well equipped with amenities. There is another indoor pool on the premises and a fitness center, as well as the full-service Galleria Restaurant. The Catzz Lounge features live music and complimentary hors d'oeuvres.

THE INN AT CHACHALACA BEND, *20 Chachalaca Bend Drive, Los Fresnos. Tel. 956/233-1180, Fax 956/233-1932, Toll free 888/612-6800, Website: www.chachalaca.com. 6 Rooms. Rates $100-195. Credit cards accepted.*

You'll enjoy your stay at this bed and breakfast no matter who you are, but if you're a birder you'll think you've died and gone to heaven. This newly-constructed inn offers accommodation in a unique natural setting where you can hike a 14-acre birding trail or scan 27 acres of prairie from a 40-foot observation tower. Tropical birds are plentiful here – you might see Green Jays, Roseate Spoonbills, and Altamira Orioles.

The rooms possess charms equal to their environment. Each is named after a bird you might expect to see during your stay, and each is uniquely furnished and decorated. Materials such as terra cotta tile, slate, wood, and tumbled marble further connect both building and occupants to the natural glory all about them. A country buffet breakfast along with freshly ground espresso and cappuccino is served each morning in the dining room from 7:30am to 9:30am. The town of Los Fresnos is about seven miles north of Brownsville.

RAMADA LIMITED FORT BROWN, *1900 East Elizabeth Street. Tel 956/ 541-2921, Fax 956/541-2695, Toll free 888/298-2054, Website: www.the.ramada.com/brownsville02482. 104 Rooms. Rates: $47-125.*

The Ramada Limited stands on over 10 acres of grounds landscaped with hundreds of palm trees, and is surrounded by a *resaca*, or waterway. It's only a two-block walk to the Gateway International Bridge and Mexico from here. There is a playground for children, exercise room, heated pool, hot tub, and complimentary continental breakfast. The University of Texas at Brownsville campus is nearby. Rooms include continental breakfast and the hotel has tennis courts and a pool.

Where to Eat

GIO'S VILLA ITALIAN RESTAURANT, *2325 Central Boulevard. Tel. 956/542-5054. Open Wednesday through Sunday 5pm-11:30pm, closed Monday and Tuesday. Credit cards accepted.*

There is something about the tomato sauce at Gio's that makes the meal. It's zesty, it's fresh, and whether on pizza or pasta it has made Gio's a Valley favorite for over 30 years. Some of the best Italian food south of San Antonio is right here. The best bets are Gio's crispy-crusted pizza, tossed salad with the house Italian dressing, and minestrone soup that is comfort food at its finest.

EL PATO MEXICAN FOOD, *1631 East Price Road. Tel. 956/541-0241.*

Try El Pato for good Tex-Mex, and have a plate of soft tacos with various fillings like potatoes, refritos, chorizo, avocado, and carne guisada wrapped up in fresh tortillas.

PALM COURT RESTAURANT, *2200 Boca Chica Boulevard. Tel. 956/ 542-3575. Open Monday-Saturday 11am-3pm, closed Sunday. Credit cards accepted.*

The Palm Court offers a slightly more ambitious menu than is the norm for these parts, and for the most part it succeeds. There's no question that the restaurant is visually pleasing, with its courtyard ambiance and crystal chandelier. Gazpacho, tortilla, and black bean soups are all good, and you can't go wrong with desserts like coco mocho pie. The Palm Court serves only lunch.

Seeing the Sights

The remains of the fort that started all the trouble between the United States and Mexico, **Fort Brown**, *600 International Boulevard*, are now part of the campus of Texas Southmost College. The post hospital is now used as the administrative building. Other fort structures still standing are the post commander's home, the morgue, and the cavalry barracks.

In 1928, the Southern Pacific Depot was built for the first rail line through Brownsville. The design reflects the Spanish and Mexican heritage of the region. Today, this historic building houses the **Historic Brownsville Museum**, *641 East Madison Street, Tel. 956/548-1313, Monday-Saturday 10am-4:30pm, Sunday 2pm-5pm, admission $2 for adults*, which traces the history of the border, and Brownsville in particular, through photos, documents and historic objects. This museum offers a concise but illuminating picture of South Texas.

The **Immaculate Conception Church**, *1218 East Jefferson Street*, stands in dramatic contrast to most of the buildings in the area, which have rounded mission-style facades with ornate Spanish designs. This church was built by French missionaries in 1859 and has dramatic neo-Gothic lines. You can walk through the church, which is open during the day.

Another landmark from the mid-nineteenth century is the **Stillman House**, *1305 East Washington Street, Tel. 956/542-3929*. The man credited with founding Brownsville, Charles Stillman, built this one-story pink brick house in 1850. The Stillman family donated many of the items on exhibit to the museum. One of the oldest pieces in the collection is a Wedgwood chandelier from 1770. The Stillman House is listed in the National Register of Historic Places.

The **Gladys Porter Zoo**, *500 Ringgold Street, Tel. 956/ 546-7187, open daily 9am to sundown, Admission $6.50 for adults, $5 for senior citizens, $3.25 for children under 14, children under 2 admitted free*, is consistently named one of the top ten zoos in the country. Although the zoo is small, only 31 acres, it has been carefully designed and landscaped to hold a diverse collection of animals from five continents. The zoo is divided into geographical areas, and in each one the animals live either in small natural habitats on islands or larger spaces bordered by moats – there are no bars or cages. The aviary is a tropical free-flight oasis and bursts with the sound of singing birds. A special area for children lets them explore and learn interactively. You can scoot around the zoo in style on the Zoofari Express train. To get to the zoo from Highway 77, take the 6th Street exit.

At the time of Spanish colonization, much of the land of the Rio Grande Valley may have resembled the **Sabal Palm Audubon Center & Sanctuary**, *Farm Road 1419, Tel. 956/541-8034, Visitor Center open 9am-5pm daily*. This remarkable ecosystem is a rare palm forest. The Audubon Society conducts research in the 527-acre Sabal Palm Grove and oversees its preservation and revegetation. There are three trails that wind through the preserve – observation decks and walkways provide places where you can just sit and listen to the sounds of the forest. At the wildlife viewing area you can watch for birds and other animals. From Brownsville, take International Boulevard east to Farm Road 1419. Continue on FM 1419 for six miles and look for the entrance sign on your right.

Nightlife & Entertainment

The **University of Texas at Brownsville**, *80 Fort Brown, Tel. 956/544-8247*, sponsors a fine arts program which bring touring musicians to the area. Pianists, vocalists and other classical musicians of international quality grace the stage. The season runs from late September through May. Free concerts are offered during the season.

Cobbleheads Bar and Grill, *3154 Central Boulevard, Tel. 956/546-6224*, is a popular hangout and offers live music on occasion. The sandwiches are beloved by regulars, particularly the Philly cheese-steak.

Sports & Recreation

You will know that you are playing golf near the coast since the majority of holes have water traps. The **Brownsville Golf and Recreation Center**, *Farm Road 802 between US 77/83 and Farm Road 1847, Tel. 956/541-2582*, has an 18-hole par 70 course. To reach the course, take Highway 77 north and go east on Farm Road 802.

Excursions & Day Trips

The southernmost shoreline in Texas is a 45,000 acre tropical sanctuary, the **Laguna Atascosa National Wildlife Refuge**, *Farm Road 1847, Rio Hondo, Tel. 956/748-3608, open October to April, daily 10am to 4pm*. The visitor center will provide a map of two road tours though the refuge. Hiking trails through the park remain open until sunset. From Brownsville, take Highway 77 north. At Harlingen, turn east onto Farm Road 106. Continue past Rio Hondo for 18 miles, then turn north onto the Refuge. The Visitor Center is three miles from the highway.

Another favorite back to nature escape is the **Bensten Rio Grande Valley State Park**, *Park Road 43, Mission, Tel. 956/519-6448 (tours) or 800/792-1112 (camping), open Sunday to Saturday 7am to 10pm*. Once part of a private land holding, the 580-acre park was opened to the public in 1944. The park is a favorite of birdwatchers, as migrating and rare birds are found here. Excellent all-day tours are conducted daily from December to March. The park employees lead a bus tour combined with easy walking and introduce participants to the many unique plants and seasonal wildlife. The popularity of the tours means you should make reservations well in advance. Camping facilities include sites with full hook-ups, showers and picnic areas.

PORT ISABEL

Port Isabel offers extraordinary fishing. The small surfside city is on the mainland just across the water from the resorts of South Padre Island. The city sits on a peninsula in the calm Laguna Madre Bay. Many vacationers choose Port Isabel to escape the higher prices and crowds of tourist on South Padre Island.

If you just pass through on your way to South Padre Island, stop at the **Port Isabel Lighthouse**, *Highway 100, Tel. 512/943-1172, open daily 10am to noon and 1pm to 5pm, admission $1*, and climb to the top for a spectacular view. The lighthouse stands 82 feet high and was built in 1852; it guided ships until 1902. This is one of the few lighthouses on the Texas coast, and th only one open to the public.

You can arrange accommodations or receive more information from the **Port Isabel Chamber of Commerce**, *213 Yturia Street, Tel. 512/943-2262 or 800/527-6102*. From Brownsville, take Highway 48 east to Port Isabel.

MATAMOROS, MEXICO

Most tourists that cross the border to **Matamoros, Mexico** go for a short day trip. The city offers bargain shopping and a colorful, hectic atmosphere. Be sure to take identification with you in the form of a driver's license or voter's registration card. The easiest way by far to cross the Rio Grande border is on foot. Public parking is available in downtown Brownsville. As you approach the **Gateway International Bridge**, take the last turn west. The lot is only one block from the pedestrian walkway. There is another pedestrian bridge further south at Perl Boulevard (East 12th Street). Both bridges end in Matamoros at Avenida Alvaro Obregon, a major thoroughfare. Simply walk across either bridge and you are in the heart of the tourist center.

As you walk down the main street you will find yourself at the markets. One favorite shop is **Barbara de Matamoros**, *37 Avenida Alvaro Obregon*, where you can buy life-sized brass animals, jewelry, ceramics, enormous papier-mâché parrots and macaws, and any number of items that are sure to make eyes pop come Christmastime. **Mercado Juarez**, *Matamoros at Calle Nueve (9ᵗʰ Street)*, is a true market; a collection of many small shops under one low roof. Don't be intimidated by the aggressive hawkers and salespeople – that's actually a good indication that they're interested in bargaining. You may be hesitant to haggle over price at first, but once you've tried it you'll find yourself eager to track down the next bargain.

Walking through the colorful marketplaces both old and new can be fun, but you will find some of the best shopping at the city's most famous store, **Garcia's**, *Avenida Alvaro Obregon, near the bridge*. Prices at Garcia's may be somewhat higher than in the market, but you will find better selection and quality. At the elegant restaurant upstairs, Garcia's serves lunch and dinner with nightly specials. Steak dinner costs less than $10, and of course, the margaritas are good. If you're more in the mood for a party, you can eat at **Blanca White's**, *49 Avenida Alvaro Obregon*, a raucous cantina serving fajitas, enchiladas, and other border specialties.

To enjoy a slice of Mexico's culture, visit **Casa Mata Fort and City Museum**, *Guatemala y Santos Degollado Streets, Tuesday to Sunday 10am to 5pm*. This fort was built in 1845 as a reaction to the United States presence Brownsville and was used during the Mexican-American War. The small building now serves as a museum, housing, among other interesting items, a *charro* suit that belonged to Pancho Villa. Catch a taxi to the museum, which is about one mile from the bridge.

Practical Information

You can get information about Brownsville and Matamoros at the **Brownsville Visitor Information Center**, *Highway 77/83 at the FM 802 exit, Tel. 956/546-3721 or 800/626-2639*. On the web, visit *www.brownsville.org*.

South texas

Chapter 19

Beautiful **South Texas** comprises a dramatic patch-work of cultures. The stark coastal plains are the birthplace of the American cowboy and the majestic Longhorn cattle. The rich Latino heritage contributes a vibrant cultural flare that characterizes the area.

San Antonio

San Antonio marks the border of central and south Texas. The city offers the benefits of both regions—beautiful central Texas hill country and the rich history of the Texas-Mexico border. With its major theme parks surrounding an appealing and culturally unique central district, San Antonio is the most popular travel destination in the state of Texas. San Antonio has always been situated at the crossroads of many cultures. The city has been a part of Mexico, a center of German immigrant settlement, and a major trade center for North America. The patchwork quilt of history lives on in the historic residential districts, picturesque downtown, and thriving arts scene.

The San Antonio area was one of the first areas to be settled during the Spanish colonization of North America. Catholic missionaries braved the rugged terrain and long dry summers to establish religious centers. The city absorbed many armed conflicts during the birth of the state of Texas. The famous **Alamo** still stands at the center of the city. The Mexican Army marched on San Antonio twice in 1842, with one significant battle resulting, the Battle of Salado Creek.

Although San Antonio played an important role as a point on the trade route that connected Mexico and North

America, for decades it remained little more than a frontier town with mud streets. After Texas independence was won, San Antonio grew up around the cattle industry and became the southern end of the Chisholm Trail. Downtown Houston Street was part of the Old San Antonio Highway, the route for traffic traveling to Mexico City. In the late 1800s, mule-drawn trolleys provided public transportation downtown.

Today San Antonio is the eighth largest city in the United States, with a population of over one million. The metropolitan area sustains slow, consistent growth, allowing the city to maintain its turn-of-the-century demeanor. The center of tourism lies downtown along the famous **River Walk**. The factories and rail-yards that once dominated the city are now incorporated into its metropolitan character. San Antonio is home to five military bases and is a major Air Force and medical center.

San Antonio hosts conventions throughout the year, with the spring (from February to April) being high season. On certain weekends, such as Valentine's Day or Easter, you may find all the hotels downtown booked full. San Antonio celebrates the many aspects of its rich history with festivals throughout the year. The **San Antonio Stock Show & Rodeo**, *Tel. 210/225-0612, Website: www.sarodeo.com*, is held each February, and is the major rodeo on the South Texas circuit.

The ten-day long **Fiesta** lights up the city in April. Fiesta is like San Antonio's version of Mardi Gras – it started over a hundred years ago as a fete in honor of President Benjamin Harrison. The President was a no-show, but the city enjoyed the party so much that it became an annual event. Concerts, parades, outdoor activities and festivals fill the days. La Villita is the site of "A Night in Old San Antonio," a celebration of the city's history and culture. A number of formal dances and balls are held. Some events are free to the public, and admission prices vary for others. For a complete schedule of events contact the **Fiesta San Antonio Commission**, *2611 Broadway, San Antonio 78215, Tel. 210/227-5191, Toll free 877/723-4378, Website: www.fiesta-sa.org*.

Every summer, the **Institute of Texan Cultures**, *801 South Bowie Street, Tel. 210/458-2300, Website: www.texancultures.utsa.edu/tff*, holds the **Texas Folklife Festival** to celebrate multiculturalism in Texas and the traditions of the many peoples of the state. Over 10,000 participants from 103 cities come to share crafts, foods, music, storytelling, dance, and other cultural treasures with 100,000 festivalgoers.

Christmas brings a number of celebrations throughout the city. Two of the most popular and picturesque of these events occur downtown. Shortly after Thanksgiving each year the **River Parade and Lighting Ceremony** takes place. 80,000 lights that will shine until New Year's Day illuminate the River Walk. In early December, the holiday season is welcomed with **Las Posadas**, a candle-lit procession of singers along the River Walk that ends with a pinata party.

Arrivals & Departures

San Antonio International Airport, *9800 Airport Boulevard, Website: www.sanantonio.gov/airport*, is conveniently located only 13 miles from downtown and is seldom crowded. The number for airport information is *Tel. 210/207-3411*. For parking information, the number is *Tel. 210/207-3465*. The airport is located at the intersection of Highways 281 and 410, in north central San Antonio. A taxicab from the airport to the downtown area will usually cost an average of $15-17, plus tip. Up to four people may share a cab with no extra charge.

SATrans, *Tel. 210/281-9900, Toll free 800/868-7707, Website: www.saairportshuttle.com*, runs a shuttle from the airport to downtown hotels for $8, $14 round trip. Shuttle kiosks are located outside either terminal, and credit cards are accepted. The **Star Shuttle Service**, *Tel. 210/341-6000, Toll free 800/341-6000, Website: www.starshuttle.com*, runs mini-vans between the airport and the San Antonio area. Shuttle pick-up is just outside the baggage claim area of either terminal.

The **Amtrak** Station, *1174 East Commerce Street, Tel. 210/223-3226 or 800/872-7245*, is located downtown. Trains run to Dallas/Fort Worth, Houston, and El Paso and connect to out-of-state routes.

To get to the **Greyhound Bus Station**, *500 N St. Mary Street, Tel. 800/231-2222*, from Interstate Highway 35, take the Lexington Street Exit, turn left and cross under the highway. Continue on Lexington Street for five blocks, and then turn right onto St. Mary's Street; the station is three blocks down. **Kerrville Bus Company**, *Tel. 210/227-5669 or 800/335-3722*, serves South Texas with regular routes, charters and tours.

Orientation

In Texas, all roads lead to San Antonio. Both Interstate Highway 35, which bisects the state from north to south, and Interstate Highway 10, which cuts across from east to west, run through central San Antonio. Interstate Highway 35 branches off into Interstate Highway 37, which continues on to the Texas Gulf Coast.

Loop 410 circles the city and provides access to many major attractions that lie outside the center. Highway 281 is a picturesque road connecting downtown to the airport and the parks in the northwest areas.

The San Antonio River runs north/south through the center of the city. The downtown area contains the **River Walk**, a developed canal loop lined by hotels, restaurants and bars, located near the **Alamo**. Large trees provide shade along the 20-block pedestrian zone that sits below street level. This is the city's center of tourism, entertainment and recreation. In the evening, music floats through the air as the bars and nightclubs come alive.

Just south of downtown, off St. Mary's Street, is the historic neighborhood of the **King William District**. First settled by German merchants when

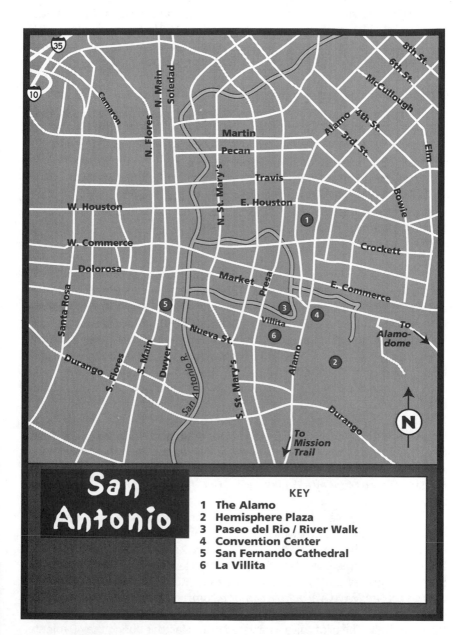

San Antonio

KEY

1 The Alamo
2 Hemisphere Plaza
3 Paseo del Rio / River Walk
4 Convention Center
5 San Fernando Cathedral
6 La Villita

the territory was part of Mexico, the 25-block area is chock-full of marvelous restored Victorian homes, some of which are open to the public. The King William Conservation Society sponsors walking tours of the area. The **Mission Trail** is found just south of the King William District. North of downtown you will find **Fort Sam Houston** and the lovely **McNay** and **San Antonio Museums**, **Botanical Garden**, and **San Antonio Zoo**.

Getting Around Town

If you plan to stay only a few days in San Antonio, you may decide a car is not necessary. Most points of interest are within walking distance of the River Walk and public transportation provides excellent service to tourist attractions outside the immediate downtown area.

Local car rental agencies include:
- **A & P Recreational Vehicle Rentals**, *Tel. 210/667-1838*
- **Capps Rent A Car**, *Tel. 210/822-8655*
- **Chuck's Rent-A-Clunker**, *Tel. 210/922-9464*
- **Rent-A-Van**, *Tel. 210/340-8267*

Taxis in San Antonio charge $1.60 for the first one-fifth of a mile and $.30 for each one-fifth of a mile following. There's a minimum charge of $3 during the day, $4 at night. Two companies that serve the San Antonio area are **United Cab**, *Tel. 210/737-9380* and **Yellow Cab**, *Tel. 210/226-4242*.

San Antonio has an excellent, modern bus system, **VIA Metropolitan Transport**, which has nearly 100 routes across the city and streetcar-style buses that serve the central tourist district. Downtown Streetcar fares are $.50 each way, and one-day passes are available at many downtown hotels. Other bus fares are $.80. Route 7 serves the Alamo, McNay Art Museum, Witte Museum, Zoo and Botanical Gardens. Route 40 runs from the Alamo to the historic San Antonio Missions in the southern suburbs. Special express buses run to Sea World and Six Flags Amusement Park. The VIA Metropolitan Transport Information Office is located close to the River Walk, *260 East Houston Street, Monday to Friday 7am to 6pm and Saturday 9am to 2pm; Tel. 210/362-2020*.

Generally people do not take a horse drawn carriage to actually get somewhere but just to enjoy the ride. In San Antonio, the carriages are most easily found at the plaza in front of the Alamo. They generally take a route along the older streets of downtown. Two services that can be hired are **Lone Star Carriage**, *Tel. 210/656-7527*, and **Yellow Rose Carriage**, *Tel. 210/225-6490, Website: www.yellowrosecarriage.com*.

Deck-boat river cruises are a pleasant and popular way to sightsee along the River Walk. The pilots give a narrated historical tour during the 40-minute cruise. Unfortunately, on busy weekends you may have to stand in line longer than 40 minutes just to get on a boat. Standard fare is $5.25 for adults and

$1 for children under the age of 5 years. You can also buy an all-day River Taxi pass for $10 that allows you to hop on and off the boats at your own pace. For more information or to charter your own boat for a special event call **Yanaguana River Cruise**, *Tel. 210/244-5700 or 800/417-4139, Website: www.sarivercruise.com.*

Bus tours of San Antonio and specific tours of the Mission Trail are offered by **Gray Line of San Antonio**, *Tel. 210/226-1706 or 800/472-9546*. Gray Line also ventures to Laredo, Texas and Nuevo Laredo, Mexico for shopping trips and conducts tours of the Texas Hill Country. The Gray Line information office is located across the street from the Alamo.

Where to Stay
DOWNTOWN

In San Antonio, "downtown" is usually synonymous with the River Walk. However, there are several excellent choices a few blocks removed from the action. On weekends, downtown can be noisy if you're anywhere close to the water.

Expensive

THE FAIRMOUNT, *401 South Alamo Street. Tel. 210/224-8800, Fax 210/475-0082, Toll free reservations 800/WYNDHAM, Website: www.wyndham.com/Fairmount. 37 Rooms, 17 Suites. Rates: $164-269. Credit cards accepted.*

This charming hotel was moved from its former site to preserve the building. Much of the hotel is the original building from 1906. The lobby and restaurant are accented with authentic period lamps and crystal chandeliers. The Fairmount provides a luxurious and secluded setting in the heart of the city. The location, a block away from La Villita, is serene and picturesque, in contrast to many of the larger and louder establishments over on the River Walk. Even the hotel restaurant, Polo's, is a bit more dignified and sedate than its rowdier neighbors.

The courtyard provides a garden setting, while the rooms provide a haven of luxury. Each room of the Fairmount is uniquely furnished in turn-of-the-century style. Canopied beds and marble baths are kept sparkling with twice-daily maid service. The master suite is an entire extravagant apartment, with a spa bath, hardwood floors and two bathrooms.

ADAM'S MARK SAN ANTONIO—RIVERWALK, *111 Pecan Street East. Tel. 210/354-2800, Fax 210/354-2700, Toll free reservations 800/444-2326, Website: www.adamsmark.com. 410 Rooms. Rates: $145-210. Credit cards accepted.*

This newer high-rise hotel, opened in 1997, stands at the south end of the River Walk, not far from the convention center. The recreational facilities on the premises include a full health club with an indoor spa and outdoor pool.

The hotel restaurant Marbella features New World cuisine with a Mediterranean accent; two bars provide entertainment into the night. The rooms are up to the usual high standard of the Adam's Mark chain, as is the service. The hotel offers both a parking lot and valet service.

THE CAMBERLEY GUNTER, *205 East Houston Street. Tel. 210/227-3241, Fax 210/227-3299, Toll free reservations 800/999-2089, Website: http://www.gunterhotel.com. 334 Rooms. Rates: $145-165, Suites $225-700, seasonal and promotional rates also available. Credit cards accepted.*

The Gunter Hotel has a rich history that reflects the character of San Antonio itself. When the hotel opened in 1909, not only was it the mainstay of the San Antonio skyline, but it was hailed as the most stylish hotel between the east and west coasts. The Gunter cost one million to build, and the price tag itself made news. The spot where the hotel stands has a long history. It was the site of San Antonio's first inn in 1837, first military barracks in 1851, and two subsequent hotels. The Mahncke Hotel was famous as the home of newly arrived German immigrants. San Antonio's social scene quickly found its hub in the Gunter. Famous guests include President Harry S. Truman, John Wayne and Mae West.

The Gunter has been designated a Historic Hotel of America by the National Trust for Historic Preservation. It underwent a $5 million renovation in 1997. The hotel is located across from the Majestic Theater, just a block away from the River Walk. Living history surrounds you on the street. From the moment you enter the lobby, you are surrounded by the exuberant elegance of a cattle baron's palace. Even the guest rooms are done in a cattleman motif. During the afternoon you can enjoy high tea; in the evening Muldoon's Bar serves cocktails. There is an outdoor heated pool and whirlpool as well as a fitness center for guests to enjoy.

HILTON PALACIO DEL RIO, *200 South Alamo Street. Tel. 210/222-1400, Fax 210/226-4123, Toll free reservations 800/774-1500, Website: www.hilton.com/hotels/SATPDHH/index.html. Rates: $145-250. Credit cards accepted.*

The tall Hilton stands on the River Walk; many of its rooms have balconies that overlook the river and downtown. This was one of the first high-rise hotels on the San Antonio River, and the entire building was recently renovated. The hotel is convenient to the convention center and Alamodome.

SAINT ANTHONY HOTEL, *300 East Travis Street. Tel. 210/227-4392, Fax 210/222-1896, Toll free reservations 800/227-6963, Website: www.stanthonyhotel.com. 352 Rooms. Rates $145-215. Credit cards accepted.*

The Saint Anthony is a beautiful hotel just off the River Walk. It retains the aura it must have had when it opened in 1909. Guests have included First Lady Eleanor Roosevelt, President Eisenhower, and Prince Rainier and Princess Grace of Monaco. The lovely hotel restaurant, The Madrid Room, serves breakfast, lunch, and dinner in Old World ambiance. The truly elegant Peacock Alley lobby is drenched in bronze statuary and French Empire antiques. The rooms are extremely spacious and attractive. There is a heated rooftop swimming pool just to round out your movie star fantasy.

THE MENGER, *204 Alamo Plaza. Tel 210/223-4361, Fax 210/228-0022, Toll free reservations 800/345-9285, Website: www.mengerhotel.com. 350 Rooms. Rates: $132-142, Suites $225-589, promotional rates and discounts available. Credit cards accepted.*

When the Menger was built in 1859, it had fifty rooms and two stories. Eight subsequent additions expanded the hotel. The 1909 renovation added much of the decoration that makes the Menger famous, including marble, columns and ornamentation. The halls leading to the reception area are lined with photos of the hotel's rich history. General Robert E. Lee rode his horse into the hotel lobby; Teddy Roosevelt recruited Rough Riders in the Menger bar. The baby grand player piano in the lobby fills the air with haunting music in the evenings.

Yet another of San Antonio's historical gems, the Menger has also received the title of Historic Hotel of America bestowed by the National Trust for Historic Preservation. The hotel itself is a rambling conglomeration of additions. Requesting a room in the 19th Century wing will give you the best location and Victorian decor. The hotel is built around two large gardens and has lots of windows. Just across the street you will find the Alamo and the River Walk.

HYATT REGENCY RIVER WALK, *123 Losoya Street. Tel. 210/222-1234, Toll free reservations 800/233-1234. Rates: $195-220. Credit cards accepted.*

The Hyatt is one of the most convenient places to stay on the River Walk because the lower floors of the hotel have a lovely miniature mall with fountains, food, and the area's foremost jazz club, Jim Cullum's Landing. The hotel was a landmark when it was built because it incorporated the River Walk into a modern high-rise. A series of fountains runs though the hotel, bringing the feeling of the river through the building.

LA MANSION DEL RIO, *112 College Street. Tel. 210/225-2581, Fax 210/226-0389, Toll free reservations 800/292-7300. Rates: $165-290. Credit cards accepted.*

This beautiful hotel offers guests the warmth of traditional Mexican style. From the tiled floors to the whitewashed walls, you step into the atmosphere of a refined hacienda. The Mexican decor carries into the spacious and comfortable rooms. Las Canarias, the hotel's main restaurant serves authentic Mexican food. La Mansion offers the most beautiful views of San Antonio's River Walk from the outdoor seating at the restaurant. Even if you don't stay here, stop in for coffee and dessert.

EMILY MORGAN RAMADA, *705 East Houston Street. Tel 210/225-8486, Fax 210/225-7227, Toll free reservations 800/824-6674, Website: pw1.netcom.com/~ramadaem/index.html. 177 Rooms. Rates: $129-179. Credit cards accepted.*

The historic building, which dates from the mid-1920s, was constructed as the city's first medical center. In 1985 it was renovated into a modern hotel. The Emily Morgan offers an excellent location near the Alamo and some of the most reasonable rates downtown. Most of the rooms have a spa bathtub and all have hair dryers and irons. You can wake up to complimentary coffee and newspapers in lobby each morning. The Yellow Rose dining room serves buffets at breakfast and lunch. Room service is also offered. The hotel has a full health club and sauna rooms.

PLAZA SAN ANTONIO MARRIOTT, *555 South Alamo. Tel. 210/229-1000, Fax 210/229-1418, Toll free reservations 800/421-1172, Website: www.plazasa.com. 252 Rooms. Rates: $139-249. Credit cards accepted.*

This Marriott emphasizes the blend of Mexican and American aspects of San Antonio. Sitting on six acres of manicured grounds, the refreshing Plaza offers the feeling of a resort in the center of town. The excellent health club has an indoor gym and outdoor tennis courts, croquet area and jogging routes. The rooms are thoroughly modern with a western style that emphasizes comfort. This hotel places a premium on service with two standard room cleanings per day and an evening turndown service to prepare your bed. All rooms receive morning coffee and a daily newspaper.

MARRIOTT RIVERCENTER, *101 Bowie Street. Tel. 210/224-4555, Tll free reservations 800/228-9290, Website: www.marriott.com/marriott/SATRC. 1000 Rooms. Rates: $179-235. Credit cards accepted.*

The Marriott River Center can be seen when approaching the city; the huge hotel is a major part of the River Center Mall. A variety of activities go on each night in the mall; just a few steps away is the River Walk. This hotel is very popular with large tour groups and conventions.

MARRIOTT RIVER WALK, *711 East River Walk. Tel. 210/224-4555, Fax 210/224-2754, Toll free reservations 800/228-9290, Website: www.marriott.com/marriott/SATDT. 503 Rooms. Rates: $179-235. Credit cards accepted.*

The older Marriott of the two, this one is half the size of the newer hotel. It's non-descript in its decor, but remains an adequate travel center. The indoor pool is under a glass atrium and many of the rooms have a pool view.

Moderate

CROCKETT HOTEL, *320 Bonham. Tel 210/225-6500, Fax 210/225-6251, Toll free 800/292-1050, Website: www.crocketthotel.com. 204 Rooms, 2 Suites. Rates: $85-150. Credit cards accepted.*

The Crockett is a downtown landmark, distinguished most of all by the large neon sign that spelled out its name. The property was built in 1907 by a fraternal organization known as the International Order of Odd Fellows. The Crockett was painstakingly restored in the 1980's to replicate the grandeur of the days when it was constructed. Currently operated by Holiday Inn, the hotel overlooks the Alamo and offers very comfortable accommodations at good rates. There is a humdrum addition behind the original building, so be sure to get a room in the old historic part of the hotel. Holiday Inn operates six other hotels in San Antonio, including one near Sea World.

ALAMO INN, *2203 East Commerce Street. Tel. 210/227-2203, Fax 210/ 222-2869, Toll free reservations 888/222-7666, Website: www.alamo-inn.com. 15 Rooms. Rates: $55-99. Credit cards accepted.*

This is a good find for travelers looking for comfortable accommodations at reasonable prices. The Alamo Inn is located just east of Interstate Highway 37, about a three-minute drive to the historic area of downtown. The inn runs a free shuttle to and from the River Walk, airport, and convention center.

WEST & NORTH
Expensive
HYATT REGENCY HILL COUNTRY RESORT, *9800 Resort Drive. Tel. 210/647 1234, Fax 210/681-9681. Rates: $190 to $425. Suites $485-1700. Credit cards accepted.*

Each morning you greet the day with a splendid breakfast and set off to enjoy all the recreational pleasures of the Hill Country. The Hyatt resort stands on 200 acres west of San Antonio. Designed in the style of a stately ranch house, the resort gives a majestic elegance to the serene hill country setting. The splendid pools have a naturalistic area that includes a beach and river for floating. The 18-hole golf course has spectacular views

For those who want true rest, the day spa offers facials, massage and salon services such as manicures and hair cuts. The resort is an ideal retreat for families; special children's activities are held each day. And guests under the age of 18 years can stay free with their parents. Package prices are offered throughout the year.

Moderate
BULLIS HOUSE INN, *621 Pierce Street. Tel. 210/223-9426, Fax 210/229-1479, Toll free reservations 877/477-4100. 10 Rooms. Rates: $55-$115.*

This historic three-story house with its high ceilings provides an elegant night's lodging at a surprisingly good rate. Breakfast is included in your stay. The most popular room is the Corner Room, with its decorative white iron bed. There is a swimming pool for guests to use, a delightful veranda, and sometimes the hosts will hold a movie night with snacks. Not all the rooms have private baths, so if that's important to you, be sure to ask ahead of time.

The International Youth Hostel of San Antonio is attached to this property, and offers dormitory-style lodging for $16-18 per person.

FAMILY GARDEN SUITES, *2382 Northeast Loop 410. Tel. 210/599-4204, Fax 210/599-4648, Toll free reservations 800/314-3824. 191 Rooms. Rates: $69-75. Credit cards accepted.*

This unusual motel is a top choice for families with traveling with children or those interested in an extended stay. Low-rise buildings surround a central swimming pool, making the place feel more like a neighborhood than a motel. Every room is a suite with a sitting room, refrigerator, microwave, and even a porch to sit on. The complex has its own grocery store, a coin-operated laundry room, an on-site playground, and (best of all) three whirlpool spas.

DOUBLETREE CLUB HOTEL, *1111 North East Loop 410. Tel. 210/828-9031 or 888/444-CLUB, Fax 210/828-3066. 227 Rooms. Rates: $59-124. Credit cards accepted.*

This newly renovated hotel is close to the San Antonio International Airport. A fitness room and outdoor pool provide recreation. Business facilities include a lounge with data port computer hook-ups at each table. Informal dining is available throughout the day. The rooms are large and have areas for working. There is plenty of free parking available.

Inexpensive

QUALITY INN AND CONFERENCE CENTER, *10811 Interstate Highway 35. Tel 210/590-4646 or 800/797-1234, Fax 210/967-6717. Credit cards accepted.*

The Quality Inn is conveniently located on the major north/south thoroughfare. This is truly not your typical economy lodging. The grounds are lovely include a large outdoor pool and a chapel for wedding ceremonies. The motel has only 128 rooms, many are suites and all are spacious. Business travelers will find everything for life on the road including in-room hair dryers, coffee makers microwaves alarm clocks and irons. Breakfast is included with all rooms; airport shuttle service available.

King William District/South

The King William District is a charming historic neighborhood filled with lovely Victorian-era cottages. Many of these houses have been converted into Bed & Breakfast Inns.

ADAMS HOUSE, *231 Adams Street. Tel. 210/224-4791, Toll free reservations 800/666-4810, Website: www.san-antonio-texas.com. Rates $99-$139, off-season and single traveler discounts available.*

Four verandahs and pretty grounds shaded by pecan trees make this an appealing choice for the discriminating traveler. Each room has a queen-sized bed and private bath – the Verandah room has a jacuzzi, refrigerator, and work area. Harold the cat welcomes you to his domain on the back verandah, while a hearty gourmet breakfast welcomes you each morning.

BED AND BREAKFAST ON THE RIVER, *129 Woodward Place. Tel. 210/ 225-6333 or 800/730-0019. Rates: $99-150. Credit cards accepted.*

The stately old home stands just over the San Antonio River, offering the only bed and breakfast rooms in the center of town. Inside you enter a comfortable Victorian setting with antique accents. The charming rooms have private baths, some have spa baths and balconies. The large penthouse room on the top floor has a large spa bath and French doors that open to a private balcony.

A YELLOW ROSE, *229 Madison Street. Tel. 210/229-9903 or 800/ 950-9903. Rates: $95-145. Credit cards accepted.*

When the Mueller House was built in 1878, it was a grand residence. Today you can relive a bygone era when you stay at A Yellow Rose. The five rooms each are finished with antique furnishings, and have private baths. The largest, the Magnolia Rooms, can accommodate four adults. Breakfast is served at 9am and prepared with the inn's own recipes.

BECKMANN INN AND CARRIAGE HOUSE, *222 East Guenther. Tel. 210/229-1449 or 800/945-1449. Rates: $90-130. Credit cards accepted.*

This historic inn built in 1886 has five guest rooms, three in the main house and two in the separate carriage house. This elegant home was the resident of one of San Antonio's most prominent families and is on the National Register of Historic places. You can enjoy the beautifully landscaped yard from the front porch, which wraps around the house. The rooms in the carriage house each have a sitting area. All rooms have queen size beds, private baths and refrigerators. The gourmet breakfast is served in the main dining room. A two night minimum stay is required on weekends.

VICTORIAN LADY, *421 Howard Street. Tel. 210/224-2524 or 800/879-7116, Fax 210/224-2524. Rates: $70. Credit cards accepted.*

The stately Victorian home has seven guest rooms, each furnished in the period style. The home was constructed in 1898, at the height of the fancy architecture for which the Victorian period is famous. Children under the age of nine years may not stay at the house.

Where to Eat
RIVER WALK

Although the River Walk is a wonderful place to sit by the water, have a drink, watch the passers-by, or indulge in coffee and dessert, for truly fine dining you should look elsewhere in the city. That said, there's nothing wrong with stopping for a burger or a salad when your feet start to fail you, and there are a couple of excellent restaurants in this tourist-y part of town.

Expensive

BOUDRO'S, *421 East Commerce Street. Tel. 210/224-8484. Sunday-Thursday 11am-11pm, Friday and Saturday 11am-2am. Reservations accepted. Credit cards accepted.*

This is one of the few restaurants on the River Walk that merits a visit just for the sake of the food. The aroma of steaks hot off the grill whets the appetite upon entering this restaurant. The repertoire featured on the menu is not that of an ordinary steak house. Boudro's has moved with the times, and when the Cajun craze died out some years ago they shifted the focus of their menu to Southwestern/New American-style dishes. However, the best item on the menu remains the blackened prime rib.

THE FIG TREE, *515 Villita. Tel. 210/224-1976, Website: www.figtreerestaurant.com. Open daily 6pm-10pm. Reservations recommended. Credit cards accepted.*

This is one of the few other restaurants on the River Walk that merits a visit based on cuisine alone. The Fig Tree, housed in a historic stone house, is part of the restored La Villita Shopping Center. Since 1971 it has occupied a place in the hearts of San Antonians as a luxurious "special occasion" spot. Although the menu still features traditional Continental dishes like chateaubriand, chef Tan Nguyen has updated the preparation, incorporating subtle Asian and New American flavors. The menu is pricey; the décor is very elegant, and the table settings exquisite with fine linens, china, and crystal. The undisputed champion favorite dish here is the beef Wellington.

Moderate

ACAPULCO SAM'S BURGER JOINT, *212 College Street. Tel. 210/212-SAMS. Credit cards accepted.*

Thick, juicy burgers are featured here. A variety of appetizers such as nachos go with seven fruity types of frozen margaritas. The huge warehouse style restaurant attracts many who want the festive atmosphere of a nightclub. This is a good place to come for an informal meal and a few hours of noisy fun.

THE BAYOUS RIVERSIDE, *517 North Prensa. Tel. 210/223-6403. Monday to Thursday and Sunday 11:30am to 11pm; Friday and Saturday 11:30 to midnight. Credit cards accepted.*

A mild touch of Louisiana flavors mixes with the unusual combination of Creole and southwestern spices. The seafood of The Bayous Riverside is fresh and specialties include fresh fish from the Gulf of Mexico. The riverside patio seating is an excellent place to enjoy a long Sunday brunch is served every Sunday from 11:30am to 3pm.

CASA RIO, *430 East Commerce. Tel. 210/225-6718. Open daily 11am to 11pm. Credit cards accepted.*

You are sure to eat genuine Tex-Mex food here-Casa Rio practically invented it. The restaurant first opened in 1946 and is one of the first establishments on the River Walk. The recipes reputedly have been passed down in the family.

DICK'S LAST RESORT, *406 Navarro Street. Tel. 210/224-0026. Open daily, 11am to 2am. Credit cards accepted.*

Be certain to bring your sense of humor to Dick's, where both beer and ribs are served by the bucketful. The informal atmosphere, rows of picnic tables, and offbeat wait staff make for a fun, informal meal. You can chow down on just about any fried treat imaginable, such as "Fried Shrimpies" and onion rings. The sandwiches are the best on part of the menu; the Marinated Chicken Breast is best with the bacon and cheese option. The burgers are inexpensive (for this part of town) and downright juicy. This is the rowdiest establishment on the River Walk.

IBIZA PATIO BAR & RESTAURANT, *715 River Walk. Tel. 210/270-0773. Monday to Thursday and Sunday 6:30am to midnight; Friday and Saturday 6:30am to 2am. Credit cards accepted.*

This is one of the few Spanish restaurants in San Antonio. The menu offers dishes with a Mediterranean flair. Tapas are the specialty, and there is no better place to enjoy tapas and cocktails than the brightly colored restaurant. The full menu includes breakfast, lunch and dinner. Bands perform on weekends. Round off your meal with the excellent cappuccino and luscious deserts.

PAESANO'S, *111 East Commerce. Tel. 210/22-PASTA.*

The first Paesano's opened its doors in 1969 and quickly became the standard of Italian food in south Texas. The best dishes on the menu are still the traditional Italian specialties, such as Veal Marsala and Osso Buco Milanese. Fish, pizza and a long list of pasta give all tastes a good deal of choice. The wine selection includes Italian reds that perfectly accompany the food.

PRESIDIO, *245 East Commerce Street #101. Tel. 210/472-2265. Sunday to Wednesday 11am to 11pm; Thursday to Saturday 11am to midnight. Credit cards accepted.*

Italian cooking highlighted with Mediterranean influences compose the menu. Non-traditional use of spices and sauces bring together European and Mexican cooking for such creations as Grilled Game Hen Mole. The distinct tastes come together for bold and pleasing creations. The Snapper Ancho has a spicy sauce of ancho chiles and pesto with artichoke hearts and shitake mushrooms on top. Presidio offers an extensive selection of wine and cigars.

ZUNI GRILL, *223 Losoya. Tel 210/227-0864. Credit cards accepted.*

Zuni Grill brings together the flavor of Mexico and New Mexico. The menu is a eclectic collection of nuevo Tex-Mex cuisine. The mesquite smoke flavored salsa exemplifies how Zuni takes a standard (like red salsa) and puts a Texan twist to it (with smoked flavor). You will find surprises on the menu, like the appetizer of Applewood Smoked Salmon served with bagels. The food is lighter and probably far healthier than traditional Tex-Mex cooking. The Blue Corn Enchiladas are a sure bet, with smoked chicken and spicy green sauce. Vegetarians will find the Grilled Vegetable Fajitas flavorful and more than filling.

CENTRAL
Expensive
SILO, *1133 Austin Highway. Tel. 210/824-8686. Credit cards accepted. Reservations recommended for dinner.*

Located over the small boutique grocery "Farm to Market," Silo claims to serve "elevated cuisine." They do. This is perhaps the best dining to be had in San Antonio. Chef Mark Bliss serves new American cuisine in this warm, sleek establishment. The atmosphere is casual, the service is engaging, yet professional, and the food is divine. Tuck into upscale comfort food such as roasted chicken breast or peppered yellowfin tuna on steak fries. Many of the wines on the excellent wine list are available by the glass. Chicken-fried oysters on sautéed spinach are a don't-miss appetizer, and chocolate souffle cake is mandatory for dessert.

Moderate
EARL ABEL'S, *4200 Broadway. Tel. 210/822-3358. Open daily, 6:30am to 1am. Credit cards accepted.*

Since 1933, Earl Abel's has been serving the flavor of home-cooked meals in a neighborhood setting. The decoration dates from the same era as the beehive hairdos that some of the waitresses have. Long-time customers know the staff on a personal basis, and they come in for leisurely conversations with their meals. Oatmeal, pancakes and eggs highlight the breakfast selections. Heartier appetites will enjoy the hot roast beef sandwich or the Hand Breaded Beef Cutlet; both come with fluffy mashed potatoes. But the real centerpiece of the menu is the list of desserts. The lemon chess pie and the chocolate icebox pie are legendary. All the deserts are made at Earl Abel's. Take Broadway north from downtown to get to Earl Abel's.

CARRANZA'S, *701 Austin Street. Tel. 210/223-0903. Open Monday to Saturday, lunch 11am-2pm (weekdays only), dinner 5pm-11pm. Credit cards accepted.*

Carrranza's stands alone, both in the dining experience it provides and location. The restaurant is in the family store, a building that dates from 1920 and is located in an area that was once an industrial and railroad center. The unusual location is enhanced by the unique interior — walls made of rough limestone and tall old west-style windows that overlook the neighboring train tracks. The menu offers fish, mesquite smoked barbecue and Tex-Mex and Italian dishes. The variety does not lower the quality. The fish is accented with you choice of six delicate sauces. The scallops are best with Venustiano sauce, a lemon butter sauce. Try the Vera Cruz, a spicy tomato sauce, with the Red snapper. The Italian cuisine is bursting with flavor. During lunch you can order brisket, pork ribs or combination plates. Downstairs the deli serves food-to-go. Carranza's is just southeast of the intersection of Interstate Highway 35 and Highway 281.

LA MARGARITA, *120 Produce Row. Tel. 210/227-7140. Credit cards accepted.*

La Margarita is known for serving large plates of fajitas, giant margaritas and blazingly spicy salsa. The tables outdoors give diners a festive atmosphere right on the Market Square. The food is moderately priced and tame enough for the most sensitive palates.

MI TIERRA, *218 Produce Row. Tel. 210/225-1262. Open daily, 24 hours. Credit cards accepted.*

You can satisfy your Tex-Mex craving anytime at Mi Tierra, the restaurant is open round the clock. This family-owned establishment has been serving food since 1941. Mariachis stroll through the restaurant offering serenades during dinner and lunch. Mi Tierra is a tradition for natives and tourists alike. The food is known as good, standard Tex-Mex; the chicken mole enchiladas are the most exotic dish on the menu. Be sure to visit the colorful Mexican bakery inside with its eye-popping array of pastries and cookies.

PECAN STREET MARKET DELI, *152 East Pecan Street. Tel. 210/227-3226. Monday to Friday 7:30am to 5pm; Saturday 10am to 6pm.*

Hams and sausage hang in the window, giving away the fact that this is an authentic old-fashioned deli. In the heart of San Antonio's business district, Pecan Street Deli caters to the hurried business crowd. This does not mean they serve fast food. The mufallettas are overstuffed, and the vegetarian pita will not disappoint. Mediterranean specialties such as humus, couscous and Greek salads round out the menu.

SEA ISLAND, *322 West Rector. Tel. 210/342-7771. Credit cards accepted.*

This informal seafood house is no secret to locals, who crowd in for lunch and dinner. The secret recipes for the breading, the highest quality seafood and large charcoal grills come together for seafood that surpasses most formal restaurants. The Coho Salmon is a large fillet with lemon and butter, and Lemon Pepper Fish almost melt right into your taste buds. The Charcoal Broiled Shrimp Platter is three kabob skewers full of shrimp grilled to perfection. The platter is almost more food than one can eat, with French fries, cole slaw and hush puppies. You can always substitute a baked potato or corn on the cob. The excellent lunch specials draw a crowd large enough to cause a 30-minute wait even on weekdays. Sea Island is located next to North Star Mall.

Inexpensive

SCHILO'S , *424 East Commerce Street. Tel. 210/223-6692. Monday to Saturday 7am-8:30pm.*

At Schilo's you can get a taste of San Antonio's German Heritage. Schilo's serves Weiner schnitzel, bratwurst and their very own root beer. This is a San Antonio tradition you should not miss. You can hear live German music here on Friday and Saturday night.

Seeing the Sights
The Alamo

The **Alamo** is a place to use your imagination. I think many first-time visitors expect a large, dramatic, isolated monument, and a common reaction to seeing the small stone building buried in downtown San Antonio is, "That's it?" But look closer at the heavy doors riddled with bullet holes and think about what each mark means.

The Alamo is located at *300 Alamo Plaza at Houston Street, in the center of downtown near the River Walk. Tel 210/225-1391, open Monday to Saturday 9am to 5:30pm; in the summer hours are extended until 6:30pm. Admission free; donations accepted.*

Even to the outside world, the Battle of the Alamo symbolizes the great sacrifice and courage that contributed to the freedom of Texas.

The 189 defenders of the Alamo heroically faced certain death against 5,000 Mexican troops under the command of General Santa Anna. Several of the founding fathers of Texas died in the battle, most notably Colonel James Bowie and Colonel William B. Travis. Many of the defenders of the Alamo were not Texans, including Davy Crockett and his Tennessee Boys. A number of women and one child survived the attack. Some 600 Mexican soldiers were killed. On March 6, 1836 the Alamo fell after a 13-day siege. The vicious slaughter and mutilation of their fellow rebels enraged Texans throughout the state, and their cry for revenge echoed at the victorious Battle of San Jacinto, "Remember the Alamo!"

The Alamo is actually the **Mission San Antonio de Valero**, the first of five colonial structures built in the area in the early 1700s. The name "Alamo" comes from the commander of Mexican forces who used the Alamo as a military camp at the turn of the nineteenth century. A museum presents a multimedia account of the siege of the Alamo. Parts of the grounds are reconstructed to show the daily life of the clergy and Native Americans who inhabited the mission. The Alamo Library is open to the public for research and photocopy services.

When you visit the Alamo, you see the famous inner building that has been portrayed in movies and novels. This small stone structure actually stood in the center of the Alamo grounds, surrounded by the outer walls. In the park in front of the Alamo stands a modern monument to the defenders. The names of the 189 men who died defending the Alamo are engraved on the monument.

The River Walk

The main entrance of the **River Walk**, *315 East Commerce Street*, is located across the street from the Alamo. The pedestrian thoroughfare follows the San Antonio River through the downtown area. Tour deck-boats scoot along the river all day and into the night. Restaurants, shops and bars line the way. The **Rivercenter Mall**, *100 Alamo Plaza*, has a multitude of department and specialty stores, restaurants and entertainment. The **IMAX Theater**, *River Center Mall, Tel. 210/225-4629*, shows special IMAX films and occasionally runs new releases.

For the flavor of the past and the shopping and dining experiences of today, visit **La Villita**, *418 Villita, Tel. 210/ 207-8610. Daily 10am to 6pm*, - the Little Village. It is a group of twenty adobe and wood homes that date from the period of Mexican rule. The buildings have been restored; some are shops and an historical exhibit. Large shade trees make this a comfortable retreat from the afternoon sun. Along the River Walk you will see the tiered park that serves as outdoor seating for the **Arneson Open Air Theater**. The stage is across the river in the rock wall. During the summer frequent musical performances grace the stage. La Villita is located across the street from the convention center. You can reach La Villita by the River Walk or downtown between South Alamo and Nueva Streets.

The Missions of San Antonio

Just south of downtown you can visit the sites of some of the first colonization in Texas. The Spanish missions are the legacy of the Franciscans. The Alamo was the first mission founded on the San Antonio River, but is now regarded more as a war memorial than a religious settlement. While the Alamo is a State Historic Site and is maintained by the Daughters of the Republic of Texas, the remaining missions comprise a National Historic Park. This chain forms the largest collection of Catholic missions in North America. You can learn more about the Spanish missions on the web at *www.nps.gov/ saan*.

To reach the **Mission Trail** from Highway 281/Interstate Highway 37 south, take Highway 90/Interstate Highway 10 west. Exit Mission Road and follow the Mission Trail signs. From downtown, take Alamo Street south to South St. Mary's Street, and follow the Mission Trail signs.

From north to south you will find:
• Nuestra Senora de la Purisima Concepcion
• San Jose y San Miguel de Aguayo
• San Juan Capistrano
San Francisco de la Espada

Each is described below:

The **Nuestra Senora de la Purisima Conception Mission**, *807 Mission Street, Open daily 9am to 6pm; admission free*, is partially restored and there are no tours of the grounds or services held in the church. Due to this, the mission is less frequented by visitors than the others, and this adds to its charm. The mission was settled in 1731, but took 20 years to build. The massive stone church on the mission grounds accounts for the many years that went into construction. This is one of the oldest stone churches in North America. Anyone interested in not only seeing, but truly feeling the history of the mission settlements will enjoy a peaceful stop at Conception Mission.

San Jose y San Miguel de Aguayo Mission, *6539 San Jose Street, Tel. 210/932-1001, open daily 8am to 5pm, admission free*, is the largest of the missions and the first to be established. In the year 1720 ground broke on the famous mission, but the main building phase did not conclude until over 60 years later when the church was completed in 1782 after 14 years of construction. This was a working mission, with granary facilities, a flourmill and various workshops on the grounds. Tours of the grounds, which include quarters for Native Americans, offer a glimpse of a bygone era.

Mass is held daily at 8am. On Sunday the service is in Spanish at 7:45am and in English at 9am, 10:30am. At noon **Mariachi Mass** is held featuring traditional Mariachi music.

The beautiful grounds of **San Juan Capistrano Mission**, *9101 Graf Street, open daily 9am to 6pm, admission free*, are an idyllic setting for an afternoon picnic. There are no tours of the mission, but the buildings are lovely. Mass in English is held Monday to Wednesday, 6:30pm; Saturday, 5pm. Spanish Mass is held Friday 6:30pm; and Sunday 10:30am.

The smallest of the missions, **San Francisco do la Espada Mission**, *Espada Road, open daily 9am to 5pm, admission free*, is not completely reconstructed. The mission was built in 1731. The grounds overlooking a creek are probably the loveliest of all the missions. You can walk among the ruins of the original walls and housing quarters. The church is restored but public services are not held. Tours are available. To reach the mission, take Espada Road to the very end; it leads directly to the mission.

King William Historic District

The **San Antonio Conservation Society**, *107 King William Street, Tel 210/224-6163*, provides brochures that detail a walking tour of the King William District and describe the history of the area. After working hours you may pick up a brochure from the box on the front gate of the Conservation Society office.

San Antonio is home to one of the nation's largest flourmills, Pioneer Flour. The **Guenther House**, *205 East Guenther, Tel. 210/227-1061, open Monday to Saturday 9am to 5pm, Sunday 8am to 2pm, admission free*, holds a collection of historic items that trace the history of the mill. This house is one of the historic German mansions of the King William Historic District, and viewing the Guenther House alone is well worth the trip. The museum restaurant is open during regular museum hours. This is a pleasant setting for a light lunch or afternoon coffee.

The **Steves Homestead Museum**, *509 King William Street, Tel. 210/ 225-5924, open daily 10am to 4:15pm*, provides a glimpse into the daily life of the prestigious German merchant community of the nineteenth century. This Victorian house has been restored to its original splendor. The furnishings represent the period and the grounds are maintained according to the original style.

Museums

The **San Antonio Museum of Art**, *200 West Jones Avenue, Tel 210/978-8100, website: www.sa-museum.org, open Monday to Saturday 10am to 5pm, Tuesday 10am to 9pm, Sunday noon to 5pm, admission varies, free on Tuesday from 3pm to 9pm*, boasts an exceptional representation of art from around the world as well as excellent traveling exhibitions. The permanent collection includes Latin American and European masterpieces in oil and some sculpture. The impressive new Nelson A. Rockefeller wing houses a world-class collection of Latin Art. The museum is housed in the former Lone Star Brewery. The renovation is a beautiful mix of rough, old texture and modern improvements.

The small but impressive collection of the **McNay Art Museum**, *6000 North New Braunfels Road, Tel. 210/824-5368, closed Monday, open Tuesday to Saturday 10am to 5pm; Sunday noon to 5pm, admission*, includes work from the masters Picasso, Van Gogh and Monet, among others. The beautiful museum was once a private home. The grounds are a relaxing park-like setting with flowers and fountains. Be careful not to trip over all the wedding photographers on the grounds. Touring exhibits of painting, photography and are featured throughout the year. The McNay Museum is located at the intersection of US highway 81 and New Braunfels Road.

The **San Antonio Children's Museum**, *305 East Houston Street, Tel. 210/21-CHILD, closed Monday, open Tuesday to Saturday 9am to 6pm; Sunday noon to 5pm, admission*, features exhibits that encourage children to participate and learn. Children from as young as two years old to the age of ten will find something of interest at this museum. The goal of the museum is to encourage children to participate in learning about the cultures of San Antonio.

What could be more fun than climbing a giant tree house? This is just one of the interesting exhibits at the **Witte Museum**, *3801 Broadway, Tel. 210/ 357-1900, open Monday to Saturday 9am to 6pm*. This science museum has a number of permanent displays that deal with the history and wildlife of

Texas. The ancient rock paintings of the Pecos Valley are featured. You can tour the three restored historic homes on the museum grounds.

The Texas rangers are a legendary part of Texas history. Their story is displayed at the **Pioneer, Trail Drivers and Texas Rangers Memorial Museum**, *3805 Broadway Street, Tel. 210/822-9011, open daily 11am to 4pm, admission, children under five years of age free*. The cattle drives that shaped the lore of Texas are documented in this museum housed in the historic Memorial Building dating from 1936. The ruggedness of the frontier is portrayed with displays featuring guns and weapons, accounts of the Texas Rangers stories and a memorial to Rangers who died in the line of duty. The museum is located in Brackenridge Park, next to the Witte Museum.

One of the only museums dedicated to the lonely life of the frontier, **The Cowboy Museum**, *209 Alamo Plaza, Tel. 210/229-1257, open daily 10am to 7pm, admission*, is a private collection of memorabilia. The museum contains a replica of a frontier town.

In the heart of downtown San Antonio, you will find the **Hertzberg Circus Museum**, *210 Market Street, Tel. 210/207-7810 or 207-7819, open Monday to Saturday 10am to 5pm; from June to August open Sunday 1pm to 5pm; closed Sunday during other months*, an entertaining tribute to the history of the traveling circus of yesteryear. The museum has unique pieces from turn-of-the-century circus shows. On weekends the Hertzberg Museum sponsors films, and entertainment such as shows of juggling and magic. The Hertzberg museum is on the corner of South Prensa and West Market Streets.

The various cultures that make up Texas are represented at the **Institute of Texan Cultures**, *801 South Bowie Street, Tel. 210/558-2300, closed Monday, open Tuesday to Sunday 9am to 5pm, $5 admission includes 2 hours parking*. The Institute is far more than a museum portraying the life of the Texas frontier. This is a learning experience, very worthwhile for anyone who wants to gain a greater understanding of the foundations of modern Texan culture. You will see replicas of frontier families and the homes in which they lived. The Native American cultures of the Texas territory are well represented. The Institute is part of the University of Texas at San Antonio and publishes excellent books about the peoples of Texas. The Dome Show, a multimedia show, gives insight to the diversity of the people of Texas. The Institute of Texan Culture is located at the HemisFair Park, at the corner of Bowie and Durango Streets.

The **Lone Star Brewery**, *600 Lone Star Boulevard, Tel. 210/270-9467, open daily 9:30am to 5pm, admission*, has two museums on its grounds. You can tour the brewery and enjoy a drink afterward, then visit the museums. The **Buckhorn Hall of Horns, Fins and Feathers** has on display 3,500 stuffed animals that have been hunted throughout the world. The Hall of Feathers features game birds, and likewise, the Hall of Fins exhibits fish. The **Texas History Wax Museum** and the San Antonio home of William Sidney Porter,

O. Henry House, are on the brewery grounds.

One of San Antonio's more unusual collections is housed in the **Texas Transportation Museum**, *11731 Wetmore Road, Tel. 210/490-3554, open Thursday to Sunday 9am to 4pm, donations accepted*. Horse-drawn carriages and trains show the development of transportation, which was crucial in the taming of the Texas frontier. The museum is located in McAllister Park.

Military Sights & Military Museums

San Antonio has a long history as a military stronghold in the southern United States. The military bases in the area specialize in aviation and medical training. Military buffs will find hours of fascinating displays at the museums housed at San Antonio's military bases.

The **Fort Sam Houston Museum**, *Harry Wurzbach Road, Building 123, Fort Sam Houston, Tel. 210/221-1886, open Wednesday to Sunday 10am to 4pm*, traces the history of the United States military in the San Antonio area. Fort Sam Houston is a piece of history as well. The base first began operations in the mid-1800s as a cavalry headquarters. The officers quarters are grand old homes from the first half of this century. The museum is located on the corner of Harry Wurzbach Road and Stanley Road.

Across the street you will find the **U. S. Army Medical Department Museum**, *Harry Wurzbach and Stanley Roads, Fort Sam Houston, Tel. 210/221-6358, closed Monday, open Tuesday to Sunday 10am to 4pm, admission free*, which shows how medical care was administered during wartime. Displays feature medical equipment from foreign countries including Russia, Germany and China.

The displays inside the **Lackland Aviation Museum**, *Lackland Air Force Base, Tel. 210/671-3055, open Tuesday to Saturday, 8am to 4:45pm, closed Sunday and Monday, admission free*, show the inner workings of airplanes and the history of early military aviation. Outside you will find the planes themselves, a collection of 43 historic planes on display throughout Lackland Air Force Base. You can walk through military aviation history at the park-like display of planes. Among the older planes are the C119 Flying Boxcar and P38 World War II fighters. This is one of the few places you can see an SR71 Blackbird, the fastest plane developed, which was used for high-level aerial reconnaissance during the Cold War.

To reach the base from Interstate Highway 10 west, take Highway 90 west, exit Military Drive and follow the signs to Lackland Air Force Base. The military police officer at the gate will ask you to present photo identification and will provide directions.

The **Edward H. White Memorial Museum**, *Brooks Air Force Base, Tel. 210/536-2203 or 531-9767, open Monday to Friday, 8am to 4pm; closed weekends, admission free*, also known as **Hangar 9**, traces the history of modern military medicine and aviation. Of particular interest is the section that deals with the development of aerospace medicine. Attached to the museum is the Flight Nursing Annex, which shows the history of flight nurses. The hangar itself is a museum piece, built entirely of wood and dating from the World War I period. The museum is named for Edward White, who was the first astronaut to walk in space.

Parks

The largest park in San Antonio, **Brackenridge Park**, is the home of the **San Antonio Zoo**, *3900 Saint Mary's Street, open daily 9:30am to 5pm, admission $6 adults, $4 children*. The zoo has the third largest animal population of all the zoos in the United States. The wildlife of each continent is represented. You can ride atop a camel during the summer. The zoo has an aquarium section that takes you under the sea.

Various climates of Texas are represented in the city's 33 acre **Botanical Gardens**, *555 Funston Street, open Tuesday to Sunday 9am to 6pm*. Wildflowers, a fragrance garden and a biblical garden are featured. The gardens have a 90,000 square foot conservatory that replicates desert and tropical environments. The tearoom is a quiet place to relax and enjoy greenery.

A lovely, tranquil place for a stroll is the **Japanese Tea Garden**, *3800 North Saint Mary's Street, Tel. 210/821-3120, open daily 8am until nightfall, admission free*. Paths and water features offset the native Texas plants arranged in a Japanese-style setting.

Nightilfe & Entertainment

CHAMPION'S SPORTS BAR, *Rivercenter Mall. Tel. 210/226-7171*.

Champion's is the armchair quarterbacks' retreat. The walls are full of antique sports memorabilia, and the modern sports scene is represented with 16 television sets which bring the latest events via satellite. Should you not want to sit inside and watch sports, the bar has outdoor tables along the River Walk. On weekends a DJ plays loud dance tunes. Open daily from 11am to 2am.

JIM CULLUM'S LANDING, *123 Losoya Street. Tel. 210/223-7266*.

The Landing brings sophistication to the River Walk. This small jazz club is brimming over with talent. Inside every night except Sundays you can hear the modern jazz great Jim Cullum and his band. Standard bar drinks and light fare is served. The small outdoor patio has its own band. Monday to Friday 4pm to 1am; Saturday and Sunday noon to 1am.

HARD ROCK CAFE, *111 Crockett Street. Tel. 210/224-ROCK. Credit cards accepted*.

The gingham tablecloths in the Hard Rock Cafe give this chain restaurant an even-more-than casual feeling. The food is standard, and service not always up to par. Naturally most of the clientele are tourists. The entrance is near the River Walk. Open daily 11am to 2am.

MAD DOG'S BRITISH PUB, *123 Losoya Street. Tel. 210/222-0220.*

A pub in San Antonio stands out as different from the usual bar. This is just the place to sip on a single malt scotch or a pint of British brew. British-style pub food served until midnight. Open daily 10am to 2am.

THE LABORATORY BREWING COMPANY, *7310 Jones Maltsberger. Tel. 210/824-1997.*

The Laboratory is located in an historical building that was formerly the Alamo Cement Company. The brewpub always offers six varieties on tap. The signature brews such as Alamo Amber Ale are made by one of the best brewmasters in the region. On Wednesdays and weekends you can enjoy live music.

MAJESTIC THEATER, *212 East Houston Street. Tel. 210/226-3333.*

The Majestic is an historic theater that is home for the San Antonio Symphony. The theater is on Houston Street, which was a major street in the early part of the century. The beautiful old buildings show off the glamour of yesteryear.

SIX FLAGS FIESTA TEXAS, *17000 West Interstate Highway 10. Tel. 210/697-5050. Tel 210/697-5050. Admission adults $31; children $21.*

This theme park has thrilling rides and a water park, but the center of the entertainment is the shows. The cartoon character theme shows are performed on five stages. The latest addition to the park is the Joker's Revenge Roller-coaster. Or you can choose a less exciting zip through cartoon land on the Roadrunner Express ride. Special celebrations are held for Cinco de Mayo, the Fourth of July and Labor Day. Take Interstate Highway west from San Antonio to Loop 1604. The park is at Exit 555.

SEA WORLD, *10500 Sea World Drive. Tel. 210/523-3611. Admission Adults $29.95, children $19.95.*

This is the only Sea World theme park in Texas. The huge complex is part zoo, part amusement park. Free shuttles, *Tel. 210/228-9776*, are available from downtown San Antonio.

RIPLEY'S BELIEVE IT OR NOT THEATER OF WAX, *301 Alamo Plaza. Sunday to Thursday 9am to 7pm; Friday and Saturday 9am to 10pm. Tel. 210/224-9299.*

There's more good clean fun to be had at Ripley's Believe It or Not Theater of Wax. You can tour over 200 wax figures of the famous and infamous. The museum contains a collection of cartoon-related memorabilia from Ripley's own collection.

Sports & Recreation
Spectator Sports

The **Alamodome**, *100 Montana Street, Tel. 210/207-3663*, is the largest arena in south Texas. The enormous stadium seating 65,000 hosts events and concerts. Sports events, including football games are held here. This is the home turf of San Antonio's professional basketball team, the Spurs. You can reach the Alamodome from Interstate Highway 37 at the Market Street exit.

Just north of San Antonio, **La Retama Race Track**, *One Retama Parkway, Selma, Tel. 210/ 651-7000*, has horse racing from June through November. Admission ranges from $2.50 to $20. Races are run throughout the day and races from other tracks around the nation are shown in the building. The complex has restaurants, private rooms and club seating. Take exit 174-A from Interstate Highway 35.

The **San Antonio Dragons**, the city's International Hockey League (IHL) team, set the ice ablaze from October to March. They play against the 10 teams of the western conference, which includes the Houston Aeros. Tickets cost from $8 to $12 and can be purchased from the Dragon's Box Office, *Tel. 210/229-1524*, on the day of the game until 3pm. The **Dragon's Souvenir Shop**, *600 East Market Street*, also sells tickets.

Shopping

Near the Alamo you will find a store which sells Texas memorabilia. **The History Shop**, *713 East Houston Street, Tel 210/229-9855*, has interesting items and historical reproductions, which are not your average souvenirs.

The **Rivercenter Mall**, *849 East Commerce Street, Tel. 210/225-0000*, stands proudly in the center of the city. The mall is an entertainment center on the River Walk, with many restaurants including **Morton's of Chicago**, an IMAX Theater and outdoor stage. Over 1300 stores and shops provide plenty of shopping for everyone.

The most exclusive shopping center in San Antonio is **North Star Mall**, *Loop 410 at McCullogh, Tel. 210/340-6627*. There are over 200 stores and shops including some of the country's best department stores, Neiman Marcus, Saks Fifth Avenue and Marshall Field's. The mall is open Monday to Saturday 10am to 9pm and Sunday noon to 6pm.

La Villita, the "Little Village," was a group of twenty modest homes dating from the nineteenth century. Today La Villita retains its historical look while offering an upscale shopping area featuring art galleries and restaurants.

Excursions & Day Trips

Fishermen should not miss **Choke Canyon Reservoir**, *Callihan, Tel. 512/ 786-3868*. The early spring is best for catching largemouth bass, and white crappie is abundant in the late spring. This is one of the few places with water clear enough for nighttime bow fishing. Camping facilities from primitive sites to camper hookups are available. Play areas for children, swimming areas and nature trails offer pastimes other than fishing. From San Antonio, take

Highway 281 west, exit Highway 72 and travel west for 11 miles. Take Park Road 8 to the entrance of the park.

Practical Information

The Visitors Bureau, *121 North Alamo Street, Tel. 800/447-3372*, can provide specific information about almost any attraction or event in the area.

San Antonio operates an information and reservation service for hotel and motel rooms. Contact the **Lodging Line**, *Tel. 800/858-4303*, for assistance in booking a room.

You might also need:

- **American Automobile Association** (AAA), *13431 San Pedro Avenue. Tel. 210/736-4691*
- **Time and Temperature**, *Tel. 210/226-3232*
- **Travel advisories and road conditions**, *Tel. 210/533-9171*
- **Main Post Office**, *10410 Perrin Beitel Street, Tel. 210/657-8300*

Castroville

The small town of **Castroville**, about 20 miles west of San Antonio, is one of the oldest settlements of European immigrants in Texas. Henri Castro, a Jewish Frenchman of Portuguese descent, received a land grant and founded the town in 1842. The first settlers in the town hailed from the Alsace region shared by France and Germany and came to Texas in 1844. They brought the architecture and food of their homeland, and these traditions have withstood the test of time. The local Alsatian Club keeps the language a living part of the community.

Nearly 100 historic buildings fill the center of town. Many are the original handiwork of the settlers who carved a life out of the rugged riverfront territory. The quaint shops are a blend of European and Mexican frontier styles.

Arrivals & Departures

Little Castroville does have its own **Municipal Airport**, which is really a landing strip in the middle of some farmland. The airport is used for private air traffic and is located on Farm Road 471, just south of Highway 90 East.

Castroville is served by the **Kerrville Bus Company**, *Tel. 800/256-4723*, and **Greyhound/Trailways Bus Company**, *Tel. 800/231-2222*.

The **Castro Garden Club**, *Tel. 830/931-2298*, hosts walking tours of selected historic homes. These tours can be arranged for a large or small group by appointment.

Where to Stay

LANDMARK INN, *402 East Florence Street. Tel. 830/931-2133, Fax 538-3858. 8 Rooms. Rate: $45 to $55. Credit cards accepted.*

This was once a stagecoach stop for adventurers on El Camino Real, the King's Highway. The Inn, built in 1849, is part of a state historical park with other historic buildings, a museum, and the beautiful Medina River. The inn offers eight rooms, six of which are air-conditioned; all furnished with Depression-era and Early American antiques. The 1981 renovation brought the rooms up to date, but you should still expect some quirks – four rooms share bathrooms, for instance. Rooms 7 and 8 are ideal for those wishing a more private setting, as they are housed in a separate building, the Old Bath House. All rooms include a self-serve breakfast as well as a pantry open round the clock for snack attacks. By prior arrangement, you can treat yourself or someone you love to breakfast in bed. There aren't any televisions, but you can draw up a rocking chair on the porch and watch small-town life instead. The Landmark Inn is not always open for visitors. Make a reservation well in advance of your expected stay.

The Landmark Inn State Park has camping facilities as well. You may camp at a primitive site or choose a cabin with electricity and water. Cabin rates range from $35 to $79 per night.

THE ALSATIAN INN, *1650 Highway 90 West. Tel. 830/538-2262 or 800/446-8528. Rates: $59 to $74. Credit cards accepted.*

The Alsatian Inn used to be a Best Western Hotel, so you have the comfort of a modern room and facilities for your stay. The decor is true to the Alsatian theme, with French doors in each room, and historic photos of the region decorating the walls. The inn has an outdoor pool and can arrange transportation to the city golf course. Britschs' is the restaurant at the inn. The good American food is accented by a casual dining room. Entrees range from $6 to $10. The restaurant is open ffom 7am to 9pm each day.

Where to Eat

THE ALSATIAN, *402 Angelo Street. Tel. 830/931-3260, Fax 931-3259. Open daily for lunch 11am-2pm, dinner Thursday-Sunday 5pm-9pm. Credit cards accepted.*

The Alsatian is a step back in time. Located in an historical home, the restaurant serves delicious European cuisine. The sauces, which enhance both seafood and steak, are made from Alsatian recipes. The wine selection offers a good variety of vintages, and the imported beer accompanies the heartier menu selections well. This is the most intimate spot for a meal in Castroville.

LA NORMANDIE, *1302 Fiorella. Tel. 830/538-3070.* Wednesday-Friday 5pm-9pm, Saturday 11am-2pm and 5pm-9pm, Sunday 11:30am-8pm. *Credit cards accepted.*

La Normandie is true to its name. Traditional French food constitutes the main part of the menu. German dishes provide the right blend to make this a representation of Alsace. The romantic interior compliments the historic dwelling that houses the restaurant. La Normandie is at the corner of Fiorella and Paris Streets.

HABY'S BAKERY, *207 Highway 290 East. Monday-Saturday 5:30am-7pm, closed Sunday. Credit cards accepted.*

This small bakery warms the stomach and soul with Alsatian delicacies such as cookies and pastries. The fresh bread is delicious and would be a welcome addition to a picnic. If you are passing through town, this is a good place for a coffee stop.

DAN'S MEAT MARKET, *1303 Lorenzo Street. Tel. 830/931-2049. Monday-Friday 8am-6pm, Saturday 8am-5pm.*

You can escape from Texas barbecue with a visit to Dan's Meat Market. The front of the store has a deli with a full selection of European-style meats and cheeses. In the back of the market is an old world beer hall where you can cool off with your favorite brew.

Seeing the Sights

The section of town known as Old Castroville is a designated National Historic District. There are nearly 100 structures that are recognized as historic landmarks, and many historical markers around town that explain their significance. Old Castroville is roughly ten blocks in size and lies at the heart of the town. From Highway 90, take either Angelo Street or Fiorella Street; these are respectively the western and eastern boundaries of the town center. Madrid Street in the north and Florence Street in the south enclose this imaginary rectangle.

The center of Alsatian heritage is **Houston Square**, at the corner of Angelo and Madrid Streets. From March to September, on the second Saturday of each month **Market Trail Days**, a large crafts market, is held.

Religion has been at the center of life in Castroville since the first European settlers arrived. The oldest churches in the area are still used for services. The **Saint Louis Catholic Church**, which stands across from Houston Square, is one of the most predominant landmarks in Castroville. The tall sturdy steeple stands accents the somber Gothic lines of this simple church. Much of its unique character comes from the local limestone that gives the church a style reflecting the roughness of the land. You can see the layers of change in the cuts of limestone cubes over the two years of construction. The church was completed in 1870 and the pews and altars from that time remain in use. Services are held on Sunday at 8am and 10:30am. The church is open to visitors daily from 8am to 4pm.

St. Louis Day Celebration

Every year the town of Castroville remembers its founding and shares its traditions with the **St. Louis Day Celebration**, held on the third Sunday of August. Alsatian food and drink, which most closely resembles German, is plentiful and made in the old-fashioned manner. Traditional costumes and music enliven the dances and festivities.

The older and far more humble **First Saint Louis Church**, on Moye Square, was built in 1844. The single room rectangle was used as a church by the founders of Castroville and then became a school. The rock and wood on the church are all original.

You would never guess that the adorable white home at the corner of Florence and Angelo Streets was ordered from a catalog. The **Sears and Roebuck House** stands as proudly as it did when it was built from a mail-order kit in 1911. The house is two streets south of Highway 90 on Angel Street.

Nightilfe & Entertainment

Country Gold is a Texas dance hall located on the highway just outside Castroville. Live music twangs through the air and the dance floor is often full on Saturday nights. This is an informal sort of place, so bring your own bottle and kick up your heels. Country Gold is open from 9pm to 2am and usually charges a $5 cover.

Practical Information

The **Castroville Chamber of Commerce**, *802 London Street, Tel. 830/538-3142*, publishes a comprehensive Visitor's Guide that lists current events, details a self-guided walking tour, and even includes Alsatian recipes. The guide is free to the public.

You can book a room through **Castroville's First Bed & Breakfast Registry**, *Tel. 830/538-9622*, which has an extensive list of the area's accommodations.

Seguin

Rich in history and beauty, **Seguin** is a popular retreat for weekend travelers. The town is on the border region where the hills of central Texas blend toward the coastal plains. A sense of small town pride is the hallmark of Seguin, which is named after a leader of the Texas Revolution.

Texas Lutheran University is located in Seguin, and offers cultural performances throughout the year.

Arrivals & Departures

Seguin is 34 miles east of San Antonio between Highway 46 and Highway 123. When traveling on Interstate Highway 10, take either of these highway exits to Seguin.

Orientation

The center of town is the courthouse square, which is on Court Street. Historic buildings line the streets around the courthouse

Where to Stay

COTTONTAIL CREEK RANCH BED AND BREAKFAST, *3767 South State Highway 46. Tel. 830/379-1693, Website: www.neworleansseafood.net/ Cottontail. 2 Rooms. Please call for rates.*

The Cottontail Creek Ranch is five miles from Seguin. With only two guest rooms, grazing cattle, and a resident donkey on the land, the ranch is a true escape. The friendly hosts will make you feel as though you are visiting your Texas family. The Louisiana Room has a quaint dormer window and decorations from New Orleans. The Texas Room is packed with memorabilia from the Lone Star State. Your day starts with a hearty and delicious breakfast. Afterwards, stroll along the creek on one of the nature trails or sit on the porch – you've got your choice of two. Arrangements can be made for lunch or dinner meals. From Seguin take either Highway 46 or Highway 123 south to their intersection at Austin Street. Cash or checks are accepted.

WEINERT HOUSE, *1207 North Austin Street. Tel. and fax 830/372-0422, Toll free 888/303-0912, Website: www.weinerthouse.com. Rates per night: $135-165 for one-night stays, $125-150 for two-night stays. Credit cards accepted.*

The breathtaking Weinert home was a landmark when it was built in 1890, and remains so today. The stately Victorian house displays all the fanciful trim that Victorian-era architecture is famous for. Each of the four rooms has a private bath, is furnished with antiques, and features some unique characteristic such as a turret or a private sun porch. Your hosts ply you with luxuries like homemade chocolates and custom bath salts. The Weinert house is centrally located, within walking distance of the historic town center and close to golfing and shopping. Children under the age of nine years are not accepted as guests.

BEST WESTERN, *1603 Interstate Highway 10. Tel. 830/379-9631. Rates: $50 to $75. Credit cards accepted.*

This 84-room motel is located at the intersection of Interstate Highway 10 and Highway 46. Fitness facilities include an outdoor pool. The hotel restaurant is open around the clock.

Where to Eat

EL RANCHITO, *983 North Highway at the 123 Bypass. Tel. 830/303-7802*.

For over two generations, El Ranchito has been serving the best Tex-Mex food in the area. The casual restaurant prepares large plates of enchiladas, fajitas and other regional favorites. The large, fresh margaritas are a good way to start your meal. Or visit Ciro's, the restaurant's bar, for a nightcap.

Seeing the Sights

Los Nogales Museum, *415 South River Street*. The tiny building that holds the collection is more interesting than the artifacts on display inside. In 1849 it was constructed from hand-made bricks and used as a house. The building is registered as a state and national historic landmark.

One of the earliest hotels you will find in Texas is the **Magnolia Hotel**, located on Crocket Street between Donegan and Nolte Streets, built in 1842. Stagecoaches traveling the route between Austin and Houston used the hotel.

The **Guadalupe County Courthouse**, *Court Street*, built in 1935, is a boxy limestone building reflecting the modern design movement of the time. In front of the courthouse is a large carving of a pecan, which claims that Seguin is "Home of the World's Largest Pecan."

If you would rather learn about the unknown, you can pay a visit to the **International Headquarters of the Mutual UFO Network**, *628 North 123, Tel 830/379-9216*. The center provides informative exhibits about local and international sightings of Unidentified Flying Objects. You must make an appointment for a visit and tour of the International Headquarters.

Nightilfe & Entertainment

Local and touring theatrical performances are held at **The Wupperman Little Theater**, *Texas Lutheran University, 1000 West Court Street, Tel. 210/372-8180*. The regional theater company, **One Seguin Art Center**, produces musicals on a regular basis.

The **Teatro de Artes de Juan Seguin**, *901 West New Braunfels Street, Tel. 210/401-0232*, sponsors performances of Latino folk singing and dancing. The **Noche de Gala**, an annual competition of ballet folklorico and mariachi music, is held in the beginning of the year.

Excursions & Day Trips
PANNA MARIA

The town of **Panna Maria** is the oldest Polish settlement in the United States. The name is Polish for "Virgin Mary." The town reflects the character of the European Silesian heritage of the original 100 families who settled Panna Maria in 1850. The church is the focal point of the community still.

The most significant building in the old town is the **Church of Saint Mary**, which was built in 1877 after the first church burned down. The interior of the church has much of the original woodwork and some interesting treasures. Poland gave President Johnson a mosaic, which he donated to the church, and Pope John Paul II gave the town a golden chalice.

You may attend mass, held every Sunday at 10am. The annual church fund-raiser, held on the second Sunday of October, is a festive cultural feast. The town prepares a real dinner for over 2500 people, and everyone is invited.

To visit the church and museum, simply ask in the **Visitor's Center**, *Ranch Road 81, Tel. 830/780-4471, open Wednesday to Saturday, 10am to 4pm, Sunday 1pm to 5pm*. The building that houses the center is the Pilcaczyk Store; the structure dates from 1875.

GOLIAD & GONZALEZ

The city of **Goliad** was a major settlement during the days of Spanish colonization. The **Presidio La Bahia** was constructed in 1749, and is the nation's only completely restored Spanish fort. It is also the site of one of the

The Goliad Massacre

The events that led to **the Goliad Massacre** began in October 1835, when a group of Texas citizens led by Captain George Collinsworth successfully wrested possession of the presidio from a Mexican garrison. A few months later, in December, the first Declaration of Texas Independence was formally declared, signed, and distributed.

In March, 1836, Colonel James Walker Fannin, Jr., and his men were vastly outnumbered at the nearby Battle of Coleto, so they negotiated a surrender with General Jose de Urrea in which they would be treated as prisoners of war and released back to the United States. They were marched back to Goliad where they were held with other Texan prisoners. On March 27, 1836 – Palm Sunday – Santa Anna rejected the terms of the surrender and ordered the execution of Fannin and all of the other prisoners. They were marched out in groups along the road, believing that they were being taken to Matamoros, and then slaughtered by gunfire, bayonet, and lance. The prisoners too sick or gravely wounded to march, including Colonel Fannin, were put to death back at the presidio. The death toll of 342 at Goliad exceeds that of the Alamo twice over.

The Goliad Massacre so enraged and inspired the Texans and, indeed, people all over the country, that the cry "Remember Goliad" was taken up and uttered at every battle for Texas Independence until Santa Anna was defeated at San Jacinto.

bloodiest and most tragic battles in Texas history. Standing by the rugged building in the silence and the stillness, you get a sense of the site's sorrowful history and profound significance.

The large, sturdy building remains much as it may have looked when missionaries used it. The Presidio chapel still serves as a community church. On the grounds stands a museum that documents the Spanish period of Texas. From Seguin, take Interstate Highway 10 east to Highway 183. Go south to Goliad.

North of Goliad, on Highway 183 is another town of great importance to the Spanish and to Texans, **Gonzales**. The battle for independence is said to have begun in Gonzales. It was here that the army of General Santa Anna demanded the residents return a cannon that was given to them by the Mexican government. When the request was refused, shots were fired.

If you're thinking of building your dream house or just remodeling the one you're stuck with, don't miss **Discovery Architectural Antiques**, *409 St. Francis Street, Tel. 830/672-2428, Toll free 888/686-2966, Website: www.discoverys.net*. The proprietors of this unique store salvage and sell vintage building materials as well as antiques. Old House buffs rejoice, for everything at Discovery is original – no reproductions. Here you can find anything from vintage wood floor planking and tin ceilings to doorknobs and claw foot tubs. The stained glass windows are an inspiration if you're bogged down with the redecorating blahs.

Texans talk about making the "pilgrimage" to the town of **Shiner**, just east of Gonzales on Alternate Highway 90. The site that inspires such devotion is **The Spoetzl Brewery**, *603 East Brewery Street, Shiner, Tel. 361/594-3383, Website: www.shiner.com*. This is where Shiner Beer has been brewed, one kettle at a time, since 1909. Kosmos Spoetzl, a Bavarian brewmaster, created Shiner Bock, a full-flavored beer that has achieved cult status among savvy suds lovers. Stop by for a taste at the white brick brewery, which has been designated a historical landmark by a grateful State of Texas. Tours are given Monday-Friday at 11 am and 1:30 pm. If you happen to be around in mid-October, be sure to look into Bocktoberfest, complete with fireworks, food, and the best live bands in Texas.

Practical Information

A unique way to see the area is the **"True Women" Tour** of the region. The tour is based on the novel of the same name, and is available guided or self-guided. For more information about the tour and general travel activities, contact the **Seguin Area Convention & Visitors Bureau**, *427 North Austin Street, Tel. 830/379-6382, Toll free 800/580-7322, Website: www.visitseguin.com*.

Del Rio

On Saint Philips Day in 1635, a group of Spanish missionaries arrived on the banks of the Rio Grande and founded a settlement known as San Felipe del Rio. Over the next two centuries the name shortened to **Del Rio**. The charming town and its neighbor across the Rio Grande, **Ciudad Acuna, Mexico** are full of history. They remain free of the hordes of tourists that frequent the towns of the Lower Rio Grande Valley, and make excellent destinations for leisurely trips.

The natural beauty of the area is a striking blend of the rough Hill Country and the stark desert land of West Texas. The Rio Grande has carved amazing landscapes in the canyons just north of Del Rio. **Lake Amistad** is one of the largest lakes in the state and is a favorite spot for boating, camping and diving. **Seminole Canyon** has breathtaking walking and hiking trails and at least 300 groups of ancient cave paintings.

Although he never lived in Del Rio, Judge Roy Bean, the "Law West of the Pecos" is closely associated with the town. The judge's reputation is somewhat glorified compared to historical accounts of his life. Although Judge Roy Bean actually lived in **Langtry** (see Excursions section, below), his grave was moved to Del Rio in 1964.

Del Rio is the home of **Laughlin Air Force Base**, which is located six miles east of town on Highway 90. Since World War I, military flights have come through the area. The base officially began operations in 1942 as a training facility. The flat landscape and clear skies make the area perfect for pilot training. When driving east, you may see some plane racing across the sky.

During the first weekend in May, **Ciudad Acuna, Mexico** is the site of an unusual festival called **Calcutta**. The point of this tradition is to bet on riders for the Del Rio Rodeo. Since gambling was illegal in Texas for many years, the bets were taken in the sister city of Acuna. The fun and frolicking that goes along with the Rodeo still goes on when people go to Calcutta in the evening.

Arrivals & Departures

Del Rio is located on Highway 90, west of San Antonio. Highway 90 approaches from the east, then shoots northwesterly. Lake Amistad is about 10 miles northwest of Del Rio.

Orientation

Near the center of town, Main Street crosses Highway 90, which becomes Avenue F within the city. The old downtown area stands on Main Street. The historic neighborhood streets of Del Rio run parallel to and are on the west of Main Street. To get to the Mexican border, take Main Street south from Highway 90 to Highway 277. Heading west on Highway 277 will take you to the crossing.

Getting Around Town

You can take a **City Taxi**, *Tel. 830/775-6344*, around town or across the border. The **Del Rio Taxi Service**, *Tel. 830/775-4448*, also serves the area.

The **Lake Amistad Guide Service**, *Tel. 830/774-3484*, offers guides to show you the natural highlights and sportsman's opportunities on the lake. **Forever Resorts**, *Highway 90 West HCR-3, Tel. 830/774-4157 or 800/255-5561*, offers houseboat and deck cruiser rentals on Lake Amistad.

Del Rio Public Transportation, *Tel. 830/774-8670*, has information about city bus routes that serve Del Rio and the surrounding area.

Where to Stay

VILLA DEL RIO BED AND BREAKFAST, *123 Hudson Drive. Tel. 830/768-1100, Toll free 800/995-1877, Website: http://www.villadelrio.com/. 4 Rooms. Rates: $85-195. Credit cards accepted.*

Nestled in the city's oldest and most stately neighborhood, Villa Del Rio elegantly demonstrates the Mexican and European roots of the area's settlers. The house is built in the Mexican style with porches surrounding stucco walls. The bright, tile floors were shipped from Italy, and the wide beamed ceiling is Mediterranean cypress wood. Large magnolia and pecan trees shade the two acre yard. The interior is a beautiful blend of original antiques and modern renovation. A series of small murals lines the main rooms; the previous owner, Mrs. Mary Foster, painted these.

The rooms are large and artfully decorated. The cheerful Yellow Rose of Texas room shares a connecting bath with the homey Southern Comfort room; these can be combines to form a suite. The largest room, the Peacock Suite, has a large private bath and a private sun porch. The three upstairs rooms have queen size-beds. If you're craving a king-size bed on which to sprawl, rent the Adobe Cottage, a separate two-bedroom building set back against the vineyard.

Allow ample time in your day to relax and savor the atmosphere of this historic house, which was built in 1887. Afternoon tea and breakfast features homemade bread and fresh juice.

THE 1890 HOUSE, *609 Griner Street. Tel. 830/775-8061 or 800/282-1306, Fax 830/775-4667. Rates: $75 to $105. Credit cards accepted.*

The lovely 1890 house combines southern comfort and tropical charm. The superbly landscaped grounds have old shade trees and graceful palm trees. Each room is furnished with Victorian decor and modern beds and baths. The in room spa bathtubs are a particularly pleasurable amenity. The four guest rooms on the second floor of the house are fresh and homey. The largest, the Victorian suite, has a luxurious bed and spacious modern bath. Breakfast is served in the downstairs dining room. In the evenings, guests gather in the living room to enjoy drinks and listen to piano music.

RAMADA INN, *2101 Avenue F (Highway 90). Tel. 830/775-1511 or 800/ 272-6232. Rates: $64 to $72. Credit cards accepted.*

The Ramada has a gym, heated pool and jogging track on the premises. All rooms have amenities such as hair dryers and coffee makers. The motel is located close to the center of town and a short drive from the International Bridge.

DAYS INN, *3808 Avenue F (Highway 90) West. Tel. 830/775-0585 or 800/DAYS-INN, Fax 830/775-1981. Rates: $36 to $58. Credit cards accepted.*

The Days Inn offers good budget accommodations just outside the center of the city. The hotel offers two bedroom suites with kitchenettes or standard rooms. A picnic area with grills is located on the hotel grounds. Continental breakfast included with each room.

Where to Eat

TEXAS ROSE RESTAURANT, *Highway 90 at Laughlin Air Force Base. Tel. 830/298-2286. Credit cards accepted.*

The Texas Rose is a favorite among the military families of the area. Although the building looks like a roadhouse saloon, inside its a family restaurant. The casual atmosphere and variety of the menu is a crowd pleaser. The house specialty is barbecue, and a plate of brisket comes with beans potato salad, onion rings and toast. Or choose from the pasta fetuccini alfredo or salmon fillet. The food here is simple and good, a home run for the unadventurous palate. To reach Texas Rose, take Highway 90 east from town, toward Laughlin Air Force Base. The restaurant is on the highway, just before the turn-off to Laughlin. Monday to Saturday 11am to 9pm; closed Sunday.

JITRA THAI CUISINE, *800 East Gibbs Street. Tel. 830/775-7553. Credit cards accepted.*

The restaurant advertises that Thai-Chinese-Japanese food is served. The Thai part of the deal is authentic, and by far the best choice. Pad Thai, or rice noodles with shrimp and chicken, is light and aromatic and the Pad See-eew, wide noodles with meat and vegetables, are excellent. Traditional Thai salads such as Yum nuea, beef salad, and yum woon sen, glass-noodle salad can be prepared as spicy as you dare to try. A variety of vegetarian dishes are available. Lunch specials run daily and include salad and soup; the special dinner menu is smaller and entrees includes the same sides. Sunday to Thursday 11 am to 9pm; Friday and Saturday 11am to 10pm; closed Tuesday.

BETTY'S RANCH HOUSE CAFE, *1312 Avenue F. Tel. 830/775-5457. Credit cards accepted.*

This is a gem of a diner. The walls are adorned with little vases and bottles, so you feel as if you are eating in Betty's own house. Betty has run the place for years, and often is around to tell stories of the history of the building, and the town. Breakfast includes real southern grits and firm biscuits. You can order breakfast throughout the day or choose from standard south Texas fare, like enchiladas. The pies are home made and a different type is featured each day. If you are lucky enough to be there on a pecan pie day, do not pass it up- it surpasses even grandma's.

MEMO'S, *804 Losoya. Tel. 830/775-8104. Credit cards accepted.*

Memo's is virtually a landmark in Del Rio. The owner, a musician and local celebrity, brings in bands and plays for patrons on Tuesday nights. The food is reputed to be the best in the city. The Tex-Mex recipes at Memo's have been passed down in the family. The casual and thoroughly authentic atmosphere at Memo's brings visitors in touch with the people who have lived in Del Rio for generations.

Seeing the Sights

The oldest winery in the state, and the only one to operate legally during Prohibition is the **Val Verde Winery**, *100 Qualia Drive, Tel. 830/775-9714, Monday to Saturday 9am to 5pm*. One of the secrets of the rich port wine produced here are the Lonoir grapes, a black Spanish grape which grows wild in the area. The family immigrated from Italy in 1883, and you can see the family history on display in photographs on the walls. When you stop by, you can tour the small reserve area and taste the current selections. This is probably the most interesting and worthwhile stop on a wine connoisseur's tour.

The heavy limestone walls and imposing architecture of the **Val Verde County Courthouse**, *400 Pecan Street*, dominates the courthouse square. In the northeast corner of the square, the jail, built in 1885 is preserved. The Victorian building was constructed in 1887 by Italian masons. Just south of the courthouse, the **Sacred Heart Church**, *310 Mills Street*, still stands, but is closed to the public.

The **Whitehead Memorial Museum**, *1308 South Main Street, Tel. 830/ 7747568, admission $3 adults, $2 children*, was once a store. Today the building is a haberdashery of historic memorabilia from the area. Outside stands a replica of the saloon where Judge Roy Bean held court in Langtry. The graves of the Judge and his son were moved to the museum in the 1960s. Another building on the museum grounds is a barn and livery. Although the displays do concern the past, the museum is a hodgepodge of history borrowed from surrounding towns.

Nightlife & Entertainment

The most entertaining way to spend an evening is to visit **Ciudad Acuna, Mexico**; see *Excursions & Day Trips*, below.

Sports & Recreation

Enjoyed by the United States and Mexico, **Lake Amistad National Recreation Area**, *Highway 90, Tel. 830/775-7491*, provides 67,000 acres of water and over 850 miles of shoreline. The lake, populated by bass, crappie and perch and drum, is very popular with fishermen. During certain times of the year hunting of small game and birds is permitted. Three swimming beaches, picnic areas and campgrounds are located throughout the Amistad are open to the public. Walking trails and boat launches are located throughout the park.

A number of archaeological sites can be visited. **Seminole Canyon State Park**, *Highway 90, Comstock, Tel. 915/292-4464*, offers easily accessible and impressive cave paintings. The one-mile guided tour offered daily at 10am and 3pm visits a site that was inhabited for thousands of years. The Native Americans who lived in the canyon left amazing pictographs of people, animals and mysterious symbols. The park has 30 campsites, most with full hook-ups, and eight miles of hiking trails. Mountain biking is allowed on the six-mile canyon overlook trail. Seminole Canyon is 45 miles northwest of Del Rio.

Eco-Educational Tourism

To thoroughly explore the archaeology of the region, contact the **Rock Art Foundation, Inc.**, *4833 Fredericksburg Road, San Antonio, Tel. 210/525-9907 or 888/525-9907*. The group, which is primarily concerned with education and preservation, conducts tours of the area's many rock art sites. You can learn from members about the research and lore associated with the ancient Native American history. Regular tours are held on the first weekend of each month. Tours usually include one site in the area and last one day. Some strenuous hiking may be required.

Another group that conducts seminars about the Seminole Canyon and surrounding area is the **Big Bend Natural History Association**, *P. O. Box 196, Big Bend, 79834, Tel. 915/477-2236*. The topics of the seminars are diverse - from astronomy to photography - and are held at points of interest throughout West Texas. Former topics include Edible and useful plants of the Amistad National Recreation Area and Rock Art and Archaeology.

Excursions & Day Trips
BRACKETTVILLE

If you simply drive through, **Bracketville** may look like a ghost town. Small white houses, many deserted, line the sleepy streets. And it may be hard to find an open store or gas station. But stop in Bracketville for history and you will not be disappointed. Black Seminoles, former slaves who lived and migrated with the Seminole Indians, settled the town.

The town grew up around **Fort Clark**, which was built in 1852 and remained an active military post for over 100 years. The fort stands on the southwestern frontier of Texas, about 20 miles from the Rio Grande. Here the military stood strong against Comanche raids on settlers and helped secure the Texas-Mexico border. Fort Clark was home to some of the famous Buffalo Soldiers, the African-American cavalrymen who served in western forts after the Civil War. Bracketville and Fort Clark are located on Highway 90, 32 miles east of Del Rio.

Today visitors to Fort Clark can learn history and enjoy recreational facilities. The **Fort Clark Springs Association**, *Box 345, Brackettville, Tel. 830/ 563-2493*, offers camp sites, two golf courses and a spring-fed pool. The Officers Club, built in 1939, has been renovated into a restaurant.

A total of 15 caves make up the **Kickapoo Caverns**, *P. O. Box 705, Brackettville, Tel. 830/563-2342 or 800/792-1112*, an undeveloped state park area. Kickapoo Caverns are open to the public by tours guided by Texas State Park personnel. One of the largest caves, Green Cave, is a habitat for migrating Brazilian Freetail Bats throughout the summer months until October. Visitors can ride fourteen miles of rigorous mountain bike trails. **Kickapoo Caverns State Park** is near Brackettville, which is on Highway 90 west of San Antonio. When taking Highway 90 to Brackettville, take Ranch Road 674 north from Brackettville. Clock 22 miles, then look for a gate which is just past the Edwards County line. Be certain to make reservations for a guided tour. The park is closed to regular visitors and used as a hunting area in the fall.

If the real version of the Alamo in San Antonio just is not enough for you, there is the **Alamo Village**, *Ranch Road 674, Brackettville*, a movie set with a reproduction of the Alamo. The site does not keep regular hours.

UVALDE

Further east, in **Uvalde**, you will find one of the best-kept art secrets in the country. The **First State Bank**, *200 East Nopal Street, Uvalde, Tel. 830/ 278-6231*, has an amazing collection of art on display in the lobby. Most notable is an original Rembrandt, the centerpiece of the collection that was donated by Dolph Briscoe, a former state governor. You may view the collection during regular bank hours, 9am to 3pm on weekdays.

The **Uvalde Grand Opera House**, *104 West North Street, Uvalde, Tel. 830/278-4184*, built in 1891, is still used for occasional performances. Most of the building has been used as offices for decades, but part of the opera house is a museum and you can take a free tour of the frontier building.

LANGTRY

Northwest of Del Rio, in the small town of **Langtry**, is the former site of the "Law West of the Pecos." The **Judge Roy Bean Visitor Center** is located on the site where the famous saloon that doubled as a courthouse stood. The

SOUTH TEXAS 395

saloon, The Jersey Lily, and the town were named after a famous actor of the time, Lily Langtry, whom the Judge admired. A small museum has dioramas that show scenes from Langtry in the 1880's.

CIUDAD ACUNA, MEXICO

Those who have seen the movie *El Mariachi* will recognize **Ciudad Acuna, Mexico**. The colorful buildings and quiet streets are a pleasure for a casual stroll. The first eight blocks of the main street, Calle Miguel Hidalgo, is a pedestrian thoroughfare that leads to the border crossing. Neon signs advertising restaurants and bars hang over the street and buzz to life at dusk. The small shops along the street carry the usual arts and crafts, and a few have ceramics, hand-made furniture and sterling silver jewelry of high quality.

If you want to stay overnight and grab a meal, try:

HOTEL SAN ANTONIO, *300 Calle Hidalgo, Acuna, Mexico. Rates $45 to $60. Credit cards accepted.*

This Spanish-style hotel has clean, comfortable rooms with modern baths. Of the two wings, the old section is actually more comfortable and is just over the main building. The new wing, across the parking lot, has rooms that are slightly larger. The friendly staff speaks English and caters to American tourists. The restaurant on the premises serves good, inexpensive food. A Mexican breakfast costs about $2 U S. The parking lot is in the center of the hotel and is a safe place to leave your vehicle.

CROSBY'S, *Calles Hidalgo y Matamoros, Acuna, Mexico. Credit cards accepted.*

This is the most famous restaurant and bar in Acuna, and by far has the most personality of any of the bars on the border. The restaurant, with its white tablecloths and attentive service, is excellent. You can order the standard enchiladas or try something different such as a steak or fresh fish fillet. A meal including desert is under $20. Next-door, the cozy bar gets absolutely rowdy on some weekends and the friendly crowd often contains faces from all over the world. The giant margaritas are the most requested drink, but the best on the menu is the blue Hawaiian.

Across the street is the **Corona Club**, a large bar that stays open late for dancing if the crowd is large enough.

Practical Information

The **Del Rio Chamber of Commerce**, *1915 Avenue F, Del Rio, Tel. 830/ 775-3551 or 800/889-8149*, publishes a number of informative brochures about the area history and tourist information.

Laredo

Laredo stands on the Texas-Mexico border. Interstate Highway 35 passes through Laredo and continues south as the major Mexican highway to Mexico City. As the gateway to the United States, Laredo is a busy center of trade and commerce. In the last few years truck and car traffic across the border has increased dramatically.

Laredo and **Nuevo Laredo, Mexico** used to be one city. They split after the United States-Mexico War. Laredo was founded early in the Spanish attempt to colonize their northern territory. In 1755, the San Augustin Plaza, or Town Square, was the core of the community. Later the business district took over as a downtown area. Today the older parts of the city are in decline, while the suburban malls and shopping centers blossom.

Every year Laredo throws a big celebration for the Birthday of George Washington. The tradition stems from the celebration of the end of Spanish and European rule on the continent. For nearly 100 years parades, celebrations and a lot of home cooking have paid homage to Washington and freedom.

Arrivals & Departures

The Laredo Airport is to the north of the city. Take Loop 20 from Interstate Highway 35. American, Continental, Conquest and the Mexican carrier TAESA serve Laredo.

Orientation

The main access to Laredo is via Interstate Highway 35, which runs south from San Antonio. Highway 59 connects Laredo to Houston from the northeast.

Getting Around Town

Ole Tours, *Tel. 956/726-4290*, takes groups on sightseeing and shopping tours of Laredo and Nuevo Laredo. The four and one-half hour tour rate includes hotel pick-up. They also have daily tours to Monterey, Mexico.

The **Laredo Municipal Transit System**, *401 Scott Street, Tel. 956/722-0951*, operates the city bus service.

Where to Stay

LA POSADA, *1000 Zaragoza Street. Tel. 956/722-1701, Fax 956/722-4758. Rates $79 to $300. Credit cards accepted.*

The premier hotel in Laredo stands on the historic San Augustine Plaza. La Posada offers the charm of an historical setting and the luxury of first-class accommodations. The building was a convent in the nineteenth century and retains its historical character. The hotel boasts beautiful Mexican decoration and elegant surroundings. The floorplan centers around a serene courtyard, a traditional Spanish setting. Each of the 204 rooms and suites is comfortably furnished. You can expect the highest standard of service. Many of the rooms overlook the pool and tropical courtyard. The Tack Room, the hotel restaurant, is popular with local diners; El Cafe serves less formal, Mexican_meals. La Posada provides free airport shuttle service to all guests.

CONEXION BED AND BREAKFAST, *907 Zaragoza Street. Tel. 956/725-7563. Rates: $75.*

The Conexion stands just off Laredo's historic old square. The location is ideal for tourists who want to walk to Nuevo Laredo; the International Bridge is only a few blocks away. The comfortable rooms are on the second floor of an old home. The shared baths and large kitchen let you feel right at home. The rooms have tall ceilings, hardwood floors and plenty of windows. A long balcony overlooks the Rio Grande.

HOLIDAY INN CIVIC CENTER, *800 Garden Street. Tel. 956/727-5800 or 800/HOLIDAY, Fax 956/727-0278. Rates: $59 to $85. Credit cards accepted.*

The Holiday Inn is a short drive from the border, and offers the comfort and convenience of nearby retail shopping centers. Two restaurants, one that remains open around the clock, a small gym and indoor parking are on premises. Children under the age of 12 stay free with parents, and during certain seasons they eat free at the hotel restaurant. The hotel is located just across from the Laredo Civic Center, close to Interstate Highway 35.

BEST WESTERN FIESTA INN, *5240 San Bernardo Street. Tel. 956/723-3603 or 800/460-1176, Fax 956/724-7697. Rates: $55.*

The Fiesta Inn offers the best service-oriented budget accommodation in the area. Located near Interstate Highway 35, about four miles from the border, this is a good choice for travelers passing through. Each room includes continental breakfast. The large pool in the center of the courtyard-style hotel is a great way to cool off after along day of sight-seeing. Free shuttles to the border and airport are provided.

Where to Eat

CHEZ MAURICETTE, *500 Flores Avenue. Credit cards accepted.*

This French restaurant offers a break from the Mexican-influenced food of south Texas. The servings are large and the food more hearty than typical French fare. The highlight is your choice of eight superb soups. The aromatic garlic soup perfectly accompanies rib-eye steak in wine sauce. Monday to Friday 11:30am to 5:30pm and Thursday to Saturday 7pm to 11pm.

ROSITA'S, *1402 San Bernadino. Tel. 956/722-4599.*

This simple cafe serves homemade Tex-Mex food. Here you can taste the flavors that south Texans grow up with, like the rich chicken-broth of the caldo, or soup, and the heavy enchiladas. Prices are reasonable. Closed on Sunday.

Seeing the Sights

San Augustin Plaza has been the center of town since the days of Spanish Rule. When approaching from Interstate Highway 35, Zaragoza Street veers west just before International Bridge 1; San Augustine Plaza is only two blocks from the highway.

The **San Augustin Roman Catholic Church** stands on San Augustin Plaza, the city's historic district. The white walls of the church are an element of understatement in the simple Gothic-style design. Inside beautiful wooden carvings and vivid stained glass windows provide aesthetic tranquillity.

In the midst of turmoil on the frontier, a group of ranchers, lawyers and businessmen decided to take politics into their own hands. They declared the region an independent state, free from the governments of Mexico and Texas, and Laredo was the capital. The **Capital of the Republic of the Rio Grande Museum**, *1009 Zaragoza Street, Tel. 956/727-3480, open Tuesday to Saturday 9am to 4pm, Sunday 1pm to 4pm*, is the only institution that pays tribute to these brave individuals. Three rooms document the battles, and are furnished with pieces from the nineteenth century. The small republic attempted to operate as an independent state from 1839 to 1841. The declaration of independence was signed at a constitutional convention on a ranch near Zapata, Texas. The "revolution" received far less attention than that of the larger Republic of Texas, which was at war with Mexico at the time. The museum holds free Historic Walking Tours of Laredo every Friday and Saturday at 10:30am and 1:30pm.

Nightlife & Entertainment

Most head to the bars of Nuevo Laredo across the border for entertainment and nightlife.

Sports & Recreation

Laredo has a modest horseracing track at the **Laredo International Fair and Exposition Grounds**, *Highway 59, Tel. 956/722-5662*.

Excursions & Day Trips
NUEVO LAREDO, MEXICO

International Bridge 1 is the main pedestrian and passenger car route into Laredo. Taxis always can be found near the border crossing. Rates are not fixed and meters are not used, so set your rate before accepting a ride. If you choose to walk, park in the free public lot at Water Street and Salinas Avenue. Just after you cross the bridge, continue straight on Avenida Gurrero. This is the center of shops for tourists, and the streets with recommended restaurants cross this road.

I recommend the following restaurants in town:

VICTORIA, *Calle Victoria No. 3020, Nuevo Laredo. Tel. 871/2-69-00 or 3-30-20*.

The colorful decoration of Victoria puts you in the mood for some festive, truly Mexican food. This restaurant serves the type of cuisine you would expect in an international city, and the menu comes in English. The sauces are flavorful and not shy with the spice, and the appetizers are not to be missed. The bean soup is creamy and delicious; queso flameado, white cheese with peppers and mushrooms eaten in tortillas, is excellent. The main dishes will not disappoint. The selection includes steak, chicken and shrimp specialties that are made with the rich sauces and styles of southern Mexico. For desert, round your meal off with flan, custard in caramel sauce and a cup of cafe Mexicana, dark coffee with cinnamon and spice. An entire meal including drinks costs under $20. The restaurant is located to the west of the main street that connects to the border.

EL DORADO, *Avenida Ocampo and Calle Belden, Nuevo Laredo*.

To Texans, this is still the Cadillac Bar, the famous restaurant that concocted the Ramos Gin Fizz. Many long nights have begun in this unassuming restaurant-bar. The food is good, an authentic version of what Tex-Mex should be. And the atmosphere is always festive, since the clientele are tourists. The hunting trophies on the walls betray the origins of this bar as one of the favorites of Texas hunters and ranchers since 1926.

SENOR FROG'S, *351 Avienida Ocampo, Nuevo Laredo. Tel. 87/13-30-31 or 13-30-11*.

Nuevo Laredo's link in the infamous Carlos n' Charlies' restaurant chain is just across the street from the time-honored El Dorado. Senor Frogs serves good food, and better drinks with the brightly colored "in-your-face" style of fun for which they are famous.

Shopping

Just two blocks from the International Bridge, on *Calle Victoria* you will find **El Mercado**, the city's marketplace. The festive atmosphere will entertain even those who do not want to buy the artifacts. The **Plaza de Toros**, city bullring, holds bullfights every second Sunday from February through October.

Practically the entire town of Nuevo Laredo is an open shop, especially along Gurrero Street. There are small alleyways lined with shops, merchants calling you in, and markets old and new. The finest of all shops on the border is **Marti's**, *2923 Calle Victoria, Tel. 87/12-3337 or 12-21-83*. Three floors are packed with the finest crafts from all over Mexico. The top floor holds lovely, rustic hacienda-style furnishings, sculpture and decorations. The second floor has an array of ceramics and glass. The first floor has cases of gold and silver jewelry, clothes and accessories. You can rest assured that the items are the finest quality, and credit cards are accepted.

For a more adventurous approach to shopping, visit the **El Cid Glass Factory**, *3861 Avenida Reforma, Nuevo Laredo*, where you can watch the pieces being hand-blown. The shop, which is open daily, is located about two miles from the border.

SAN YGNACIO

A short drive south from Laredo on Highway 83 is **San Ygnacio, Texas**, a border hamlet founded in the eighteenth century. The town was little more than a large ranch and reflects the architecture of northern Mexico of the time. Small stucco buildings accented with Spanish-style decoration dating from the nineteenth century compose an historic district. To reach the historic district, from Highway 83, exit to Mina Street.

Every September the town throws the **San Ygnacio Anniversary Celebration**, a small yet jubilant festival providing a glimpse into the current life and history along the Rio Grande. The town grew up around and received protection from the Jesus Trevino Fort, 1830-1871. The main threats to frontier life were hostile bandits that roamed the desolate borderlands. Armed rebellion was a common occurrence on the Texas frontier. The **Our Lady of Refuge Church** dates from 1875. The preservation in the town is remarkable, considering that the historic sites are not open for tourists.

The Falcon Reservoir is surrounded by **Falcon State Park**, which offers fishing, swimming, boating and camping. Known primarily as a location for bass fishing, Falcon Reservoir also is a birdwatchers paradise. Highway 83 runs along the eastern coast of the reservoir.

Practical Information

American Automobile Association (AAA), *7100 San Bernando Avenue, Tel. 956/727-3527.*

Both the **Laredo Convention & Visitors Bureau**, *501 San Augustine, Tel. 956/795-2200 or 800/361-3360; Fax 956/795-2185* and the **Laredo-Webb County Chamber of Commerce**, *2310 San Bernardo Avenue, Tel. 956/722-9895 or 800/292-2122*, provide tourist and historical information.

A **Texas Department of Highways Travel Information Center** is located on Interstate Highway 35, six miles north of Laredo. Blue signs indicate the exit.

McAllen

The town of **McAllen**, with a population of 100,000, is a popular destination for winter tourists. For this reason, the city has a good deal of large shopping centers and chain restaurants. **Reynosa, Mexico** is about 8 miles from McAllen. Reynosa is a charming town offering a bit of Mexico.

Arrivals & Departures

McAllen is at the intersection of Highway 281, which runs north to San Antonio, and Highway 83, which runs a east-west route along the Rio Grande. The **McAllen Miller International Airport**, *Tel. 956/682-9101*, is located just south of the city.

Orientation

Most of what you will need to find in McAllen is along Highway 83, which crosses through the center of town. Highway 336, which runs to Hidalgo and the Mexico border, is also called 10th Street.

Where to Stay

DOUBLETREE CLUB HOTEL CASA DE PALMAS, *101 North Main Street. Tel. 956/631-1101, 800/222-8733. 158 Rooms. Rates: $49-99. Credit cards accepted.*

This historic building underwent a complete renovation in 1989. The three-story hotel combines the excellent service and comfort of a Doubletree with the historic charm of McAllen. Mexican tile floors and large, arched doorways highlight the Spanish style. The center courtyard, the focus of the hotel, adds breezy comfort even in the hottest season. Each room has a coffee maker and hair-dryer; some have views of the outdoor pool. The hotel has a restaurant and a lounge. The Doubletree is downtown. Complimentary shuttle service takes guests to the nearby golf course and airport.

McALLEN AIRPORT HILTON, *2721 South 10th Street. Tel. 956/687-1161 or 800/346-2878, Fax 956-687-8651. Rates: $64-74. Credit cards accepted.*

The 149 room hotel is located in close proximity to the airport. The fitness facilities include a tennis court and an outdoor pool. The hotel can arrange access to a nearby golf course. The shine has somewhat faded from this Hilton, although it remains the business traveler's choice for service and convenience.

COURTYARD BY MARRIOTT, *2131 South 10th Street. Tel. 956/668-7800 or 800/321-2211, Fax 956/668-7801. Rates: $75.*

The Courtyard is at the corner of 10th Street and Wichita Street. This rather new hotel offers a gym and outdoor pool. Children under the age of 17 stay free of charge with parents.

Where to Eat

COUNTRY OMELETTE, *2025 North 10th Street. Tel. 956/687-6461. Credit cards accepted.*

When you sit down for a meal at the Country Omelette, you get a slice of local life. The waitresses know almost everyone in the restaurant by name. So, you can catch up on the local gossip while you await a No Imagination

Omelet (one ingredient) or Super Omelet (five ingredients). The menu includes lunch and dinner. Beef fajitas and Chicken Fried Steak are reputed to be the local favorites. The daily "happy hour" lets you fill up on all the ice tea or coffee you can drink for $.65. The lottery tickets sold here are a major pastime and point of conversation.

1318 CAFE & PATIO, *1318 North 10th Street. Tel. 956/687-2520. Credit cards accepted.*

The 1318 serves lunch only, and does an exemplary job of it. A number of classic sandwiches are offered such as Ham and Cheese, but the menu beckons you to try something wild. Unusual combinations come together for Tony's Sandwich (hard boiled eggs and avocado with cucumber yogurt sauce), and the Po Boy (made with chicken breast and spicy chile orange mayonnaise). The soup is made from scratch each day.

LA GUACAMAYA GRILL, *400 Nolana Street. Tel. 956/668-7230. Credit cards accepted.*

For a real adventure in dining, try La Guacamaya Grill. You may begin your meal at the salad bar, which is always fresh. The seafood entrees are not shy in flavor. Bold flavors borrowed from Mexican cooking such as strong garlic and spicy peppers accent the entrees.

Seeing the Sights

For over 28 years the **McAllen International Museum**, *1900 Nolana, Tel. 956/682-1564, open Tuesday to Saturday 10am to 5pm, Sunday 1pm to 5pm, admission adult $2, students $1; Saturdays 9am to 1pm admission free*, has celebrated the culture of the Rio Grande Valley. Much of the museum focuses on modern art. The folk art collection focuses on arts and crafts that have developed in northern Mexico and the Rio Grande Valley. The permanent collection includes pieces from Europe and Latin America. This museum is a necessary stop for anyone who is interested in the development of folk art in the Rio Grande Valley. The emphasis of many of the museum's programs is to nurture the artistic expression of the area's youth. The museum also has educational science collections aimed at teaching children.

The **Texas Air Museum**, *Farm Road 106, Rio Hondo, Tel. 956/748-2112 Monday to Saturday 9am to 4pm, admission $4 adults, $2 children, $1 ages 11 and under*, holds all sorts of military air craft from World Wars I and II, the Korean War, and the Vietnamese conflict. And there are some history lessons you might not expect. Exhibits and a film illustrate the battle of the Alamo and nineteenth century Texas' fight for independence from Mexico.

For a look at the indigenous flora, walk along one of the trails at the **McAllen Nature Center**, *4101 West Business 83, Tel. 956/682-1517, open daily 8am to dark*. The center is the home of some of the beautiful coastal birds that inhabit the Valley.

Excursions & Day Trips
REYNOSA, MEXICO

Reynosa is about eight miles south of McAllen. Take Highway 336 (10th Street) south to Hidalgo. There is a shopping center and parking lots just to the west of the International Bridge.

Once you cross over the bridge you will be in the shopping area. Continue down the main street and you will reach the town square. If you cut across the square a large pedestrian street to the left leads you along the city marketplace for residents. Here you can buy music, food and various sundries. As you move away from the square the merchandise becomes more utilitarian and the crowd thickens. Should you want to stay the night in Reynosa, the hotels on the town square are clean and reasonably safe.

HOTEL SAN CARLOS, *970 Plaza Hidalgo, Reynosa. Tel. 89/22-12-80 or 22-40-00. Credit cards accepted. Rates: $28 to $35.*

This five-story hotel over looks the main plaza. The rooms are clean and comfortable, and the friendly staff speaks some English. The hotel restaurant serves good, inexpensive food. And you are just two blocks away from the cafes on Zaragoza Street.

HOTEL MIRABEL, *830 Plutarco Elias Calles, Reynosa. Tel. 89/22-25-90 or 89/22-26-30. Rates: $30. Credit cards accepted.*

This 53-room hotel is just around the block from the main street that leads to the border crossing. The neighborhood setting is quiet and just a four block walk to Plaza Hidalgo, the main square.

CAFE SANCHEZ, *Calle Zaragoza, Reynosa. Open daily 8am to 7pm.*

This small diner is packed with locals grabbing a quick meal. The food is good and the atmosphere authentic. The best part of the place is that there probably will not be other tourists. Do not expect anything exceptional, and you will be very satisfied.

CAFE PARIS, *Calle Zaragoza, Reynosa. Open daily 7am to 7pm.*

This upscale cafe serves excellent breakfast. You can buy fresh pastry, muffins and sweetbread to take away or eat there with coffee. For lunch and dinner, each day a different set menu special features soup, a meat dish (like chicken and peppers) with rice and beans.

TREVINO'S, *30 Virreges, Reynosa. Tel. 89/22-14-44.*

This is the best-known bar, and the one most frequented by tourists. It is stumbling distance from the border, and it earned its reputation by making excellent margaritas. On weekend nights Trevino's still gets festive, although it can be empty on weeknights.

Practical Information

The **McAllen Convention & Visitors Bureau**, *Tel. 800/250-2591*, can answer questions about city attractions.

Harlingen & the Rio Grande Valley

Harlingen, founded in 1905, is a hub of the area vegetable and citrus farmers. The city derives its name from the Dutch language, but its demeanor is purely south Texan. Harlingen has a regional airport that makes it a favorite destination for people who want to tour south Texas. It is located in the Rio Grande Valley, near South Padre Island.

Even more interesting than Harlingen itself are the many small towns that surround the city. The personality of the Rio Grade Valley comes into focus with a visit to nearby **Mission** or **Alamo** (not to be confused with the much more famous Alamo Mission in San Antonio).

Arrivals & Departures

The **Valley International Airport**, *Tel. 956/430-8605; Fax 956/430-8619 http://www.iflyharlingen.com*, lets you fly into the heart of the lower Rio Grande Valley. Southwest Airlines has regular flights to Harlingen.

Shuttles services such as **Surftran**, *Tel. 800/962-8497*, and **Gray Line Tours**, *Tel. 800/321-8720*, connect with South Padre Island, McAllen and other cities.

Where to Stay

COURTYARD BY MARRIOTT, *1725 West Filmore Avenue, Harlingen. Tel. 956/412-7800 or 888/267-8927 Rates: $62-$79. Credit cards accepted.*

The Courtyard is a comfortable hotel ideally located for visitors who want to tour the Rio Grande Valley. This new hotel offers guests a pool, gym and indoor whirlpool area.

Seeing the Sights

The **Rio Grand Valley Museum**, *Harlingen Industrial Park, Harlingen, Tel. 956/430-8500, open Wednesday to Saturday 10am to 4pm, Sunday 1pm to 4pm, closed Monday*, gives an interpretive look at life in south Texas. History is traced through art, recreations of businesses and photos of documents. The museum helps visitors understand history through the perspective of the residents of the Rio Grande Valley. The enthusiastic guides relate stories and folklore. From McAllen, take Highway 83 east to Loop 499 in Harlingen. The museum is across from Texas State Technical College.

Rio Grande City has one of the more unusual landmarks in south Texas, a **Lourdes Grotto Replica**, *305 North Britton Street, Rio Grande City*. Father Gustave built the grotto over a period of time from 1927 to 1928. Tranquil recorded music gives a haunting quality to the 90-foot tall stone grotto. From the Highway, turn toward the courthouse.

La Borde House, *601 East Main Street, Rio Grande City*, was the house of a French businessman, and today is a lovely inn. The establishment may not be open, but this curiosity is worth a stop, simply to appreciate the historic French architecture that is so unusual in the area. La Borde House has the charm of French style and the beauty of a preserved landmark. The rooms are richly furnished in antiques and the restaurant downstairs has a patio for drinks and dining.

The town of **Alamo** has nothing to do with the famous mission in San Antonio; it was named for a local agricultural firm, Alamo Land and Sugar Company. Lovers of uncultivated nature will want to visit the **Santa Ana National Wildlife Refuge**, *Farm Road 907, Alamo, Tel. 956/787-3079*. Thousands of acres of sub-tropical forest are home to many animals seen more commonly in Mexico. Nature trails run through the preserve, and a tram takes visitors on tours (fare adult $3 children $1) with a skilled guide. From McAllen, travel west on Highway 83 to Alamo. Take Farm Road 907 south to Highway 281, then head west.

In January, **Mission** is the site of the **Texas Citrus Festival**. This celebration of fruit culminates in a parade that features entire floats made from citrus-peel, leaves and seeds.

A few miles south of Mission, **La Lomita Chapel**, *Farm Road 1016, Mission*, is a worthwhile side trip. The small, white chapel with a shingle roof was a rest stop for travelers along the Rio Grande. Built in 1865, the chapel is not only standing but occasionally used for religious services. In 1899 the building was moved to its present location. From McAllen, take Highway 83 west; go south on Farm Road 1016.

The small town of **Los Ebanos** has a bit of living history connecting the United States and Mexico. This is the site of a hand drawn ferry. You may cross the Rio Grande with your car or on foot. The small boat holds two average-sized vehicles. The ferry conductor stands at the front and pulls the ferry across, hand over hand. There is nothing of interest on the Mexican side of the border, just a dirt road that leads to a village. From McAllen, take Highway 83 west 14 miles past Mission to Farm Road 886. Turn south and this road leads to the ferry.

Sports & Recreation

Harlingen Country Club, *5500 El Camino Real, Harlingen, Tel. 956/412-4110*, is open to the public for a fee. The 18-hole golf course is par 72. Golf carts are available so you can traverse the over 6,500 yard course in comfort. The club also offers five lighted tennis courts. Pro shops and lessons available for both golf and tennis. Facilites include locker rooms and club house.

Practical Information

Harlingen has its own **Chamber of Commerce**, *311 East Taylor Avenue, Tel. 956/423-5440 or 800/531-7346, www.harlingen.com*.

Chapter 20

Although many people think of **West Texas** as something you fly over on your way to Phoenix, it can be the most rewarding area of the state to travel. Nowhere else is there such a mixture of historic and cultural significance, breathtaking natural beauty, solitude if you wish it, and hospitality when you need it.

When they sing "the stars at night/are big and bright," West Texas is the place they're thinking of. The dry climate and lack of city lights make for absolutely stunning night skies. The University of Texas operates the **McDonald Observatory** in the Davis Mountains, which is open to the public at day and night for stargazing.

The **Rio Grande** (literally "Big River") marks the border between Texas and Mexico. The snaking waterway cuts through the mountains of the **Big Bend** area, carving canyons and creating flood plains. Driving distances through West Texas are long. While Interstate Highway 10 is seldom empty, smaller roads may often be deserted.

The largest urban area in this vast expanse of land is cosmopolitan **El Paso**, at the very western edge of the state. Numerous quirky communities are scattered through the desert and tucked like wildflowers amongst the mountains, and further east are the oil-producing powerhouses of **Midland** and **Odessa**.

El Paso

El Paso, known as the "the pass to the north" to the Spanish who settled it, sits high in the Franklin Mountains at an elevation of 3,500 feet. **Juarez, Mexico**, El Paso's

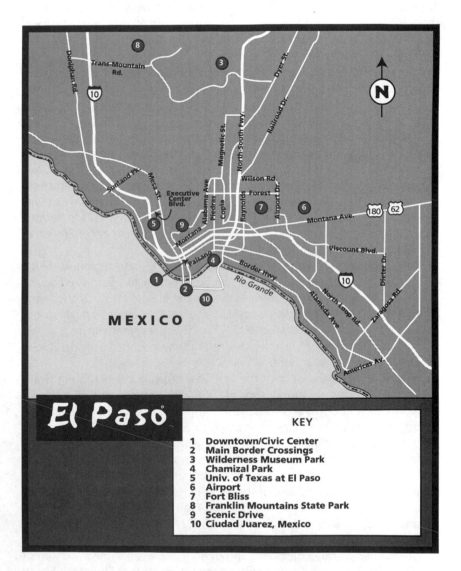

El Paso

KEY

1 Downtown/Civic Center
2 Main Border Crossings
3 Wilderness Museum Park
4 Chamizal Park
5 Univ. of Texas at El Paso
6 Airport
7 Fort Bliss
8 Franklin Mountains State Park
9 Scenic Drive
10 Ciudad Juarez, Mexico

twin city, is connected to the United States by five international bridges spanning the Rio Grande River.

El Paso is the largest city on the Mexican border in the United States. It is also unique in that it belongs to a different time zone than the majority of the state. When driving to El Paso on Interstate Highway 10, the time zone changes from Central to Mountain at Van Horn, about 40 miles east of El Paso.

The surrounding **Franklin Mountains** offer one of the most beautiful evening skylines one could imagine. The scenic hills overlook an expanse of city lights that stretch across the entire horizon. El Paso and sister city Juarez seem to disregard the international borders in the light of day as well. Mexican and United States customs and culture mingle on both sides of the border, giving these two cities a unique international feel.

Long before Pancho Villa or Billy the Kid roamed the Chihuahuan desert near El Paso, the Spanish claimed the land. Some of the first explorers and settlers traversed the lands of El Paso in their drives for conquest, riches, and the spread of Christianity. The first Spanish colony in El Paso was a seventeenth century missionary settlement occupied by the Tigua Indians. It was not until the railroads brought Americans from the east and west that El Paso became an English-speaking community. Today you are likely to hear either English or Spanish on either side of the border.

The railroad is the element that reshaped the El Paso region. In 1881, railroad developers brought together the Southern Pacific, Santa Fe and the Texas and Pacific Rail Lines. The lines met at the El Paso Union Station, and Americans began to flood the sleepy village of in their quest to move goods between the east and west coasts. The city maintained its role as an international crossroads when the Mexican railway extended a line to El Paso Union Station a few years later.

The city claims the right of the first Thanksgiving celebration in North America. According to the legend, 400 Spanish settlers and missionaries arrived in El Paso after a treacherous five-month journey through the Chihuahuan Desert, from the town of Santa Barbara, Mexico. Their destination was Santa Fe, but the waters of the Rio Grande provided a diversion and rest stop. The leader, Don Juan de Onate, claimed the land for the Spanish crown then held a feast of thanks. Every April, El Paso celebrates the **First Thanksgiving** in commemoration. A recreation of the event in period costume is followed by musical performances. The **El Paso Mission Trail Association**, *P.O. Box 3789, El Paso, 79923, Tel. 915/534-0677 or 800/351-6024, Email: Epmissions@aol.com*, organizes the First Thanksgiving and provides information about the event.

A number of other festivities throughout the year highlight different aspects of life in El Paso. The **Southwestern International Livestock Show & Rodeo** is held in February at the *El Paso County Coliseum and Fairgrounds, Tel. 915/532-1401*. The **International Balloon Festival**, *Tel. 915/886-2222*, falls on Memorial Day weekend, when dozens of hot air balloons take to the skies. A celebration of Latino culture, the **Fiesta de las Flores**, *Tel. 915/542-3464*, takes place on Labor Day Weekend at the El Paso County Coliseum. The **EL Paso Chamber Music Festival**, *Pro-Musica, P.O. Box 13328, El Paso, 79913, Tel. 915/833-9400*, highlights the talent of young musicians from all over the world. The festival takes place in the first weeks of January and has been featured on National Public Radio.

Arrivals & Depatures

The **El Paso International Airport**, *Tel. 915/780-4749, Website: www.elpasointernationalairport.com*, is served by American Airlines, America West, Continental, Delta, Southwest and United. The airport is located just east of the center of the city. From Interstate Highway 10, take the Airway Boulevard Exit.

The historic El Paso Union Station is the **Amtrak Station**, *700 San Francisco Avenue, Tel. 915/545-2247 for station information only, or 800/872-7245*. This downtown depot was restored in 1982. Eastbound trains stop in El Paso on Monday, Wednesday and Saturday; westbound trains stop Tuesday, Thursday and Sunday. Just around the corner is the **Greyhound Bus Station**, *200 West San Antonio Avenue, Tel. 800/231-2222*.

Orientation

El Paso is on Interstate Highway 10. Highway 54 runs north to Ruidoso, New Mexico, and Highways 62 and 180 go northeast to Carlsbad, New Mexico. Interstate Highway 25 runs north to Las Cruces, New Mexico. Just south of El Paso is Juarez, Mexico. The main international crossing points, the Santa Fe and Stanton Bridges, are downtown. They handle pedestrian and motor traffic.

Getting Around Town

The most convenient way for tourists to enjoy the attractions of El Paso is by taking the trolley tours offered by **Sun Metro**, *El Paso Union Station, 700-A San Francisco Avenue, Tel. 915/533-3333*. The "trolleys" are motor-driven buses reminiscent of years past in design only. True trolleys served the cities of El Paso and Juarez from 1885 to 1960, mule-driven until the turn of the century.

Trolley routes run north/south and east/west through the downtown and historic visitors' areas of the city. The fare for regular city routes is 25 cents one-way. The trolleys run every 15 minutes during the day; service halts in the evening.

The **El Paso-Juarez Trolley Co.**, *Tel. 915/544-0062, Toll free 800/259-6284*, operates routes between El Paso and Juarez, Mexico and along the El Paso Mission Trail. The "Border Jumper" to Juarez makes numerous stops in

Juarez and leaves on the hour from the Civic Center. You can return at any time of the day; the fare is $11. During the Christmas season a two and one-half hour tour takes visitors through the city to view the decorations that light up the city with holiday spirit.

The trolley office is located at the Civic Center. To reach the Civic Center from Interstate Highway 10, exit Mesa and go south. Turn west onto Main then go south on Santa Fe. The large Civic Center has a parking garage entrance on Santa Fe Street.

Taxi services in El Paso include:
- **Border Taxi**, *Tel. 915/533-4282*
- **Checker Cab**, *Tel. 915/532-2626*
- **El Paso Cab**, *Tel. 915/598-9702*
- **Sun City Cab**, *Tel. 915/544-2211*
- **United Independent Cab**, *Tel. 915/590-8294*
- **Yellow Cab**, *Tel. 915/533-3433*

Where to Stay
Central

CAMINO REAL HOTEL EL PASO, *101 South El Paso Street. Tel. 915/534-3000, Fax 915/534-3024, Toll free reservations 800/722-6466, Website: www.caminoreal.com/elpaso/default_i.htm. 359 Rooms. Rates: $80-295. Credit cards accepted.*

The El Paso Camino Real has changed hands and is now operated by Hilton. It remains the city's finest accommodation. The 17-story red brick building is the most distinctive peak on the downtown skyline, and is located next to the Convention and Performing Arts Center and the El Paso Art Museum. From here it is an easy walk to the Mexican border.

The architectural highlight of the interior is a stunning Tiffany glass dome the color of azure over the lounge area. The building was constructed in 1912 and has undergone extensive renovation and addition since. The rooms are pleasantly decorated, if you can tear your eyes away from the incredible views of the mountains and Mexico long enough to notice. All of the standard in-room amenities are present, although there is no hotel pool or fitness center as of yet. Two restaurants provide fine dining, and the bar under the dome is a romantic spot for a nightcap.

TRAVELODGE CITY CENTER, *409 East Missouri Street. Tel. 915/544-3333, Fax 915/533-4109, Toll free reservations 888/515-6375. 108 Rooms. Rates: $50-70. Credit cards accepted.*

The newly remodeled Travelodge is the budget hotel located closest to the city center. The hotel is directly off Interstate Highway 10 in downtown El Paso. There is a small outdoor pool, a guest laundry, and an on-site restaurant. All rooms have a private balcony, in-room coffee and tea, cable television, and weekday newspaper. This is an excellent place to stay for those who want an economic hotel close to the border and in the heart of downtown El Paso. The hotel offers free shuttle service to the airport and to the Juarez border. To get to the hotel going west on Interstate Highway 10, take Exit 19B.

SUNSET HEIGHTS BED AND BREAKFAST INN, *717 Yandell Avenue. Tel. 915/544-1743, Fax 915/544-5119, Toll free reservations 800/767-8513. Rates: $70-165. Credit cards accepted.*

This beautiful three-story red brick home provides elegant accommodations. The decor offers the romance of the Victorian Era. The four guest rooms have private baths and are furnished with period antiques. Accents such as stained-glass windows, chandeliers and fireplaces make this home one to remember. You awaken to a large gourmet breakfast in the morning and later in the day are treated to afternoon refreshments. Sunset Heights is located near downtown and the University of Texas at El Paso (UTEP) campus. From Interstate Highway 10, exit to Porfirio Diaz Street. Take a right on Yandell Street; continue until Randolph Street.

GARDNER HOTEL & YOUTH HOSTEL, *311 East Franklin Avenue. Tel. 915/532-3661, Fax 915/532-0302, Website: www.gardnerhotel.com. 32 Beds, private rooms available. Rates: $15 per person. Visa and MasterCard accepted.*

The El Paso International Hostel offers a low-budget alternative to hotel stays in a historic building. The Gardner Hotel, built in 1922, is the oldest continuously operating hotel in the city. John Dillinger stayed here in the 1930s, shortly before his capture in Tucson, Arizona. The hostel is a member of the Hostels of America and is located close to downtown El Paso and Juarez, Mexico. Either private or dormitory style rooms are available. The hostel has a full kitchen, laundry facilities and no curfew. Discounted rates are offered for hostel members and weekly stays. The hostel is in the center of downtown; from Interstate Highway 10, take exit 19; follow Franklin Street.

AIRPORT AREA

EL PASO AIRPORT HILTON, *2027 Airway Boulevard. Tel. 915/778-4241, Fax: 915/779-1276, Toll free reservations 800/774-1500. 271 Rooms. Rates: $65-195. Credit cards accepted.*

This rambling Hilton with all its rooms on two floors received a full, modern renovation in 1994. The hotel is right next to the airport, and only minutes by car from downtown. If you are in the mood for some pampering, request a suite with a private hot tub. The large outdoor pool is heated, although the water rarely needs more than the El Paso sun to keep the water warm. The featured on-site restaurant serves the cuisine of northern Italy. The lounge offers satellite television featuring sports events and serves food late into the night.

EL PASO MARRIOTT HOTEL, *1600 Airway Boulevard. Tel. 915/779-3300, Toll free reservations 800/228-9290. Rates: $115-134. Credit cards accepted.*

The Marriott is only one-quarter mile from the airport. Two restaurants and a lounge offer a variety of food service at all times of the day. Sports facilities include an indoor/outdoor pool and sauna. The rooms are large and tastefully furnished. Shuttle service between the hotel and airport is complimentary. From Interstate Highway 10, exit Airway Boulevard and go north. The hotel is two miles from the highway.

EMBASSY SUITES HOTEL, *6100 Gateway East. Tel. 915/779-6222, Toll free reservations 800/362-2779. Rates: $90-100.*

The eight-story Embassy Suites Hotel features a large atrium and substantial conference area. Each room is like an apartment in miniature, with a small kitchen and sitting area. The indoor pool is the highlight of the athletic facilities. A breakfast buffet and cocktail hour are included. From Interstate Highway 10, take the Geronimo exit. You should see the hotel on the south side of the highway.

RADISSON SUITE INN, *1770 Airway Boulevard. Tel. 915/772-3333, Fax 915/779-3323, Toll free reservations 800/333-3333. 151 Suites. Rates: $99-125.*

The Radisson Suite Inn is located minutes from the airport. Every room at this Radisson is a suite with a sitting area, refrigerator and coffee maker. Rates include breakfast. The Radisson has a lovely outdoor pool and indoor workout area. Services such as room service and shuttles to the airport are available.

HOLIDAY INN AIRPORT, *6655 Gateway Boulevard West. Tel. 915/778-6411, Toll free reservations 800/HOLIDAY. 203 Rooms. Rates: $75-80. Credit cards accepted.*

The Holiday Inn has an airy lobby and southwestern decor. The fresh renovation of the hotel included the all guest rooms, the indoor/outdoor pool, and fitness room. Courtesy shuttles will take guests to the airport or nearby shopping centers. From Interstate Highway 10, exit Airway Boulevard.

CLARION HOTEL, *6789 Boeing Drive. Tel. 915/778-6789, Fax 915/778-2288. Rates: $55-94. Credit cards accepted.*

The comfortable ranch-house style Clarion is one-quarter mile from the airport. Some rooms have fireplaces, and all offer in-room video games. The fitness area includes an outdoor pool. Airport shuttle service available and breakfast is included. From Interstate Highway 10, take Exit 25 close to the airport.

BEST WESTERN AIRPORT, *7144 Gateway East. Tel. 915/779-7700, Toll free reservations 800/528-1234. 175 Rooms. Rates: $49 to $75. Credit cards accepted.*

This large, modern Best Western offers complimentary breakfast, a pleasant courtyard setting, and an outdoor heated pool. The airport is two miles from the hotel, and a 24-hour courtesy shuttle is available. To get to the hotel, exit Interstate Highway 10 at Hawkins Boulevard.

Where to Eat
Central

ARDOVINO'S, *206 Cincinnati Avenue. Tel. 915/532-9483. Credit cards accepted.*

This wonderful deli is the place to buy genuine Italian groceries to make an authentic Italian meal. If you are ready to eat, but not to cook, Ardovino's makes terrific pizza. Try the Four Seasons pie with each quarter a different delicious variety. The fresh sandwiches made from the deli can be taken out or eaten in the cozy dining room. The shop is located near the University of Texas at El Paso (UTEP) campus, in the Kern Place shopping center. There is another Ardovino's at *865 North Resler, Tel. 915/760-6000*, with a patio and mountain view.

CASA JURADO, *226 Cincinnati Avenue, Tel. 915/532-6429 or 4772 Doniphan Street, Tel. 915/833-1151. Credit cards accepted.*

Excellent Mexican food served in elegant surroundings has been the hallmark of Casa Jurado for over a generation. Long a favorite of local diners, Casa Jurado offers a full range of specialties for all tastes. The restaurant is known for its half-dozen different types of enchiladas. The Mexican combo plate is a godsend for diners who just can't decide what they want to try. Local artists exhibit their work here.

CAFÉ CENTRAL, *One Texas Court. Tel. 915/545-CAFÉ, Website: www.cafecentral.com. Credit cards accepted.*

This is probably the trendiest restaurant in town. During dinner, music from the baby grand piano sets the mood. The décor is understated, elegant, and modern, as is the food. Each day the menu changes, while the chef highlights variations on northern Italian recipes. A number of selections such as duck and lamb are grilled to perfection. You can choose from the extensive selection of wine to compliment your meal. Café Central would be my choice for a "special occasion" meal. The restaurant is located downtown, just across the street from the Camino Real Hotel.

LA HACIENDA, *1720 West Paisano Street. Tel. 915/533-1919, Fax 915/533-3636, Website: www.shambala.net/milehigh/lahacienda. Credit cards accepted.*

This restaurant has been serving up some of the most authentic Mexican food in town since 1940. Today La Hacienda is part of a bustling border scene, but the site of this restaurant was once part of the King's Highway connecting Mexico City to San Antonio. You can sit on the large outdoor patio that overlooks Mexico and enjoy some of the finest Mexican cuisine north of the border. Seasonings from the Yucatan and central Mexico give this food its flair.

LEO'S MEXICAN FOOD, *8001 North Mesa. Tel. 915/833-5367. Credit cards accepted.*

El Paso loves Leo's so much, that the restaurants have four locations throughout the town. For over 46 years the homespun recipes of Leo's have set the standard for Tex-Mex food. The menu is huge, but a sure short cut to a good meal is to try one of the daily specials. Toasty sopapillas, small sweetbreads topped with honey, are a specialty of the house.

THE RIB HUT, *2612 North Mesa. Tel. 915/532-RIBS. Credit cards accepted.*

A favorite of college students, near the University of Texas at El Paso (UTEP) campus, this informal restaurant features (of course) ribs. Catfish and steaks are other favorites. The atmosphere is that of a well-frequented dive. Every Wednesday is dollar rib night.

MICHELINO'S, *3615 Rutherglen. Tel. 915/592-1700, Website: www.michelinos.com. Monday to Friday 11am to 2pm and 5pm to 10pm. Credit cards accepted.*

For over 23 years this restaurant has served some of the best Italian food in El Paso. The lengthy menu includes classic dishes such as eggplant parmigiana and more unusual specialties like Chicken Jerusalem. The baked manicotti is prepared with hand made pasta and a delicious blend of cheese. You cannot go wrong with the oven-fired pizzas.

CARNITAS QUERETARO, *6515 North Mesa. Tel. 915/584-9906. Credit cards accepted.*

At this modest but popular restaurant, you can order Mexican specialties such as *asado ballezano*, a thick pork stew flavored with red chile, and lamb barbecoa. The real attraction here, though, is carnitas – after all, that's the name of the restaurant. The carnitas do not disappoint, either. The pork is roasted until exquisitely tender, sliced, and served up with condiments.

Cafes

DOLCE VITA, *205 Cincinnati Street. Tel 915/533-8482. Credit cards accepted.*

Art hangs on the wall, and in the back a bulletin board lists the latest happenings. Dolce Vita has all the components of a great café, including a wide array of coffee and coffee drinks, all of which can be ordered decaffeinated. All day this cafe is filled with students seeking a comfortable repose. In the evening the crowd becomes markedly trendier, as many prefer a quiet drink and dessert instead of a loud bar. Open daily 8am to midnight.

SOUJOURNS COFFEEHOUSE, *127 Pioneer Plaza. Tel. 915/532-2817. Credit cards accepted.*

The Soujourns Coffeehouse is a refreshing place to have a light breakfast or lunch, and is conveniently located in the Pioneer Plaza. The menu offers sandwiches and soups, which will not ruin your dessert, the highlight of the visit. Monday 7:30am to 3pm; Tuesday to Thursday, 7:30am to 10pm; Friday 7:30am to midnight; Saturday 10am to midnight; closed Sunday.

Near El Paso

BILLY CREW'S, *1200 Country Club Boulevard, Santa Teresa, New Mexico. Tel. 505/589-2071. Credit cards accepted.*

This restaurant is not just out of town-it is in another state. The drive to New Mexico takes only one-half hour from the center of El Paso, and is well worth the trip for true steak lovers. Billy Crew's opened its doors in 1956 and has been a favorite of El Pasoans since then. All steak lovers will find the right cut from the extensive selection of meat on the men. Seafood and chicken are also featured. The adjoining piano bar lets you relax after your meal. From Interstate Highway 10, exit North Mesa Street and continue for three miles.

CATTLEMAN'S STEAKHOUSE, *Indian Cliff's Ranch, Fabens. Tel. 915/544-3200. Credit cards accepted.*

The Indian Cliff's Ranch is an unusual spot for an excellent restaurant. The ranch itself is a tourist attraction with exhibits of cattle, rattle snakes, and party facilities. Yet even native El Pasoans adverse to dude ranches vouch for the quality of the steaks at the Cattleman's. The secret to the barbecue is the mesquite smoking method. You can jump on the free hayrides that the ranch offers every Sunday. The ranch is about 20 miles east of El Paso. From Interstate Highway 10, travel east from downtown. Exit Fabens turn north; the ranch is five miles from the highway. Open Monday to Friday 4:30pm to 10pm; Saturday 4pm to 10pm; Sunday noon to 9pm

Seeing the Sights

Before El Paso had its name, a small settlement known as Magoffinville existed on the banks of the Rio Grande. **The Magoffin Homestead**, *1120 Magoffin Avenue, Tel. 915/533-5147, open daily 9am to 4pm*, stands as the historic landmark of that era. The Magoffin family played a major role in shaping West Texas. The original family house was destroyed in the 1868 flood of the Rio Grande. The present museum is a replica of that home, and was built in 1875. The architectural features, such as thick adobe walls, rough timber and native materials represent the blending of the traditions of Mexico and the American west.

A sister community to Magoffinville was **Hart's Mill Settlement**, *1720 West Paisano Drive*. In the mid-nineteenth century, the mill served the small communities that would later grow into El Paso. The mill no longer remains, but the small home in which Hart raised his family still stands at the site of the mill. One of the first US military installations in the area, **Old Fort Bliss**, *1844 West Paisano Drive*, stood across from Hart's Mill. Some of the original housing quarters remain.

Boot Hill, the final resting place of the folks that made El Paso part of the Old West, is found in **Concordia Cemetery**. You can visit the grave of John Wesley Hardin, the famous outlaw, who is buried on Boot Hill. The cemetery is a piece of history and its five sections contain a wealth of information for the curious. To reach the cemetery from Interstate Highway 10, exit Copia Street. The cemetery is between Yandell Street and Gateway West.

The **Chamizal National Memorial**, *800 South Marcal Street,* commemorates the solution to border disputes between the United States and Mexico. The **Paisanos Gallery**, *Tel. 915/532-7273, open daily 8am to 5pm*, exhibits art of significance to the culture and history of the area. The amphitheater is the site of free concerts and festivals.

The Missions

The El Paso missions are some of the first colonial settlements in North America. The mission settlement in the El Paso area is the result of the disputes between the Spanish and Native American tribes in New Mexico. After being forced out of the lands that today are New Mexico, Spanish Missionaries and Native Americans built three missions in Texas. The stories of the missions are full of natural disasters and struggle. The determination to maintain these religious settlements after numerous set backs and reconstructions is a tribute to the faith of the early settlers of West Texas. The missions, now in urban El Paso, are still in use, holding regular services and tours.

The **Mission Ysleta**, *9501 Socorro Road*, has transformed itself many times during its history. The site of the Corpus Christi de la Ysleta del Sur Mission was settled in 1680 as a temporary refuge camp for Native

El Paso's Scenic Drives

The rolling hills of the El Paso area are the hallmark of the city, which lies nestled in a mountain pass. For a scenic tour of the area's urban beauty, starting in downtown El Paso, take Interstate Highway 10 to the Mesa Drive exit. Follow Mesa to Rim Road and take a right. Rim Road winds along a hillside then turns into **Scenic Drive**. There are parking areas on these roads, which are very popular as evening rendezvous spots.

Another scenic route, **Transmountain Road**, cuts through Franklin Mountain State Park and part of Fort Bliss. This road will show you the natural beauty of the area as it winds along the mountain pass known as Smuggler's Gap. To the east of the state park is Casner Range, a large land preserve which is part of Fort Bliss. To reach Transmountain Road, take Interstate Highway 10 west, away from the city. Exit Loop 375.

Americans fleeing conflict in northern New Mexico. After a decade of occupation, a Mission building was constructed. However, this would not prove to be permanent, because floodwaters from the Rio Grande destroyed the mission in 1742, then again in 1821. The mission was renamed the San Antonio de la Ysleta after the first reconstruction, then again renamed Our Lady of Mount Carmel. Despite the many changes in the appearance and name of Mission Ysleta, the occupation has been constant for centuries and parts of the mission grounds have been worked for over three centuries.

Mission Ysleta is in an urban part of El Paso. From Interstate Highway 10, take the Zaragoza Exit. Signs will indicate the way to Mission Ysleta, which is south of the highway, near the intersection of Zaragoza and Socorro Road.

Only one year after the Ysleta Mission, the **Nuestra Senora de la Limpia Conception de Socorro del Sur**, *Socorro Road, Tel. 915/859-7718*, was established. The name, which means "Our Lady of the Immaculate Conception of Socorro of the South," is usually shortened to simply "Socorro." The history of the mission is no less complicated than the name. The Socorro Mission moved from its original location to the present day grounds because the Spanish feared the Native Americans living at the mission might revolt. Two floods, in 1692 and 1829, completely destroyed the mission. At different times Franciscans, secular leaders and Jesuits have administered the Socorro Mission.

Parts of the early structure are preserved in the mission. The large beams in the ceiling pre-date the building and exemplify the craftsmanship of the Native Americans who built and inhabited the mission. To reach Mission Socorro from Interstate Highway 10, exit Zaragoza and travel south on Zaragoza Street for four miles. Turn onto Socorro Road. Signs will indicate the way to the mission.

The chapel of the **Presidio San Elizario**, *Socorro Road, Tel. 915/851-2333*, first stood on the San Elizario Fort, some 37 miles to the south of its present location. The chapel was part of a fort built in 1777 that protected the Camino Real, the major road linking El Paso to San Antonio. During the United States war with Mexico in the mid-seventeenth century the fort was demolished. The church was rebuilt in 1877, but fell victim to a fire in 1935, which destroyed the interior. The church remains true to the original architecture of the small adobe church. Presidio San Elizario is located 6 miles east of the Socorro Mission.

Daily tours of the missions depart from the El Paso Civic Center, *1 Civic Center Plaza, Tel. 915/544-0062*, every day at 10:30 am. From the comfort of an air-conditioned trolley-style bus you can learn the history of the area and have free time to tour the mission complexes and shop in the gift shops. The tour lasts about four hours, and includes a stop for lunch.

The **Tigua Indian Reservation**, *305 Yaya Road, Tel. 915/859-5287, open Tuesday to Sunday 8am to 4pm; closed Monday*, is the result of the settlements that established the missions in El Paso. During the weekend, visitors can watch scheduled dance performances by the Tigua. The reservation's visitor center, the **Ysleta del Sur Pueblo**, has a museum and cafe. The museum documents the Tigua culture and visually chronicles the tribal history in Texas. The Cacique Cafe serves traditional Tigua food as well as regional fare. The Tigua Indian Reservation is on the Mission Trail. From Interstate Highway 10 east, exit Zaragosa and go south to Socorro Drive. Travel east on Socorro Drive to the intersection of Yaya Road.

Civic Center Area

The rich history and culture unique to the area is a source of pride for El Paso natives. The **Americana Museum**, *5 Civic Center Plaza, Tel. 915/542-0394, open Tuesday to Saturday, 10am to 5pm; closed Sunday and Monday*, exhibits a collection of the artifacts and art of early Native Americans. The extensive collection includes pieces from Meso-American cultures. Painted murals depict the life of the Native Americans of nearby Hueco Tanks, which is now a state park. The museum provides an interesting educational experience, and is housed in the Performing Art Center in the Civic Center Plaza. To reach the Civic Center, from Interstate Highway 10, exit Mesa and go south. Turn west onto Main, then go south on Santa Fe. The large Civic Center has a parking garage entrance on Santa Fe Street.

The centerpiece of the Arts District is the **El Paso Museum of Art**, *across from the Civic Center, Tel 915/541-4040, open Tuesday to Saturday 10am to 5pm; Sunday 1pm to 5pm; closed Monday, admission free*. The impressive new home of the El Paso Art Museum opened in 1998. A variety of temporary exhibits grace the walls, and the museum's permanent exhibits include the Kress Collection of Old European masterpieces as well as American and Mexican paintings. The Mexican collection is one of the most extensive to be found anywhere and includes colonial art from the sixteenth century to modern works.

Museums

The **Bridge for Contemporary Arts**, *1112 East Yandell, Pioneer Plaza, Tel. 915/532-6707, open Tuesday to Friday 11am to 6pm; Saturday 11am to 4pm; closed Sunday*, strives to promote local artists of all disciplines including painting, film, music and theater. The exhibits and performances vary greatly in content. Recent activities include poetry readings, the unveiling of a mural and a one-woman dramatic performance. Admission fees vary with events.

Insights, the El Paso Science Museum, *505 North Santa Fe Street, Tel. 915/542-2990, open Tuesday to Saturday 9am to 5pm*, lets kids and grown-ups learn about the science that surrounds us through hands-on participation. The 104 exhibits allow visitors to interact with science using every sense. The museum provides an overview of the technology that shapes our society and the future.

One of the most worthwhile museums in the state is the **Wilderness Museum**, *2000 Transmountain Road, Tel. 915/755-4332, open Tuesday to Sunday 9am to 5pm, admission free*. The indoor/outdoor exhibits do not have much to do with wilderness. Instead the material culture of Native Americans is displayed in detail. Archaeological sites of Mexico and the United States Southwest are brought into context with maps, artifacts and historic descriptions. Paintings depict the daily life of the tribes of West Texas. Visitors gain valuable insight to the petroglyphs and painted pottery and material culture of the area's first inhabitants.

The outdoor displays grant a unique glimpse into the life of the region before colonization. The nature trail stretches for one mile and has recreations of various houses including a pithouse, a partially underground structure with a twig roof, and a pueblo, an early agricultural settlement.

One of the most unusual collections traces the legacy of the officers who patrol the international border. The **Border Patrol Museum**, *4315 Transmountain, Tel. 915/759-6060*, is the only museum of its type in Texas. A collection of the memorabilia relating to the United States Border Patrol may at first seem to be a dry, even unenjoyable subject for a museum. However, the border between the United States and Mexico was not always marked by fences, customs posts and bridges as it is today. The borderland was a nearly unexplored frontier, harsh and inhospitable. The story of the early lawmen in this area is a unique and insightful glimpse of part of the American story. The Border Patrol Museum is located next to the Wilderness Museum.

The collection of the **El Paso Museum of History**, *Interstate Highway 10 east, exit Avenue of the Americas, Tel. 915/858-1928, open Tuesday to Sunday 9am to 4:30pm; closed Monday, admission free*, traces the history of the El Paso area from the time of the Native Americans, through the colonial conquest to the present day. The majority of exhibits portray the lives of the rugged frontiersmen who claimed and attempted to tame the land. The museum sponsors classes and lectures for all ages throughout the year. The museum is located at the intersection of Interstate Highway 10 and Avenue of the Americas.

Regional history is further explored at the **Centennial Museum**, *The University of Texas at El Paso (UTEP), Tel 915/747-5565, open Tuesday to Saturday 10am to 4pm; closed Sunday and Monday*. The collection traces the history of the El Paso region through art, historical artifacts, and local geology. Temporary exhibits are featured.

The tranquil grounds of **the El Paso Holocaust Museum and Study Center**, *401 Wallenberg Drive, Tel. 915/833-5656*, give visitors opportunity to reflect on the emotionally powerful exhibits. The collection includes a good deal of artifacts from the European Jewish ghettos and concentration camps of World War II. Visitors are educated about the Holocaust and reminded of the brutality of history. Tours are free for individuals and groups. Modern art adorns the museum and conveys the feelings of pain and perseverance of persecuted peoples. The Study Center sponsors speakers and provides resource materials for study of the Holocaust. To reach the museum from Interstate Highway 10, exit Executive Center and follow that road north. After 1.5 miles, turn Left on Mesa Drive; turn left onto Festival Street and then right onto Mardi Gras Street. This street will turn into Wallenberg Street.

The **El Paso Zoo**, *4001 Paisano, Tel. 915/541-4600, open daily, 9:30am to dusk, admission $3 adults, children 12 years and younger, $1.50*, stretches across 18 acres and is the home of over 400 varieties of animals. The zoo is known for its outstanding collection of reptiles and the beautiful park-like atmosphere of the grounds. Endangered animals have a special home at the zoo, which is active in preservation of rare species. The aviary recreates a tropical South American environment with a variety of flora and fauna. The Grasslands Cafe serves lunch, snacks and ice cream during the normal hours of the zoo. From Interstate Highway 10, exit Paisano and travel south. The zoo is located at the intersection of Evergreen and Paisano streets. Signs will lead you to the zoo entrance.

Military Museums of Fort Bliss

El Paso has been important to the military since Texas entered the Union. The earliest military role was to protect settlers from attacks by Native American warriors and bandits. **Fort Bliss** was established in 1848 to fulfill this mission. In time, Fort Bliss gained importance as an Air Force training center. A number of museums at Fort Bliss provide insight to the role of the United States military on the Western frontier. To reach the museums, take Airway Boulevard to the Robert E. Lee gate of Fort Bliss. The guard will give directions to the museums.

The **Artillery Museum**, *Mount Pleasanton Road, Building 5000, Fort Bliss, open daily 9am to 4:30pm*, documents the history of aviation defense in the Army. This is an appropriate topic for Fort Bliss, since it was one of the first and most significant air training grounds. Many of the displays are interactive.

The **Fort Bliss Museum**, *Pleasanton and Sheridan Roads, Fort Bliss, open daily 9am to 4:30pm*, is a recreation of what a frontier fort of the late 1800's would have looked like. The buildings are based on the plans of the Magoffinsville fort, which was an early part of Fort Bliss. The Third Cavalry has been stationed near El Paso for nearly 150 years, and their history is documented at this museum.

Fort Bliss' tribute to the soldiers who have served the area is the **Museum of the Non-Commissioned Officer**, *Biggs Army Airfield, Building 11331, Monday to Friday 9am to 4pm; Saturday to Sunday noon to 4pm*. The displays chronicle the large picture of military service; some of the artifacts pre-date the founding of the fort.

Nightlife & Entertainment

The **El Paso Symphony**, *10 Civic Center Plaza, Tel. 915/532-3776*, presents concerts during the fall and spring. Performances are held at the **Performing Arts Center** at the Civic Center. **Music Ballet El Paso**, *Tel. 915/533-2200*, also uses this venue.

McKelligan Canyon Theater, *McKelligan Canyon, Tel. 915/532-3776*, brings music, ballet and theater to the beautiful outdoors. Throughout the year the canyon theater hosts a variety of performances including the El Paso Symphony, the annual Shakespeare on the Rocks Festival, and Viva! El Paso.

Viva! El Paso is a musical extravaganza that tells the history of the settlement of the southwest. The musical runs during the summer months from June to August, and attracts over 60,000 attendees during that short season. Even the native El Pasoans turn out for the show. Performances begin at 8:30pm; a pre-show barbecue dinner is served at 7pm (reservations required).

Independence Day is celebrated with **Canyon Fest**, an all-day event featuring music, food and family activities. A new twist to the traditional fireworks is added with a laser show just after dark. The El Paso Association for the Performing Arts sponsors Canyon Fest every Fourth of July.

A completely different annual festival is **Ballet Under the Stars**, which is held at the McKelligon Canyon Amphitheater on Memorial Day weekend. The ballet performances are for three days only and tickets range in price from $8 to $15, with discounts for students, children and senior citizens.

On Sunday nights from June through August, free concerts are held at the **Chamizal National Memorial Amphitheater**, *800 South San Marcial, Tel. 915/541-4481*. A wide variety of music is featured from reggae to classical to Latin. This annual series known as Music Under the Stars includes comedy and dance performances. The concerts are free of charge and sponsored by the city of El Paso.

Bars & Clubs

SPEAKING ROCK CASINO AND ENTERTAINMENT CENTER, *122 South Old Pueblo Road, Ysleta. Tel. 915/860-7777. Credit cards accepted.*

The Tigua Indian Reservation operates the Lucky Eagle Casino and Restaurant. Blackjack, poker and low stakes baccarat are played at tables in the card room. The bingo room can seat 850 players, and the stakes can go as high as $50,000 per game. Wyngs Restaurant serves Tex-Mex food on from 11am to 10:30pm with an adjoining bar open until 2am. The restaurant and bar are closed on Monday and Tuesday. From Interstate Highway 10, exit

Zaragoza and go south. Turn east onto Alameda Street. Speaking Rock is located on Old Pueblo Road, just past the Ysleta Mission. The casino is open daily 1pm to 4am.

JAXON'S BREWERY, *4799 North Mesa, Tel. 915/542-0281, or 1135 Airway, Tel. 915/778-9696. Credit cards accepted.*

The two locations of this brewpub quickly became a tradition for El Paso's beer lovers. The six beers on tap were each made by Jaxon's brewmaster. The houseblend, Black Jack Stout, has a rich, full flavor. Other selections include Star Lite, Chihuahua Brown and Cactus Jack Pale Amber. There is always a special at Jaxon's. The grill cooks up southwestern food, which is featured at Brewer Diners. The Mesa location is at the intersection of Mesa and Westside Streets.

CINCINNATI CLUB, *209 Cincinnati Street. Tel. 915/532-5592.*

This bar brings the old west theme of Cincinnati to the street of the same name. The dark wood interior is reminiscent of family room decoration in the 1970s. But the clientele come here for the extremely large margaritas and the relatively quiet atmosphere. Pub food such as fish and chips and hamburgers is served.

HEMINGWAY'S, *214 Cincinnati Street. Tel. 915/532-7333. Credit cards accepted.*

This small college hang out is a favorite of the unpretentious set. Whether you wear a suit or a pair of shorts and tee-shirt, you will not be out of place here. The front room feels like someone's back-yard patio and often becomes standing-room-only crowded. The back area has larger tables and more breathing space. Hemingway's serves 132 types of bottled beer, and has twenty draft beer taps.

Sports & Recreation

A hiker could spend weeks on the trails that lead through the mountains of the Chihuahuan Desert in the **Franklin Mountains State Park**, *Transmountain Road, Tel. 915/566-6441.* The park covers 24,000 acres of mountains and desert and is located in the city at the Woodrow Bean and Transmountain Roads. From Interstate Highway 10, exit Woodrow Bean Road, continue east and this will turn into Transmountain Road and cut through the park.

Golf Courses

The fact that El Paso generally experiences less than a week of cloudy days per year makes this area excellent for golfing. A few courses for you to try are:
• **Ascarate Golf Course**, *Ascarate Park, Tel 915/772-7381*
• **Desert East Driving Range**, *1351 Lee Trevino, Tel. 915/591-4653*
• **Painted Dunes Golf Course**, *12000 McCombs, Tel. 915/533-4416*
• **Vista Hills Golf and Tennis Club**, *2210 Trawood, Tel. 915/592-4558*

Spectator Sports

The **Sun Bowl Stadium** hosts the annual college Sun Bowl Football championship. The University of Texas at El Paso football team plays here on weekends during the regular season. The large stadium occasionally has music and other performances. To reach the Sun Bowl, from Interstate Highway 10, take the University of Texas at El Paso exit. Signs will guide you to the parking lots for the Sun Bowl. For more information contact the **Sun Bowl Association**, *4100 Rio Bravo, Tel. 915/533-4416.*

Shopping

In the 1920's the Paradise hotel occupied the building that today is **Placita Santa Fe** shopping center. That the hotel was a house of ill repute is one of the less kept secrets in El Paso. A number of antique shops, import stores and art galleries fill the renovated historical building today. Some of the shops are open seven days a week.

The **El Paso Chile Company**, *909 Texas Avenue, Tel. 915/544-3434, open Monday to Friday 10am to 5pm; Saturday 10am to 2pm; closed Sunday*, lets you take the taste of Texas home. This store specializes in salsas, sauces, and spices that will add zip to your next southern meal. Gift packages and clothes, and cookbooks are also sold.

The largest mall in the El Paso area is **Cielo Vista Mall**, *Interstate Highway 10 East, Tel. 915/779-7070.* Four department stores, 140 shops and a number of informal restaurants are found in this shopping center. From Interstate 10, take the Hawkins Boulevard Exit.

Art Galleries

El Paso's vibrant art community is accessible to everyone at the many local galleries and shops. **Adair Margo Gallery**, *415 East Yandell Street, Tel. 915/533-0048*, is one of El Paso's finest galleries exhibiting modern art. The gallery is proud of its international reputation; most of the talent featured is that of local artists.

The objects at **Counterpoint**, *2626 North Stanton, Tel. 915/545-5073 or 888/CNT-POINT*, exemplify the latest and best design. Decoration from Europe merges practical function with innovative style. Lights, candleholders and games are among the accent pieces that this gallery offers. Open Monday to Saturday 11am to 6pm; closed Sunday.

The Galeria Palacio, *1716 Montana Avenue, Tel. 915/544-3589*, gives visitors insight to the regional art scene within the context of the international Latin movement. Featured artists include painters from throughout Latin America, and the focus of the gallery remains true to local artists. Serious collectors will enjoy the quality of the work displayed. Exhibits change often. Open Tuesday to Friday 11am to 6pm; Saturday noon to 5pm; closed Sunday and Monday.

Bright colors and humanistic themes highlight local artist Hal Marcus' paintings that adorn the University of Texas at El Paso and the El Paso Courthouse. Marcus showcases his work in his family home, the **Hal Marcus Gallery**, *2403 North Mesa Street, Tel. 915/533-9090*. His work is well received throughout the world. Marcus works in stained glass and illustration also. All varieties of his art are available at the gallery. Open Tuesday to Saturday 10am to 6pm; closed Sunday and Monday.

One of the best places in the state to buy art, furniture and decorations from all over the world is **Galeria San Ysidro**, *801 Texas Avenue, Tel. 915/544-4444, open Monday to Friday 9am to 5pm; Saturday 9am to 3pm; closed Sunday*. The gallery is really more like a department store because of its size- it occupies three floors of a former factory. The eclectic mix of art ranges from modern to antique. The stock changes almost daily, since new shipments are constantly arriving from all reaches of the globe. The prices are reasonable and the casual atmosphere makes shopping here a pleasure. From Interstate Highway 10, exit Mesa and go south to Texas. Travel East of Texas. The store is near the intersection of Virginia and Texas Streets.

Western Wear

The essential element of Texan fashion is a good pair of boots. Whether you want low-heeled lace-ups or the fanciest high-heeled snakeskin boots, you can find them at the large outlets in El Paso. The outlets sell discontinued and slightly defective boots for about 50 percent less than retail prices.

The oldest bootmaker in the area is Lucchese Boots at the **Lucchese Boot Outlet**, *6601 Montana, Tel. 915/778-8680*. The Duke, John Wayne, wore Lucchese boots. The Lucchese Outlet is located near the airport.

The most recognizable name in bootmaking, **Tony Lama**, has no less than three outlet stores. The largest and easiest to find is just east of downtown on Interstate Highway 10 at the Mesa Exit, *Tel. 915/581-8192*.

For custom-made boots, go to **Champion Attitude**, *505 South Cotton Street, Tel. 915/534-7783*. The bootmaking process takes three days, but you will wind up with just the right details and comfort.

Excursions & Day Trips

For centuries people have visited **Hueco Tanks**, giant granite outcroppings that form natural cisterns. To the Native Americans, the Hueco Tanks were an oasis in the west Texas desert. The area has many examples of rock art left by Native Americans over the centuries. Hikers can journey through the Hueco Tanks State Park. The extraordinary rock face is one of the best sites for rock climbing in the state. The **Hueco Tanks State Park**, *Tel. 915/857-1135, open daily 8am to 5pm*, is 22 miles northeast of El Paso. The park offers picnic facilities, 20 campsites, and wildlife observation areas. To reach the park from El Paso, take Highway 62 north.

The lower end of the Guadalupe Mountains extends from New Mexico into northwestern Texas. The **Guadalupe Mountains National Park**, *Highways 62 and 189, Pine Springs, Tel. 915/828-3251*, covers over 86,000 acres, the majority of which is in New Mexico. The environment of the mountains is dramatically different than the surrounding land in west Texas. Many of the mountains reach heights of over 8000 feet, and pine forest covers the area. Elk, deer and forest animals inhabit the park, which has a cooler environment than the surrounding desert. Although this is a popular area for backpacking, there are no facilities at the park; all overnight visitors must stay at backcountry campsites. Park Rangers present educational evening programs from April through September. Many tourists stop by the park on the way to Carlsbad Caverns, New Mexico, which is 55 miles north.

For the adventurous traveler who wants to journey south of the border, **Pan American Tours**, *P. O. Box 9401, El Paso, 79984. Tel. 800/876-3942 or 351-1612*, offer tours of Mexico's spectacular **Copper Canyon** and the southern **Baja Peninsula**. Most tours include travel on the famous Chihuahua/Pacific Railway, which cuts through the mountains of the northwest Mexican state of Chihuahua. Packages range in length from four to eight days.

Practical Information

For car assistance or information, contact the **American Automobile Association**, *1201 Airport Boulevard, Suite A1, Tel 915/778-9521*.

The **Texas Department of Transportation** operates a large travel information center just outside El Paso. The information provided at the center deals with the entire state of Texas and is free. The travel information center is located on Interstate Highway 10 at the border of Texas and New Mexico.

Juarez, Mexico

Juarez is not a typical Mexican city, especially for a border town. Much of the city looks like a city in the US, with traffic congestion, new shopping centers and office buildings. The city has a population of about 1.4 million, and some estimate the growth as high as 100,000 people per year.

Arrivals & Depatures

Most people who travel between El Paso and Juarez go by car. Of course, tourists are not most people, and the traffic problems on the international bridges are reason enough to not take your car across. Unlike other towns on the Texas-Mexico border, walking across the border is not the simplest solution. Juarez is very spread-out and you may want to visit a number of areas in the city.

The **El Paso-Juarez Trolley Company**, *One Civic Center Plaza, El Paso, Tel. 915/544-0061 or 800/259-6284*, is the best way to see the city and get around. Adult fare is $11, children four to twelve years old $8.50 and children under three ride free. The trolleys run hourly from April to October, Sunday to Tuesday 9am to 4pm, Wednesday to Saturday, 9am to 5pm. From November to March, daily 9am to 4pm.

Orientation
The areas of interest to tourists are small compared to the entire city, which stretches out from the border with rapidly expanding neighborhoods.

Getting Around Town
The trolley crosses the international bridge close to downtown El Paso and continues across the Rio Grande, past Chamizal National Park (Mexico). During most times of the year, tourists prefer to take taxis and not walk around the city, because of the intense heat and noticeable automobile exhaust fumes. Use only taxis that are clearly marked and always negotiate the price for the ride before you get in, even if you are at a restaurant or hotel. Usually you can negotiate the price to half the original quote for the ride.

The El Paso Juarez Trolley makes 11 stops in Mexico and one in the United States, at the Civic Center. In El Paso, to reach the Civic Center, from Interstate Highway 10, exit Mesa and go south. Turn west onto Main, then go south on Santa Fe. The large Civic Center has a parking garage entrance on Santa Fe Street.

The trolley stops at a number of shops and restaurants and the museum area of Juarez. The next-to-the-last stop in Juarez is the City Market, where you can find souvenirs galore.

Where to Stay
HOTEL LUCERNA, *3976 Paseo Triunfo de la Republica, Juarez City, Chihuahua, Mexico. Tel. 91/800-66-300 (in Mexico) or 800/LUCERNA (in the United States). Rates: $77 to $82. Credit cards accepted.*

The large, modern hotel Lucerna has a five star rating. Enjoy the style and flavor of Mexico in comfort here. The two restaurants and lobby bar offer good food and atmosphere. The pool is in the center of a traditional Mexican-style patio courtyard. All rooms have television and phones that are suitable for business travelers. This hotel is directly across the street from the Holiday Inn.

Where to Eat
CHIHUAHUA CHARLIE'S, *2525 Plaza de la Republica, Juarez. Tel. 13-12-54.*

The Carlos n' Charlie's restaurants have managed to provide Juarez with the best food and most fun you will find on the border. You could easily ruin your appetite with the fresh margaritas and basket of hot-from-the-oven bread. But you would not want to miss the entrees. The Pollo Yucateco is chicken prepared with mild spices from the Yucatan region of Mexico. The Filete Reyes, a beef fillet with garlic and mild peppers prepared at your table, is entertainment as well as good food. The dessert line-up includes caramel or mango crepes, and cakes prepared on site. On the weekends the bar is hopping and live music fills the air. Breakfast is served all day, every day.

Seeing the Sights

Juarez differs from other Mexican border towns in the newness of many of the shopping centers. You might mistake being in the United States in the crowded city streets and up-scale strip malls. The trolley runs a circular route and covers the major points of interest.

The **City Cathedral**, at the *Plaza de Armas* (the main square), is worth a visit. The streets surrounding the plaza are closed to traffic and lined with vendors selling everything from household goods to curios.

The older bars are lined up along Avenida Juarez, a pedestrian street that begins at the international bridge and continues to the main square. This is where you will find the typical border-town diversions such as campy souvenirs and dusty bars that smell like tequila.

The **Juarez Racetrack**, *Avenida El Galgodromo, Tel 915/542-1942*, has greyhound racing all year long. The Jockey Club is a comfortable restaurant with a view of the track.

Shopping

The last stop on the trolley route in Juarez is the **City Market**, a new tourist market. In general prices are unnecessarily high, and much of the silver is not sterling. The shops just outside the market sell nice pottery, glassware and liquor for reasonable prices. *The City Market is on Avenida de 16 Septiembre, about one mile from the international bridge.*

If you are searching for high-end retail shopping, try the **Export Free Store**, *Avenida Juarez 114-A, Tel. 16/12-31-50*. This duty free store resembles those found in airports, and caters to clientele shopping for liquor and tobacco. The store does not charge any Mexican tax. They clam to have the best prices on cigars, sunglasses and perfume. Of course, you are subject to alcohol and tobacco duties and restrictions when returning to the United States.

Practical Information

The **Juarez Tourist Bureau** can be reached by calling the office in Mexico, *Tel. 16/14-06-07 or 29-33-00*, or through the United States office, *Tel. 800/406-3491*.

Big Bend National Park

Not too long ago, when people said they were going to "Big Bend," they meant they were going to Big Bend National Park, and perhaps a few of the surrounding towns on either side of the border. Today, however, Big Bend is comprised of not only the famed national facility, but the newer 275,000 acre state preserve known as the Big Bend Ranch State Natural Area. In other words, the Big Bend is now the HUGE Bend, and the appreciative traveler could spend weeks exploring it, so we've added a section following this one for surrounding areas.

Big Bend National Park, a rugged slice of heaven 1,100 square miles in size, is home to over 400 species of wildlife roaming both mountain and desert regions. The bend in the Rio Grande for which the park is named curves through three canyons. The park hotel is located in the basin of the tall Chisos Mountains. Camping areas are located throughout the park and range from full hook-ups to primitive; reservations are not taken for campsites.

You'll find the state's most spectacular scenery in this park. Hiking offers the best opportunity to catch a glimpse of deer, javelina, birds, and even mountain lions. There are 14 hiking trails, ranging in difficulty from very easy paved trails to difficult climbs. The longest trail is 20 miles and the shortest less than one-third mile.

A driving tour of the park will also provide you with magnificent views and wildlife sightings. Roads run thorough all regions of the park; many are paved while some are rough backcountry trails.

Arrivals & Departures

When traveling on Interstate Highway 10, the main entrance to the park is on Highway 385, south of Marathon. You can reach the west entrance by taking Highway 118 south from Alpine and turning east on Highway 170. Maps of roads, campsites and trails are available from the any park ranger station. Paved roads lead to the major campsites and ranger stations.

Ranger Stations in Big Bend

A ranger station is located at the northernmost entrance to the park, at Persimmon gap on Highway 385. The **Park Headquarters** is located in the center of the park at Panther Junction. The Chisos Basin, where the only hotel in the park is located, is just west of Panther Junction. Boquillas Canyon and nearby Rio Grande Village, which has picnic areas and campsites, are on the eastern end of the park. Castolon and the ranger station, near Santa Elena Canyon, is in the southwestern area.

Getting Around the Park

Some of the auto-trails cross rugged terrain, but do not require four-wheel-drive vehicles. All roads and auto trails are clearly marked.

Where to Stay & Eat

CHISOS MOUNTAIN LODGE, *Big Bend National Park. Tel. 915/477-2291, Fax 477-2352. Rates: $54 to $77. Credit cards accepted.*

This is the only hotel in Big Bend. It stands in the basin of the Chisos Mountains and is by far the best place to stay in the area. The location of the hotel alone is worth trip to Big Bend. The road that leads to the hotel offers some of the most spectacular views in the park. A small paved trail leads to a favorite sunset overlook in the park. The trails and canyons in the park are easily accessible from the hotel, and a number of trails begin at the hotel itself.

The rooms are modern and comfortable with phones, but no television. Each room has a balcony and views of the mountains and forest. Rooms A1 to A12 have balconies that overlook the spectacular sunset view. Make reservations well in advance of your stay; the hotel is often booked months in advance. Even more fun to stay in are the stone cottages just up the mountain trail from the hotel. Ask for Cottage Number 103 – it has the best view.

Attached to the lodge is a state-run restaurant. The restaurant and coffee shop serve meals throughout the day and are open to the public. As is the case with most of the state-operated concessions in Texas, the food is good for what it is, which is reasonably priced (if somewhat institutional) cuisine.

Seeing the Sights

A rich variety of animals inhabit the park including black bears, mountain lions and (at last count) 434 species of birds. The park rangers offer weekend hikes for wildlife watching. Many of the hiking trails have self-guided nature information posted on the route or available at the ranger stations.

The mighty **Rio Grande** snakes and curves its way for 1,896 miles. In the United States it is second in size to the Mississippi only. You can travel for over 100 miles along the river by canoe or rage. Of the three canyons in the Big Bend area-Santa Elena, Mariscal and Boquillas-**Santa Elena Canyon** is the most spectacular. Its rock walls rise to over 1500 feet, and narrow passages mark the curving water. The emotion of the river changes with the subtleties of the seasons, so hiring a guide is preferred. You can cross the Rio Grande by rowboat to visit the tiny Mexican villages along the way, and stop by the cantina for an icy cold cerveza.

Big Bend Ranch State Natural Area & El Camino Del Rio

One of the newer and less well-known state parks of Texas, the **Big Bend Ranch State Natural Area** combines desert and river in truly grand fashion.

You'll never forget the sixty-mile drive along the River Road, more commonly known as **El Camino del Rio**.

The tallest point in the park is known as **Solitario**. It is a dome of molten rock measuring almost 8 miles across and reaches a height of 5,128 feet. This is one of the largest formations of its type in the world, and one of the few nearly symmetrical natural structures. Solitario is found in the northeastern area of the park.

The **Warnock Environmental Education Center**, *Highway 170 (just east of Lajitas), Tel. 915/424-3327*, occasionally sponsors art shows and displays of relevance to the Big Bend area, such as photography exhibits.

Fort Leaton, *Ranch Road 170, Presidio, Tel 915/229-3613, open daily 8am to 4:30pm*, may be the only walled fort in the state. In fact, it may be the only nationally recognized fort that was not an army outpost. This was a private building occupied by the Texas Rangers for a short time.

Sports & Recreation

Even if you are not a hearty outdoors person, Big Bend can be the adventure of a lifetime for those who want to see the real West Texas. **Lajitas Stables**, *Star Route 70, Terlingua, Tel. 915/424-3238 or 888/508-7667*, arranges combination trips of horseback riding and river rafting. Overnight trips include horses, camping equipment and a guide; prices start at $100 per day. Hourly trail rides include lunch ($16 per hour); three-day trips into the borderlands of Mexico are a specialty of Lajitas Stables.

You can visit Big Bend on horseback with **Turquoise Trailriders**, *Big Bend Motor Inn, Terlingua, Tel. 915/371-2212*. The tour company offers a variety of riding experiences for the novice or expert rider. Overnight camp-outs, half or full day trips or even excursions by the hour will let you see west Texas the way the cowboys did-from atop a horse. The guides provide local insight to the history, folklore and nature of the area. Bicycle rentals and tours may also be arranged.

Desert Sports, *Highway 170, Terlingua, Tel. 915/371-2727 or 888/989-6900, www.desertsportstx.com*, outfits tours that include camping expeditions, trips down the Rio Grande and mountain bike adventures. You can experience the hidden beauty of the canyons and mountains of Big Bend the country with the experienced guides. Desert Sports is located on Highway 170 four miles west of the intersection with Highway 118.

Big Bend River Tours, *Highway 170, Lajitas, Tel. 915/424-3219 or 800/545-4240*, offers year-round professionally guided backcountry tours by river raft or 4x4 Jeeps. You may choose from one-day tours that can last from 4 to 12 hours, or overnight trips of up to 10 days, and this outfitter promises that all trips are suitable for novices.

Other tour companies in the area include:

- **San Carlos Excursions**, *Tel. 915/424-3221*, for easy day tours of Big Bend
- **Far Flung Adventures**, *Tel. 800/359-4138*, specializes in rafting trips down the Rio Grande
- **Big Bend Rivers Tours**, *915/424-3234 or 800/545-4240*, to get far off the beaten path
- **Texas River Expeditions**, *Tel. 800/839-4138* or **Rio Grande Adventures**, *Tel. 800/343-1640*, both located in Study Butte.

Practical Information

For tourist information, contact **Big Bend National Park General Information**, *Tel. 915/477-2251*.

The **Big Bend Natural History Association**, *Tel. 915/424-3252*, sponsors workshops about bird watching.

The **Big Bend Touring Society**, *Tel. 915/371-2548*, plans tours designed to your specifications.

The Fort Davis State Bank has an **ATM** at the Big Bend Motor Inn.

Visitor registration and information can be found at the **Barton Warnock Environmental Education Center**, *just east of Lajitas on Farm Road 170, 915/424-3327, open 8am-5pm daily*. A sales area contains numerous natural and historical guides to the region.

Fort Leaton State Historical Park, *4 miles southeast of Presidio on Farm Road 170, Tel. 915/229-3613*, also serves as a visitor's center.

Big Bend Area Towns

The towns outside the park – **Terlingua**, **Lajitas** and **Study Butte** – are small villages that cater to park visitors. Tour companies and hotels in these towns offer rafting, horseback riding and hiking guided tours. Terlingua and Study Butte were small mining towns in the late nineteenth century. Some visitors stay in **Marathon**, which is 78 miles north of Big Bend on Highway 385. The Gage Hotel, in Marathon, is a first-rate establishment, but the long drive does not allow the serious nature lover adequate time to enjoy the scenery of the park.

Every November the winter heats up with the **Terlingua Chili Cook-off**. The event promises to be the largest chili competition in the world. The event draws over 5,000 chili fans from all over the globe.

Lajitas is the product of the vision of a developer who saw a dude-ranch sort of oasis in the desert. The town is a modern rendition of an Old West street. The hotels are part of a large conference center that offers a variety of recreational activities, including a nine hole golf course, pool and saloon and dance hall.

One of the only ghost towns in the state is in Terlingua. The small adobe homes of miners stand abandoned on a hillside overlooking the cemetery. Nearby **Presidio** also has a ghost town that was once an adobe mining camp for the Presidio Mining Company. The town was abandoned in 1931 with the demise of the silver mines. Presidio is 45 miles west of Terlingua on Highway 170.

Where to Stay

To arrange the rental of a house in the Big Bend Area, contact **Lajitas on the Rio Grande**, *Star Route 70, Box 400, Lajitas 79852. Tel. 915/424-3471 or 800/944-9907.*

BADLANDS HOTEL, *Star Route 70, Lajitas. Tel. 915/424-3452 or 800/ 944-9907. $30 to $110 Credit cards accepted.*

The main accommodations facility of Lajitas offers motel rooms, modern cabins and apartments. Guests may use the nine-hole golf course and pool. A frontier fortress-style inn stands on the spot of a former cavalry fort. The single story motel has a Mexican adobe theme exterior. A dozen shops and restaurants on the main street offer entertainment nearby. If you come here on the off-season, it is best to travel to this resort with a large group of friends, otherwise you may feel like you are visiting a ghost town. The campground offers full hookups for tents or recreational vehicles. The hotel is 13 miles form Big Bend.

BIG BEND MOTOR INN, *Terlingua. Tel. 915/371-2218 or 800/848-BEND. Rates: $59.95 to $79.95. Credit cards accepted.*

This motel has simple rooms with microwave ovens and refrigerators. The accommodations are sparse and suited for the most economical of travelers. The location is convenient to Big Bend and the motel can arrange outdoor excursions in the park.

THE GAGE HOTEL, *102 Highway 90 West, Marathon. Tel. 915/386-4205 or 800/884-GAGE, Fax 915/386-4510. Rates: $65 to 100. Credit cards accepted.*

The Gage Hotel was built in 1920, on the half-million acre ranch owned by Alfred Gage. The hotel has been renovated into a modern facility with a restaurant and outdoor pool. Adobe walls, Mexican furnishings and rough timber ceilings accent the 37 rooms. The southwestern decoration is a posh atmosphere for a respite in the badlands of west Texas. Many choose to stay here when visiting Big Bend, although the park is 78 miles away.

You can stroll around Marathon to visit some of the turn-of-the-century buildings occupying the five blocks north and south of the post office. The Gage Hotel pretty much constitutes the entire city of Marathon. So when the hotel and its adjoining cafe shuts down for afternoon siesta, there is nothing to do but get gasoline and get out of town. The Cafe Cenizo has a menu that offers a bit of variety from the standard west Texas fare. The Croque Macho, is served on French bread (croissants are not macho) and comes with a side of onion rings. Big Ed's Chicken Fried Steak is large and comes with potato salad and cole slaw. Shirley makes four varieties of home-cooked pies. The cafe is closed from 2pm to 6pm daily.

Alpine

The city of **Alpine** has intellect, art and natural beauty. Area ranches raised mohair sheep and depended on Alpine as a center of commerce. Alpine now relies primarily on art and tourism for its sustenance. You can see the mohair warehouses by the railroad station. They are among the numerous historic buildings in the town. Alpine is the seat of the largest county in Texas, Brewster.

After the railroad tamed the frontier, Alpine became a whistle stop on the transcontinental line. Time and again fires devastated the community. In 1888, 1907, 1911, and 1946 fires destroyed major parts of the city. Many of the old buildings are now artists' studios and shops.

Sul Ross University casts a stately shadow upon the city. For over ten years the university has been the site of the **Texas Cowboy Poetry Gathering**. Local ranchers and cowhands share true stories in the form of poetry, song and narrative. The event lasts three days and usually is held on the first weekend of March.

Arrivals & Depatures

The regional airport is served by **Dallas Express Airlines**, *Tel. 800/529-0925*, a small commuter airline that flies into Dallas Love Field four times a week. The charter airline **Skies of Texas**, *Tel. 915/837-2290*, based in Alpine, offers flights by special arrangement.

You can step off the train at the **Amtrak Station**, *102 West Holland Street, Tel. 800/USA-RAIL*, right in the center of the historic downtown. This is a good point for a break in the long journey across west Texas.

By car, you can reach Alpine from Interstate Highway 10 by heading south on Highway 90.

Orientation

Alpine is on the northern ridge of the Glass Mountains, on Highway 90. Highway 118 runs from Big Bend (Study Butte entrance) in the south through Fort Davis and the Davis Mountains in the north. Alpine is the only stop on the Amtrak Train line between Del Rio and El Paso.

Where to Stay

WHITE HOUSE INN, *2003 Fort Davis Highway. Tel. 915/837-1401, Fax 837-2197. Rates: $75. Credit cards accepted.*

This stately southern home has six rooms for guests, each with a private bath. The traditional decor invites relaxation, as do the large porches which run the length of the house, and the beautiful tree-filled yard. Breakfast is included with each room, and lunch or dinner can be ordered for an additional charge.

Where to Eat

REATA, *203 North Hwy 118 (5th Street). Tel. 915/837-9232. Credit cards accepted.*

The restaurant is named after the ranch in "Giant," and the gigantic flavors of the west accent the excellent food. The tenderloin tamale appetizer is outstanding, as is the basket full of flaky biscuits and spiced flatbread that comes to each table. Chef Grady Spears prepares faultless cowboy classics, but takes chances as well. The chicken fried steak and ribeye are always dead on, but for exciting flavor try the game of the day special entree or the bar-b-cue shrimp enchiladas. Striking paintings and western paraphernalia decorate the interior, or you can dine outside on the patio beneath the enormous mural. Open for dinner six days a week (closed Sunday); lunch Wednesday-Saturday. The bar remains open until midnight.

ALPINE BAKERY, *302 East Holland. Tel. 915/837-7297.*

The Alpine Bakery has a complete selection of breakfast pastries and muffins as well as fresh coffee. Lunch is served Monday to Saturday until 3pm. Baked potatoes, quiche and fresh sandwiches are featured.

Seeing the Sights

Many of the buildings still in use today are living history lessons. The **Holland Hotel** was constructed in 1928 and was the center of social activity in the town. The train station has been in continuous use since before the present building went up in 1946.

The span of history-from the first traces of Native Americans to the present towns-is documented at the **Museum of the Big Bend**, *Sul Ross University, Tel. 915/ 837-8143, open Tuesday to Saturday 9am to 5pm, Sunday 1pm to 5pm, admission free*. Many of the exhibits showcase artistic depictions of life in the Big Bend area. From Highway 290, take Entrance #2 into the University. The museum is to the west of the entrance.

Shopping

Downtown, many artists exhibit and sell their crafts at the **Arts and Crafts Mall of the Big Bend**, *101 West Holland Avenue, Tel. 915/837-7486*. Clothing, jewelry and paintings are among the offerings. Nearby, **Front**

Street Books, *121 Holland Avenue, Tel. 915/837-3360*, sells maps, books about Big Bend and West Texas, regional newspapers and an excellent selection of nature and history books.

Excursions & Day Trips
MARFA

Marfa was put on the map, or rather the big screen, in 1955, when the movie Giant was filmed in the city. The cast, including James Dean and Elizabeth Taylor, stayed in the **El Paisano Hotel** in the center of the city. The El Paisano was built in 1928. The Spanish-style architecture is unique to the area The movie Come Back to the Five and Dime, Jimmy Dean, Jimmy Dean is a fictional account of the personal aftermath of the filming of Giant, and might be set in Marfa.

But today, the city is more famous for the **Marfa Lights**. The lights are unexplained globes of light that appear on the horizon shortly after sundown. Residents first spotted the lights in the late 1800s. Speculation about the cause of the lights abounds. Many believe that phosphorus gas is the cause; some opt for the ghost light theory, while others are convinced that the only explanation is otherworldly intrigue. Science offers no solution.

Marfa sits high in the mountains at an altitude of over 4,000 feet. The **Marfa Municipal Golf Course** may have only nine holes, but can call itself the highest golf course in Texas.

Most visitors come to see the Marfa lights, which appear shortly after sundown on clear nights. The city has a parking area for viewing the lights. Take Highway 90 east of Marfa. Nine miles outside of the city you will see a small parking area and an historical marker. Probably there will be a number of cars as well. The lights appear throughout the night; many spectators spend hours watching the ghost lights. Marfa is 26 miles west of Alpine on Highway 90.

Practical Information

The **Alpine Chamber of Commerce**, *106 North Third Street, Tel. 915/837-2326*, provides tourist information for the city and the surrounding area.

The **Marfa Chamber of Commerce**, *Tel. 915/729-4942*, provides tourist information.

Fort Davis

Fort Davis was founded in 1856 as a United States military post. Ranchers began to tame the surrounding area in the late 1800s. The beautiful mountains and desert combine to make a stunning landscape. The area is popular with campers, hikers and hunters.

The altitude, clear skies and open ranges give the Davis Mountain region the best conditions for stargazing. And this is why the University of Texas chose Fort Davis as the site for the **McDonald Observatory**. The facility is open to the public for tours and sun and stargazing.

On the Saturday of Labor Day Weekend, the **Fort Davis Festival** is held on the grounds of the national park. History buffs will enjoy the participants who dress in period costume. For more information about these events contact the Superintendent of Fort Davis National Historical Park, *P. O. Box 1456, Fort Davis 79734, Tel. 915/426-3224.*

Arrivals & Depatures

Fort Davis is located at the intersection of Highways 118 and 17. From Interstate Highway 10, take Highway 17 south at Balmorhea; form Highway 90 take Highway 118 north from Alpine or Highway 17 north from Marfa. The town is very small; the hotels are located in the center of the city. The points of interest are just northwest of the city, on Highway 118.

Where to Stay

HOTEL LIMPIA, *On the Town Square, P.O. Box 1341. Tel. 915/426-3237, Fax 915/426-3983, Toll free 800/662-5517, Website: www.hotellimpia.com. 36 Rooms. Rates: $69-150. Credit cards accepted.*

The Limpia is an entire complex of lodgings that includes the historic hotel, the adjoining Limpia West, and three guesthouses in the older sections of town. The hotel still has the fancy touches that made it a first-rate accommodation in 1912—decorative tin ceilings, moldings and period furniture. There are 12 suites available, some with kitchens and living areas. The sun porch overlooks the main square.

You cannot miss the Limpia; it is the largest building in town and dominates the town square. The Hotel Limpia houses the only drinking establishment in the county, Sutler's Club. The casual yet refined western bar serves drinks and food. You must purchase a membership to the club for a nominal charge. Also on the premises is the best restaurant in town (see Where to Eat) as well as an excellent gift shop.

THE DRUGSTORE AND OLD TEXAS INN, *Box 822 Main Street. Tel. 915/426-3118 or 800/DAVIS-MT. Rates: $60 to $75. Credit cards accepted.*

The only place on the town square besides the Hotel Limpia to hang your hat for the night is the Old Texas Inn. The 6 rooms upstairs from the Drugstore are large and furnished with homey, old-western decor. The friendly atmosphere and comfortable decor make a welcoming environment. The central living area has a large television and comfortable couch. In the morning, have the best breakfast in west Texas style, downstairs at the Drugstore. The Drugstore sells western memorabilia, a selection of interesting books about

Texana and souvenirs. On the weekends locals fill the restaurant, indulging in the hearty and inexpensive breakfast specials.

INDIAN LODGE, *Davis Mountains State Park, Park Road 3, Fort Davis. Tel. 915/426-3254. Rates: $65-80. Mastercard, Visa, Personal checks accepted.*

The Indian Lodge is like a back-to-nature resort. The hotel is built in the style of Pueblo Native American settlements. The beautiful white adobe walls stand out against the mountainous desert backdrop of the secluded setting. An outdoor pool and patios accent the different levels of the rambling building. Rooms in the historical section of the lodge, built by the CCC in the 1930s, have river cane ceilings, adobe fireplaces and their original rough-hewn cedar furnishings.

All 39 rooms have modern amenities such as telephones, televisions and central heat and air conditioning. You can pass your days hiking the park trails through the Davis Mountains and your evenings stargazing at the almost always clear skies. The Black Bear Restaurant is housed in the same complex. Make reservations well in advance to ensure a room at this popular getaway.

PRUDE GUEST RANCH, *Highway 118, Fort Davis. Tel. 915/426-3202 or 800/458-6232, Fax 915/426-3502, Rates: $65-75. Credit cards accepted.*

This little dude ranch in the big mountains of west Texas offers a taste of Texas. The cowboy theme runs through the dining hall decoration. A rodeo area and a scattering of exotic animals provide the ranch feeling. The guest lodges are the better rooms, and are located some distance from the main entrance of the ranch. Family Bunk rooms offer dormitory style accommodations. The Ranch Bunkhouse can hold from 8 to 20 people per room and no sheet or towels are provided. Near the entrance you will find rows of camp sites with full hook-ups. Meals can be purchased. Take Highway 118 northwest from Fort Davis for six miles.

Where to Eat

HOTEL LIMPIA DINING ROOM, *On the Town Square. Tel. 915/426-3241. Credit cards accepted.*

The intimate country-style dining room at the Hotel Limpia serves some of the best food in West Texas. The bread is a source of pride for the restaurant, which makes all of its rolls on-site. Entrees include beef and pasta specialties cooked to perfection with excellent sauces. The Burgundy Marinated Roast Beef is succulent. Fried Beef Tenderloin is a gourmet version of chicken fried steak. Lasagne Roll-up is a vegetarian option. Sunday lunch features a Prime Rib Special. You can have seconds on vegetables and side dishes, but why ruin your appetite for dessert? The pies and cakes are baked in-house.

BLUE MOUNTAIN GOURMET DINER, *Intersection of Highways 118 and 17. Tel. 915/426-2479.*

Delicious breakfasts and satisfying sandwiches are the reason locals come to the Blue Mountain. The appellation "Gourmet" Diner may seem like an oxymoron, but rest assured that it isn't. This is one of the only places to get a great cup of coffee in all of West Texas. Local art adorns the wall, and the staff is most welcoming.

BLACK BEAR RESTAURANT, *Indian Lodge State Park, Park Road 3, Fort Davis. Tel. 915/426-3254.*

If you're staying at the Indian Lodge, the Black Bear is a convenient place to fortify yourself with breakfast for a day of hiking though the park's nature trails. However, if you have the time to make the short trek into town, there are better places to eat. The food at this state-run concession is plain, filling, and uninspired, but the prices are reasonable. The exception to the routine fare is the Sunday buffet, which is popular enough to attract even the locals. For less than ten dollars you can have all you want of tasty fried catfish, pork loin, salads, beverages and dessert. Open for breakfast 7-10 am Monday–Saturday, 7-9:30 am; Sunday lunch and dinner are available from 11am-2pm and 5-8pm, Monday–Saturday noon-2:30 pm and 5-8pm on Sunday.

Seeing the Sights

The **Fort Davis National Historic Park**, *Highways 17 and 118, Tel. 915/426-3224, Fax 426-3122*, is only a few blocks from the center of the town. When the United States government established the fort in 1861, it had already been in operation since 1854. Its mission was to protect travelers on the road that connected San Antonio to El Paso. The fort was intended to curb the threat of the outlaw raiders who plagued this no-man's-land. At the time, as a visitor can well imagine, there was little other settlement in the region. The dry desert and foreboding landscape stretched as far as the eye could see.

The entire national park encompasses about 460 acres. Visitors can take a self-guided tour through the restored enlisted men's barracks buildings and four other buildings dating from the 1880s. Foundations of the military buildings remain uncovered from archaeological investigation and hiking trails are also accessible.

Fort Davis is open daily from 8am to 6pm; during the winter months the closing time moves ahead to 5pm. Other historical programs and lectures are held during the year, especially in the summer months. Evening tours are conducted in the fall and winter. To reach Fort Davis, take Highway 17 south from Interstate Highway 10 for 39 miles. Admission to the museum is $2 per person; children and educational groups admitted free.

The **Davis Mountain State Park**, *Highway 118, Tel. 915/426-3254*, has over 18,000 acres of preserved land with hiking trails and campsites. The Indian Lodge is located on the park grounds. During the summer months, park rangers host educational seminars in the park amphitheater and guide nature walks. The park is located six miles west of Fort Davis on Highway 118.

If you continue along Highway 118, then climb Spur 78, you will reach the summit of Mt. Locke in the Davis Mountains, 6,800 miles above sea level, and home to the **University of Texas at Austin McDonald Observatory**, *Tel. 915/426-3640, Website: www.as.utexas.edu/mcdonald/mcdonald.html*. The Visitors' Information Center is open daily from 9am-5pm. You can get up close and marvel at the large reflecting telescopes, which do not actually observe celestial objects, but gather light and data. Visitors can watch an orientation film at the visitors' center, then tour the three enormous telescopes. Self–guided tours are free, or you can take a guided tour for a small fee. After the tour a question and answer session is held.

On Tuesday, Friday, and Saturday nights, Star Parties are held. Besides the public observatory telescopes, visitors often have access to dozens of tele-scopes brought by enthusiastic local astronomers who share their favorite celestial views with everyone. Star Party admission is $4 for adults, $3 for children, or $10 for an entire family. Weather permitting, the sun can be viewed daily through a special telescope at 11am and 3:30pm. Solar viewing is free to the public. Visitors can look to the heavens through the largest telescope once a month, usually on the Wednesday closest to the full moon. The fee is $10 per individual or $20 per family, and reservations are required. The observation sessions should be booked well in advance, especially in spring and summer.

Excursions & Day Trips

Some of the mysteries of the desert are explained at the **Chihuahuan Desert Research Institute**, *Highway 118, open daily 1pm to 5pm*. This is the only desert research institute in the state. The visitor's center gives information about the desert habitat and how man has used the native resources. The institute is located three and one-half miles south of Fort Davis.

The San Solomon Springs feed a warm, deep pool in **Balmorhea State Park**. The absolutely clear water which is full of fish-some of which are endangered species-is a favorite place for scuba divers and snorkelers. The water remains a constant 70 degrees Fahrenheit, regardless of the winter cold or summer heat. You can camp in the state park, which has campsites with full hook-ups including cable television. A small motel with 18 units is available for rental. The state park is located four miles west of Balmorhea city. From Interstate Highway 10, go south of Highway 17 to the park entrance.

Practical Information

The **Fort Davis Chamber of Commerce** is located in the Hotel Limpia lobby, *Main Street on the Square, Tel. 915/426-3237*.

Fort Stockton

The area around **Fort Stockton** is an oasis in the brutal arid climate. In 1859, Fort Stockton was settled on what was then the Old San Antonio Road, a trade route linking San Antonio with El Paso. Today, as in the previous century, Fort Stockton is a rest stop for weary travelers.

The downtown area retains the quiet charm of years past. Historic buildings such as the 1883 schoolhouse and Catholic Church built in 1875 surround the county courthouse.

Arrivals & Depatures

Fort Stockton is a popular rest stop for travelers heading toward Big Bend. The town is about 110 miles north of Big Bend at the intersection of Interstate Highway 10 and Highway 290.

Orientation

Main Street begins at Highway 290. At this intersection an 11-foot tall roadrunner statue, "Paisano Pete" greets visitors. Follow Main Street down to the center of the city. On the left of downtown stands old Fort Stockton, which has a short audio presentation that works at all times.

Getting Around Town

Roadrunner Bus Tours, *open daily 11am to 6pm, Tel. 915/336-8052*, offers a tour of Fort Stockton, or you can purchase an audio cassette and drive yourself.

Where to Stay

GLASS MOUNTAIN BED AND BREAKFAST, *Highway 385. Tel/Fax: 915/395-2435 or 800/695-8249. Rates: $75. Credit cards accepted.*

Escape to the open west Texas country life. Only the stars provide faint outdoor light at Glass Mountain Manor, and the sounds you hear will be cattle or horses. Guests stay in the small original ranch house that was built at the turn of the 19th century. The seclusion and privacy of the entire house are yours; only one set of guests is accommodated at a time and you have the run of the house. All the fixings for breakfast are left in the house. Glass Mountain Manor is located on Highway 385, 26 miles south of Fort Stockton.

BEST WESTERN SWISS CLOCK INN, *3201 West Dickinson. Tel. 915/336-8521 or 800/528-1234. Rates: $40-60. Credit cards accepted.*

This is a comfortable motel with a homey atmosphere. A lounge and cafe are in the motel, and there is an outdoor pool. The inn is about three miles from the center of town. From Interstate 10, take exit 256 south.

DAYS INN, *1408 North Highway 285. Tel. 915/336-7500 or 800/ DAYS-INN, Fax 915/336-7501. Rates: $40-60. Credit cards accepted.*

This 50-room motel has a hair salon and outdoor pool. There is plenty of parking space for recreational vehicles. Guests may bring their pets. Continental breakfast is included with all rooms.

LA QUINTA, *2601 Interstate Highway 10 West. Tel. 915/336-9781 or 800/531-5900, Fax 915/336-3634. Rates: $60-70. Credit cards accepted.*

La Quinta offers breakfast and airport shuttle service to all guests. Both families and business travelers will find adequate facilities here. Phones have computer connections for modem use and dry cleaning service is available. Recreational facilities include an outdoor pool. The motel offers both a restaurant and room service. Children under the age of 18 stay free in parents' room.

KOA CAMPGROUND, *Interstate Highway 10 at exit 264. Tel. 915/395-2494. Rates: $17.50 per night.*

The KOA campground has all the facilities you need to make roughing-it seem like a pleasure trip. The facilities for the 85 campsites include a restaurant, store and pool.

Where to Eat

FORT STOCKTON BAKERY, *600 West Dickinson. Tel. 915/336-7232.*

This small bakery serves fresh, delicious pastry and cinnamon rolls. The Mexican specialties include huge cookies cinnamon rolls. When you walk in, take a metal tray and pair of tongs and help yourself to the selections along the wall. For lunch you can have tortas, rolls with fillings of brisket, ham or hamburger baked in.

Seeing the Sights

Fort Stockton, *300 East 3rd Street, Tel 915/336-2400, open Monday to Saturday 10am to 1pm and 2pm to 5pm*, the military fort that gave its name to this town, was in use for only 28 years, from 1858 to 1886. A number of the original 35 stone buildings remain including the prison, barracks and officers houses. The museum has a display of the gear and uniforms worn by the cavalry. Fort Stockton, like other Texas frontier forts, was the home of Buffalo Soldiers. The displays, especially the audio presentation in the jail building, gives insight to the difficult conditions the soldiers faced. You can walk around the historic buildings even when the fort complex is closed. As you walk up to the front porch of the old jail, a recorded story describes life in the frontier forts.

Anne Riggs was a hotelier from 1877 until 1931. The **Anne Riggs Memorial Museum**, *301 South Main Street, Tel. 915/336-2167, open Monday to Saturday 10am to noon and 1:30pm to 5pm, Sunday 1:30 to 5pm;*

Admission $1 adults, $.50 children, was once the city's hotel. The rooms hold displays about the history and culture of Fort Stockton. One room remains furnished as it would have been for hotel guests in 1905. The museum provides a unique glimpse into the frontier life of west Texas. During the summer months of June, July and August, the museum remains open until 8pm.

The town also has a modern landmark of interest. The **Ste. Genevieve Winery** produces inexpensive yet high quality table wine. The winery is a project of private winemakers and University of Texas researchers. The Domaine Corridor Vineyard and facility is in the Escondido Valley. A visit to the winery provides education about high-tech winemaking and a general course on wine tasting. The winery is just off Interstate Highway 10 at McKenzie Road Exit 285.

Shopping

Beautiful hand-made pottery is sold at **In the Round**, *204 West 2nd Street, Tel. 915/336-3542, Monday to Saturday 9am to 6pm*. The pieces reflect the simplicity of the southwest and are designed for daily use.

Practical Information

The **Fort Stockton Visitor Center** is located in the historic city train station at the intersection of Business Highway 10 and Main Street.

Midland/Odessa

Midland stands on the rocky Texas plains, halfway between El Paso and Dallas. The city is a vibrant, modern haven with an active cultural scene. Midland has weathered the roughest historic and economic storms. The city was in the thick of battles between Comanches and settlers. With the oil boom, prosperity flooded the region. Consequently, when Texas oil went bad, the city faced rough times.

Midland and **Odessa** are practically twin cities, located ten miles apart on Interstate Highway 20.

Arrivals & Departures

Midland is served by Southwest Airlines and the commuter services of American and Continental Airlines. The **Midland International Airport** is between Midland and Odessa; from Interstate Highway 20, exit Highway 1788.

Greyhound Bus, *Toll free reservations Tel. 800/231-2222*, provides transportation through Midland, *1308 West Front Street, Tel. 915/682-2761*, and Odessa, *500 North Jackson Street, Tel. 915/332-5711*.

Orientation

Both Midland and Odessa are on business loops of Interstate Highway 20. Odessa is the more western of the two cities

In Midland, Highway 250 forms a loop around the north of the city. Highway 349, or Rankin Highway, bisects the city center from north to south. Loop 338 encircles Odessa, and Highway 385 becomes Grant Avenue, the main north-south street in the city center.

Getting Around Town

Major auto rental agencies such as **Budget**, *Tel. 915/563-1352*, and **Enterprise**, *Tel. 915/689-9500*, serve Midland. The local **agency AA Auto Rentals**, *Tel. 915/694-8275*, can provide cars for local trips.

There is no public transportation service in Midland. Visitors must rely on their own transportation or use one of the area taxi services such as **A1 Taxi**, *Tel. 915/ 697-2521*, or **Yellow Checker Cab**, *Tel. 915/682-1661*.

Where to Stay

MIDLAND HILTON AND TOWERS, *117 West Wall Avenue, Midland. Tel. 915/683-6131 or 800/774-1500, Fax 915/683-0985. 256 Rooms. Rates: $70-255. Credit cards accepted.*

You can walk downtown from the Hilton, although you will feel as though you are already in the heart of cosmopolitan Midland in this 11-story hotel. You may see a genuine Texas oilman, since the concierge caters to guests of the local oil industry. Three restaurants in the hotel offer southwestern and traditional American cuisine. The local museums are only a few blocks away. The hotel offers a good fitness center.

MELLIE VAN HORN'S INN, *903 North Sam Houston Street, Midland. Tel. 915/337-3000. Rates: $69-99. Credit cards accepted.*

The inn was built in 1938 and used as dormitory-style accommodation for single teachers working in Midland schools. After the boarding house closed in 1975, the building was renovated into a bed and breakfast type inn. Each of the sixteen rooms has a private bath and is decorated with antique furnishings. Breakfast is included. The central location makes this an ideal place to stay if you want to get a feel for old-time Midland.

BEST WESTERN GARDEN OASIS, *110 West Interstate Highway 20, Odessa. Tel. 915/337-3006 or 800/528-1234, Fax 915/332-1956. Rates: $48-58. Credit cards accepted.*

This hotel strives to be an oasis in the desert with a large atrium and heated pool. The recreational facilities include a spa and sauna. Guests may take advantage of the free shuttle service to Midland International Airport.

MIDLAND DAYS INN, *4717 Highway 80, Midland. Tel. 915/699-7727, Fax 915/699-7813. 90 Rooms. Rates: $32-47. Credit cards accepted.*

The Midland Days Inn was recently remodeled and redecorated. Recreational facilities include an outdoor pool and use of a golf course. A barbershop and safe-deposit boxes are on the premises.

ODESSA DAYS INN, *3075 East Business Loop 20, Odessa. Tel. 915/335-8000 or 800/DAYS-INN, Fax 915/335-9562. Rates: $44-56. Credit cards accepted.*

The hotel has a lounge and an outdoor pool for guests. Extra perks include coffee at any time for guests, and coffee and donuts every morning. This is a simple motel convenient for those passing through the area on a road trip.

Where to Eat

WALL STREET BAR AND GRILL, *115 East Wall Street, Midland. Tel. 915/684-8686. Credit cards accepted.*

You will be able to find many national chain restaurants in Midland, but this is the only place you will find truly excellent cuisine. When you walk into Wall Street Bar and Grill, it seems that the old west comes alive again. The interior of this bar is straight out of a saloon scene in a movie. What makes the atmosphere incredible is that the decorations are all authentic antiques. The menu includes steaks and the city's freshest and best fish. The food is prepared with traditional recipes. On the weekends a brunch comes with fresh fruit and home-baked sweet rolls.

Seeing the Sights

The substance that put Odessa on the map is the focus of the **Petroleum Museum**, *1500 Interstate Highway 20 West, Midland, Tel. 915/683-4403, open Monday to Saturday 9am to 5pm, Sunday 2pm to 5pm*. But this museum includes an entire history of the area, showing the role that oil production played in the development of Midland and Odessa.

The **Confederate Flight Museum**, *9600 Wright Drive, Midland, Tel. 915/563-1000, open Monday to Saturday 9am to 5pm, Sunday noon to 5pm*, is all about aircraft, but has nothing to do with the Civil War. The museum houses an extensive collection of planes and military equipment from World War II. Every October the museum holds an air show that relives the battle flying of World War II. Explosions, fire and sirens are all part of the staged spectacle.

The office of the president of the United States is honored at the **Presidential Museum**, *622 North Lee Street, Odessa, Tel. 915/332-7123 or 800/862-7123, open Tuesday to Saturday 10am to 5pm, closed Sunday and Monday, admission free*. Permanent exhibits include campaign posters (including "Pat Paulsen for President"), White House memorabilia and a library of over 3500 volumes. Temporary exhibits are featured throughout the year. The museum is located in downtown Odessa, just north of Highway 80.

Just six miles south of Odessa you will find a meteor crater so large that you can walk through a nature trail within its circumference. The **Odessa Meteor Crater**, *Interstate Highway 20 West, Odessa*, measures 500 feet in diameter. It is located six miles south of Odessa. From Odessa, travel west on Interstate Highway 20, exit Farm Road 1936 and travel south for three and one-half miles.

Nightlife & Entertainment

THE GLOBE THEATER, *Odessa College, 2308 Shakespeare Road, Odessa. Tel. 915/332-1586.*

Odessa has an active arts scene and some of the best theater west of the Dallas/Fort Worth area. Although a western city may seem an unlikely place for Shakespeare, the Globe Theater presents Shakespeare's plays in a setting that is designed to replicate the original Globe Theater in England. The theater is also used for traditional country music performances. Every April, Odessa College presents the Shakespeare Festival. The theater and Shakespearean library are open daily from 9am to 5pm.

PERMIAN PLAYHOUSE, *310 West 42nd Street, Odessa. Tel. 915/362-2329.*

Odessa Community Theater presents dramatic, musical and youth productions throughout the year. This theater has received national recognition for the quality of its productions. Do not miss the chance to see excellent community theater when in the area.

Sports & Recreation

The last week of August brings the **Permian Basin Open** to Odessa. The $200,000 purse attracts some of the best-but as yet not well known-professional golfers. The **Club at Mission Dorado**, *Tel. 915/561-8811*, hosts the competition.

Excursions & Day Trips

The town of **Monahans** sprang up as a watering hole for the railroad, and grew with he oil industry of the early twentieth century. This is a rest stop for those weary of long miles of bland highway or thirsty for a taste of absurdity: the small has an unusual museum, the **Million Barrel Museum**, *Highway 80, Monahans, closed Monday, open Tuesday to Saturday, 10am to 6pm; Sunday 2pm to 6pm; free admission*. What does a city do with a one million barrel storage facility of oil when there is no need to fill it? Open a recreational park, of course. The tank is actually more of a man-made crater. One small corner has a 400 seat theater. In the historic part of the park is a turn-of-the-century hotel, the old city jail-house and some agricultural machinery. The Million Barrel Museum is just east of Monahans on Highway 80-you cannot miss it.

You will not find an ocean in West Texas, but there sure are sand dunes. The **Monahans Sandhills State Park**, *Park Road 41, Monahans, Tel. 915/ 943-2092 or 800/792-1112*, has over 3800 acres of sand dunes, some reaching 70 feet in height. The park has picnic areas, camping facilities and trailer hook-ups. You'll find unusual flora and fauna that maintain the ecosystem of the dunes. Over 600 acres are reserved for horseback riding. The Visitor's Center has exhibits explaining the natural phenomena of the desert dunes. Tours by four-wheel-drive vehicle are available.

Visitors can take a short, self-guided walking tour. During the summer, park rangers host campfire lectures in the evening. From Interstate Highway 20, exit Park Road 41 (mile marker 86).

Practical Information

Tourism information is available from the **Midland Chamber Convention and Visitors Bureau**, *109 North Main, Midland, Tel. 915/683-3381 or 800/624-6435*.

The **Odessa Cultural Council**, *Tel. 915/337-1492*, provides information and schedules of upcoming cultural events at the Permian Playhouse, the Globe Theater and many other theater and music events in the city.

Texas Guide

i
n
d
e
x

Things Change!

Phone numbers, prices, addresses, quality of food, etc, all change. If you come across any new information, we'd appreciate hearing from you. No item is too small! Drop us an email note at: Jopenroad@aol.com, or write us at:

Texas Guide
Open Road Publishing, P.O. Box 284
Cold Spring Harbor, NY 11724

travel notes